iOS 8 App Development Essentials

i

iOS 8 App Development Essentials – First Edition

ISBN-13: 978-1505586411

Rev 1.0b

 eBookFrenzy

Table of Contents

λ

1. Start Here

The goal of this book is to teach the skills necessary to create iOS applications using the iOS 8 SDK, Xcode 6 and the Swift programming language.

How you make use of this book will depend to a large extent on whether you are new to iOS development, or have worked with iOS 7 and need to get up to speed on the features of iOS 8 and the Swift programming language. Rest assured, however, that the book is intended to address both category of reader.

1.1 For New iOS Developers

If you are entirely new to iOS development then the entire contents of the book will be relevant to you.

Beginning with the basics, this book provides an outline of the steps necessary to set up an iOS development environment. An introduction to the architecture of iOS 8 and programming in Swift is provided, followed by an in-depth look at the design of iOS applications and user interfaces. More advanced topics such as file handling, database management, in-app purchases, graphics drawing and animation are also covered, as are touch screen handling, gesture recognition, multitasking, iAds integration, location management, local notifications, camera access and video and audio playback support. Other features are also covered including Auto Layout, Twitter and Facebook integration, App Store hosted in-app purchase content, collection views, Sprite Kit-based game development, local map search and user interface animation using UIKit dynamics.

The key new features of the iOS 8 SDK and Xcode 6 are also covered, including Swift playgrounds, universal user interface design using size classes, app extensions, Interface Builder Live Views, embedded frameworks, CloudKit data storage and TouchID authentication.

The aim of this book, therefore, is to teach you the skills necessary to build your own apps for iOS 8. Assuming you are ready to download the iOS 8 SDK and Xcode, have an Intel-based Mac and ideas for some apps to develop, you are ready to get started.

1.2 For iOS 7 Developers

If you have already read the iOS 7 edition of this book, or have experience with the iOS 7 SDK then you might prefer to go directly to the new chapters in this iOS 8 edition of the book.

Start Here

All chapters have been updated to reflect the changes and features introduced as part of iOS 8 and Xcode 6. Chapters included in this edition that were not contained in the previous edition, or have been significantly rewritten for iOS 8 and Xcode 6 are as follows:

- *An Introduction to Swift Playgrounds*
- *Swift Data Types, Constants and Variables*
- *Swift Operators and Expressions*
- *Swift Flow Control*
- *The Swift Switch Statement*
- *An Overview of Swift Functions and Closures*
- *The Basics of Object Oriented Programming in Swift*
- *An Introduction to Swift Inheritance*
- *Working with Array and Dictionary Collections in Swift*
- *Using Size Classes to Design Universal iOS User Interfaces*
- *An Introduction to CloudKit Data Storage on iOS 8*
- *An iOS 8 CloudKit Example*
- *An iOS 8 CloudKit Subscription Example*
- *Implementing TouchID Authentication in iOS 8 Apps*
- *Interface Builder Live Views and iOS 8 Embedded Frameworks*
- *An Introduction to Extensions in iOS 8*
- *An iOS 8 Today Extension Widget Tutorial*
- *Creating an iOS 8 Photo Editing Extension*
- *Creating an iOS 8 Action Extension*
- *Receiving Data from an iOS 8 Action Extension*

In addition the following changes have also been made:

- All chapters have been updated where necessary to reflect the changes made to Xcode 6.
- All chapters and examples have been rewritten to use Swift instead of Objective-C.
- TableView examples have been updated to cover self-sizing table cells and dynamic type.
- The SpriteKit chapters have been updated to use the new Xcode 6 SpriteKit Level Editor environment.
- The SQLite chapters have been updated to make use of the FMDB wrapper classes.
- The video playback chapter has been rewritten to use the AVPlayerViewControler and AVPlayer classes.

1.3 **Source Code Download**

The source code and Xcode project files for the examples contained in this book are available for download at:

http://www.ebookfrenzy.com/print/ios8/

1.4 Feedback

We want you to be satisfied with your purchase of this book. If you find any errors in the book, or have any comments, questions or concerns please contact us at *feedback@ebookfrenzy.com*.

1.5 Errata

Whilst we make every effort to ensure the accuracy of the content of this book, it is inevitable that a book covering a subject area of this size and complexity may include some errors and oversights. Any known issues with the book will be outlined, together with solutions at the following URL:

http://www.ebookfrenzy.com/errata/ios8.html

In the event that you find an error not listed in the errata, please let us know by emailing our technical support team at *feedback@ebookfrenzy.com*.

2. Joining the Apple iOS Developer Program

The first step in the process of learning to develop iOS 8 based applications involves gaining an understanding of the differences between *Registered Apple Developers* and *iOS Developer Program Members*. Having gained such an understanding, the next choice is to decide the point at which it makes sense for you to pay to join the iOS Developer Program. With these goals in mind, this chapter will cover the differences between the two categories of developer, outline the costs and benefits of joining the developer program and, finally, walk through the steps involved in obtaining each membership level.

2.1 Registered Apple Developer

There is no fee associated with becoming a registered Apple developer. Simply visit the following web page to begin the registration process:

http://developer.apple.com/programs/register/

An existing Apple ID (used for making iTunes or App Store purchases) is usually adequate to complete the registration process.

Once the registration process is complete, access is provided to developer resources such as online documentation and tutorials. Registered developers are also able to download older versions of the iOS SDK and Xcode development environment.

2.2 Downloading Xcode 6 and the iOS 8 SDK

The latest versions of both the iOS SDK and Xcode can be downloaded free of charge from the Mac App Store. Since the tools are free, this raises the question of whether to upgrade to the iOS Developer Program, or to remain as a Registered Apple Developer. It is important, therefore, to understand the key benefits of the iOS Developer Program.

2.3 iOS Developer Program

Membership in the iOS Developer Program currently costs $99 per year. As previously mentioned, membership includes access to the latest versions of the iOS SDK and Xcode development environment. The benefits of membership, however, go far beyond those offered at the Registered Apple Developer level.

One of the key advantages of the developer program is that it permits the creation of certificates and provisioning profiles to test applications on physical devices. Although Xcode includes device simulators which allow for a significant amount of testing to be performed, there are certain areas of functionality, such as location tracking, TouchID authentication and device motion, which can only fully be tested on a physical device. Of particular significance is the fact that some aspects of iCloud access, Reminders and In-App Purchasing can only be tested when applications are running on physical devices.

Of further significance is the fact that iOS Developer Program members have unrestricted access to the full range of guides and tutorials relating to the latest iOS SDK and, more importantly, have access to technical support from Apple's iOS technical support engineers (though the annual fee covers the submission of only two support incident reports).

By far the most important aspect of the iOS Developer Program is that membership is a mandatory requirement in order to publish an application for sale or download in the App Store.

Clearly, developer program membership is going to be required at some point before your application reaches the App Store. The only question remaining is when exactly to sign up.

2.4 **When to Enroll in the iOS Developer Program?**

Clearly, there are many benefits to iOS Developer Program membership and, eventually, membership will be necessary to begin selling applications. As to whether or not to pay the enrollment fee now or later will depend on individual circumstances. If you are still in the early stages of learning to develop iOS applications or have yet to come up with a compelling idea for an application to develop then much of what you need is provided in the Registered Apple Developer package. As your skill level increases and your ideas for applications to develop take shape you can, after all, always enroll in the developer program at a later date.

If, on the other hand, you are confident that you will reach the stage of having an application ready to publish or know that you will need to test the functionality of the application on a physical device as opposed to a simulator then it is worth joining the developer program sooner rather than later.

2.5 **Enrolling in the iOS Developer Program**

If your goal is to develop iOS applications for your employer then it is first worth checking whether the company already has membership. That being the case, contact the program administrator in your company and ask them to send you an invitation from within the iOS Developer Program Member Center to join the team. Once they have done so, Apple will send you an email entitled *You Have Been Invited to Join an Apple Developer Program* containing a link to activate your membership. If you or your company is not already a program member, you can enroll online at:

http://developer.apple.com/programs/ios/

Apple provides enrollment options for businesses and individuals. To enroll as an individual you will need to provide credit card information in order to verify your identity. To enroll as a company you must have legal signature authority (or access to someone who does) and be able to provide documentation such as Articles of Incorporation and a Business License.

Acceptance into the developer program as an individual member typically takes less than 24 hours with notification arriving in the form of an activation email from Apple. Enrollment as a company can take considerably longer (sometimes weeks or even months) due to the burden of the additional verification requirements.

Whilst awaiting activation you may log into the Member Center with restricted access using your Apple ID and password at the following URL:

http://developer.apple.com/membercenter

Once logged in, clicking on the *Your Account* tab at the top of the page will display the prevailing status of your application to join the developer program as *Enrollment Pending*:

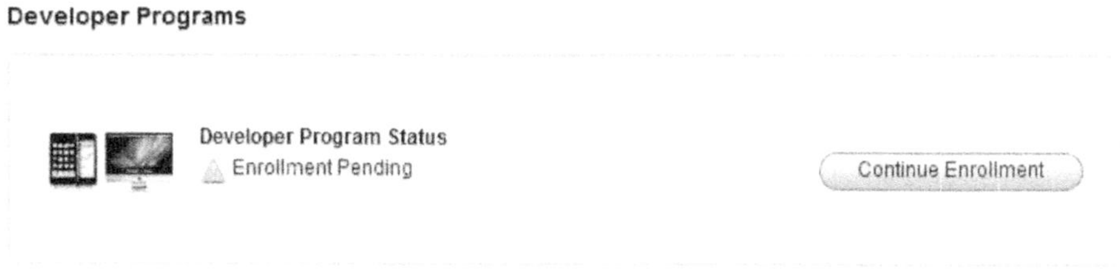

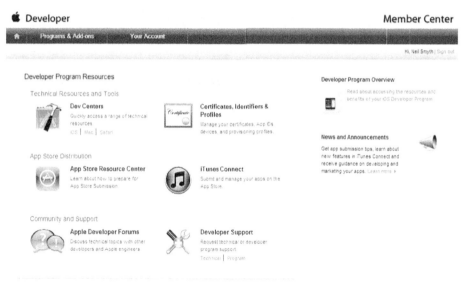

Figure 2-1

Once the activation email has arrived, log into the Member Center again and note that access is now available to a wide range of options and resources as illustrated in Figure 2-2:

Figure 2-2

2.6 **Summary**

An important early step in the iOS 8 application development process involves registering as an Apple Developer and identifying the best time to upgrade to iOS Developer Program membership. This chapter has outlined the differences between the two programs, provided some guidance to keep in mind when considering developer program membership and walked briefly through the enrollment process. The next step is to download and install the iOS 8 SDK and Xcode 6 development environment.

3. Installing Xcode 6 and the iOS 8 SDK

iOS apps are developed using the iOS SDK in conjunction with Apple's Xcode 6.x development environment. Xcode 6 is an integrated development environment (IDE) within which you will code, compile, test and debug your iOS applications. The Xcode 6 environment also includes a feature called Interface Builder which enables you to graphically design the user interface of your application using the components provided by the UIKit Framework.

In this chapter we will cover the steps involved in installing both Xcode 6 and the iOS 8 SDK on Mac OS X.

3.1 Identifying if you have an Intel or PowerPC based Mac

Only Intel based Mac OS X systems can be used to develop applications for iOS. If you have an older, PowerPC based Mac then you will need to purchase a new system before you can begin your iOS app development project. If you are unsure of the processor type inside your Mac, you can find this information by clicking on the Apple menu in the top left hand corner of the screen and selecting the *About This Mac* option from the menu. In the resulting dialog check the *Processor* line. Figure 3-1 illustrates the results obtained on an Intel based system.

If the dialog on your Mac does not reflect the presence of an Intel based processor then your current system is, sadly, unsuitable as a platform for iOS app development.

In addition, the iOS 8 SDK with Xcode 6 environment requires that the version of Mac OS X running on the system be version 10.9.4 or later. If the "About This Mac" dialog does not indicate that Mac OS X 10.9.4 or later is running, click on the *Software Update...* button to download and install the appropriate operating system upgrades.

Figure 3-1

3.2 **Installing Xcode 6 and the iOS 8 SDK**

The best way to obtain the latest versions of Xcode and the iOS SDK is to download them from the Apple Mac App Store. Launch the App Store on your Mac OS X system, enter Xcode into the search box and click on the *Free* button to initiate the installation.

The download is several Gigabytes in size and may take a number of hours to complete depending on the speed of your internet connection.

3.3 **Starting Xcode**

Having successfully installed the SDK and Xcode, the next step is to launch it so that we can create a sample iOS 8 application. To start up Xcode, open the Finder and search for *Xcode*. Since you will be making frequent use of this tool take this opportunity to drag and drop it into your dock for easier access in the future. Click on the Xcode icon in the dock to launch the tool. The first time Xcode runs you may be prompted to install additional components. Follow these steps, entering your username and password when prompted to do so.

Once Xcode has loaded, and assuming this is the first time you have used Xcode on this system, you will be presented with the *Welcome* screen from which you are ready to proceed:

Figure 3-2

Having installed the iOS 8 SDK and successfully launched Xcode 6 we can now look at Xcode 6 in more detail.

4. A Guided Tour of Xcode 6

Just about every activity related to developing and testing iOS applications involves the use of the Xcode environment. This chapter is intended to serve two purposes. Primarily it is intended to provide an overview of many of the key areas that comprise the Xcode development environment. In the course of providing this overview, the chapter will also work through the creation of a very simple iOS application project designed to display a label which reads "Hello World" on a colored background.

By the end of this chapter you will have a basic familiarity with Xcode and your first running iOS application.

4.1 Starting Xcode 6

As with all iOS examples in this book, the development of our example will take place within the Xcode 6 development environment. If you have not already installed this tool together with the latest iOS SDK refer first to the *Installing Xcode 6 and the iOS 8 SDK* chapter of this book. Assuming that the installation is complete, launch Xcode either by clicking on the icon on the dock (assuming you created one) or use the Mac OS X Finder to locate Xcode in the Applications folder of your system.

When launched for the first time, and until you turn off the *Show this window when Xcode launches* toggle, the screen illustrated in Figure 4-1 will appear by default:

Figure 4-1

If you do not see this window, simply select the *Window -> Welcome to Xcode* menu option to display it. From within this window, click on the option to *Create a new Xcode project*. This will display the main Xcode 6 project window together with the *project template* panel where we are able to select a template matching the type of project we want to develop:

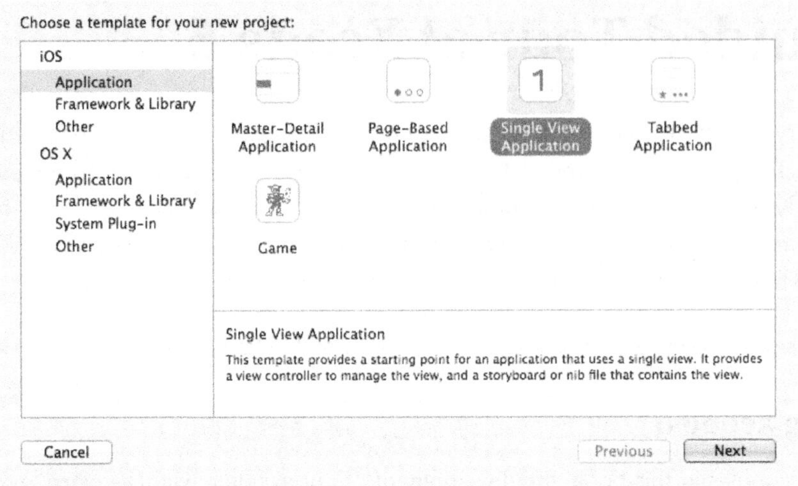

Figure 4-2

The panel located on the left hand side of the window allows for the selection of the target platform, providing options to develop an application either for iOS based devices or Mac OS X.

Begin by making sure that the *Application* option located beneath *iOS* is selected. The main panel contains a list of templates available to use as the basis for an application. The options available are as follows:

- **Master-Detail Application** – Used to create a list based application. Selecting an item from a master list displays a detail view corresponding to the selection. The template then provides a *Back* button to return to the list. You may have seen a similar technique used for news based applications, whereby selecting an item from a list of headlines displays the content of the corresponding news article. When used for an iPad based application this template implements a basic split-view configuration.

- **Page-based Application** – Creates a template project using the page view controller designed to allow views to be transitioned by turning pages on the screen.

- **Tabbed Application** – Creates a template application with a tab bar. The tab bar typically appears across the bottom of the device display and can be programmed to contain items that, when selected, change the main display to different views. The iPhone's built-in *Phone* user interface, for example, uses a tab bar to allow the user to move between favorites, contacts, keypad and voicemail.

- **Single View Application** – Creates a basic template for an application containing a single view and corresponding view controller.

- **Game** – Creates a project configured to take advantage of Sprite Kit, Scene Kit, OpenGL ES and Metal for the development of 2D and 3D games.

For the purposes of our simple example, we are going to use the *Single View Application* template so select this option from the new project window and click *Next* to configure some more project options:

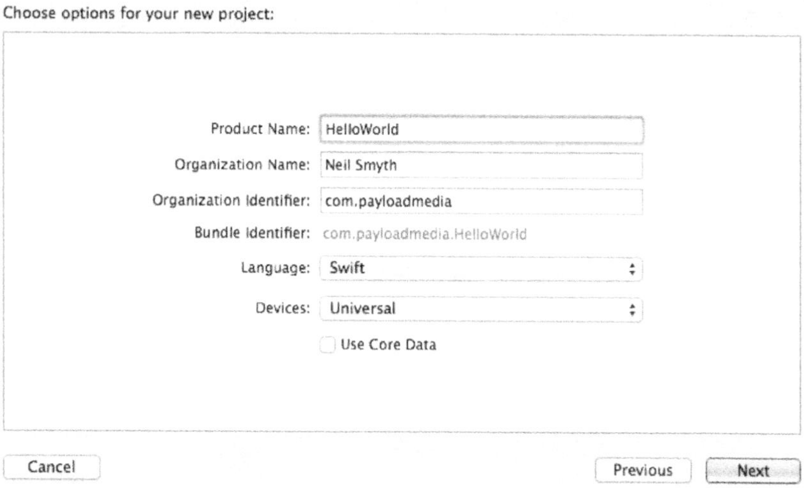

Choose options for your new project:

Product Name:	HelloWorld
Organization Name:	Neil Smyth
Organization Identifier:	com.payloadmedia
Bundle Identifier:	com.payloadmedia.HelloWorld
Language:	Swift
Devices:	Universal
	☐ Use Core Data

Cancel   Previous   Next

Figure 4-3

On this screen, enter a Product name for the application that is going to be created, in this case "HelloWorld". The company identifier is typically the reversed URL of your company's website, for example "com.mycompany". This will be used when creating provisioning profiles and certificates to enable applications to be tested on a physical iPhone or iPad device (covered in more detail in *Testing Apps on iOS 8 Devices with Xcode 6*).

The iOS ecosystem now includes a variety of devices and screen sizes. When creating a new project it is possible to indicate that the project is intended to target either the iPhone or iPad family of devices. With the gap between iPad and iPhone screen sizes now reduced by the introduction of the iPad Mini and iPhone 6 Plus it no longer makes sense to create a project that targets just one device family. A much more sensible approach is to create a single project that addresses all device types and screen sizes. In fact, as will be shown in later chapters, Xcode 6 and iOS 8 include a number of features designed specifically to make the goal of *universal* application projects easy to achieve. With this in mind, make sure that the *Devices* menu is set to *Universal*.

Along with iOS 8 and Xcode 6, Apple has also introduced a new programming language named *Swift*. Whilst it is still possible to program using the older Objective-C language, Apple considers Swift to be the future of iOS development. All the code examples in this book are written in Swift, so make sure that the *Language* menu is set accordingly before clicking on the *Next* button.

On the final screen, choose a location on the file system for the new project to be created and click on *Create*.

Once the new project has been created, the main Xcode window will appear as illustrated in Figure 4-4:

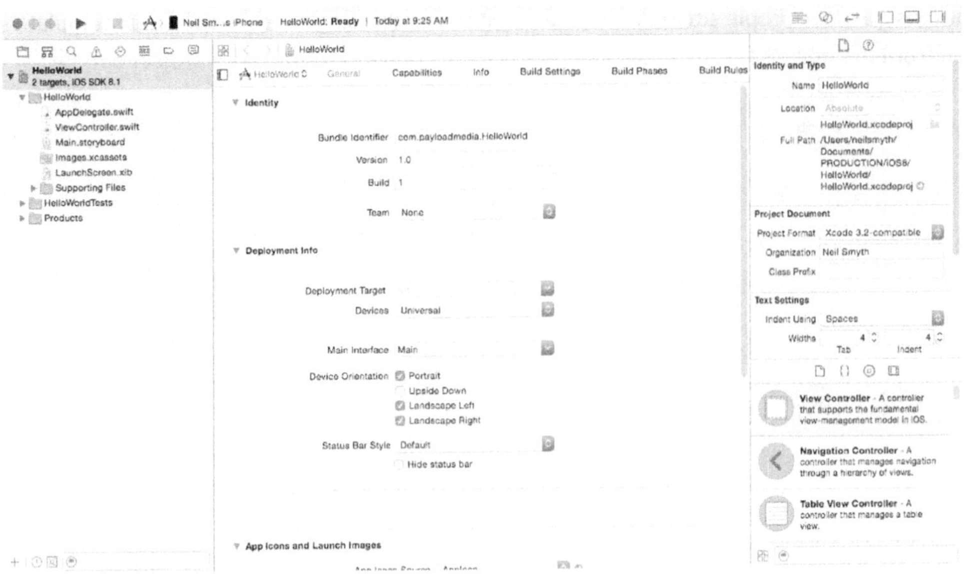

Figure 4-4

Before proceeding we should take some time to look at what Xcode has done for us. Firstly it has created a group of files that we will need to create our application. Some of these are Swift source code files (with a .swift extension) where we will enter the code to make our application work.

In addition, the *Main.storyboard* file is the save file used by the Interface Builder tool to hold the user interface design we will create. A second Interface builder file named *LaunchScreen.xib* will also have been added to the project. This contains the user interface layout design for the screen which appears on the device while the application is loading.

Also present will be one or more files with a .plist file extension. These are *Property List* files which contain key/value pair information. For example, the *Info.plist* file in the *Supporting Files* folder contains resource settings relating to items such as the language, executable name and app identifier. The list of files is displayed in the *Project Navigator* located in the left hand panel of the main Xcode project window. A toolbar at the top of this panel contains options to display other information such as build and run history, breakpoints and compilation errors.

By default, the center panel of the window shows a general summary of the settings for the application project. This includes the identifier specified during the project creation process and the target device. Options are also provided to configure the orientations of the device that are to be supported by the application together with options to upload icons (the small images the user selects on the device screen to launch the application) and launch screen images (displayed to the user while the application loads) for the application.

In addition to the General screen, tabs are provided to view and modify additional settings consisting of Capabilities, Info, Build Settings, Build Phases and Build Rules. As we progress through subsequent chapters of this book we will explore some of these other configuration options in greater detail. To return to the project settings panel at any future point in time, make sure the *Project Navigator* is selected in the left hand panel and select the top item (the application name) in the navigator list.

When a source file is selected from the list in the navigator panel, the contents of that file will appear in the center panel where it may then be edited. To open the file in a separate editing window, simply double click on the file in the list.

4.2 Creating the iOS App User Interface

Simply by the very nature of the environment in which they run, iOS apps are typically visually oriented. As such, a key component of just about any app involves a user interface through which the user will interact with the application and, in turn, receive feedback. Whilst it is possible to develop user interfaces by writing code to create and position items on the screen, this is a complex and error prone process. In recognition of this, Apple provides a tool called Interface Builder which allows a user interface to be visually constructed by dragging and dropping components onto a canvas and setting properties to configure the appearance and behavior of those components. Interface Builder was originally developed some time ago for creating Mac OS X applications, but has now been updated to allow for the design of iOS app user interfaces.

As mentioned in the preceding section, Xcode pre-created a number of files for our project, one of which has a .storyboard filename extension. This is an Interface Builder storyboard save file and the file we are interested in for our HelloWorld project is named *Main.storyboard.* To load this file into Interface Builder simply select the file name in the list in the left hand panel. Interface Builder will subsequently appear in the center panel as shown in Figure 4-5:

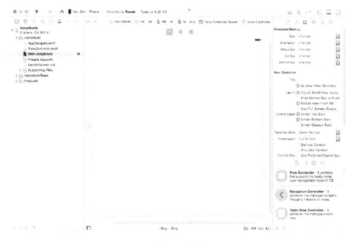

Figure 4-5

In the center panel a visual representation of the user interface of the application is displayed. Initially this consists solely of the UIView object. This *UIView* object was added to our design by Xcode when we selected the Single View Application option during the project creation phase. We will construct the user interface for our HelloWorld app by dragging and dropping user interface objects onto this UIView object. Designing a user interface consists primarily of dragging and dropping visual components onto the canvas and setting a range of properties and settings. In order to access objects and property settings it is necessary to display the Xcode right hand panel (if it is not already displayed). This panel is referred to as the *Utilities panel* and can be displayed by selecting the right hand button in the right hand section of the Xcode toolbar:

Figure 4-6

The Utilities panel, once displayed, will appear as illustrated in Figure 4-7:

Figure 4-7

Along the top edge of the panel is a row of buttons which change the settings displayed in the upper half of the panel. By default the *File Inspector* is displayed. Options are also provided to display quick help, the *Identity Inspector*, *Attributes Inspector*, *Size Inspector* and *Connections Inspector*. Before proceeding, take some time to review each of these selections to gain some familiarity with the configuration options each provides. Throughout the remainder of this book extensive use of these inspectors will be made.

The lower section of the panel may default to displaying the file template library. Above this panel is another toolbar containing buttons to display other categories. Options include frequently used code snippets to save on typing when writing code, the Object Library and the Media Library. For the purposes of this tutorial we need to display the Object Library so click on the appropriate toolbar button (represented by the circle with a small square in the center). This will display the UI components that can be used to construct our user interface. Move the cursor to the line above the lower toolbar and click and drag to increase the amount of space available for the library if required. The layout of the items in the library may also be switched from a single column of objects with descriptions to multiple columns without descriptions by clicking on the button located in the bottom left hand corner of the panel and to the left of the search box.

4.3 **Changing Component Properties**

With the property panel for the View selected in the main panel, we will begin our design work by changing the background color of this view. Start by making sure the View is selected and that the Attributes Inspector (*View -> Utilities -> Show Attributes Inspector*) is displayed in the Utilities panel. Click on the white rectangle next to the *Background* label to invoke the *Colors* dialog. Using the color selection tool, choose a visually pleasing color and close the dialog. You will now notice that the view window has changed from white to the new color selection.

4.4 **Adding Objects to the User Interface**

The next step is to add a Label object to our view. To achieve this, either scroll down the list of objects in the Object Library panel to locate the Label object or, as illustrated in Figure 4-8, enter *Label* into the search box beneath the panel:

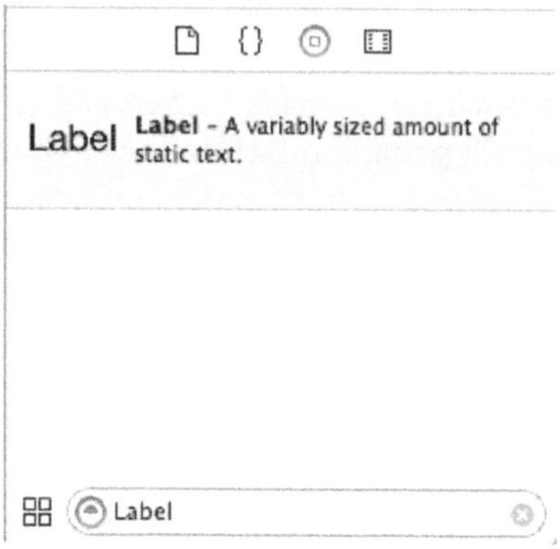

Figure 4-8

Having located the Label object, click on it and drag it to the center of the view so that the vertical and horizontal center guidelines appear. Once it is in position release the mouse button to drop it at that location. Cancel the Object Library search by clicking on the "x" button on the right hand edge of the search field. Select the newly added label and stretch it horizontally so that it is approximately three times the current width. With the Label still selected, click on the centered alignment button in the Attributes Inspector (*View -> Utilities -> Show Attributes Inspector*) to center the text in the middle of the label view.

Figure 4-9

Double click on the text in the label that currently reads "Label" and type in "Hello World". Locate the font setting property in the Attributes Inspector panel and click on the "T" button next to the font name to display the font selection menu. Change the Font setting from *System – System* to *Custom* and choose a larger font setting, for example a Georgia bold typeface with a size of 24 as shown in Figure 4-10:

Figure 4-10

The final step is to add some layout constraints to ensure that the label remains centered within the containing view regardless of the size of screen on which the application ultimately runs. This involves the use of the Auto Layout capabilities of iOS, a topic which will be covered extensively in later chapters. For this example, simply select the Label object, display the Align menu as shown in Figure 4-11 and enable both the *Horizontal Center in Container* and *Vertical Center in Container* options before clicking on the *Add 2 Constraints* button.

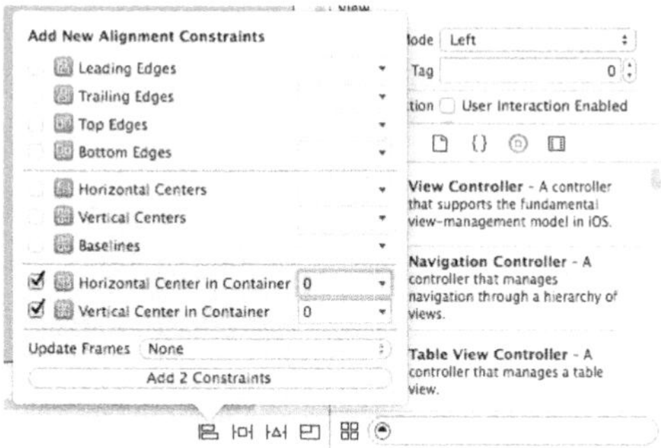

Figure 4-11

With the label still selected, display the *Pin* menu, enable the *Width* constraint and set the *Update Frames* menu to *All Frames in Container* before clicking on the *Add 1 Constraint* button. This will set the label to a specific width and update the storyboard view so that these new constraints are reflected in the layout.

Figure 4-12

At this point, your View window will hopefully appear as outlined in Figure 4-13 (allowing, of course, for differences in your color and font choices).

Figure 4-13

Before building and running the project it is worth taking a short detour to look at the Xcode *Document Outline* panel. This panel appears by default to the left of the Interface Builder panel and is controlled by the small button in the bottom left hand corner (indicated by the arrow in Figure 4-14) of the Interface Builder panel.

Figure 4-14

When displayed, the document outline shows a hierarchical overview of the elements that make up a user interface layout together with any constraints that have been applied to views in the layout.

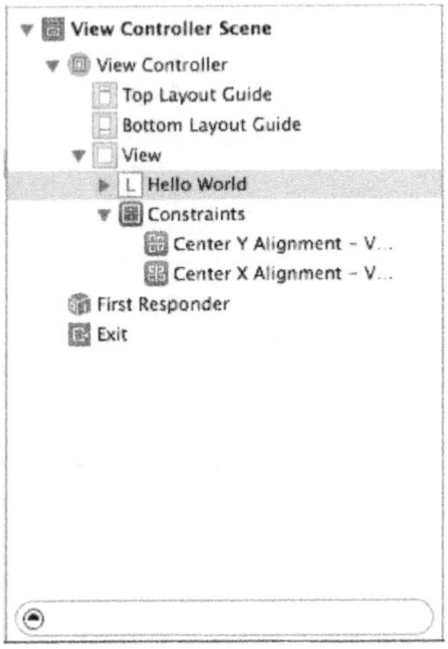

Figure 4-15

4.5 Building and Running an iOS 8 App in Xcode 6

Before an app can be run it must first be compiled. Once successfully compiled it may be run either within a simulator or on a physical iPhone, iPad or iPod Touch device. The process for testing an app on a physical device requires some additional steps to be performed involving developer certificates and provisioning profiles and will be covered in detail in *Testing Apps on iOS 8 Devices with Xcode 6*. For the purposes of this chapter, however, it is sufficient to run the app in the simulator.

Within the main Xcode 6 project window, make sure that the menu located in the top left hand corner of the window (marked C in Figure 4-16) has the *iPhone 6* simulator option selected:

Figure 4-16

Click on the *Run* toolbar button (A) to compile the code and run the app in the simulator. The small panel in the center of the Xcode toolbar (D) will report the progress of the build process together with any problems or errors that cause the build process to fail. Once the app is built, the simulator will start and the HelloWorld app will run:

Figure 4-17

Note that the user interface appears as designed in the Interface Builder tool. Click on the stop button (B), change the target menu from iPhone 6 to iPad Air 2 and run the application again. Once again, the label will appear centered in the screen even with the larger screen size. Finally, verify that the layout is correct in landscape orientation by using the *Hardware -> Rotate Left* menu option. This indicates that the Auto Layout constraints are working and that we have designed a *universal* user interface for the project.

4.6 **Dealing with Build Errors**

As we have not actually written or modified any code in this chapter it is unlikely that any errors will be detected during the build and run process. In the unlikely event that something did get inadvertently changed thereby causing the build to fail it is worth taking a few minutes to talk about build errors within the context of the Xcode environment.

If for any reason a build fails, the status window in the Xcode toolbar will report that an error has been detected by displaying "Build" together with the number of errors detected and any warnings. In addition, the left hand panel of the Xcode window will update with a list of the errors. Selecting an error from this list will take you to the location in the code where corrective action needs to be taken.

4.7 **Monitoring Application Performance**

Another useful feature of Xcode is the ability to monitor the performance of an application while it is running. This information is accessed by displaying the *Debug Navigator*.

When Xcode is launched, the project navigator is displayed in the left hand panel by default. Along the top of this panel is a bar with a range of other options. The sixth option from the left displays the debug navigator when selected as illustrated in Figure 4-18. When displayed, this panel shows a number of real-time statistics relating to the performance of the currently running application such as memory, CPU usage, disk access, network activity and iCloud storage access.

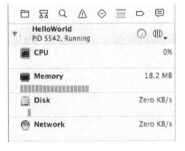

Figure 4-18

When one of these categories is selected, the main panel (Figure 4-19) updates to provide additional information about that particular aspect of the application's performance:

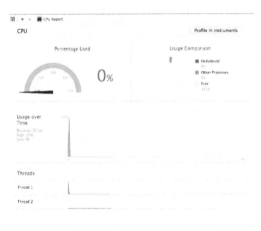

Figure 4-19

Yet more information can be obtained by clicking on the *Profile in Instruments* button in the top right hand corner of the panel.

4.8 An Exploded View of the User Interface Layout Hierarchy

Xcode 6 also provides an option to break the user interface layout out into a rotatable 3D view that shows how the view hierarchy for a user interface is constructed. This can be particularly useful for identifying situations where one view object is obscured by another appearing on top of it or a layout is not appearing as intended. To access the View Hierarchy in this mode, run the application and click on the *Debug View Hierarchy* button highlighted in Figure 4-20:

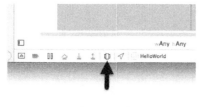

Figure 4-20

Once activated, a 3D "exploded" view of the layout will appear and may be used for design and debugging work. Figure 4-21 shows an example layout in this mode for a slightly more complex user interface than that created in this chapter:

Figure 4-21

4.9 Summary

Applications are primarily created within the Xcode development environment. This chapter has served to provide a basic overview of the Xcode environment and to work through the creation of a very simple example application. Finally, a brief overview was provided of some of the performance monitoring features in Xcode 6. Many more features and capabilities of Xcode and Interface Builder will be covered in subsequent chapters of the book.

5. Testing Apps on iOS 8 Devices with Xcode 6

In the chapter entitled *A Guided Tour of Xcode 6* we were able to run an application in the iOS Simulator environment bundled with the iOS 8 SDK. Whilst this is fine for most cases, in practice there are a number of areas that cannot be comprehensively tested in the simulator. For example, no matter how hard you shake your computer (not something we actually recommend) or where in the world you move it to, neither the accelerometer nor GPS features will provide real world results within the simulator (though the simulator does have the option to perform a basic virtual shake gesture and to simulate location data). If we really want to test an iOS application thoroughly in the real world, therefore, we need to install the app onto a physical iOS device.

Many new features have been added to Xcode 6 to make the task of the developer easier. One of these features makes it considerably easier to obtain the signing certificates and provisioning profiles that are necessary to perform testing of applications on physical iOS devices.

A previous edition of this book, which was based on Xcode 4, dedicated no less than 11 pages to the process of obtaining a developer certificate, App ID and provisioning profile to test an application on a physical iOS device. Much of this work is now performed automatically by Xcode resulting in a much simpler path to testing applications on iOS devices.

5.1 Configuring Xcode with Apple IDs

The first step in setting up a fully configured development environment involves entering the Apple ID associated with your Apple Developer Program membership.

To enter this information, start Xcode and select the *Xcode -> Preferences...* menu option. From within the preferences window, select the *Accounts* tab as illustrated in Figure 5-1:

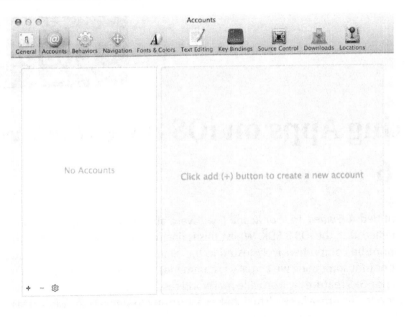

Figure 5-1

To add an Apple ID, click on the + button in the lower left hand corner and select *Add Apple ID...* from the drop down menu. When prompted to do so (Figure 5-2), either enter the Apple ID and password associated with your Apple Developer Program membership, or click on the *Join a Program...* button if you are not yet a member.

Figure 5-2

Repeat these steps to add additional Apple IDs if you are associated with more than one development team. Once the information has been entered, the accounts will be listed in the preferences window.

5.2 Generating Signing Identities

Before an application can be run on a physical iOS device for testing purposes it must first be signed with a *developer signing identity*. When the application is finished and ready to be placed on sale in the App Store it must then be signed with a *distribution signing identity*. Signing identities are comprised of a certificate and a private key.

Signing identities can be generated from within the Xcode account preferences panel. Begin by selecting the Apple ID for which the identities are to be generated before clicking on the *View Details...* button located in the lower right hand corner of the window. This will display a list of signing identities and any provisioning profiles associated with those identities. If no valid signing identities are listed (as is the case in Figure 5-3), the next step is to generate them.

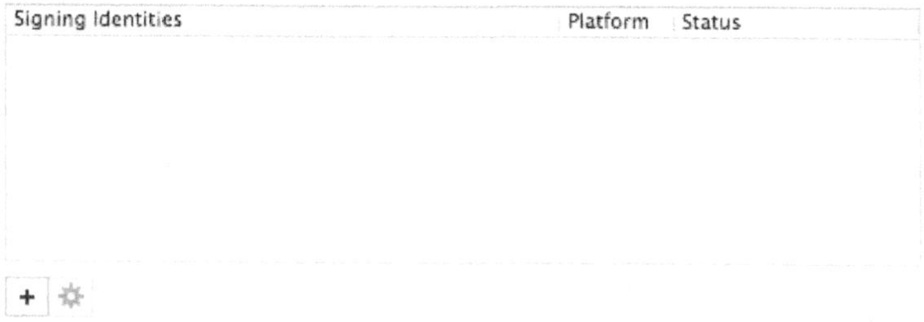

Signing Identities	Platform	Status

+ ☼

Figure 5-3

Begin by clicking on the + button and selecting the *iOS Development* option from the resulting menu. Xcode will then contact the Apple Developer Member Center portal and request and download a developer signing identity. Repeat these steps, this time selecting *iOS Distribution* from the menu to create and download a distribution signing identity. Once completed, the two identities should now be listed as shown in Figure 5-4:

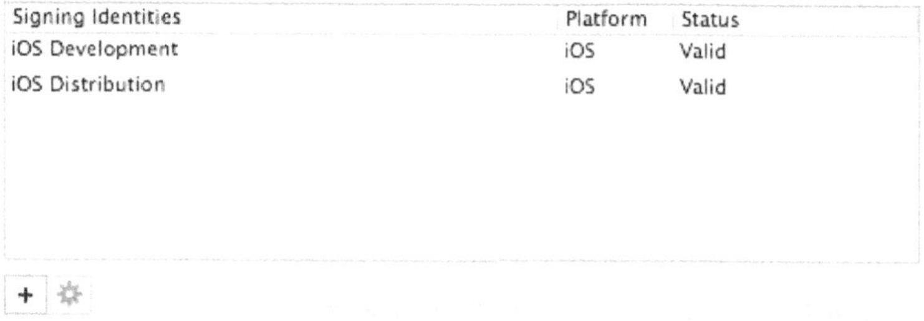

Signing Identities	Platform	Status
iOS Development	iOS	Valid
iOS Distribution	iOS	Valid

+ ☼

Figure 5-4

Once created, signing identities and account information can be migrated to other development computer systems by clicking on the button displaying a gear cog on the first account settings page and selecting the *Export Accounts...* menu option. On the destination system repeat these steps, this time selecting the *Import Accounts...* option.

It is worth noting that the certificates associated with the signing identities can also be viewed and created within the Apple Developer Member Center portal. Within a browser, navigate to the following URL and log in using your Apple ID credentials:

https://developer.apple.com/membercenter

Within the member center, click on the Certificates, Identifiers and Profiles option and choose *Certificates* from the list of options under the *iOS Apps* category. On the resulting page, the certificates for both signing identifiers should be listed. Clicking on a certificate will display details such as the expiration date as outlined in Figure 5-5:

Figure 5-5

As can be seen in the left hand panel of Figure 5-5, the member center also provides options to manually create App IDs and Provisioning Profiles. With Xcode 6, however, these are typically created automatically.

5.3 Device Registration

Having generated signing identities the next step is to register a device for testing purposes. With the introduction of Xcode 6, device registration takes place automatically when an iPhone or iPad device is connected to the development system. Simply run Xcode, attach the device to the computer and wait for it to appear as an option on the *run destinations* menu. Figure 5-6, for example, shows two physical devices available for testing together with the standard iOS Simulator options:

Figure 5-6

Details of the devices connected to the system can be obtained via the Xcode Devices window (*Window -> Devices*) as shown in Figure 5-7:

Figure 5-7

To exclude a connected device from the list of potential targets on the device scheme menu, select the device from the Devices screen and use the settings menu in the bottom left hand corner of the window to deselect the *Show in Run Destinations Menu* option:

Figure 5-8

5.4 **Manually Adding Test Devices**

In addition to allowing Xcode to automatically register connected devices for testing purposes, it is also possible to manually enter devices from within the Developer Portal. This is a useful option when the device is not currently available to be attached to the development system for registration (perhaps it belongs to a co-worker who has volunteered to perform some app testing).

To manually register a device, the UDID of that device is required. This can be obtained from the Xcode Devices window or from within iTunes when the device is attached. To find the UDID from within iTunes, connect the device, select it in iTunes and display the Summary screen. By default the summary screen will display the device serial number. Clicking on this number will cycle through a number of different values, eventually listing the UDID:

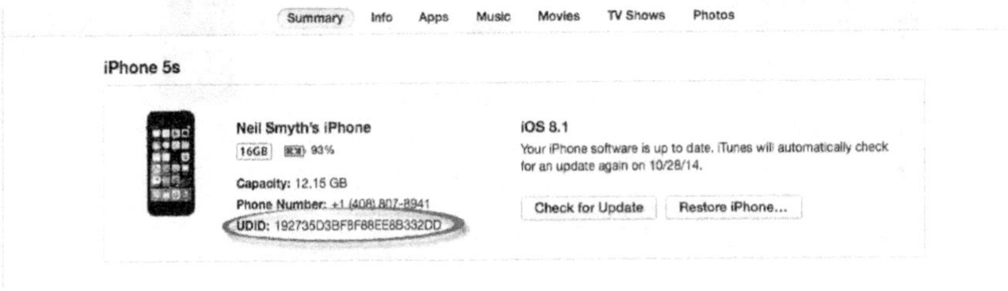

Figure 5-9

Once the UDID of the device has been obtained, log into the Apple Developer Member Center portal, select the *Certificates, Identifiers & Profiles* option and on the resulting page choose the *Devices* option listed under *iOS Apps*.

On the *iOS Devices* screen, click on the + button to add a new device and enter a name for the device and the UDID into the *Register Device* section:

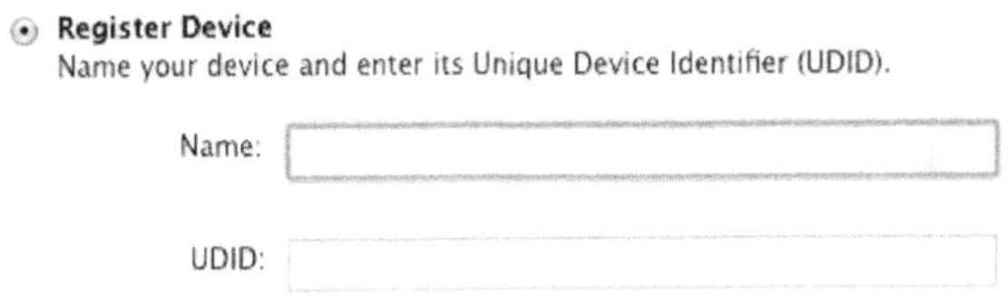

Register Device
Name your device and enter its Unique Device Identifier (UDID).

Name:

UDID:

Figure 5-10

5.5 Running an Application on a Registered Device

With a registered device connected to the development system, and an application ready for testing, refer to the device menu located in the Xcode toolbar. There is a reasonable chance that this will have defaulted to one of the iOS Simulator configurations (in the case of Figure 5-11, this is the iPhone 6 simulator).

Figure 5-11

Switch to the physical device by selecting this menu and changing it to the device name as shown in Figure 5-12:

Figure 5-12

Xcode will request a provisioning profile that matches the App ID of the application and includes permission to run on the specified device, build the application using the developer signing identity before installing the application and provisioning profile on the device. Finally the application will be launched on the device.

5.6 Summary

Without question, the iOS Simulator included with the iOS 8 SDK is an invaluable tool for testing applications during the development process. There are, however, a number of situations where it is necessary to test an application on a physical iOS device. In this chapter we have covered the steps involved in provisioning applications for installation and testing on iPhone and iPad devices.

6. An Introduction to Swift Playgrounds

Along with iOS 8 and Xcode 6, Apple has introduced the new Swift programming language. Intended as a replacement for Objective-C as the basis for developing iOS apps, the significance of this new language is such that nine chapters of this book are dedicated solely to introducing the basics of Swift. In addition, all of the code examples in this book have been developed entirely using this new programming language.

Before introducing the Swift programming language in the chapters that follow, however, it is first worth learning about a feature known as *Swift playgrounds*. Playgrounds are another new feature introduced in Xcode 6 that make learning Swift and experimenting with the iOS 8 SDK much easier. The concepts covered in this chapter can be put to use when experimenting with many of the introductory Swift code examples contained in the chapters that follow.

6.1 What is a Swift Playground?

A playground is an interactive environment where Swift code can be entered and executed with the results appearing in real-time. This makes an ideal environment in which to learn the syntax of Swift without the need to work continuously through the edit/compile/run/debug cycle that would ordinarily accompany a standard Xcode iOS project.

6.2 Creating a New Swift Playground

To create a new Playground, start Xcode and select the *Get started with a playground* option from the welcome screen or select the *File -> New -> Playground* menu option. On the resulting options screen, name the playground *LearnSwift* and set the Platform menu to *iOS*. Click *Next* and choose a suitable file system location into which the playground should be saved.

Once the playground has been created, the following screen will appear ready for Swift code to be entered:

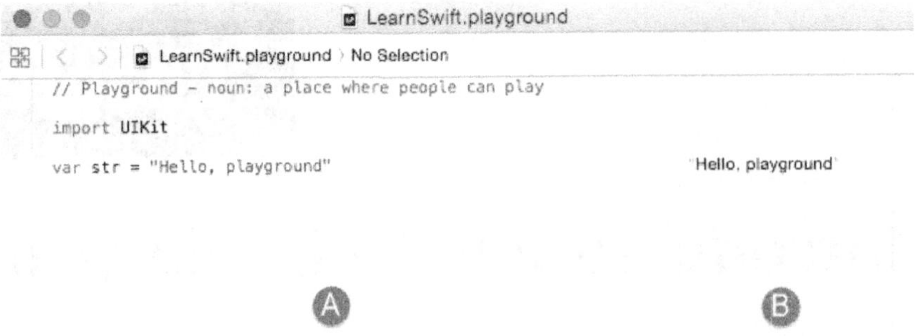

```
                                    LearnSwift.playground
        <    >    LearnSwift.playground > No Selection
        // Playground - noun: a place where people can play

        import UIKit

        var str = "Hello, playground"                                    Hello, playground
```

Ⓐ   Ⓑ

Figure 6-1

The panel on the left hand side of the window (marked A in Figure 6-1) is the *playground editor* where the lines of Swift code are entered. The right hand panel (marked B) is referred to as the *results panel* and is where the results of each Swift expression entered into the playground editor panel are displayed.

By far the quickest way to gain familiarity with the playground environment is to work through some simple examples.

6.3 **A Basic Swift Playground Example**

Perhaps the simplest of examples in any programming language (that at least does something tangible) is to write some code to output a single line of text. Swift is no exception to this rule so, within the playground window, begin by deleting the current Swift expression from the editor panel:

```
var str = "Hello, playground"
```

Next, enter a line of Swift code that reads as follows:

```
println("Welcome to Swift")
```

All that the code does is make a call to the built-in Swift *println* function which takes as a parameter a string of characters to be displayed on the console. Those familiar with other programming languages will note the absence of a semi-colon at the end of the line of code. In Swift, semi-colons are optional and generally only used as a separator when multiple statements occupy the same line of code.

Note that after entering the line of code, the results panel to the right of the editing panel is now showing the output from the println call as highlighted in Figure 6-2:

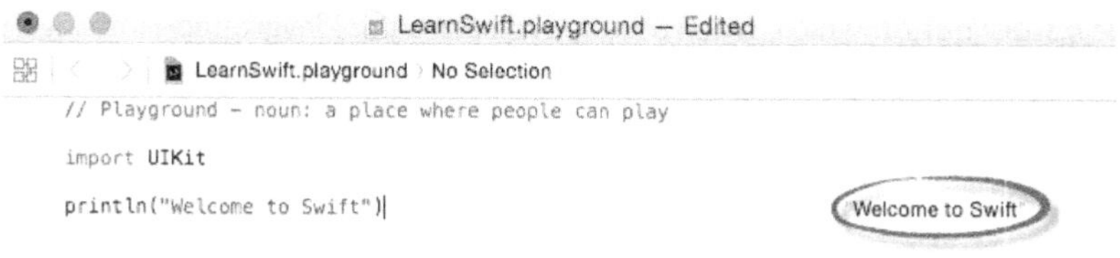

```
●  ●  ●                    ⬚ LearnSwift.playground — Edited
⊞    ⟨    ⟩  ⬚ LearnSwift.playground ⟩ No Selection
     // Playground - noun: a place where people can play

     import UIKit

     println("Welcome to Swift")|                                    ⬭ Welcome to Swift ⬭
```

Figure 6-2

6.4 Playground Timelines

Playgrounds are particularly useful when working and experimenting with Swift algorithms. This can be of particular use when combined with the Playground Timeline Assistant. Remaining within the playground editor, enter the following lines of code beneath the existing println statement:

```
var x = 10

for index in 1...20 {
        let y = index * x--
}
```

This expression repeats a loop 20 times, performing an arithmetic expression on each iteration of the loop. Once the code has been entered into the editor, the playground will execute the loop and display in the results panel the number of times the loop was performed. More interesting information, however, may be obtained by hovering the mouse pointer over the results line so that two additional buttons appear as shown in Figure 6-3:

Figure 6-3

The left most of the two buttons is the *quick look* button which, when selected, will show a popup panel displaying the results. In this context it simply displays the "(20 times)" message again but, as will be shown later, becomes more useful when working with user interface views or graphics drawing code. The right-most button is the *value history* button which, when selected, displays the Playground Timeline Assistant panel. In this case, the timeline panel displays a graph plotting the result values generated within the loop:

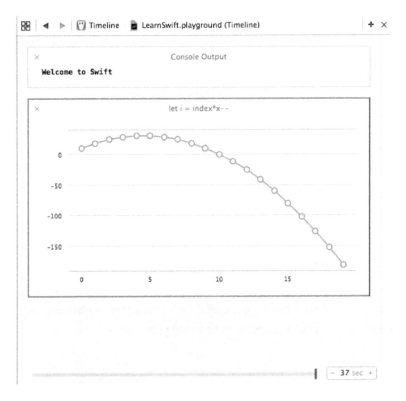

Figure 6-4

The timeline records and displays the value history for all of the expressions in the playground editor panel. Note, for example, that an entry is included for the earlier println statement.

The slider along the bottom edge of the timeline panel can be moved to view the prevailing results at different points in the timeline. Sliding it to the left, for example, will highlight and display the different values in the graph:

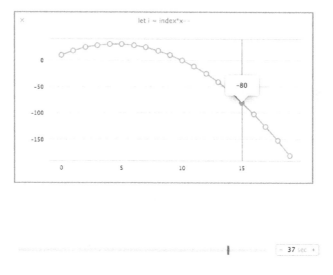

Figure 6-5

6.5 **Working with UIKit in Playgrounds**

The playground environment is not restricted to simple Swift code statements. Much of the power of the iOS 8 SDK is also available for experimentation within a playground.

When the playground used in this chapter was created, it included a line to import the iOS UIKit Framework. The UIKit Framework contains most of the classes necessary to implement user interfaces for iOS applications and is an area which will be covered in significant detail throughout the book. An extremely powerful feature of playgrounds is that it is also possible to work with UIKit along with many of the other Frameworks that comprise the iOS 8 SDK.

The following code, for example, creates a UILabel instance and sets color, text and font properties on it:

```
let myLabel = UILabel(frame: CGRectMake(0, 0, 200, 50))
myLabel.backgroundColor = UIColor.redColor()
myLabel.text = "Hello Swift"
myLabel.textAlignment = .Center
myLabel.font = UIFont(name: "Georgia", size: 24)
myLabel
```

Enter this code into the playground editor and note that the label object appears in the timeline:

Figure 6-6

This is a good example of how the quick look feature can be useful. Each line of the example Swift code configures a different aspect of the appearance of the UILabel instance. Clicking on the quick look button for the first line of code will display an empty view (since the label exists but has yet to be given any visual attributes). Clicking on the quick look button in the line of code which sets the background color, on the other hand, will show the red label:

Figure 6-7

Similarly, the quick look for the line where the text property is set will show the red label with the "Hello Swift" text left aligned:

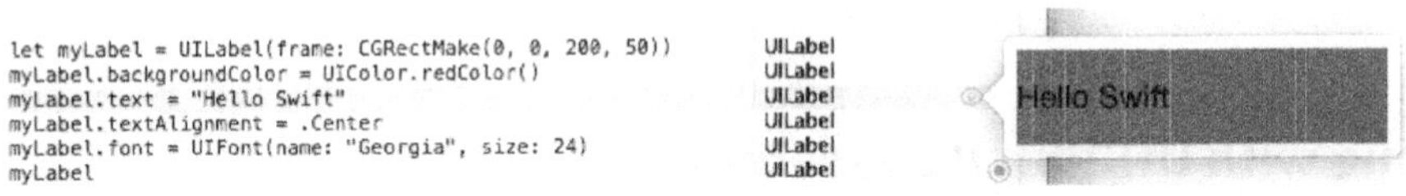

Figure 6-8

The font setting quick look on the other hand displays the UILabel with centered text and the larger Georgia font:

Figure 6-9

6.6 **When to Use Swift Playgrounds**

Clearly Swift Playgrounds provide an ideal environment for learning to program using the Swift programming language and the use of playgrounds in the Swift introductory chapters that follow is recommended.

It is also important to keep in mind that playgrounds will remain useful long after the basics of Swift have been learned and will become increasingly useful when moving on to more advanced areas of iOS development.

The iOS 8 SDK is a vast collection of Frameworks and classes and it is not unusual for even experienced developers to need to experiment with unfamiliar aspects of iOS development before adding code to a project. Historically this has involved creating a temporary iOS Xcode project and then repeatedly looping through the somewhat cumbersome edit, compile, run cycle to arrive at a programming solution. Rather than fall into this habit, consider having a playground on standby to carry out experiments during your project development work.

6.7 **Summary**

This chapter has introduced the concept of Swift playgrounds. Playgrounds provide an environment in which Swift code can be entered and the results of that code viewed dynamically. This provides an excellent environment both for learning the Swift programming language and for experimenting with many of the classes and APIs included in the iOS 8 SDK without the need to create Xcode projects and repeatedly edit, compile and run code.

7. Swift Data Types, Constants and Variables

Prior to the introduction of iOS 8, the stipulated programming language for the development of iOS 8 applications was Objective-C. When Apple announced iOS 8, however, the company also introduced an alternative to Objective-C in the form of the new Swift programming language.

Due entirely to the popularity of iOS, Objective-C has become one of the most widely used programming languages today. With origins firmly rooted in the 40 year-old C Programming Language, however, and in spite of recent efforts to modernize some aspects of the language syntax, Objective-C was beginning to show its age.

Swift, on the other hand, is an entirely new programming language designed specifically to make programming easier, faster and less prone to programmer error. Starting with a clean slate and no burden of legacy, Swift is a new and innovative language with which to develop applications for both iOS and Mac OS X with the advantage that much of the syntax will be familiar to those with experience of other programming languages.

The introduction of Swift aside, it is still perfectly acceptable to continue to develop applications using Objective-C. Indeed, it is also possible to mix both Swift and Objective-C within the same application code base. That being said, Apple clearly sees the future of iOS and Mac OS X development in terms of Swift rather than Objective-C. In recognition of this fact, all of the examples in this book are implemented using Swift. Before moving on to those examples, however, the next several chapters will provide an overview and introduction to Swift programming. The intention of these chapters is to provide enough information so that you can begin to confidently program using Swift. For an exhaustive and in-depth guide to all the features, intricacies and capabilities of Swift, some time spent reading Apple's excellent book entitled "The Swift Programming Language" (available free of charge from within the Apple iBookStore) is strongly recommended.

7.1 Using a Swift Playground

Both this and the following few chapters are intended to introduce the basics of the Swift programming language. As outlined in the previous chapter, entitled *An Introduction to Swift Playgrounds*, the best way to learn Swift is to experiment within a Swift playground environment. Before starting this chapter, therefore, create a new playground and use it to try out the code in both this and the other Swift introduction chapters that follow.

7.2 **Swift Data Types**

When we look at the different types of software that run on computer systems and mobile devices, from financial applications to graphics intensive games, it is easy to forget that computers are really just binary machines. Binary systems work in terms of 0 and 1, true or false, set and unset. All the data sitting in RAM, stored on disk drives and flowing through circuit boards and buses are nothing more than sequences of 1s and 0s. Each 1 or 0 is referred to as a *bit* and bits are grouped together in blocks of 8, each group being referred to as a *byte*. When people talk about 32-bit and 64-bit computer systems they are talking about the number of bits that can be handled simultaneously by the CPU bus. A 64-bit CPU, for example, is able to handle data in 64-bit blocks, resulting in faster performance than a 32-bit based system.

Humans, of course, don't think in binary. We work with decimal numbers, letters and words. In order for a human to easily (easily being a relative term in this context) program a computer, some middle ground between human and computer thinking is needed. This is where programming languages such as Swift come into play. Programming languages allow humans to express instructions to a computer in terms and structures we understand, and then compile that down to a format that can be executed by a CPU.

One of the fundamentals of any program involves data, and programming languages such as Swift define a set of *data types* that allow us to work with data in a format we understand when programming. For example, if we want to store a number in a Swift program we could do so with syntax similar to the following:

```
var mynumber = 10
```

In the above example, we have created a variable named *mynumber* and then assigned to it the value of 10. When we compile the source code down to the machine code used by the CPU, the number 10 is seen by the computer in binary as:

```
1010
```

Similarly, we can express a letter, the visual representation of a digit ('0' through to '9') or punctuation mark (referred to in computer terminology as *characters*) using the following syntax:

```
var myletter = "c"
```

Once again, this is understandable by a human programmer, but gets compiled down to a binary sequence for the CPU to understand. In this case, the letter 'c' is represented by the decimal number 99 using the ASCII table (an internationally recognized standard that assigns numeric values to human readable characters). When converted to binary, it is stored as:

```
10101100011
```

Now that we have a basic understanding of the concept of data types and why they are necessary we can take a closer look at some of the more commonly used data types supported by Swift.

7.2.1 Integer Data Types

Swift integer data types are used to store whole numbers (in other words a number with no decimal places). Integers can be *signed* (capable of storing positive, negative and zero values) or *unsigned* (positive and zero values only).

Swift provides support for 8, 16, 32 and 64 bit integers (represented by the Int8, Int16, Int32 and Int64 types respectively). The same variants are also available for unsigned integers (UInt8, UInt16, UInt32 and UInt64).

In general, Apple recommends using the *Int* data type rather than one of the above specifically sized data types. The Int data type will use the appropriate integer size for the platform on which the code is running.

All integer data types contain bounds properties which can be accessed to identify the minimum and maximum supported values of that particular type. The following code, for example, outputs the minimum and maximum bounds for the 32-bit signed integer data type:

```
println("Int32 Min = \(Int32.min) Int32 Max = \(Int32.max)")
```

When executed, the above code will generate the following output:

```
Int32 Min = -2147483648 Int32 Max = 2147483647
```

7.2.2 Floating Point Data Types

The Swift floating point data types are able to store values containing decimal places. For example, 4353.1223 would be stored in a floating point data type. Swift provides two floating point data types in the form of *Float* and *Double*. Which type to use depends on the size of value to be stored and the level of precision required. The Double type can be used to store up to 64-bit floating point numbers with a level of precision of 15 decimal places or greater. The Float data type, on the other hand, is limited to 32-bit floating point numbers and offers a level of precision as low as 6 decimal places depending on the native platform on which the code is running.

7.2.3 Bool Data Type

Swift, like other languages, includes a data type for the purpose of handling true or false (1 or 0) conditions. Two Boolean constant values (*true* and *false*) are provided by Swift specifically for working with Boolean data types.

7.2.4 Character Data Type

The Swift Character data type is used to store a single Unicode character such as a letter, numerical digit, punctuation mark or symbol. For example, the following lines assign a variety of different characters to Character type variables:

```
var myChar1 = "f"
var myChar2 = ":"
var myChar3 = "X"
```

7.2.5 String Data Type

The String data type is a sequence of characters that typically make up a word or sentence. In addition to providing a storage mechanism, the String data type also includes a range of string manipulation features allowing strings to be searched, matched, concatenated and modified.

Strings can also be constructed using combinations of strings, variables, constants, expressions, and function calls using a concept referred to as *string interpolation*. For example, the following code creates a new string from a variety of different sources using string interpolation before outputting it to the console:

```
var userName = "John"
var inboxCount = 25
let maxCount = 100

var message = "\(userName) has \(inboxCount) message. Message capacity
remaining is \(maxCount - inboxCount)"

println(message)
```

When executed, the code will output the following message:

```
John has 25 messages. Message capacity remaining is 75 messages.
```

7.2.6 Special Characters/Escape Sequences

In addition to the standard set of characters outlined above, there is also a range of *special characters* (also referred to as *escape sequences*) available for specifying items such as a new line, tab or a specific Unicode value within a string. These special characters are identified by prefixing the character with a backslash (a concept referred to as *escaping*). For example, the following assigns a new line to the variable named newline:

```
var newline = "\n"
```

In essence, any character that is preceded by a backslash is considered to be a special character and is treated accordingly. This raises the question as to what to do if you actually want a backslash character. This is achieved by *escaping* the backslash itself:

```
var backslash = "\\"
```

Commonly used special characters supported by Swift are as follows:

- \n - New line
- \r - Carriage return
- \t - Horizontal tab
- \\ - Backslash
- \" - Double quote (used when placing a double quote into a string declaration)
- \' - Single quote (used when placing a single quote into a string declaration)

- **\u{*nn*}** – Single byte Unicode scalar where *nn* is replaced by two hexadecimal digits representing the Unicode character.
- **\u{*nnnn*}** – Double byte Unicode scalar where *nnnn* is replaced by four hexadecimal digits representing the Unicode character.
- **\U{*nnnnnnnn*}** – Four byte Unicode scalar where *nnnnnnnn* is replaced by four hexadecimal digits representing the Unicode character.

7.3 **Swift Variables**

Variables are essentially locations in computer memory reserved for storing the data used by an application. Each variable is given a name by the programmer and assigned a value. The name assigned to the variable may then be used in the Swift code to access the value assigned to that variable. This access can involve either reading the value of the variable, or changing the value. It is, of course, the ability to change the value of variables which gives them the name *variable*.

7.4 **Swift Constants**

A constant is similar to a variable in that it provides a named location in memory to store a data value. Constants differ in one significant way in that once a value has been assigned to a constant it cannot subsequently be changed.

Constants are particularly useful if there is a value which is used repeatedly throughout the application code. Rather than use the value each time, it makes the code easier to read if the value is first assigned to a constant which is then referenced in the code. For example, it might not be clear to someone reading your Swift code why you used the value 5 in an expression. If, instead of the value 5, you use a constant named interestRate the purpose of the value becomes much clearer. Constants also have the advantage that if the programmer needs to change a widely used value, it only needs to be changed once in the constant declaration and not each time it is referenced.

As with variables, constants have a type, a name and a value. Unlike variables, however, once a value has been assigned to a constant, that value cannot subsequently be changed.

7.5 **Declaring Constants and Variables**

Variables are declared using the *var* keyword and may be initialized with a value at creation time. If the variable is declared without an initial value it must be declared as being *optional* (a topic which will be covered later in this chapter). The following, for example, is a typical variable declaration:

```
var userCount = 10
```

Constants are declared using the *let* keyword. A value must be assigned to a constant at the point at which it is declared and, once initialized, the assigned value cannot subsequently be changed:

```
let maxUserCount = 20
```

For greater code efficiency and execution performance, Apple recommends the use of constants rather than variables whenever possible.

7.6 **Type Annotations and Type Inference**

Swift is categorized as a *type safe* programming language. This essentially means that once the data type of a variable has been identified, that variable cannot subsequently be used to store data of any other type without inducing a compilation error. This contrasts to *loosely typed* programming languages where a variable, once declared, can subsequently be used to store other data types.

There are two ways in which the type of a constant or variable will be identified. One approach is to use a *type annotation* at the point the variable or constant is declared in the code. This is achieved by placing a colon after the constant or variable name followed by the type declaration. The following line of code, for example, declares a variable named userCount as being of type Int:

```
var userCount: Int = 10
```

In the absence of a type annotation in a declaration, the Swift compiler uses a technique referred to as *type inference* to identify the type of the constant or variable. When relying on type inference, the compiler looks to see what type of value is being assigned to the constant or variable at the point that it is initialized and uses that as the type. Consider, for example, the following variable and constant declarations:

```
var signalStrength = 2.231
let companyName = "My Company"
```

During compilation of the above lines of code, Swift will infer that the signalStrength variable is of type Double (type inference in Swift defaults to Double for all floating point numbers) and that the companyName constant is of type String.

7.7 **Type Casting and Type Checking**

When writing Swift code, situations will occur where the compiler is unable to identify the specific type of a value. This is often the case when a value of ambiguous or unexpected type is returned from a method or function call. In this situation it may be necessary to let the compiler know the type of value that your code is expecting or requires using the *as* keyword (a concept referred to as *type casting*). The following code, for example, lets the compiler know that the value returned from the *objectForKey* method needs to be treated as a String type:

```
let myValue = record.objectForKey("comment") as String
```

It is also possible to *type check* a value using the *is* keyword. The following code, for example, checks that a specific object is an instance of a class named MyClass:

```
if myobject is MyClass {
        // myobject is an instance of MyClass
}
```

7.8 **The Swift Tuple**

Before proceeding, now is a good time to introduce the Swift tuple. The tuple is perhaps one of the simplest, yet most powerful features of the Swift programming language. A tuple is, quite simply, a way to temporarily group together multiple values into a single entity. The items stored in a tuple can be of any type and there are no restrictions requiring that those values all be of the same type. A tuple could, for example, be constructed to contain an Int value, a Float value and a String as follows:

```
let myTuple = (10, 432.433, "This is a String")
```

The elements of a tuple can be accessed using a number of different techniques. A specific tuple value can be accessed simply by referencing the index position (with the first value being at index position 0). The code below, for example, extracts the string resource (at index position 2 in the tuple) and assigns it to a new string variable:

```
let myTuple = (10, 432.433, "This is a String")
var myString = myTuple.2
println(myString)
```

Alternatively, all of the values in a tuple may be extracted and assigned to variables or constants in a single statement:

```
let (myInt, myFloat, myString) = myTuple
```

This same technique can be used to extract selected values from a tuple whilst ignoring others by replacing the values to be ignored with an underscore character. The following code fragment extracts the integer and string values from the tuple and assigns them to variables, but ignores the floating point value:

```
var (myInt, _, myString) = myTuple
```

When creating a tuple it is also possible to assign a name to each value:

```
let myTuple = (count: 10, length: 432.433, message: "This is a String")
```

The names assigned to the values stored in a tuple may then be used to reference those values in code. For example to output the *message* string value from the myTuple instance, the following line of code could be used:

```
println(myTuple.message)
```

Perhaps the most powerful use of tuples is, as will be seen in later chapters, the ability to return multiple values from a function.

7.9 **The Swift Optional Type**

The Swift optional data type is a new concept that does not exist in most other programming languages. The purpose of the optional type is to provide a safe and consistent approach to handling situations where a variable or constant may not have any value assigned to it.

Variables are declared as being optional by placing a ? character after the type declaration. The following code declares an optional Int variable named index:

```
var index: Int?
```

The variable *index* can now either have an integer value assigned to it, or have nothing assigned to it. Behind the scenes, and as far as the compiler and runtime are concerned, an optional with no value assigned to it actually has a value of nil.

An optional can easily be tested (typically using an if statement) to identify whether or not it has a variable assigned to it as follows:

```
var index: Int?

if index != nil {
    // index variable has a value assigned to it
} else {
    // index variable has no value assigned to it
}
```

If an optional has a value assigned to it, that value is said to be "wrapped" within the optional. The value wrapped in an optional may be accessed using a concept referred to as *forced unwrapping*. This simply means that the underlying value is extracted from the optional data type, a procedure that is performed by placing an exclamation mark (!) after the optional name.

To explore this concept of unwrapping optional types in more detail, consider the following code:

```
var index: Int?

index = 3

var treeArray = ["Oak", "Pine", "Yew", "Birch"]

if index != nil {
    println(treeArray[index!])
} else {
    println("index does not contain a value")
}
```

The code simply uses an optional variable to hold the index into an array of strings representing the names of tree types (Swift arrays will be covered in more detail in the chapter entitled *Working with Array and Dictionary Collections in Swift*). If the index optional variable has a value assigned to it, the tree name at that location in the array is printed to the console. Since the index is an optional type, the value has been unwrapped by placing an exclamation mark after the variable name:

```
println(treeArray[index!])
```

Had the index not been unwrapped (in other words the exclamation mark omitted from the above line), the compiler would have issued an error similar to the following:

```
Value of optional type Int? not unwrapped
```

As an alternative to forced unwrapping, the value assigned to an optional may be allocated to a temporary variable or constant using *optional binding*, the syntax for which is as follows:

```
if let constantname = optionalName {

}

if var variablename = optionalName {

}
```

The above constructs perform two tasks. In the first instance, the statement ascertains whether or not the designated optional contains a value. Secondly, in the event that the optional has a value, that value is assigned to the declared constant or variable and the code within the body of the statement is executed. The previous forced unwrapping example could, therefore, be modified as follows to use optional binding instead:

```
var index: Int?

index = 3

var treeArray = ["Oak", "Pine", "Yew", "Birch"]

if let myvalue = index {
    println(treeArray[myvalue])
} else {
    println("index does not contain a value")
}
```

In this case the value assigned to the index variable is unwrapped and assigned to a temporary constant named *myvalue* which is then used as the index reference into the array. Note that the myvalue constant is described as temporary since it is only available within the scope of the if statement. Once the if statement completes execution, the constant will no longer exist.

It is also possible to declare an optional as being *implicitly unwrapped*. When an optional is declared in this way, the underlying value can be accessed without having to perform forced unwrapping or optional binding. An optional is declared as being implicitly unwrapped by replacing the question mark (?) with an exclamation mark (!) in the declaration. For example:

```
var index: Int! // Optional is now implicitly unwrapped

index = 3

var treeArray = ["Oak", "Pine", "Yew", "Birch"]

if index != nil {
    println(treeArray[index])

} else {
    println("index doex not contain a value")
}
```

With the index optional variable now declared as being implicitly unwrapped, it is no longer necessary to unwrap the value when it is used as an index into the array in the above println call.

One final observation with regard to optionals in Swift is that only optional types are able to have no value or a value of nil assigned to them. In Swift it is not, therefore, possible to assign a nil value to a non-optional variable or constant. The following declarations, for instance, will all result in errors from the compiler since none of the variables are declared as optional:

```
var myInt = nil // Invalid code
var myString: String = nil // Invalid Code
let myConstant = nil // Invalid code
```

7.10 Summary

This chapter has begun the introduction to Swift by exploring data types together with an overview of how to declare constants and variables. The chapter has also introduced concepts such as type safety, type inference and optionals, each of which is an integral part of Swift programming and designed specifically to make code writing less prone to error.

8. Swift Operators and Expressions

So far we have looked at using variables and constants in Swift and also described the different data types. Being able to create variables is only part of the story however. The next step is to learn how to use these variables and constants in Swift code. The primary method for working with data is in the form of *expressions*.

8.1 Expression Syntax in Swift

The most basic Swift expression consists of an *operator*, two *operands* and an *assignment*. The following is an example of an expression:

```
var myresult = 1 + 2
```

In the above example, the (+) operator is used to add two operands (1 and 2) together. The *assignment operator* (=) subsequently assigns the result of the addition to a variable named *myresult*. The operands could just have easily been variables (or a mixture of constants and variables) instead of the actual numerical values used in the example.

In the remainder of this chapter we will look at the basic types of operators available in Swift.

8.2 The Basic Assignment Operator

We have already looked at the most basic of assignment operators, the = operator. This assignment operator simply assigns the result of an expression to a variable. In essence, the = assignment operator takes two operands. The left hand operand is the variable or constant to which a value is to be assigned and the right hand operand is the value to be assigned. The right hand operand is, more often than not, an expression which performs some type of arithmetic or logical evaluation, the result of which will be assigned to the variable or constant. The following examples are all valid uses of the assignment operator:

```
var x: Int? // Declare an optional Int variable
var y = 10 // Declare and initialize a second Int variable

x = 10 // Assign a value to x
x = x! + y // Assign the result of x + y to x
x = y // Assign the value of x to y
```

8.3 **Swift Arithmetic Operators**

Swift provides a range of operators for the purpose of creating mathematical expressions. These operators primarily fall into the category of *binary* operators in that they take two operands. The exception is the *unary negative operator* (-) which serves to indicate that a value is negative rather than positive. This contrasts with the *subtraction operator* (-) which takes two operands (i.e. one value to be subtracted from another). For example:

```
var x = -10 // Unary - operator used to assign -10 to variable x
x = x - 5 // Subtraction operator. Subtracts 5 from x
```

The following table lists the primary Swift arithmetic operators:

Operator	Description
-(unary)	Negates the value of a variable or expression
*	Multiplication
/	Division
+	Addition
-	Subtraction
%	Remainder/Modulo

Note that multiple operators may be used in a single expression.

For example:

```
x = y * 10 + z - 5 / 4
```

8.4 **Compound Assignment Operators**

In an earlier section we looked at the basic assignment operator (=). Swift provides a number of operators designed to combine an assignment with a mathematical or logical operation. These are primarily of use when performing an evaluation where the result is to be stored in one of the operands. For example, one might write an expression as follows:

```
x = x + y
```

The above expression adds the value contained in variable x to the value contained in variable y and stores the result in variable x. This can be simplified using the addition compound assignment operator:

```
x += y
```

The above expression performs exactly the same task as *x = x + y* but saves the programmer some typing.

Numerous compound assignment operators are available in Swift. The most frequently used of which are outlined in the following table:

Operator	Description
x += y	Add x to y and place result in x
x -= y	Subtract y from x and place result in x
x *= y	Multiply x by y and place result in x
x /= y	Divide x by y and place result in x
x %= y	Perform Modulo on x and y and place result in x
x && y	Assign to x the result of logical AND operation on x and y
x || y	Assign to x the result of logical OR operation on x and y

8.5 **Increment and Decrement Operators**

Another useful shortcut can be achieved using the Swift increment and decrement operators (also referred to as *unary operators* because they operate on a single operand). Consider the code fragment below:

```
x = x + 1 // Increase value of variable x by 1
x = x - 1 // Decrease value of variable x by 1
```

These expressions increment and decrement the value of x by 1. Instead of using this approach, however, it is quicker to use the ++ and -- operators. The following examples perform exactly the same tasks as the examples above:

```
x++ // Increment x by 1
x-- // Decrement x by 1
```

These operators can be placed either before or after the variable name. If the operator is placed before the variable name, the increment or decrement operation is performed before any other operations are performed on the variable. For example, in the following code, x is incremented before it is assigned to y, leaving y with a value of 10:

```
var x = 9
var y = ++x
```

In the next example, however, the value of x (9) is assigned to variable y *before* the decrement is performed. After the expression is evaluated the value of y will be 9 and the value of x will be 8.

```
var x = 9
var y = x--
```

8.6 **Comparison Operators**

Swift also includes a set of logical operators useful for performing comparisons. These operators all return a Boolean result depending on the result of the comparison. These operators are *binary operators* in that they work with two operands.

Comparison operators are most frequently used in constructing program flow control logic. For example an *if* statement may be constructed based on whether one value matches another:

```
if x == y {
      // Perform task
}
```

The result of a comparison may also be stored in a *Bool* variable. For example, the following code will result in a *true* value being stored in the variable result:

```
var result: Bool?
var x = 10
var y = 20

result = x < y
```

Clearly 10 is less than 20, resulting in a *true* evaluation of the $x < y$ expression. The following table lists the full set of Swift comparison operators:

Operator	Description
x == y	Returns true if x is equal to y
x > y	Returns true if x is greater than y
x >= y	Returns true if x is greater than or equal to y
x < y	Returns true if x is less than y
x <= y	Returns true if x is less than or equal to y
x != y	Returns true if x is not equal to y

8.7 Boolean Logical Operators

Swift also provides a set of so called logical operators designed to return Boolean *true* or *false* values. These operators both return Boolean results and take Boolean values as operands. The key operators are NOT (!), AND (&&), OR (||) and XOR (^).

The NOT (!) operator simply inverts the current value of a Boolean variable, or the result of an expression. For example, if a variable named *flag* is currently true, prefixing the variable with a '!' character will invert the value to false:

```
var flag = true // variable is true
var secondFlag = !flag // secondFlag set to false
```

The OR (||) operator returns true if one of its two operands evaluates to true, otherwise it returns false. For example, the following code evaluates to true because at least one of the expressions either side of the OR operator is true:

```
if (10 < 20) || (20 < 10) {
      println("Expression is true")
}
```

The AND (&&) operator returns true only if both operands evaluate to be true. The following example will return false because only one of the two operand expressions evaluates to true:

```
if (10 < 20) && (20 < 10) {
    println("Expression is true")
}
```

The XOR (^) operator returns true if one and only one of the two operands evaluates to true. For example, the following code will return true since only one operator evaluates to be true:

```
if ((10 < 20) ^ (20 < 10)){
    println("Expression is true")
}
```

If both operands evaluated to be true or both were false the expression would return false.

8.8 **Range Operators**

Swift includes two useful operators that allow ranges of values to be declared. As will be seen in later chapters, these operators are invaluable when working with looping in program logic.

The syntax for the *closed range operator* is as follows:

x...y

This operator represents the range of numbers starting at x and ending at y where both x and y are included within the range. The range operator 5...8, for example, specifies the numbers 5, 6, 7 and 8.

The *half-closed range operator*, on the other hand uses the following syntax:

x..<y

In this instance, the operator encompasses all the numbers from x up to, but not including, y. A half closed range operator 5..<8, therefore, specifies the numbers 5, 6 and 7.

8.9 **The Ternary Operator**

Swift supports the *ternary operator* to provide a shortcut way of making decisions within code. The syntax of the ternary operator (also known as the conditional operator) is as follows:

```
condition ? true expression : false expression
```

The way the ternary operator works is that *condition* is replaced with an expression that will return either *true* or *false*. If the result is true then the expression that replaces the *true expression* is evaluated. Conversely, if the result was *false* then the *false expression* is evaluated. Let's see this in action:

```
var x = 10
```

```
var y = 20

println("Largest number is \(x > y ? x : y)")
```

The above code example will evaluate whether x is greater than y. Clearly this will evaluate to false resulting in y being returned to the println call for display to the user:

```
Largest number is 20
```

8.10 Bitwise Operators

As previously discussed, computer processors work in binary. These are essentially streams of ones and zeros, each one referred to as a bit. Bits are formed into groups of 8 to form bytes. As such, it is not surprising that we, as programmers, will occasionally end up working at this level in our code. To facilitate this requirement, Swift provides a range of *bit operators*.

Those familiar with bitwise operators in other languages such as C, C++, C#, Objective-C and Java will find nothing new in this area of the Swift language syntax. For those unfamiliar with binary numbers, now may be a good time to seek out reference materials on the subject in order to understand how ones and zeros are formed into bytes to form numbers. Other authors have done a much better job of describing the subject than we can do within the scope of this book.

For the purposes of this exercise we will be working with the binary representation of two numbers. Firstly, the decimal number 171 is represented in binary as:

```
10101011
```

Secondly, the number 3 is represented by the following binary sequence:

```
00000011
```

Now that we have two binary numbers with which to work, we can begin to look at the Swift bitwise operators:

8.10.1 Bitwise NOT

The Bitwise NOT is represented by the tilde character and has the effect of inverting all of the bits in a number. In other words, all the zeros become ones and all the ones become zeros. Taking our example 3 number, a Bitwise NOT operation has the following result:

```
00000011 NOT
========
11111100
```

The following Swift code, therefore, results in a value of -4:

```
var y = 3
```

```
var z = ~y

println("Result is \(z)")
```

8.10.2 Bitwise AND

The Bitwise AND is represented by a single ampersand (&). It makes a bit by bit comparison of two numbers. Any corresponding position in the binary sequence of each number where both bits are 1 results in a 1 appearing in the same position of the resulting number. If either bit position contains a 0 then a zero appears in the result. Taking our two example numbers, this would appear as follows:

```
10101011 AND
00000011
========
00000011
```

As we can see, the only locations where both numbers have 1s are the last two positions. If we perform this in Swift code, therefore, we should find that the result is 3 (00000011):

```
var x = 171
var y = 3
var z = x & y

println("Result is \(z)")
```

8.10.3 Bitwise OR

The bitwise OR also performs a bit by bit comparison of two binary sequences. Unlike the AND operation, the OR places a 1 in the result if there is a 1 in the first or second operand. The operator is represented by a single vertical bar character (|). Using our example numbers, the result will be as follows:

```
10101011 OR
00000011
========
10101011
```

If we perform this operation in a Swift example the result will be 171:

```
var x = 171
var y = 3
var z = x | y

println("Result is \(z)")
```

8.10.4 Bitwise XOR

The bitwise XOR (commonly referred to as *exclusive OR* and represented by the caret '^' character) performs a similar task to the OR operation except that a 1 is placed in the result if one or other corresponding bit positions in the two numbers is 1. If both positions are a 1 or a 0 then the corresponding bit in the result is set to a 0. For example:

```
10101011  XOR
00000011
========
10101000
```

The result in this case is 10101000 which converts to 168 in decimal. To verify this we can, once again, try some Swift code:

```
var x = 171
var y = 3
var z = x ^ y

println("Result is \(z)")
```

When executed, we get the following output from println:

```
Result is 168
```

8.10.5 Bitwise Left Shift

The bitwise left shift moves each bit in a binary number a specified number of positions to the left. Shifting an integer one position to the left has the effect of doubling the value.

As the bits are shifted to the left, zeros are placed in the vacated right most (low order) positions. Note also that once the left most (high order) bits are shifted beyond the size of the variable containing the value, those high order bits are discarded:

```
10101011  Left Shift one bit
========
101010110
```

In Swift the bitwise left shift operator is represented by the '<<' sequence, followed by the number of bit positions to be shifted. For example, to shift left by 1 bit:

```
var x = 171
var z = x << 1

println("Result is \(z)")
```

When compiled and executed, the above code will display a message stating that the result is 342 which, when converted to binary, equates to 101010110.

8.10.6 Bitwise Right Shift

A bitwise right shift is, as you might expect, the same as a left except that the shift takes place in the opposite direction. Shifting an integer one position to the right has the effect of halving the value.

Note that since we are shifting to the right there is no opportunity to retain the lower most bits regardless of the data type used to contain the result. As a result the low order bits are discarded. Whether or not the vacated high order bit positions are replaced with zeros or ones depends on whether the *sign bit* used to indicate positive and negative numbers is set or not.

```
10101011 Right Shift one bit
========
01010101
```

The bitwise right shift is represented by the '>>' character sequence followed by the shift count:

```
var x = 171
var z = x >> 1

println("Result is \(z)")
```

When executed, the above code will report the result of the shift as being 85, which equates to binary 01010101.

8.11 Compound Bitwise Operators

As with the arithmetic operators, each bitwise operator has a corresponding compound operator that allows the operation and assignment to be performed using a single operator:

Operator	Description
x &= y	Perform a bitwise AND of x and y and assign result to x
x |= y	Perform a bitwise OR of x and y and assign result to x
x ^= y	Perform a bitwise XOR of x and y and assign result to x
x <<= n	Shift x left by n places and assign result to x
x >>= n	Shift x right by n places and assign result to x

8.12 Summary

Operators and expressions provide the underlying mechanism by which variables and constants are manipulated and evaluated within Swift code. This can take the simplest of forms whereby two numbers are added using the addition operator in an expression and the result stored in a variable using the assignment operator. Operators fall into a range of categories, details of which have been covered in this chapter.

9. Swift Flow Control

Regardless of the programming language used, application development is largely an exercise in applying logic, and much of the art of programming involves writing code that makes decisions based on one or more criteria. Such decisions define which code gets executed, how many times it is executed and, conversely, which code gets by-passed when the program is executing. This is often referred to as *flow control* since it controls the *flow* of program execution. Flow control typically falls into the categories of *looping control* (how often code is executed) and *conditional flow control* (whether or not code is executed). This chapter is intended to provide an introductory overview of both types of flow control in Swift.

9.1 Looping Flow Control

This chapter will begin by looking at flow control in the form of loops. Loops are essentially sequences of Swift statements which are to be executed repeatedly until a specified condition is met. The first looping statement we will explore is the *for* loop.

9.2 The Swift *for* Statement

Swift provides two types of *for* loop, namely the *condition-increment* for loop and the *for-in* loop:

9.2.1 The Condition-Increment for Loop

The condition-increment for loop uses the following syntax:

```
for initializer; conditional expression; increment expression {
    // statements to be executed
}
```

The *initializer* typically initializes a variable to act as the counter for the loop. Traditionally the variable name *i* is used for this purpose, though any valid variable name will do. For example:

```
var i = 0
var nameCount = 0
```

The *conditional expression* specifies the test that is to be executed on each loop iteration to verify whether the loop has been performed the required number of times. For example, if a loop is to be performed 10 times:

```
i < 10
```

Finally the *loop expression* specifies the action to be performed on the counter variable. For example to increment by 1:

```
++i
```

The body of statements to be executed on each iteration of the loop is contained within the code block defined by the opening ({) and closing (}) braces.

Bringing this all together we can create a *for* loop to perform a task a specified number of times:

```
for var i = 0; i < 10; ++i {
      println("Value of i is \(i)")
}
```

9.2.2 The for-in Loop

The *for-in* loop is used to iterate over a sequence of items contained in a collection or number range and provides a simpler alternative to the condition-increment looping technique previously described.

The syntax of the for-in loop is as follows:

```
for constant name in collection or range {
        // code to be executed
}
```

In this syntax, *constant name* is the name to be used for a constant that will contain the current item from the collection or range through which the loop is iterating. The code in the body of the loop will typically use this constant name as a reference to the current item in the loop cycle. The *collection or range* references the item through which the loop is iterating. This could, for example, be an array of string values, a range operator or even a string of characters (the topic of collections will be covered in greater detail within the chapter entitled *Working with Array and Dictionary Collections in Swift*).

Consider, for example, the following for-in loop construct:

```
for index in 1...5 {
      println("Value of index is \(index)")
}
```

The loop begins by stating that the current item is to be assigned to a constant named *index*. The statement then declares a closed range operator to indicate that the for loop is to iterate through a range of numbers, starting at 1 and ending at 5. The body of the loop simply prints out a message to the console panel indicating the current value assigned to the *index* constant, resulting in the following output:

```
Value of index is 1
Value of index is 2
Value of index is 3
Value of index is 4
```

```
Value of index is 5
```

The for-in loop can be used with any data that contains more than one element. The following code, for example, outputs each of the characters contained within a string literal:

```
for char in "This is a string" {
     println(char)
}
```

As will be demonstrated in the *Working with Array and Dictionary Collections in Swift* chapter of this book, the *for-in* loop is of particular benefit when working with collections such as arrays and dictionaries.

The declaration of a constant name in which to store a reference to the current item is not mandatory. In the event that a reference to the current item is not required in the body of the *for* loop, the constant name in the *for* loop declaration can be replaced by an underscore character. For example:

```
var count = 0

for _ in "This is a string" {
     // No reference to the current character is required.
     ++count
}
```

9.2.3 The while Loop

The Swift *for* loop described previously works well when it is known in advance how many times a particular task needs to be repeated in a program. There will, however, be instances where code needs to be repeated until a certain condition is met, with no way of knowing in advance how many repetitions are going to be needed to meet that criteria. To address this need, Swift provides the *while* loop.

Essentially, the *while* loop repeats a set of tasks until a specified condition is met. The *while* loop syntax is defined as follows:

```
while condition {
     // Swift statements go here
}
```

In the above syntax, *condition* is an expression that will return either *true* or *false* and the *// Swift statements go here* comment represents the code to be executed while the *condition* expression is *true*. For example:

```
var myCount = 0

while  myCount < 100 {
     ++myCount
}
```

In the above example, the *while* expression will evaluate whether the *myCount* variable is less than 100. If it is already greater than 100, the code in the braces is skipped and the loop exits without performing any tasks.

If, on the other hand, *myCount* is not greater than 100 the code in the braces is executed and the loop returns to the *while* statement and repeats the evaluation of *myCount*. This process repeats until the value of *myCount* is greater than 100, at which point the loop exits.

9.3 The *do ... while* loop

It is often helpful to think of the *do ... while* loop as an inverted *while* loop. The *while* loop evaluates an expression before executing the code contained in the body of the loop. If the expression evaluates to *false* on the first check then the code is not executed. The *do ... while* loop, on the other hand, is provided for situations where you know that the code contained in the body of the loop will *always* need to be executed at least once. For example, you may want to keep stepping through the items in an array until a specific item is found. You know that you have to at least check the first item in the array to have any hope of finding the entry you need. The syntax for the *do ... while* loop is as follows:

```
do
{
        // Swift statements here
} while conditional expression
```

In the *do ... while* example below the loop will continue until the value of a variable named *i* equals 0:

```
var i = 10

do {
        --i
} while (i > 0)
```

9.4 Breaking from Loops

Having created a loop, it is possible that under certain conditions you might want to break out of the loop before the completion criteria have been met (particularly if you have created an infinite loop). One such example might involve continually checking for activity on a network socket. Once activity has been detected it will most likely be necessary to break out of the monitoring loop and perform some other task.

For the purpose of breaking out of a loop, Swift provides the *break* statement which breaks out of the current loop and resumes execution at the code directly after the loop. For example:

```
var j = 10

for var i = 0; i < 100; ++i
{
    j += j
```

```
    if j > 100 {
        break
    }

    println("j = \(j)")
}
```

In the above example the loop will continue to execute until the value of j exceeds 100 at which point the loop will exit and execution will continue with the next line of code after the loop.

9.5 The *continue* Statement

The *continue* statement causes all remaining code statements in a loop to be skipped, and execution to be returned to the top of the loop. In the following example, the println function is only called when the value of variable *i* is an even number:

```
var i = 1

while i < 20
{
        ++i

        if (i % 2) != 0 {
            continue
        }

        println("i = \(i)")
}
```

The *continue* statement in the above example will cause the println call to be skipped unless the value of *i* can be divided by 2 with no remainder. If the *continue* statement is triggered, execution will skip to the top of the while loop and the statements in the body of the loop will be repeated (until the value of *i* exceeds 19).

9.6 Conditional Flow Control

In the previous chapter we looked at how to use logical expressions in Swift to determine whether something is *true* or *false*. Since programming is largely an exercise in applying logic, much of the art of programming involves writing code that makes decisions based on one or more criteria. Such decisions define which code gets executed and, conversely, which code gets by-passed when the program is executing. This is often referred to as *flow control* since it controls the *flow* of program execution.

9.7 **Using the if Statement**

The *if* statement is perhaps the most basic of flow control options available to the Swift programmer. Programmers who are familiar with C, Objective-C, C++ or Java will immediately be comfortable using Swift *if* statements.

The basic syntax of the Swift *if* statement is as follows:

```
if boolean expression {
    // Swift code to be performed when expression evaluates to true
}
```

Unlike some other programming languages, it is important to note that the braces ({}) are mandatory in Swift, even if only one line of code is executed after the *if* expression.

Essentially if the *Boolean expression* evaluates to *true* then the code in the body of the statement is executed. The body of the statement is enclosed in braces ({}). If, on the other hand, the expression evaluates to *false* the code in the body of the statement is skipped.

For example, if a decision needs to be made depending on whether one value is greater than another, we would write code similar to the following:

```
var x = 10

if x > 9 {
    println("x is greater than 9!")
}
```

Clearly, x is indeed greater than 9 causing the message to appear in the console panel.

9.8 **Using if ... else ... Statements**

The next variation of the *if* statement allows us to also specify some code to perform if the expression in the *if* statement evaluates to *false*. The syntax for this construct is as follows:

```
if boolean expression {
// Code to be executed if expression is true
} else {
// Code to be executed if expression is false
}
```

Using the above syntax, we can now extend our previous example to display a different message if the comparison expression evaluates to be *false*:

```
var x = 10
```

```
if x > 9 {
        println("x is greater than 9!")
} else {
        println("x is less than 9!")
}
```

In this case, the second println statement would execute if the value of x was less than 9.

9.9 Using if ... else if ... Statements

So far we have looked at *if* statements which make decisions based on the result of a single logical expression. Sometimes it becomes necessary to make decisions based on a number of different criteria. For this purpose, we can use the *if ... else if ...* construct, an example of which is as follows:

```
var x = 9;

if x == 10 {
        println("x is 10");
} else if x == 9 {
        println("x is 9");
} else if x == 8 {
        println("x is 8");
}
```

This approach works well for a moderate number of comparisons, but can become cumbersome for a larger volume of expression evaluations. For such situations, the Swift *switch* statement provides a more flexible and efficient solution. For more details on using the *switch* statement refer to the next chapter entitled *The Swift Switch Statement*.

9.10 Summary

The term *flow control* is used to describe the logic that dictates the execution path that is taken through the source code of an application as it runs. This chapter has looked at the two types of flow control provided by Swift (looping and conditional) and explored the various Swift constructs that are available to implement both forms of flow control logic.

Chapter 10

10. The Swift Switch Statement

In *Swift Flow Control* we looked at how to control program execution flow using the *if* and *else* statements. Whilst these statement constructs work well for testing a limited number of conditions, they quickly become unwieldy when dealing with larger numbers of possible conditions. To simplify such situations, Swift has inherited the *switch* statement from the C programming language. Those familiar with the switch statement from other programming languages should be aware, however, that the Swift switch statement has some key differences from other implementations. In this chapter we will explore the Swift implementation of the *switch* statement in detail.

10.1 Why Use a switch Statement?

For a small number of logical evaluations of a value the *if ... else if ...* construct is perfectly adequate. Unfortunately, any more than two or three possible scenarios can quickly make such a construct both time consuming to write and difficult to read. For such situations, the *switch* statement provides an excellent alternative.

10.2 Using the switch Statement Syntax

The syntax for a basic Swift *switch* statement implementation can be outlined as follows:

```
switch expression
{
    case match1:
        statements

    case match2:
        statements

    case match3, match4:
        statements

    default:
        statements
}
```

In the above syntax outline, *expression* represents either a value, or an expression which returns a value. This is the value against which the *switch* operates.

For each possible match a *case* statement is provided, followed by a *match* value. Each potential match must be of the same type as the governing expression. Following on from the *case* line are the Swift statements that are to be executed in the event of the value matching the case condition.

Finally, the *default* section of the construct defines what should happen if none of the case statements present a match to the *expression*.

10.3 **A Swift switch Statement Example**

With the above information in mind we may now construct a simple *switch* statement:

```
var value = 4

switch (value)
{
      case 0:
        println("zero")

      case 1:
        println("one")

      case 2:
        println("two")

      case 3:
        println("three")

      case 4:
        println("four")

      case 5:
        println("five")

      default:
        println("Integer out of range")
}
```

10.4 **Combining case Statements**

In the above example, each case had its own set of statements to execute. Sometimes a number of different matches may require the same code to be executed. In this case, it is possible to group case matches together with a common set of statements to be executed when a match for any of the cases is found. For example, we can modify the switch construct in our example so that the same code is executed regardless of whether the value is 0, 1 or 2:

```
var value = 1

switch (value)
{
      case 0, 1, 2:
        println("zero, one or two")

      case 3:
        println("three")

      case 4:
        println("four")

      case 5:
        println("five")

      default:
        println("Integer out of range")
}
```

10.5 Range Matching in a switch Statement

The case statements within a switch construct may also be used to implement range matching. The following switch statement, for example, checks a temperature value for matches within three number ranges:

```
var temperature = 83

switch (temperature)
{
      case 0...49:
        println("Cold")

      case 50...79:
        println("Warm")

      case 80...110:
        println("Hot")

      default:
        println("Temperature out of range")
}
```

10.6 **Using the where statement**

The *where* statement may be used within a switch case match to add additional criteria required for a positive match. The following switch statement, for example, checks not only for the range in which a value falls, but also whether the number is odd or even:

```
var temperature = 54

switch (temperature)
{
    case 0...49 where temperature % 2 == 0:
        println("Cold and even")

    case 50...79 where temperature % 2 == 0:
        println("Warm and even")

    case 80...110 where temperature % 2 == 0:
        println("Hot and even")

    default:
        println("Temperature out of range or odd")
}
```

10.7 **Fallthrough**

Those familiar with switch statements in other languages such as C and Objective-C will notice that it is no longer necessary to include a *break* statement after each case declaration. Unlike other languages, Swift automatically breaks out of the statement when a matching case condition is met. The fallthrough effect of other switch implementations (whereby the execution path continues through the remaining case statements) can be emulated using the *fallthrough* statement:

```
var temperature = 10

switch (temperature)
{
    case 0...49 where temperature % 2 == 0:
        println("Cold and even")
        fallthrough

    case 50...79 where temperature % 2 == 0:
        println("Warm and even")
        fallthrough

    case 80...110 where temperature % 2 == 0:
        println("Hot and even")
```

```
        fallthrough

    default:
        println("Temperature out of range or odd")
}
```

Although *break* is less commonly used in Swift switch statements, it is useful when no action needs to be taken for the default case. For example:

```
        .
        .
        .

    default:
        break
}
```

10.8 Summary

Whilst the *if.. else..* construct serves as a good decision making option for small numbers of possible outcomes, this approach can become unwieldy in more complex situations. As an alternative method for implementing flow control logic in Swift when many possible outcomes exist as the result of an evaluation, the *switch* statement invariably makes a more suitable option. As outlined in this chapter, however, developers familiar with switch implementations from other programming languages should be aware of some subtle differences in the way that the Swift switch statement works.

11. An Overview of Swift Functions and Closures

Swift functions and closures are a vital part of writing well-structured and efficient code and provide a way to organize programs and avoid code repetition. In this chapter we will look at how functions and closures are declared and used within Swift.

11.1 What is a Function?

A function is a named block of code that can be called upon to perform a specific task. It can be provided data on which to perform the task and is capable of returning results to the code that called it. For example, if a particular arithmetic calculation needs to be performed in a Swift program, the code to perform the arithmetic can be placed in a function. The function can be programmed to accept the values on which the arithmetic is to be performed (referred to as *parameters*) and to return the result of the calculation. At any point in the program code where the calculation is required, the function is simply called and, parameter values passed through as *arguments* and the result returned.

The terms *parameter* and *argument* are often used interchangeably when discussing functions. There is, however, a subtle difference. The values that a function is able to accept when it is called are referred to as *parameters*. At the point that the function is actually called and passed those values, however, they are referred to as *arguments*.

11.2 How to Declare a Swift Function

A Swift function is declared using the following syntax:

```
func <function name> (<para name>: <para type>, <para name>: <para type>,
... ) -> <return type> {
        // Function code
}
```

Explanations of the various fields of the function declaration are as follows:

- **func** – The prefix keyword used to notify the Swift compiler that this is a function.
- **<function name>** - The name assigned to the function. This is the name by which the function will be referenced when it is called from within the application code.

- **<para name>** - The name by which the parameter is to be referenced in the function code.
- **<para type>** - The type of the corresponding parameter.
- **<return type>** - The data type of the result returned by the function. If the function does not return a result then no return type is specified.
- **Function code** - The code of the function that does the work.

As an example, the following function takes no parameters, returns no result and simply displays a message:

```
func sayHello() {
    println("Hello")
}
```

The following sample function, on the other hand, takes an integer and a string as parameters and returns a string result:

```
func buildMessage(name: String, count: Int) -> String {
    return("\(name), you are customer number \(count)")
}
```

11.3 **Calling a Swift Function**

Once declared, functions are called using the following syntax:

```
<function name> (<arg1>, <arg2>, ... )
```

Each argument passed through to a function must match the parameters the function is configured to accept. For example, to call a function named *sayHello* that takes no parameters and returns no value, we would write the following code:

```
sayHello()
```

To call a function named *buildMessage* that takes two parameters and returns a result, on the other hand, we might write the following code:

```
var message = buildMessage("John", 100)
```

In the above example, we have created a new variable called *message* and then used the assignment operator (=) to store the result returned by the function.

11.4 **Declaring External Parameter Names**

When the preceding example functions were declared, they were configured with parameters that were assigned names which, in turn, could be referenced within the body of the function code. When declared in this way, the names are local to the function and cannot be referenced when making a function call.

In order to make code easier to read and more self-explanatory, it can be useful to be able to reference the parameter names when a function is called. This can be achieved by declaring the parameter names as being *external* and involves prefixing the name with a # in the function declaration. Taking the *buildMessage* function as an example, this would involve the following declaration:

```
func buildMessage(#name: String, #count: Int) -> String {
       return("\(name), you are customer number \(count)")
}
```

Once external names have been declared, they must be referenced when calling the function:

```
var message = buildMessage(name: "John", count: 100)
```

In the event that the local and external names need to be different, external names can be declared preceding the local name in the function declaration:

```
func buildMessage(customerName name: String,
                  customerCount count: Int) -> String {

    return ("\(name), you are customer number \(count)")
}

var message = buildMessage(customerName: "John", customerCount: 100)
```

In this case, the local names are used to reference the parameters within the body of the function, while the external names are used to pass the arguments through when calling the function.

11.5 Declaring Default Function Parameters

Swift provides the ability to designate a default parameter value to be used in the event that the value is not provided as an argument when the function is called. This simply involves assigning the default value to the parameter when the function is declared. When using default parameters, it is important that the parameters for which a default is being declared be placed at the end of the parameter list so that the compiler does not become confused about which parameters have been omitted during a function call. Swift also provides a default external name based on the local parameter name for defaulted parameters (unless one is already provided) which must then be used when calling the function.

To see default parameters in action the *buildMessage* function will be modified so that the string "Customer" is used as a default in the event that a customer name is not passed through as an argument:

```
func buildMessage(count: Int, name: String = "Customer") -> String {
    return ("\(name), you are customer number \(count)")
}
```

The function can now be called without passing through a customer name value:

```
var message = buildMessage(100)
println(message)
```

When executed, the above function call will generate output to the console panel which reads:

```
Customer, you are customer 100
```

In order to call the function with a customer name, however, it will now be necessary to reference the automatically created parameter name to avoid a syntax error from the compiler:

```
var message = buildMessage(100, name: "John")
```

11.6 Returning Multiple Results from a Function

A function can return multiple result values by wrapping those results in a tuple. The following function takes as a parameter a measurement value in inches. The function converts this value into yards, centimeters and meters, returning all three results within a single tuple instance:

```
func sizeConverter (length: Float) -> (yards: Float, centimeters: Float,
meters: Float) {

    var yards = length * 0.0277778
    var centimeters = length * 2.54
    var meters = length * 0.0254

    return (yards, centimeters, meters)
}
```

The return type for the function indicates that the function returns a tuple containing three values named yards, centimeters and meters respectively, all of which are of type Float:

```
-> (yards: Float, centimeters: Float, meters: Float)
```

Having performed the conversion, the function simply constructs the tuple instance and returns it.

Usage of this function might read as follows:

```
var lengthTuple = sizeConverter(20)

println(lengthTuple.yards)
println(lengthTuple.centimeters)
println(lengthTuple.meters)
```

11.7 Variable Numbers of Function Parameters

It is not always possible to know in advance the number of parameters a function will need to accept when it is called within application code. Swift handles this possibility through the use of *variadic parameters*. Variadic parameters are declared using three periods (...) to indicate that the function accepts zero or more parameters of a specified data type. Within the body of the function, the parameters are made available in the form of an array object. The following function, for example, takes as parameters a variable number of String values and then outputs them to the console panel:

```
func displayStrings(strings: String...)
{
    for string in strings {
        println(string)
    }
}

displayStrings("one", "two", "three", "four")
```

11.8 Parameters as Variables

All parameters accepted by a function are declared constants by default preventing changes being made to those parameter values within the function code. If changes to parameters need to be made within the function body, those parameters must be specifically declared as being variable within the function declaration. The following function, for example, is passed length and width parameters in inches and converts those parameters (which have been declared as variables) to centimeters before calculating and returning the area value:

```
func calcuateArea (var length: Float, var width: Float) -> Float {
    length = length * 2.54
    width = width * 2.54
    return length * width
}

println(calcuateArea(10, 20))
```

11.9 Working with In-Out Parameters

When the value assigned to a variable is passed through as an argument to a function, and that function both declares the parameter as a variable, and specifically changes that value, the question arises as to whether that change is reflected in the original variable. Consider the following code:

```
var myValue = 10

func doubleValue (var value: Int) -> Int {
    value += value
    return(value)
}

println("Before function call myValue = \(myValue)")

println("doubleValue call returns \(doubleValue(myValue))")
```

```
println("Before function call myValue = \(myValue)")
```

The code begins by declaring a variable named *myValue* initialized with a value of 10. A new function is then declared which accepts a single integer parameter which is declared as being a variable. Within the body of the function, the value of the parameter is doubled and returned.

The remaining lines of code display the value of the *myValue* variable before and after the function call is made. When executed, the following output will appear in the console:

```
Before function call myValue = 10
doubleValue call returns 20
After function call myValue = 10
```

Clearly, the function has made no change to the original myValue variable, even though it was passed through to the function as an argument.

In order to make any changes made to a parameter persist after the function has returned, the parameter must be declared as an *in-out parameter* within the function declaration. To see this in action, modify the *doubleValue* function to prefix the parameter with the *inout* keyword as follows:

```
func doubleValue (inout value: Int) -> Int {
    value += value
    return(value)
}
```

Finally, when calling the function, the inout parameter must now be prefixed with an & modifier:

```
println("doubleValue call returned \(doubleValue(&myValue))")
```

Having made these changes, a test run of the code should now generate output clearly indicating that the function modified the value assigned to the original *myValue* variable:

```
Before function call myValue = 10
doubleValue call returns 20
After function call myValue = 20
```

11.10 Functions as Parameters

An interesting feature of functions within Swift is that they can be treated as data types. It is perfectly valid, for example, to assign a function to a constant or variable as illustrated in the declaration below:

```
func inchesToFeet (inches: Float) -> Float {

    return inches * 0.0833333
}
```

```
let toFeet = inchesToFeet
```

The above code declares a new function named *inchesToFeet* and subsequently assigns that function to a constant named *toFeet*. Having made this assignment, a call to the function may be made using the constant name instead of the original function name:

```
var result = toFeet(10)
```

On the surface this does not seem to be a particularly compelling feature. Since we could already call the function without assigning it to a constant or variable data type it does not seem that much has been gained.

The possibilities that this feature offers become more apparent when we consider that a function assigned to a constant or variable now has the capabilities of many other data types. In particular, a function can now be passed through as an argument to another function, or even returned as a result from a function.

Before we look at what is, essentially, the ability to plug one function into another, it is first necessary to explore the concept of function data types. The data type of a function is dictated by a combination of the parameters it accepts and the type of result it returns. In the above example, since the function accepts a floating point parameter and returns a floating point result, the function's data type conforms to the following:

```
(Float) -> Float
```

A function which accepts an Int and a Double as parameters and returns a String result, on the other hand, would have the following data type:

```
(Int, Double) -> String
```

In order to accept a function as a parameter, the receiving function simply declares the data type of the function it is able to accept.

For the purposes of an example, we will begin by declaring two unit conversion functions and assigning them to constants:

```
func inchesToFeet (inches: Float) -> Float {

    return inches * 0.0833333
}

func inchesToYards (inches: Float) -> Float {

    return inches * 0.0277778
}
```

```
let toFeet = inchesToFeet
let toYards = inchesToYards
```

The example now needs an additional function, the purpose of which is to perform a unit conversion and print the result in the console panel. This function needs to be as general purpose as possible, capable of performing a variety of different measurement unit conversions. In order to demonstrate functions as parameters, this new function will take as a parameter a function type that matches both the inchesToFeet and inchesToYards function data type together with a value to be converted. Since the data type of these functions is equivalent to (Float) -> Float, our general purpose function can be written as follows:

```
func outputConversion(converterFunc: (Float) -> Float, value: Float) {

    var result = converterFunc(value)

    println("Result of conversion is \(result)")
}
```

When the outputConversion function is called, it will need to be passed a function matching the declared data type. That function will be called to perform the conversion and the result displayed in the console panel. This means that the same function can be called to convert inches to both feet and yards, simply by "plugging in" the appropriate converter function as a parameter. For example:

```
outputConversion(toYards, 10) // Convert to Yards
outputConversion(toFeet, 10) // Convert to Inches
```

Functions can also be returned as a data type simply by declaring the type of the function as the return type. The following function is configured to return either our toFeet or toYards function type (in other words a function which accepts and returns a Float value) based on the value of a Boolean parameter:

```
func decideFunction (feet: Bool) -> (Float) -> Float
{
    if feet {
        return toFeet
    } else {
        return toYards
    }
}
```

11.11 Closure Expressions

Having covered the basics of functions in Swift it is now time to look at the concept of *closures* and *closure expressions*. Although these terms are often used interchangeably there are some key differences.

Closure expressions are self-contained blocks of code. The following code, for example, declares a closure expression and assigns it to a constant named sayHello and then calls the function via the constant reference:

```
let sayHello = { println("Hello") }
sayHello()
```

Closure expressions may also be configured to accept parameters and return results. The syntax for this is as follows:

```
{(<para name>: <para type>, <para name> <para type>, ... ) -> <return
type> in
        // Closure expression code here
}
```

The following closure expression, for example, accepts two integer parameters and returns an integer result:

```
let multiply = {(val1: Int, val2: Int) -> Int in
      return val1 * val2
}
let result = multiply(10, 20)
```

Note that the syntax is similar to that used for declaring Swift functions with the exception that the closure expression does not have a name, the parameters and return type are included in the braces and the *in* keyword is used to indicate the start of the closure expression code. Functions are, in fact, simply named closure expressions.

Closure expressions are often used when declaring completion handlers for asynchronous method calls. In other words, when developing iOS applications it will often be necessary to make calls to the operating system where the requested task is performed in the background allowing the application to continue with other tasks. Typically in such a scenario, the system will notify the application of the completion of the task and return any results by calling the completion handler that was declared when the method was called. Frequently the code for the completion handler will be implemented in the form of a closure expression. Consider the following code from an example used later in the book:

```
eventStore?.requestAccessToEntityType(EKEntityTypeReminder, completion:
{(granted: Bool, error: NSError!) -> Void in
                if !granted {
                    println(error.localizedDescription)
                }
})
```

When the tasks performed by the *requestAccessToEntityType* method call are complete it will execute the closure expression declared as the *completion:* parameter. The completion handler is required by the method to accept a Bool value and an NSError object as parameters and return no results, hence the following declaration:

```
{(granted: Bool, error: NSError!) -> Void in
```

In actual fact, the Swift compiler already knows about the parameter and return value requirements for the completion handler for this method call, and is able to infer this information without it being declared in the closure expression. This allows a simpler version of the closure expression declaration to be written:

```
eventStore?.requestAccessToEntityType(EKEntityTypeReminder, completion:
{(granted, error) in
                if !granted {
                    println(error.localizedDescription)
                }
})
```

11.12 Closures in Swift

A *closure* in computer science terminology generally refers to the combination of a self-contained block of code (for example a function or closure expression) and one or more variables that exist in the context surrounding that code block. Consider, for example the following Swift function:

```
func functionA() -> () -> Int {

    var counter = 0

    func functionB() -> Int {
        return counter + 10
    }
    return functionB
}

let myClosure = functionA()
let result = myClosure()
```

In the above code, *functionA* returns a function named *functionB*. In actual fact functionA is returning a closure since functionB relies on the *counter* variable which is declared outside the functionB's local scope. In other words, functionB is said to have *captured* or *closed over* (hence the term closure) the counter variable and, as such, is considered a closure in the traditional computer science definition of the word.

To a large extend, and particularly as it relates to Swift, the terms *closure* and *closure expression* have started to be used interchangeably. The key point to remember, however, is that both are supported in Swift.

11.13 Summary

Functions, closures and closure expressions are self-contained blocks of code that can be called upon to perform a specific task and provide a mechanism for structuring code and promoting reuse. This chapter has introduced the concepts of functions and closures in terms of declaration and implementation.

Chapter 12

12. The Basics of Object Oriented Programming in Swift

Swift provides extensive support for developing object-oriented iOS applications. The subject area of object oriented programming is, however, large. It is not an exaggeration to state that entire books have been dedicated to the subject. As such, a detailed overview of object oriented software development is beyond the scope of this book. Instead, we will introduce the basic concepts involved in object oriented programming and then move on to explaining the concept as it relates to Swift application development. Once again, whilst we strive to provide the basic information you need in this chapter, we recommend reading a copy of Apple's *The Swift Programming Language* book for more extensive coverage of this subject area.

12.1 What is an Object?

Objects (also referred to as instances) are self-contained modules of functionality that can be easily used, and re-used as the building blocks for a software application.

Objects consist of data variables (called *properties*) and functions (called *methods*) that can be accessed and called on the object or instance to perform tasks and are collectively referred to as *class members*.

12.2 What is a Class?

Much as a blueprint or architect's drawing defines what an item or a building will look like once it has been constructed, a class defines what an object will look like when it is created. It defines, for example, what the methods will do and what the properties will be.

12.3 Declaring a Swift Class

Before an object can be instantiated, we first need to define the class 'blueprint' for the object. In this chapter we will create a bank account class to demonstrate the basic concepts of Swift object oriented programming.

In declaring a new Swift class we specify an optional *parent class* from which the new class is derived and also define the properties and methods that the class will contain. The basic syntax for a new class is as follows:

```
class NewClassName: ParentClass {
    // Properties
    // Instance Methods
```

```
    // Type methods
}
```

The *Properties* section of the declaration defines the variables and constants that are to be contained within the class. These are declared in the same way that any other variable or constant would be declared in Swift.

The *Instance methods* and *Type methods* sections define the methods that are available to be called on the class and instances of the class. These are essentially functions specific to the class that perform a particular operation when called upon and will be described in greater detail later in this chapter.

To create an example outline for our BankAccount class, we would use the following:

```
class BankAccount {

}
```

Now that we have the outline syntax for our class, the next step is to add some instance properties to it.

12.4 **Adding Instance Properties to a Class**

A key goal of object oriented programming is a concept referred to as *data encapsulation*. The idea behind data encapsulation is that data should be stored within classes and accessed only through methods defined in that class. Data encapsulated in a class are referred to as *properties* or *instance variables*.

Instances of our BankAccount class will be required to store some data, specifically a bank account number and the balance currently held within the account. Properties are declared in the same way any other variables and constants are declared in Swift. We can, therefore, add these variables as follows:

```
class BankAccount {
    var accountBalance: Float = 0
    var accountNumber: Int = 0
}
```

Having defined our properties, we can now move on to defining the methods of the class that will allow us to work with our properties while staying true to the data encapsulation model.

12.5 **Defining Methods**

The methods of a class are essentially code routines that can be called upon to perform specific tasks within the context of that class.

Methods come in two different forms, *type methods* and *instance methods*. Type methods operate at the level of the class, such as creating a new instance of a class. Instance methods, on the other hand, operate only on the instances of a class (for example performing an arithmetic operation on two property variables and returning the result).

Instance methods are declared within the opening and closing braces of the class to which they belong and are declared using the standard Swift function declaration syntax.

Type methods are declared in the same way as instance methods with the exception that the declaration is preceded by the *class* keyword.

For example, the declaration of a method to display the account balance in our example might read as follows:

```swift
class BankAccount {

    var accountBalance: Float = 0
    var accountNumber: Int = 0

    func displayBalance()
    {
        println("Number \(accountNumber)")
        println("Current balance is \(accountBalance)")
    }
}
```

The method is an *instance method* so it is not preceded by the *class* keyword.

When designing the BankAccount class it might be useful to be able to call a type method on the class itself to identify the maximum allowable balance that can be stored by the class. This would enable an application to identify whether the BankAccount class is suitable for storing details of a new customer without having to go through the process of first creating a class instance. This method will be named *getMaxBalance* and is implemented as follows:

```swift
class BankAccount {

    var accountBalance: Float = 0
    var accountNumber: Int = 0

    func displayBalance()
    {
        println("Number \(accountNumber)")
        println("Current balance is \(accountBalance)")
    }

    class func getMaxBalance() -> Float {
        return 100000.00
    }
}
```

12.6 **Declaring and Initializing a Class Instance**

So far all we have done is define the blueprint for our class. In order to do anything with this class, we need to create instances of it. The first step in this process is to declare a variable to store a reference to the instance when it is created. We do this as follows:

```
var account1: BankAccount = BankAccount()
```

When executed, an instance of our BankAccount class will have been created and will be accessible via the *account1* variable.

12.7 **Initializing and Deinitializing a Class Instance**

A class will often need to perform some initialization tasks at the point of creation. These tasks can be implemented by placing an *init* method within the class. In the case of the BankAccount class, it would be useful to be able to initialize the account number and balance properties with values when a new class instance is created. To achieve this, the *init* method could be written in the class as follows:

```
class BankAccount {

    var accountBalance: Float = 0
    var accountNumber: Int = 0

    init(number: Int, balance: Float)
    {
        accountNumber = number
        accountBalance = balance
    }

    func displayBalance()
    {
       println("Number \(accountNumber)")
       println("Current balance is \(accountBalance)")
    }

}
```

When creating an instance of the class, it will now be necessary to provide initialization values for the account number and balance properties as follows:

```
var account1 = BankAccount(number: 12312312, balance: 400.54)
```

Conversely, any cleanup tasks that need to be performed before a class instance is destroyed by the Swift runtime system can be performed by implementing the deinitializer within the class definition:

```
class BankAccount {
```

```
    var accountBalance: Float = 0
    var accountNumber: Int = 0

    init(number: Int, balance: Float)
    {
        accountNumber = number
        accountBalance = balance
    }

    deinit {
        // Perform any necessary clean up here
    }

    func displayBalance()
    {
        println("Number \(accountNumber)")
        println("Current balance is \(accountBalance)")
    }
}
```

12.8 Calling Methods and Accessing Properties

Now is probably a good time to recap what we have done so far in this chapter. We have now created a new Swift class named *BankAccount*. Within this new class we declared some properties to contain the bank account number and current balance together with an initializer and a method to display the current balance information. In the preceding section we covered the steps necessary to create and initialize an instance of our new class. The next step is to learn how to call the instance methods and access the properties we built into our class. This is most easily achieved using *dot notation*.

Dot notation involves accessing an instance variable, or calling an instance method by specifying a class instance followed by a dot followed in turn by the name of the property or method:

```
classInstance.propertyName
classInstance.instanceMethod()
```

For example, to get the current value of our *accountBalance* instance variable:

```
var balance1 = account1.accountBalance
```

Dot notation can also be used to set values of instance properties:

```
account1.accountBalance = 6789.98
```

The same technique is used to call methods on a class instance. For example, to call the *displayBalance* method on an instance of the BankAccount class:

```
account1.displayBalance()
```

Type methods are also called using dot notation, though they must be called on the class type instead of a class instance:

```
ClassName.typeMethod()
```

For example, to call the previously declared *getMaxBalance* type method, the BankAccount class is referenced:

```
var maxAllowed = BankAccount.getMaxBalance()
```

12.9 **Stored and Computed Properties**

Class properties in Swift fall into two categories referred to as *stored properties* and *calculated properties*. Stored properties are those values that are contained within a constant or variable. Both the account name and number properties in the BankAccount example are stored properties.

A calculated property, on the other hand, is a value that is derived based on some form of calculation or logic at the point at which the property is set or retrieved. Computed properties are implemented by creating *getter* and optional corresponding *setter* methods containing the code to perform the computation. Consider, for example, that the BankAcccount class might need an additional property to contain the current balance less any recent banking fees. Rather than use a stored property, it makes more sense to use a computed property which calculates this value on request. The modified BankAccount class might now read as follows:

```
class BankAccount {

    var accountBalance: Float = 0
    var accountNumber: Int = 0;
    let fees: Float = 25.00

    var balanceLessFees: Float {
        get {
            return accountBalance - fees
        }
    }

    init(number: Int, balance: Float)
    {
        accountNumber = number
        accountBalance = balance
    }
```

.

.

.

```
}
```

The above code adds a getter that returns a computed property based on the current balance minus a fee amount. An optional setter could also be declared in much the same way to set the balance value less fees:

```
var balanceLessFees: Float {
    get {
        return accountBalance - fees
    }

    set(newBalance)
    {
            accountBalance = newBalance - fees
    }
}
```

The new setter takes as a parameter a floating point value from which it deducts the fee value before assigning the result to the current balance property. Regardless of the fact that these are computed properties, they are accessed in the same way as stored properties using dot-notation. The following code gets the current balance less fees value before setting the property to a new value:

```
var balance1 = account1.balanceLessFees
account1.balanceLessFees = 12123.12
```

12.10 Using self in Swift

Programmers familiar with other object oriented programming languages may be in the habit of prefixing references to properties and methods with *self* to indicate that the method or property belongs to the current class instance. The Swift programming language also provides the *self* property type for this purpose and it is, therefore, perfectly valid to write code which reads as follows:

```
class MyClass {
    var myNumber = 1

    func addTen() {
        self.myNumber += 10
    }
}
```

In this context, the *self* prefix indicates to the compiler that the code is referring to a property named *myNumber* which belongs to the MyClass class instance. When programming in Swift, however, it is no longer necessary to use self in most situations since this is now assumed to be the default for references to properties and methods. To quote The Swift Programming Language guide published by Apple, "in practice you don't need to write *self* in your code very often". The function from the above example, therefore, can also be written as follows with the self reference omitted:

```
func addTen() {
    myNumber += 10
}
```

In most cases, use of self is optional in Swift. That being said, one situation where it is still necessary to use *self* is when referencing a property or method from within a closure expression. The use of self, for example, is mandatory in the following closure expression:

```
document?.openWithCompletionHandler({ (success: Bool) -> Void in
    if success {
        self.ubiquityURL = resultURL
    }
})
```

It is also necessary to use self to resolve ambiguity such as when a function parameter has the same name as a class property. In the following code, for example, the first println statement will output the value passed through to the function via the myNumber parameter while the second println statement outputs the number assigned to the myNumber class property (in this case 10):

```
class MyClass {

    var myNumber = 10 // class property

    func addTen(myNumber: Int) {
        println(myNumber) // Output the function parameter value
        println(self.myNumber) // Output the class property value
    }
}
```

Whether or not to use self in most other situations is largely a matter of programmer preference. Those who prefer to use self when referencing properties and methods can continue to do so in Swift. Code that is written without use of the self property type (where doing so is not mandatory) is, however, just as valid when programming in Swift.

12.11 Summary

Object oriented programming languages such as Swift encourage the creation of classes to promote code reuse and the encapsulation of data within class instances. This chapter has covered the basic concepts of classes and instances within Swift together with an overview of stored and computed properties and both instance and type methods.

Chapter 13

13. An Introduction to Swift Inheritance

In the *Basics of Object Oriented Programming in Swift* we covered the basic concepts of object-oriented programming and worked through an example of creating and working with a new class using Swift. In that example, our new class was not derived from any base class and, as such, did not inherit any traits from a parent or super class. In this chapter we will provide an introduction to the concepts of subclassing and inheritance in Swift.

13.1 Inheritance, Classes and Subclasses

The concept of inheritance brings something of a real-world view to programming. It allows a class to be defined that has a certain set of characteristics (such as methods and properties) and then other classes to be created which are derived from that class. The derived class inherits all of the features of the parent class and typically then adds some features of its own.

By deriving classes we create what is often referred to as a *class hierarchy*. The class at the top of the hierarchy is known as the *base class* or *root class* and the derived classes as *subclasses* or *child classes*. Any number of subclasses may be derived from a class. The class from which a subclass is derived is called the *parent class* or *super class*.

Classes need not only be derived from a root class. For example, a subclass can also inherit from another subclass with the potential to create large and complex class hierarchies.

In Swift a subclass can only be derived from a single direct parent class. This is a concept referred to as *single inheritance*.

13.2 A Swift Inheritance Example

As with most programming concepts, the subject of inheritance in Swift is perhaps best illustrated with an example. In *The Basics of Object Oriented Programming in Swift* we created a class named *BankAccount* designed to hold a bank account number and corresponding current balance. The BankAccount class contained both properties and instance methods. A simplified declaration for this class is reproduced below:

```
class BankAccount {

    var accountBalance: Float
```

```
    var accountNumber: Int

    init(number: Int, balance: Float)
    {
        accountNumber = number
        accountBalance = balance
    }

    func displayBalance()
    {
        println("Number \(accountNumber)")
        println("Current balance is \(accountBalance)")
    }
}
```

Though this is a somewhat rudimentary class, it does everything necessary if all you need it to do is store an account number and account balance. Suppose, however, that in addition to the BankAccount class you also needed a class to be used for savings accounts. A savings account will still need to hold an account number and a current balance and methods will still be needed to access that data. One option would be to create an entirely new class, one that duplicates all of the functionality of the BankAccount class together with the new features required by a savings account. A more efficient approach, however, would be to create a new class that is a *subclass* of the BankAccount class. The new class will then inherit all the features of the BankAccount class but can then be extended to add the additional functionality required by a savings account.

To create a subclass of BankAccount that we will call SavingsAccount, we simply declare the new class, this time specifying BankAccount as the parent class:

```
class SavingsAccount: BankAccount {

}
```

Note that although we have yet to add any instance variables or methods, the class has actually inherited all the methods and properties of the parent BankAccount class. We could, therefore, create an instance of the SavingsAccount class and set variables and call methods in exactly the same way we did with the BankAccount class in previous examples. That said, we haven't really achieved anything unless we actually take steps to extend the class.

13.3 Extending the Functionality of a Subclass

So far we have been able to create a subclass that contains all the functionality of the parent class. In order for this exercise to make sense, however, we now need to extend the subclass so that it has the features we need to make it useful for storing savings account information. To do this, we simply add the properties and methods that provide the new functionality, just as we would for any other class we might wish to create:

```
class SavingsAccount: BankAccount {

    var interestRate: Float

    func calculateInterest() -> Float
    {
        return interestRate * accountBalance
    }
}
```

13.4 Overriding Inherited Methods

When using inheritance it is not unusual to find a method in the parent class that almost does what you need, but requires modification to provide the precise functionality you require. That being said, it is also possible you'll inherit a method with a name that describes exactly what you want to do, but it actually does not come close to doing what you need. One option in this scenario would be to ignore the inherited method and write a new method with an entirely new name. A better option is to *override* the inherited method and write a new version of it in the subclass.

Before proceeding with an example, there are two rules that must be obeyed when overriding a method. Firstly, the overriding method in the subclass must take exactly the same number and type of parameters as the overridden method in the parent class. Secondly, the new method must have the same return type as the parent method.

In our BankAccount class we have a method named *displayBalance* that displays the bank account number and current balance held by an instance of the class. In our SavingsAccount subclass we might also want to output the current interest rate assigned to the account. To achieve this, we simply declare a new version of the *displayBalance* method in our SavingsAccount subclass, prefixed with the *override* keyword:

```
class SavingsAccount: BankAccount {

    var interestRate: Float

    func calculateInterest() -> Float
    {
        return interestRate * accountBalance
    }

    override func displayBalance()
    {
        println("Number \(accountNumber)")
        println("Current balance is \(accountBalance)")
        println("Prevailing interest rate is \(interestRate)")
    }
```

}

It is also possible to make a call to the overridden method in the super class from within a subclass. The *displayBalance* method of the super class could, for example, be called to display the account number and balance, before the interest rate is displayed, thereby eliminating further code duplication:

```
override func displayBalance()
{
        super.displayBalance()
        println("Prevailing interest rate is \(interestRate)")
}
```

13.5 Initializing the Subclass

As the SavingsAccount class currently stands, it inherits the init initializer method from the parent BankAccount class which was implemented as follows:

```
init(number: Int, balance: Float)
{
        accountNumber = number
        accountBalance = balance
}
```

Clearly this method takes the necessary steps to initialize both the account number and balance properties of the class. The SavingsAccount class, however, contains an additional property in the form of the interest rate variable. The SavingsAccount class, therefore, needs its own initializer to ensure that the interestRate property is initialized when instances of the class are created. This method can perform this task and then make a call to the *init* method of the parent class to complete the initialization of the remaining variables:

```
class SavingsAccount: BankAccount {

    var interestRate: Float

    init(number: Int, balance: Float, rate: Float)
    {
        interestRate = rate
        super.init(number: number, balance: balance)
    }
    .
    .
    .
}
```

Note that to avoid potential initialization problems, the *init* method of the superclass must always be called *after* the initialization tasks for the subclass have been completed.

13.6 **Using the SavingsAccount Class**

Now that we have completed work on our SavingsAccount class, the class can be used in some example code in much the same way as the parent BankAccount class:

```
var savings1 = SavingsAccount(number: 12311, balance: 600.00,
                                              rate: 0.07)

println(savings1.calculateInterest())
savings1.displayBalance()
```

13.7 **Summary**

Inheritance extends the concept of object re-use in object oriented programming by allowing new classes to be derived from existing classes, with those new classes subsequently extended to add new functionality. When an existing class provides some, but not all, of the functionality required by the programmer, inheritance allows that class to be used as the basis for a new subclass. The new subclass will inherit all the capabilities of the parent class, but may then be extended to add the missing functionality.

14. Working with Array and Dictionary Collections in Swift

Arrays and dictionaries in Swift are objects that contain collections of other objects. In this chapter, we will cover some of the basics of working with arrays and dictionaries in Swift.

14.1 Mutable and Immutable Collections

Collections in Swift come in mutable and immutable forms. The contents of immutable collection instances cannot be changed after the object has been initialized. To make a collection immutable, assign it to a *constant* when it is created. Collections are mutable, on the other hand, if assigned to a *variable*.

14.2 Swift Array Initialization

An array is a data type designed specifically to hold multiple values in a single ordered collection. An array, for example, could be created to store a list of String values. A single Swift based array is only able to store values that are of the same type. An array of String values, therefore, could not also contain an Int value. The type of an array can be specified specifically using type annotation, or left to the compiler to identify using type inference.

An array may be initialized with a collection of values (referred to as an *array literal*) at creation time using the following syntax:

var variableName: [type] = [value 1, value2, value3, ...]

The following code creates a new array assigned to a variable (thereby making it mutable) that is initialized with three string values:

```
var treeArray = ["Pine", "Oak", "Yew"]
```

Alternatively, the same array could have been created immutably by assigning it to a constant:

```
let treeArray = ["Pine", "Oak", "Yew"]
```

In the above instance, the Swift compiler will use type inference to decide that the array contains values of String type and prevent values of other types being inserted into the array elsewhere within the application code.

Alternatively, the same array could have been declared using type annotation:

```
var treeArray: [String] = ["Pine", "Oak", "Yew"]
```

Arrays do not have to have values assigned at creation time. The following syntax can be used to create an empty array:

```
var variableName = [type]()
```

Consider, for example, the following code which creates an empty array designated to store floating point values and assigns it to a variable named priceArray:

```
var priceArray = [Float]()
```

Another useful initialization technique allows an array to be initialized to a certain size with each array element pre-set with a specified default value:

```
var nameArray = [String](count: 10, repeatedValue: "My String")
```

When compiled and executed, the above code will create a new 10 element array with each element initialized with a string that reads "My String".

Finally, a new array may be created by adding together two existing arrays (assuming both arrays contain values of the same type). For example:

```
var firstArray = ["Red", "Green", "Blue"]
var secondArray = ["Indigo", "Violet"]

var thirdArray = firstArray + secondArray
```

14.3 **Working with Arrays in Swift**

Once an array exists, a wide range of methods and properties are provided for working with and manipulating the array content from within Swift code, a subset of which is as follows:

14.3.1 Array Item Count

A count of the items in an array can be obtained by accessing the array's count property:

```
var treeArray = ["Pine", "Oak", "Yew"]
var itemCount = treeArray.count

println(itemCount)
```

Whether or not an array is empty can be identified using the array's Boolean *isEmpty* property as follows:

```
var treeArray = ["Pine", "Oak", "Yew"]
```

```
if treeArray.isEmpty {
    // Array is empty
}
```

14.3.2 Accessing Array Items

A specific item in an array may be accessed or modified by referencing the item's position in the array index (where the first item in the array has index position 0) using a technique referred to as *index subscripting*. In the following code fragment, the string value contained at index position 2 in the array (in this case the string value "Yew") is output by the println call:

```
var treeArray = ["Pine", "Oak", "Yew"]

println(treeArray[2])
```

This approach can also be used to replace the value at an index location:

```
treeArray[1] = "Redwood"
```

The above code replaces the current value at index position 1 with a new String value that reads "Redwood".

14.4 Appending Items to an Array

Items may be added to an array using either the *append* method or + and += operators. The following, for example, are all valid techniques for appending items to an array:

```
treeArray.append("Redwood")
treeArray += ["Redwood"]
treeArray += ["Redwood", "Maple", "Birch"]
```

14.4.1 Inserting and Deleting Array Items

New items may be inserted into an array by specifying the index location of the new item in a call to the array's *insert(atIndex:)* method. An insertion preserves all existing elements in the array, essentially moving them to the right to accommodate the newly inserted item:

```
treeArray.insert("Maple", atIndex: 0)
```

Similarly, an item at a specific array index position may be removed using the *removeAtIndex* method call:

```
treeArray.removeAtIndex(2)
```

To remove the last item in an array, simply make a call to the array's *removeLast* method as follows:

```
treeArray.removeLast()
```

14.4.2 Array Iteration

The easiest way to iterate through the items in an array is to make use of the for-in looping syntax. The following code, for example, iterates through all of the items in a String array and outputs each item to the console panel:

```
var treeArray = ["Pine", "Oak", "Yew", "Maple", "Birch", "Myrtle"]

for tree in treeArray {
    println(tree)
}
```

Upon execution, the following output would appear in the console:

```
Pine
Oak
Yew
Maple
Birch
Myrtle
```

14.5 **Swift Dictionary Collections**

String dictionaries allow data to be stored and managed in the form of key-value pairs. Dictionaries fulfill a similar purpose to arrays, except each item stored in the dictionary has associated with it a unique key (to be precise, the key is unique to the particular dictionary object) which can be used to reference and access the corresponding value. Currently only String, Int, Double and Bool data types are suitable for use as keys within a Swift dictionary.

14.6 **Swift Dictionary Initialization**

A dictionary is a data type designed specifically to hold multiple values in a single unordered collection. Each item in a dictionary consists of a key and an associated value. The data types of the key and value elements type may be specified specifically using type annotation, or left to the compiler to identify using type inference.

A new dictionary may be initialized with a collection of values (referred to as a *dictionary literal*) at creation time using the following syntax:

var *variableName*: [*key type*: *value type*] = [*key 1: value 1, key 2: value2 ....*]

The following code creates a new array assigned to a variable (thereby making it mutable) that is initialized with four key-value pairs in the form of ISBN numbers acting as keys for corresponding book titles:

```
var bookDict = ["100-432112" : "Wind in the Willows",
                "200-532874" : "Tale of Two Cities",
```

```
              "202-546549" : "Sense and Sensibility",
              "104-109834" : "Shutter Island"]
```

In the above instance, the Swift compiler will use type inference to decide that both the key and value elements of the dictionary are of String type and prevent values or keys of other types being inserted into the dictionary.

Alternatively, the same array could have been declared using type annotation:

```
var bookDict: [String: String] =
              ["100-432112" : "Wind in the Willows",
               "200-532874" : "Tale of Two Cities",
               "202-546549" : "Sense and Sensibility",
               "104-109834" : "Shutter Island"]
```

As with arrays, it is also possible to create an empty dictionary, the syntax for which reads as follows:

var *variableName* = [*key type*: *value type*]()

The following code creates an empty dictionary designated to store integer keys and string values:

```
var myDictionary = [Int: String]()
```

14.6.1 Dictionary Item Count

A count of the items in a dictionary can be obtained by accessing the dictionary's count property:

```
var bookDict: [String: String] =
              ["100-432112" : "Wind in the Willows",
               "200-532874" : "Tale of Two Cities",
               "202-546549" : "Sense and Sensibility",
               "104-109834" : "Shutter Island"]


println(bookDict.count)
```

14.6.2 Accessing and Updating Dictionary Items

A specific value may be accessed or modified using key subscript syntax to reference the corresponding key. The following code references a key known to be in the bookDict dictionary and outputs the associated value (in this case the book entitled "A Tale of Two Cities"):

```
println(bookDict["200-532874"])
```

A similar approach can be used when updating the value associated with a specified key, for example, to change the title of the same book from "At Tale of Two Cities" to "Sense and Sensibility"):

```
bookDict["200-532874"] = "Sense and Sensibility"
```

The same result is also possible by making a call to the *updateValue(forKey:)* method, passing through the key corresponding to the value to be changed:

```
bookDict.updateValue("The Ruins", forKey: "200-532874")
```

14.6.3 Adding and Removing Dictionary Entries

Items may be added to a dictionary using the following key subscripting syntax:

dictionaryVariable[key] = value

For example, to add a new key-value pair entry to the books dictionary:

```
bookDict["300-898871"] = "The Overlook"
```

Removal of a key-value pair from a dictionary may be achieved either by assigning a *nil* value to the entry, or via a call to the *removeValueForKey* method of the dictionary instance. Both code lines below achieve the same result of removing the specified entry from the books dictionary:

```
bookDict["300-898871"] = nil
bookDict.removeValueForKey("300-898871")
```

14.6.4 Dictionary Iteration

As with arrays, it is possible to iterate through the entries by making use of the for-in looping syntax. The following code, for example, iterates through all of the entries in the books dictionary, outputting both the key and value for each entry panel:

```
for (bookid, title) in bookDict {
  println("Book ID: \(bookid) Title: \(title)")
}
```

Upon execution, the following output would appear in the console:

```
Book ID: 100-432112 Title: Wind in the Willows
Book ID: 200-532874 Title: The Ruins
Book ID: 104-109834 Title: Shutter Island
Book ID: 202-546549 Title: Sense and Sensibility
```

14.7 Summary

Collections in Swift take the form of either dictionaries or arrays. Both provide a way to collect together multiple items within a single object. Arrays provide a way to store an ordered collection of items where those items are accessed by an index value corresponding to the item position in the array. Dictionaries provide a platform for storing key-value pairs, where the key is used to gain access to the stored value. Iteration through the elements of Swift collections can be achieved using the for-in loop construct.

15. The iOS 8 Application and Development Architecture

So far we have covered a considerable amount of ground intended to provide a sound foundation of knowledge on which to begin building iOS 8 based apps. Before plunging into more complex apps, however, it is vital that you have a basic understanding of some key methodologies associated with the overall architecture of iOS applications.

These methodologies, also referred to as *design patterns,* clearly define how your applications should be designed and implemented in terms of code structure. The patterns we will explore in this chapter are *Model View Controller (MVC)*, *Subclassing*, *Delegation* and *Target-Action*.

It is also useful to gain an understanding of how iOS 8 itself is structured in terms of operating system layers.

If you are new to these concepts this can seem a little confusing to begin with. Much of this will become clearer, however, once we start working on some examples in subsequent chapters.

15.1 An Overview of the iOS 8 Operating System Architecture

iOS consists of a number of different software layers, each of which provides programming frameworks for the development of applications that run on top of the underlying hardware.

These operating system layers can be presented diagrammatically as illustrated in Figure 15-1:

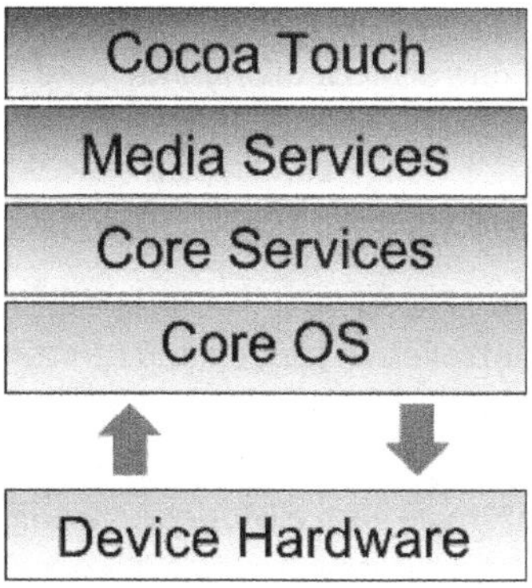

Figure 15-1

Some diagrams designed to graphically depict the iOS software stack show an additional box positioned above the Cocoa Touch layer to indicate the applications running on the device. In the above diagram we have not done so since this would suggest that the only interface available to the app is Cocoa Touch. In practice, an app can directly call down to any of the layers of the stack to perform tasks on the physical device.

That said, however, each operating system layer provides an increasing level of abstraction away from the complexity of working with the hardware. As an iOS developer you should, therefore, always look for solutions to your programming goals in the frameworks located in the higher level iOS layers before resorting to writing code that reaches down to the lower level layers. In general, the higher level of layer you program to, the less effort and fewer lines of code you will have to write to achieve your objective. And as any veteran programmer will tell you, the less code you have to write the less opportunity you have to introduce bugs.

15.2 **Model View Controller (MVC)**

In the days before object-oriented programming (and even for a time after object-oriented programming became popular) there was a tendency to develop applications where the code for the user interface was tied tightly to the code containing the application logic and data handling. This coupling made application code difficult to maintain and locked the application to a single user interface. If, for example, an application written for Microsoft Windows needed to be migrated to Mac OS, all the code written specifically for the Windows UI toolkits had to be ripped out from amongst the data and logic code and replaced with the Mac OS equivalent. If the application then needed to be turned into a web based solution, the process would have to be repeated again. Attempts to achieve this feat were usually found to be prohibitively expensive and ultimately ended up with the applications being completely re-written each time a new platform needed to be targeted.

The goal of the MVC design pattern is to divorce the logic and data handling code of an application from the presentation code. In this concept, the Model encapsulates the data for the application, the View presents and manages the user interface and the Controller provides the basic logic for the application and acts as the go-between, providing instructions to the Model based on user interactions with the View and updating the View to reflect responses from the Model. The true value of this approach is that the Model knows absolutely nothing about the presentation of the application. It just knows how to store and handle data and perform certain tasks when called upon by the Controller. Similarly, the View knows nothing about the data and logic model of the application.

Within the context of an object-oriented programming environment such as the iOS 8 SDK and Swift, the Model, View and Controller components are objects. It is also worth pointing out that applications are not restricted to a single model, view and controller. In fact, an app can consist of multiple view objects, controller objects and model objects.

The way that a view controller object interacts with a Model is through the methods and properties exposed by that model object. This, in fact, is no different from the way one object interacts with another in any object-oriented programming environment.

In terms of the view controller's interactions with the view, however, things get a little more complicated. In practice, this is achieved using the *Target-Action pattern*, together with *Outlets* and *Actions.*

15.3 **The Target-Action pattern, IBOutlets and IBActions**

When you create an iOS 8 app you will typically design the user interface (the view) using the Interface Builder tool and write the view controller and model code in Swift using the Xcode code editor. The previous section looked briefly at how the view controller interacts with the model. In this section we will look at how the view created in Interface Builder and our view controller code interact with each other.

When a user interacts with objects in the view, for example touching and releasing a button control, an *event* is triggered (in this case the event is called a *Touch Up Inside* event). The purpose of the *Target-Action* pattern is to allow you to specify what happens when such events are triggered. In other words, this is how you connect the objects in the user interface you have designed in the Interface Builder tool to the back end Swift code you have written in the Xcode environment. Specifically, this allows you to define which method of which controller object gets called when a user interacts in a certain way with a view object.

The process of wiring up a view object to call a specific method on a view controller object is achieved using something called an *Action*. An action is a method defined within a view controller object that is designed to be called when an event is triggered in a view object. This allows us to connect a view object created within Interface Builder to the code that we have written in the view controller class. This is one of the ways that we bridge the separation between the *View* and the *Controller* in our MVC design pattern. As we will see in *Creating an Interactive iOS 8 App*, action methods are declared using the *IBAction* keyword.

The opposite of an *Action* is the *Outlet*. As previously described, an Action allows a view object to call a method on a controller object. An Outlet, on the other hand, allows a view controller object method to directly access the properties of a view object. A view controller might, for example, need to set the text on a UILabel object. In order to do so an Outlet must first have been defined using the *IBOutlet* keyword. In programming terms, an *IBOutlet* is simply an instance variable that references the view object to which access is required.

15.4 **Subclassing**

Subclassing is an important feature of any object-oriented programming environment and the iOS SDK is no exception to this rule. Subclassing allows us to create a new class by deriving from an existing class and then extending the functionality. In so doing we get all the functionality of the parent class combined with the ability to extend the new class with additional methods and properties.

Subclassing is typically used where a pre-existing class does most, but not all, of what you need. By subclassing we get all that existing functionality without having to duplicate it and simply add on the functionality that was missing.

We will see an example of subclassing in the context of iOS 8 development when we start to work with view controllers. The UIKit Framework contains a class called the UIViewController. This is a generic view controller from which we will create a subclass so that we can add our own methods and properties.

15.5 **Delegation**

Delegation allows an object to pass the responsibility for performing one or more tasks on to another object. This allows the behavior of an object to be modified without having to go through the process of subclassing it.

A prime example of delegation can be seen in the case of the UIApplication class. The UIApplication class, of which every iOS application must have one (and only one) instance, is responsible for the control and operation of the application within the iOS environment. Much of what the UIApplication object does happens in the background. There are, however, instances where it gives us the opportunity to include our own functionality into the mix. UIApplication allows us to do this by delegating some methods to us. As an example, UIApplication delegates the *didFinishLaunchingWithOptions* method to us so that we can write code to perform specific tasks when the app first loads (for example taking the user back to the point they were at when they last exited). If you still have a copy of the Hello World project created earlier in this book you will see the template for this method in the *AppDelegate.swift* file.

15.6 **Summary**

In this chapter we have provided an overview of a number of design patterns and discussed the importance of these patterns in terms of structuring iOS 8 applications. Whilst these patterns may seem unclear to some, the relevance and implementation of such concepts will become clearer as we progress through the examples included in subsequent chapters of this book.

16. Creating an Interactive iOS 8 App

In the previous chapter we looked at the design patterns that we will need to learn and use regularly in the course of developing iOS 8 based applications. In this chapter we will work through a detailed example intended to demonstrate the View-Controller relationship together with the implementation of the Target-Action pattern to create an example interactive iOS 8 application.

16.1 Creating the New Project

The purpose of the application we are going to create is to perform unit conversions from Fahrenheit to Centigrade. Obviously the first step is to create a new Xcode project to contain our application. Start Xcode and on the Welcome screen select *Create a new Xcode project.* On the template screen choose the *Application* option located under *iOS* in the left hand panel and select *Single View Application.* Click *Next,* set the product name to *UnitConverter,* enter your company identifier and make sure that the *Devices* menu is set to *Universal* so that the user interface will be suitable for deployment on all iPhone and iPad screen sizes. Before clicking *Next,* change the *Language* menu to Swift. On the final screen, choose a location in which to store the project files and click on *Create* to proceed to the main Xcode project window.

16.2 Creating the User Interface

Before we begin developing the logic for our interactive application we are going to start by designing the user interface. When we created the new project, Xcode generated a storyboard file for us and named it *Main.storyboard.* It is within this file that we will create our user interface, so select this file from the project navigator in the left hand panel to load it into Interface Builder.

Figure 16-1

From the Object Library panel, drag a Text Field object onto the View design area. Resize the object and position it so that it appears as outlined in Figure 16-2.

Figure 16-2

Within the Attributes Inspector panel (*View -> Utilities -> Show Attributes Inspector*), type the words *Enter temperature* into the *Placeholder* text field. This text will then appear in a light gray color in the text field as a visual cue to the user. Since only numbers and decimal points will be required to be input for the temperature, locate the *Keyboard Type* property in the Attributes Inspector panel and change the setting to *Numbers and Punctuation*.

Now that we have created the text field into which the user will enter a temperature value, the next step is to add a Button object which may be pressed to initiate the conversion. To achieve this, drag and drop a *Button* object from the Object Library to the View. Double click the button object so that it changes to text edit mode and type the word *Convert* onto the button. Finally, select the button and drag it beneath the text field until the blue dotted line appears indicating it is centered horizontally in relation to the containing view before releasing the mouse button.

The last user interface object we need to add is the label where the result of the conversion will be displayed. Add this by dragging a Label object from the Object Library panel to the View and position it beneath the button. Stretch the width of the label so that it is approximately a third of the overall width of the view and reposition it using the blue guidelines to ensure it is centered in relation to the containing view. Modify the Alignment attribute for the label object so that the text is centered.

Double click on the label to highlight the text and press the backspace key to clear it (we will set the text from within a method of our View Controller class when the conversion calculation has been performed). Though the label is now no longer visible it is still present in the view. If you click where it is located it will be highlighted with the resize dots visible.

In order for the user interface design layout to adapt to the many different iPad and iPhone screen sizes it will be necessary to add some Auto Layout constraints to the views in the storyboard. Auto Layout will be covered in detail in subsequent chapters, but for the purposes of this example, we will request that Interface Builder add what it considers to be the appropriate constraints for this layout. In the lower right hand corner of the Interface Builder panel is a toolbar. Click on the background view of the current scene and click on the *Resolve Auto Layout Issues* button as highlighted in Figure 16-3:

Figure 16-3

From the menu, select the *Reset to Suggested Constraints* option listed under *All Views in View Controller*:

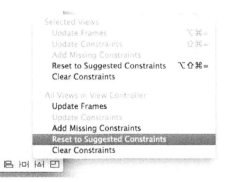

Figure 16-4

At this point the user interface design phase of our project is complete and the view should appear as illustrated in Figure 16-5. We now are ready to try out a test build and run.

Figure 16-5

16.3 Building and Running the Sample Application

Before we move on to implementing the view controller code for our application and then connecting it to the user interface we have designed we should first perform a test build and run of the application so far. Click on the run button located in the toolbar (the triangular "play" button) to compile the application and run it in the simulator. If you are not happy with the way your interface looks feel free to reload it into Interface Builder and make improvements. Assuming the user interface appears to your satisfaction in the simulator we are ready to start writing some Swift code to add some logic to our controller.

16.4 Adding Actions and Outlets

When the user enters a temperature value into the text field and touches the convert button we need to trigger an action which will perform a calculation to convert the temperature. The result of that calculation will then be presented to the user via the label object. The *Action* will be in the form of a method which we will declare and implement in our View Controller class. Access to the text field and label objects from the view controller method will be implemented through the use of *Outlets*.

Before we begin, now is a good time to highlight an example of the use of subclassing as previously described in *The iOS 8 Application and Development Architecture*, the UIKit Framework contains a class called UIViewController which provides the basic foundation for adding view controllers to an application. In order to create a functional application, however, we inevitably need to add functionality specific to our application to this generic view controller class. This is achieved by subclassing the UIViewController class and extending it with the additional functionality we need.

When we created our new project, Xcode anticipated our needs and automatically created a subclass of UIViewController and named it ViewController. In so doing, Xcode also created a source code file named *ViewController.swift*.

Selecting the *ViewController.swift* file in the Xcode project navigator panel will display the contents of the file in the editing pane:

```
import UIKit

class ViewController: UIViewController {

    override func viewDidLoad() {
        super.viewDidLoad()
        // Do any additional setup after loading the view, typically from
a nib.
    }

    override func didReceiveMemoryWarning() {
        super.didReceiveMemoryWarning()
        // Dispose of any resources that can be recreated.
    }


}
```

As we can see from the above code, a new class called ViewController has been created that is a subclass of the UIViewController class belonging to the UIKit framework.

The next step is to extend the subclass to include the two outlets and our action method. This could be achieved by manually declaring the outlets and actions within the *ViewController.swift* file. A much easier approach is to use the Xcode Assistant Editor to do this for us.

With the *Main.storyboard* file selected, display the Assistant Editor by selecting the *View -> Assistant Editor -> Show Assistant Editor* menu option. Alternatively, it may also be displayed by selecting the center button (the one containing an image of interlocking circles) of the row of Editor toolbar buttons in the top right hand corner of the main Xcode window as illustrated in the following figure:

Figure 16-6

In the event that multiple Assistant Editor panels are required, additional tiles may be added using the *View -> Assistant Editor -> Add Assistant Editor* menu option.

By default, the editor panel will appear to the right of the main editing panel in the Xcode window. For example, in Figure 16-7 the panel to the immediate right of the Interface Builder panel is the Assistant Editor:

Figure 16-7

By default, the Assistant Editor will be in *Automatic* mode, whereby it automatically attempts to display the correct source file based on the currently selected item in Interface Builder. If the correct file is not displayed, use the toolbar along the top of the editor panel to select the correct file. The small instance of the Assistant Editor icon in this toolbar can be used to switch to *Manual* mode allowing the file to be selected from a pull-right menu containing all the source files in the project.

Make sure that the *ViewController.swift* file is displayed in the Assistant Editor and establish an outlet for the Text Field object by Ctrl-clicking on the Text Field object in the view and dragging the resulting line to the area immediately beneath the class declaration line in the Assistant Editor panel as illustrated in Figure 16-8:

Figure 16-8

Upon releasing the line, the configuration panel illustrated in Figure 16-9 will appear requesting details about the outlet to be defined.

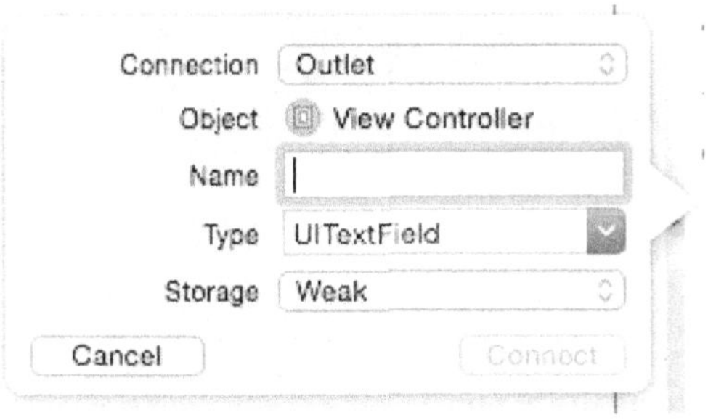

Figure 16-9

Since this is an outlet, the *Connection* menu should be left as *Outlet*. The type and storage values are also correct for this type of outlet. The only task that remains is to enter a name for the outlet, so in the *Name* field enter *tempText* before clicking on the *Connect* button.

Once the connection has been established, select the *ViewController.swift* file and note that the outlet property has been declared for us by the assistant:

```
import UIKit

class ViewController: UIViewController {

    @IBOutlet weak var tempText: UITextField!
    .
    .
    .
}
```

Repeat the above steps to establish an outlet for the Label object named *resultLabel*.

Next we need to establish the action that will be called when the user touches the Convert button in our user interface. The steps to declare an action using the Assistant Editor are essentially the same as those for an outlet. Once again, select the *Main.storyboard* file, but this time Ctrl-click on the button object. Drag the resulting line to the area beneath the existing *viewDidLoad* method in the Assistant Editor panel before releasing it. The connection box will once again appear. Since we are creating an action rather than an outlet, change the *Connection* menu to *Action*. Name the action *convertTemp* and make sure the *Event* type is set to *Touch Up Inside*:

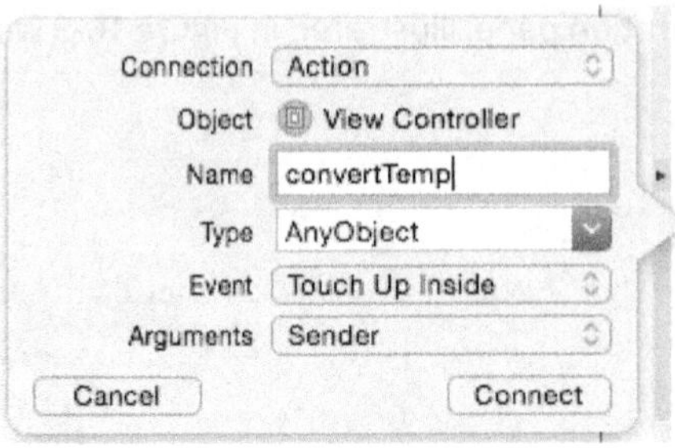

Figure 16-10

Click on the *Connect* button to create the action.

Select the *ViewController.swift* file and note that a stub method for the action has now been declared for us by the assistant:

```
@IBAction func convertTemp(sender: AnyObject) {
}
```

All that remains is to write the Swift code in the action method to perform the conversion:

```
@IBAction func convertTemp(sender: AnyObject) {
    let fahrenheit = (tempText.text as NSString).doubleValue
    let celsius = (fahrenheit - 32)/1.8
    let resultText = "Celsius \(celsius)"
    resultLabel.text = resultText
}
```

Before we proceed it is probably a good idea to pause and explain what is happening in the above code. Those already familiar with Swift, however, may skip the next few paragraphs.

In this file we are implementing the *convertTemp* method, a template for which was created for us by the Assistant Editor. This method takes as a single argument a reference to the *sender.* The sender is the object that triggered the call to the method (in this case our Button object). Whilst we won't be using this object in the current example, this can be used to create a general purpose method in which the behavior of the method changes depending on how (i.e. via which object) it was called. We could, for example, create two buttons labeled *Convert to Fahrenheit* and *Convert to Celsius* respectively, each of which calls the same *convertTemp* method. The method would then access the *sender* object to identify which button triggered the event and perform the corresponding type of unit conversion.

Within the body of the method we use dot notation to access the *text* property (which holds the text displayed in the text field) of the UITextField object to access the text in the field. This property is itself an object of type NSString. The NSString class has an instance method named *doubleValue* that converts the string value to a double number value. We therefore call this method on the text property and assign the result to a new constant named *fahrenheit*.

Having extracted the text entered by the user and converted it to a number, we then perform the conversion to Celsius and store the result in another constant named *celsius*. Next, we create a new string object and initialize it with text comprising the word Celsius and the result of our conversion. In doing so, we declare a constant named *resultText*.

Finally, we use dot notation to assign the new string to the text property of our UILabel object so that it is displayed to the user.

16.5 **Building and Running the Finished Application**

From within the Xcode project window click on the run button located in the Xcode toolbar (the triangular "play" style button) to compile the application and run it in the simulator. Once the application is running, click inside the text field and enter a Fahrenheit temperature. Next, click on the Convert button to display the equivalent temperature in Celsius. Assuming all went to plan your application should appear as outlined in the following figure:

Figure 16-11

16.6 **Hiding the Keyboard**

The final step in the application implementation is to add a mechanism for hiding the keyboard. Ideally, the keyboard should withdraw from view when the user touches the background view or taps the return key on the keyboard.

To achieve this, we will begin by implementing the *touchesBegan* event handler method on the view controller in the *ViewController.swift* file as follows:

```
override func touchesBegan(touches: NSSet, withEvent event: UIEvent) {
    tempText.endEditing(true)
```

}

When the background view is touched by the user, the keyboard will now be hidden.

The next step is to hide the keyboard when the return key is tapped. To do this, display the Assistant Editor and Ctrl-click and drag from the Text Field to a position beneath the *viewDidLoad* method within the *ViewController.swift* file. On releasing the line, change the settings in the connection dialog to establish an Action connection named *textFieldReturn* for the *Did End on Exit* event as shown in Figure 16-12 and click on the *Connect* button to establish the connection.

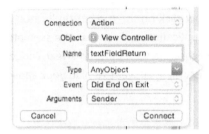

Figure 16-12

Select the *ViewController.swift* file in the project navigator, locate and edit the *textFieldReturn* stub method so that it now reads as follows:

```
@IBAction func textFieldReturn(sender: AnyObject) {
    sender.resignFirstResponder()
}
```

In the above method we are making a call to the *resignFirstResponder* method of the object that triggered the event. The *first responder* is the object with which the user is currently interacting (in this instance, the virtual keyboard displayed on the device screen).

Save the code and then build and run the application. When the application starts up, select the text field so that the keyboard appears. Touching any area of the background or tapping the return key should cause the keyboard to disappear.

16.7 Summary

In this chapter we have put into practice some of the theory covered in previous chapters, in particular the separation of the view from the controller, the use of subclassing and the implementation of the Target-Action pattern through the use of actions and outlets.

The next chapter also provided steps on how to hide the keyboard when either the keyboard Return key or the background view are touched by the user.

17. Understanding iOS 8 Views, Windows and the View Hierarchy

In the preceding chapters we have created a number of user interfaces in the course of building our example iOS 8 applications. In doing so, we have been using *views* and *windows* without actually providing much in the way of explanation. Before moving on to other topics, however, it is important to have a clear understanding of the concepts behind the way that iOS user interfaces are constructed and managed. In this chapter we will cover the concepts of *views, windows* and *view hierarchies*.

17.1 An Overview of Views

Views are visual objects that are assembled to create the user interface of an iOS application. They essentially define what happens within a specified rectangular area of the screen, both visually and in terms of user interaction. All views are subclasses of the UIKit UIView class and include items such as the label (UILabel) and image view (UIImageView) and controls such as the button (UIButton) and text field (UITextField).

Another type of view that is of considerable importance is the UIWindow class.

17.2 The UIWindow Class

If you have developed (or even used) applications for desktop systems such as Windows or Mac OS X you will be familiar with the concept of windows. A typical desktop application will have multiple windows, each of which has a title bar of some sort containing controls that allow you to minimize, maximize or close the window. Windows in this context essentially provide a surface area on the screen onto which the application can present information and controls to the user.

The UIWindow class provides a similar function for iOS based applications in that it also provides the surface on which the view components are displayed. There are, however, some differences in that an iOS app typically only has one window, the window must fill the entire screen and it lacks the title bar we've come to expect on desktop applications.

As with the views described previously, UIWindow is also a subclass of the UIView class and sits at the root of the view hierarchy which we will discuss in the next section. The user does not see or interact directly with the UIWindow object. These windows may be created programmatically, but are typically created automatically by Interface Builder when you design your user interface.

17.3 **The View Hierarchy**

iOS 8 user interfaces are constructed using a hierarchical approach whereby different views are related through a parent/child relationship. At the top of this hierarchy sits the UIWindow object. Other views are then added to the hierarchy. If we take the example from the chapter entitled *Creating an Interactive iOS 8 App* we have a design that consists of a window, a view, a text field, a button and a label. The view hierarchy for this user interface would be drawn as illustrated in Figure 17-1:

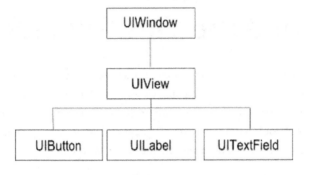

Figure 17-1

In this example, the UIWindow object is the parent or *superview* of the UIView instance and the UIView is the child, or *subview* of the UIWindow. Similarly, the text, label and button objects are all *subviews* of the UIView. A subview can only have one direct parent. As shown in the above example, however, a superview may have multiple subviews.

In addition, view hierarchies can be nested to any level of depth. Consider, for example, the following hierarchy diagram:

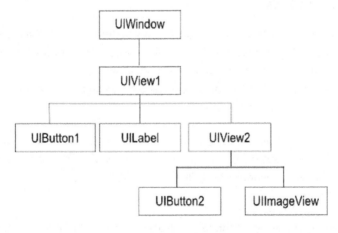

Figure 17-2

The hierarchical structure of a user interface has significant implications for how the views appear and behave. Visually, subviews always appear on top of and within the visual frame of their corresponding parent.

The button in the above example, therefore, appears on top of the parent view in the running application. Furthermore, the resizing behavior of subviews (in other words the way in which the views change size when the device is rotated) is defined in relation to the parent view. Superviews also have the ability to modify the positioning and size of their subviews.

If we were to design the above nested view hierarchy in Interface Builder it might appear as illustrated in Figure 17-3.

In this example, the UIWindow instance is not visible because it is fully obscured by the UIView1 instance. Displayed on top of, and within the frame of UIView1, are the UIButton1, UILabel and UIView2 subviews. Displayed on top of, and within the frame of, UIView2 are its respective subviews, namely UIButton2 and UIImageView.

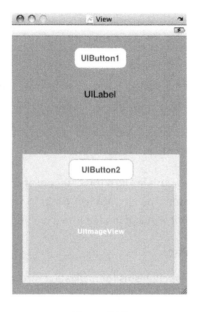

Figure 17-3

The view hierarchy also defines how events are handled when a user interacts with the interface, essentially defining something called the *responder chain*. If, for example, a subview receives an event that it cannot handle, that event is passed up to the immediate superview. If that superview is also unable to handle the event it is passed up to the next parent and so on until it reaches a level within the responder chain where it can be dealt with.

17.4 **View Types**

Apple groups the various views included in the UIKit Framework into a number of different categories:

17.4.1 The Window

The UIWindow is the root view of the view hierarchy and provides the surface on which all subviews draw their content.

17.4.2 Container Views

Container views enhance the functionality of other view objects. The UIScrollView class, for example, provides scrollbars and scrolling functionality for the UITableView and UITextView classes. Another example is the UIToolbar view which serves to group together multiple controls in a single view.

17.4.3 Controls

The controls category encompasses views that both present information and respond to user interaction. Control views inherit from the UIControl class (itself a subclass of UIView) and include items such as buttons, sliders and text fields.

17.4.4 Display Views

Display views are similar to *controls* in that they provide visual feedback to the user, the difference being that they do not respond to user interaction. Examples of views in this category include the UILabel and UIImageView classes.

17.4.5 Text and Web Views

The UITextView and UIWebView classes both fall into this category and are designed to provide a mechanism for displaying formatted text to the user. The UIWebView class, for example, is designed to display HTML content formatted so that it appears as it would if loaded into a web browser.

17.4.6 Navigation Views and Tab Bars

Navigation views and tab bars provide mechanisms for navigating through an application user interface. They work in conjunction with the view controller and are typically created from within Interface Builder.

17.4.7 Alert Views

Views in this category are designed specifically for prompting the user with urgent or important information together with optional buttons to call the user to action.

17.5 Summary

In this chapter we have explored the concepts of using views in terms of constructing an iOS application user interface and also how these views relate to each other within the context of a view hierarchy. We have also discussed how the view hierarchy dictates issues such as the positioning and resize behavior of subviews and defines the response chain for the user interface.

18. An Introduction to Auto Layout in iOS 8

Arguably one of the most important parts of designing the user interface for an application involves getting the layout correct. In an ideal world, designing a layout would simply consist of dragging view objects to the desired location on the screen and fixing them at these positions using absolute X and Y screen coordinates. In reality, the world of iOS devices is more complex than that and a layout must be able to adapt to variables such as the device rotating between portrait and landscape modes, dynamic changes to content and differences in screen resolution and size.

Prior to the release of iOS 6, layout handling involved use of a concept referred to as *autosizing*. Autosizing involves the use of a series of "springs" and "struts" to define, on a view by view basis, how a subview will be resized and positioned relative to the superview in which it is contained. Limitations of autosizing, however, typically meant that considerable amounts of coding were required to augment the autosizing in response to orientation or other changes.

Perhaps one of the most significant new features in iOS 6 was the introduction of Auto Layout, which has continued to evolve with the release of iOS 8. Auto Layout is an extremely large subject area allowing layouts of just about any level of flexibility and complexity to be created once the necessary skills have been learned.

The goal of this and subsequent chapters will be to introduce the basic concepts of Auto Layout, work through some demonstrative examples and provide a basis on which to continue learning about Auto Layout as your application design needs evolve. Auto layout introduces a lot of new concepts and can, initially, seem a little overwhelming. By the end of this sequence of chapters, however, it should be clearer how the pieces fit together to provide a powerful and flexible layout management system for iOS based user interfaces.

18.1 An Overview of Auto Layout

The purpose of Auto Layout is to allow the developer to describe the behavior that is required from the views in a layout independent of the device screen size and orientation. This behavior is implemented through the creation of *constraints* on the views that comprise a user interface screen. A button view, for example, might have a constraint that tells the system that it is to be positioned in the horizontal center of its superview. A second constraint might also declare that the bottom edge of the button should be positioned a fixed distance from the bottom edge of the superview. Having set these constraints, no matter what happens to the superview, the button will always be centered horizontally and a fixed distance from the bottom edge.

Unlike autosizing, Auto Layout allows constraints to be declared not just between a subview and superview, but between subviews. Auto layout, for example, would allow a constraint to be configured such that two button views are always positioned a specific distance apart from each other regardless of changes in size and orientation of the superview. Constraints can also be configured to cross superview boundaries to allow, for example, two views with different superviews (though in the same screen) to be aligned. This is a concept referred to as *cross-view hierarchy constraints*.

Constraints can also be explicit or variable (otherwise referred to in Auto Layout terminology as *equal* or *unequal*). Take for example, a width constraint on a label object. An explicit constraint could be declared to fix the width of the label at 70 points. This might be represented as a constraint equation that reads as follows:

```
myLabel.width = 70
```

This explicit width setting might, however, become problematic if the label is required to display dynamic content. An attempt to display text on the label that requires a greater width will result in the content being clipped.

Constraints can, however, also be declared using *less-than or equal to* or *greater than or equal to* controls. For example the width of a label could be constrained to any width as long as it is less than or equal to 800:

```
myLabel.width <= 800
```

The label is now permitted to grow in width up to the specified limit, allowing longer content to be displayed without clipping.

Auto layout constraints are by nature interdependent and, as such, situations can arise where a constraint on one view competes with a constraint on another view to which it is connected. In such situations it may be necessary to make one constraint *stronger* and the other *weaker* in order to provide the system with a way of arriving at a layout solution. This is achieved by assigning *priorities* to constraints.

Priorities are assigned on a scale of 0 to 1000 with 1000 representing a *required constraint* and lower numbers equating to *optional constraints*. When faced with a decision between the needs of a required constraint and an optional constraint, the system will meet the needs of the required constraint exactly while attempting to get as close as possible to those of the optional constraint. In the case of two optional constraints, the needs of the constraint with the higher priority will be addressed before those of the lower.

18.2 **Alignment Rects**

When working with constraints it is important to be aware that constraints operate on the content of a view, not the frame in which a view is displayed. This content is referred to as the *alignment rect* of the view. Alignment constraints such as those that cause the center of one view to align with that of another will do so based on the alignment rects of the views, disregarding any padding that may have been configured for the frame of the view.

18.3 **Intrinsic Content Size**

Some views also have what is known as an *intrinsic content size*. This is the preferred size that a view itself believes it needs to be to display its content to the user. A Button view, for example, will have an intrinsic content size in terms of height and width that is based primarily on the text or image it is required to display and internal rules on the margins that should be placed around that content. When a view has an intrinsic content size, Auto Layout will automatically assign two constraints for each dimension for which the view has indicated an intrinsic content size preference (i.e. height and/or width). One constraint is intended to prevent the size of the view becoming larger than the size of the content (otherwise known as the *content hugging* constraint). The other constraint is intended to prevent the view from being sized smaller than the content (referred to as the *compression resistance* constraint).

18.4 **Content Hugging and Compression Resistance Priorities**

The resize behavior of a view with an intrinsic content size can be controlled by specifying compression resistance and content hugging priorities. A view with a high compression resistance priority and a low content hugging priority will be allowed to grow but will resist shrinking in the corresponding dimension. Similarly, a high compression resistance priority in conjunction with a high content hugging priority will cause the view to resist any form of resizing, keeping the view as close as possible to its intrinsic content size.

18.5 **Three Ways to Create Constraints**

There are three ways in which constraints in a user interface layout can be created:

- **Interface Builder** – Interface Builder has been modified extensively to provide support for the visual implementation of Auto Layout constraints in user interface designs. Examples of using this approach are covered in the *Working with iOS 8 Auto Layout Constraints in Interface Builder* and *An iOS 8 Auto Layout Example* chapters of this book.
- **Visual Format Language** – The visual format language defines a syntax that allows constraints to be declared using a sequence of ASCII characters that visually approximate the nature of the constraint being created with the objective of making constraints in code both easier to write and understand. Use of the visual format language is documented in the chapter entitled *Understanding the iOS 8 Auto Layout Visual Format Language*.
- **Writing API code** – This approach involves directly writing code to create constraints using the standard programming API calls, the topic of this is covered in *Implementing iOS 8 Auto Layout Constraints in Code*.

Wherever possible, Interface Builder is the recommended approach to creating constraints. When creating constraints in code, the visual format language is generally recommended over the API based approach.

18.6 **Constraints in more Detail**

A constraint is created as an instance of the NSLayoutConstraint class which, having been created, is then added to a view. The rules for a constraint can generally be represented as an equation, the most complex form of which can be described as follows:

```
view1.attribute = multiplier * view2.attribute2 + constant
```

In the above equation, a constraint relationship is being established between two views named view1 and view2 respectively. In each case an attribute is being targeted by the constraint. Attributes are represented by NSLayoutAttribute*<name>* constants where *<name>* is one of either Left, Right, Top, Bottom, Leading, Trailing, Width, Height, CenterX, CenterY or Baseline (i.e. NSLayoutAttribute.Width). The multiplier and constant elements are floating point values used to modify the constraint.

A simple constraint that dictates that view1 and view2 should, for example, be the same width would be represented using the following equation:

```
view1.width = view2.width
```

Similarly, the equation for a constraint to align the horizontal center of view1 with the horizontal center of view 2 would read as follows:

```
view1.centerX = view2.centerX
```

A slightly more complex constraint to position view1 so that its bottom edge is positioned a distance of 20 points above the bottom edge of view2 would be expressed as follows:

```
view1.bottom = view2.bottom - 20
```

The following constraint equation specifies that view1 is to be twice the width of view2 minus a width of 30 points:

```
view1.width = view2.width * 2 - 30
```

So far the examples have focused on equality. As previously discussed, constraints also support inequality in the form of <= and >= operators. For example:

```
view1.width >= 100
```

A constraint based on the above equation would limit the width of view1 to any value greater than or equal to 100.

The reason for representing constraints in the form of equations is less obvious when working with constraints within Interface Builder but will become invaluable when setting constraints in code either using the API or the visual format language.

18.7 **Summary**

Auto layout involves the use of constraints to descriptively express the geometric properties, behavior and relationships of views in a user interface.

Constraints can be created using Interface Builder, or in code using either the visual format language or the standard SDK API calls of the NSLayoutConstraint class.

Constraints are typically expressed using a linear equation, an understanding of which will be particularly beneficial when working with constraints in code.

Having covered the basic concepts of Auto Layout, the next chapter will introduce the creation and management of constraints within Interface Builder.

19. Working with iOS 8 Auto Layout Constraints in Interface Builder

By far the most productive and intuitive way to work with constraints is to do so using the auto layout features of Interface Builder. Not only does this avoid the necessity to write time consuming code (though for complex layout requirements some code will be inevitable) but it also provides instant visual feedback on constraints as they are configured.

Within this chapter, a simple example will be used to demonstrate the effectiveness of Auto Layout together with an in-depth look at the Auto Layout features of Interface Builder. The chapter will then move on to demonstrate the concepts of content hugging and constraint priorities.

19.1 A Simple Example of Auto Layout in Action

Before digging deeper into the Auto Layout features of Interface Builder, the first step in this chapter will be to quickly demonstrate the basic concept of Auto Layout. Begin, therefore, by creating a new Xcode project using the *Single View Application* template, entering *AutoLayoutExample* as product name and choosing *iPhone* from the devices menu.

19.2 Enabling and Disabling Auto Layout in Interface Builder

By default, Auto Layout is switched on for user interface design files, both for storyboard and individual XIB files. Begin by selecting the *Main.storyboard* file from the project navigator panel and then display the File Inspector panel (*View -> Utilities-> Show File Inspector*). Located within this inspector is an option labeled *Use Autolayout* as illustrated in Figure 19-1.

Figure 19-1

Below the *Use Auto Layout* option is another item titled *Use Size Classes*. Size classes are a new feature of Xcode 6 and iOS 8 that enable different Auto Layout settings to be configured for different device screen sizes from within a single storyboard file. So that this chapter can focus solely on Auto Layout, and to avoid the confusion of learning two concepts at once, turn off the *Use Size Classes* option for this project. When the confirmation panel appears (Figure 19-2), verify that the *Keep size data for* menu is set to *iPhone* before clicking on the *Disable Size Classes* button. Rest assured that size classes and their relationship to Auto Layout constraints will be covered in considerable detail in the chapter entitled *Using Size Classes to Design Universal iOS User Interfaces*.

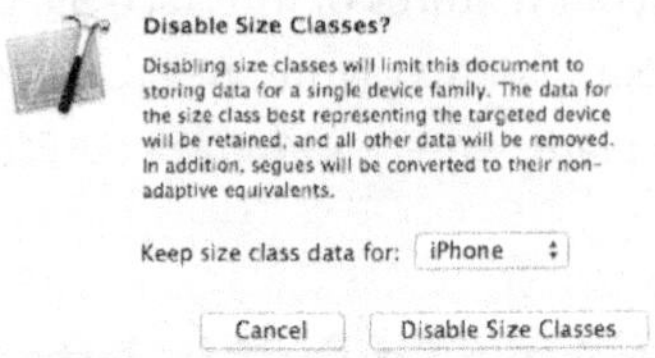

Figure 19-2

Although Auto Layout is enabled by default, the Interface Builder tool does not automatically apply any default constraints as views are added to the layout. Views are instead positioned using absolute x and y coordinates. To see this in action, drag a label view from the Object Library and position it towards the bottom of the view in the horizontal center of the view canvas so the vertical blue guideline appears indicating that it is centered before dropping the view into place. In actual fact, the location of the view has just been defined using hard coded absolute x and y coordinates on the screen. As far as the view is concerned, the label is positioned perfectly as long as the device remains in portrait orientation:

Figure 19-3

A problem arises, however, when the device rotates to landscape orientation. This can be demonstrated by compiling and running the application on a physical iPhone or iPad device or iOS Simulator in the usual way. Alternatively, the effect of an orientation change can be tested within the Interface Builder environment using a feature known as *simulated metrics*. To access these settings, begin by selecting the view controller in the storyboard canvas. This can be achieved by clicking on the view controller item in the toolbar above the view as illustrated in Figure 19-4:

Figure 19-4

With the view controller selected, display the Attributes Inspector in the utility panel on the far right. Under the *Simulated Metrics* heading, locate the *Orientation* option and change the menu setting from *Inferred* to *Landscape* as outlined in Figure 19-5.

Figure 19-5

As illustrated in Figure 19-6, the label is no longer visible. This is because it remains positioned at the same geographical coordinates in relation to the parent view, which in landscape orientation, is outside the visible bounds of the parent view.

Figure 19-6

Similar problems can occur when the application runs on different sizes of iPhone device. Whilst this can be tested using the *Size* menu on the *Simulated Metrics* panel, another useful tool is the Preview screen. The Preview screen is accessed from within the Assistant Editor which can be accessed either from the *View -> Assistant Editor -> Show Assistant Editor* menu option, or by clicking on the button showing interlocking circles in the Xcode toolbar and allows the layout to be reviewed simultaneously on multiple screen sizes.

Once the Assistant Editor is displayed, click on the *Automatic* item in the upper bar across the panel and select *Preview -> Main.storyboard* as shown in Figure 19-7:

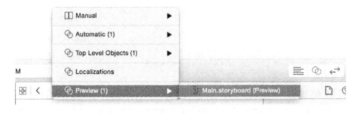

Figure 19-7

Once selected, a preview of the user interface layout will appear for the iPhone 4-inch model. Using the + button located in the bottom left hand corner of the panel allows previews of other device configurations to be displayed. The following figure, for example, shows previews for the layout as it will appear on 4, 4.7 and 5.5-inch iPhone devices:

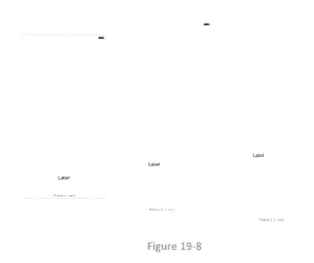

Figure 19-8

To change the orientation of a device preview, move the mouse pointer over the preview outline and click on the rotation button shown in Figure 19-9:

Figure 19-9

Note that on larger display form factors in portrait orientation, the label is once again positioned incorrectly. Clearly layout is important, not only for handling device orientation, but also to ensure correct user interface appearance on different device models.

Prior to the introduction of Auto Layout, options to address this would have either involved using springs and struts or writing code to detect the rotation of the device and to move the label to the new location on the screen. Now, however, the problem can be solved using Auto Layout.

Begin by closing the preview panel and returning the view to portrait orientation in the simulated metrics settings so that the label is once again visible and select the label within the view canvas. Xcode provides a number of different ways to add constraints to a layout. These options will be covered later in this chapter but by far the easiest is to use the Auto Layout toolbar. With the label selected, click on the *Pin* menu (Figure 19-10):

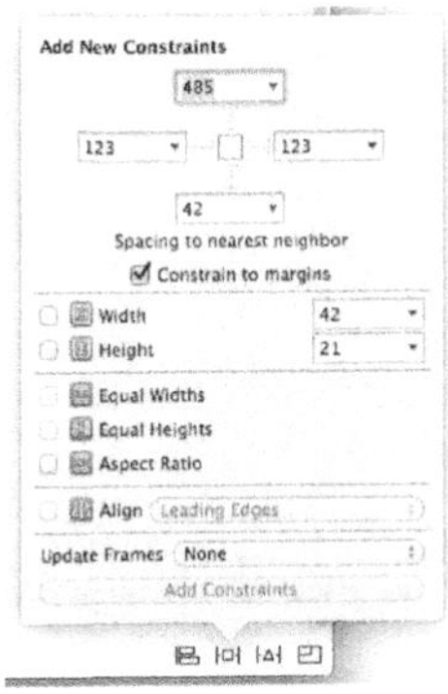

Figure 19-10

The goal for this example is to add a constraint to the label such that the bottom edge of the label is always positioned the same distance from the bottom of the containing superview and so that it remains centered horizontally. To do this we are first interested in the *Spacing to nearest neighbor* section of this panel. This provides a visual representation of the view in question (in this case the label) which is represented by the square in the middle. Extending from each side of the square are faded and dotted I-beam icons that connect with fields containing values. The fact that the I-beams are dotted and faded indicates that these are constraints that have not been set. The values indicate the current distances within the layout of the corresponding side to the nearest neighbor. The "nearest neighbor" will either be the nearest view to that side of the currently selected view, or the corresponding side of the superview.

Select the constraint I-beam icon located beneath the view so that it appears in solid red (as shown in Figure 19-11) to indicate that the constraint is now set before clicking on the *Add 1 Constraint* button to add the constraint to the view.

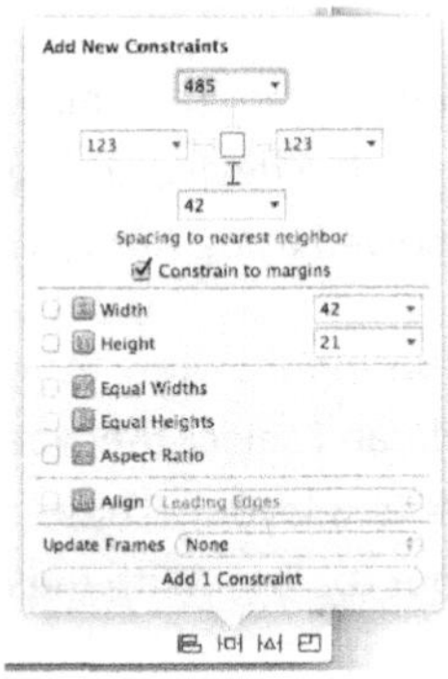

Figure 19-11

Having added a constraint, Auto Layout now knows that the bottom edge of the label must always be positioned a fixed distance from the bottom edge of the containing superview. The layout is still missing a constraint to designate the horizontal position of the label in the superview. One way to add this constraint is to make use of the *Align* menu. With the label still selected in the view canvas and the Align menu panel displayed, enable the checkbox next to the *Horizontal Center in Container* property (Figure 19-12). Since no offset from the center is required, leave the offset value at 0.

Figure 19-12

With the constraint appropriately configured, click on the *Add 1 Constraint* button to add the constraint to the view.

Having configured some constraints, rotate the orientation once again, noting this time that the label is visible and positioned sensibly. Testing different display form factors in the Preview screen should also demonstrate that the constraints are working to keep the label correctly positioned for different devices.

Figure 19-13

In this example so far only a small subset of the Auto Layout features provided by Xcode 6 has been used. In actual fact, Xcode 6 provides a wide range of options and visual cues that are designed to ease the task of creating Auto Layout constraints.

19.3 The Auto Layout Features of Interface Builder

A number of features are provided in Xcode 6 in order to assist in the implementation of Auto Layout based constraints. This section will present a guided tour of many of these features.

19.3.1 Suggested Constraints

When objects are added to a layout canvas, Interface Builder does not implement any default constraints on those views leaving the developer to add constraints as needed. There is, however, the option to have

Interface Builder apply suggested constraints. When this option is used, Interface Builder will apply what it believes to be the correct constraints for the layout based on the positioning of the views. Suggested constraints can be added either to the currently selected view objects, or to an entire scene layout.

In situations where constraints are missing from a layout resulting in warnings, Interface Builder also provides the option to automatically add the constraints that it believes are missing.

The options to perform these tasks are accessed via the *Resolve Auto Layout Issues* menu in the toolbar as illustrated in Figure 19-14.

The top section of the menu represents tasks that relate to the currently selected views in the canvas, whilst the options in the lower section apply to all views in the currently selected view controller scene.

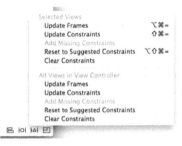

Figure 19-14

Most of the time, the suggested constraints will exactly match the required layout behavior and occasionally, the suggested constraints will be incorrect. Most of the time, however, the suggested constraints provide an excellent starting point for implementing Auto Layout. A typical process for designing a user interface might, therefore, involve positioning the views by dragging and dropping them into place, applying suggested constraints and then editing and fine tuning those constraints to perfect the layout.

To see suggested constraints in action, select the label view in the AutoLayoutExample project and select the *Clear Constraints* option from the *Resolve Auto Layout Issues* menu. At this point there are no constraints in the layout and the old positioning problem appears when the view is rotated. With the label still selected, choose the *Reset to Suggested Constraints* menu option. A review of the view canvas, and change of orientation should demonstrate that Interface Builder has suggested and applied the exact same constraints that we previously added manually.

19.3.2 Visual Cues

Interface Builder includes a number of visual cues in the layout canvas to highlight the constraints currently configured on a view and to draw attention to areas where problems exist. When a view is selected within the layout canvas, the constraints that reference that view will be represented visually. Consider, for example, the label view created in our *AutoLayoutExample* application. When selected in the canvas, a number of additional lines appear as shown in Figure 19-15:

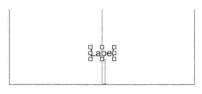

Figure 19-15

The vertical line that runs through the center of the label indicates the presence of a constraint that positions the label in the horizontal center of the parent view (analogous to the NSLayoutAttribute.CenterX attribute). If expressed as an equation, therefore, this would read as:

```
label.NSLayoutAttribute.CenterX = superview.NSLayoutAttribute.CenterX
```

The I-beam line running from the bottom edge of the label view to the bottom edge of the parent view indicates that a vertical space constraint is in place between the two views. The absence of any additional visual information on the line indicates that this is an *equality* constraint. Figure 19-16 shows an example of a "greater than or equal to" horizontal constraint between two button views:

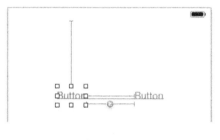

Figure 19-16

The horizontal line running beneath the Button label text indicates that constraints are in place to horizontally align the content baseline (represented by NSLayoutAttributeBaseline) of the two buttons.

Width constraints are indicated by an I-beam line running parallel to the edge of the view in the corresponding dimension. The text view object in Figure 19-17, for example, has a "greater than or equal to" width constraint configured:

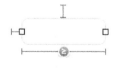

Figure 19-17

19.3.3 Highlighting Constraint Problems

Interface Builder also uses a range of visual cues and decorations to indicate that constraints are either missing, ambiguous or in conflict. Valid and complete Auto Layout configurations are drawn using blue lines. When part of a layout is ambiguous the constraint lines are orange.

Ambiguity typically occurs when a constraint is missing. Take for example the label view used earlier in the chapter. If only the horizontal center constraint is set, that constraint line will appear in orange because Auto Layout does not know where to position the view in the vertical plane. Once the second constraint is set between the bottom edge of the label and the bottom of the superview the constraint line will turn blue to indicate that the layout is no longer ambiguous.

Red constraint lines are used to indicate that constraints are in conflict. Consider, for example, a view object on which two width constraints have been configured, each for a different width value. The Auto Layout system categorizes such a situation as a constraint conflict and Interface Builder draws the offending constraint lines on the layout canvas in red. Figure 19-18, for example, illustrates a conflict where one constraint is attempting to set the width of a view to 110 points while a second constraint dictates that the width must be greater than or equal to 120 points:

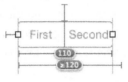

Figure 19-18

The layout canvas does not dynamically update the positions and sizes of the views that make up a user interface as constraints are added. It is possible, therefore, to have constraints configured that will result in layout behavior different to that currently displayed within the canvas. When such a situation arises, Interface Builder will draw a dotted orange outline indicating the actual size and location of the frame for the currently selected item. This is, perhaps, best demonstrated with an example. Within the *AutoLayoutExample* project, add a Text View object to the layout so that it is positioned near to the top of the view and to the right of the horizontal center as shown in Figure 19-19:

Figure 19-19

Select the new Text View object and, using the *Pin* menu, establish a *Spacing to nearest neighbor* constraint from the top of the text view to the top of the superview. Using the *Align* menu, add another constraint that aligns the view with the horizontal center in the container. Having established these constraints, review the constraint lines within the view canvas. As outlined in Figure 19-20, the horizontal center constraint appears in orange with a number assigned to it. A dotted box also appears on this line, level with the text view object. Interface Builder is attempting to warn us that the size and position of this view is going to resemble the dotted orange box at run time, and not the size and position currently shown for the view in the canvas. The number on the horizontal center constraint tells us that the horizontal position of the object is going to be 84.5 points to the left of the current position.

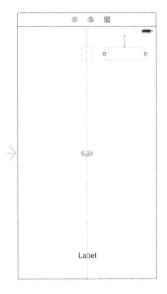

Figure 19-20

To reset the view to the size and position dictated by the constraints so that the canvas matches the runtime layout, simply select the Text View object, display the *Resolve Auto Layout Issues* menu and select the *Update Frames* menu option. The canvas will subsequently update to reflect the correct layout appearance (Figure 19-21). Alternatively, the *Update All Frames* menu option can be used to update all the frames in the current view controller scene.

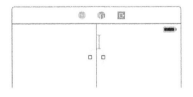

Figure 19-21

19.3.4 Viewing, Editing and Deleting Constraints

All of the constraints currently set on the views of a user interface may be viewed at any time from within the Document Outline panel that is positioned to the left of the Interface Builder canvas area. Hidden by default, this panel can be displayed by clicking on the button in the bottom left hand corner of the storyboard canvas (marked by the arrow in Figure 19-22).

Figure 19-22

Within this outline, a category listed as *Constraints* will be present which, when unfolded, will list all of the constraints currently configured for the layout. Note that when more than one container view is present in the view hierarchy there will be a separate constraints list for each one. Figure 19-23, for example, lists the constraints for the user interface represented in Figure 19-15 above:

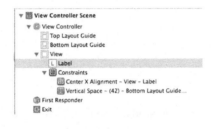

Figure 19-23

As each constraint is selected from the outline list, the corresponding visual cue element will highlight within the layout canvas.

The details of a particular constraint may be viewed and edited at any time using a variety of methods. One method is simply to double click on the constraint line in the canvas to display a constraint editing panel:

Figure 19-24

Another option is to select the constraint either from within the layout canvas or in the Document Outline panel. Once selected, display the Attributes Inspector in the Utilities panel (*View -> Utilities -> Show Attributes Inspector*) to view and edit the properties of the constraint. Figure 19-25 illustrates the settings for an equality spacing constraint.

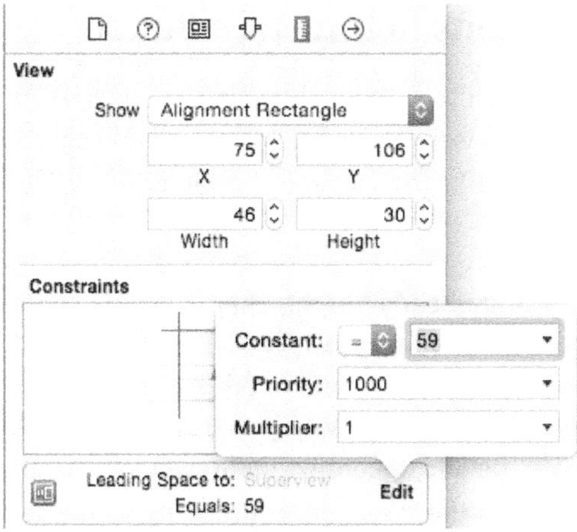

Figure 19-25

A listing of the constraints associated with a specific view can be obtained by selecting that view in the layout canvas and displaying the Size Inspector in the Utilities panel. Figure 19-26, for example, lists two constraints that reference the currently selected view. Clicking on the edit button on any constraint will provide options to edit the constraint properties. In addition, constraints can be removed by selecting them in the layout canvas and pressing the keyboard Delete key.

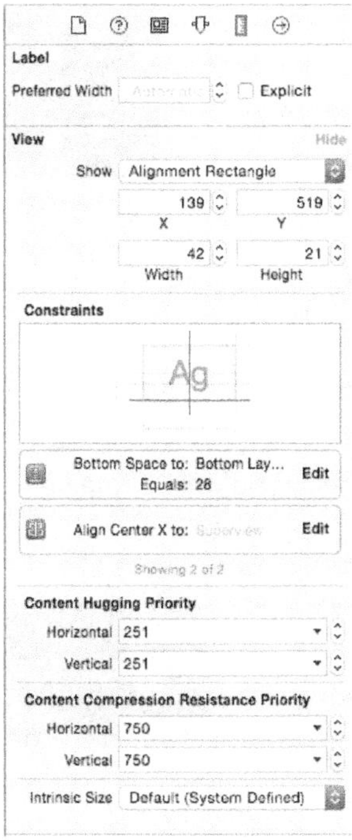

Figure 19-26

19.4 **Creating New Constraints in Interface Builder**

New user constraints can be created in Interface Builder using a variety of approaches, keeping in mind that constraints can relate to more than one view at a time. For example to configure an alignment constraint, all of the views which are to be included in the alignment operation must be selected before creating the constraints.

One of the easiest ways, as demonstrated earlier in this chapter, is to use the various options in the toolbar in the bottom right hand corner of the storyboard canvas.

Another useful option is simply to Ctrl-click within a view and then drag the resulting line outside of the boundary of the view. On releasing the line, a context menu will appear providing constraint options. The menu options provided will depend on the direction in which the line was dragged. If the line is dragged downwards, for example, the menu will include options to add a constraint to the bottom of the view, or to center vertically within the container. Dragging horizontally, on the other hand, provides the option to attach to the corresponding edge of the container or to center horizontally. Dragging the line to another view in the canvas will provide options (Figure 19-27) to set up spacing, alignment and size equality constraints between those views.

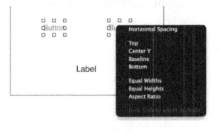

Figure 19-27

19.5 **Adding Aspect Ratio Constraints**

The height and width of a view can be constrained to retain aspect ratio by Ctrl-clicking in the view, dragging diagonally and then releasing. In the resulting menu, selecting *Aspect Ratio* ensures that regardless of whether the view shrinks or grows, the current aspect ratio will be retained.

Figure 19-28

19.6 **Resolving Auto Layout Problems**

Another advantage of implementing Auto Layout constraints in Xcode is that a number of features are available in Xcode 6 to assist in resolving problems.

In the first instance, descriptions of current issues can be obtained by clicking on the yellow warning triangle in the top right hand corner of the canvas area:

Figure 19-29

Solutions to some problems may be implemented by using the options in the *Resolve Auto Layout Issues* menu to perform tasks such as automatically adding missing constraints or resetting to suggested constraints.

More detailed resolution options are available from within the document outline panel. When issues need to be resolved, a red circle with a white arrow appears next to the corresponding view controller name in the outline panel as shown in Figure 19-30:

Figure 19-30

Clicking on the red circle displays all current layout issues listed by category:

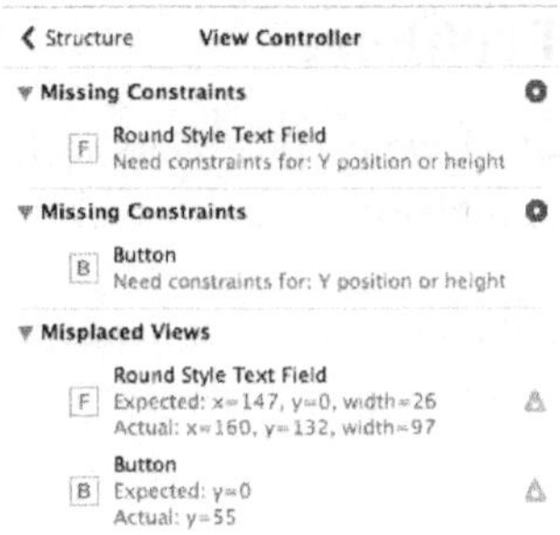

Figure 19-31

Hovering over a category title (for example Missing Constraints) will display an information symbol which, when clicked, will display a detailed description of the problem type.

Clicking on the error or warning symbol will display a panel providing one or more possible solutions together with a button to apply the selected change:

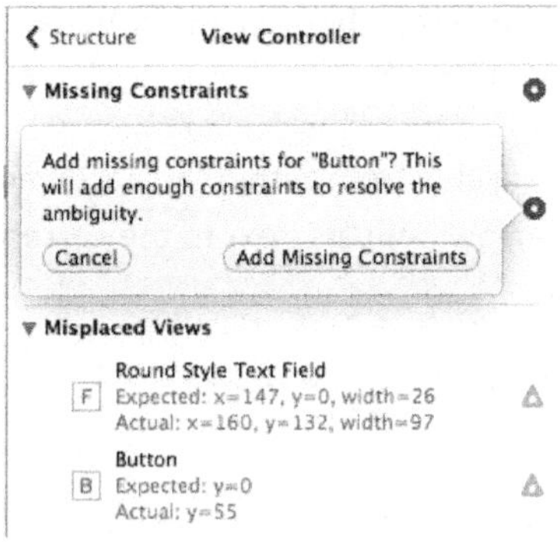

Figure 19-32

19.7 Summary

Within this chapter we have looked at a very simplistic example of the benefits of using Auto Layout in iOS 8 user interface design. The remainder of the chapter has been dedicated to providing an overview of the Auto Layout features that are available in Interface Builder.

20. An iOS 8 Auto Layout Example

Having covered the basics of Auto Layout and the Auto Layout features of Interface Builder in the preceding chapters, this chapter will work through an example user interface design intended to demonstrate the use of Interface Builder to create Auto Layout constraints. This example will also include a demonstration of constraint priorities.

20.1 Preparing the Project

Launch Xcode and load the *AutoLayoutExample* project created in the previous chapter. Once loaded, select the *Main.storyboard* file and remove the Label view and any other views added whilst working through the chapter.

20.2 Designing the User Interface

Initially, the user interface will simply require two Label views and a second View object. Begin, however, by selecting the *Main.storyboard* file and selecting the background view canvas. Display the Attributes Inspector in the Utilities panel and change the background color to a light shade of gray.

Drag a Label view from the Object Library and position it so that it is centered horizontally and on the top margin guideline as indicated in Figure 20-1. Drag a second Label view and position it to the left of the first label.

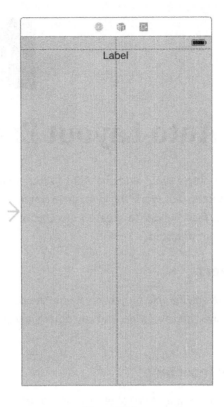

Figure 20-1

Finally, locate the View object in the Object Library. As a shortcut, type the word "UIView" into the search bar located immediately beneath the Object Library panel (Figure 20-2) to narrow the search criteria and then scroll to find the View object.

Figure 20-2

Drag and drop the View object onto the layout and resize it to fill the space below the two labels with appropriate margins from the outer edges of the screen. Cancel the Object Library search filter by clicking on the "x" at the right hand edge of the search box.

Figure 20-3

20.3 Adding Auto Layout Constraints

A number of constraints now need to be added to the layout so that it resizes and positions the views correctly when the device is rotated.

Select the view object in the layout and display the *Pin* menu from the toolbar in the bottom right hand corner of the storyboard canvas. In the *Spacing to nearest neighbor* section of the panel enable constraints on each of the four sides of the view with the *Constrain to margins* option enabled as outlined in Figure 20-4:

Figure 20-4

With the settings entered, click on the *Add 4 Constraints* button to implement the constraints.

Next, select the right most of the two labels, display the *Pin* menu and enable the *Spacing to nearest neighbor* constraint for the top edge of the view. Instead of entering a point value into the spacing field, use the drop down menu to select *Use Standard Value.* Note that this menu also provides the option to set the constraint to the top edge of the *View* or to the *Top Layout Guide.* The top layout guide is the blue dotted line that appears when a view is moved close to the edge of the containing view (the horizontal line in Figure 20-1). For the purposes of this example, leave the *Top Layout Guide* option selected.

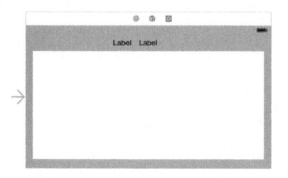

Figure 20-5

With the label still selected, use the *Align* menu to constrain the label to the horizontal center of the container.

All that now remains is to establish some constraints between the two labels. Ctrl-click on the left most label and drag the line to the right hand label before releasing the line. From the resulting menu, hold down the Shift key on the keyboard and select the *Baseline* and *Horizontal Spacing* options to align the content baselines of the two labels and to add a spacing constraint. With both options selected, hit the keyboard return key to add the constraints.

Rotate the canvas display into landscape mode by selecting the view controller and clicking on the left most icon in the layout scene toolbar so that the view is highlighted in blue. Display the Attributes Inspector in the Utilities panel and change the *Orientation* value under *Simulated Metrics* to *Landscape.* Note that the layout now re-organizes to accommodate the orientation change:

Figure 20-6

20.4 **Adjusting Constraint Priorities**

Up until this point, the layout is behaving correctly using basic constraints with default priorities. We are now going to introduce some problems that cannot be handled adequately by the constraints as they currently stand. With the view still in landscape mode, double click on the left hand label and change the text so that it reads *Customer Record:*. Using the Attributes Inspector, change the Alignment property so that the text is right aligned.

With the view in landscape mode the label appears correctly positioned. Rotate the view to portrait orientation, however, and the label is clearly being clipped by the left hand edge of the parent view:

Figure 20-7

Clearly there is some work to be done to make the user interface appear correctly in both orientations. The first step is to consider the constraints that are currently set on the label views. The right hand label has a constraint that forces it to be centered horizontally in the parent view. The left hand label, on the other hand, has a constraint that connects its trailing edge to the leading edge of the second label. The absence of a constraint on the left hand edge of the Customer Record label is resulting in the label being pushed off the screen in portrait mode.

One possible solution to this problem might be to create a new constraint on the Customer Record label that puts some space between the left hand edge of the customer record label and the left hand edge of the parent view. To add this constraint, rotate the view back to landscape so that the label is fully visible, select the Customer Record label, display the *Pin* menu, turn off the *Constrain to margins* option and establish a *standard* space constraint between the left hand edge of the view and the nearest neighbor. Before adding the constraint, change the *Update Frames* option from *None* to *Items of New Constraints* so that the frame for the view is updated to reflect the new constraint when it is added.

Now rotate to Portrait mode and note that the label is, unfortunately, now clipped on the right hand edge.

Figure 20-8

The reason for this problem is that the right hand label contains a constraint which forces it to be centered horizontally within the super view with a priority of 1000. Similarly, the customer record label has constraints that dictate that the leading and trailing edges of the label must be the standard width from the superview and right hand label respectively. Since these also have a priority of 1000, the system has no choice but to clip the label in order to satisfy the constraints. In order for the label to be fully visible, one of these priorities needs to be reduced.

We already know from experience that without the constraint on the leading edge of the customer record label, the left hand edge will be clipped by the superview window when the device is in portrait orientation. Another option is to lower the priority on the space constraint between the two labels. Unfortunately, this will just cause the left hand label to overlap the right hand label within the layout.

The only remaining constraint to experiment with is the horizontal center constraint on the right hand label. Select this label so that the constraints for that view are drawn on the canvas and double click on the horizontal center constraint (the vertical blue line) to display the constraint settings as shown in Figure 20-9. Using the drop down menu, reduce the priority by selecting the *Prevent "Customer Record:" From Clipping* menu option. When this option is selected, Xcode will calculate the optimal priority to ensure the label is not clipped.

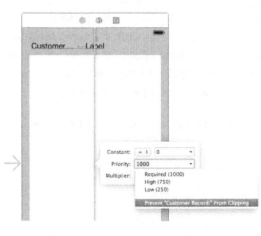

Figure 20-9

As a result of this setting, the label will only be centered when another constraint with a higher priority does not require that the label be moved. As such, the label will be centered when the device is in landscape mode but will be pushed off center when the space is needed by the Customer Record label in portrait orientation.

Figure 20-10

20.5 Testing the Application

Throughout this tutorial, the behavior of the user interface layout in response to orientation changes has been performed using simulated metrics within Xcode. As a full test of the layout, build and run the application either on a physical iPhone device or the iOS Simulator and check that the layout handles device rotation. This involves both a visual check that the views appear as intended and a review of the console to ensure no errors are reported with relation to the Auto Layout constraints.

20.6 Summary

Within this chapter, a sequence of steps have been outlined demonstrating the creation of an application that uses Auto Layout constraints to design a user interface that responds sensibly to orientation changes of the device. The example also introduced practical examples of the importance of constraint priorities.

Now that the implementation of Auto Layout constraints in Interface Builder has been covered, the next chapter will begin to explore the creation of constraints in code.

21. Implementing iOS 8 Auto Layout Constraints in Code

I n addition to using Interface Builder, it is also possible to create Auto Layout constraints directly within the code of an application. These approaches, however, are not necessarily mutually exclusive. There are, for example, situations where a layout will be constructed using a combination of Interface Builder and manual coding. Furthermore, some types of constraint cannot yet be implemented in Interface Builder, constraints that cross view hierarchies being a prime example. Interface Builder is also of limited use when user interfaces are created dynamically at run time.

Given these facts, an understanding of how to create Auto Layout constraints in code is an important skill, and is the focus of this chapter.

21.1 Creating Constraints in Code

Implementing constraints in code is a two-step process which involves first creating the constraint, and then adding the constraint to a view.

In order to create a constraint, an instance of the NSLayoutConstraint class must be created and initialized with the appropriate settings for the Auto Layout behavior it is to implement. This is achieved by calling the *constraintWithItem* method and passing through a set of arguments for the constraint.

When considering this syntax, it is helpful to recall the way in which constraints can be represented using linear equations (as outlined in *An Introduction to Auto Layout in iOS 8*) because the elements of the equation match the arguments used to create an NSLayoutConstraint instance.

Consider, for example, the following constraint expressed as an equation:

```
view1.bottom = view2.bottom - 20
```

The objective of this constraint is to position view1 so that its bottom edge is positioned a distance of 20 points above the bottom edge of view2. This same equation can be represented in code as follows:

```
var myConstraint =
        NSLayoutConstraint(item: view1,
            attribute: NSLayoutAttribute.Bottom,
```

```
           relatedBy: NSLayoutRelation.Equal,
           toItem: view2,
           attribute: NSLayoutAttribute.Bottom,
           multiplier: 1.0,
           constant: -20)
```

As we can see, the arguments to the method exactly match those of the equation (with the exception of the multiplier which is absent from the equation and therefore equates to 1 in the method call).

The following equation sets the width of a Button view named *mybutton* to be 5 times the width of a Label view named *mylabel:*

```
var myConstraint =
           NSLayoutConstraint(item: mybutton,
               attribute: NSLayoutAttribute.Width,
               relatedBy: NSLayoutRelation.Equal,
               toItem: mylabel,
               attribute: NSLayoutAttribute.Width,
               multiplier: 5.0,
               constant: 0)
```

So far the examples shown in this chapter have been *equality* based constraints and, as such, the *relatedBy:* argument has been set to NSLayoutRelation.Equal. The following equation uses a greater than or equal to operator:

```
mybutton.width >= 200
```

Translated into code, this reads as follows:

```
var myConstraint =
           NSLayoutConstraint(item: mybutton,
               attribute: NSLayoutAttribute.Width,
               relatedBy: NSLayoutRelation.GreaterThanOrEqual,
               toItem: nil,
               attribute: NSLayoutAttribute.Width,
               multiplier: 1.0,
               constant: 200)
```

Note that since this constraint is not related to another view, the *toItem:* argument is set to *nil.*

21.2 Adding a Constraint to a View

Once a constraint has been created, it needs to be assigned to a view in order to become active. This is achieved by passing it through as an argument to the *addConstraint* method of the view instance to which it is being added. In the case of multiple constraints, each is added by a separate call to the *addConstraint* method. This leads to the question of how to decide which view the constraint should be added to.

In the case of a constraint that references a single view, the constraint must be added to the immediate parent of the view. When a constraint references two views, the constraint must be applied to the closest ancestor of the two views. Consider, for the purposes of an example, the view hierarchy illustrated in Figure 21-1.

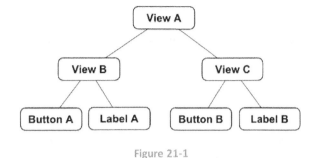

Figure 21-1

A constraint referencing only *Label A* should be added to the immediate parent, in this case *View B*. A constraint referencing *Button B* and *Label B*, on the other hand, must be added to the nearest common ancestor, which in this case is *View C*. A constraint referencing *Button A* and *Button B* must, once again, be added to the nearest common ancestor which equates to *View A*.

For the purposes of an example, the following code excerpt creates a new constraint and adds it to a view:

```
var myConstraint =
            NSLayoutConstraint(item: mybutton,
                attribute: NSLayoutAttribute.Width,
                relatedBy: NSLayoutRelation.Equal,
                toItem: mylabel,
                attribute: NSLayoutAttribute.Width,
                multiplier: 5.0,
                constant: 0)

self.view.addConstraint(myConstraint)
```

21.3 Turning off Auto Resizing Translation

When adding views to a layout in code the toolkit will, by default, attempt to convert the autosizing mask for that view to Auto Layout constraints. Unfortunately those auto-generated constraints will conflict with any constraints added within the application code. It is essential, therefore, that translation be turned off for views to which constraints are to be added in code. This is achieved by calling the *setTranslatesAutoresizingMaskIntoConstraints* method of the target view, passing through *false* as an argument. For example, the following code creates a new Button view, turns off translation and then adds it to the parent view:

```
let mybutton = UIButton()

mybutton.setTitle("My Button", forState: UIControlState.Normal)
```

```
mybutton.setTranslatesAutoresizingMaskIntoConstraints(false)

self.view.addSubview(mybutton)
```

21.4 An Example Application

Create a new Xcode project using the *Single View Application* template. Select *Universal* from Devices menu and *Swift* from the language menu, entering *AutoLayoutCode* as the product name.

21.5 Creating the Views

For the purpose of this example, the code to create the views and constraints will be added to the *viewDidLoad* method of the *AutoLayoutCode* view controller. Select the *ViewController.swift* file, locate this method and modify it to create a button and a label and add them to the main view:

```
override func viewDidLoad() {
    super.viewDidLoad()

    let superview = self.view

    let mylabel = UILabel()
    mylabel.setTranslatesAutoresizingMaskIntoConstraints(false)
    mylabel.text = "My Label"

    let mybutton = UIButton()

    mybutton.setTitle("My Button", forState: UIControlState.Normal)
    mybutton.backgroundColor = UIColor.blueColor()
    mybutton.setTranslatesAutoresizingMaskIntoConstraints(false)

    superview.addSubview(mylabel)
    superview.addSubview(mybutton)
}
```

21.6 Creating and Adding the Constraints

Constraints will be added to position the label in the horizontal and vertical center of the superview. The button will then be constrained to be positioned to the left of the label with the baselines of both views aligned. To achieve this layout, the *viewDidLoad* method needs to be modified as follows:

```
override func viewDidLoad() {
    super.viewDidLoad()

    let superview = self.view
```

```
let mylabel = UILabel()
mylabel.setTranslatesAutoresizingMaskIntoConstraints(false)
mylabel.text = "My Label"

let mybutton = UIButton()

mybutton.setTitle("My Button", forState: UIControlState.Normal)
mybutton.backgroundColor = UIColor.blueColor()
mybutton.setTranslatesAutoresizingMaskIntoConstraints(false)

superview.addSubview(mylabel)
superview.addSubview(mybutton)

var myConstraint =
        NSLayoutConstraint(item: mylabel,
            attribute: NSLayoutAttribute.CenterY,
            relatedBy: NSLayoutRelation.Equal,
            toItem: superview,
            attribute: NSLayoutAttribute.CenterY,
            multiplier: 1.0,
            constant: 0)

superview.addConstraint(myConstraint)

myConstraint =
    NSLayoutConstraint(item: mylabel,
        attribute: NSLayoutAttribute.CenterX,
        relatedBy: NSLayoutRelation.Equal,
        toItem: superview,
        attribute: NSLayoutAttribute.CenterX,
        multiplier: 1.0,
        constant: 0)

superview.addConstraint(myConstraint)

myConstraint =
    NSLayoutConstraint(item: mybutton,
        attribute: NSLayoutAttribute.Trailing,
        relatedBy: NSLayoutRelation.Equal,
        toItem: mylabel,
        attribute: NSLayoutAttribute.Leading,
        multiplier: 1.0,
        constant: -10)
```

```
    superview.addConstraint(myConstraint)

myConstraint =
    NSLayoutConstraint(item: mybutton,
        attribute: NSLayoutAttribute.Baseline,
        relatedBy: NSLayoutRelation.Equal,
        toItem: mylabel,
        attribute: NSLayoutAttribute.Baseline,
        multiplier: 1.0,
        constant: 0)

    superview.addConstraint(myConstraint)
}
```

When the application is compiled and run, the layout of the two views should match that illustrated in Figure 21-2.

Figure 21-2

21.7 Removing Constraints

Whilst it has not been necessary to do so in this example, it is important to be aware that it is also possible to remove constraints from a view. This can be achieved simply by calling the *removeConstraint* method of the view to which the constraint was added, passing through as an argument the NSLayoutConstraint object matching the constraint to be removed:

```
self.myview.removeConstraint(myconstraint)
```

It is also worth knowing that constraints initially created in Interface Builder can be connected to outlet properties, thereby allowing them to be referenced in code. The steps involved in creating an outlet for a constraint are covered in more detail in *Implementing Cross-Hierarchy Auto Layout Constraints in iOS 8*.

21.8 **Summary**

Whilst Interface Builder is the recommended method for implementing Auto Layout constraints, there are still situations where it may be necessary to implement constraints in code. This is typically necessary when dynamically creating user interfaces, or in situations where specific layout behavior cannot be achieved using Interface Builder (a prime example of this being constraints that cross view hierarchies as outlined in the next chapter).

Constraints are created in code by instantiating instances of the NSLayoutConstraint class, configuring those instances with the appropriate constraint settings and then adding the constraints to the appropriate views in the user interface.

22. Implementing Cross-Hierarchy Auto Layout Constraints in iOS 8

O ne of the few types of Auto Layout constraint that cannot be implemented within the Interface Builder environment is one that references views contained in different view hierarchies. Constraints of this type must, therefore, be implemented in code. Fortunately, however, the steps to achieve this are quite simple. The objective of this chapter is to work through an example that demonstrates the creation of a cross-view hierarchy Auto Layout constraint.

22.1 The Example Application

For the purposes of this example, a very simple user interface will be created consisting of two Views, a Button and a Label. In terms of the physical view hierarchy, the user interface will be constructed as outlined in Figure 22-1.

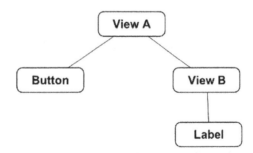

Figure 22-1

The goal will be to implement a constraint that aligns the centers of the Button and Label which are part of different view hierarchies - the button being part of the hierarchy contained by View A and the label being part of the View B sub-hierarchy.

In terms of visual layout, the user interface should appear as illustrated in Figure 22-2. Key points to note are that the label should have constraints associated with it which horizontally and vertically center it within View B and the button view should be positioned so that it is off center in the horizontal axis:

Figure 22-2

Begin by launching Xcode and selecting the options to create a new iOS application based on the *Single View Application* template. Enter *CrossView* as the product name and set the Device and Language menus to *Universal* and *Swift* respectively.

Select the *Main.storyboard* file from the project navigator panel, select the view and change the background color to a light shade of grey using the Attributes Inspector. Drag and drop UIView, Button and Label views onto the design canvas as illustrated in Figure 22-2, making sure to center the label object horizontally and vertically within the parent view.

Select the newly added view object, click on the *Resolve Auto Layout Issues* menu from the toolbar in the lower right hand corner of the canvas and select the *Reset to Suggested Constraints* option listed under *All Views in View Controller*.

22.2 Establishing Outlets

In order to set a cross hierarchy constraint within code, it will be necessary to implement some outlets. Since the constraint will need to reference both the button and the label, outlets need to be configured for these views. Select the label object and display the Assistant Editor using the *View -> Assistant Editor -> Show Assistant Editor* menu option or by selecting the center button (the one containing an image of two interlocking circles) of the row of Editor toolbar buttons in the top right hand corner of the main Xcode window.

Make sure that the Assistant Editor is showing the *ViewController.swift* file. Ctrl-click on the Label object in the view and drag the resulting line to the area immediately beneath the class declaration directive in the Assistant Editor panel. Upon releasing the line, the connection panel will appear. Configure the connection as an *Outlet* named *myLabel* and click on the *Connect* button. Repeat the above steps to add an outlet for the button object named *myButton.*

As currently constrained, the label object is centered horizontally within the view we are referring to as View B. In place of this constraint, we need the label to be aligned with the center of the button object. This will involve removing the CenterX constraint and replacing it with a new constraint referencing the button. This requires outlets for both the View B instance and the CenterX constraint.

Ctrl-click on the View B parent of the label object and drag the resulting line to the area immediately beneath the previously declared outlets in the Assistant Editor. Release the line and configure an outlet named *viewB*.

Next, select the label object so that the associated constraint lines appear. Click on the vertical line passing through the label view so that it highlights. Ctrl-click on the constraint line and drag to the Assistant Editor panel (Figure 22-3) and create a new outlet for this object named *centerConstraint*.

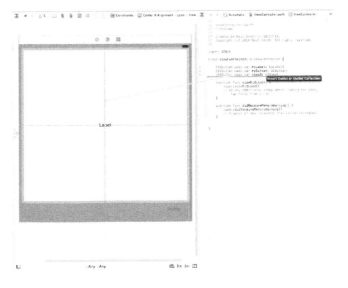

Figure 22-3

22.3 Writing the Code to Remove the Old Constraint

With the necessary outlets created, the next step is to write some code to remove the center constraint from the label object. For the purposes of this example, all code will be added to the *viewDidLoad* method of the view controller. Select the *ViewController.swift* file and locate and modify the method as follows:

```
override func viewDidLoad() {
    super.viewDidLoad()
    viewB.removeConstraint(centerConstraint)
}
```

All that the code is doing is calling the *removeConstraint* method of view B using the previously configured outlet, passing through a reference to the CenterX constraint, once again using the previously configured outlet to that object.

22.4 Adding the Cross Hierarchy Constraint

All that remains is to add the constraint to align the centers of the label and button. With the appropriate outlets already configured, this is simply a matter of creating the NSLayoutConstraint object with the appropriate values, and adding it to the closest common ancestor:

```
override func viewDidLoad() {
    super.viewDidLoad()

    viewB.removeConstraint(centerConstraint)

    let constraint =
        NSLayoutConstraint(item: myLabel,
            attribute: NSLayoutAttribute.CenterX,
            relatedBy: NSLayoutRelation.Equal,
            toItem: myButton,
            attribute: NSLayoutAttribute.CenterX,
            multiplier: 1.0,
            constant: 0.0)

    self.view.addConstraint(constraint)
}
```

22.5 Testing the Application

Compile and run the application either on a physical iOS device, or using the iOS Simulator. When the application is running, the label view should be aligned with the button and this alignment should be maintained when the device is rotated into landscape orientation.

22.6 Summary

The current version of Interface Builder does not provide a way to select two views that reside in different view-hierarchies and configure a constraint between them. The desired result can, as outlined in this chapter, be achieved in code. Of key importance in this process is the fact that constraints, just like any other view object in a user interface, may be connected to an outlet and accessed via code.

23. Understanding the iOS 8 Auto Layout Visual Format Language

The third and final option for the creation of Auto Layout constraints involves a combination of code and the visual format language. The goal of this chapter is to provide an introduction to the visual format language and to work through some code samples that demonstrate the concept in action.

23.1 Introducing the Visual Format Language

The visual format language is not a new programming language in the way that C++, Java and Swift are all programming languages. Instead, the visual format language defines a syntax through which Auto Layout constraints may be created using sequences of ASCII characters. These visual format character sequences are then turned into constraints by passing them through to the *constraintsWithVisualFormat* method of the NSLayoutConstraint class.

What makes the language particularly appealing and intuitive is that the syntax used to define a constraint involves characters sequences that, to a large extent, visually represent the constraint that is being created.

23.2 Visual Language Format Examples

By far the easiest way to understand the concepts behind the visual format language is to look at some examples of the syntax. Take for example, visual format language syntax to describe a view object:

```
[mybutton]
```

As we can see, view objects are described in the visual format language by surrounding the view name with square brackets ([]).

Two views may be constrained to be positioned flush with each other by placing the views side by side in the visual format string:

```
[mybutton1][mybutton2]
```

Similarly, a horizontal spacer between two view objects is represented by a hyphen:

```
[mybutton1]-[mybutton2]
```

The above example instructs the Auto Layout system to create a constraint using the standard spacing for views. The following construct, on the other hand, specifies a spacing distance of 30 points between the two views:

```
[mybutton1]-30-[mybutton2]
```

By default, constraints of the type outlined above are assumed to be horizontal constraints. Vertical constraints are declared using a *V:* prefix. For example, the following syntax establishes a vertical spacing constraint between two views:

```
V:[mylabel]-50-[mybutton]
```

For consistency and completeness, horizontal constraints may, optionally, be prefixed with *H:*.

The width of a view can be set specifically as follows:

```
[mybutton(100)]
```

Alternatively, inequality can be used:

```
[mybutton(<=100)]
```

Using similar syntax, the width of one view can be constrained to match that of a second view:

```
[mylabel(==mybutton2)]
```

When using the visual format language, the superview of the view for which the constraint is being described is represented by the | character. For example, the following visual format language construct declares a constraint for the mybutton1 view that attaches the leading and trailing edges of the view to the left and right edges of the containing superview with a spacing of 20 and 30 points respectively:

```
|-20-[mybutton1]-30-|
```

The language also allows priorities to be declared. The following excerpt specifies that the width of mybutton1 must be greater than, or equal to 70 points with a priority value of 500:

```
[mybutton1(>=70@500)]
```

Of particular importance, however, is the fact that the language may be used to construct multiple constraints in a single sequence, for example:

```
V:|-20-[mybutton1(>=70@500)]-[mybutton2(==mybutton1)]-30-[mybutton3]-|
```

23.3 Using the constraintsWithVisualFormat Method

As previously described, visual language format based constraints are created via a call to the *constraintsWithVisualFormat* method of the NSLayoutConstraint class. There are, however a number of other arguments that the method is able to accept. The syntax for the method is as follows:

```
NSLayoutConstraint.constraintsWithVisualFormat(<visual format string>,
        options: <options>,
        metrics: <metrics>,
        views: <views dictionary>)
```

The <visual format string> is, of course, the visual format language string that describes the constraints that are to be created. The <options> are required to be set when the constraint string references more than one view. The purpose of this is to indicate how the views are to be aligned and the value must be of type NSLayoutFormatOptions, for example .AlignAllLeft, .AlignAllRight, .AlignAllTop, .AlignAllBaselines etc.

The <metrics> argument is an optional NSDictionary object containing the corresponding values for any constants referenced in the format string.

Finally, the <views dictionary> is an NSDictionary object that contains the view objects that match the view names referenced in the format string.

When using a visual format string that will result in the creation of multiple constraints, the options should include an alignment directive such as NSLayoutFormatOptions.AlignAllBaseLines.

Since the method is able to create multiple constraints based on the visual format string, it returns an array of NSLayoutConstraint objects, one for each constraint, which must then be added to the appropriate view object.

Some sample code to create views and then specify multiple constraints using a visual format language string, would, therefore, read as follows:

```
// Get a reference to the superview
let superview = self.view

//Create a label
let myLabel = UILabel()
myLabel.setTranslatesAutoresizingMaskIntoConstraints(false)
myLabel.text = "My Label"

//Create a button
let myButton = UIButton()
myButton.backgroundColor = UIColor.redColor()
myButton.setTitle("My Button", forState: UIControlState.Normal)
myButton.setTranslatesAutoresizingMaskIntoConstraints(false)

// Add the button and label to the superview
superview.addSubview(myLabel)
superview.addSubview(myButton)
```

```
// Create the views dictionary
let viewsDictionary = ["myLabel": myLabel, "myButton": myButton]

// Create and add the vertical constraints
superview.addConstraints(NSLayoutConstraint.constraintsWithVisualFormat("
V:|-[myButton]-|",
                options: NSLayoutFormatOptions.AlignAllBaseline,
                metrics: nil,
                views: viewsDictionary))

// Create and add the horizontal constraints
superview.addConstraints(NSLayoutConstraint.constraintsWithVisualForma
("|-[myButton]-[myLabel(==myButton)]-|",
                options: NSLayoutFormatOptions.AlignAllBaseline,
                metrics: nil,
                views: viewsDictionary))
```

23.4 Summary

The visual format language allows Auto Layout constraints to be created using sequences of characters that have been designed to visually represent the constraint that is being described. Visual format strings are converted into constraints via a call to the *constraintsWithVisualFormat* method of the NSLayoutConstraints class which, in turn, returns an array containing an NSLayoutConstraint object for each new constraint created as a result of parsing the visual format string.

24. Using Size Classes to Design Universal iOS User Interfaces

In 2007 developers only had to design user interfaces for a single screen size and resolution (that of the first generation iPhone). Taking into consideration the range of iOS devices, screen sizes and resolutions available today, the task of designing a single user interface layout to target the full range of device configurations now seems a much more daunting task.

Although eased to some degree by the introduction of Auto Layout, designing a user interface layout that would work on both iPhone and iPad device families (otherwise known as a *universal interface*) typically involved the creation and maintenance of two storyboard files, one for each device type.

iOS 8 and Xcode 6 have introduced a new concept in user interface design referred to as *size classes* intended specifically to allow a user interface layout for multiple screen sizes and orientations to be designed within a single storyboard file. In this chapter of iOS 8 App Development Essentials, the concept of size classes will be covered together with a sample application that demonstrates how to use them to create a universal user interface.

24.1 Understanding Size Classes

Size classes categorize the various screen areas that an application user interface is likely to encounter during execution. Rather than represent specific screen dimensions and orientations, size classes represent width and height in terms of being *compact* or *regular*.

An iPhone display in portrait orientation, for example, is represented by the regular height and compact width size class. The same device in landscape, on the other hand, is considered to be of compact height and regular width.

In terms of size class categorization, the iPad family of devices is considered to be of regular height and regular width in both portrait and landscape orientation.

24.2 Size Classes in Interface Builder

Interface Builder in Xcode 6 allows different Auto Layout constraints to be configured for different size class settings within a single storyboard file. In other words, size classes allow a single user interface file to store multiple sets of layout data, with each data set targeting a particular size class. At runtime, the application will use the layout data set for the size class that matches the device and prevailing orientation on which it is executing, ensuring that the user interface appears correctly.

Any Auto Layout constraints that are assigned while Interface Builder is in regular height, compact width mode, for example, will only be applied to the views in the user interface when the app encounters such an environment that matches the size class (in this case an iPhone device in portrait orientation).

Similarly, switching Interface Builder to a different size class mode (such as regular height and width) within the same storyboard file will allow entirely different Auto Layout constraints to be defined within the same layout storyboard file which will take effect only when the app is running on an iPad.

Customizing a user interface for different size classes goes beyond the ability to configure different Auto Layout constraints for different size classes. Size classes may also be used to designate which views in a layout are visible within each class, and also which version of a particular image is displayed to the user. A smaller image may be used when an app is running on an iPhone, for example, or extra buttons might be made to appear to take advantage of the larger iPad screen.

24.3 Setting "Any" Defaults

When designing user interfaces using size classes, there will often be situations where particular Auto Layout constraints or view settings will be appropriate for all size classes. Rather than having to configure these same settings for each size class, these can, instead be configured within the *Any* category. Settings configured with Interface Builder in *Any* mode will be picked up by default by all other size classes unless specifically overridden within those classes.

In fact, the recommended approach to designing universal user interfaces using Interface Builder is to begin by designing for a particular target device (for example the iPad) with all of the settings applied to the *Any* category. Once the layout is complete, any exceptions should then be specified in the other size classes. Using this approach, it is only necessary to override those settings that need to change to meet the requirements of the other size classes. Essentially, the Any settings can be thought of as the *base values* which apply to all size classes.

24.4 Working with Size Classes in Interface Builder

Size classes are an optional feature within Interface Builder and can be turned on and off on a per storyboard file basis. Whether or not a storyboard file has size classes enabled can be verified by loading the file into the Interface Builder environment and displaying the *File Inspector* in the Utilities panel. Figure 24-1, for example, shows the size class and Auto Layout settings for a storyboard file:

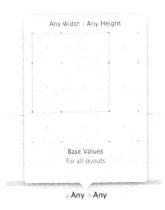

Figure 24-1

When a storyboard file has size classes enabled, an extra option appears along the bottom edge of the Interface Builder file indicating the currently selected size class. Figure 24-2, for example, shows that size classes are enabled for the current storyboard file and that the Any category is selected for both height and width size classes:

Figure 24-2

Clicking on the size class setting in the status bar will display the panel shown in Figure 24-3. This panel displays a grid with each cell representing a width and height size class combination. This grid serves to provide a visual representation of the current size class selection whilst also providing a mechanism for selecting a different size class. In the case of Figure 24-3, the Any Width and Any Height classes are selected. Consequently, any layout settings performed in the storyboard canvas in this mode will be used in all other size class configurations unless specifically overridden.

Figure 24-3

When in Any mode, the layout canvas for the view controllers in the storyboard are sized at 480 x 480 to indicate that layout settings configured in this mode are not specific to any particular size class.

As the mouse pointer is moved over the size class selection grid, the blue area will change to reflect different size classes. Hovering the mouse pointer over the bottom left hand square within the grid (Figure 24-4), for example, displays the traits of the corresponding size class and provides the opportunity to change to the Compact Width and Regular Height size class.

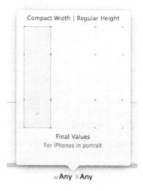

Figure 24-4

Clicking within the grid location will make this size class the active class and the view controller layout canvas in the storyboard will change size to represent an iPhone screen in portrait orientation. Once a size class has been selected, layout changes made to the storyboard will apply only to that class. Note also that the size class indicator now changes to "wCompact hRegular" (Figure 24-5), reflecting the currently selected size class. It is also worth noting that the status bar has changed to a blue background. This is intended as a subtle reminder that the layout is no longer in the "wAny hAny" mode and that layout changes will not apply to all size classes.

Figure 24-5

24.5 A Universal User Interface Tutorial

The remainder of this chapter will work through the creation of a universal layout example.

Create a new Xcode Single View Application project named *UniversalDemo* with the language option set to Swift and the Devices menu set to *Universal*. Once the project has been created, select the *Main.storyboard* file, display the File Inspector in the Utilities panel and make sure that both the *Use Auto Layout* and *Use Size Classes* options are enabled.

24.6 **Designing the iPad Layout**

The iPad layout will serve as the base configuration for the user interface, so begin by making sure that the size class settings for Interface Builder are currently set to "wAny hAny".

Add an ImageView and two Buttons to the view controller layout so that the user interface layout resembles that of Figure 24-6. Edit the text on the button views to read "Send" and "Edit" respectively:

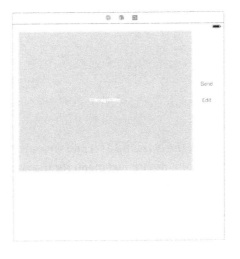

Figure 24-6

Select the Image View instance in the layout and use the *Pin* menu to set constraints on the top and left edges of the view of 0 with the *Constrain to margins* option enabled as shown in Figure 24-7 and click on the Add 2 Constraints button:

Figure 24-7

Ctrl-click and drag diagonally across the Image View as shown in Figure 24-8. On releasing the line, select *Aspect Ratio* from the resulting menu.

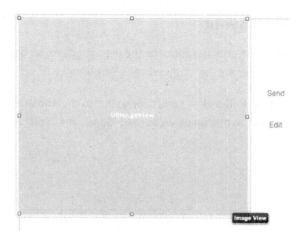

Figure 24-8

With the Image View still selected, display the *Pin* menu a second time and enable the right hand edge spacing to nearest neighbor constraint. Click on the drop down menu for the constraint value and select the View option (Figure 24-9) so that the constraint is relative to the parent view and not one of the Button views. Click on the Add 1 Constraint button to commit the change.

Figure 24-9

With the Image View still selected, Shift-click on the Edit button so that both views are selected. Display the Auto Layout Align menu, enable the *Vertical Centers* constraint option and add the constraint.

Select just the Edit button and, using the *Pin* menu, configure spacing to nearest neighbor constraints for both the trailing and leading edges of the view with the *Constrain to margins* option disabled.

Finally, select the Send button, display the *Pin* menu and configure leading, trailing and bottom spacing to nearest neighbor constraints using the current values with the *Constrain to margins* option disabled.

Use the size classes menu to change the current size class to "wRegular hRegular" and verify that the layout appears correctly. Return to "wAny hAny" and make any necessary adjustments.

Be sure to return the size classes setting to "wAny hAny" before proceeding with the tutorial.

24.7 Adding Universal Image Assets

The next step in the tutorial is to add some image assets to the project. The images can be found in the *universal_images* directory of the code samples download which can be obtained from:

http://www.ebookfrenzy.com/print/ios8/

Within the project navigator panel, locate and click on the *Images.xcassets* entry and, once loaded, select the *Editor -> New Image Set* menu option. Double click on the new image set which will have been named *Image* and rename it to *Sunset*.

Locate the *sunset_wAny_hAny.png* file in a Finder window and drag and drop it onto the 1x image box as illustrated in Figure 24-10:

Figure 24-10

Return to the *Main.storyboard* file, select the Image View and display the Attributes Inspector panel. Click on the down arrow at the right of the Image field and select *Sunset* from the resulting menu. The Image View in the view controller canvas will update to display the sunset image from the asset catalog.

Perform a test run of the app on a physical iPad device or iPad simulator and verify that the user interface matches that designed in Interface Builder.

24.8 Designing the iPhone Layout

Use the size classes menu to switch Interface Builder into "Wcompact hRegular" mode so that the view controller canvas changes to represent the size proportions for the iPhone device family in portrait mode.

The iPhone layout in this example will differ from the iPad layout in a number of ways. In the first instance the Edit button will be absent from the iPhone layout. To achieve this, select the Edit button, display the Attributes Inspector and scroll down to the last attribute setting which consists of a check box labelled *Installed*.

Click on the + button to the left of the installed check box and, from the resulting menu, select the *Compact Width | Regular Height (current)* menu option (Figure 24-11):

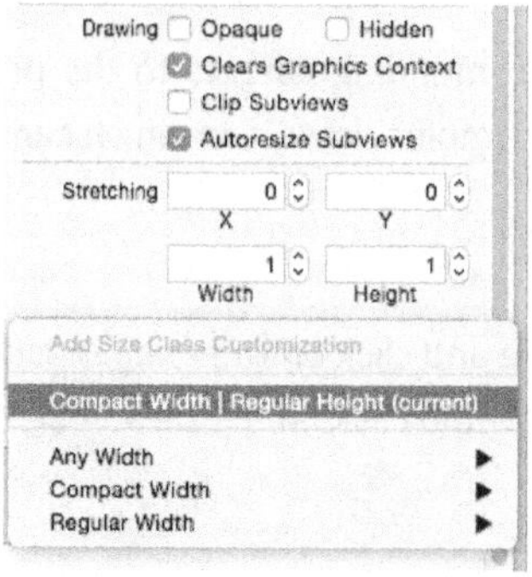

Figure 24-11

An option will now be available to control whether or not the selected view is installed in the current size class. To uninstall the view, uncheck the "wC hR" option as shown in Figure 24-12. Once the option has been disabled, the Edit button will no longer be present in the current size class. Temporarily switch back to "wAny hAny" mode and verify that the button will still be visible on the iPad before switching back to the "wCompact hRegular" size class.

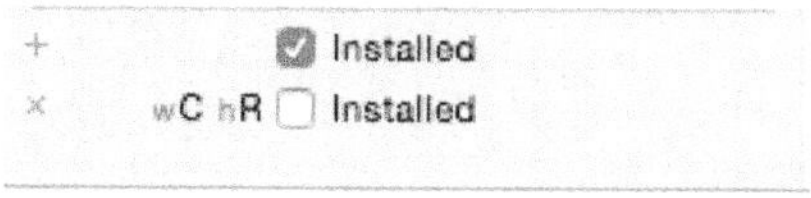

Figure 24-12

24.9 Adding a Size Class Specific Image File

The iPhone portrait variant of the user interface layout is going to use an image file that is more appropriate to the size of the screen. Once again, select *Images.xcassets* from the project navigator panel and, with the *Sunset* image set selected, display the Attributes Inspector and change the Width attribute to *Any & Compact*. Within the Sunset image set, an additional row of image options will appear. Once again, locate the images in the sample source code download, this time dragging and dropping the *sunset_wCompact_hRegular.png* file onto the 1x image well in the compact row as shown in Figure 24-13:

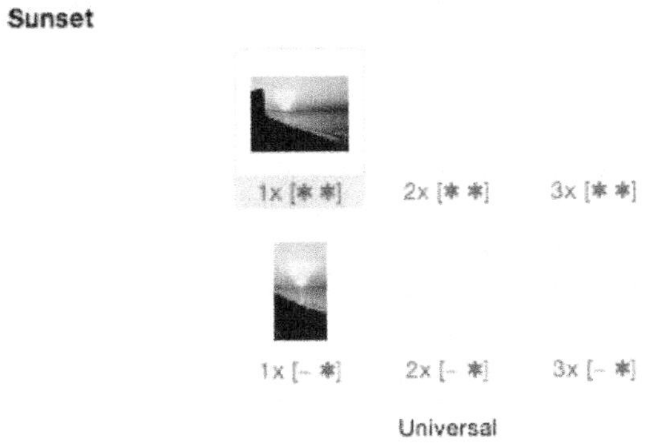

Sunset

1x [✱ ✱]   2x [✱ ✱]   3x [✱ ✱]

1x [– ✱]   2x [– ✱]   3x [– ✱]

Universal

Figure 24-13

Return to the storyboard file and note that the new image is now displayed on the current size class (the "wAny hAny" class will continue to display the previous image).

Shift-click on both the Image View and Send button and select *Clear Constraints* from the Auto Layout *Resolve Auto Layout Issues* menu. Display the *Resolve Auto Layout Issues* menu a second time, this time choosing the *Update Frames* menu option.

Within the view controller layout canvas, re-design the layout to match that of Figure 24-14 below:

Send

Figure 24-14

Select the Image View, display the *Pin* menu and set *spacing to nearest neighbor* constraints with the *Constrain to margins* option enabled as follows:

- Top – 0
- Left – 0
- Right – 0
- Bottom – Select drop down menu and choose Bottom Layout Guide, using the current value

Click on the *Add 4 Constraints* button to commit the changes to the layout.

Select the Send button and, using the Align menu, select and apply a *Horizontal Center in Container* constraint. Using the *Pin* menu, set a top edge spacing to nearest neighbor constraint using the currently displayed value.

Select the view controller background, display the Attributes Inspector and change the background color to Black Color.

24.10 **Removing Redundant Constraints**

In a previous step, the Edit button was uninstalled from the "wCompact hRegular" size class for the storyboard layout. When the view was uninstalled, however, a number of constraints that referenced the view were left in place. This may result in warnings when the app is compiled and run. As the final task before testing the app, these constraints will need to be uninstalled for the current size class.

If it is not already displayed, show the Xcode Document Outline panel by clicking on the button indicated by the arrow in Figure 24-15:

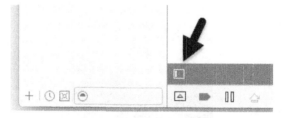

Figure 24-15

Within the Document Outline, unfold the section entitled *Constraints* located under the entry for the Edit button and Shift-click on the constraints that refer to the Edit button:

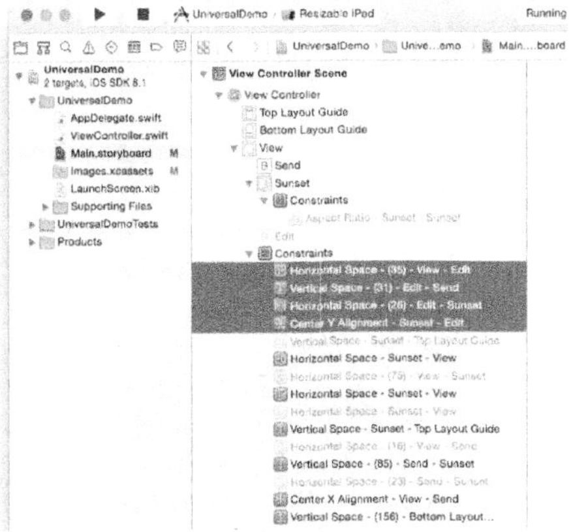

Figure 24-16

Display the Attributes Inspector and click on the + button to the left of the *Installed* setting and, from the menu, select *Compact Width | Regular Height (current)*. A new option will appear labelled "wC hR". Turn off the check box for this size class. Note that the selected constraints in the document outline panel are now grayed out. This indicates that the constraints still exist for other size classes but are uninstalled in the current size class.

24.11 Previewing Layouts

A storyboard layout can be previewed in a variety of device configurations using the Xcode preview tool. To preview the current layout, display the Assistant Editor panel either using the *View -> Assistant Editor -> Show Assistant Editor* menu option, or by clicking on the Xcode toolbar button showing the image of interlocking circles.

From within the Assistant Editor panel, click on the entry in the navigation bar along the top of the panel (this will currently display either *Automatic* or *Manual*). From the resulting menu, select the *Preview (1) -> Main.storyboard (Preview)* option. The editor will subsequently change to display a preview of the user interface as it will appear on a 4-inch iPhone device.

To preview on other device formats, click on the + button in the bottom left hand corner of the Assistant Editor panel and select a different device from the list as shown in Figure 24-17:

Figure 24-17

To remove a preview from the Assistant Editor simply select it and tap the keyboard delete key.

24.12 **Testing the Application**

For all of the convenience of the preview panel, there is no substitute for testing a layout running on either a physical device or an iOS Simulator session. Perform test runs of the application on different device families and note that, depending on the target device and orientation, the appropriate layout is adopted. When running on an iPhone it is also worth noting that rotating the device into landscape mode causes the app to display the "wAny hAny" layout since the iPhone layout was, of course, targeted only at iPhone devices in portrait orientation.

24.13 **Summary**

The range of iOS device screen sizes and resolutions is much more diverse that it was when the original iPhone was introduced in 2007. Today, developers need to be able to target an increasingly wide range of display sizes when designing user interface layouts for iOS applications. Prior to the release of iOS 8 and Xcode 6, it was often necessary to design a separate storyboard layout for each device category. With the introduction of size classes, it is now possible to target all screen sizes, resolutions and orientations from within a single storyboard. This chapter has outlined the basics of size classes and worked through a simple example user interface layout designed for both the iPad and iPhone device families.

25. Using Storyboards in Xcode 6

Storyboarding is a feature built into Xcode that allows both the various screens that comprise an iOS application and the navigation path through those screens to be visually assembled. Using the Interface Builder component of Xcode, the developer simply drags and drops view and navigation controllers onto a canvas and designs the user interface of each view in the normal manner. The developer then drags lines to link individual trigger controls (such as a button) to the corresponding view controllers that are to be displayed when the control is selected by the user. Having designed both the screens (referred to in the context of storyboarding as *scenes*) and specified the transitions between scenes (referred to as *segues*) Xcode generates all the code necessary to implement the defined behavior in the completed application. The style of transition for each segue (page fold, cross dissolve etc) may also be defined within Interface Builder. Further, segues may also be triggered programmatically in situations where behavior cannot be defined graphically using Interface Builder.

The finished design is saved by Xcode to a *storyboard file*. Typically, an application will have a single storyboard file, though there is no restriction preventing the use of multiple storyboard files within a single application.

The remainder of this chapter will work through the creation of a simple application using storyboarding to implement multiple scenes with segues defined to allow user navigation.

25.1 Creating the Storyboard Example Project

Begin by launching Xcode and creating a new project named *Storyboard* using the *Single View Application* template with the device and language menus set to *Universal* and *Swift* respectively. Save the project to a suitable location by clicking on the *Create* button.

25.2 Accessing the Storyboard

Upon creation of the new project, Xcode will have created what appears to be the usual collection of files for a single view application, including a storyboard file named *Main.storyboard*. Select this file in the project navigator panel to view the storyboard canvas as illustrated in Figure 25-1:

Figure 25-1

The view displayed on the canvas is the view for the *ViewController* class created for us by Xcode when we selected the *Single View Application* template. The arrow pointing inwards to the left side of the view indicates that this is the initial view controller and will be the first view displayed when the application launches. To change the initial view controller simply drag this arrow to any other scene in the storyboard and drop it in place.

Objects may be added to the view in the usual manner by dragging and dropping items from the Object Library (*View -> Utilities -> Show Object Library*) onto the view canvas. For the purposes of this example, drag a label and a button onto the view canvas. Using the properties panel, change the label text to *Scene 1* and the button text to *Go to Scene 2*. Resize the label so that it extends horizontally to the blue guidelines at the sides of the containing view and configure centered text alignment.

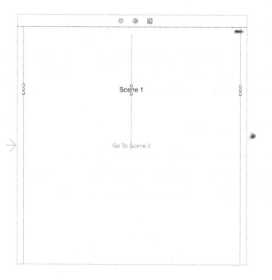

Figure 25-2

Using the *Resolve Auto Layout Issues* menu, select the *Reset to Suggested Constraints* option listed under *All Views in View Controller.*

In order to manipulate text displayed on the label object from within the application code it will be necessary to first establish an outlet. Select the label in the storyboard canvas and display the Assistant Editor (*View -> Assistant Editor -> Show Assistant Editor*). Check that the Assistant Editor is showing the content of the *ViewController.swift* file and then Ctrl-click on the label and drag the resulting line to just below the class declaration line in the Assistant Editor panel. In the resulting connection dialog, enter *scene1Label* as the outlet name and click on the *Connect* button. Upon completion of the connection, the top of the *ViewController.swift* file should read as follows:

```
import UIKit

class ViewController: UIViewController {

    @IBOutlet weak var scene1Label: UILabel!
```

25.3 Adding Scenes to the Storyboard

To add a second scene to the storyboard, simply drag a View Controller object from the Object Library panel onto the canvas. Figure 25-3 shows a second scene added to a storyboard:

Figure 25-3

Drag and drop a label and a button into the second scene and configure the objects so that the view appears as follows, making sure to stretch the label horizontally so that it extends to the blue margin guidelines with centered text alignment. Repeat the steps performed for the first scene to configure the necessary Auto Layout constraints on the two views.

Figure 25-4

As many scenes as necessary may be added to the storyboard, but for the purposes of this exercise we will use just two scenes. Having implemented the scenes the next step is to configure segues between the scenes.

25.4 **Configuring Storyboard Segues**

As previously discussed, a segue is the transition from one scene to another within a storyboard. Within the example application, touching the *Go To Scene 2* button will segue to scene 2. Conversely, the button on scene 2 is intended to return the user to scene 1. To establish a segue, hold down the Ctrl key on the keyboard, click over a control (in this case the button on scene 1) and drag the resulting line to the scene 2 view. Upon releasing the mouse button a menu will appear. Select the *show* menu option to establish the segue.

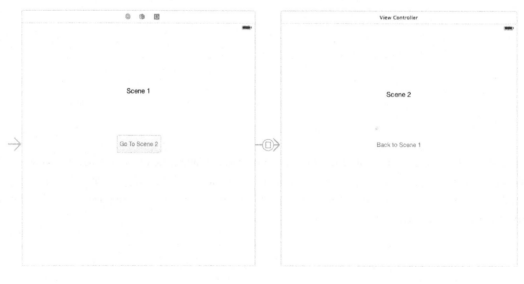

Figure 25-5

As more scenes are added to a storyboard, it becomes increasingly difficult to see more than a few scenes at one time on the canvas. To zoom out double click on the canvas. To zoom back in again simply double click once again on the canvas. Ctrl-clicking on the storyboard canvas background will provide a menu containing a number of zoom level options.

25.5 Configuring Storyboard Transitions

Xcode provides the option to change the visual appearance of the transition that takes place during a segue. By default a *Cover Vertical* transition is performed whereby the new scene slides vertically upwards from the bottom of the view to cover the currently displayed scene. To change the transition, select the corresponding segue line, display the Attributes Inspector (*View -> Utilities -> Show Attributes Inspector*) and modify the *Transition* setting. In Figure 25-6 the transition has been changed to *Cross Dissolve*:

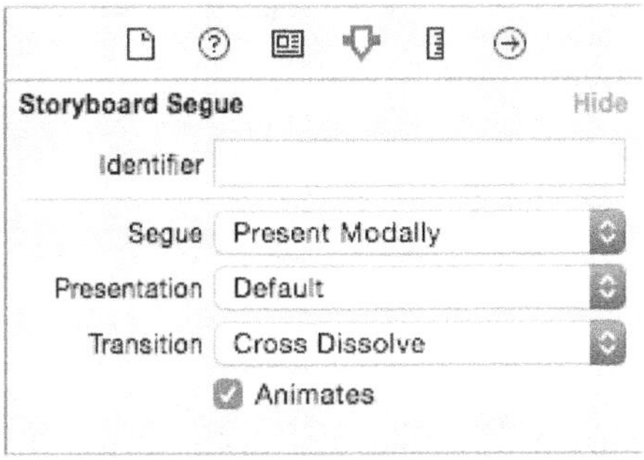

Figure 25-6

If animation is not required during the transition, turn off the *Animates* option. To delete a segue from a storyboard simply select the segue line in the storyboard canvas and press the keyboard delete key.

Compile and run the application. Note that touching the "Go to Scene 2" button causes Scene 2 to appear.

25.6 Associating a View Controller with a Scene

At this point in the example we have two scenes but only one view controller (the one created by Xcode when we selected *Single View Application*). Clearly in order to be able to add any functionality behind scene 2 it too will need a view controller. The first step, therefore, is to add the class source file for a view controller to the project. Ctrl-click on the *Storyboard* target at the top of the project navigator panel and select *New File...* from the resulting menu. In the new file panel, select *Source* listed under *iOS* in the left hand panel followed by *Cocoa Touch Class* in the main panel and click *Next* to proceed. On the options screen verify that the *Subclass of* menu is set to *UIViewController* and that the *Also create XIB file* option is deselected (since the view already exists in the storyboard there is no need for an XIB user interface file) and name the class *Scene2ViewController*.

Select the *Main.storyboard* file in the project navigator panel and select the View Controller button located in the panel beneath the Scene 2 view as shown in Figure 25-7:

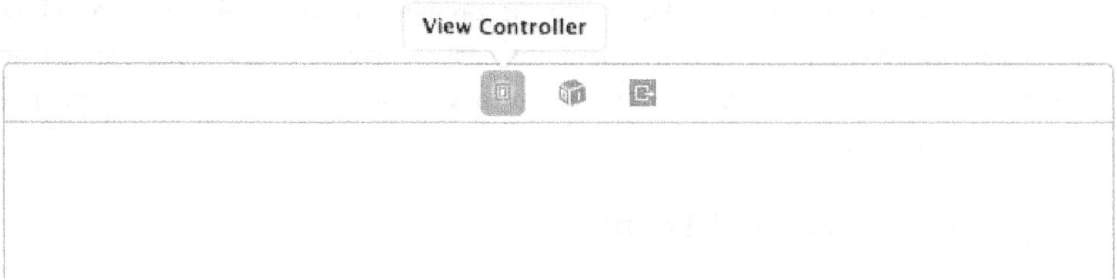

Figure 25-7

With the view controller for scene 2 selected within the storyboard canvas, display the Identity Inspector (*View -> Utilities -> Identity Inspector*) and change the *Class* from *UIViewController* to *Scene2ViewController*:

Custom Class

Class Scene2ViewController

Module Current – Storyboard

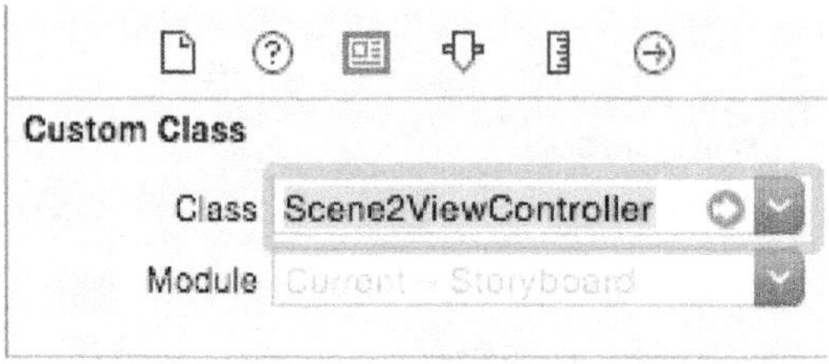

Figure 25-8

Scene 2 now has a view controller and corresponding Swift source file where code may be written to implement any required functionality.

Select the label object in scene 2 and display the Assistant Editor. Make sure that the *Scene2ViewController.swift* file is displayed in the editor and then establish an outlet for the label named *scene2Label*.

25.7 Passing Data Between Scenes

One of the most common requirements when working with storyboards involves the transfer of data from one scene to another during a segue transition. This is achieved using the *prepareForSegue* method.

Before a segue is performed by the storyboard runtime environment, a call is made to the *prepareForSegue* method of the current view controller. If any tasks need to be performed prior to the segue taking place simply implement this method in the current view controller and add code to perform any necessary tasks. Passed as an argument to this method is a segue object from which a reference to the destination view controller may be obtained and subsequently used to transfer data.

To see this in action, begin by selecting *Scene2ViewController.swift* and adding a new variable property:

```
import UIKit

class Scene2ViewController: UIViewController {
```

```
@IBOutlet weak var scene2Label: UILabel!

var labelText: String?
```

.

.

.

This property will hold the text to be displayed on the label when the storyboard transitions to this scene. As such, some code needs to be added to the *viewDidLoad* method located in the *Scene2ViewController.swift* file:

```
override func viewDidLoad() {
    super.viewDidLoad()
    scene2Label.text = labelText
}
```

Finally, select the *ViewController.swift* file and implement the *prepareForSegue* method as follows:

```
override func prepareForSegue(segue: UIStoryboardSegue, sender:
AnyObject?) {
    let destination = segue.destinationViewController
                                    as Scene2ViewController
    destination.labelText = "Arrived from Scene 1"
}
```

All this method does is obtain a reference to the destination view controller and then assigns a string to the *labelText* property of the object so that it appears on the label.

Compile and run the application once again and note that when scene 2 is displayed the new label text appears. We have, albeit using a very simple example, transferred data from one scene to the next.

25.8 Unwinding Storyboard Segues

The next step is to configure the button on scene 2 to return to scene 1. It might seem as though the obvious choice is to simply implement a segue from the button on scene 2 to scene 1. Instead of returning the original instance of scene 1, however, this would create an entirely new instance of the ViewController class. If a user were to perform this transition repeatedly the application would continue to use more memory and would eventually be terminated by the operating system.

The application should instead make use of the Storyboard *unwind* feature. This involves implementing a method in the view controller of the scene to which the user is to be returned and then connecting a segue to that method from the source view controller. This enables an unwind action to be performed across multiple levels of scene.

To implement this in our example application, begin by selecting the *ViewController.swift* file and implementing a method to be called by the unwind segue named *returned:*

```
@IBAction func returned(segue: UIStoryboardSegue) {
    scene1Label.text = "Returned from Scene 2"
}
```

All that is required of this method for this example is that it set some new text on the label object of scene 1. Once the method has been added, it is important to save the *ViewController.swift* file before continuing.

The next step is to establish the unwind segue. To achieve this, locate scene 2 within the storyboard canvas and Ctrl-click and drag from the button view to the "exit" icon (the orange button with the white square and the right facing arrow pointing outward shown in Figure 25-9) in the panel located along the top edge of the scene view. Release the line and select the *returned* method from the resulting menu:

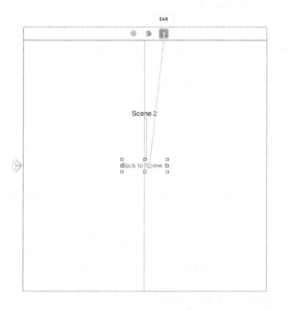

Figure 25-9

Once again, run the application and note that the button on scene 2 now returns to scene 1 and, in the process, calls the *returned* method resulting in the label on scene 1 changing.

25.9 Triggering a Storyboard Segue Programmatically

In addition to wiring up controls in scenes to trigger a segue, it is also possible to initiate a preconfigured segue from within the application code. This can be achieved by assigning an identifier to the segue and then making a call to the *performSegueWithIdentifier* method of the view controller from which the segue is to be triggered.

To set the identifier of a segue, select it in the storyboard canvas, display the Attributes Inspector (*View -> Utilities -> Show Attributes Inspector*) and set the value in the *Identifier* field.

Assuming a segue with the identifier of *SegueToScene1*, this could be triggered from within code as follows:

```
self.performSegueWithIdentifier("SegueToScene1", sender: self)
```

25.10 **Summary**

The Storyboard feature of Xcode allows for the navigational flow between the various views in an iOS application to be visually constructed without the need to write code. In this chapter we have covered the basic concepts behind storyboarding and worked through the creation of an example iOS application using storyboards and, in doing so, also explored the storyboard unwind feature.

26. Using Xcode 6 Storyboards to Create an iOS 8 Tab Bar Application

Having worked through a simple Storyboard based application in the previous chapter, the goal of this chapter will be to create a slightly more complex storyboard example.

So far in this book we have worked primarily with applications that present a single view to the user. In practice, however, it is more likely that an application will need to display a variety of different content depending on the actions of the user. This is typically achieved by creating multiple views (often referred to as content views) and then providing a mechanism for the user to navigate from one view to another. One of a number of mechanisms for achieving this involves the use of either the UINavigationBar or UITabBar components. In this chapter we will begin by using the storyboard feature of Xcode to implement a multiview application using a Tab Bar.

26.1 An Overview of the Tab Bar

The UITabBar component is typically located at the bottom of the screen and presents an array of tabs containing text and an optional icon that may be selected by the user to display a different content view. Typical examples of the tab bar in action include the iPhone's built-in Music and Phone applications. The Music application, for example, presents a tab bar with options to display playlists, artists, songs and videos. Depending on the selection made from the tab bar, a different content view is displayed to the user.

26.2 Understanding View Controllers in a Multiview Application

In preceding chapters we have talked about the model-view-controller concept in relation to each view having its own view controller (for additional information on this read the chapter entitled *The iOS 8 Application and Development Architecture*). In a multiview application, on the other hand, each content view will still have a view controller associated with it to handle user interaction and display updates. Multiview applications, however, also require an additional controller.

Multiview applications need a visual control that will be used by the user to switch from one content view to another, and this often takes the form of a tab or navigation bar. Both of these components are also *views* and as such also need to have a *view controller*. In the context of a multiview application, this is known as the *root controller* and is responsible for controlling which content view is currently displayed to the user. As an app developer you are free to create your own root controller by subclassing from the UIViewController class, but in practice it usually makes more sense to use an instance of either the UIKit UITabBarController or UINavigationController classes.

Regardless of the origins of your chosen root controller, it is the first controller that is loaded by the application when it launches. Once loaded, it is responsible for displaying the first content view to the user and then switching the various content views in and out as required based on the user's subsequent interaction with the application.

Since this chapter is dedicated to the creation of a tab bar based application we will be using an instance of the UITabBarController as our root controller.

26.3 Setting up the Tab Bar Example Application

The first step in creating our example application is to create a new Xcode project. To do so, launch Xcode and select the option to *Create a new Xcode project.*

Amongst the new project template options provided by Xcode is the *Tabbed Application* template. When selected, this template creates a pre-configured application consisting of a Tab Bar application with two content views. Whilst we could have used this template in this chapter, to do so would fail to convey a number of skills that will be essential when developing more complicated applications using storyboards. Whilst it is useful, therefore, to be aware of this template option for future reference, in the interest of providing a sound knowledge foundation we will be using the *Single View Application* template in this example.

On the template selection screen, select *Single View Application* and click *Next* to proceed. On the next screen enter *TabBar* as the product name, make sure that the *Devices* menu is set to *Universal* and that *Swift* is selected as the language. Proceed to the final screen and browse to a suitable location for the project files before clicking on the *Create* button.

26.4 Reviewing the Project Files

Based on our selections during the project creation process, Xcode has pre-populated the project with a number of files. In addition to the standard application delegate files it has, for example, provided the file necessary for a single view controller based application named *ViewController.swift*. A *Main.storyboard* file has also been created.

To start with an entirely clean project, select the *ViewController.swift* file in the project navigator panel and press the keyboard Delete key to remove the file from the project, choosing the option to move the file to the trash when prompted to do so.

26.5 Adding the View Controllers for the Content Views

The ultimate goal of this chapter is to create a tab bar based application consisting of two tabs with corresponding views, each of these will require a view controller. The first step, therefore, is to add the view controller for the first view. To achieve this, select the *File -> New -> File...* menu option and, on the resulting panel, select *Source* from beneath the *iOS* heading in the left hand panel and *Cocoa Touch Class* from the list of templates. Click *Next* and on the next screen, name the new class *Tab1ViewController* and change the *Subclass of* menu to *UIViewController*. Ensure that the *Also create XIB file* option is switched off before clicking *Next*. Select the desired location for the creation of the class files before clicking on *Create*.

Repeat the above steps to add a second view controller class named *Tab2ViewController*.

The scene within the storyboard file now needs to be associated with one of these view controller classes. Select the *Main.storyboard* file and select the scene added by Xcode so that it is highlighted with a blue border before displaying the Identity Inspector panel (*View -> Utilities -> Show Identity Inspector*). Within the inspector panel change the *Class* setting from *UIViewController* to *Tab1ViewController*.

The second view controller may be added to the storyboard simply by dragging and dropping one from the Object Library panel (*View -> Utilities -> Show Object Library*) onto the storyboard canvas. Once it has been added, follow the same steps to change the view controller class within the Identity Inspector panel, this time selecting *Tab2ViewController* in the *Class* field.

26.6 Adding the Tab Bar Controller to the Storyboard

As previously explained, the navigation between view controllers in a Tab Bar based interface is handled by a Tab Bar Controller. It will be necessary, therefore, to add one of these to our storyboard. Begin by selecting the *Main.storyboard* file in the Xcode project navigator panel.

In order to add a Tab Bar Controller to the storyboard, select the Tab1ViewController in the storyboard design area and select the *Editor -> Embed In -> Tab Bar Controller* menu option. The Tab Bar Controller will subsequently appear in the storyboard already connected to the Tab 1 View Controller as shown in Figure 26-1:

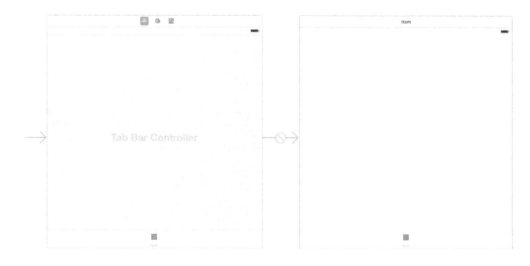

Figure 26-1

A relationship now needs to be established between the *Tab2ViewController* class and the Tab Bar Controller. To achieve this simply Ctrl-click on the Tab Bar Controller object in the storyboard canvas and drag the line to the *Tab2ViewController* scene. Upon releasing the line select the *view controllers* menu option listed under *Relationship Segue* as illustrated in Figure 26-2. This will add the *Tab2ViewController* to the *viewControllers* property of the Tab Bar Controller object so that it will be included in the tab navigation.

Figure 26-2

At this point in the design process the storyboard should now consist of one Tab Bar Controller with relationships established with both *Tab1ViewController* and *Tab2ViewController*. Allowing for differences in positioning of the storyboard elements, the canvas should now appear as shown in the following figure:

Figure 26-3

All that remains in order to complete the application is to configure the tab bar items and design rudimentary user interfaces for the two view controllers.

26.7 Designing the View Controller User interfaces

In order to visually differentiate the two view controllers we will add labels to the views and change the background colors. If you are currently zoomed out of the canvas begin by zooming in (if the canvas is zoomed out it will not be possible to make changes to the views). Begin by selecting the view of the Tab1ViewController scene. Within the Attributes Inspector panel (*View -> Utilities -> Show Attributes Inspector*) click on the white rectangle next to the *Background* label and select a shade of red from the resulting Colors dialog. Next, drag and drop a Label object from the Object Library panel and position it in the center of the red view. Double click on the label so that it becomes editable and change the text to *Screen One.* With the label still selected, use the Auto Layout Align menu to establish Horizontal and Vertical *Center in Container* constraints.

Once completed, the Tab1ViewController storyboard scene should appear as shown in Figure 26-4:

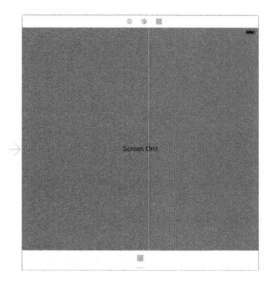

Figure 26-4

Repeat the above steps to change the background of the Tab2ViewController view to green and to add a label displaying text that reads *Screen Two.*

26.8 Configuring the Tab Bar Items

As is evident from the tab bars shown across the bottom of the two view controller elements, the tab items are currently configured to display text which reads "Item". The final task prior to compiling and running the application, therefore, is to rectify this issue. Begin by double clicking on the word "Item" in the tab bar of Tab1ViewController so that the text highlights and enter *Screen One.* Repeat this step to change the text of the tab bar item for Tab2ViewController to *Screen Two.*

In the event that you already have some icons suitable to be displayed on the tab bar items feel free to use them for this project. Alternatively, example icons can be found in the *tabicons* folder of the sample code archive which can be downloaded from the following URL:

http://www.ebookfrenzy.com/print/ios8

The icon archive contains two PNG format icon images named *first.png* and *second.png*. Locate these files (or any two other icons you have chosen to use) in a Finder window and drag and drop them onto the *Supporting Files* entry in the Xcode project navigator panel. With the icons added to the project, click on the placeholder icon in the tab bar of the Tab1ViewController and in the Attributes Inspector panel use the *Image* drop down menu to select *first.png* as the image file:

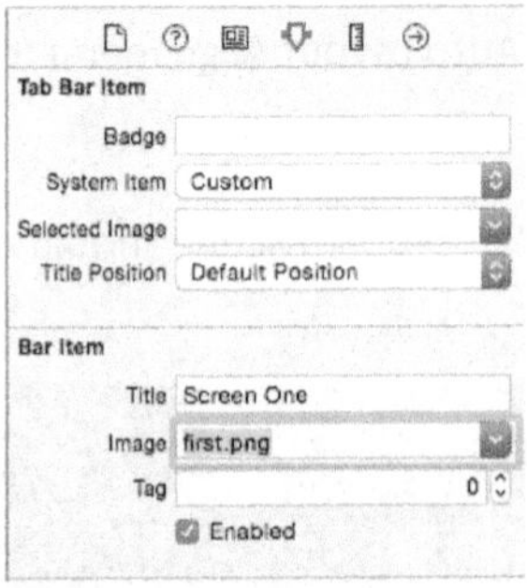

Figure 26-5

Note that it is also possible to display a different image when a tab is selected by providing an image for the *Selected Image* setting.

Perform the same steps to specify *second.png* as the image file for Tab2ViewController.

26.9 Building and Running the Application

The design and implementation of the example application is now complete and all that remains is to build and run it. Click on the run button located in the Xcode toolbar and wait for the code to compile and the application to launch within the iOS Simulator environment. The application should appear with the Tab1ViewController active and the two tab items in the tab bar visible across the bottom of the screen. Clicking on the Screen Two tab will navigate to the Tab2ViewController view:

Figure 26-6

26.10 **Summary**

The Storyboard feature of Xcode allows Tab Bar based navigation to be quickly and easily built into applications. Perhaps the most significant point to make is that the example project created in this chapter was implemented without the need to write a single line of Swift code.

27. An Overview of iOS 8 Table Views and Xcode 6 Storyboards

I f you have spent an appreciable amount of time using iOS on an iPhone the chances are good that you have interacted with a UIKit Table View object. Table Views are the cornerstone of the navigation system for many iOS iPhone applications. For example, both the iPhone *Mail* and *Settings* applications make extensive use of Table Views to present information to users in a list format and to enable users to drill down to more detailed information by selecting a particular list item.

Historically, table views have been one of the more complex areas of iOS user interface implementation. In recognition of this fact, Apple introduced ways to implement table views through the use of the Xcode Storyboard feature.

The goal of this chapter is to provide an overview of the concept of the UITableView class together with an introduction to the ways in which storyboards can be used to ease the table view implementation process. Once these basics have been covered a series of chapters, starting with *Using Xcode 6 Storyboards to Build Dynamic TableViews with Prototype Table View Cells*, will work through the creation of example projects intended to demonstrate the use of storyboards in the context of table views.

27.1 An Overview of the Table View

Table Views present the user with data in a list format and are represented by the UITableView class of the UIKit framework. The data is presented in rows, whereby the content of each row is implemented in the form of a UITableViewCell object. By default, each table cell can display a text label (textLabel), a subtitle (detailedTextLabel) and an image (imageView). More complex cells can be created by either adding subviews to the cell, or subclassing UITableViewCell and adding your own custom functionality and appearance.

27.2 Static vs. Dynamic Table Views

When implementing table views using an Xcode storyboard it is important to understand the distinction between *static* and *dynamic* tables. Static tables are useful in situations when a fixed number of rows need to be displayed in a table. The settings page for an application, for example, would typically have a predetermined number of configuration options and would be an ideal candidate for a static table.

Dynamic tables (also known as *prototype-based* tables), on the other hand, are intended for use when a variable number of rows need to be displayed from a data source. Within the storyboard editor, Xcode allows you to visually design a prototype table cell which will then be replicated in the dynamic table view at runtime in order to display data to the user.

27.3 The Table View Delegate and dataSource

Each table view in an application needs to have a *delegate* and a *dataSource* associated with it (with the exception of static tables which do not have a data source). The dataSource implements the UITableViewDataSource protocol, which basically consists of a number of methods that define title information, how many rows of data are to be displayed, how the data is divided into different sections and, most importantly, supplies the table view with the cell objects to be displayed. The delegate implements the UITableViewDelegate protocol and provides additional control over the appearance and functionality of the table view including detecting when a user touches a specific row, defining custom row heights and indentations and also implementation of row deletion and editing functions.

27.4 Table View Styles

Table views may be configured to use either *plain* or *grouped* style. In the grouped style, the rows are grouped together in sections separated by optional headers and footers. For example, Figure 27-1 shows a table view configured to use the grouped style:

Figure 27-1

In the case of the plain style, the items are listed without separation and using the full width of the display:

Figure 27-2

Table Views using plain style can also be *indexed*, whereby rows are organized into groups according to specified criteria, such as alphabetical or numerical sorting.

27.5 Self-Sizing Table Cells

iOS 8 has introduced a new feature of table views in the form of "self-sizing" cells. With self-sizing, each row of a table is sized according to the content of the corresponding cell based on the Auto Layout constraints applied to the cell contents. Self-sizing will be demonstrated in the next chapter entitled *Using Xcode 6 Storyboards to Build Dynamic TableViews with Prototype Table View Cells*, but is of particular importance when the labels in a cell are configured to use dynamic type.

27.6 Dynamic Type

iOS 7 provided a way for the user to select a preferred text size which applications are expected to adopt when displaying text. The current text size can be configured on a device via the *Settings -> Display & Brightness -> Text Size* screen which provides a slider to adjust the font size as shown in Figure 27-3:

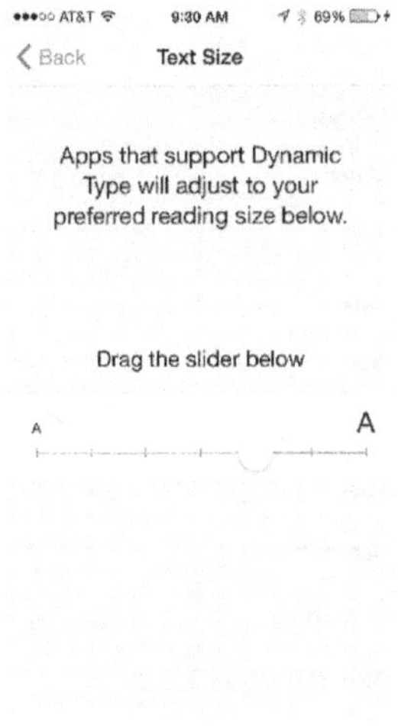

Figure 27-3

Almost without exception, the built-in iOS apps adopt the font size setting selected by the user when displaying text. Apple also recommends that third-party apps also conform to the user's text size selection and with iOS 8, support for dynamic type has been extended to table views. This is achieved by specifying a preferred text style setting for the font of any custom labels in a cell. iOS specifies a variety of different preferred text styles for this purpose including headings, sub-headings, body, captions and footnotes. The text style used by a label can be configured using Interface Builder or in code. To configure the text style in Interface Builder, select the label, display the Attributes Inspector and click on the "T" button in the font setting field as demonstrated in Figure 27-4. From the drop-down menu click on the Font menu button and select an item from the options listed under the *Text Styles* heading:

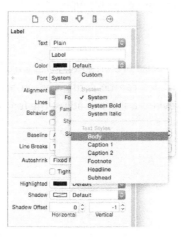

Figure 27-4

The preferred font is configured in code by setting the *preferredFontForTextStyle* property to one of the following pre-configured text style values:

• UIFontTextStyleHeadline
• UIFontTextStyleSubheadline

- UIFontTextStyleBody
- UIFontTextStyleFootnote
- UIFontTextStyleCaption1
- UIFontTextStyleCaption2

The following code, for example, sets a dynamic type font on a label using the headline font style:

```
cell.myLabel.font =
        UIFont.preferredFontForTextStyle(UIFontTextStyleHeadline)
```

Clearly, the text size selected by a user will dictate the size of any cells containing labels that use dynamic type, hence the importance of using self-sizing to ensure the table rows are displayed using an appropriate height.

27.7 **Table View Cell Styles**

In addition to the style of the Table View itself, different styles may also be specified for the individual table cells (unless custom table cells are being used). The iOS 8 SDK currently supports four different cell styles:

- **UITableViewCellStyleDefault** – only the labelText in black and left aligned.

- **UITableViewCellStyleSubtitle** – labelText in black and left aligned with the detailLabelText positioned beneath it in a smaller font using a gray foreground.

- **UITableViewCellStyleValue1** – labelText in black left aligned and the smaller detailLabelText in blue, on the same line and right aligned.

- **UITableViewCellStyleValue2** – labelText in blue on left side of cell, right aligned and detailedLabelText on right of cell, left aligned and black.

27.8 **Table View Cell Reuse**

A table view is, at the basic level, comprised of a UITableView object and a UITableViewCell for each row to be displayed. The code for a typical iOS 8 application using a table view will not directly create instances of a cell. The reasoning behind this becomes evident when performance and memory requirements are taken into consideration. Consider, for example, a table view that is required to display 1000 photo images. It can be assumed with a reasonable degree of certainty that only a small percentage of cells will be visible to the user at any one time. If the application was permitted to create each of the 1000 cells in advance the device would very quickly run into memory and performance limitations.

Instead, the application begins by registering with the table view object the class to be used for cell objects, along with the *reuse identifier* previously assigned to that class. If the cell class was written in code, the registration is performed using the *registerClass* method of UITableView object. For example:

```
self.tableView.registerClass(AttractionTableViewCell.self,
                    forCellReuseIdentifier: "MyTableCell")
```

In the event that the cell is contained within an Interface Builder NIB file, the *registerNib* method is used instead.

Perhaps the most important point to remember from this chapter is that if the cell is created using prototypes within a storyboard it is not necessary to register the class and, in fact, doing so will prevent the cell or view from appearing when the application runs.

As the table view initializes, it calls the *cellForRowAtIndexPath* method of the datasource class passing through the index path for which a cell object is required. This method will then call the *dequeueReusableCellWithReuseIdentifier* method of the table view object, passing through both the index path and the reuse ID assigned to the cell class when it was registered, to find out if there is a reusable cell object in the queue that can be used for this new cell. Since this is the initialization phase and no cells have been deemed eligible for reuse, the method will create a new cell and return it. Once all the visible cells have been created, the table view will stop asking for more cells. The code for *cellForCellAtIndexPath* will typically read as follows (the code to customize the cell before returning it will be implementation specific):

```
override func tableView(tableView: UITableView, cellForRowAtIndexPath
indexPath: NSIndexPath) -> UITableViewCell {

    let cell =
        tableView.dequeueReusableCellWithIdentifier("MyTableCell",
                forIndexPath: indexPath) as MyTableViewCell

    // Configure the cell here
    return cell
}
```

As the user scrolls through the table view, some cells will move out of the visible frame. When this happens, the table view places them on the reuse queue. As cells are moving out of view, new ones are likely to be coming into view. For each cell moving into the view area, the table view will call *cellForRowAtIndexPath*. This time, however, when a call to the *dequeueReusableCellWithReuseIdentifier* method is made, it is most likely that an existing cell object will be returned from the reuse queue, thereby avoiding the necessity to create a new object.

27.9 **Summary**

Whilst table views provide a popular mechanism for displaying data and implementing view navigation within applications, implementation has historically been a complex process. That changed with the introduction of storyboard support in Xcode. Xcode now provides a mechanism for visually implementing a considerable amount of Table View functionality with minimal coding. Such table views can be implemented as either *static* or *dynamic* depending on the requirements of the table and the nature of the data being displayed.

28. Using Xcode 6 Storyboards to Build Dynamic TableViews with Prototype Table View Cells

Arguably one of the most powerful features of Xcode storyboards involves the implementation of table views through the concept of prototype table cells. This allows the developer to visually design the user interface elements that will appear in a table cell (such as labels, images etc) and then replicate that prototype cell on demand within the table view of the running application. Prior to the introduction of Storyboards, this would have involved a considerable amount of coding work combined with trial and error.

The objective of this chapter is to work through a detailed example designed to demonstrate dynamic table view creation within a storyboard using table view prototype cells. Once this topic has been covered, the next chapter (entitled *Implementing iOS 8 TableView Navigation using Storyboards in Xcode 6*) will explore the implementation of table view navigation and the passing of data between scenes using storyboards.

28.1 Creating the Example Project

Start Xcode and create a Single View Application project named *TableViewStory* with the Devices menu set to *Universal* and with the Swift programming language option selected.

A review of the files in the project navigator panel will reveal that, as requested, Xcode has created a view controller subclass for us named ViewController. In addition, this view controller is represented within the Storyboard file, the content of which may be viewed by selecting the *Main.storyboard* file.

In order to fully understand the steps involved in creating a Storyboard based TableView application we will start with a clean slate by removing the view controller added for us by Xcode. Within the storyboard canvas, select the *View Controller* scene so that it is highlighted in blue and press the Delete key on the keyboard. Next, select and delete the corresponding *ViewController.swift* file from the project navigator panel. In the resulting panel select the option to move the file to trash.

At this point we have a template project consisting solely of a storyboard file and the standard app delegate code file and are ready to begin building a storyboard based application using the UITableView and UITableViewCell classes.

28.2 Adding the TableView Controller to the Storyboard

From the perspective of the user, the entry point into this application will be a table view containing a list of tourist attractions, with each table view cell containing the name of the attraction and corresponding image. As such, we will need to add a Table View Controller instance to the storyboard file. Select the *Main.storyboard* file so that the canvas appears in the center of the Xcode window. From within the Object Library panel (accessible via the *View -> Utilities -> Show Object Library* menu option) drag a *Table View Controller* object and drop it onto the storyboard canvas as illustrated in Figure 28-1:

Figure 28-1

With the new view controller selected in the storyboard, display the Attributes Inspector and enable the *Is initial View Controller* attribute as shown in Figure 28-2. Without this setting, the system will not know which view controller to display when the application launches.

Figure 28-2

Within the storyboard we now have a table view controller instance. Within this instance is also a prototype table view cell that we will be able to configure to design the cells for our table. At the moment these are generic UITableViewCell and UITableViewController classes that do not give us much in the way of control within our application code. So that we can extend the functionality of these instances we need to declare them as being subclasses of UITableViewController and UITableViewCell respectively. Before doing so, however, we need to actually create those subclasses.

28.3 **Creating the UITableViewController and UITableViewCell Subclasses**

We will be declaring the Table View Controller instance within our storyboard as being a subclass of UITableViewController named AttractionTableViewController. At present, this subclass does not exist within our project so clearly we need to create it before proceeding. To achieve this, select the *File -> New -> File...* menu option and in the resulting panel select the option to create a new iOS Source Cocoa Touch class. Click *Next* and on the subsequent screen, name the class AttractionTableViewController and change the *Subclass of* menu to *UITableViewController*. Make sure that the *Also create XIB file* option is turned off and click *Next*. Select a location into which to generate the new class files before clicking the *Create* button.

Within the Table View Controller added to the storyboard in the previous section, Xcode also added a prototype table cell. Later in this chapter we will add a label and an image view object to this cell. In order to extend this class it is necessary to, once again, create a subclass. Perform this step by selecting the *File -> New -> File....* menu option. Within the new file dialog select *Cocoa Touch Class* and click *Next.* On the following screen, name the new class *AttractionTableViewCell*, change the *Subclass of* menu to *UITableViewCell* and proceed with the class creation. Select a location into which to generate the new class files and click on *Create*.

Next, the items in the storyboard need to be configured to be instances of these subclasses. Begin by selecting the *Main.storyboard* file and select the Table View Controller scene so that it is highlighted in blue. Within the Identity Inspector panel (*View -> Utilities -> Show Identity Inspector*) use the *Class* drop down menu to change the class from *UITableViewController* to *AttractionTableViewController* as illustrated in Figure 28-3:

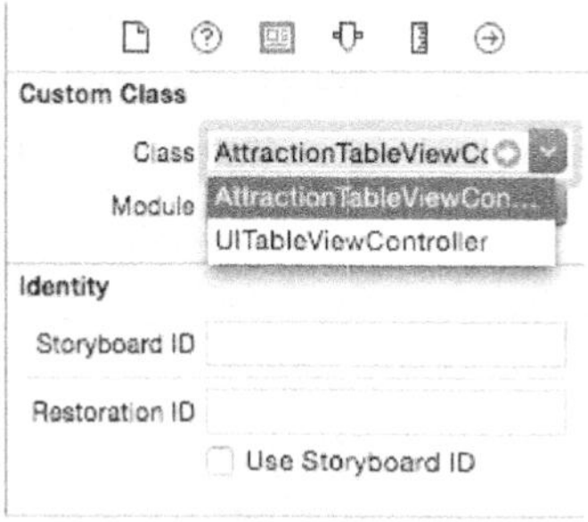

Figure 28-3

Similarly, select the prototype table cell within the table view controller storyboard scene and change the class from *UITableViewCell* to the new *AttractionTableViewCell* subclass.

With the appropriate subclasses created and associated with the objects in the storyboard, the next step is to design the prototype cell.

28.4 **Declaring the Cell Reuse Identifier**

Later in the chapter some code will be added to the project to replicate instances of the prototype table cell. This will require that the cell be assigned a reuse identifier. With the storyboard still visible in Xcode, select the prototype table cell and display the Attributes Inspector. Within the inspector, change the *Identifier* field to *AttractionTableCell*:

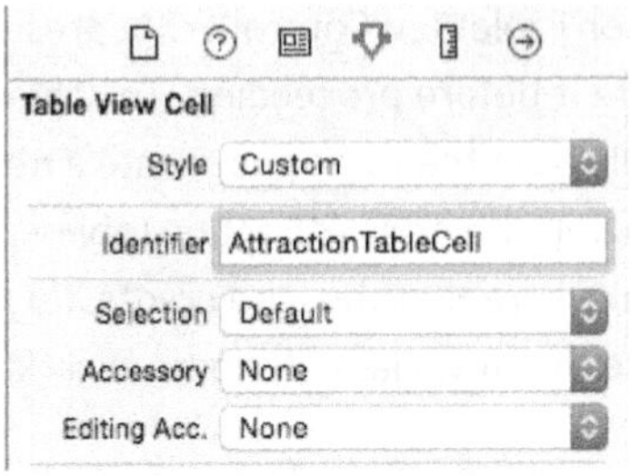

Figure 28-4

28.5 Designing a Storyboard UITableView Prototype Cell

Table Views are made up of multiple cells, each of which is actually either an instance of the UITableViewCell class or a subclass thereof. A useful feature of storyboarding allows the developer to visually construct the user interface elements that are to appear in the table cells and then replicate that cell at runtime. For the purposes of this example each table cell needs to display an image view and a label which, in turn, will be connected to outlets that we will later declare in the *AttractionTableViewCell* subclass. Much like any other Interface Builder layout, components may be dragged from the Object Library panel and dropped onto a scene within the storyboard. Note, however, that this is only possible when the storyboard view is zoomed in. With this in mind, verify that the storyboard is zoomed in and then drag and drop a Label and an Image View object onto the prototype table cell. Resize and position the items so that the cell layout resembles that illustrated in Figure 28-5, making sure to stretch the label object so that it extends toward the mid-point of the cell width.

Figure 28-5

Select the Image View and, using the Auto Layout Pin menu, set *Spacing to nearest neighbor* constraints on the top, left and bottom edges of the view with the *Constrain to margins* option switched off. Before adding the constraints, also enable the *Width* constraint.

Select the Label view, display the Auto Layout Align menu and add a *Vertical Center in Container* constraint to the view. With the Label still selected, display the Pin menu and add a *Spacing to nearest neighbor* constraint on the left hand edge of the view with the *Constrain to margins* option off.

Having configured the storyboard elements for the table view portion of the application it is time to begin modifying the table view and cell subclasses.

28.6 Modifying the AttractionTableViewCell Class

Within the storyboard file, a label and an image view were added to the prototype cell which, in turn, has been declared as an instance of our new AttractionTableViewCell class. In order to manipulate these user interface objects from within our code we need to establish two outlets connected to the objects in the storyboard scene. Begin, therefore, by selecting the image view object, displaying the Assistant Editor and making sure that it is displaying the content of the *AttractionTableViewCell.swift* file. If it is not, use the bar across the top of the editor panel to select this file.

Ctrl-click on the image view object in the prototype table cell and drag the resulting line to a point just below the class declaration line in the Assistant Editor window. Release the line and use the connection panel to establish an outlet named *attractionImage*.

Repeat these steps to establish an outlet for the label named *attractionLabel*.

28.7 Creating the Table View Datasource

Dynamic Table Views require a *datasource* to provide the data that will be displayed to the user within the cells. By default, Xcode has designated the *AttractionTableViewController* class as the datasource for the table view controller in the storyboard. Consequently, it is within this class that we can build a very simple data model for our application consisting of a number of arrays. The first step is to declare these as properties in the *AttractionTableViewController.swift* file:

```
import UIKit

class AttractionTableViewController: UITableViewController {

    var attractionImages = [String]()
    var attractionNames = [String]()
    var webAddresses = [String]()
    .
    .
    .
```

In addition, the arrays need to be initialized with some data when the application has loaded, making the *viewDidLoad* method an ideal location. Select the *AttractionTableViewController.swift* file within the project navigator panel and modify the method as outlined in the following code fragment:

```
override func viewDidLoad() {
    super.viewDidLoad()

    attractionNames = ["Buckingham Palace",
                       "The Eiffel Tower",
                       "The Grand Canyon",
```

```
                            "Windsor Castle",
                            "Empire State Building"]

        webAddresses = ["http://en.wikipedia.org/wiki/Buckingham_Palace",
                        "http://en.wikipedia.org/wiki/Eiffel_Tower",
                        "http://en.wikipedia.org/wiki/Grand_Canyon",
                        "http://en.wikipedia.org/wiki/Windsor_Castle",
                        "http://en.wikipedia.org/wiki/Empire_State_Building"]

        attractionImages = ["buckingham_palace.jpg",
                            "eiffel_tower.jpg",
                            "grand_canyon.jpg",
                            "windsor_castle.jpg",
                            "empire_state_building.jpg"]

        tableView.estimatedRowHeight = 50
}
```

In addition to initializing the arrays, the code also sets an estimated row height for the table view. This will prevent the row heights from collapsing when table view navigation is added later in the tutorial and also improves the performance of the table rendering.

For a class to act as the datasource for a table view controller a number of methods must be implemented. These methods will be called by the table view object in order to obtain both information about the table and also the table cell objects to display. When we created the AttractionTableViewController class we specified that it was to be a subclass of UITableViewController. As a result, Xcode created templates of these data source methods for us within the *AttractionTableViewController.swift* file. To locate these template datasource methods, scroll down the file until the *// MARK: – Table view data source* marker comes into view. The first template method, named *numberOfSectionsInTableView* needs to return the number of sections in the table. For the purposes of this example we only need one section so will simply return a value of 1 (note also that the #warning line needs to be removed):

```
override func numberOfSectionsInTableView(tableView: UITableView!) -> Int
{
    return 1
}
```

The next method is required to return the number of rows to be displayed in the table. This is equivalent to the number of items in our attractionNames array so can be modified as follows:

```
override func tableView(tableView: UITableView, numberOfRowsInSection
section: Int) -> Int {
    return attractionNames.count
}
```

The above code returns the *count* property of the *attractionNames* array object to obtain the number of items in the array and returns that value to the table view.

The final datasource method that needs to be modified is *cellForRowAtIndexPath*. Each time the table view controller needs a new cell to display it will call this method and pass through an index value indicating the row for which a cell object is required. It is the responsibility of this method to return an instance of our *AttractionTableViewCell* class and extract the correct attraction name and image file name from the data arrays based on the index value passed through to the method. The code will then set those values on the appropriate outlets on the AttractionTableViewCell object. Begin by removing the comment markers from around the template of this method and then re-write the method so that it reads as follows:

```
override func tableView(tableView: UITableView, cellForRowAtIndexPath
indexPath: NSIndexPath) -> UITableViewCell {

    let cell =
        self.tableView.dequeueReusableCellWithIdentifier(
            "AttractionTableCell", forIndexPath: indexPath)
                        as AttractionTableViewCell

    let row = indexPath.row
    cell.attractionLabel.font =
        UIFont.preferredFontForTextStyle(UIFontTextStyleHeadline)
    cell.attractionLabel.text = attractionNames[row]
    cell.attractionImage.image = UIImage(named: attractionImages[row])
    return cell
}
```

Before proceeding with this tutorial we need to take some time to deconstruct this code to explain what is actually happening.

The code begins by calling the *dequeueReusableCellWithIdentifier* method of the table view object passing through the cell identifier assigned to the cell (AttractionTableCell) and index path as arguments. The system will find out if an AttractionTableViewCell cell object is available for reuse, or create a new one and return it to the method:

```
let cell = tableView.dequeueReusableCellWithIdentifier(
                "AttractionTableCell", forIndexPath: indexPath)
                        as AttractionTableViewCell
```

Having either created a new cell, or obtained an existing reusable cell the code simply uses the outlets previously added to the AttractionTableViewCell class to set the label with the attraction name, using the row from the index path as an index into the data array. Because we want the text displayed on the label to reflect the preferred font size selected by the user within the Settings app, the font on the label is set to use the preferred font for headline text.

The code then creates a new UIImage object configured with the image of the current attraction and assigns it to the image view outlet. Finally, the method returns the modified cell object to the table view:

```
let row = indexPath.row
cell.attractionLabel.font =
        UIFont.preferredFontForTextStyle(UIFontTextStyleHeadline)
cell.attractionLabel.text = attractionNames[row]
cell.attractionImage.image = UIImage(named: attractionImages[row])
return cell
```

28.8 Downloading and Adding the Image Files

Before a test run of the application can be performed the image files referenced in the code need to be added to the project. An archive containing the images may be found in the *attractionImages* folder of the code sample archive which can be downloaded from the following URL:

http://www.ebookfrenzy.com/print/ios8

Once the file has been downloaded, unzip the files and then drag and drop them from a Finder window onto the *Supporting Files* folder in the Xcode project navigator panel.

28.9 Compiling and Running the Application

Now that the storyboard work and code modifications are complete the final step in this chapter is to run the application by clicking on the run button located in the Xcode toolbar. Once the code has compiled the application will launch and execute within an iOS Simulator session as illustrated in Figure 28-6.

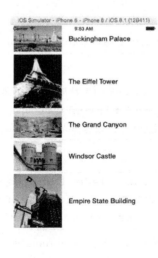

Figure 28-6

Clearly the table view has been populated with multiple instances of our prototype table view cell, each of which has been customized through outlets to display different text and images. Note that the new self-sizing rows feature of iOS 8 has caused the rows to automatically size to accommodate the attraction images.

As a final step, verify that the preferred font size code is working by running the app on a physical iOS device, displaying *Settings -> Display & Brightness -> Text Size* and dragging the slider to change the font size. Stop and restart the application and note that the attraction names are now displayed using the newly selected font size.

The next step, which will be outlined in the following chapter entitled *Implementing iOS 8 TableView Navigation using Storyboards in Xcode 6* will be to use the storyboard to add navigation capabilities to the application so that selecting a row from the table results in a detail scene appearing to the user.

28.10 **Summary**

The Storyboard feature of Xcode significantly eases the process of creating complex table view based interfaces within iOS 8 applications. Arguably the most significant feature is the ability to visually design the appearance of a table view cell and then have that cell automatically replicated at run time to display information to the user in table form. iOS 8 also introduced support for automatic table cell sizing and the adoption of the user's preferred font setting within table views.

29. Implementing iOS 8 TableView Navigation using Storyboards in Xcode 6

The objective of this chapter is to extend the application created in the previous chapter (entitled *Using Xcode 6 Storyboards to Build Dynamic TableViews with Prototype Table View Cells*) and, in so doing, demonstrate the steps involved in implementing table view navigation within a storyboard. In other words, we will be modifying the attractions example from the previous chapter such that selecting a row from the table view displays a second scene in which a web page providing information about the chosen location will be displayed to the user. As part of this exercise we will also explore the transfer of data between different scenes in a storyboard.

29.1 Understanding the Navigation Controller

Navigation based applications present a hierarchical approach to displaying information to the user. Such applications typically take the form of a navigation bar (UINavigationBar) and a series of Table based views (UITableView). Selecting an item from the table list causes the view associated with that selection to be displayed. The navigation bar will display a title corresponding to the currently displayed view together with a button that returns the user to the previous view when selected. For an example of this concept in action, spend some time using the iPhone *Mail* or *Music* applications.

When developing a navigation-based application, the central component of the architecture is the *navigation controller*. In addition, each scene has a view and a corresponding view controller. The navigation controller maintains a stack of these view controllers. When a new view is displayed it is *pushed* onto the navigation controller's stack and becomes the currently active controller. The navigation controller automatically displays the navigation bar and the "back" button. When the user selects the button in the navigation bar to move back to the previous level, that view controller is *popped* off the stack and the view controller beneath it moved to the top becoming the currently active controller.

The view controller for the first table view that appears when the application is started is called the *root view controller*. The root view controller cannot be popped off the navigation controller stack.

29.2 Adding the New Scene to the Storyboard

For the purposes of this example we will be adding a new View Controller to our storyboard to act as the second scene. With this in mind, begin by loading the *TableViewStory* project created in the previous chapter into Xcode.

Once the project has loaded we will need to add a new UIViewController subclass to our project files so select the *File -> New -> File...* menu item and choose the *Cocoa Touch Class* option from the *iOS Source* category. On the options screen, make sure that the *Subclass of* menu is set to UIViewController, name the new class *AttractionDetailViewController* and make sure that the *Also create XIB file* option is switched off. Click *Next* before clicking on *Create*.

Next, select the *Main.storyboard* file from the project navigator so that the storyboard canvas is visible. From the Object Library, select a View Controller and drag and drop it to the right of the existing table view controller as outlined in Figure 29-1. With the new view controller added, select it and display the identity inspector (*View -> Utilities -> Show Identity Inspector*) and change the class setting from UIViewController to AttractionDetailViewController.

Figure 29-1

The detail scene has now been added and assigned to the newly created subclass where code can be added to bring the scene to life.

29.3 Adding a Navigation Controller

Once the application is completed, selecting a row from the Table View will trigger a segue to display the detail view controller. The detail view will contain a button which, when selected by the user, will navigate back to the table view. This functionality will be made possible by the addition of a Navigation Controller to the storyboard. This can be added by selecting the Attraction Table View Controller item in the storyboard so that it highlights in blue, and then selecting the Xcode *Editor -> Embed In -> Navigation Controller* menu option. Once performed, the storyboard will appear as outlined in Figure 29-2:

Figure 29-2

29.4 Establishing the Storyboard Segue

When the user selects a row within the table view, a segue needs to be triggered to display the attraction detail view controller. In order to establish this segue, Ctrl-click on the *prototype cell* located in the Attraction Table View Controller scene and drag the resulting line to the Attraction Detail View Controller scene. Upon releasing the line, select the *show* option from the resulting menu. The storyboard will update to display a segue connection between the table view cell and the view controller. In code that will be implemented later in this chapter it will be necessary to reference this specific segue. In order to do so it must, therefore, be given an identifier. Click on the segue connection between Attraction Table View Controller and Attraction Detail View Controller, display the Attributes Inspector (*View -> Utilities -> Show Attributes Inspector*) and change the Identifier value to *ShowAttractionDetails*.

In addition, a toolbar should have appeared in both scenes. Double click on the center of the Attraction Table View Controller toolbar and change the title to "Attractions". Next, drag a Navigation Item view from the Object Library and drop it onto the toolbar of the Attraction Detail View Controller. Double click on the Title and change it to "Attraction Details":

Figure 29-3

Build and run the application and note that selecting a row in the table view now displays the second view controller which, in turn, has a button in the toolbar to return to the "Attractions" table view. Clearly, we now need to do some work on the AttractionDetailViewController class so that information about the selected tourist location is displayed in the view.

29.5 Modifying the AttractionDetailViewController Class

For the purposes of this example application, the attraction detail view is going to display a web view loaded with a web page relating to the selected tourist attraction. In order to achieve this, the class is going to need a UIWebView object which will later be added to the view.

In addition to the web view, the class is also going to need an internal data model that contains the URL of the web page to be displayed. It will be the job of the table view controller to update this variable prior to the segue occurring so that it reflects the selected attraction. For the sake of simplicity, the data model will take the form of a String object. Select the *AttractionDetailViewController.swift* file and modify it as follows to declare this variable:

```
import UIKit

class AttractionDetailViewController: UIViewController {

    var webSite: String?
.
.
.
```

The next step is to add the Web View to the view controller. Select the storyboard file in the project navigator, ensure that the view is zoomed in and drag and drop a Web View from the Object Library onto the Attraction Detail scene. Resize the view so that it fills the entire scene area as illustrated in Figure 29-4:

Figure 29-4

With the Web View selected in the storyboard canvas, display the Auto Layout Pin menu and add *Spacing to nearest neighbor* constraints on all four sides of the view with the *Constrain to margins* option disabled.

Display the Assistant Editor panel and verify that the editor is displaying the contents of the *AttractionDetailViewController.swift* file. Ctrl-click on the Web View and drag to a position just below the class declaration line in the Assistant Editor. Release the line and in the resulting connection dialog establish an outlet connection named *webView*.

When the detail view appears, the Web View will need to load the web page referenced by the *webSite* string variable. This can be achieved by adding code to the *viewDidLoad* method of the *AttractionDetailViewController.swift* file as follows:

```
override func viewDidLoad() {
    super.viewDidLoad()

    if let address = webSite {
        let webURL = NSURL(string: address)
        let urlRequest = NSURLRequest(URL: webURL!)
        webView.loadRequest(urlRequest)
    }
}
```

29.6 Using prepareForSegue to Pass Data between Storyboard Scenes

The last step in the implementation of this project is to add code so that the data model contained within the AttractionDetailViewController class is updated with the URL of the selected attraction when a table view row is touched by the user. As previously outlined in *Using Storyboards in Xcode 6*, the *prepareForSegue* method on an originating scene is called prior to a segue being performed. This is the ideal place to add code to pass data between source and destination scenes. The *prepareForSegue* method needs to be added to the *AttractionTableViewController.swift* file as outlined in the following code fragment:

```
override func prepareForSegue(segue: UIStoryboardSegue,
                             sender: AnyObject?) {

    if segue.identifier == "ShowAttractionDetails" {
        let detailViewController = segue.destinationViewController
                    as AttractionDetailViewController

        let myIndexPath = self.tableView.indexPathForSelectedRow()
        let row = myIndexPath?.row
        detailViewController.webSite = webAddresses[row!]
    }
}
```

The first task performed by this method is to check that the triggering segue is the *ShowAttractionDetails* segue we added to the storyboard. Having verified that to be the case the code then obtains a reference to the view controller of the destination scene (in this case an instance of our AttractionDetailViewController class). The table view object is then interrogated to find out the index of the selected row which, in turn, is used to prime the URL string variable in the AttractionDetailViewController instance.

29.7 **Testing the Application**

The final step is to compile and run the application. Click on the run button located in the Xcode toolbar and wait for the application to launch. Select an entry from the table and watch as the second view controller appears and loads the appropriate web page:

Figure 29-5

29.8 **Summary**

A key component of implementing table view navigation using storyboards involves the use of segues and the transfer of data between scenes. In this chapter we have used a segue to display a second scene based on table view row selections. The use of the *prepareForSegue* method as a mechanism for passing data during a segue has also been explored and demonstrated.

30. An iOS 8 Split View Master-Detail Example

Whilst it is possible to use the UITableView class as both an information display and application navigation tool on iPhone applications, it is extremely inefficient in terms of the use of screen space when used on an iPad or iPhone 6 Plus. In recognition of this fact, Apple introduced the Split View and Popover concepts for use when developing iOS applications specifically for the iPad and carried this functionality to the iPhone 6 Plus device.

The purpose of this chapter is to provide an overview of Split Views and Popovers followed by a tutorial that implements these concepts in a simple example iPad application.

30.1 An Overview of Split View and Popovers

When an iPad or iPhone 6 Plus is in landscape mode, the UISplitViewController class divides the screen into two side-by-side panels which implement a *master-detail* model. Within this model, the left hand panel is the *master* panel and presents a list of items to the user. The right hand panel is the *detail* panel and displays information relating to the currently selected item in the *master* panel.

A prime example of this concept in action can be seen with the iPad Mail app which lists messages in the master panel and displays the content of the currently selected message in the detail panel.

When an iPad or iPhone 6 Plus device is in portrait mode, however, the Split View Controller hides the master panel so that the detail panel is able to utilize the entire screen. In this instance, the master panel is provided in the form of a full screen table view which segues to the detail view when items are selected from the list. When the device is rotated back to landscape orientation, the master and detail panels appear side by side once again. When in this "split view" mode, a button is provided to hide the master panel, leaving the full screen available for use by the detail panel.

When a split view user interface is run on a smaller iPhone screen, it behaves in the same way as when running on an iPad or iPhone 6 Plus in portrait mode.

The UISplitterViewController is essentially a container to which two child view controllers are added to act as the master (also referred to as the *root view controller*) and detail views.

In the remainder of this chapter we will work through a tutorial that involves the creation of a simple iOS application that demonstrates the use of a split view configuration.

30.2 **About the Example Split View Project**

The goal of this tutorial is to create an application containing a split view user interface. The master panel will contain a table view listing a number of web site addresses. When a web site URL is selected from the list, the detail panel will load the corresponding web site and display it using a UIWebView component.

30.3 **Creating the Project**

Begin by launching Xcode and creating a new application using the *Master-Detail Application* template. Enter *SplitView* as the product name, select *Universal* from the Devices menu, *Swift* from the language menu and verify that the *Use Core Data* option is switched off.

By using this template we save a lot of extra coding effort in the implementation of the split view behavior. Much of the code generated for us is standard boilerplate code that does not change from one split view implementation to another. In fact, much of this template can be copied even if you plan to hand code split view behavior in future applications. That said, there are some unusual aspects to the template which will need to be modified during the course of this tutorial.

30.4 **Reviewing the Project**

The Split View template has created a number of project files for us. The most significant of these are the files relating to the Master View Controller and Detail View Controller classes. These classes correspond to the master and detail views and are named MasterViewController and DetailViewController respectively.

Xcode has also created a custom *didFinishLaunchingWithOptions* method located within the *AppDelegate* class. Whilst the custom *didFinishLaunchingWithOptions* method fits perfectly with our requirements, the template actually creates a simple application in which the date and time may be added to the master view and then displayed in the detail view when selected. Since this is not quite the behavior we need for our example it will be necessary to delete some of this template code as our project progresses.

Finally, a *Main.storyboard* file has been created configured with the following elements:

- A UISplitViewController
- A View Controller named DetailViewController for the detail pane
- A Table View Controller named MasterViewController for the master pane
- Two navigation controllers

This represents the standard storyboard configuration for a typical split view implementation. The only changes to this storyboard that will be necessary for this example will be to change the user interface of the detail view pane and to modify the title of the master pane. The rest of the storyboard will remain unchanged. To change the title of the master pane, locate it within the storyboard canvas, double click on the title text which currently reads "Master" and enter "Favorite Web Sites" as the new title as outlined in Figure 30-1:

Figure 30-1

30.5 Configuring Master View Items

The master view controller created for us by Xcode is actually a subclass of UITableView. The next step, therefore, is to configure the table view to display the list of web sites. For this purpose we will need to configure two array objects to store the web site names and corresponding URL addresses. Select the *MasterViewController.swift* file and modify it as follows to declare these two arrays:

```
import UIKit

class MasterViewController: UITableViewController {

    var siteNames: [String]?
    var siteAddresses: [String]?

    var detailViewController: DetailViewController? = nil
    var objects = NSMutableArray()
.
.
.
```

Having declared the arrays, modify the *MasterViewController.swift* file further to initialize the arrays in the *viewDidLoad* method. Note that Xcode has already added some code to the *viewDidLoad* method for the template example so be sure to remove this before adding the new code below:

```
override func viewDidLoad() {
    super.viewDidLoad()

    siteNames = ["Yahoo", "Google", "Apple", "eBookFrenzy"]
    siteAddresses = ["http://www.yahoo.com", "http://www.google.com",
"http://www.apple.com", "http://www.ebookfrenzy.com"]

    if let split = splitViewController {
        let controllers = split.viewControllers
        detailViewController =
                controllers[controllers.count-1].topViewController
                        as? DetailViewController
```

```
    }
}
```

There are a number of methods that must be implemented in order for the items to appear within the table view object. Fortunately, Xcode has already placed template methods for us to use in the *MasterViewController.swift* file. First, modify the *numberOfRowsInSection* method to notify the table view of the number of items to be displayed (in this case, a value equal to the number of items in our siteNames array). Since there is only one section in the table also modify the *numberOfSectionsInTableView* method accordingly. Note that Xcode has, once again, added some code for the template example so be sure to remove this code where necessary:

```
-  (NSInteger)numberOfSectionsInTableView:(UITableView *)tableView
{
     return 1
}


-  (NSInteger)tableView:(UITableView *)tableView
numberOfRowsInSection:(NSInteger)section
{
     return siteNames!.count
}
```

Next, modify the *cellForRowAtIndexPath* method to return the item to be displayed, using the row number argument as an index into the siteNames array:

```
override func tableView(tableView: UITableView, cellForRowAtIndexPath
indexPath: NSIndexPath) -> UITableViewCell {

    let cell = tableView.dequeueReusableCellWithIdentifier("Cell",
        forIndexPath: indexPath) as UITableViewCell

    cell.textLabel.text = siteNames![indexPath.row]
    return cell
}
```

Click on the run button located in the Xcode toolbar to test the current state of the application, using a physical iPad or iPhone 6 Plus device, or a corresponding simulator as the target. Once the application loads, rotate the device into landscape mode (using the *Hardware -> Rotate Left* menu if running on a simulator):

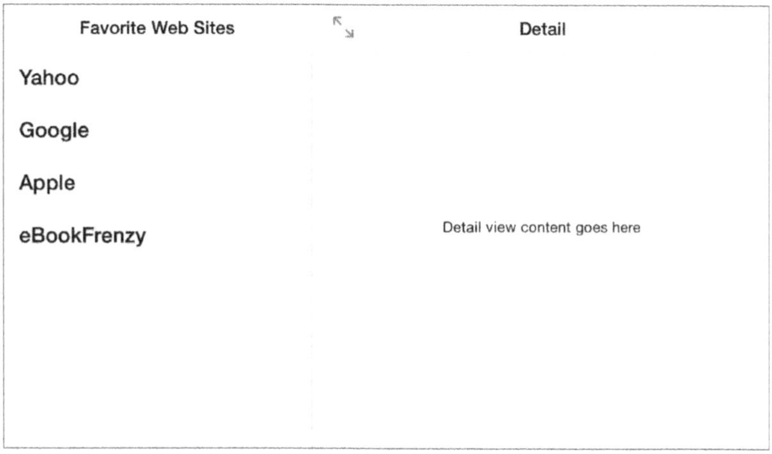

| Favorite Web Sites | ↖↘ | Detail |

Yahoo

Google

Apple

eBookFrenzy

Detail view content goes here

Figure 30-2

At this point the items in the master panel actually load the detail view onto the master panel when selected and the detail panel still displays the place holder label provided by Xcode when the project was first created. The next step is to change this behavior and add the web view to the detail view controller.

30.6 Configuring the Detail View Controller

When a user selects a web site item from the master panel, the detail panel will load the selected web site into a web view object.

Begin by selecting the *Main.storyboard* file, locate the DetailViewController scene, click on the placeholder label that reads "Detail view content goes here" and press the Delete key. Drag and drop a UIWebView object from the object library (*View -> Utilities -> Show Object Library*) onto the view and resize it so that it fills the entire view area. With the Web View instance selected in the storyboard, use the Auto Layout Pin menu to set *Spacing to nearest neighbor* constraints on all four sides of the view with the *Constrain to margins* option disabled.

Select the web view object, display the Assistant Editor panel and verify that the editor is displaying the contents of the *DetailViewController.swift* file. Ctrl-click on the web view again and drag to a position just below the class declaration line in the Assistant Editor. Release the line and in the resulting connection dialog establish an outlet connection named *webView*.

30.7 Connecting Master Selections to the Detail View

The next task is to configure the detail panel to update based on selections made in the master panel. When a user makes an item selection from the table view the *prepareForSegue* method in the master view controller is triggered. This template method needs to be modified to assign the selected URL to the *detailItem* property of the DetailViewController class. Select the *MasterViewController.swift* file and locate the method. Once again, Xcode has added code to the template example so remove the current code and modify the method as follows:

```
override func prepareForSegue(segue: UIStoryboardSegue,
                        sender: AnyObject?) {
```

```
if segue.identifier == "showDetail" {
    if let indexPath = self.tableView.indexPathForSelectedRow() {
        let urlString = siteAddresses?[indexPath.row]

        let controller = (segue.destinationViewController
            as UINavigationController).topViewController
                as DetailViewController

        controller.detailItem = urlString
        controller.navigationItem.leftBarButtonItem =
            splitViewController?.displayModeButtonItem()
        controller.navigationItem.leftItemsSupplementBackButton =
true
    }
  }
}
```

The method begins by verifying that this is the segue associated with the transition to the detail view before identifying the URL of the selected web site by using the selected row as an index into the siteAddresses array. A reference to the destination view controller is then obtained and the *detailItem* property of that instance set to the URL of the web page to be displayed. Finally, a bar button item is added to the detail navigation bar. The button added is the UISplitViewController's "display mode" button. This button provides the user with the option to expand the detail view to fill the entire display, causing the master panel to be hidden from view.

30.8 Modifying the DetailViewController Class

The DetailViewController class created by Xcode is designed to display some text on a Label view. Given that the Label view has now been replaced by a Web View, some changes to the class will inevitably need to be made. Locate the *DetailViewController.swift* file in the project navigator panel and locate and modify the *configureView* method so that it now reads as follows:

```
func configureView() {
    // Update the user interface for the detail item.

    if let detail: AnyObject = detailItem {

        if let myWebview = webView {
            let url = NSURL(string: detailItem as String)
            let request = NSURLRequest(URL: url!)
            myWebview.scalesPageToFit = true
            myWebview.loadRequest(request)
        }
    }
}
```

```
}
```

The code checks to make sure that the detailItem variable has a value assigned to it, verifies that the webView view has been created and then performs a number of steps to load the designated URL into the view. Note that in order to make the web page scale to fit the detail view area the scalePagesToFit property of the UIWebView object is set to true.

30.9 **Testing the Application**

All that remains is to test the application so select a suitable iPad or iPhone 6 Plus device or simulator as the target, click on the Xcode run button and wait for the application to load. In portrait mode only the master panel should be visible. Selecting an item from the master list should trigger the segue to the detail panel within which the selected web page should load into the web view instance.

Tapping the "Master" button in the detail panel should return back to the master panel.

Select the *Hardware -> Rotate Left* menu option to switch the device into landscape mode and note that both the master and detail panels are now visible:

Figure 30-3

Tapping the display mode button located in the top left hand corner of the detail panel navigation bar will cause the detail view to expand to fill the entire screen.

30.10 **Summary**

Split views provide iOS applications with a master-detail interface paradigm designed to make better use of the larger screen space of the device. Where ever possible, this approach should be taken in favor of the table view based navigation common in iPhone based applications. In this chapter we have explored split views in general and worked through the implementation of an example application.

31. Implementing a Page based iOS 8 Application using UIPageViewController

The UIPageViewController class was introduced into the iOS 5 SDK as a mechanism to implement a page turning style of user interface in iOS applications. This chapter will provide a brief overview of the concepts behind the page view controller before working through the development of an example application in the next chapter.

31.1 The UIPageViewController Class

The UIPageViewController class highlights the distinction between a *view controller* and a *container controller*. A view controller is responsible for managing a user interface view, typically in the form of a view hierarchy contained within a storyboard or Interface Builder XIB file. Creating a *Single View Application* with Xcode, for example, will create a single view controller class with a corresponding entry in the storyboard file.

A *container controller*, on the other hand, is a class designed to contain and manage multiple *view controllers*, usually providing a mechanism for switching from one view controller to another, either programmatically or in response to user interaction.

The UIPageViewController class is a *container controller* designed to facilitate navigation through multiple views using a page curling visual transition. When implemented, this allows users to page through content using screen based gestures, much in the same way Apple's iBooks application allows a user to move backwards and forwards within the pages of an eBook using page turning gestures. Each page displayed to the user is actually a view controller created on demand for the page controller by a *data source*.

31.2 The UIPageViewController DataSource

In order to function, a UIPageViewController instance must be assigned a data source which, in turn, is responsible for providing view controller objects as required for each page. The data source takes the form of a class instance that implements the UIPageViewControllerDataSource protocol which, at a minimum, must implement the following two methods:

- **viewControllerAfterViewController** - This method is passed a view controller representing the currently displayed page and is required to return the view controller corresponding to the next page in the paging sequence.
- **viewControllerBeforeViewController** - This method is passed the view controller representing the currently displayed page and is required to return the view controller corresponding to the previous page in the paging sequence.

The mechanism used to create the requested view controllers and the content therein will generally be application specific and is at the discretion of the developer. Apple does, however, recommend that in order to ensure optimal performance and minimal resource usage, the view controllers be created on an as-needed basis rather than pre-created.

When a UIPageViewController object is initialized, a number of configuration options may be specified to configure the appearance and behavior of the contained views.

31.3 **Navigation Orientation**

The page controller is capable of transitioning between views using either a vertical or horizontal paradigm. In the case of horizontal navigation, page transitions take place in the same way pages are turned in a physical book by sweeping a finger on the screen either left or right.

In the case of horizontal navigation, pages are turned by making vertical gestures in much the same way the pages of a wall calendar are flipped. These options are configured using the following constants:

- UIPageViewControllerNavigationOrientation.Horizontal
- UIPageViewControllerNavigationOrientation.Vertical

31.4 **Spine Location**

The UIPageViewController class allows for the location of the *spine* to be configured. The term *spine* in this context is analogous to the spine of a book and dictates the location of the axis on which each page will turn.

The behavior of the spine location settings vary depending on the navigation orientation setting. For example, the default for most configurations is UIPageViewControllerSpineLocation.Min which places the spine on the left hand side or top of the screen depending on whether the navigation orientation is horizontal or vertical. Similarly, the UIPageViewControllerSpineLocation.Max setting will position the spine at the right or bottom edge of the display. In order to display two pages simultaneously the UIPageViewControllerSpineLocationMid setting should be used.

The view controller may also be configured to treat pages as being double sided via the doubleSided property.

Note that when using UIPageViewControllerSpineLocationMid spine location it will be necessary to provide the page controller with two view controllers (one for the left hand page and one for the right) for each page turn. Similarly, when using either the min or max spine location together with the double sided setting, view controllers for both the front and back of the current page will be required for each page.

31.5 **The UIPageViewController Delegate Protocol**

In addition to a data source, instances of the UIPageViewController class may also be assigned a delegate which, in turn, may implement the following delegate methods:

- **spineLocationForInterface** - The purpose of this delegate method is to allow the spine location to be changed in the event that the device is rotated by the user. An application might, for example, switch to UIPageViewControllerSpineLocationMid layout when the device is placed in a landscape orientation. The method is passed the new orientation and must return a corresponding spine location value. Before doing so it may, for example, also set up two view controllers if a switch is being made to a UIPageViewControllerSpineLocationMid spine location.

- **transitionComplete** - This method is called after the user initiates a page transition via a screen based gesture. The success or otherwise of the transition may be identified through the implementation of a completion handler.

31.6 **Summary**

The UIPageViewController class is categorized as a container controller in that it is responsible for containing view controllers and managing which view is displayed to the user. The main purpose of the UIPageViewController is to allow the user to navigate through different views using a page curl transition style. Implementation of this functionality requires the configuration of navigation orientation, spine location and a number of data source methods.

The theory covered in this chapter will be put into practice in the next chapter entitled *An Example iOS 8 UIPageViewController Application*.

32. An Example iOS 8 UIPageViewController Application

The previous chapter entitled *Implementing a Page based iOS 8 Application using UIPageViewController* covered the theory behind implementing page curling view transitions using the UIPageViewController class. This chapter will work through the creation of an application designed to demonstrate this class in action.

32.1 The Xcode Page-based Application Template

When creating a new project within the Xcode environment, an option is provided to base the project on the *Page-based Application* template. When selected, this option generates a project containing an application designed to display a page for each month of the year. This is somewhat strange and something of an anomaly in that this is the only instance where Xcode provides a template that goes beyond providing a basic foundation on which to build and actually provides a sample application. Whilst this is useful for initial learning, unless an application with 12 pages labeled with months of the year is what you need, effort will need to be invested removing existing functionality from the template before it can be used for other purposes.

Rather than use Xcode's Page-based Application template, this chapter will work through the implementation of page based behavior using the *Single View Application* template as a starting point. The reasons for this are two-fold. Firstly, implementing UIPageViewController functionality without recourse to the page-based template provides the reader with a better understanding of how the implementation actually works. Secondly, it will typically be quicker to implement the UIPageViewController code by hand than to attempt to repurpose the example application provided by the Page-based Application template.

32.2 Creating the Project

Begin by launching Xcode and creating a new iOS Single View Application project with a product name of *PageApp*, the device menu set to *Universal* and using Swift as the programming language.

32.3 Adding the Content View Controller

The example application will use instances of a single view controller class to display pages to the user. The view will contain a UIWebView object onto which different HTML content will be displayed depending on the currently selected page. The view controller class will also need a data object property that will be used to hold the HTML content for the view.

To add the content view controller, select the Xcode *File -> New -> File...* menu option and create a new iOS Cocoa Touch class. Configure the class to be a subclass of UIViewController without an XIB file and name the class *ContentViewController.* On the final screen, select a location for the new class files before clicking on *Create*.

Select the *ContentViewController.swift* file from the project navigator panel and add a reference to the data object:

```
import UIKit

class ContentViewController: UIViewController {

    var dataObject: AnyObject?
    .
    .
    .
```

Next, select the *Main.storyboard* file and drag and drop a new View Controller object from the Object Library to the storyboard canvas. Display the Identity Inspector (*View -> Utilities -> Show Identity Inspector*) and change the *Class* setting to *ContentViewController.* In the *Identity* section beneath the Class setting, specify a *Storyboard ID* of *contentView.*

Drag and drop a Web View object from the Object Library to the ContentViewController view in the storyboard canvas and size and position it so that it fills the entire view as illustrated in Figure 32-1. With the Web View object selected in the canvas, use the Auto Layout Pin menu to configure *Spacing to nearest neighbor* constraints on all four sides of the view with the *Constrain to margins* option switched off.

Select the Web View object in the storyboard panel, display the Assistant Editor panel and verify that the editor is displaying the contents of the *ContentViewController.swift* file. Ctrl-click on the web view object and drag to a position just below the class declaration line in the Assistant Editor. Release the line and in the resulting connection dialog establish an outlet connection named *webView.*

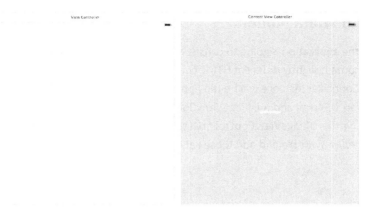

Figure 32-1

With the user interface designed, select the *ContentViewController.swift* file. Each time the user turns a page in the application, the data source methods for a UIPageViewController object are going to create a new instance of our ContentViewController class and set the *dataObject* property of that instance to the HTML that is to be displayed on the web view object. As such, the *viewWillAppear* method of ContentViewController needs to assign the value stored in the *dataObject* property to the web view object. To achieve this behavior, add the *viewWillAppear* method to assign the HTML to the web view:

```
import UIKit

class ContentViewController: UIViewController {

    var dataObject: AnyObject?

    @IBOutlet weak var webView: UIWebView!
.
.
.

    override func viewWillAppear(animated: Bool) {
        super.viewWillAppear(animated)

        webView.loadHTMLString(dataObject as String,
            baseURL: NSURL(string: ""))
    }
.
.
.
```

At this point work on the content view controller is complete. The next step is to create the data model for the application.

32.4 **Creating the Data Model**

The data model for the application is going to consist of an array object containing a number of string objects, each configured to contain slightly different HTML content. For the purposes of this example, the data source for the UIPageViewController instance will be the application's *ViewController* class. This class will, therefore, need references to an NSArray and a UIPageViewController object. It will also be necessary to declare this class as implementing the UIPageViewControllerDataSource and UIPageViewControllerDelegate protocols. Select the *ViewController.swift* file and add these references as follows:

```
import UIKit

class ViewController: UIViewController, UIPageViewControllerDataSource,
UIPageViewControllerDelegate {

    var pageController: UIPageViewController?
    var pageContent = NSArray()
    .
    .
    .
```

The final step in creating the model is to add a method to the *ViewController.swift* file to add the HTML strings to the array and then call that method from *viewDidLoad:*

```
import UIKit

class ViewController: UIViewController, UIPageViewControllerDataSource,
UIPageViewControllerDelegate {
    .
    .
    .
    override func viewDidLoad() {
        super.viewDidLoad()
        createContentPages()
    }

    func createContentPages() {

        var pageStrings = [String]()

        for i in 1...11
        {
            let contentString = "<html><head></head><body><br><h1>Chapter
\(i)</h1><p>This is the page \(i) of content displayed using
UIPageViewController in iOS 8.</p></body></html>"
```

```
        pageStrings.append(contentString)
    }
    pageContent = pageStrings
}
```

.

.

.

The application now has a content view controller and a data model from which the content of each page will be extracted by the data source methods. The next logical step, therefore, is to implement those data source methods. As previously outlined in *Implementing a Page based iOS 8 Application using UIPageViewController*, instances of the UIPageViewController class need a data source. This takes the form of two methods, one of which is required to return the view controller to be displayed after the currently displayed view controller, and the other the view controller to be displayed before the current view controller. Since the *ViewController* class is going to act as the data source for the page view controller object, these two methods, together with two convenience methods (which we will borrow from the Xcode Page-based Application template) will need to be added to the *ViewController.swift* file. Begin by adding the two convenience functions:

```
func viewControllerAtIndex(index: Int) -> ContentViewController? {

    if (pageContent.count == 0) ||
        (index >= pageContent.count) {
        return nil
    }

    let storyBoard = UIStoryboard(name: "Main",
                bundle: NSBundle.mainBundle())
    let dataViewController =
storyBoard.instantiateViewControllerWithIdentifier("contentView") as
ContentViewController

    dataViewController.dataObject = pageContent[index]
    return dataViewController
}

func indexOfViewController(viewController: ContentViewController) -> Int
{

    if let dataObject: AnyObject = viewController.dataObject {
        return pageContent.indexOfObject(dataObject)
    } else {
        return NSNotFound
    }
}
```

The *viewControllerAtIndex* method begins by checking to see if the page being requested is outside the bounds of available pages by checking if the index reference is zero (the user cannot page back beyond the first page) or greater than the number of items in the *pageContent* array. In the event that the index value is valid, a new instance of the ContentViewController class is created and the dataObject property set to the contents of the corresponding item in the pageContent array of HTML strings.

Since the view controller is stored in the storyboard file, the following code is used to get a reference to the storyboard and to create a new ContentViewController instance:

```
let storyBoard = UIStoryboard(name: "Main",
                    bundle: NSBundle.mainBundle())
let dataViewController =
    storyBoard.instantiateViewControllerWithIdentifier("contentView")
            as ContentViewController
```

The *indexOfViewController* method is passed a viewController object and is expected to return the index value of the controller. It does this by extracting the dataObject property of the view controller and finding the index of the matching element in the pageContent array.

All that remains to be implemented as far as the data source is concerned are the two data source protocol methods which, in turn, make use of the two convenience methods to return the view controllers before and after the current view controller:

```
func pageViewController(pageViewController: UIPageViewController,
viewControllerBeforeViewController viewController: UIViewController) ->
UIViewController? {

    var index = indexOfViewController(viewController
                            as ContentViewController)

    if (index == 0) || (index == NSNotFound) {
        return nil
    }

    index--
    return viewControllerAtIndex(index)
}

func pageViewController(pageViewController: UIPageViewController,
viewControllerAfterViewController viewController: UIViewController) ->
UIViewController? {

    var index = indexOfViewController(viewController
        as ContentViewController)
```

```
    if index == NSNotFound {
        return nil
    }

    index++
    if index == pageContent.count {
        return nil
    }
    return viewControllerAtIndex(index)
}
```

With the data source implemented, the next step is to create and initialize an instance of the UIPageViewController class.

32.5 Initializing the UIPageViewController

All that remains is to create the UIPageViewController instance and initialize it appropriately. Since this needs to be performed only once per application invocation a suitable location for this code is the *viewDidLoad* method of the ViewController class. Select the *ViewController.swift* file and modify the *viewDidLoad* method so that it reads as follows:

```
override func viewDidLoad() {
    super.viewDidLoad()

    createContentPages()

    pageController = UIPageViewController(
            transitionStyle: .PageCurl,
            navigationOrientation: .Horizontal,
            options: nil)

    pageController?.delegate = self
    pageController?.dataSource = self

    let startingViewController: ContentViewController =
            viewControllerAtIndex(0)!

    let viewControllers: NSArray = [startingViewController]
    pageController!.setViewControllers(viewControllers,
            direction: .Forward,
            animated: false,
            completion: nil)
```

```
        self.addChildViewController(pageController!)
        self.view.addSubview(self.pageController!.view)

        var pageViewRect = self.view.bounds
        pageController!.view.frame = pageViewRect
        pageController!.didMoveToParentViewController(self)
}
```

All the code for the application is now complete. Before compiling and running the application some time needs to be taken to deconstruct and analyze the code in the *viewDidLoad* method.

After constructing the data model with the call to the *createContentPage* method an instance of the UIPageViewController class is created specifying page curling and horizontal navigation orientation. Since the current class is going to act as the datasource and delegate for the page controller this also needs to be configured:

```
pageController = UIPageViewController(
        transitionStyle: .PageCurl,
        navigationOrientation: .Horizontal,
        options: nil)

pageController?.delegate = self
pageController?.dataSource = self
```

Before the first page can be displayed a view controller must first be created. This can be achieved by calling our *viewControllerAtIndex* convenience method. Once a content view controller has been returned it needs to be assigned to an array object:

```
let startingViewController: ContentViewController =
        viewControllerAtIndex(0)!

let viewControllers: NSArray = [startingViewController]
```

Note that only one content view controller is needed because the page controller is configured to display only one, single sided page at a time. Had the page controller been configured for two pages (with a mid-location spine) or for double sided pages it would have been necessary to create two content view controllers at this point and assign both to the array.

With an array containing the content view controller ready, the array needs to be assigned to the view controller with the navigation direction set to forward mode:

```
pageController!.setViewControllers(viewControllers,
        direction: .Forward,
        animated: false,
        completion: nil)
```

Finally, the standard steps need to be taken to add the page view controller to the current view. Code is also included to ensure that the pages fill the entire screen:

```
self.addChildViewController(self.pageController!)
self.view.addSubview(pageController!.view)

var pageViewRect = self.view.bounds
pageController!.view.frame = pageViewRect
pageController!.didMoveToParentViewController(self)
```

32.6 **Running the UIPageViewController Application**

Click on the *Run* button to compile and launch the application in the iOS Simulator or on a physical device. Once loaded, the first content page should appear. A right to left gesture motion on the screen will cause the page to transition to the second page of content and reversing the gesture direction will page backwards:

Figure 32-2

32.7 **Summary**

The goal of this chapter has been to work through an example application designed to implement the page turning transition view provided by the UIPageViewController class.

33. Working with Directories in Swift on iOS 8

It is sometimes easy to forget that iOS is an operating system much like that running on many other computers today. Given this fact, it should come as no surprise that iOS has a file system much like any other operating system allowing applications to store persistent data on behalf of the user. Much like other platforms, the iOS file system provides a directory based structure into which files can be created and organized.

Since the introduction of iOS 5 the iOS app developer has had two options in terms of storing data. Files and data may now be stored on the file system of the local device or remotely using Apple's iCloud service. In practice, however, it is most likely that an application will utilize iCloud storage to augment, rather than replace, the use of the local file system so familiarity with both concepts is still a necessity.

The topic of iCloud based storage will be covered in detail beginning with the chapter entitled *Preparing an iOS 8 App to use iCloud Storage*. The goal of this chapter, however, is to provide an overview of how to work with local file system directories from within an iOS 8 application. Topics covered include identifying the application's document and temporary directories, finding the current working directory, creating, removing and renaming directories and obtaining listings of a directory's content. Once the topic of directory management has been covered, we will move on to handling files in *Working with Files in Swift on iOS 8*.

33.1 The Application Documents Directory

An iPhone or iPad user can install multiple applications on a single device. The iOS platform is responsible for ensuring that these applications cannot interfere with each other, both in terms of memory usage and data storage. As such, each application is restricted in terms of where it can store data on the file system of the device. iOS achieves this by allowing applications to read and write only to their own *Documents* and *tmp* directories. Within these two directories the corresponding application can create files and also sub-directories to any required level of depth. This area constitutes the application's *sandbox* and the application cannot usually create or modify files or directories outside of these directories unless using the UIDocumentPickerViewController class.

33.2 The NSFileManager, NSFileHandle and NSData Classes

The Foundation Framework provides three classes that are indispensable when it comes to working with files and directories:

- **NSFileManager** - The *NSFileManager* class can be used to perform basic file and directory operations such as creating, moving, reading and writing files and reading and setting file attributes. In addition, this class provides methods for, amongst other tasks, identifying the current working directory, changing to a new directory, creating directories and listing the contents of a directory.
- **NSFileHandle** - The *NSFileHandle* class is provided for performing lower level operations on files, such as seeking to a specific position in a file and reading and writing a file's contents by a specified number of byte chunks and appending data to an existing file. This class will be used extensively in the chapter entitled *Working with Files in Swift on iOS 8*.
- **NSData** - The *NSData* class provides a useful storage buffer into which the contents of a file may be read, or from which dynamically stored data may be written to a file.

33.3 **Understanding Pathnames in Swift**

As with Mac OS X, iOS defines pathnames using the standard UNIX convention. As such each component of a path is separated by a forward slash (/). When an application starts, the current working directory is the file system's *root directory* represented by a single /. From this location, the application must navigate to its own *Documents* and *tmp* directories in order to be able to write files to the file system. Path names that begin with a / are said to be *absolute path names* in that they specify a file system location relative to the root directory. For example, */var/mobile* is an absolute path name.

Paths that do not begin with a slash are interpreted to be *relative* to a current working directory. For example, if the current working directory is */User/demo* and the path name is *mapdata/local.xml* then the file is considered to have an equivalent full, absolute pathname of */User/demo/mapdata/local.xml*.

33.4 **Obtaining a Reference to the Default NSFileManager Object**

The NSFileManager class contains a class method named *defaultManager* that is used to obtain a reference to the application's default file manager instance:

```
let filemgr = NSFileManager.defaultManager()
```

Having obtained the object reference we can begin to use it to work with files and directories.

33.5 **Identifying the Current Working Directory**

As previously mentioned, when an application first loads, its current working directory is the application's root directory, represented by a / character. The current working directory may be identified at any time by accessing the *currentDirectoryPath* property of the file manager object. For example, the following code fragment identifies the current working directory:

```
let currentPath = filemgr.currentDirectoryPath
```

33.6 **Identifying the Documents Directory**

Each iOS application on a device has its own private *Documents* and *tmp* directories into which it is permitted to read and write data. Because the location of these directories is different for each application the only way to find the correct path is to ask iOS. In fact, the exact location will also differ depending on whether the application is running on a physical iPhone or iPad device or in the iOS Simulator. The *Documents* directory for an application may be identified by making a call to a C function named *NSSearchPathForDirectoriesInDomains*, passing through an argument (in this case NSDocumentDirectory) indicating that we require the path to the Documents directory. Since this is a C function, as opposed to a method of a Swift class, there is no need for us to establish an instance of a Foundation class such as NSFileManager before making the call. That said, the function does return an object in the form of an NSArray containing the results of the request. We can, therefore, obtain the path to the current application's Documents directory as follows:

```
let dirPaths = NSSearchPathForDirectoriesInDomains(.DocumentDirectory,
                    .UserDomainMask, true)

let docsDir = dirPaths[0] as String
```

When executed, the above code will assign the path to the *Documents* directory to the docsDir constant.

When executed within the iOS Simulator environment, the path returned will take the form of:

```
/Users/<user name>/Library/Developer/CoreSimulator/Devices/<device
id>/data/Containers/Data/Application/<app id>/Documents
```

Where *<user name>* is the name of the user currently logged into the Mac OS X system on which the simulator is running, *<device id>* is the unique ID of the device on which the app is running and *<app id>* is the unique ID of the app, for example:

```
06A3AEBA-8C34-476E-937F-A27BDD2E450A
```

Clearly this references a path on your Mac OS X system so feel free to open up a Finder window and explore the file system sandbox areas for your iOS applications.

When executed on a physical iOS device, however, the path returned by the function call will take the following form:

```
/var/mobile/Containers/Data/Application/<app id>/Documents
```

33.7 **Identifying the Temporary Directory**

In addition to the *Documents* directory, iOS applications are also provided with a *tmp* directory for the storage of temporary files. The path to the current application's temporary directory may be ascertained with a call to the *NSTemporaryDirectory* C function as follows:

```
let tmpDir = NSTemporaryDirectory() as String
```

Once executed, the string object referenced by tmpDir will contain the path to the temporary directory for the application.

33.8 Changing Directory

Having identified the path to the application's document or temporary directory the chances are good that you will need to make that directory the current working directory. The current working directory of a running iOS application can be changed with a call to the *changeCurrentDirectoryPath* method of an NSFileManager instance. The destination directory path is passed as an argument to the instance method in the form of a String object. Note that this method returns a Boolean *true* or *false* result to indicate if the requested directory change was successful or not. A failure result typically indicates either that the specified directory does not exist, or that the application lacks the appropriate access permissions:

```
let filemgr = NSFileManager.defaultManager()

let dirPaths = NSSearchPathForDirectoriesInDomains(.DocumentDirectory,
                              .UserDomainMask, true)

let docsDir = dirPaths[0] as String

if filemgr.changeCurrentDirectoryPath(docsDir) {
    // Success
} else {
    // Failure
}
```

In the above example, the path to the *Documents* directory is identified and then used as an argument to the *changeCurrentDirectoryPath* method of the file manager object to change the current working directory to that location.

33.9 Creating a New Directory

A new directory on an iOS device is created using the *createDirectoryAtPath* instance method of the NSFileManager class, once again passing through the pathname of the new directory as an argument and returning a Boolean success or failure result. The second argument to this method defines whether any intermediate directory levels should be created automatically. For example, if we wanted to create a directory with the path */var/mobile/Containers/Data/Application/<app id>/Documents/mydata/maps* and the *mydata* subdirectory does not yet exist, setting the *withIntermediateDirectories* argument to *true* will cause this directory to be created automatically before then creating the *maps* sub-directory within it. If this argument is set to *false,* then the attempt to create the directory will fail because *mydata* does not already exist and we have not given permission for it to be created on our behalf.

This method also takes additional arguments in the form of a set of attributes for the new directory. Specifying *nil* will use the default attributes.

The final argument provides the option to reference an NSError object to contain error information in the event of a failure. If this is not required, *nil* may be specified for this argument.

The following code fragment identifies the documents directory and creates a new sub-directory named *data* in that directory:

```
let filemgr = NSFileManager.defaultManager()

let dirPaths = NSSearchPathForDirectoriesInDomains(.DocumentDirectory,
                       .UserDomainMask, true)

let docsDir = dirPaths[0] as String
let newDir = docsDir.stringByAppendingPathComponent("data")

var error: NSError?

if !filemgr.createDirectoryAtPath(newDir,
            withIntermediateDirectories: true,
            attributes: nil,
            error: &error) {

    println("Failed to create dir: \(error!.localizedDescription)")
}
```

33.10 Deleting a Directory

An existing directory may be removed from the file system using the *removeItemAtPath* method, passing through the path of the directory to be removed as an argument. For example, to remove the data directory created in the preceding example we might write the following code:

```
var error: NSError?

if !filemgr.removeItemAtPath(newDir, error: &error) {
        println("Failed to delete directory:
 \(error!.localizedDescription)")
}
```

33.11 Listing the Contents of a Directory

A listing of the files contained within a specified directory can be obtained using the *directoryContentsAtPath* method. This method takes the directory pathname as an argument and returns an array object containing the names of the files and sub-directories in that directory. The following example obtains a listing of the contents of the root directory (/) and displays each item in the Xcode console panel during execution:

```
let filemgr = NSFileManager.defaultManager()
let filelist = filemgr.contentsOfDirectoryAtPath("/", error: &error)

for filename in filelist! {
    println(filename)
}
```

33.12 Getting the Attributes of a File or Directory

The attributes of a file or directory may be obtained using the *attributesOfItemAtPath* method. This takes as arguments the path of the directory and an optional NSError object into which information about any errors will be placed (may be specified *as nil* if this information is not required). The results are returned in the form of an NSDictionary dictionary object. The keys for this dictionary are as follows:

```
NSFileType

NSFileTypeDirectory

NSFileTypeRegular

NSFileTypeSymbolicLink

NSFileTypeSocket

NSFileTypeCharacterSpecial

NSFileTypeBlockSpecial

NSFileTypeUnknown

NSFileSize

NSFileModificationDate

NSFileReferenceCount

NSFileDeviceIdentifier

NSFileOwnerAccountName

NSFileGroupOwnerAccountName

NSFilePosixPermissions

NSFileSystemNumber

NSFileSystemFileNumber

NSFileExtensionHidden

NSFileHFSCreatorCode

NSFileHFSTypeCode
```

NSFileImmutable

NSFileAppendOnly

NSFileCreationDate

NSFileOwnerAccountID

NSFileGroupOwnerAccountID

For example, we can extract the file type for the */Applications* directory using the following code excerpt:

```
let filemgr = NSFileManager.defaultManager()

var error: NSError?

let attribs: NSDictionary? = filemgr.attributesOfItemAtPath(
                    "/Applications", error: &error)

if let fileattribs = attribs {
    let type = fileattribs["NSFileType"] as String
    println("File type \(type)")
}
```

When executed, results similar to the following output will appear in the Xcode console:

```
File type NSFileTypeDirectory
```

34. Working with Files in Swift on iOS 8

In the chapter entitled *Working with Directories in Swift on iOS 8* we looked at the NSFileManager, NSFileHandle and NSData Foundation Framework classes and discussed how the NSFileManager class in particular enables us to work with directories when developing iOS 8 based applications. We also spent some time covering the file system structure used by iOS and, in particular, looked at the temporary and *Documents* directories assigned to each application and how the location of those directories can be identified from within the application code.

In this chapter we move on from working with directories to covering the details of working with files within the iOS 8 SDK. Once we have covered file handling topics in this chapter, the next chapter will work through an application example that puts theory into practice.

34.1 Creating an NSFileManager Instance

Before proceeding, first we need to recap the steps necessary to obtain a reference to the application's NSFileManager instance. As discussed in the previous chapter, the NSFileManager class contains a class method named *defaultManager* that is used to obtain a reference. For example:

```
let filemgr = NSFileManager.defaultManager()
```

Once a reference to the file manager object has been obtained it can be used to perform some basic file handling tasks.

34.2 Checking for the Existence of a File

The NSFileManager class contains an instance method named *fileExistsAtPath* which checks whether a specified file already exists. The method takes as an argument an NSString object containing the path to the file in question and returns a Boolean value indicating the presence or otherwise of the specified file:

```
if filemgr.fileExistsAtPath("/Applications") {
    println("File exists")
} else {
    println("File not found")
}
```

34.3 **Comparing the Contents of Two Files**

The contents of two files may be compared for equality using the *contentsEqualAtPath* method. This method takes as arguments the paths to the two files to be compared and returns a Boolean result to indicate whether the file contents match:

```
if filemgr.contentsEqualAtPath(filepath1, andPath: filepath2) {
    println("File contents match")
} else {
    println("File contents do not match")
}
```

34.4 **Checking if a File is Readable/Writable/Executable/Deletable**

Most operating systems provide some level of file access control. These typically take the form of attributes designed to control the level of access to a file for each user or user group. As such, it is not a certainty that your program will have read or write access to a particular file, or the appropriate permissions to delete or rename it. The quickest way to find out if your program has a particular access permission is to use the *isReadableFileAtPath*, *isWritableFileAtPath*, *isExecutableFileAtPath* and *isDeletableFileAtPath* methods. Each method takes a single argument in the form of the path to the file to be checked and returns a Boolean result. For example, the following code excerpt checks to find out if a file is writable:

```
if filemgr.isWritableFileAtPath(filepath1) {
    println("File is writable")
} else {
    println("File is read-only")
}
```

To check for other access permissions simply substitute the corresponding method name in place of *isWritableFileAtPath* in the above example.

34.5 **Moving/Renaming a File**

A file may be renamed (assuming adequate permissions) using the *moveItemAtPath* method. This method returns a Boolean result and takes as arguments the pathname for the file to be moved, the destination path and an optional NSError object into which information describing any errors encountered during the operation will be placed. If no error description information is required, this argument may be set to *nil*. Note that if the destination file path already exists this operation will fail.

```
var error: NSError?

if filemgr.moveItemAtPath(filepath1, toPath: filepath2, error: &error) {
    println("Move successful")
} else {
    println("Moved failed with error: \(error!.localizedDescription)")
```

```
}
```

34.6 Copying a File

File copying can be achieved using the *copyItemAtPath* method. As with the *move* method, this takes as arguments the source and destination pathnames and an optional NSError object. Success of the operation is indicated by the returned Boolean value:

```
var error: NSError?

if filemgr.copyItemAtPath(filepath1, toPath: filepath2, error: &error) {
    println("Copy successful")
} else {
    println("Copy failed with error: \(error!.localizedDescription)")
}
```

34.7 Removing a File

The *removeItemAtPath* method removes the specified file from the file system. The method takes as arguments the pathname of the file to be removed and an optional NSError object. The success of the operation is, as usual, reported in the form of a Boolean return value:

```
var error: NSError?

if filemgr.removeItemAtPath(filepath1, error: &error) {
    println("Remove successful")
} else {
    println("Remove failed: \(error!.localizedDescription)")
}
```

34.8 Creating a Symbolic Link

A symbolic link to a particular file may be created using the *createSymbolicLinkAtPath* method. This takes as arguments the path of the symbolic link, the path to the file to which the link is to refer and an optional NSError object:

```
var error: NSError?

if filemgr.createSymbolicLinkAtPath(filepath2,
                withDestinationPath: filepath1, error: &error) {
    println("Link successful")
} else {
    println("Link failed: \(error!.localizedDescription)")
}
```

34.9 **Reading and Writing Files with NSFileManager**

The NSFileManager class includes some basic file reading and writing capabilities. These capabilities are somewhat limited when compared to the options provided by the NSFileHandle class, but can be useful nonetheless.

First, the contents of a file may be read and stored in an NSData object through the use of the *contentsAtPath* method:

```
let databuffer = filemgr.contentsAtPath(filepath1)
```

Having stored the contents of a file in an NSData object that data may subsequently be written out to a new file using the *createFileAtPath* method:

```
filemgr.createFileAtPath(filepath2, contents: databuffer,
                         attributes: nil)
```

In the above example we have essentially copied the contents from an existing file to a new file. This, however, gives us no control over how much data is to be read or written and does not allow us to append data to the end of an existing file. If the file in the above example had already existed it, and any data it contained, would have been overwritten by the contents of the source file. Clearly some more flexible mechanism is required. This is provided by the Foundation Framework in the form of the NSFileHandle class.

34.10 **Working with Files using the NSFileHandle Class**

The NSFileHandle class provides a range of methods designed to provide a more advanced mechanism for working with files. In addition to files, this class can also be used for working with devices and network sockets. In the following sections we will look at some of the more common uses for this class.

34.11 **Creating an NSFileHandle Object**

An NSFileHandle object can be created when opening a file for reading, writing or updating (in other words both reading and writing). Having opened a file, it must subsequently be closed when we have finished working with it using the *closeFile* method. If an attempt to open a file fails, for example because an attempt is made to open a non-existent file for reading, these methods return *nil*.

For example, the following code excerpt opens a file for reading and then closes it without actually doing anything to the file:

```
let file: NSFileHandle? = NSFileHandle(forReadingAtPath: filepath1)

    if file == nil {
        println("File open failed")
    } else {
        file?.closeFile()
```

```
}
```

34.12 **NSFileHandle File Offsets and Seeking**

NSFileHandle objects maintain a pointer to the current position in a file. This is referred to as the *offset*. When a file is first opened the offset is set to 0 (the beginning of the file). This means that any read or write operations performed using the NSFileHandle instance methods will take place at offset 0 in the file. To perform operations at different locations in a file (for example to append data to the end of the file) it is first necessary to *seek* to the required offset. For example to move the current offset to the end of the file, use the *seekToEndOfFile* method. Alternatively, *seekToFileOffset* allows you to specify the precise location in the file to which the offset is to be positioned. Finally, the current offset may be identified using the *offsetInFile* method. In order to accommodate large files, the offset is stored in the form of an unsigned 64-bit integer.

The following example opens a file for reading and then performs a number of method calls to move the offset to different positions, outputting the current offset after each move:

```
let file: NSFileHandle? = NSFileHandle(forReadingAtPath: filepath1)

if file == nil {
    println("File open failed")
} else {
    println("Offset = \(file?.offsetInFile)")
    file?.seekToEndOfFile()
    println("Offset = \(file?.offsetInFile)")
    file?.seekToFileOffset(30)
    println("Offset = \(file?.offsetInFile)")
    file?.closeFile()
}
```

File offsets are a key aspect of working with files using the NSFileHandle class so it is worth taking extra time to make sure you understand the concept. Without knowing where the current offset is in a file it is impossible to know the location in the file where data will be read or written.

34.13 **Reading Data from a File**

Once a file has been opened and assigned a file handle, the contents of that file may be read from the current offset position. The *readDataOfLength* method reads a specified number of bytes of data from the file starting at the current offset. For example, the following code reads 5 bytes of data from offset 10 in a file. The data read is returned encapsulated in an NSData object:

```
let file: NSFileHandle? = NSFileHandle(forReadingAtPath: filepath1)

if file == nil {
    println("File open failed")
```

```
} else {
    file?.seekToFileOffset(10)
    let databuffer = file?.readDataOfLength(5)
    file?.closeFile()
}
```

Alternatively, the *readDataToEndOfFile* method will read all the data in the file starting at the current offset and ending at the end of the file.

34.14 **Writing Data to a File**

The *writeData* method writes the data contained in an NSData object to the file starting at the location of the offset. Note that this does not insert data but rather overwrites any existing data in the file at the corresponding location.

To see this in action, let's assume the existence of a file named *quickfox.txt* containing the following text:

```
The quick brown fox jumped over the lazy dog
```

Next, we will write code that opens the file for updating, seeks to position 10 and then writes some data at that location:

```
let file: NSFileHandle? = NSFileHandle(forUpdatingAtPath: filepath1)

if file == nil {
    println("File open failed")
} else {
    let data = ("black dog" as
                    NSString).dataUsingEncoding(NSUTF8StringEncoding)
    file?.seekToFileOffset(10)
    file?.writeData(data!)
    file?.closeFile()
}
```

When the above program is compiled and executed the contents of the *quickfox.txt* file will have changed to:

```
The quick black dog jumped over the lazy dog
```

34.15 **Truncating a File**

A file may be truncated at the specified offset using the *truncateFileAtOffset* method. To delete the entire contents of a file, specify an offset of 0 when calling this method:

```
let file: NSFileHandle? = NSFileHandle(forUpdatingAtPath: filepath1)

if file == nil {
```

```
    println("File open failed")
} else {
    file?.truncateFileAtOffset(0)
    file?.closeFile()
}
```

34.16 **Summary**

Much like other operating systems, iOS provides a file system for the purposes of locally storing user and application files and data. In this and the preceding chapter, details of file and directory handling have been covered in some detail. The next chapter, entitled *iOS 8 Directory Handling and File I/O in Swift – A Worked Example* will work through the creation of an example designed specifically to demonstrate iOS file and directory handling.

35. iOS 8 Directory Handling and File I/O in Swift – A Worked Example

In the *Working with Directories in Swift on iOS 8* and *Working with Files in Swift on iOS 8* chapters of this book we discussed in some detail the steps involved in working with the iOS 8 file system in terms of both file and directory handling from within iOS applications. The goal of this chapter is to put theory into practice by working through the creation of a simple application that demonstrates some of the key concepts outlined in the preceding chapters.

35.1 The Example Application

The steps in this chapter walk through the creation of an iOS 8 application consisting of a text field and a button. When the user touches the button after entering text into the text field, that text is saved to a file. The next time the application is launched the content of the file is read by the application and pre-loaded into the text field.

35.2 Setting up the Application Project

The first step in creating the application is to set up a new project. To do so, start the Xcode environment and select the option to create a new project (or select the *File -> New -> Project* menu option if Xcode is already running or the welcome screen does not appear by default).

Select the *Single View Application* template, choose the *Universal* option from the *Devices* menu, *Swift* as the language and name the product *FileExample.*

35.3 Designing the User Interface

The example application is going to consist of a button and a text field. To begin the user interface design process, select the *Main.storyboard* file to load it into the Interface Builder environment. Drag a Button and then a Text Field from the Object Library panel (*View -> Utilities -> Show Object Library*) onto the view. Double click on the button and change the text to *Save*. Position the components and resize the width of the text field so that the layout appears as illustrated in Figure 35-1:

Figure 35-1

Shift-click on the Text Field and Button so that both views are selected and use the Auto Layout Align menu to add a *Horizontal Center in Container* constraint. Select only the Text Field view and use the Auto Layout Pin menu to add a *Spacing to nearest neighbor* constraint on the top edge of the view and enable the *Width* constraint. After adding these constraints, select the Button view and use the Pin menu once again to add a *Spacing to nearest neighbor* constraint on the top edge of the view.

Select the Text Field object in the view canvas, display the Assistant Editor panel and verify that the editor is displaying the contents of the *ViewController.swift* file. Ctrl-click on the text field object and drag to a position just below the class declaration line in the Assistant Editor. Release the line and in the resulting connection dialog establish an outlet connection named *textBox*.

Ctrl-click on the button object and drag the line to the area immediately beneath the *viewDidLoad* method in the Assistant Editor panel. Release the line and, within the resulting connection dialog, establish an Action method on the *Touch Up Inside* event configured to call a method named *saveText*.

35.4 Checking the Data File on Application Startup

Each time the application is launched by the user it will need to check to see if the data file already exists (if the user has not previously saved any text, the file will not have been created). If the file does exist, the contents need to be read by the application and displayed within the text field. A good place to put initialization code of this nature is in the *viewDidLoad* method of the view controller. With this in mind, select the *ViewController.swift* file, declare some variables that will be needed in the code and scroll down to the *viewDidLoad* method and edit it as follows:

```
import UIKit

class ViewController: UIViewController {

    @IBOutlet weak var textBox: UITextField!
```

```
var fileMgr: NSFileManager = NSFileManager.defaultManager()
var docsDir: String?
var dataFile: String?

override func viewDidLoad() {
    super.viewDidLoad()

    let dirPaths = NSSearchPathForDirectoriesInDomains(
            .DocumentDirectory, .UserDomainMask, true)

    docsDir = dirPaths[0] as? String
    dataFile =
        docsDir?.stringByAppendingPathComponent("datafile.dat")

    if fileMgr.fileExistsAtPath(dataFile!) {
        let databuffer = fileMgr.contentsAtPath(dataFile!)
        var datastring = NSString(data: databuffer!,
                                encoding: NSUTF8StringEncoding)
        textBox.text = datastring
    }
}
```

.

.

.

Before proceeding we need to take some time to talk about what the above code is doing. First, we declare some variables that will be used in the method and create an instance of the NSFileManager class. Because each iOS application on a device has its own *Documents* directory, we next make the appropriate calls to identify the path to that directory and assign the result to the *docsDir* variable. Once we know where the documents directory is located we construct the full path to our file (which is named *datafile.dat*) before checking whether the file already exists. If it exists, we read the contents of the file and assign it to the *text* property of our text field object so that it is visible to the user. Finally, we release the file manager object.

Now that we have the initialization code implemented, we need to write the code for our action method.

35.5 Implementing the Action Method

When the user enters text into our text field component and touches the save button, the text needs to be saved to the *datafile.dat* file located in the application's *Documents* directory. In order to make this happen we need, therefore, to implement the code in our *saveText* action method. Select the *ViewController.swift* file if it is not already open and modify the template *saveText* method we created previously so that it reads as follows:

```
@IBAction func saveText(sender: AnyObject) {
```

```
    let databuffer = (textBox.text as
                NSString).dataUsingEncoding(NSUTF8StringEncoding)

    fileMgr.createFileAtPath(dataFile!, contents: databuffer,
                        attributes: nil)
}
```

This code converts the text contained in the text field object and assigns it to an NSData object, the contents of which are written to the data file by calling the *createFileAtPath* method of the file manager object.

35.6 Building and Running the Example

Once the appropriate code changes have been made, test the application by clicking on the run button located in the toolbar of the main Xcode project window.

When the application has loaded, enter some text into the text field and click on the *Save* button. Next, stop the app by clicking on the stop button in the Xcode toolbar and then restart the app by clicking the run button again. On loading for a second time the text field will be primed with the text saved during the previous session:

iOS Simulator – iPhone 5 – iPhone 5 / iOS 8.0...

Carrier 🔋   3:43 PM   ▉▉▉

Welcome to iOS 8|

Save

Figure 35-2

36. Preparing an iOS 8 App to use iCloud Storage

From the perspective of the average iPhone or iPad owner, iCloud represents a vast remote storage service onto which device based data may be backed up and music stored for subsequent streaming to multiple iCloud supported platforms and devices.

From the perspective of the iOS application developer, on the other hand, iCloud represents a set of programming interfaces and SDK classes that facilitate the storage of files and data on iCloud servers hosted at Apple's data centers from within an iOS application.

This chapter is intended to provide an overview of iCloud and to walk through the steps involved in preparing an iOS 8 application to utilize the services of iCloud.

36.1 iCloud Data Storage Services

The current version of the iOS SDK provides support for three types of iCloud based storage, namely *iCloud Document Storage*, *iCloud Key-Value Data Storage* and *CloudKit Data Storage*.

iCloud document storage allows data files and documents on the user's device to be stored on iCloud. Once stored, these files may be subsequently retrieved from iCloud storage via any supported device or platform using the owner's iCloud account details.

The iCloud key-value storage service allows small amounts of data packaged in key/value format to be stored in the cloud. This service is intended to provide a way for the same application to synchronize user settings and status when installed on multiple devices. A user might, for example, have the same game application installed on both an iPhone and an iPad. The game application would use iCloud key-value storage to synchronize the player's current position in the game and the prevailing score, thereby allowing the user to switch between devices and resume the game from the same state.

CloudKit data storage is a new feature introduced with iOS 8 that provides applications with access to the iCloud servers hosted by Apple and provides an easy to use way to store, manage and retrieve data and other asset types (such as large binary files, videos and images) in a structured way. This provides a way for users to store private data and access it from multiple devices, and also for the developer to provide data that is publicly available to all the users of an application. CloudKit data storage is covered in detail beginning with the chapter entitled *An Introduction to CloudKit Data Storage on iOS 8*.

36.2 **Preparing an Application to Use iCloud Storage**

In order for an application to be able to use iCloud services it must be code signed with an App ID with iCloud support enabled. In addition to enabling iCloud support within the App ID, the application itself must also be configured with specific entitlements to enable one or both of the two iCloud storage methods outlined in the preceding section of this chapter.

Fortunately, both of these tasks can be performed within the *Capabilities* screen within Xcode 6.

Clearly, iOS developers who are not yet members of the iOS Developer Program will need to enroll before implementing any iCloud functionality. Details on enrolling in this program are outlined in the *Joining the Apple iOS Developer Program* chapter of this book.

36.3 **Enabling iCloud Support for an iOS 8 Application**

In order to enable iCloud support for an application, load the project into Xcode and select the application name target from the top of the project navigator panel. From the resulting project settings panel, select the *Capabilities* tab and locate and switch on *iCloud* support as outlined in Figure 36-1, selecting a Development Team to use for the provisioning profile if prompted to do so:

Figure 36-1

The iCloud capabilities section provides options to enable key-value storage, iCloud Documents and CloudKit services.

Enabling iCloud support will have automatically added the iCloud entitlement to the application's App ID, and also created an entitlements file to the project containing the application's iCloud container identifiers.

36.4 **Reviewing the iCloud Entitlements File**

Once iCloud capabilities have been enabled for an application within Xcode, a new file will appear in the project named *<product name>*.entitlements. Any applications that intend to use iCloud storage in any way must obtain entitlements appropriate to the iCloud features to be used. These entitlements are placed into this *entitlements file* and built into the application at compile time.

If the application is intended to make use of iCloud document storage then the entitlements file must include a request for the *com.apple.developer.icloud-container-identifiers* entitlement. Similarly, if the key-value store is to be used then the *com.apple.developer.ubiquity-kvstore-identifier* entitlement must be included. Applications that require both forms of iCloud storage must include both entitlements.

The entitlements file is an XML file in which the requests are stored in a key-value format. The keys are the entitlement identifiers outlined above and the values are represented by one or more *container identifiers* comprised of the developer's ID and a custom string that uniquely identifies the application (the corresponding application's App ID is generally recommended, though not mandatory, for this value).

The entitlements file may be created either manually or, as outlined above, automatically from within the Xcode environment. When using the *Capabilities* settings, the entitlements file will appear in the project navigator panel.

A single iCloud container is added to the entitlements file by default when using the *Capabilities* panel. Additional containers may be added by selecting the *Specify custom containers* option and clicking on the '+' button located beneath the *Containers* list.

36.5 **Accessing Multiple Ubiquity Containers**

The *ubiquity-container-identifiers* value is an array that may reference multiple iCloud containers. If an application requires access to more than one ubiquity container it will need to specifically reference the identifier of the required container. This is achieved by specifying the container identifier when constructing URL paths to documents within the iCloud storage. For example, the following code fragment defines a container identifier constant and then uses it to obtain the URL of the container in storage:

```
let UBIQUITY_CONTAINER_URL = "ABCDEF12345.com.yourdomain.icloudapp"

ubiquityURL = filemgr.URLForUbiquityContainerIdentifier(
    UBIQUITY_CONTAINER_URL)?.URLByAppendingPathComponent("Documents")
```

If *nil* is passed through as an argument in place of the container identifier the method will simply return the URL of the first container in the *ubiquity-container-identifiers* array of the entitlements file:

```
ubiquityURL = filemgr.URLForUbiquityContainerIdentifier(
    nil)?.URLByAppendingPathComponent("Documents")
```

36.6 **Ubiquity Container URLs**

When documents are saved to the cloud they will be placed in sub folders of a folder on iCloud using the following path:

```
/private/var/mobile/Library/Mobile Documents/<ubiquity container id>/
```

36.7 **Summary**

iCloud brings cloud based storage and application data synchronization to iOS 8 based applications. Before an application can take advantage of iCloud it must first be provisioned with an iCloud enabled profile and built against an appropriately configured entitlements file.

37. Managing Files using the iOS 8 UIDocument Class

U se of iCloud to store files requires a basic understanding of the UIDocument class. Introduced as part of the iOS 5 SDK, the UIDocument class is the recommended mechanism for working with iCloud based file and document storage.

The objective of this chapter is to provide a brief overview of the UIDocument class before working through a simple example demonstrating the use of UIDocument to create and perform read and write operations on a document on the local device file system. Once these basics have been covered the next chapter will extend the example to store the document using the iCloud document storage service.

37.1 An Overview of the UIDocument Class

The iOS UIDocument class is designed to provide an easy to use interface for the creation and management of documents and content. Whilst primarily intended to ease the process of storing files using iCloud, UIDocument also provides additional benefits in terms of file handling on the local file system such as reading and writing data asynchronously on a background queue, handling of version conflicts on a file (a more likely possibility when using iCloud) and automatic document saving.

37.2 Subclassing the UIDocument Class

UIDocument is an *abstract class*, in that it cannot be directly instantiated from within code. Instead applications must create a subclass of UIDocument and, at a minimum, override two methods:

- **contentsForType(_:error:)** - This method is called by the UIDocument subclass instance when data is to be written to the file or document. The method is responsible for gathering the data to be written and returning it in the form of an NSData or NSFileWrapper object.
- **loadFromContents(_:ofType:error:)** - Called by the subclass instance when data is being read from the file or document. The method is passed the content that has been read from the file by the UIDocument subclass and is responsible for loading that data into the application's internal data model.

37.3 Conflict Resolution and Document States

Storage of documents using iCloud means that multiple instances of an application can potentially access the same stored document consecutively. This considerably increases the risk of a conflict occurring when application instances simultaneously make different changes to the same document. One option is to simply let the most recent save operation overwrite any changes made by the other application instances. A more user friendly alternative, however, is to implement conflict detection code in the application and present the user with the option to resolve the conflict. Such resolution options will be application specific but might include presenting the file differences and letting the user choose which one to save, or allowing the user to merge the conflicting file versions.

The current state of a UIDocument subclass object may be identified by accessing the object's *documentState* property. At any given time this property will be set to one of the following constants:

- **UIDocumentState.Normal** – The document is open and enabled for user editing.
- **UIDocumentState.Closed** – The document is currently closed. This state can also indicate an error in reading a document.
- **UIDocumentState.InConflict** – Conflicts have been detected for the document.
- **UIDocumentState.SavingError** – An error occurred when an attempt was made to save the document.
- **UIDocumentState.EditingDisabled** – The document is busy and is not currently safe for editing.

Clearly one option for detecting conflicts is to periodically check the *documentState* property for a UIDocumentStateInConflict value. That said, it only really makes sense to check for this state when changes have actually been made to the document. This can be achieved by registering an observer on the *UIDocumentStateChangedNotification* notification. When the notification is received that the document state has changed the code will need to check the *documentState* property for the presence of a conflict and act accordingly.

37.4 **The UIDocument Example Application**

The remainder of this chapter will focus on the creation of an application designed to demonstrate the use of the UIDocument class to read and write a document locally on an iOS 8 based device or simulator.

To create the project, begin by launching Xcode and create a new product named *iCloudStore* using the *Single View Application* template, the Swift programming language and configured with the *Universal* device setting.

37.5 **Creating a UIDocument Subclass**

As previously discussed, UIDocument is an abstract class that cannot be directly instantiated. It is necessary, therefore, to create a subclass and to implement some methods in that subclass before using the features that UIDocument provides. The first step in this project is to create the source file for the subclass so select the Xcode *File -> New -> File…* menu option and in the resulting panel select the *Source* category listed under *iOS* in the left hand panel and the *Cocoa Touch Class* template before clicking on *Next*. On the options panel, set the *Subclass of* menu to *UIDocument,* name the class *MyDocument* and click *Next* to create the new class.

With the basic outline of the subclass created the next step is to begin implementing the user interface and the corresponding outlets and actions.

37.6 **Designing the User Interface**

The finished application is going to consist of a user interface comprising a UITextView and UIButton. The user will enter text into the text view and initiate the saving of that text to a file by touching the button.

Select the *Main.storyboard* file and display the Interface Builder Object Library (*View -> Utilities -> Show Object Library*). Drag and drop the Text View and Button objects into the view canvas, resizing the text view so that it occupies only the upper area of the view. Double click on the button object and change the label text to "Save":

Figure 37-1

Click on the Text View so that it is selected and use the Auto Layout Pin menu to add *Spacing to nearest neighbor* constraints on the top, left and right hand edges of the view with the *Constrain to margins* option switched on. Before adding the nearest neighbor constraints, also enable the *Height* constraint so that the height of the view is preserved at runtime.

Having configured the constraints for the Text View, select the Button view and use the Auto Layout Align menu to configure a *Horizontal Center in Container* constraint. With the Button view still selected, display the Pin menu and add a *Spacing to nearest neighbor* constraint on the top edge of the view using the current value and with the *Constrain to margins* option switched off.

Remove the example Latin text from the text view object by selecting it in the view canvas and deleting the value from the *Text* property in the Attributes Inspector panel. Replace the text with a string which reads "Sample Text".

With the user interface designed it is now time to connect the action and outlet. Select the Text View object in the view canvas, display the Assistant Editor panel and verify that the editor is displaying the contents of the *ViewController.swift* file. Ctrl-click on the Text View object and drag to a position just below the "class

ViewController" declaration line in the Assistant Editor. Release the line and in the resulting connection dialog establish an outlet connection named *textView*.

Finally, Ctrl-click on the button object and drag the line to the area immediately beneath the *viewDidLoad* method declaration in the Assistant Editor panel. Release the line and, within the resulting connection dialog, establish an Action method on the *Touch Up Inside* event configured to call a method named *saveDocument*.

37.7 Implementing the Application Data Structure

So far we have created and partially implemented a UIDocument subclass named *MyDocument* and designed the user interface of the application together with corresponding actions and outlets. As previously discussed, the *MyDocument* class will require two methods that are responsible for interfacing between the *MyDocument* object instances and the application's data structures. Before we can implement these methods, however, we first need to implement the application data structure. In the context of this application the data simply consists of the string entered by the user into the text view object. Given the simplicity of this example we will declare the data structure, such as it is, within the *MyDocument* class where it can be easily accessed by the *contentsForType* and *loadFromContents* methods. To implement the data structure, albeit a single data value, select the *MyDocument.swift* file and add a declaration for a String object:

```
import UIKit

class MyDocument: UIDocument {

    var userText: String? = "Some Sample Text"
}
```

Now that the data model is defined it is now time to complete the *MyDocument* class implementation.

37.8 Implementing the contentsForType Method

The *MyDocument* class is a subclass of UIDocument. When an instance of MyDocument is created and the appropriate method is called on that instance to save the application's data to a file, the class makes a call to its *contentsForType* instance method. It is the job of this method to collect the data to be stored in the document and to pass it back to the MyDocument object instance in the form of an NSData object. The content of the NSData object will then be written to the document. Whilst this may sound complicated most of the work is done for us by the parent UIDocument class. All the method needs to do, in fact, is get the current value of the *userText* NSString object, put it into an NSData object and return it.

Select the *MyDocument.swift* file and add the *contentsForType* method as follows:

```
override func contentsForType(typeName: String,
            error outError: NSErrorPointer) -> AnyObject {

    if let content = userText {
```

```
        var length =
            content.lengthOfBytesUsingEncoding(NSUTF8StringEncoding)
        return NSData(bytes:content, length: length)

    } else {
        return NSData()
    }
}
```

37.9 Implementing the loadFromContents Method

The *loadFromContents* instance method is called by an instance of MyDocument when the object is instructed to read the contents of a file. This method is passed an NSData object containing the content of the document and is responsible for updating the application's internal data structure accordingly. All this method needs to do, therefore, is convert the NSData object contents to a string and assign it to the *userText* object:

```
override func loadFromContents(contents: AnyObject,
    ofType typeName: String, error outError: NSErrorPointer) -> Bool {

    if let userContent = contents as? NSData {
        userText = NSString(bytes: contents.bytes,
                    length: userContent.length,
                    encoding: NSUTF8StringEncoding)
    }
    return true
}
```

The implementation of the MyDocument class is now complete and it is time to begin implementing the application functionality.

37.10 Loading the Document at App Launch

The ultimate goal of the application is to save any text in the text view to a document on the local file system of the device. When the application is launched it needs to check if the document exists and, if so, load the contents into the text view object. If, on the other hand, the document does not yet exist it will need to be created. As is usually the case, the best place to perform these tasks is the *viewDidLoad* method of the view controller.

Before implementing the code for the *viewDidLoad* method we first need to perform some preparatory work. First, both the *viewDidLoad* and *saveDocument* methods will need access to an NSURL object containing a reference to the document and also an instance of the *MyDocument* class, so these need to be declared in the view controller implementation file. With the *ViewController.swift* file selected in the project navigator, modify the file as follows:

```
import UIKit

class ViewController: UIViewController {

    @IBOutlet weak var textView: UITextView!

    var document: MyDocument?
    var documentURL: NSURL?
    .

    .

    .

}
```

The first task for the *viewDidLoad* method is to identify the path to the application's *Documents* directory (a task outlined in *Working with Directories in Swift on iOS 8*) and construct a full path to the document which will be named *savefile.txt*. The method will then need to create an NSURL object based on the path to the document and use it to create an instance of the *MyDocument* class. The code to perform these tasks can be implemented as outlined in the following code fragment:

```
let dirPaths = NSSearchPathForDirectoriesInDomains(.DocumentDirectory,
                        .UserDomainMask, true)

let docsDir = dirPaths[0] as String
let dataFile = docsDir.stringByAppendingPathComponent("savefile.txt")

documentURL = NSURL(fileURLWithPath: dataFile)
document = MyDocument(fileURL: documentURL!)
document!.userText = ""
```

The next task for the method is to create an NSFileManager instance and use it to identify whether the file exists. In the event that it does, the *openWithCompletionHandler* method of the *MyDocument* instance object is called to open the document and load the contents (thereby automatically triggering a call to the *loadFromContents* method created earlier in the chapter).

The *openWithCompletionHandler* method allows for a code block to be written to which is passed a Boolean value indicating the success or otherwise of the file opening and reading process. On a successful read operation this handler code simply needs to assign the value of the *userText* property of the *MyDocument* instance (which has been updated with the document contents by the *loadFromContents* method) to the text property of the *textView* object, thereby making it visible to the user.

In the event that the document does not yet exist, the *saveToURL* method of the *MyDocument* class will be called using the argument to create a new file:

```
if filemgr.fileExistsAtPath(dataFile) {
```

```
document?.openWithCompletionHandler({ (success: Bool) -> Void in
    if success {
        println("File open OK")
        self.textView.text = self.document?.userText
    } else {
        println("Failed to open file")
    }
})
} else {
    document?.saveToURL(documentURL!,
            forSaveOperation: .ForCreating,
            completionHandler: { (success: Bool) -> Void in
        if success {
            println("File created OK")
        } else {
            println("Failed to create file")
        }
    })
}
}
```

Note that for the purposes of debugging, println calls have been made at key points in the process. These can be removed once the application is verified to be working correctly.

Bringing the above code fragments together results in the following, fully implemented *viewDidLoad* method:

```
override func viewDidLoad() {
    super.viewDidLoad()

    let dirPaths =
        NSSearchPathForDirectoriesInDomains(.DocumentDirectory,
                        .UserDomainMask, true)

    let docsDir = dirPaths[0] as String

    let dataFile =
            docsDir.stringByAppendingPathComponent("savefile.txt")

    documentURL = NSURL(fileURLWithPath: dataFile)
    document = MyDocument(fileURL: documentURL!)
    document!.userText = ""

    let filemgr = NSFileManager.defaultManager()
```

```
if filemgr.fileExistsAtPath(dataFile) {

    document?.openWithCompletionHandler({(success: Bool) -> Void in
        if success {
            println("File open OK")
            self.textView.text = self.document?.userText
        } else {
            println("Failed to open file")                    }
    })
} else {
    document?.saveToURL(documentURL!, forSaveOperation:
        .ForCreating,
         completionHandler: {(success: Bool) -> Void in
        if success {
            println("File created OK")
        } else {
            println("Failed to create file ")
        }
    })
}
}
```

37.11 Saving Content to the Document

When the user touches the application's save button the content of the text view object needs to be saved to the document. An action method has already been connected to the user interface object for this purpose and it is now time to write the code for this method.

Since the *viewDidLoad* method has already identified the path to the document and initialized the *document* object, all that needs to be done is to call that object's *saveToURL* method using the *UIDocumentSaveForOverwriting* option. The *saveToURL* method will automatically call the *contentsForType* method implemented previously in this chapter. Prior to calling the method, therefore, it is important that the *userText* property of the *document* object be set to the current text of the *textView* object.

Bringing this all together results in the following implementation of the *saveDocument* method:

```
@IBAction func saveDocument(sender: AnyObject) {
    document!.userText = textView.text

    document?.saveToURL(documentURL!,
        forSaveOperation: .ForOverwriting,
        completionHandler: {(success: Bool) -> Void in
        if success {
            println("File overwrite OK")
```

```
    } else {
        println("File overwrite failed")
    }
})
}
```

37.12 Testing the Application

All that remains is to test that the application works by clicking on the Xcode run button. Upon execution, any text entered into the text view object should be saved to the *savefile.txt* file when the Save button is touched. Once some text has been saved, click on the stop button located in the Xcode toolbar. On subsequently restarting the application the text view should be populated with the previously saved text.

37.13 Summary

Whilst the UIDocument class is the cornerstone of document storage using the iCloud service it is also of considerable use and advantage in terms of using the local file system storage of an iOS device. As an abstract class, UIDocument must be subclassed and two mandatory methods implemented within the subclass in order to operate. This chapter worked through an example of using UIDocument to save and load content using a locally stored document. The next chapter will look at using UIDocument to perform cloud based document storage and retrieval.

38. Using iCloud Storage in an iOS 8 Application

The two preceding chapters of this book were intended to convey the knowledge necessary to begin implementing iCloud based document storage in iOS 8 based applications. Having outlined the steps necessary to enable iCloud access in the chapter entitled *Preparing an iOS 8 App to use iCloud Storage*, and provided an overview of the UIDocument class in *Managing Files using the iOS 8 UIDocument Class*, the next step is to actually begin to store documents using the iCloud service.

Within this chapter the *iCloudStore* application created in the previous chapter will be re-purposed to store a document using iCloud storage instead of the local device based file system. The assumption is also made that the project has been enabled for iCloud document storage following the steps outlined in *Preparing an iOS 8 App to use iCloud Storage*.

38.1 iCloud Usage Guidelines

Before implementing iCloud storage in an application there are a few rules that must first be understood. Some of these are mandatory rules and some are simply recommendations made by Apple:

- Applications must be associated with a provisioning profile enabled for iCloud storage.
- The application projects must include a suitably configured entitlements file for iCloud storage.
- Applications should not make unnecessary use of iCloud storage. Once a user's initial free iCloud storage space is consumed by stored data the user will either need to delete files or purchase more space.
- Applications should, ideally, provide the user with the option to select which documents are to be stored in the cloud and which are to be stored locally.
- When opening a *previously created* iCloud based document the application should never use an absolute path to the document. The application should instead search for the document by name in the application's iCloud storage area and then access it using the result of the search.
- Documents stored using iCloud should be placed in the application's *Documents* directory. This gives the user the ability to delete individual documents from the storage. Documents saved outside the *Document* folder can only be deleted in bulk.

38.2 **Preparing the iCloudStore Application for iCloud Access**

Much of the work performed in creating the local storage version of the *iCloudStore* application in the previous chapter will be reused in this example. The user interface, for example, remains unchanged and the implementation of the UIDocument subclass will not need to be modified. In fact, the only methods that need to be rewritten are the *saveDocument* and *viewDidLoad* methods of the view controller.

Load the *iCloudStore* project into Xcode and select the *ViewController.swift* file. Locate the *saveDocument* method and remove the current code from within the method so that it reads as follows:

```
@IBAction func saveDocument(sender: AnyObject) {
}
```

Next, locate the *viewDidLoad* method and modify it accordingly to match the following fragment:

```
override func viewDidLoad() {
    super.viewDidLoad()
}
```

38.3 **Configuring the View Controller**

Before writing any code there are a number of variables that need to be defined within the view controller's *ViewController.swift* file in addition to those implemented in the previous chapter.

It will also now be necessary to create a URL to the document location in the iCloud storage. When a document is stored on iCloud it is said to be *ubiquitous* since the document is accessible to the application regardless of the device on which it is running. The object used to store this URL will, therefore, be named *ubiquityURL.*

As previously stated, when opening a stored document, an application should search for the document rather than directly access it using a stored path. An iCloud document search is performed using an *NSMetaDataQuery* object which needs to be declared in the view controller class, in this instance using the name *metaDataQuery*. Note that declaring the object locally to the method in which it is used will result in the object being released by the automatic reference counting system (ARC) before it has completed the search.

To implement these requirements, select the *ViewController.swift* file in the Xcode project navigator panel and modify the file as follows:

```
import UIKit

class ViewController: UIViewController {

    @IBOutlet weak var textView: UITextView!

    var document: MyDocument?
```

```
var documentURL: NSURL?
var ubiquityURL: NSURL?
var metaDataQuery: NSMetadataQuery?
.
.
.
}
```

38.4 Implementing the viewDidLoad Method

The purpose of the code in the view controller *viewDidLoad* method is to identify the URL for the ubiquitous version of the file to be stored using iCloud (assigned to *ubiquityURL*). The ubiquitous URL is constructed by calling the *URLForUbiquityContainerIdentifier* method of the NSFileManager passing through *nil* as an argument to default to the first container listed in the entitlements file. Since it is recommended that documents be stored in the *Documents* sub-directory, this needs to be appended to the URL path:

```
ubiquityURL = filemgr.URLForUbiquityContainerIdentifier(nil)!.
                     URLByAppendingPathComponent("Documents")
```

The next step is to append the document name (*savefile.txt*) to the end of the *ubiquityURL* path:

```
ubiquityURL = ubiquityURL!.URLByAppendingPathComponent("savefile.txt")
```

The final task for the *viewDidLoad* method is to initiate a search in the application's iCloud storage area to find out if the *savefile.txt* file already exists and to act accordingly subject to the result of the search. The search is performed by calling the methods on an instance of the *NSMetaDataQuery* object. This involves creating the object, setting a predicate to indicate the files to search for and defining a ubiquitous search scope (in other words instructing the object to search within the Documents directory of the app's iCloud storage area). Once initiated, the search is performed on a separate thread and issues a notification when completed. For this reason, it is also necessary to configure an observer to be notified when the search is finished. The code to perform these tasks reads as follows:

```
metaDataQuery?.predicate =
        NSPredicate(format: "%K like 'savefile.txt'",
                NSMetadataItemFSNameKey)
metaDataQuery?.searchScopes =
        [NSMetadataQueryUbiquitousDocumentsScope]

NSNotificationCenter.defaultCenter().addObserver(self,
    selector: "metadataQueryDidFinishGathering:",
    name: NSMetadataQueryDidFinishGatheringNotification,
    object: metaDataQuery!)

metaDataQuery!.startQuery()
```

Once the *startQuery* method is called, the search will run and call the *metadataQueryDidFinishGathering* method once the search is complete. The next step, therefore, is to implement the *metadataQueryDidFinishGathering* method. Before doing so, however, note that the *viewDidLoad* method is now complete and the full implementation should read as follows:

```
override func viewDidLoad() {
    super.viewDidLoad()

        let filemgr = NSFileManager.defaultManager()

        ubiquityURL =
            filemgr.URLForUbiquityContainerIdentifier(
                nil)!.URLByAppendingPathComponent("Documents")

        ubiquityURL =
            ubiquityURL?.URLByAppendingPathComponent("savefile.txt")

        metaDataQuery = NSMetadataQuery()

        metaDataQuery?.predicate =
            NSPredicate(format: "%K like 'savefile.txt'",
                NSMetadataItemFSNameKey)
        metaDataQuery?.searchScopes =
            [NSMetadataQueryUbiquitousDocumentsScope]

        NSNotificationCenter.defaultCenter().addObserver(self,
            selector: "metadataQueryDidFinishGathering:",
            name: NSMetadataQueryDidFinishGatheringNotification,
            object: metaDataQuery!)

        metaDataQuery!.startQuery()
}
```

38.5 Implementing the metadataQueryDidFinishGathering Method

When the meta data query was triggered in the *viewDidLoad* method to search for documents in the Documents directory of the application's iCloud storage area, an observer was configured to call a method named *metadataQueryDidFinishGathering* when the initial search completed. The next logical step is to implement this method. The first task of the method is to identify the query object that caused this method to be called. This object must then be used to disable any further query updates (at this stage the document either exists or doesn't exist so there is nothing to be gained by receiving additional updates) and stop the search. It is also necessary to remove the observer that triggered the method call. Combined, these requirements result in the following code:

```
let query: NSMetadataQuery = notification.object as NSMetadataQuery

query.disableUpdates()

NSNotificationCenter.defaultCenter().removeObserver(self,
            name: NSMetadataQueryDidFinishGatheringNotification,
            object: query)

query.stopQuery()
```

The next step is to extract the array of documents located during the search:

```
let results = query.results
```

A more complex application would, in all likelihood, need to implement a *for* loop to iterate through more than one document in the array. Given that the iCloudStore application searched for only one specific file name we can simply check the array element count and assume that if the count is 1 then the document already exists. In this case, the ubiquitous URL of the document from the query object needs to be assigned to our *ubiquityURL* member property and used to create an instance of our MyDocument class called *document*. The *openWithCompletionHandler* method of the *document* object is then called to open the document in the cloud and read the contents. This will trigger a call to the *loadFromContents* method of the *document* object which, in turn, will assign the contents of the document to the *userText* property. Assuming the document read is successful the value of *userText* needs to be assigned to the *text* property of the text view object to make it visible to the user. Bringing this together results in the following code fragment:

```
if query.resultCount == 1 {
    let resultURL =
        results[0].valueForAttribute(NSMetadataItemURLKey) as NSURL

    document = MyDocument(fileURL: resultURL)

    document?.openWithCompletionHandler({ (success: Bool) -> Void in
        if success {
            println("iCloud file open OK")
            self.textView.text = self.document?.userText
            self.ubiquityURL = resultURL
        } else {
            println("iCloud file open failed")
        }
    })
} else {
}
```

In the event that the document does not yet exist in iCloud storage the code needs to create the document using the *saveToURL* method of the *document* object passing through the value of *ubiquityURL* as the destination path on iCloud:

.

.

```
} else {
    document = MyDocument(fileURL: ubiquityURL!)

    document?.saveToURL(ubiquityURL!,
        forSaveOperation: .ForCreating,
        completionHandler: {(success: Bool) -> Void in
        if success {
            println("iCloud create OK")
        } else {
            println("iCloud create failed")
        }
    })
}
```

The individual code fragments outlined above combine to implement the following *metadataQueryDidFinishGathering* method which should be added to the *ViewController.swift* file:

```
func metadataQueryDidFinishGathering(notification: NSNotification) ->
Void
{
    let query: NSMetadataQuery = notification.object as NSMetadataQuery

    query.disableUpdates()

    NSNotificationCenter.defaultCenter().removeObserver(self,
            name: NSMetadataQueryDidFinishGatheringNotification,
            object: query)

    query.stopQuery()

    let results = query.results

    if query.resultCount == 1 {
        let resultURL =
        results[0].valueForAttribute(NSMetadataItemURLKey) as NSURL

        document = MyDocument(fileURL: resultURL)
```

```
document?.openWithCompletionHandler({ (success: Bool) -> Void in
    if success {
        println("iCloud file open OK")
        self.textView.text = self.document?.userText
        self.ubiquityURL = resultURL
    } else {
        println("iCloud file open failed")
    }
})
} else {
    document = MyDocument(fileURL: ubiquityURL!)

    document?.saveToURL(ubiquityURL!,
        forSaveOperation: .ForCreating,
        completionHandler: { (success: Bool) -> Void in
            if success {
                println("iCloud create OK")
            } else {
                println("iCloud create failed")
            }
    })
}
}
}
```

38.6 Implementing the saveDocument Method

The final task before building and running the application is to implement the *saveDocument* method. This method simply needs to update the *userText* property of the *document* object with the text entered into the text view and then call the *saveToURL* method of the *document* object, passing through the *ubiquityURL* as the destination URL using the *UIDocumentSaveForOverwriting* option:

```
@IBAction func saveDocument(sender: AnyObject) {

    document!.userText = textView.text

    document?.saveToURL(ubiquityURL!,
                    forSaveOperation: .ForOverwriting,
            completionHandler: { (success: Bool) -> Void in
        if success {
            println("Save overwrite OK")
        } else {
            println("Save overwrite failed")
        }
```

```
    })
}
```

All that remains now is to build and run the iCloudStore application on an iOS device, but first some settings need to be checked.

38.7 **Enabling iCloud Document and Data Storage**

When testing iCloud on an iOS Simulator session, it is important to make sure that the simulator is configured with a valid Apple ID within the account settings app. To configure this, launch the simulator, load the Settings app and click on the iCloud option. If no account information is configured on this page, enter a valid Apple ID and corresponding password before proceeding with the testing.

Whether or not applications are permitted to use iCloud storage on an iOS device or Simulator is controlled by the iCloud settings. To review these settings, open the Settings application on the device or simulator and select the *iCloud* category. Scroll down the list of various iCloud related options and verify that the *iCloud Drive* option is set to *On*:

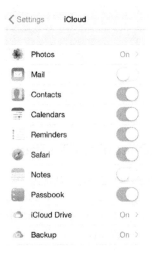

Figure 38-1

38.8 **Running the iCloud Application**

Test the iCloudStore app by connecting a suitably provisioned device or using an iOS Simulator, selecting it from the Xcode target menu and clicking on the run button. Edit the text in the text view and touch the *Save* button. In the Xcode toolbar click on the stop button to exit the application followed by the run button to re-launch the application. On the second launch the previously entered text will be read from the document in the cloud and displayed in the text view object.

38.9 **Reviewing and Deleting iCloud Based Documents**

The files currently stored in a user's iCloud account may be reviewed or deleted from the iOS Settings app running on a physical device. To review the currently stored documents select the *iCloud* option from the main screen of the *Settings* app. On the *iCloud* screen select the *Storage* option and, on the resulting screen, select *Manage Storage* followed by the name of the application for which stored documents are to be listed. A list of documents stored using iCloud for the selected application will then appear including the current file size:

Figure 38-2

To delete the document, select the *Edit* button located in the toolbar. All listed documents may be deleted using the *Delete All* button, or deleted individually.

38.10 **Making a Local File Ubiquitous**

In addition to writing a file directly to iCloud storage as illustrated in this example application, it is also possible to transfer a pre-existing local file to iCloud storage, thereby making it ubiquitous. This can be achieved using the *setUbiquitous* method of the NSFileManager class. Assuming that *documentURL* references the path to the local copy of the file, and *ubiquityURL* the iCloud destination, a local file can be made ubiquitous using the following code:

```
let filemgr = NSFileManager.defaultManager()
var error: NSError?

if filemgr.setUbiquitous(true, itemAtURL: documentURL,
            destinationURL: ubiquityURL, error: &error) {
    println("setUbiquitous OK")
} else {
```

```
        println("setUbiquitous failed: \(error!.localizedDescription)")
}
```

38.11 Summary

The objective of this chapter was to work through the process of developing an application that stores a document using the iCloud service. Both techniques of directly creating a file in the iCloud storage, and making an existing locally created file ubiquitous were covered. In addition, some important guidelines that should be observed when using iCloud were outlined.

39. Synchronizing iOS 8 Key-Value Data using iCloud

When considering the use of iCloud in an application it is important to note that the Apple ecosystem is not limited to the iOS platform. In fact, it also encompasses a range of Mac OS X based laptop and desktop computer systems, all of which have access to iCloud services. This increases the chance that a user will have the same app in one form or another on a number of different devices and platforms. Take, for the sake of an example, a hypothetical news magazine application. A user may have an instance of this application installed on both an iPhone and an iPad. If the user begins reading an article on the iPhone instance of the application and then switches to the same app on the iPad at a later time, the iPad application should take the user to the position reached in the article on the iPhone so that the user can resume reading.

This kind of synchronization between applications is provided by the Key-Value data storage feature of iCloud. The goal of this chapter is to provide an overview of this service and work through a very simple example of the feature in action in an iOS 8 application.

39.1 An Overview of iCloud Key-Value Data Storage

The primary purpose of iCloud Key-Value data storage is to allow small amounts of data to be shared between instances of applications running on different devices, or even different applications on the same device. The data may be synchronized as long as it is encapsulated in either an array, dictionary, string, NSDate, NSData, Boolean or NSNumber object.

iCloud data synchronization is achieved using the NSUbiquitousKeyValueStore class introduced as part of the iOS 5 SDK. Values are saved with a corresponding key using the setter method corresponding to the data type, the format for which is set*<datatype>* where *<datatype>* is replaced by the type of data to be stored (e.g. the *setString* method is used to save a string value). For example, the following code fragment creates an instance of an NSUbiquitousKeyValueStore object and then saves a string value using the key "MyString":

```
var keyStore = NSUbiquitousKeyValueStore()
keyStore.setString("Saved String", forKey: "MyString")
```

Once key-value pairs have been saved locally they will not be synchronized with iCloud storage until a call is made to the *synchronize* method of the NSUbiquitousKeyValueStore method:

```
keyStore.synchronize()
```

It is important to note that a call to the synchronize method does not result in an immediate synchronization of the locally saved data with the iCloud store. iOS will, instead, perform the synchronization at what the Apple documentation refers to as "an appropriate later time".

A stored value may be retrieved by a call to the appropriate method corresponding to the data type to be retrieved (the format of which is *<datatype>*forKey) and passing through the key as an argument. For example, the stored string in the above example may be retrieved as follows:

```
let storedString = keyStore.stringForKey("MyString")
```

39.2 Sharing Data Between Applications

As with iCloud document storage, key-value data storage requires the implementation of appropriate iCloud entitlements. In this case the application must have the *com.apple.developer.ubiquity-kvstore-identifier* entitlement key configured in the project's entitlements file. The value assigned to this key is used to identify which applications are able to share access to the same iCloud stored key-value data.

If, for example, the *ubiquity-kvstore-identifier* entitlement key for an application named *MyApp* is assigned a value of *ABCDE12345.com.mycompany.MyApp* (where ABCDEF12345 is developer's unique team or individual ID) then any other applications using the same entitlement value will also be able to access the same stored key-value data. This, by definition, will be any instance of the *MyApp* running on multiple devices, but applies equally to entirely different applications (for example *MyOtherApp*) if they also use the same entitlement value.

39.3 Data Storage Restrictions

iCloud key-value data storage is provided to meet the narrow requirement of performing essential synchronization between application instances, and the data storage limitations imposed by Apple clearly reflect this.

The amount of data that can be stored per key-value pair is 1MB. The per-application key-value storage limit is 1024 individual keys which, combined, must also not exceed 1MB in total.

39.4 Conflict Resolution

In the event that two application instances make changes to the same key-value pair, the most recent change is given precedence.

39.5 Receiving Notification of Key-Value Changes

An application may register to be notified when stored values are changed by another application instance. This is achieved by setting up an observer on the *NSUbiquitousKeyValueStoreDidChangeExternallyNotification* notification. This notification is triggered when a change is made to any key-value pair in a specified key value store and is passed an array of strings containing the keys that were changed together with an NSNumber indicating the reason for the change. In the event that the available space for the key-value storage has been exceeded this number will match the *NSUbiquitousKeyValueStoreQuotaViolationChange* constant value.

39.6 **An iCloud Key-Value Data Storage Example**

The remainder of this chapter is devoted to the creation of an application that uses iCloud key-value storage to store a key with a string value using iCloud. In addition to storing a key-value pair, the application will also configure an observer to receive notification when the value is changed by another application instance.

Begin the application creation process by launching Xcode and creating a new *Single View Application* project named *iCloudKeys* with the device menu set to *Universal* and *Swift* selected as the programming language.

39.7 **Enabling the Application for iCloud Key Value Data Storage**

A mandatory step in the development of the application is to configure the appropriate iCloud entitlement. This is achieved by selecting the application target at the top of the Xcode project navigator panel and selecting the *Capabilities* tab in the main project settings panel. Switch on iCloud support and enable the *Key-value storage* option:

Figure 39-1

Once selected, Xcode will create an entitlements file for the project named *iCloudKeys.entitlements* containing the appropriate iCloud entitlements key-value pairs. Select the entitlements file from the project navigator and note the value assigned to the *ubiquity-kvstore-identity* key. By default this is typically comprised of your team or individual developer ID combined with the application's Bundle identifier. Any other applications that use the same value for the entitlement key will share access to the same iCloud based key-value data stored by this application.

39.8 **Designing the User Interface**

The application is going to consist of a text field into which a string may be entered by the user and a button which, when selected, will save the string to the application's iCloud key-value data store. Select the *Main.storyboard* file, display the object library (*View -> Utilities -> Show Object Library*) and drag and drop the two objects into the view canvas. Double click on the button object and change the text to *Store Key*. The completed view should resemble Figure 39-2:

Figure 39-2

Click on the background View component in the layout, display the *Resolve Auto Layout Issues* menu and select the *Reset to Suggested Constraints* option listed under *All Views in the View Controller*.

Select the text field object in the view canvas, display the Assistant Editor panel and verify that the editor is displaying the contents of the *ViewController.swift* file. Ctrl-click on the text field object and drag to a position just below the class declaration line in the Assistant Editor. Release the line and in the resulting connection dialog establish an outlet connection named *textField*.

Finally, Ctrl-click on the button object and drag the line to the area immediately beneath the newly created outlet in the Assistant Editor panel. Release the line and, within the resulting connection dialog, establish an Action method on the *Touch Up Inside* event configured to call a method named *saveKey*.

39.9 Implementing the View Controller

In addition to the action and outlet references created above, an instance of the NSUbiquitousKeyStore class will be needed. Choose the *ViewController.swift* file, therefore, and modify it as follows:

```
class ViewController: UIViewController {

    var keyStore: NSUbiquitousKeyValueStore?

    @IBOutlet weak var textField: UITextField!
.
.
.
```

39.10 Modifying the viewDidLoad Method

The next step is to modify the *viewDidLoad* method of the view controller. Remaining within the *ViewController.swift* file, locate the *viewDidLoad* method and modify it so that it reads as follows:

```
override func viewDidLoad() {
```

```
super.viewDidLoad()

keyStore = NSUbiquitousKeyValueStore()

let storedString = keyStore?.stringForKey("MyString")

if let stringValue = storedString {
    textField.text = stringValue
}

NSNotificationCenter.defaultCenter().addObserver(self,
    selector: "ubiquitousKeyValueStoreDidChange:",
    name: NSUbiquitousKeyValueStoreDidChangeExternallyNotification,
    object: keyStore)
}
```

The method begins by allocating and initializing an instance of the NSUbiquitousKeyValueStore class and assigning it to the keyStore variable. Next, the *stringForKey* method of the keyStore object is called to check if the *MyString* key is already in the key-value store. If the key exists, the string value is assigned to the *text* property of the text field object via the textField outlet.

Finally, the method sets up an observer to call the *ubiquitousKeyValueStoreDidChange* method when the stored key value is changed by another application instance.

Having implemented the code in the *viewDidLoad* method the next step is to write the *ubiquitousKeyValueStoreDidChange* method.

39.11 Implementing the Notification Method

Within the context of this example application the *ubiquitousKeyValueStoreDidChange* method, which is triggered when another application instance modifies an iCloud stored key-value pair, is provided to notify the user of the change via an alert message and to update the text in the text field with the new string value. The code for this method, which needs to be added to the *ViewController.swift* file is as follows:

```
func ubiquitousKeyValueStoreDidChange(notification: NSNotification) {

    let alert = UIAlertController(title: "Change detected",
            message: "iCloud key-value-store change detected",
        preferredStyle: UIAlertControllerStyle.Alert)

    let cancelAction = UIAlertAction(title: "OK",
            style: .Cancel, handler: nil)

    alert.addAction(cancelAction)
```

```
    self.presentViewController(alert, animated: true,
            completion: nil)
    textField.text = keyStore?.stringForKey("MyString")
}
```

39.12 Implementing the saveData Method

The final coding task involves implementation of the *saveData* action method. This method will be called when the user touches the button in the user interface and needs to be implemented in the *ViewController.swift* file:

```
@IBAction func saveKey(sender: AnyObject) {
    keyStore?.setString(textField.text, forKey: "MyString")
    keyStore?.synchronize()
}
```

The code for this method is quite simple. The *setString* method of the keyStore object is called, assigning the current text property of the user interface textField object to the "MyString" key. The synchronize method of the keyStore object is then called to ensure that the key-value pair is synchronized with the iCloud store.

39.13 Testing the Application

Click on the run button in the Xcode toolbar and, once the application is installed and running on the device or iOS Simulator, enter some text into the text field and touch the *Store Key* button. Stop the application from running by clicking on the stop button in the Xcode toolbar then re-launch by clicking the run button. When the application reloads, the text field should be primed with the saved value string.

In order to test the change notification functionality, install the application on both a device and the iOS simulator. With the application running on both, change the text on the iOS Simulator instance and save the key. After a short delay the device based instance of the app will detect the change, display the alert and update the text field to the new value:

Figure 39-3

Chapter 40

40. iOS 8 Data Persistence using Archiving

In the previous chapters of this book we have looked at some basic file and directory handling operations which can be performed within an iOS 8 application. In the chapter entitled *Working with Files in Swift on iOS 8* we looked at creating files and reading and writing data from within an iOS application before looking at iCloud based storage in subsequent chapters. In this chapter we will look at another form of data persistence on iOS 8 using a more object oriented approach known as *archiving*.

40.1 An Overview of Archiving

iOS applications are inherently object oriented in so much as they are developed using Swift or Objective-C and consist of any number of objects designed to work together to provide the required functionality. As such, it is highly likely that any data created or used within an application will be held in memory encapsulated in an object. It is also equally likely that the data encapsulated in an object may need to be saved to the device's file system so that it can be restored on future invocations of the application. One approach might be to write code that extracts each data element from an object and writes it to a file. Similarly, code would need to be written to read the data from the file, create an instance of the original object and then assign the data to that object accordingly. Whilst this can be achieved, it can quickly become complex and time consuming to implement.

An alternative is to use a mechanism called *archiving*. Archiving involves encoding objects into a format that is written to a file. Data may subsequently be decoded (or *unarchived)* and used to automatically rebuild the object. This concept is somewhat analogous to *serialization* as supported by languages such as Java.

A number of approaches to archiving are supported by the Foundation Framework. Arguably the most flexible option is that provided by the NSKeyedArchiver class. This class provides the ability to encode an object into the form of a *binary property list* that is written to file and may subsequently be decoded to recreate the object using the NSKeyedUnarchiver class.

An alternative option is to use the *writeToFile:anatomically* method available with a subset Foundation class. This mechanism writes the object data to file in the form of an *XML property list* file. This approach, however, is limited to array, dictionary, string, NSData, NSDate and NSNumber based objects.

In the remainder of this chapter we will work through an example of archiving using the NSKeyedArchiver and NSKeyedUnarchiver classes.

40.2 The Archiving Example Application

The end product of this chapter is an application that prompts the user for a name, address and phone number. Once this data has been entered, pressing a button causes the contact data to be stored in an array object which is then archived to a binary property file. On a subsequent reload of the application this data is unarchived and used to recreate the array object. The restored data is then extracted from the array object and presented to the user.

Begin by launching Xcode and create a new project named *Archive* using the *Single View Application* template. Select *Universal* from the device menu and choose *Swift* as the programming language. Once the main Xcode project window appears populated with the template files, it is time to start developing the application.

40.3 Designing the User Interface

The user interface for our application is going to consist of three Labels, three TextFields and a single Button. Select *Main.storyboard* in the Xcode project navigator and display the Object Library panel (*View -> Utilities -> Show Object Library*) if it is not already visible. Drag, drop, resize, position and configure objects on the View window canvas until your design approximates that illustrated in Figure 40-1:

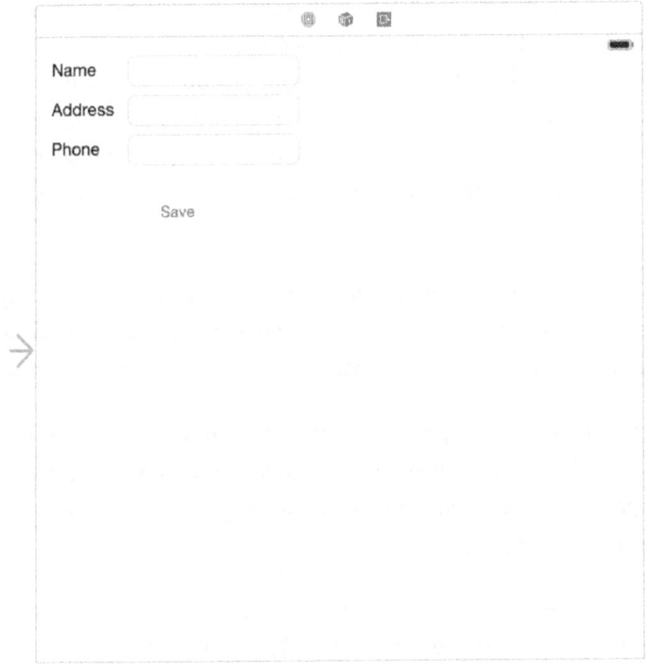

Figure 40-1

The next step is to establish the connections to our action and outlets.

Select the top most text field object in the view canvas, display the Assistant Editor panel and verify that the editor is displaying the contents of the *ViewController.swift* file. Ctrl-click on the text field object and drag to a position just below the class declaration line in the Assistant Editor. Release the line and in the resulting connection dialog establish an outlet connection named *name*.

Repeat the above steps to establish outlet connections for the remaining text fields to properties named *address* and *phone* respectively.

Ctrl-click on the button object and drag the line to the area immediately beneath the *viewDidLoad* method in the Assistant Editor panel. Release the line and, within the resulting connection dialog, establish an Action method on the *Touch Up Inside* event configured to call a method named *saveData*.

Close the Assistant Editor, select the *ViewController.swift* file and add an additional variable to store a reference to the path to the archive data file:

```
import UIKit

class ViewController: UIViewController {

    @IBOutlet weak var name: UITextField!
    @IBOutlet weak var address: UITextField!
    @IBOutlet weak var phone: UITextField!

    var dataFilePath: String?
.
.
.
```

40.4 Checking for the Existence of the Archive File on Startup

Each time the application is launched by the user, the code will need to identify whether the archive data file exists from a previous session. In the event that it does exist, the application will need to read the contents to recreate the original array object from which the archive was created. Using this newly recreated array object, the array elements will then be extracted and used to populate the name, address and phone text fields.

The traditional location for placing such initialization code is in the *viewDidLoad* method of the view controller class. Within the project window, therefore, select the *ViewController.swift* file and scroll down the contents of this file until you reach the *viewDidLoad* method. Having located the method, modify it as outlined in the following code fragment:

```
override func viewDidLoad() {
    super.viewDidLoad()
```

```
        let filemgr = NSFileManager.defaultManager()
        let dirPaths =
                NSSearchPathForDirectoriesInDomains(.DocumentDirectory,
                                    .UserDomainMask, true)

        let docsDir = dirPaths[0] as String
        dataFilePath =
                docsDir.stringByAppendingPathComponent("data.archive")

        if filemgr.fileExistsAtPath(dataFilePath!) {
            let dataArray =
                    NSKeyedUnarchiver.unarchiveObjectWithFile(dataFilePath!)
                                            as [String]
            name.text = dataArray[0]
            address.text = dataArray[1]
            phone.text = dataArray[2]
        }
    }
}
```

Within this method a number of variables are declared before creating an instance of the NSFileManager class.

A call is then made to the *NSSearchPathForDirectoriesInDomains* function and the path to the application's *Documents* directory extracted from the returned array object. This path is then used to construct the full pathname of the archive data file, which in turn is stored in the *dataFilePath* instance variable we previously added to the view controller class.

Having identified the path to the archive data file, the file manager object is used to check for the existence of the file. If it exists, the file is "unarchived" into a new array object using the *unarchiveObjectWithFile* method of the NSKeyedUnarchiver class. The data is then extracted from the array and displayed in the corresponding text fields.

With this code implemented, select the Xcode run toolbar button to compile and execute the application in the simulator. Assuming no problems are encountered, the next step is to implement the action method. Once the app has launched successfully, exit from the iOS Simulator and return to the main Xcode project window.

40.5 Archiving Object Data in the Action Method

The *Save* button in the user interface design is connected to the *saveData* method of the view controller class. Edit the *ViewController.swift* file and modify the template action method as follows:

```
@IBAction func saveData(sender: AnyObject) {
    var contactArray = [name.text, address.text, phone.text]
```

```
NSKeyedArchiver.archiveRootObject(contactArray,
                                  toFile: dataFilePath!)
}
```

When triggered, this method creates a new array and assigns the content of each text field to an element of that array. The array object is then archived to the predetermined data file using the *archiveRootObject* method of the NSKeyedArchiver class. The instance data of the array object is now saved to the archive ready to be loaded next time the application is executed.

40.6 **Testing the Application**

Save the code changes and build and run the application on a device or in the simulator environment. Enter a name, address and phone number into the respective text fields and press the save button. Stop the application by clicking the stop button located in the Xcode toolbar and then relaunch the application by clicking the run button. The application should re-appear with the text fields primed with the contact information saved during the previous session:

Figure 40-2

40.7 **Summary**

Whilst data can be written to files on an iOS device using a variety of mechanisms, archiving provides the ability to save the instance data of an object to file at a particular point and then restore the object to that state at any time in the future. This provides an object-oriented approach to data persistence on iOS based applications.

41. iOS 8 Database Implementation using SQLite

Whilst the preceding chapters of this book have looked at data storage within the context of iOS 8 based applications, this coverage has been limited to using basic file and directory handling and object archiving. In many instances, by far the most effective data storage and retrieval strategy requires the use of some form of database management system.

In order to address this need, the iOS 8 SDK includes everything necessary to integrate SQLite based databases into iOS applications. The goal of this chapter, therefore, is to provide an overview of how to use SQLite to perform basic database operations within your iOS application. Once the basics have been covered, the next chapter (entitled *An Example SQLite based iOS 8 Application using Swift and FMDB*) will work through the creation of an actual application that uses a SQLite database to store and retrieve data.

41.1 What is SQLite?

SQLite is an embedded, relational database management system (RDBMS). Most relational databases (Oracle and MySQL being prime examples) are standalone server processes that run independently, and in cooperation with, applications that require database access. SQLite is referred to as *embedded* because it is provided in the form of a library that is linked into applications. As such, there is no standalone database server running in the background. All database operations are handled internally within the application through calls to functions contained in the SQLite library.

The developers of SQLite have placed the technology into the public domain with the result that it is now a widely deployed database solution.

SQLite is written in the C programming language and therefore using SQLite from within Swift code either requires some complex handling of C function calls, data types and pointers, or the easier approach of using an existing SQLite wrapper as a layer between SQLite and Swift. In this chapter we will look at one such wrapper in the form of FMDB.

For additional information about SQLite refer to *http://www.sqlite.org*.

41.2 **Structured Query Language (SQL)**

Data is accessed in SQLite databases using a high level language known as Structured Query Language. This is usually abbreviated to SQL and pronounced *sequel*. SQL is a standard language used by most relational database management systems. SQLite conforms mostly to the SQL-92 standard.

Whilst some basic SQL statements will be used within this chapter, a detailed overview of SQL is beyond the scope of this book. There are, however, many other resources that provide a far better overview of SQL than we could ever hope to provide in a single chapter here.

41.3 **Trying SQLite on MacOS X**

For readers unfamiliar with databases in general and SQLite in particular, diving right into creating an iOS application that uses SQLite may seem a little intimidating. Fortunately, MacOS X is shipped with SQLite pre-installed, including an interactive environment for issuing SQL commands from within a Terminal window. This is both a useful way to learn about SQLite and SQL, and also an invaluable tool for identifying problems with databases created by applications in the iOS simulator.

To launch an interactive SQLite session, open a Terminal window on your Mac OS X system, change directory to a suitable location and run the following command:

```
sqlite3 ./mydatabase.db

SQLite version 3.6.12
Enter ".help" for instructions
Enter SQL statements terminated with a ";"
sqlite>
```

At the *sqlite>* prompt, commands may be entered to perform tasks such as creating tables and inserting and retrieving data. For example, to create a new table in our database with fields to hold ID, name, address and phone number fields the following statement is required:

```
create table contacts (id integer primary key autoincrement, name text,
address text, phone text);
```

Note that each row in a table must have a *primary key* that is unique to that row. In the above example we have designated the ID field as the primary key, declared it as being of type *integer* and asked SQLite to automatically increment the number each time a row is added. This is a common way to make sure that each row has a unique primary key. The remaining fields are each declared as being of type *text.*

To list the tables in the currently selected database use the *.tables* statement:

```
sqlite> .tables
contacts
```

To insert records into the table:

```
sqlite> insert into contacts (name, address, phone) values ("Bill Smith",
"123 Main Street, California", "123-555-2323");
sqlite> insert into contacts (name, address, phone) values ("Mike Parks",
"10 Upping Street, Idaho", "444-444-1212");
```

To retrieve all rows from a table:

```
sqlite> select * from contacts;
1|Bill Smith|123 Main Street, California|123-555-2323
2|Mike Parks|10 Upping Street, Idaho|444-444-1212
```

To extract a row that meets specific criteria:

```
sqlite> select * from contacts where name="Mike Parks";
2|Mike Parks|10 Upping Street, Idaho|444-444-1212
```

To exit from the sqlite3 interactive environment:

```
sqlite> .exit
```

When running an iOS application in the iOS Simulator environment, any database files will be created on the file system of the computer on which the simulator is running. This has the advantage that you can navigate to the location of the database file, load it into the sqlite3 interactive tool and perform tasks on the data to identify possible problems occurring in the application code. If, for example, an application creates a database file named *contacts.db* in its documents directory, the file will be located on the host system in the following folder:

```
/Users/<user>/Library/Developer/CoreSimulator/Devices/<simulator
id>/data/Containers/Data/Application/<id>/Documents
```

Where *<user>* is the login name of the user logged into the Mac OS X system, *<simulator id>* is the id of the simulator session and *<id>* is the unique ID of the application.

41.4 Preparing an iOS Application Project for SQLite Integration

By default, the Xcode environment does not assume that you will be including SQLite in your application. When developing SQLite based applications a few additional steps are required to ensure the code will compile when the application is built. First, the project needs to be configured to include the *libsqlite3.dylib* dynamic library during the link phase of the build process. To achieve this select the target entry in the Xcode project navigator (the top entry with the product name) to display the summary information. Select the *Build Phases* tab to display the build information.

The *Link Binary with Libraries* section lists the libraries and frameworks already included in the project. To add another library or framework click on the '+' button to display the full list. From this list, select the required item (in this case *libsqlite3.dylib*) and click *Add*.

41.5 **SQLite, Swift and Wrappers**

As previously discussed, SQLite is written in the C programming language. Whilst it was still possible to use the C-based SQLite API from within Objective-C code with relative ease, this is not the case when programming in Swift without dealing with complex issues when bridging the gap between C and Swift. A common solution to this dilemma involves the use of a SQLite "wrapper". A number of wrappers are now available for this purpose many of which show considerable potential. For the purposes of this book, however, we will be working with the FMDB wrapper. Although this is essentially an Objective-C wrapper, it can be used easily from within Swift code. FMDB has been chosen for the examples in this book because it has been available for some time, is considered to be stable and feature rich and will be familiar to the many developers who have previously used with it Objective-C. FMDB is an open-source project released under the terms of the MIT license.

Details on how to obtain FMDB and incorporate it into an iOS Xcode project are covered in detail in the next chapter (*An Example SQLite based iOS 8 Application using Swift and FMDB*).

41.6 **Key FMDB Classes**

When implementing a database using SQLite with FMDB it will be necessary to utilize a number of FMDB classes contained within the wrapper. A summary of the most commonly used classes is as follows:

- **FMDatabase** – Used to represent a single SQLite database. The object on which SQL statements are executed from within code.
- **FMResultSet** – Used to hold the results of a SQL query operation on an FMDatabase instance.
- **FMDatabaseQueue** – A version of FMDatabase designed to allow database queries to be performed from multiple threads.

For more detailed information, the FMDB Class Reference documentation is available online at:

http://ccgus.github.io/fmdb/html/Classes/FMDatabase.html

41.7 **Creating and Opening a Database**

Before work can commence on a database it must first be created and opened. The following code opens the database file at the path specified by *<database file path>*. If the database file does not already exist it will be created when the FMDatabase instance is initialized:

```
let myDatabase = FMDatabase(path: <database file path>)

if myDatabase == nil {
    // Database could not be found or created
} else {
    if myDatabase.open() {
        // Database is ready
```

```
        }
}
```

41.8 **Creating a Database Table**

Database data is organized into *tables*. Before data can be stored into a database, therefore, a table must first be created. This is achieved using the SQL CREATE TABLE statement. The following code example illustrates the creation of a table named *contacts* using FMDB:

```
let sql_stmt = "CREATE TABLE IF NOT EXISTS CONTACTS (ID INTEGER PRIMARY
KEY AUTOINCREMENT, NAME TEXT, ADDRESS TEXT, PHONE TEXT)"

if !myDatabase.executeStatements(sql_stmt) {
    // Table creation failed
}
```

41.9 **Extracting Data from a Database Table**

Those familiar with SQL will be aware that data is retrieved from databases using the SELECT statement. Depending on the criteria defined in the statement, it is typical for more than one data row to be returned. It is important, therefore, to learn how to retrieve data from a database using the SQLite FMDB wrapper.

In the following code excerpt, a SQL SELECT statement is used to extract the address and phone fields from all the rows of a database table named *contacts* via a call to the *executeQuery* method of the FMDatabase instance:

```
let querySQL = "SELECT address, phone FROM CONTACTS WHERE name =
'\(name.text)'"

let results:FMResultSet? = myDatabase.executeQuery(querySQL,
                withArgumentsInArray: nil)
```

On completion of the query execution, the FMResults object returned from the method call contains the results of the query. Regardless of whether one or more results are expected, the *next* method of the returned FMResultSet object must be called. A *false* return value from the *next* method call indicates either that no results were returned, or that the end of the result set has been reached.

In the event that results were returned, the data can be accessed using the column name as a key. The following code, for example, outputs the "address" and "phone" values for all of the matching records returned as the result of the above query operation:

```
while results?.next() == true {
    println(results?.stringForColumn("address"))
    println(results?.stringForColumn("phone"))
}
```

41.10 **Closing a SQLite Database**

When an application has finished working on a database it is important that the database be closed. This is achieved with a call to the *close* method of the FMDatabase instance:

```
myDatabase.close()
```

41.11 **Summary**

In this chapter we have looked at the basics of implementing a database within an iOS application using the embedded SQLite relational database management system together with the FMDB wrapper to make access to the database possible from within Swift code. In the next chapter we will put this theory into practice and work through an example that creates a functional iOS application that is designed to store data in a database.

42. An Example SQLite based iOS 8 Application using Swift and FMDB

In the chapter entitled *iOS 8 Database Implementation using SQLite* the basic concepts of integrating a SQLite based database into iOS 8 applications were discussed. In this chapter we will put this knowledge to use by creating a simple example application that demonstrates SQLite-based database implementation and management on iOS 8 using Swift and the FMDB wrapper.

42.1 About the Example SQLite Application

The focus of this chapter is the creation of a somewhat rudimentary iOS application that is designed to store contact information (names, addresses and telephone numbers) in a SQLite database. In addition to data storage, a feature will also be implemented to allow the user to search the database for the address and phone number of a specified contact name. Some knowledge of SQL and SQLite is assumed throughout the course of this tutorial. Those readers unfamiliar with these technologies in the context of iOS application development are encouraged to first read the *previous chapter* before proceeding.

42.2 Creating and Preparing the SQLite Application Project

Begin by launching the Xcode environment and creating a new iOS *Single View Application* project named *Database* configured for Swift and with the Devices menu set to *Universal*.

Once the project has been created, the next step is to configure the project to include the SQLite dynamic library *(libsqlite3.dylib)* during the link phase of the build process. Failure to include this library will result in build errors.

To add this library, select the target entry in the Xcode project navigator (the top entry with the product name) to display the *General* information panel. Select the *Build Phases* tab to display the build information. The *Link Binary with Libraries* section lists the libraries and frameworks already included in the project. To add another library or framework click on the '+' button to display the full list. From this list search for, and then select *libsqlite3.dylib* and click *Add*.

42.3 Checking Out the FMDB Source Code

In order to use FMDB, the source files for the wrapper will need to be added to the project. The source code for FMDB is stored on the GitHub source code repository and can be downloaded directly onto your development system from within Xcode (a process referred to as *checking out*). Begin by selecting the Xcode *Source Control -> Check Out...* menu option to display the Check Out dialog:

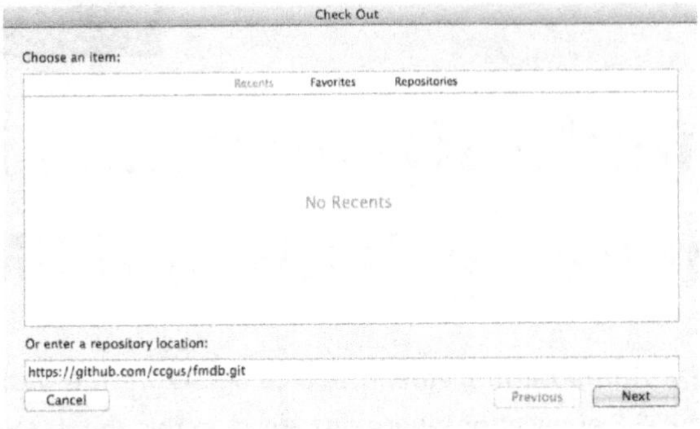

Figure 42-1

In the dialog, enter the following GitHub URL into the repository location field and click on *Next*:

https://github.com/ccgus/fmdb.git

When the list of branches appears in the dialog, select *master* and click on *Next* once again. Choose a location on your local file system into which the files are to be checked out before clicking on the *Check Out* button. Xcode will check out the files and save them at the designated location. A new Xcode project window will also open containing the FMDB source files. Within the project navigator panel, unfold the *fmdb -> Source -> fmdb* folder to list the source code files (highlighted in Figure 42-2) for the FMDB wrapper.

Figure 42-2

Shift-click on the first and last of the files in the *fmdb* folder to select all of the .h and .m files in the navigator panel and drag and drop them onto the Database project folder in the Xcode window containing the Database project. On the options panel click on the *Finish* button. Since these files are written in Objective-C rather than Swift, Xcode will offer to configure and add an *Objective-C bridging header* file as shown in Figure 42-3:

Figure 42-3

Click on the *Yes* button to add the bridging file. Once added, it will appear in the *Supporting Files* folder of the project with the name *Database-Bridging-Header.h*. Select this file and edit it to add a single line to import the FMDB.h file:

```
#import "FMDB.h"
```

With the project fully configured to support SQLite from within Swift application projects, the remainder of the project may now be completed.

42.4 **Designing the User Interface**

The next step in developing our example SQLite iOS application involves the design of the user interface. Begin by selecting the *Main.storyboard* file to edit the user interface and drag and drop components from the Object Library (*View -> Utilities -> Show Object Library*) onto the view canvas and edit properties so that the layout appears as illustrated in Figure 42-4:

Figure 42-4

Before proceeding, stretch the status label (located above the two buttons) so that it is the same width as the combined labels and text field views and change the text alignment in the Attributes Inspector so that it is centered. Finally, edit the label and remove the word "Label" so that it is blank.

Select the top most text field object in the view canvas, display the Assistant Editor panel and verify that the editor is displaying the contents of the *ViewController.swift* file. Ctrl-click on the text field object again and drag to a position just below the class declaration line in the Assistant Editor. Release the line and in the resulting connection dialog establish an outlet connection named *name*.

Repeat the above steps to establish outlet connections for the remaining text fields and the label object to properties named *address*, *phone* and *status* respectively.

Ctrl-click on the *Save* button object and drag the line to the area immediately beneath the existing *viewDidLoad* method in the Assistant Editor panel. Release the line and, within the resulting connection dialog, establish an Action method on the *Touch Up Inside* event configured to call a method named *saveData*. Repeat this step to create an action connection from the *Find* button to a method named *findContact*.

Close the Assistant Editor panel, select the *ViewController.swift* file and add a variable to store a reference to the database path:

```
class ViewController: UIViewController {

    @IBOutlet weak var name: UITextField!
    @IBOutlet weak var address: UITextField!
    @IBOutlet weak var phone: UITextField!
    @IBOutlet weak var status: UILabel!

    var databasePath = NSString()

    override func viewDidLoad() {
        super.viewDidLoad()

    }

    @IBAction func saveData(sender: AnyObject) {
    }

    @IBAction func findContact(sender: AnyObject) {
    }
    .
    .
}
```

42.5 Creating the Database and Table

When the application is launched it will need to check whether the database file already exists and, if not, create both the database file and a table within the database in which to store the contact information entered by the user. The code to perform this task can be placed in the *viewDidLoad* method of our view controller class. Select the *ViewController.swift* file, scroll down to the *viewDidLoad* method and modify it as follows:

```
override func viewDidLoad() {
    super.viewDidLoad()

    let filemgr = NSFileManager.defaultManager()
    let dirPaths =
    NSSearchPathForDirectoriesInDomains(.DocumentDirectory,
            .UserDomainMask, true)

    let docsDir = dirPaths[0] as String

    databasePath = docsDir.stringByAppendingPathComponent(
                                    "contacts.db")

    if !filemgr.fileExistsAtPath(databasePath) {

        let contactDB = FMDatabase(path: databasePath)

        if contactDB == nil {
            println("Error: \(contactDB.lastErrorMessage())")
        }

        if contactDB.open() {
            let sql_stmt = "CREATE TABLE IF NOT EXISTS CONTACTS (ID
INTEGER PRIMARY KEY AUTOINCREMENT, NAME TEXT, ADDRESS TEXT, PHONE TEXT)"
            if !contactDB.executeStatements(sql_stmt) {
                println("Error: \(contactDB.lastErrorMessage())")
            }
            contactDB.close()
        } else {
            println("Error: \(contactDB.lastErrorMessage())")
        }
    }
}
```

The code in the above method performs the following tasks:

- Identifies the application's Documents directory and constructs a path to the *contacts.db* database file.
- Creates an NSFileManager instance and subsequently uses it to detect if the database file already exists.
- If the file does not yet exist the code creates the database by creating an FMDatabase instance initialized with the database file path. If the database creation is successful it is then opened via a call to the *open* method of the new database instance.
- Prepares a SQL statement to create the *contacts* table in the database and executes it via a call to the FMDB *executeStatements* method of the database instance.
- Closes the database

42.6 Implementing the Code to Save Data to the SQLite Database

The saving of contact data to the database is the responsibility of the *saveData* action method. This method will need to open the database file, extract the text from the three text fields and construct and execute a SQL INSERT statement to add this data as a record to the database. Having done this, the method will then need to close the database.

In addition, the code will need to clear the text fields ready for the next contact to be entered, and update the status label to reflect the success or failure of the operation.

In order to implement this behavior, therefore, we need to modify the template method created previously as follows:

```
@IBAction func saveData(sender: AnyObject) {
    let contactDB = FMDatabase(path: databasePath)

    if contactDB.open() {

        let insertSQL = "INSERT INTO CONTACTS (name, address, phone)
VALUES ('\(name.text)', '\(address.text)', '\(phone.text)')"

        let result = contactDB.executeUpdate(insertSQL,
                        withArgumentsInArray: nil)

        if !result {
            status.text = "Failed to add contact"
            println("Error: \(contactDB.lastErrorMessage())")
        } else {
            status.text = "Contact Added"
            name.text = ""
            address.text = ""
            phone.text = ""
        }
    } else {
        println("Error: \(contactDB.lastErrorMessage())")
    }
}
```

The next step in our application development process is to implement the action for the find button.

42.7 Implementing Code to Extract Data from the SQLite Database

As previously indicated, the user will be able to extract the address and phone number for a contact by entering the name and touching the find button. To this end, the *Touch Up Inside* event of the find button has been connected to the *findContact* method, the code for which is outlined below:

```
@IBAction func findContact(sender: AnyObject) {
    let contactDB = FMDatabase(path: databasePath)

    if contactDB.open() {
        let querySQL = "SELECT address, phone FROM CONTACTS WHERE name =
'\(name.text)'"

        let results:FMResultSet? = contactDB.executeQuery(querySQL,
                withArgumentsInArray: nil)

        if results?.next() == true {
            address.text = results?.stringForColumn("address")
            phone.text = results?.stringForColumn("phone")
            status.text = "Record Found"
        } else {
            status.text = "Record not found"
            address.text = ""
            phone.text = ""
        }
        contactDB.close()
    } else {
        println("Error: \(contactDB.lastErrorMessage())")
    }
}
```

This code opens the database and constructs a SQL SELECT statement to extract any records in the database that match the name entered by the user into the name text field. The SQL statement is then executed via a call to the *executeQuery* method of the FMDatabase instance. The search results are returned in the form of an FMResultSet object.

The *next* method of the FMResultSet object is called to find out if at least one match was found. In the event that a match was found, the values corresponding to the address and phone columns are extracted and assigned to the text fields in the user interface.

42.8 Building and Running the Application

The final step is to build and run the application. Click on the run button located in the toolbar of the main Xcode project window. Once running, enter details for a few contacts, pressing the *Save* button after each entry. Be sure to check the status label to ensure the data is being saved successfully. Finally, enter the name of one of your contacts and click on the *Find* button. Assuming the name matches a previously entered record, the address and phone number for that contact should be displayed and the status label updated with the message "Record Found":

Figure 42-5

42.9 **Summary**

In this chapter we have looked at the basics of storing data on iOS using the SQLite database environment using the FMDB wrapper approach to using SQLite from within Swift code. For developers unfamiliar with SQL and reluctant to learn it, an alternative method for storing data in a database involves the use of the Core Data framework. This topic will be covered in detail in the next chapter entitled *Working with iOS 8 Databases using Core Data*.

43. Working with iOS 8 Databases using Core Data

The preceding chapters covered the concepts of database storage using the SQLite database. In these chapters the assumption was made that the iOS application code would directly manipulate the database using SQLite C API calls to construct and execute SQL statements. Whilst this is a perfectly good approach for working with SQLite in many cases, it does require knowledge of SQL and can lead to some complexity in terms of writing code and maintaining the database structure. This complexity is further compounded by the non-object-oriented nature of the SQLite C API functions. In recognition of these shortcomings, Apple introduced the *Core Data Framework*. Core Data is essentially a framework that places a wrapper around the SQLite database (and other storage environments) enabling the developer to work with data in terms of Swift objects without requiring any knowledge of the underlying database technology.

We will begin this chapter by defining some of the concepts that comprise the Core Data model before providing an overview of the steps involved in working with this framework. Once these topics have been covered, the next chapter will work through *An iOS 8 Core Data Tutorial*.

43.1 The Core Data Stack

Core Data consists of a number of framework objects that integrate to provide the data storage functionality. This stack can be visually represented as illustrated in Figure 43-1.

As we can see from Figure 43-1, the iOS based application sits on top of the stack and interacts with the managed data objects handled by the managed object context. Of particular significance in this diagram is the fact that although the lower levels in the stack perform a considerable amount of the work involved in providing Core Data functionality, the application code does not interact with them directly.

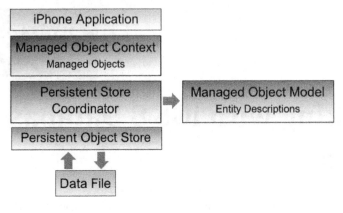

Figure 43-1

Before moving on to the more practical areas of working with Core Data it is important to spend some time explaining the elements that comprise the Core Data stack in a little more detail.

43.2 **Managed Objects**

Managed objects are the objects that are created by your application code to store data. A managed object may be thought of as a row or a record in a relational database table. For each new record to be added, a new managed object must be created to store the data. Similarly, retrieved data will be returned in the form of managed objects, one for each record matching the defined retrieval criteria. Managed objects are actually instances of the NSManagedObject class, or a subclass thereof. These objects are contained and maintained by the *managed object context*.

43.3 **Managed Object Context**

Core Data based applications never interact directly with the persistent store. Instead, the application code interacts with the managed objects contained in the managed object context layer of the Core Data stack. The context maintains the status of the objects in relation to the underlying data store and manages the relationships between managed objects defined by the *managed object model*. All interactions with the underlying database are held temporarily within the context until the context is instructed to save the changes, at which point the changes are passed down through the Core Data stack and written to the persistent store.

43.4 **Managed Object Model**

So far we have focused on the management of data objects but have not yet looked at how the data models are defined. This is the task of the *Managed Object Model* which defines a concept referred to as *entities*.

Much as a class description defines a blueprint for an object instance, entities define the data model for managed objects. In essence, an entity is analogous to the schema that defines a table in a relational database. As such, each entity has a set of attributes associated with it that define the data to be stored in managed objects derived from that entity. For example, a *Contacts* entity might contain *name, address* and *phone number* attributes.

In addition to attributes, entities can also contain *relationships, fetched properties* and *fetch requests*:

- **Relationships** – In the context of Core Data, relationships are the same as those in other relational database systems in that they refer to how one data object relates to another. Core Data relationships can be *one-to-one, one-to-many* or *many-to-many*.
- **Fetched property** – This provides an alternative to defining relationships. Fetched properties allow properties of one data object to be accessed from another data object as though a relationship had been defined between those entities. Fetched properties lack the flexibility of relationships and are referred to by Apple's Core Data documentation as "weak, one way relationships" best suited to "loosely coupled relationships".
- **Fetch request** – A predefined query that can be referenced to retrieve data objects based on defined predicates. For example, a fetch request can be configured into an entity to retrieve all contact objects where the name field matches "John Smith".

43.5 Persistent Store Coordinator

The *persistent store coordinator* is responsible for coordinating access to multiple *persistent object stores*. As an iOS developer you will never directly interact with the persistence store coordinator and, in fact, will very rarely need to develop an application that requires more than one persistent object store. When multiple stores are required, the coordinator presents these stores to the upper layers of the Core Data stack as a single store.

43.6 Persistent Object Store

The term *persistent object store* refers to the underlying storage environment in which data are stored when using Core Data. Core Data supports three disk-based and one memory-based persistent store. Disk based options consist of SQLite, XML and binary. By default, the iOS SDK will use SQLite as the persistent store. In practice, the type of store being used is transparent to you as the developer. Regardless of your choice of persistent store, your code will make the same calls to the same Core Data APIs to manage the data objects required by your application.

43.7 Defining an Entity Description

Entity descriptions may be defined from within the Xcode environment. When a new project is created with the option to include Core Data, a template file will be created named *<projectname>.xcdatamodeld*. Selecting this file in the Xcode project navigator panel will load the model into the entity editing environment as illustrated in Figure 43-2:

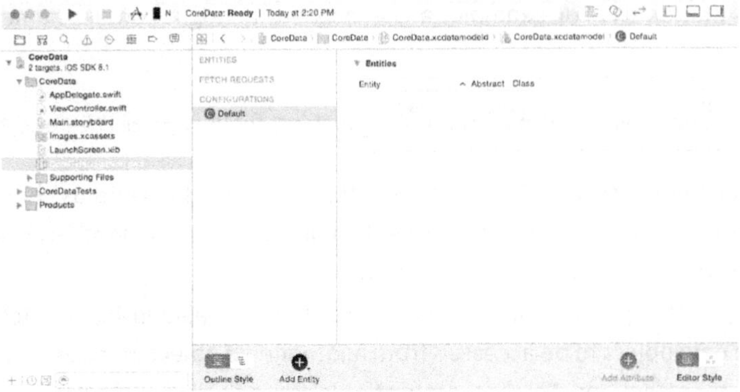

Figure 43-2

Create a new entity by clicking on the *Add Entity* button located in the bottom panel. The new entity will appear as a text box in the *Entities* list. By default this will be named *Entity*. Double click on this name to change it.

To add attributes to the entity, click on the *Add Attribute* button located in the bottom panel, or use the + button located beneath the *Attributes* section. In the *Attributes* panel, name the attribute and specify the type and any other options that are required.

Repeat the above steps to add more attributes and additional entities.

The Xcode entity environment also allows relationships to be established between entities. Assume, for example, two entities named *Contacts* and *Sales.* In order to establish a relationship between the two tables select the *Contacts* entity and click on the + button beneath the *Relationships* panel. In the detail panel, name the relationship, specify the destination as the *Sales* entity and any other options that are required for the relationship. Once the relationship has been established it is, perhaps, best viewed graphically by selecting the *Table, Graph* option in the *Editor Style* control located in the bottom panel:

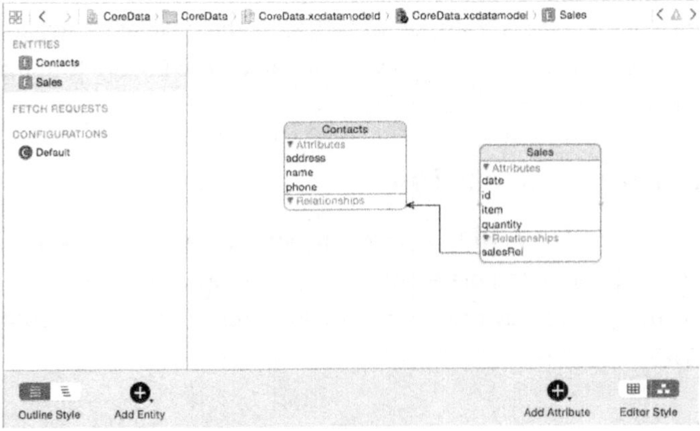

Figure 43-3

As demonstrated, Xcode makes the process of entity description creation fairly straightforward. Whilst a detailed overview of the process is beyond the scope of this book there are many other resources available that are dedicated to the subject.

43.8 Obtaining the Managed Object Context

Since many of the Core Data methods require the managed object context as an argument, the next step after defining entity descriptions often involves obtaining a reference to the context. This is achieved by first identifying the application delegate and then calling the delegate object's *managedContextObject* method:

```
let managedObjectContext = (UIApplication.sharedApplication().delegate
            as AppDelegate).managedObjectContext
```

43.9 Getting an Entity Description

Before managed objects can be created and manipulated in code, the corresponding entity description must first be loaded. This is achieved by calling the *entityForName(_:inManagedObjectContext:)* method of the NSEntityDescription class, passing through the name of the required entity and the context as arguments. The following code fragment obtains the description for an entity with the name *Contacts:*

```
let entityDescription = NSEntityDescription.entityForName("Contacts",
            inManagedObjectContext: managedObjectContext!)
```

43.10 Generating a Managed Object Subclass

As previously outlined, the data to be stored using Core Data is packaged up into Managed Object instances. Once an entity has been defined within the Xcode entity editor, Xcode can be instructed to generate a new NSManagedObject subclass for that entity. To generate a managed object class, select the entity in the entity editor and choose the *Editor -> Create NSManagedObject Subclass...* menu option. The following Swift code, for example, is a managed object class generated by Xcode for an entity named *Contacts* containing three string attributes:

```
import Foundation
import CoreData

class Contacts: NSManagedObject {

    @NSManaged var name: String
    @NSManaged var address: String
    @NSManaged var phone: String

}
```

Having obtained the managed context, and created a Managed Object class for an entity, a new managed object instance conforming to a specified entity description can be created. The following code, for example, creates a new managed object instance for the above Contacts entity class and assigns it to the managed object context so that it is ready to be saved once the object has been configured with the data to be stored:

```
let contact = Contacts(entity: entityDescription!,
        insertIntoManagedObjectContext: managedObjectContext)
```

43.11 Setting the Attributes of a Managed Object

As previously discussed, entities and the managed objects from which they are instantiated contain data in the form of attributes. Once a managed object instance has been created as outlined above, those attribute values can be used to store the data before the object is saved. Assuming a managed object named *contact* with attributes named *name, address* and *phone* respectively, the values of these attributes may be set as follows prior to the object being saved to storage:

```
contact.name = "John Smith"
contact.address = "1 Infinite Loop"
contact.phone = "555-564-0980"
```

43.12 Saving a Managed Object

Once a managed object instance has been created and configured with the data to be stored it can be saved to storage using the *save* method of the managed object context as follows:

```
var error: NSError?
managedObjectContext?.save(&error)

if let err = error {
    // handle error
}
```

43.13 Fetching Managed Objects

Once managed objects are saved into the persistent object store it is highly likely that those objects and the data they contain will need to be retrieved. Objects are retrieved by executing a fetch request and are returned in the form of an array. The following code assumes that both the context and entity description have been obtained prior to making the fetch request:

```
let request = NSFetchRequest()
request.entity = entityDescription

var error: NSError?
var results = managedObjectContext?.executeFetchRequest(request,
                                            error: &error)
```

Upon execution, the *results* array will contain all the managed objects retrieved by the request.

43.14 **Retrieving Managed Objects based on Criteria**

The preceding example retrieved all of the managed objects from the persistent object store for a specified entity. More often than not only managed objects that match specified criteria are required during a retrieval operation. This is performed by defining a *predicate* that dictates criteria that a managed object must meet in order to be eligible for retrieval. For example, the following code implements a predicate in order to extract only those managed objects where the *name* attribute matches "John Smith":

```
let request = NSFetchRequest()
request.entity = entityDescription

let pred = NSPredicate(format: "(name = %@)", "John Smith")
request.predicate = pred

var error: NSError?
var results = managedObjectContext?.executeFetchRequest(request,
                                        error: &error)
```

43.15 **Accessing the Data in a Retrieved Managed Object**

Once results have been returned from a fetch request, the data within the returned objects may be accessed using *keys* to reference the stored values. The following code, for example, accesses the first result from a fetch operation results array and extracts the values for the *name*, *address* and *phone* keys from that managed object:

```
var results = managedObjectContext?.executeFetchRequest(request,
                                        error: &error)
let match = results[0] as NSManagedObject

let nameString = match.valueForKey("name") as String
let addressString = match.valueForKey("address") as String
let phoneString = match.valueForKey("phone") as String
```

43.16 **Summary**

The Core Data Framework stack provides a flexible alternative to directly managing data using SQLite or other data storage mechanisms. By providing an object oriented abstraction layer on top of the data the task of managing data storage is made significantly easier for the iOS application developer. Now that the basics of Core Data have been covered the next chapter entitled *An iOS 8 Core Data Tutorial* will work through the creation of an example application.

44. An iOS 8 Core Data Tutorial

In the previous chapter, entitled *Working with iOS 8 Databases using Core Data*, an overview of the Core Data stack was provided, together with details of how to write code to implement data persistence using this infrastructure. In this chapter we will continue to look at Core Data in the form of a step by step tutorial that implements data persistence using Core Data in an iOS 8 application.

44.1 The Core Data Example Application

The application developed in this chapter will take the form of the same contact database application used in previous chapters, the objective being to allow the user to enter name, address and phone number information into a database and then search for specific contacts based on the contact's name.

44.2 Creating a Core Data based Application

As is often the case, we can rely on Xcode to do much of the preparatory work for us when developing an iOS application that will use Core Data. To create the example application project, launch Xcode and select the option to create a new project. In the new project window, select the *Single View Application* option. In the next screen make sure that the Devices menu is set to *Universal* and the language is set to *Swift*. Enter *CoreDataDemo* into the *Product Name* field, enable the *Use Core Data* checkbox and click *Next* to select a location to store the project files.

Xcode will create the new project and display the main project window. In addition to the usual files that are present when creating a new project, this time an additional file named *CoreDataDemo.xcdatamodeld* is also created. This is the file where the entity descriptions for our data model are going to be stored.

44.3 Creating the Entity Description

The entity description defines the model for our data, much in the way a schema defines the model of a database table. To create the entity for the Core Data application, select the *CoreDataDemo.xcdatamodeld* file to load the entity editor:

Figure 44-1

To create a new entity, click on the *Add Entity* button located in the bottom panel. Double click on the new *Entity* item that appears beneath the *Entities* heading and change the entity name to *Contacts*. With the entity created, the next step is to add some attributes that represent the data that is to be stored. To do so, click on the *Add Attribute* button. In the *Attribute* pane, name the attribute *name* and set the Type to *String*. Repeat these steps to add two other String attributes named *address* and *phone* respectively:

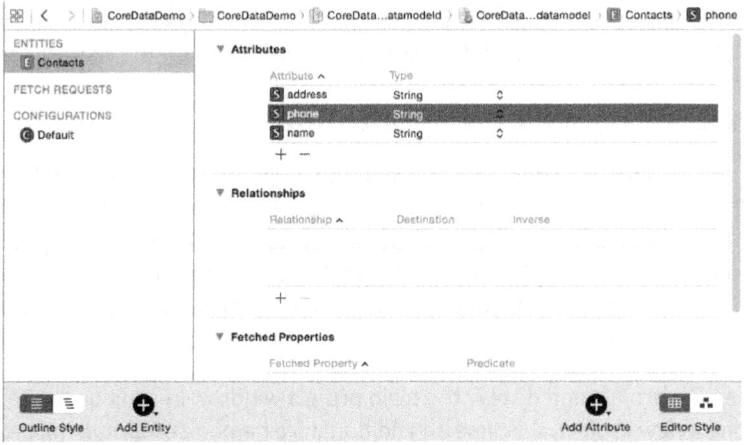

Figure 44-2

44.4 Generating the Managed Object Subclass

Within the application the data model is going to be represented by a subclass of the NSManagedObject class. Rather than manually write the code for this class, Xcode can be used to automatically generate the class on our behalf. With the Entity editor still displayed in Xcode, select the *Editor -> Create NSManagedObject Subclass...* menu option to display the dialog shown in Figure 44-3:

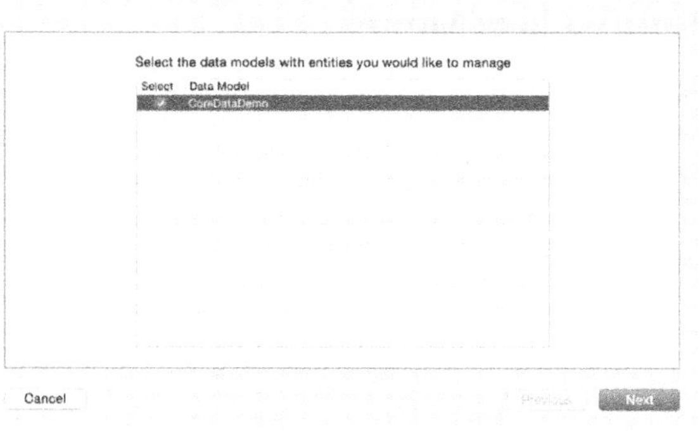

Figure 44-3

Make sure that the CoreDataDemo data model is selected before clicking on the *Next* button to display the entity selection screen (Figure 44-4):

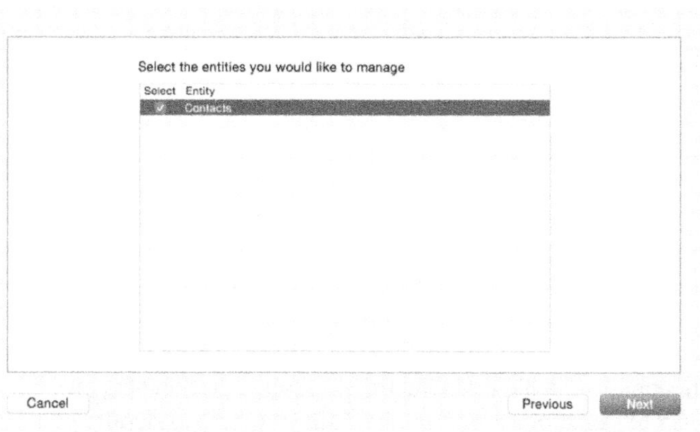

Figure 44-4

Verify that the *Contacts* entity is selected before clicking on the *Next* button once again. Within the final screen, set the Language menu to *Swift* and click on the *Create* button. A new file named *Contacts.swift* will have been added to the project containing the NSManagedObject subclass for the entity which reads as follows:

```
import Foundation
import CoreData


class Contacts: NSManagedObject {

    @NSManaged var name: String
    @NSManaged var address: String
    @NSManaged var phone: String

}
```

44.5 **Modifying the Entity Class Name**

When using Core Data within Swift based code it is important to include the application name as part of the entity class name. By default, the new entity has been assigned a class name of *Contacts*. This needs to be changed to *CoreDataDemo.Contacts*, reflecting the namespace given to the application when it was first created in Xcode. To make this change, load the *CoreDataDemo.xcdmodeld* file into the entity editor, select the *Contacts* entity name from the left hand panel and display the Data Model Inspector in the Utilities panel as illustrated in Figure 44-5:

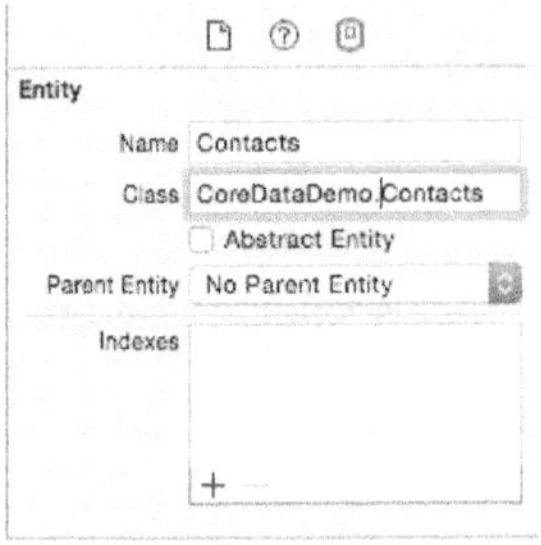

Figure 44-5

Within the *Class* field, change the name to *CoreDataDemo.Contacts*.

44.6 **Designing the User Interface**

With the entity defined, now is a good time to design the user interface and establish the outlet and action connections. Select the *Main.storyboard* file to begin the design work. The user interface and corresponding connections used in this tutorial are the same as those in previous data persistence chapters. The completed view should, once again, appear as outlined in Figure 44-6 (note that objects may be cut and pasted from the previous *Database* project to save time in designing the user interface layout):

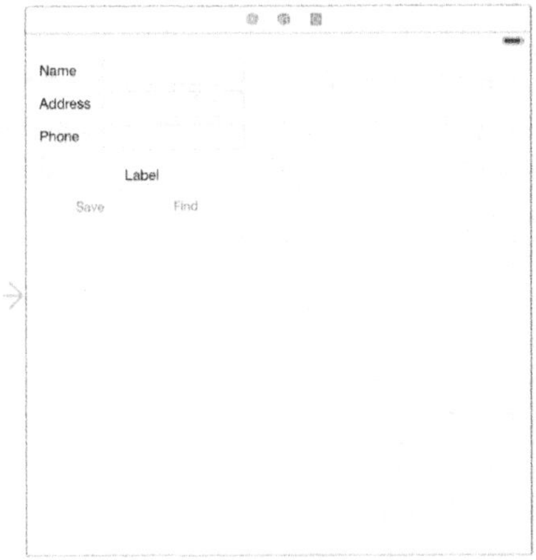

Figure 44-6

Before proceeding, stretch the status label (located above the two buttons) so that it covers most of the width of the view and configure the alignment attribute so that the text is centered. Finally, edit the label and remove the word "Label" so that it is blank.

Select the top most text field object in the view canvas, display the Assistant Editor panel and verify that the editor is displaying the contents of the *ViewController.swift* file. Ctrl-click on the text field object again and drag to a position just below the class declaration line in the Assistant Editor. Release the line and in the resulting connection dialog establish an outlet connection named *name*.

Repeat the above steps to establish outlet connections for the remaining text fields and the label object to properties named *address, phone* and *status* respectively.

Ctrl-click on the *Save* button object and drag the line to the area immediately beneath the *viewDidLoad* method in the Assistant Editor panel. Release the line and, within the resulting connection dialog, establish an Action method on the *Touch Up Inside* event configured to call a method named *saveContact*. Repeat this step to create an action connection from the *Find* button to a method named *findContact*.

44.7 Accessing the Managed Object Context

In order to store and retrieve data using Core Data a reference to the application delegate's managed object context is required. Within the *ViewController.swift* file, import the CoreData Framework and add a variable to store this reference as follows:

```
import UIKit
import CoreData

class ViewController: UIViewController {

    let managedObjectContext =
              (UIApplication.sharedApplication().delegate
                        as AppDelegate).managedObjectContext

    @IBOutlet weak var name: UITextField!
    @IBOutlet weak var address: UITextField!
    @IBOutlet weak var phone: UITextField!
    @IBOutlet weak var status: UILabel!
.
.
.
```

44.8 Saving Data to the Persistent Store using Core Data

When the user touches the Save button the *saveContact* method is called. It is within this method, therefore, that we must implement the code to create and store managed objects containing the data entered by the user. Select the *ViewController.swift* file, scroll down to the template *saveContact* method and implement the code as follows:

```
@IBAction func saveContact(sender: AnyObject) {
    let entityDescription =
            NSEntityDescription.entityForName("Contacts",
                    inManagedObjectContext: managedObjectContext!)

    let contact = Contacts(entity: entityDescription!,
            insertIntoManagedObjectContext: managedObjectContext)

    contact.name = name.text
    contact.address = address.text
    contact.phone = phone.text

    var error: NSError?

    managedObjectContext?.save(&error)

    if let err = error {
        status.text = err.localizedFailureReason
    } else {
        name.text = ""
        address.text = ""
        phone.text = ""
        status.text = "Contact Saved"
    }
}
```

The above code uses the managed object context to obtain the Contacts entity description and then uses it to create a new instance of the Contacts managed object subclass. The name, address and phone attribute values of this managed object are then set to the current text field values. Finally, the context is instructed to save the changes to the persistent store with a call to the context's *save* method. The success or otherwise of the operation is reported on the status label and, in the case of a successful outcome, the text fields are cleared ready for the next contact to be entered.

44.9 Retrieving Data from the Persistent Store using Core Data

In order to allow the user to search for a contact it is now necessary to implement the *findContact* action method. As with the save method, this method will need to identify the entity description for the Contacts entity and then create a predicate to ensure that only objects with the name specified by the user are retrieved from the store. Matching objects are placed in an array from which the attributes for the first match are retrieved using the *valueForKey* method and displayed to the user. A full count of the matches is displayed in the status field.

The code to perform these tasks is as follows:

```
@IBAction func findContact(sender: AnyObject) {
    let entityDescription =
```

```
        NSEntityDescription.entityForName("Contacts",
                inManagedObjectContext: managedObjectContext!)

    let request = NSFetchRequest()
    request.entity = entityDescription

    let pred = NSPredicate(format: "(name = %@)", name.text)
    request.predicate = pred

    var error: NSError?

    var objects = managedObjectContext?.executeFetchRequest(request,
                            error: &error)

    if let results = objects {

        if results.count > 0 {
            let match = results[0] as NSManagedObject

            name.text = match.valueForKey("name") as String
            address.text = match.valueForKey("address") as String
            phone.text = match.valueForKey("phone") as String
            status.text = "Matches found: \(results.count)"
        } else {
                status.text = "No Match"
        }
    }
}
```

44.10 Building and Running the Example Application

The final step is to build and run the application. Click on the run button located in the toolbar of the main Xcode project window. If errors are reported check the syntax of the code you have written, using the error message provided by Xcode as guidance. Once the application compiles it will launch and load into the device or iOS Simulator. Enter some test contacts (some with the same name). Having entered some test data, enter the name of the contact for which you created duplicate records and tap the Find button. The address and phone number of the first matching record should appear together with an indication in the status field of the total number of matching objects that were retrieved.

44.11 Summary

The Core Data Framework provides an abstract, object oriented interface to database storage within iOS applications. As demonstrated in the example application created in this chapter, Core Data does not require any knowledge of the underlying database system and, combined with the visual entity creation features of Xcode, allows database storage to be implemented with relative ease.

45. An Introduction to CloudKit Data Storage on iOS 8

The CloudKit Framework is one of the more remarkable developer features added to iOS 8 solely because of the ease with which it allows for the structured storage and retrieval of data on Apple's iCloud database servers.

It is not an exaggeration to state that CloudKit allows developers to work with cloud based data and media storage without any prior database experience and with a minimal amount of coding effort.

This chapter will provide a high level introduction to the various elements that make up CloudKit, build a foundation for the CloudKit tutorials presented in the next two chapters and provide a basis from which to explore other capabilities of CloudKit.

45.1 An Overview of CloudKit

The CloudKit Framework provides applications with access to the iCloud servers hosted by Apple and provides an easy to use way to store, manage and retrieve data and other asset types (such as large binary files, videos and images) in a structured way. This provides a platform for users to store private data and access it from multiple devices, and also for the developer to provide data that is publicly available to all the users of an application.

The first step in learning to use CloudKit is to gain an understanding of the key components that constitute the CloudKit framework.

45.2 CloudKit Containers

Each CloudKit enabled application has at least one container on iCloud. The container for an application is represented in the CloudKit Framework by the CKContainer class and it is within these containers that the databases reside. Containers may also be shared between multiple applications.

A reference to an application's default cloud container can be obtained via a call to the *defaultContainer* method of the CKContainer class:

```
let container = CKContainer.defaultContainer()
```

45.3 **CloudKit Public Database**

Each cloud container contains a single public database. This is the database into which is stored data that is needed by all users of an application. A map application, for example, might have a set of data about locations and routes that are applicable to all users of the application. This data would be stored within the public database of the application's cloud container.

CloudKit databases are represented within the CloudKit Framework by the CKDatabase class. A reference to the public cloud database for a container can be obtained via the *publicCloudDatabase* property of a container instance:

```
let publicDatabase = container.publicCloudDatabase
```

45.4 **CloudKit Private Databases**

Private cloud databases are used to store data that is private to each specific user. Each cloud container, therefore, will contain one private database for each user of the application. A reference to the private cloud database can be obtained via the *privateCloudDatabase* property of the container object:

```
let privateDatabase = container.privateCloudDatabase
```

45.5 **Data Storage and Transfer Quotas**

Data and assets stored in the public cloud database of an application count against the storage quota of the application. Anything stored in a private database, on the other hand, is counted against the iCloud quota of the corresponding user. Applications should, therefore, try to minimize the amount of data stored in private databases to avoid users having to unnecessarily purchase additional iCloud storage space.

At the time of writing, each application begins with 50MB of public database storage space and 5GB of space for assets free of charge. In addition, each application starts with an initial 25MB per day of free data transfer for assets and 250Kb for database data.

For each additional application user, the free storage quotas increase by 100MB and 1MB for assets and database data respectively. Data transfer quotas also increase by 0.5MB per day and 5KB per day for assets and data for each additional user. As long as these quota limits are not exceeded, the resources remain free up to a limit of 1PB for assets and 10TB for databases. Maximum data transfer quotas are 5TB per day for assets and 50GB per day for databases.

The latest quota limits can be reviewed online at:

https://developer.apple.com/icloud/documentation/cloudkit-storage/

45.6 **CloudKit Records**

Data is stored in both the public and private databases in the form of records. Records are represented by the CKRecord class and are essentially dictionaries of key-value pairs where keys are used to reference the data values stored in the record. A wide range of data types can be stored in a record including strings, numbers, dates, arrays, locations, data objects and references to other records. New key-value fields may be added to a record at any time without the need to perform any database restructuring.

Records in a database are categorized by a *record type* which must be declared when the record is created and takes the form of a string value. In practice this should be set to a meaningful value that assists in identifying the purpose of the record type. Records in a cloud database can be added, updated, queried and deleted using a range of methods provided by the CKDatabase class.

The following code demonstrates the creation of a CKRecord instance initialized with a record type of "Schools" together with three key-value pair fields:

```
let myRecord = CKRecord(recordType: "Schools")

myRecord.setObject("Silver Oak Elementary", forKey: "schoolname")
myRecord.setObject("100 Oak Street", forKey: "address")
myRecord.setObject(150, forKey: "studentcount")
```

Once created and initialized, the above record could be saved via a call to the *saveRecord* method of a database instance as follows:

```
publicDatabase.saveRecord(myRecord, completionHandler:
    ({returnRecord, error in

            if let err = error {
                // save operation failed
            } else {
                // save operation succeeded
            }

    }))
```

The method call passes through the record to be saved and specifies a completion handler in the form of a closure expression to be called when the operation returns. It is important to understand that CloudKit operations are predominantly asynchronous, enabling the calling application to continue to function while the CloudKit Framework works in the background to handle the transfer of data to and from the iCloud servers. In most cases, therefore, a call to CloudKit API methods will require that a completion handler be provided. This handler code will then be executed when the corresponding operation completes and passed results data where appropriate, or an error object in the event of a failure. Given the asynchronous nature of CloudKit operations, it is important to implement robust error handling within the completion handler.

The steps involved in creating, updating, querying and deleting records will be covered in greater detail in the next chapter entitled *An iOS 8 CloudKit Example*.

The overall concept of an application cloud container, private and public databases and records can be visualized as illustrated in Figure 45-1:

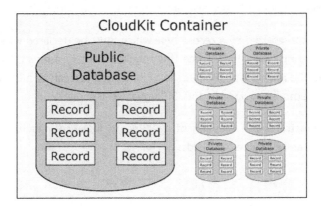

Figure 45-1

45.7 **CloudKit Record IDs**

Each CloudKit record has associated with it a unique record ID represented by the CKRecordID class. If a record ID is not specified when a record is first created, one is provided for it automatically by the CloudKit framework.

45.8 **CloudKit References**

CloudKit references are implemented using the CKReference class and provide a way to establish relationships between different records in a database. A reference is established by creating a CKReference instance for an originating record and assigning to it the record to which the relationship is to be targeted. The CKReference object is then stored in the originating record as a key-value pair field. A single record can contain multiple references to other records.

Once a record is configured with a reference pointing to a target record, that record is said to be *owned* by the target record. When the owner record is deleted, all records that refer to it are also deleted and so on down the chain of references (a concept referred to as *cascading deletes*).

45.9 **CloudKit Assets**

In addition to data, CloudKit may also be used to store larger assets such as audio or video files, large documents, binary data files or images. These assets are stored within CKAsset instances. Assets can only be stored as part of a record and it is not possible to directly store an asset in a cloud database. Once created, an asset is added to a record as just another key-value field pair. The following code, for example, demonstrates the addition of an image asset to a record:

```
let imageAsset = CKAsset(fileURL: imageURL)
```

```
let myRecord = CKRecord(recordType: "Vacations")

myRecord.setObject("London", forKey: "city")
myRecord.setObject(imageAsset, forKey: "photo")
```

At the time of writing, individual CloudKit assets are limited in size to 250Mb.

45.10 **Record Zones**

CloudKit record zones (CKRecordZone) provide a mechanism for relating groups of records within a private database. Unless a record zone is specified when a record is saved to the cloud it is placed in the *default zone* of the target database. Custom zones can be added to private databases and used to organize related records and perform tasks such as writing to multiple records simultaneously in a single transaction. Each record zone has associated with it a unique record zone ID (CKRecordZoneID) which must be referenced when adding new records to a zone.

Adding a record zone to a private database involves the creation of a CKRecordZone instance initialized with the name to be assigned to the zone:

```
let myRecordZone = CKRecordZone(zoneName: "MyRecordZone")
```

The zone is then saved to the database via a call to the *saveRecordZone* method of a CKDatabase instance, passing through the CKRecordZone instance together with a completion handler to be called upon completion of the operation:

```
privateDatabase.saveRecordZone(myRecordZone, completionHandler:
        ({returnRecord, error in
            if let err = error {
                // Zone creation failed
            } else {
                // Zone creation suceeded
            }
        }))
```

Once the record zone has been established on the cloud database, records may be added to that zone by including the zone ID of the record zone when creating CKRecord instances:

```
var myRecord = CKRecord(recordType: "Addresses",
                    zoneID: myRecordZone.zoneID)
```

When the record is subsequently saved to the database it will be associated with the designated record zone.

45.11 **CloudKit Subscriptions**

CloudKit subscriptions allow users to be notified when a change occurs within the cloud databases belonging to an installed app. Subscriptions use the standard iOS push notifications infrastructure and can be triggered based on a variety of criteria such as when records are added, updated or deleted. Notifications can also be further refined using predicates so that notifications are based on data in a record matching certain criteria. When a notification arrives, it is presented to the user in the same way as other notifications through an alert or a notification entry on the lock screen.

CloudKit subscriptions are configured using the CKSubscription class and are covered in detail in the chapter entitled *An iOS 8 CloudKit Subscription Example*.

45.12 Obtaining iCloud User Information

Within the scope of an application's cloud container, each user has a unique, application specific iCloud user ID and a user info record where the user ID is used as the record ID for the user's info record.

The record ID of the current user's info record can be obtained via a call to the *fetchUserRecordIDWithCompletionHandler* method of the container instance. Once the record ID has been obtained, this can be used to fetch the user's record from the cloud database:

```
container.fetchUserRecordIDWithCompletionHandler ({recordID,
        error in
            if let err = error {
                // Failed to get record ID
            } else {
                // Success - fetch the user's record here
            }
```

The record is of type CKRecordTypeUserRecord and is initially empty. Once fetched, it can be used to store data in the same way as any other CloudKit record.

CloudKit can also be used to perform user discovery. This allows the application to obtain an array of the users in the current user's address book who have also used the app. In order for the user's information to be provided, the user must have run the app and opted in to provide the information. User discovery is performed via a call to the *discoverAllContactUserInfosWithCompletionHandler* method of the container instance.

The discovered data is provided in the form of an array of CKApplicationUserInfo objects which contain the user's iCloud ID, first name and last name. The following code fragment, for example, performs a user discovery operation and outputs to the console the first and last names of any users that meet the requirements for discoverability:

```
container.discoverAllContactUserInfosWithCompletionHandler(
        {users, error in

            if let err = error {
                NSLog("discovery failed %@",
```

```
                          err.localizedDescription)
        } else {

            for userInfo in user {
                let userRecordID = userInfo.userRecordID
                NSLog("First Name = %@", userInfo.firstName)
                NSLog("Last Name = %@", userInfo.lastName)
            }
        }
    })
```

45.13 **CloudKit Dashboard**

The CloudKit Dashboard is a web based portal that provides an interface for managing the CloudKit options and storage for applications. The dashboard can be accessed via the *https://icloud.developer.apple.com/dashboard/* URL or using the *CloudKit Dashboard* button located in the iCloud section of the Xcode Capabilities panel for a project as shown in Figure 45-2:

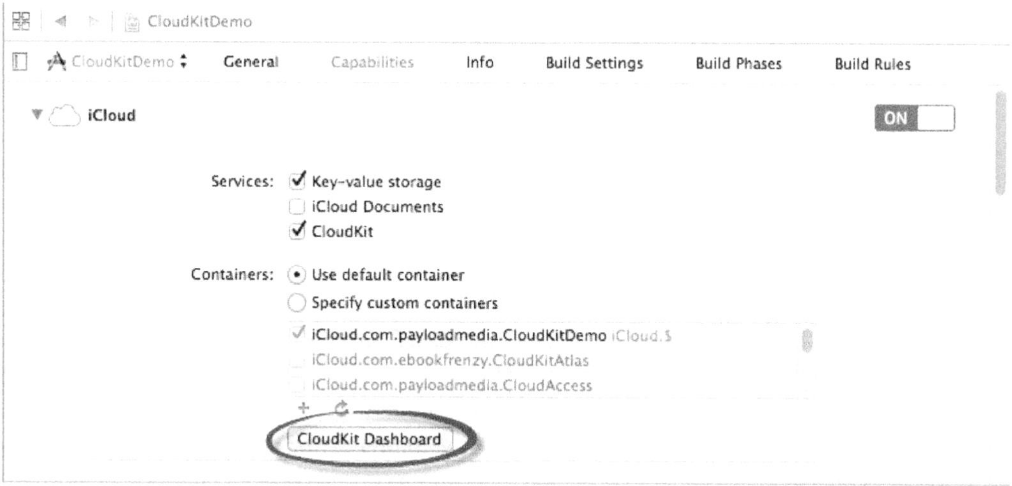

Figure 45-2

Access to the dashboard requires a valid Apple developer login and password and, once loaded into a browser window, will appear as illustrated in Figure 45-3:

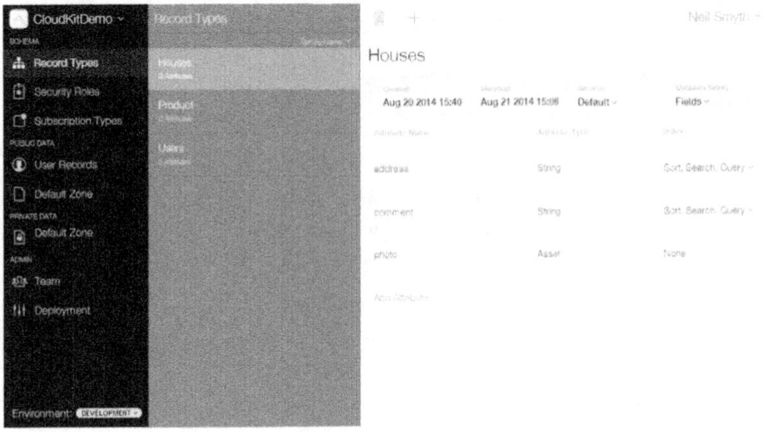

Figure 45-3

Among other features, the dashboard provides the ability to view data, add, update, query and delete records, modify database schema, view subscriptions and configure new security roles. It also provides an interface for migrating data from a development environment over to a production environment in preparation for an application to go live in the Apple App Store.

In the case of data access through the CloudKit Dashboard, it is important to be aware that private user data cannot be accessed using the dashboard interface. Only data stored in the public database and the private databases belonging to the developer account used to log into the dashboard can be viewed and modified.

45.14 Summary

This chapter has covered a number of the key classes and elements that make up the data storage features of the CloudKit framework. Each application has its own cloud container which, in turn, contains a single public cloud database in addition to one private database for each application user. Data is stored in databases in the form of records using key-value pair fields. Larger data such as videos and photos are stored as assets which, in turn, are stored as fields in records. Records stored in private databases can be grouped together into record zones and records may be associated with each other through the creation of relationships. Each application user has an iCloud user id and a corresponding user record both of which can be obtained using the CloudKit framework. In addition, CloudKit user discovery can be used to obtain, subject to permission having been given, a list of IDs for those users in the current user's address book who have also installed and run the app.

Finally, the CloudKit Dashboard is a web based portal that provides an interface for managing the CloudKit options and storage for applications.

46. An iOS 8 CloudKit Example

With the basics of the CloudKit Framework covered in the previous chapter, many of the concepts covered in that chapter will now be explored in greater detail through the implementation of an example iOS project. The app created in this chapter will demonstrate the use of the CloudKit Framework to create, update, query and delete records in a public CloudKit database. In the next chapter, the project will be extended further to demonstrate the use of CloudKit subscriptions to notify users when new records are added to the application's database.

Chapter 46

46.1 About the Example CloudKit Project

The steps outlined in this chapter are intended to make use of a number of key features of the CloudKit framework. The example will take the form of the prototype for an application designed to appeal to users while looking for a new home. The app allows the users to store the addresses, take photos and enter notes about properties visited. This information will be stored on iCloud using the CloudKit Framework and will include the ability to save, delete, update and search for records.

46.2 Creating the CloudKit Example Project

Launch Xcode and create a new Single View Application project named CloudKitDemo, with the programming language set to Swift and the Devices menu set to *Universal*.

Once the project has been created, the first step is to enable CloudKit entitlements for the application. Select the CloudKitDemo entry listed at the top of the project navigator panel and, in the main panel, click on the *Capabilities* tab. Within the resulting list of entitlements, make sure that the iCloud option is switched to the *On* position, that the *CloudKit* services option is enabled and the Containers section is configured to use the default container:

Figure 46-1

46.3 **Designing the User Interface**

The user interface layout for this project will consist of an Image View, Text Field, Text View and a Toolbar containing five Bar Button Items. Begin the design process by selecting the *Main.storyboard* file in the project navigator panel so that the storyboard loads into the Interface Builder environment.

Drag and drop views from the Object Library panel onto the storyboard canvas and resize, position and configure the views so that the layout resembles that outlined in Figure 46-2, making sure to stretch the views horizontally so that they align with the margins of the containing view (represented by the dotted blue lines that appear when resizing a view). After adding the Text View and before adding the Image View, select the Text View object, display the Auto Layout Pin menu and add a *Height* constraint.

Figure 46-2

Select the Text Field view, display the Attributes Inspector and enter *Address* into the *Placeholder* attribute field.

Click on the white background of the view controller layout so that none of the views in the layout are currently selected. Using the *Resolve Auto Layout Issues* menu located in the lower right hand corner of the Interface Builder panel, select the *Add Missing Constraints* menu option. This option will configure most of the necessary constraints with the exception of constraining the right hand edge of the Image View in relation to the containing view.

To resolve this, select the Image View in the storyboard canvas, Ctrl-click just inside the right hand edge of the view and drag the resulting line to the edge of the containing view so that the entire view highlights. Release the line and, from the popup menu, select the *Trailing Space to Container Margin* option as shown in Figure 46-3:

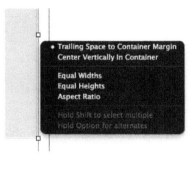

Figure 46-3

Compile and run the application on physical devices and simulators to confirm that the layout responds correctly to different screen sizes.

With the Text View selected in the storyboard, display the Attributes Inspector in the Utilities panel and delete the example Latin text.

46.4 Establishing Outlets and Actions

Display the Assistant Editor, select the Text Field view in the storyboard and Ctrl-click and drag from the view to a position beneath the "class ViewController" declaration and release the line. In the resulting connection panel, establish an outlet connection named *addressField*. Repeat these steps for the Text View and Image View, establishing Outlets named *commentsField* and *imageView* respectively.

Using the same technique establish *Action* connections from the five Bar Button Items to action methods named *saveRecord*, *performQuery*, *selectPhoto*, *updateRecord* and *deleteRecord* respectively. Once the connections have been established, the *ViewController.swift* file should read as follows:

```
import UIKit
```

```
class ViewController: UIViewController {

    @IBOutlet weak var addressField: UITextField!
    @IBOutlet weak var commentsField: UITextView!
    @IBOutlet weak var imageView: UIImageView!

    override func viewDidLoad() {
        super.viewDidLoad()
    }

    @IBAction func saveRecord(sender: AnyObject) {
    }


    @IBAction func performQuery(sender: AnyObject) {
    }


    @IBAction func selectPhoto(sender: AnyObject) {
    }


    @IBAction func updateRecord(sender: AnyObject) {
    }


    @IBAction func deleteRecord(sender: AnyObject) {
    }

    override func didReceiveMemoryWarning() {
        super.didReceiveMemoryWarning()
    }
}
```

46.5 Accessing the Public Database

Since the application is intended as a social sharing application where users can see comments posted by other users, the data entered into the application will be stored on iCloud using the application's public cloud database. Obtaining a reference to the public cloud database first involves gaining a reference to the application's container. Within the *ViewController.swift* file make the following additions, noting the inclusion of import statements for frameworks that will be needed later in the tutorial, together with variables to store the current database record and photo image URL:

```
import UIKit
```

```
import CloudKit
import MobileCoreServices

class ViewController: UIViewController {

    @IBOutlet weak var addressField: UITextField!
    @IBOutlet weak var commentsField: UITextView!
    @IBOutlet weak var imageView: UIImageView!

    let container = CKContainer.defaultContainer()
    var publicDatabase: CKDatabase?
    var currentRecord: CKRecord?
    var photoURL: NSURL?

    override func viewDidLoad() {
        super.viewDidLoad()
        publicDatabase = container.publicCloudDatabase
    }
.
.
}
```

46.6 Hiding the Keyboard

It is important to include code to ensure that the user has a way to hide the keyboard after entering text into the two text areas in the user interface. Within the *ViewController.swift* file, override the *touchesBegan* method to hide the keyboard when the user taps the background view of the user interface:

```
override func touchesBegan(touches: NSSet,
                    withEvent event: UIEvent) {
    addressField.endEditing(true)
    commentsField.endEditing(true)
}
```

46.7 Implementing the selectPhoto method

The purpose of the Photo button in the toolbar is to allow the user to include a photo in the database record. Begin by declaring that the View Controller class implements the UIImagePickerControllerDelegate and UINavigationControllerDelegate protocols, then locate the stub *selectPhoto* action method within the *ViewController.swift* file and implement the code as follows:

```
class ViewController: UIViewController, UIImagePickerControllerDelegate,
UINavigationControllerDelegate {
.
.
```

```
@IBAction func selectPhoto(sender: AnyObject) {

    let imagePicker = UIImagePickerController()

    imagePicker.delegate = self
    imagePicker.sourceType =
            UIImagePickerControllerSourceType.PhotoLibrary
    imagePicker.mediaTypes = [kUTTypeImage as NSString]

    self.presentViewController(imagePicker, animated: true,
                    completion:nil)
}
.
.
.
}
```

When executed, the code will cause the image picker view controller to be displayed from which the user can select a photo from the photo library on the device to be stored along with the current record in the application's public cloud database. The final step in the photo selection process is to implement the delegate methods which will be called when the user has either made a photo selection or cancels the selection process:

```
func imagePickerController(picker: UIImagePickerController!,
didFinishPickingMediaWithInfo info: [NSObject : AnyObject]!) {

    self.dismissViewControllerAnimated(true, completion: nil)
    let image =
            info[UIImagePickerControllerOriginalImage] as UIImage
    imageView.image = image
    photoURL = saveImageToFile(image)
}

func imagePickerControllerDidCancel(picker:
                    UIImagePickerController!) {
    self.dismissViewControllerAnimated(true, completion: nil)
}
```

In both cases the image picker view controller is dismissed from view. In the case of a photo being selected, the image is displayed within the application via the Image View instance before being written to the file system of the device and the corresponding URL stored in the *photoURL* variable for later reference. Clearly the code expects the image file writing to be performed by a method named *saveImageToFile* which must now be implemented:

```
func saveImageToFile(image: UIImage) -> NSURL
```

```
{
    let dirPaths = NSSearchPathForDirectoriesInDomains(
        .DocumentDirectory, .UserDomainMask, true)

    let docsDir: AnyObject = dirPaths[0]

    let filePath =
      docsDir.stringByAppendingPathComponent("currentImage.png")

    UIImageJPEGRepresentation(image, 0.5).writeToFile(filePath,
            atomically: true)

    return NSURL.fileURLWithPath(filePath)!
}
```

The method obtains a reference to the application's Documents directory and constructs a path to an image file named *currentImage.png*. The image is then written to the file in JPEG format using a compression rate of 0.5 in order to reduce the amount of storage used from the application's iCloud allowance. The resulting file URL is then returned to the calling method.

46.8 Saving a Record to the Cloud Database

When the user has entered an address and comments and selected a photo, the data is ready to be saved to the cloud database. This will require that code be added to the *saveRecord* method as follows:

```
@IBAction func saveRecord(sender: AnyObject) {

    if (photoURL == nil) {
        notifyUser("No Photo", message: "Use the Photo option to choose a
photo for the record")
        return
    }

    let asset = CKAsset(fileURL: photoURL!)

    let myRecord = CKRecord(recordType: "Houses")
    myRecord.setObject(addressField.text, forKey: "address")
    myRecord.setObject(commentsField.text, forKey: "comment")
    myRecord.setObject(asset, forKey: "photo")

    publicDatabase!.saveRecord(myRecord, completionHandler:
      ({returnRecord, error in
        if let err = error {
            self.notifyUser("Save Error", message:
```

```
                        err.localizedDescription)
        } else {
            dispatch_async(dispatch_get_main_queue()) {
                self.notifyUser("Success",
                    message: "Record saved successfully")
            }
                self.currentRecord = myRecord
        }
    }))
}
```

The method begins by verifying that the user has selected a photo to include in the database record. If one has not yet been selected the user is notified that a photo is required (the *notifyUser* method will be implemented in the next section).

Next a new CKAsset object is created and initialized with the URL to the photo image previously selected by the user. A new CKRecord instance is then created and assigned a record type of "Houses". The record is then initialized with the content of the Text Field and Text View and the CKAsset object containing the photo image.

Finally, the *saveRecord* method of the public cloud database is called passing through the newly created record. A completion handler then reports the success or otherwise of the save operation. Since this involves working with the user interface, it is dispatched to the main thread to prevent the application from locking up. The new record is then saved to the *currentRecord* variable where it can be referenced should the user subsequently decide to update or delete the record.

46.9 Implementing the notifyUser Method

The *notifyUser* method takes as parameters two string values representing a title and message to be displayed to the user. These strings are then used in the construction of an Alert View. Implement this method as follows:

```
func notifyUser(title: String, message: String) -> Void
{
    let alert = UIAlertController(title: title,
            message: message,
        preferredStyle: UIAlertControllerStyle.Alert)

    let cancelAction = UIAlertAction(title: "OK",
            style: .Cancel, handler: nil)

    alert.addAction(cancelAction)
    self.presentViewController(alert, animated: true,
            completion: nil)
}
```

46.10 **Testing the Record Saving Method**

Compile and run the application on a device or simulator on which an iCloud account has been configured. Enter text into the address and comments fields and select an image from the photo library (images can be added to the photo library of a simulator instance by dragging images from a Finder window and dropping them onto the simulator window).

Tap the Save button to save the record and wait for the alert to appear indicating that the record has been saved successfully. Note that CloudKit operations are performed asynchronously so the amount of time for a successful save to be reported will vary depending on the size of the record being saved, network speed and responsiveness of the iCloud servers.

Once the record has been saved, return to the Capabilities screen for the application (Figure 46-1) and click on the *CloudKit Dashboard* button. This will launch the default web browser on the system and load the CloudKit Dashboard portal. Enter your Apple developer login and password and, once the dashboard has loaded, select the CloudKitDemo application from the drop down menu (marked as A in Figure 46-4). From the navigation panel, select *Default Zone* (B) located under *PUBLIC DATA* and make sure that the *Houses* record type is selected in the record listing panel (C). The saved record should be listed and the address, comments and photo asset shown in the main panel (D):

Figure 46-4

Having verified that the record was saved, the next task is to implement the remaining action methods.

46.11 **Searching for Cloud Database Records**

The Query feature of the application allows a record matching a specified address to be retrieved and displayed to the user. Locate the template *performQuery* method in the *ViewController.swift* file and implement the body of the method to perform the query operation:

```
@IBAction func performQuery(sender: AnyObject) {
```

```
    let predicate = NSPredicate(format: "address = %@",
addressField.text)

    let query = CKQuery(recordType: "Houses", predicate: predicate)

    publicDatabase?.performQuery(query, inZoneWithID: nil,
                completionHandler: ({results, error in

        if (error != nil) {
            dispatch_async(dispatch_get_main_queue()) {
                self.notifyUser("Cloud Access Error",
                    message: error.localizedDescription)
            }
        } else {
            if results.count > 0 {

                var record = results[0] as CKRecord
                self.currentRecord = record

                dispatch_async(dispatch_get_main_queue()) {

                    self.commentsField.text =
                        record.objectForKey("comment") as String

                    let photo =
                        record.objectForKey("photo") as CKAsset

                    let image = UIImage(contentsOfFile:
                        photo.fileURL.path!)

                    self.imageView.image = image
                    self.photoURL = self.saveImageToFile(image!)
                }
            } else {
                dispatch_async(dispatch_get_main_queue()) {
                    self.notifyUser("No Match Found",
                        message: "No record matching the address was found")
                }
            }
        }
    }))
}
```

Despite the seeming complexity of this method it actually performs some very simple tasks. First a new predicate instance is configured to indicate that the query is to search for records where the address field matches the content of the address entered by the user into the application user interface. This predicate is then used to create a new CKQuery object together with the record type for which the search is to be performed.

The *performQuery* method of the public cloud database object is then called, passing through the query object together with a completion handler to be executed when the query returns (as with all CloudKit operations, queries are performed asynchronously).

In the event of an error or a failure to find a match, the user is notified via an alert. In the event that one or more matches are found, the first matching record is extracted from the results array and the data and image contained therein displayed to the user via the user interface outlet connections.

Compile and run the application, enter the address used when the record was saved in the previous section and tap the Query button. After a short delay, the display should update with the content of the record.

46.12 **Updating Cloud Database Records**

When updating existing records in a cloud database, the ID of the record to be updated must be referenced since this is the only way to uniquely identify one record from another. In the case of the CloudKitDemo application, this means that the record must already have been loaded into the application and assigned to the currentRecord variable, thereby allowing the recordID to be obtained and used for the update operation. With these requirements in mind, implement the code in the stub *updateRecord* method as follows:

```
@IBAction func updateRecord(sender: AnyObject) {

    if let record = currentRecord {

        let asset = CKAsset(fileURL: photoURL!)

        record.setObject(addressField.text, forKey: "address")
        record.setObject(commentsField.text, forKey: "comment")
        record.setObject(asset, forKey: "photo")

        publicDatabase!.saveRecord(record, completionHandler:
          ({returnRecord, error in
            if let err = error {
                dispatch_async(dispatch_get_main_queue()) {
                    self.notifyUser("Update Error",
                        message: err.localizedDescription)
                }
            } else {
                dispatch_async(dispatch_get_main_queue()) {
```

```
                    self.notifyUser("Success", message:
                            "Record updated successfully")
                }
            }
        }))
    } else {
        notifyUser("No Record Selected", message:
                "Use Query to select a record to update")
    }
}
```

This method performs similar tasks to the *saveRecord* method. This time, however, instead of creating a new CKRecord instance, the existing record assigned to the *currentRecord* variable is updated with the latest text and photo content entered by the user. When the save operation is performed, CloudKit will identify that the record has an ID that matches an existing record in the database and update that matching record with the latest data provided by the user.

46.13 Deleting a Cloud Record

CloudKit record deletions can be achieved by calling the *deleteRecordWithID* method of the CKDatabase instance, passing through as arguments the ID of the record to be deleted and a completion handler to be executed when the deletion operation returns. As with the *updateRecord* method, a deletion can only be performed when the record to be deleted has already been selected within the application and assigned to the *currentRecord* variable:

```
@IBAction func deleteRecord(sender: AnyObject) {
    if let record = currentRecord {

        publicDatabase?.deleteRecordWithID(record.recordID,
                completionHandler: ({returnRecord, error in
            if let err = error {
                dispatch_async(dispatch_get_main_queue()) {
                    self.notifyUser("Delete Error", message:
                                    err.localizedDescription)

                }
            } else {
                dispatch_async(dispatch_get_main_queue()) {
                    self.notifyUser("Success", message:
                        "Record deleted successfully")
                }
            }
        }))
    } else {
```

```
        notifyUser("No Record Selected", message:
                        "Use Query to select a record to delete")
    }
}
```

46.14 Testing the Application

With the basic functionality of the application implemented, compile and run it on a device or simulator instance and add, query, update and delete records to verify that the application functions as intended.

46.15 Summary

CloudKit provides an easy way to implement the storage and retrieval of iCloud based database records from within iOS applications. The objective of this chapter has been to demonstrate in practical terms the techniques available to save, search, update and delete database records stored in an iCloud database using the CloudKit convenience API.

One area of CloudKit that was not addressed in this chapter involves the use of CloudKit subscriptions to notify the user when changes have been made to a cloud database. In the next chapter, entitled *An iOS 8 CloudKit Subscription Example*, the CloudKitDemo application will be extended to add this functionality.

Chapter 47

47. An iOS 8 CloudKit Subscription Example

In the previous chapter, entitled *An iOS 8 CloudKit Example*, an example application was created that demonstrated the use of the iOS 8 CloudKit Framework to save, query, update and delete cloud database records. In this chapter, the CloudKitDemo application created in the previous chapter will be extended so that users of the application receive push notifications when a new record is added to the application's public database by other users.

47.1 Push Notifications and CloudKit Subscriptions

A push notification occurs when a remote server associated with an app installed on an iOS device sends a notification of importance to the user. On receipt of the notification the user will be notified either via an alert on the lock screen, or by an alert panel appearing at the top of the screen accompanied by an optional sound. Generally, selecting the notification alert will launch the associated app in a context that is relevant to the nature of the notification. When enabled, a red *badge* will also appear in the corner of the application's launch icon containing a number representing the amount of outstanding notifications received for the application since it was last launched.

Consider, for example, a news based application that is configured to receive push notifications from a remote server when a breaking news headline is available. Once the push notification is received, brief details of the news item will be displayed to the user and, in the event that the user selected the notification alert, the news app will launch and display the news article corresponding to the notification.

CloudKit subscriptions use the iOS push notifications infrastructure to enable users to receive notifications when changes occur to the data stored in a cloud database. Specifically, CloudKit subscriptions can be used to notify the user when CloudKit based records of a specific record type are created, updated or deleted. As with other push notifications, the user can select the notification and launch the corresponding application. Making the application appear in the appropriate context (for example with a newly created record loaded), however, requires some work. The remainder of this chapter will outline the steps to implement this behavior.

47.2 Registering an App to Receive Push Notifications

By default, applications installed on a user's device will not be allowed to receive push notifications until the user specifically grants permission. An application seeks this permission by registering for remote notifications. The first time this registration request occurs the user will be prompted to grant permission. Once permission has been granted, the application will be able to receive remote notifications until the user changes the notifications setting for the application in the Settings app.

To register for remote notifications for the CloudKitDemo project, locate and select the *AppDelegate.swift* file in the project navigator panel and modify the *didFinishLaunchingWithOptions* method to add the appropriate registration code. Now is also an opportune time to import the CloudKit Framework into the class:

```
import UIKit
import CloudKit

@UIApplicationMain
class AppDelegate: UIResponder, UIApplicationDelegate {

    var window: UIWindow?

    func application(application: UIApplication!,
didFinishLaunchingWithOptions launchOptions: NSDictionary!) -> Bool {

        let settings = UIUserNotificationSettings(forTypes:
            .Alert | .Badge | .Sound, categories: nil)

        application.registerUserNotificationSettings(settings)
        application.registerForRemoteNotifications()

        return true
    }
    .
    .
}
```

The code in the method configures the notification settings such that the system will display an alert to the user when an notification is received, display a badge on the application's launch icon and also, if configured, play a sound to get the user's attention. Although sound is enabled for this example, only the alert and badge settings will be used.

Having made these code changes, run the application and, when prompted, allow the application to receive notifications.

47.3 Configuring a CloudKit Subscription

A CloudKit subscription is configured using an instance of the CKSubscription class. When the CKSubscription instance is created it is passed the record type, a predicate and an option indicating whether the notifications are to be triggered when records of the specified type are created, deleted or updated. The predicate allows additional rules to be declared which the subscription must meet before the notification can be triggered. For example, a user might only be interested in notifications when records are added for houses on a particular street.

An instance of the CKNotification class is also assigned to the CKSubscription object and is used to define the information that is to be delivered to the application with the notification such as the message to be displayed in the notification alert, a sound to be played and whether or not a badge should be displayed on the application's launch icon.

Once the CKSubscription is fully configured, it is committed to the cloud database using the *saveSubscription* method of the cloud database object. For the purposes of this example, the code to implement the subscription should be implemented in the *viewDidLoad* method located in the *ViewController.swift* file:

```
override func viewDidLoad() {
    super.viewDidLoad()
    publicDatabase = container.publicCloudDatabase

    let predicate = NSPredicate(format: "TRUEPREDICATE")

    let subscription = CKSubscription(recordType: "Houses",
                        predicate: predicate,
                        options: .FiresOnRecordCreation)

    let notificationInfo = CKNotificationInfo()

    notificationInfo.alertBody = "A new House was added"
    notificationInfo.shouldBadge = true

    subscription.notificationInfo = notificationInfo

    publicDatabase?.saveSubscription(subscription,
            completionHandler: ({returnRecord, error in
        if let err = error {
            println("subscription failed %@",
                        err.localizedDescription)
        } else {
            dispatch_async(dispatch_get_main_queue()) {
                self.notifyUser("Success",
                    message: "Subscription set up successfully")
            }
        }
    }))
}
```

Note that the NSPredicate object was created using "TRUEPREDICATE". This is a special value that configures the predicate to always return a true value and is the equivalent of indicating that all records of the specified type match the predicate.

The *.FiresOnRecordCreation* option indicates that the user is to be notified whenever a new record of type "Houses" is added to the database. Other options available are *.FiresOnRecordUpdate*, *.FiresOnRecordDelete* and *.FiresOnce*. The *.FiresOnce* option causes the subscription to be deleted from the server after it has fired for the first time.

Compile and run the application on a device or simulator, then log into the iCloud Dashboard. Display the settings for the CloudKitDemo application and select the *Subscription Types* entry in the left-hand navigation panel. If the subscription was successfully configured it should be listed as shown in Figure 47-1:

Figure 47-1

47.4 Handling Remote Notifications

When the user selects a notification alert on an iOS device, the CloudKitDemo application will be launched by the operating system. At the point that the user selects the notification, the application will currently be in one of three possible states – foreground, background or not currently running.

If the application is in the background when the alert is selected, it is simply brought to the foreground. If it was not currently running, the application is launched by the operating system and brought to the foreground.

When the application is already in foreground or background state when a CloudKit notification alert is selected, the *didReceiveRemoteNotification* method of the application delegate class is called and passed as an argument an NSDictionary instance containing a CKNotification object which contains, among other information, the ID of the cloud database record that triggered the notification.

If the application was not already in the foreground or background when the alert is selected, the *didReceiveRemoteNotification* method is not called. Instead, information about the database change is passed as an argument to the *didFinishLaunchingWithOptions* method of the application delegate.

47.5 Implementing the didReceiveRemoteNotification Method

The *didReceiveRemoteNotification* method will be called when the user selects an alert and the CloudKitDemo application is either already in the foreground or currently in the background. The method will need to be implemented in the *AppDelegate.swift* file so locate this file in the project navigator panel and modify it to add this method:

```
func application(application: UIApplication, didReceiveRemoteNotification
userInfo: [NSObject : AnyObject]) {

    let viewController: ViewController =
        self.window?.rootViewController as ViewController

    let notification: CKNotification =
        CKNotification(fromRemoteNotificationDictionary: userInfo)

    if (notification.notificationType ==
                CKNotificationType.Query) {

        let queryNotification =
            notification as CKQueryNotification

        let recordID = queryNotification.recordID

        viewController.fetchRecord(recordID)
    }
}
```

The method begins by obtaining a reference to the root view controller of the application. The code then extracts the CKNotification object from the NSDictionary that was passed to the method by the operating system. The *notificationType* property of the CKNotification object is then checked to make sure it matches CKNotificationType.Query (which indicates that the notification was triggered as a result of a subscription).

The record ID is then obtained and passed to the *fetchRecord* method on the view controller. The next step is to implement the *fetchRecord* method.

47.6 Fetching a Record From a Cloud Database

Records can be fetched by record ID from a cloud database using the *fetchRecordWithID* method of the cloud database object. Within the *ViewController.swift* file, implement the *fetchRecord* method as follows:

```
func fetchRecord(recordID: CKRecordID) -> Void
{
    publicDatabase = container.publicCloudDatabase
```

```
    publicDatabase?.fetchRecordWithID(recordID,
                    completionHandler: ({record, error in
        if let err = error {
            dispatch_async(dispatch_get_main_queue()) {
                self.notifyUser("Fetch Error", message:
                    err.localizedDescription)
            }
        } else {
            dispatch_async(dispatch_get_main_queue()) {
                self.currentRecord = record
                self.addressField.text =
                    record.objectForKey("address") as String
                self.commentsField.text =
                    record.objectForKey("comment") as String
                let photo =
                    record.objectForKey("photo") as CKAsset

                let image = UIImage(contentsOfFile:
                    photo.fileURL.path!)
                self.imageView.image = image
                self.photoURL = self.saveImageToFile(image!)
            }
        }
    }))
}
```

The code obtains a reference to the public cloud database (keep in mind that this code will be executed before the *viewDidLoad* method where this has previously been obtained) and then fetches the record from the cloud database based on the record ID passed through as a parameter. If the fetch operation is successful, the data and photo are extracted from the record and displayed to the user. Since the fetched record is also now the current record, it is stored in the *currentRecord* variable.

47.7 Implementing the didFinishLaunchingWithOptions Method

As previously outlined, the *didReceiveRemoteNotification* method is only called when the user selected an alert notification and the application is already running either in the foreground or background. When the application was not already running, the *didFinishLaunchingWithOptions* method is called and passed information about the notification. In this scenario, it will be the responsibility of this method to ensure that the newly added record is displayed to the user when the application loads. Within the *AppDelegate.swift* file, locate the *didFinishLaunchingWithOptions* method and modify it as follows:

```
func application(application: UIApplication!,
didFinishLaunchingWithOptions launchOptions: NSDictionary!) -> Bool {
```

```
let settings = UIUserNotificationSettings(forTypes:
    .Alert | .Badge | .Sound, categories: nil)

application.registerUserNotificationSettings(settings)
application.registerForRemoteNotifications()

if let options: NSDictionary = launchOptions {
    let remoteNotification = options.objectForKey(
        UIApplicationLaunchOptionsRemoteNotificationKey) as?
            NSDictionary


    if let notification = remoteNotification {
        self.application(application,
            didReceiveRemoteNotification: notification)
    }
}
return true
}
```

The added source code begins by verifying that data has been passed to the method via the *launchOptions* parameter. The remote notification key is then used to obtain the NSDictionary object containing the notification data. If the key returns a value, it is passed to the *didReceiveRemoteNotification* method so that the record can be fetched and displayed to the user.

47.8 **Testing the Application**

Install and run the application on two devices or simulators (or a mixture thereof) remembering to log into iCloud on both instances via the *iCloud* screen of the *Settings* app. From one instance of the application add a new record to the database. When the notification alert appears on the other device or simulator (Figure 47-2), select it to launch the CloudKitDemo application which should, after a short delay, load and display the newly added record.

Figure 47-2

Repeat these steps both when the application on the second device is in the background and not currently running. In each case the behavior should be the same.

47.9 Summary

The iOS Push Notification system is used to notify users of events relating to applications installed on a device. This infrastructure has been integrated into CloudKit allowing applications to notify users about changes to the data stored on iCloud using CloudKit.

48. An Overview of iOS 8 Multitouch, Taps and Gestures

In terms of physical points of interaction between the device and the user, the iPhone and iPad provide four buttons, a switch and a touch screen. Without question, the user will spend far more time using the touch screen than any other aspect of the device. It is essential, therefore, that any application be able to handle gestures (touches, multitouches, taps, swipes and pinches etc) performed by the user's fingers on the touch screen.

Before writing code to handle these gestures, this chapter will spend some time talking about the responder chain in relation to touch screen events before delving a little deeper into the types of gestures an iOS application is likely to encounter.

48.1 The Responder Chain

In the chapter entitled *Understanding iOS 8 Views, Windows and the View Hierarchy* we spent some time talking about the view hierarchy of an application's user interface and how that hierarchy also defined part of the application's *responder chain*. In order to fully understand the concepts behind the handling of touch screen gestures it is first necessary to spend a little more time learning about the responder chain.

When the user interacts with the touch screen of an iPhone or iPad the hardware detects the physical contact and notifies the operating system. The operating system subsequently creates an *event* associated with the interaction and passes it into the currently active application's *event queue* where it is subsequently picked up by the *event loop* and passed to the current *first responder* object; the first responder being the object with which the user was interacting when this event was triggered (for example a UIButton or UIView object). If the first responder has been programmed to handle the type of event received it does so (for example a button may have an action defined to call a particular method when it receives a touch event). Having handled the event, the responder then has the option of discarding that event, or passing it up to the *next responder* in the *response chain* (defined by the object's *nextResponder* property) for further processing, and so on up the chain. If the first responder is not able to handle the event it will also pass it to the next responder in the chain and so on until it either reaches a responder that handles the event or it reaches the end of the chain (the UIApplication object) where it will either be handled or discarded.

Take, for example, a UIView with a UIButton subview. If the user touches the screen over the button then the button, as first responder, will receive the event. If the button is unable to handle the event it will need to be passed up to the view object. If the view is also unable to handle the event it would then be passed to the view controller and so on.

When working with the responder chain, it is important to note that the passing of an event from one responder to the next responder in the chain does not happen automatically. If an event needs to be passed to the next responder, code must be written to make it happen.

48.2 **Forwarding an Event to the Next Responder**

An event may be passed on to the next responder in the response chain by calling the *nextResponder* method of the current responder, passing through the method that was triggered by the event and the event itself. Take, for example, a situation where the current responder object is unable to handle a *touchesBegan* event. In order to pass this to the next responder, the *touchesBegan* method of the current responder will need to make a call as follows:

```
override func touchesBegan(touches: NSSet!, withEvent event: UIEvent!) {
    self.nextResponder()
}
```

48.3 **Gestures**

Gesture is an umbrella term used to encapsulate any single interaction between the touch screen and the user, starting at the point that the screen is touched (by one or more fingers) and the time that the last finger leaves the surface of the screen. *Swipes, pinches, stretches* and *flicks* are all forms of gesture.

48.4 **Taps**

A *tap*, as the name suggests, occurs when the user touches the screen with a single finger and then immediately lifts it from the screen. Taps can be single-taps or multiple-taps and the event will contain information about the number of times a user tapped on the screen.

48.5 **Touches**

A *touch* occurs when a finger establishes contact with the screen. When more than one finger touches the screen each finger registers as a touch up to a maximum of five fingers.

48.6 **Touch Notification Methods**

Touch screen events cause one of four methods on the first responder object to be called. The method that gets called for a specific event will depend on the nature of the interaction. In order to handle events, therefore, it is important to ensure that the appropriate methods from those outlined below are implemented within your responder chain. These methods will be used in the worked example contained in the *An Example iOS 8 Touch, Multitouch and Tap Application* and *Detecting iOS 8 Touch Screen Gesture Motions* chapters of this book.

48.6.1 touchesBegan method

The *touchesBegan* method is called when the user first touches the screen. Passed to this method are an argument called *touches* of type NSSet and the corresponding UIEvent object. The touches object contains a UITouch event for each finger in contact with the screen. The *tapCount* method of any of the UITouch events within the *touches* set can be called to identify the number of taps, if any, performed by the user. Similarly, the coordinates of an individual touch can be identified from the UITouch event either relative to the entire screen or within the local view itself.

48.6.2 touchesMoved method

The *touchesMoved* method is called when one or more fingers move across the screen. As fingers move across the screen this method gets called multiple times allowing the application to track the new coordinates and touch count at regular intervals. As with the *touchesBegan* method, this method is provided with an event object and an NSSet object containing UITouch events for each finger on the screen.

48.6.3 touchesEnded method

This method is called when the user lifts one or more fingers from the screen. As with the previous methods, *touchesEnded* is provided with the event and NSSet objects.

48.6.4 touchesCancelled method

When a gesture is interrupted due to a high level interrupt, such as the phone detecting an incoming call, the *touchesCancelled* method is called.

48.7 Summary

In order to fully appreciate the mechanisms for handling touch screen events within an iOS 8 application, it is first important to understand both the responder chain and the methods that are called on a responder depending on the type of interaction. We have covered these basics in this chapter. In the next chapter, entitled *An Example iOS 8 Touch, Multitouch and Tap Application* we will use these concepts to create an example application that demonstrates touch screen event handling.

49. An Example iOS 8 Touch, Multitouch and Tap Application

Having covered the basic concepts behind the handling of iOS user interaction with an iPhone or iPad touch screen in the previous chapter, this chapter will work through a tutorial designed to highlight the handling of taps and touches. Topics covered in this chapter include the detection of single and multiple taps and touches, identifying whether a user single or double tapped the device display and extracting information about a touch or tap from the corresponding event object.

49.1 The Example iOS 8 Tap and Touch Application

The example application created in the course of this tutorial will consist of a view and some labels. The view object's view controller will implement a number of the touch screen event methods outlined in *An Overview of iOS 8 Multitouch, Taps and Gestures* and update the status labels to reflect the detected activity. The application will, for example, report the number of fingers touching the screen, the number of taps performed and the most recent touch event that was triggered. In the next chapter, entitled *Detecting iOS 8 Touch Screen Gesture Motions* we will look more closely at detecting the motion of touches.

49.2 Creating the Example iOS Touch Project

Begin by launching the Xcode development environment and selecting the option to create a new project. Select the iOS Application *Single View Application* template, set the device menu *to Universal* and the language menu to *Swift*. Name the project *Touch* and, when the main Xcode project screen appears, we are ready to start writing the code for our application.

49.3 Designing the User Interface

Load the storyboard by selecting the *Main.storyboard* file. Using Interface Builder, modify the user interface by adding label components from the Object Library (*View -> Utilities -> Show Object Library*) and modifying properties until the view appears as outlined in Figure 49-1.

When adding the rightmost labels, be sure to stretch them so that the right hand edges reach approximately three quarters across the overall layout width.

Figure 49-1

Select label to the right of the "Method:" label, display the Assistant Editor panel and verify that the editor is displaying the contents of the *ViewController.swift* file. Ctrl-click on the same label object and drag to a position just below the class declaration line in the Assistant Editor. Release the line and in the resulting connection dialog establish an outlet connection named *methodStatus*.

Repeat the above steps to establish outlet connections for the remaining label objects to properties named *touchStatus* and *tapStatus*.

49.4 Enabling Multitouch on the View

By default, views are configured to respond to only single touches (in other words a single finger touching or tapping the screen at any one time). For the purposes of this example we plan to detect multiple touches. In order to enable this support it is necessary to change an attribute of the view object. To achieve this, click on the background of the *View* window, display the Attributes Inspector (*View -> Utilities -> Show Attributes Inspector*) and make sure that the *Multiple Touch* option is selected in the *Interaction* section:

Figure 49-2

49.5 **Implementing the touchesBegan Method**

When the user touches the screen, the *touchesBegan* method of the first responder is called. In order to capture these event types, we need to implement this method in our view controller. In the Xcode project navigator, select the *ViewController.swift* file and add the *touchesBegan* method as follows:

```
override func touchesBegan(touches: NSSet, withEvent event: UIEvent) {
    let touchCount = touches.count
    let touch = touches.anyObject() as UITouch
    let tapCount = touch.tapCount

    methodStatus.text = "touchesBegan"
    touchStatus.text = "\(touchCount) touches"
    tapStatus.text = "\(tapCount) taps"
}
```

This method obtains a count of the number of touch objects contained in the *touches* set (essentially the number of fingers touching the screen) and assigns it to a variable. It then gets the tap count from one of the touch objects. The code then updates the *methodStatus* label to indicate that the *touchesBegan* method has been triggered, constructs a string indicating the number of touches and taps detected and displays the information on the *touchStatus* and *tapStatus* labels accordingly.

49.6 **Implementing the touchesMoved Method**

When the user moves one or more fingers currently in contact with the surface of the touch screen, the *touchesMoved* method is called repeatedly until the movement ceases. In order to capture these events it is necessary to implement the touchesMoved method in our view controller class:

```
override func touchesMoved(touches: NSSet, withEvent event: UIEvent) {
    let touchCount = touches.count
    let touch = touches.anyObject() as UITouch
    let tapCount = touch.tapCount

    methodStatus.text = "touchesMoved"
    touchStatus.text = "\(touchCount) touches"
    tapStatus.text = "\(tapCount) taps"
}
```

Once again we report the number of touches and taps detected and indicate to the user that this time the *touchesMoved* method is being triggered.

49.7 Implementing the touchesEnded Method

When the user removes a finger from the screen the *touchesEnded* method is called. We can, therefore, implement this method as follows:

```
override func touchesEnded(touches: NSSet, withEvent event: UIEvent) {
    let touchCount = touches.count
    let touch = touches.anyObject() as UITouch
    let tapCount = touch.tapCount

    methodStatus.text = "touchesEnded"
    touchStatus.text = "\(touchCount) touches"
    tapStatus.text = "\(tapCount) taps"
}
```

49.8 Getting the Coordinates of a Touch

Although not part of this particular example, it is worth knowing that the coordinates of the location on the screen where a touch has been detected may be obtained in the form of a CGPoint structure by calling the *locationInView* method of the touch object. For example:

```
let touch = touches.anyObject() as UITouch
let point = touch.locationInView(self.view)
```

The X and Y coordinates may subsequently be extracted from the CGPoint structure by accessing the corresponding elements:

```
let pointX = point.x
let pointY = point.y
```

49.9 Building and Running the Touch Example Application

Build and run the application by clicking on the run button located in the toolbar of the main Xcode project window. The application will run in the iOS Simulator where you should be able to click with the mouse pointer to simulate touches and taps. With each click, the status labels should update to reflect the interaction:

Figure 49-3

Of course, since a mouse only has one pointer it is not possible to trigger multiple touch events using the iOS Simulator environment. In fact, the only way to try out multitouch behavior in this application is to run it on a physical iPhone or iPad device. For steps on how to achieve this, refer to the chapter entitled *Testing Apps on iOS 8 Devices with Xcode 6*.

50. Detecting iOS 8 Touch Screen Gesture Motions

The next area of iOS touch screen event handling that we will look at in this book involves the detection of gestures involving movement. As covered in a previous chapter, a *gesture* refers to the activity that takes place in the time between a finger touching the screen and the finger then being lifted from the screen. In the chapter entitled *An Example iOS 8 Touch, Multitouch and Tap Application* we dealt with touches that did not involve any movement across the screen surface. We will now create an example that tracks the coordinates of a finger as it moves across the screen.

Note that the assumption is made throughout this chapter that the reader has already reviewed the *An Overview of iOS 8 Multitouch, Taps and Gestures* chapter of this book.

50.1 The Example iOS 8 Gesture Application

This example application will detect when a single touch is made on the screen of the iPhone or iPad and then report the coordinates of that finger as it is moved across the screen surface.

50.2 Creating the Example Project

Start the Xcode environment and select the option to create a new project using the *Single View Application* template. Name the project *TouchMotion*, select the *Universal* device setting and choose *Swift* as the programming language.

50.3 Designing the Application User Interface

The application will display the X and Y coordinates of the touch and update these values in real-time as the finger moves across the screen. When the finger is lifted from the screen, the start and end coordinates of the gesture will then be displayed on two label objects in the user interface. Select the *Main.storyboard* file and, using Interface Builder, create a user interface such that it resembles the layout in Figure 50-1:

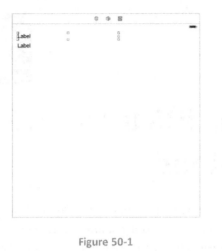

Figure 50-1

Be sure to stretch the labels so that they both extend to cover a little over half of the width of the view layout.

Select the top label object in the view canvas, display the Assistant Editor panel and verify that the editor is displaying the contents of the *ViewController.swift* file. Ctrl-click on the same label object and drag to a position just below the class declaration line in the Assistant Editor. Release the line and in the resulting connection dialog establish an outlet connection named *xCoord*. Repeat this step to establish an outlet connection to the second label object named *yCoord*.

Next, review the *ViewController.swift* file to verify that the outlets are correct, then declare a property in which to store coordinates of the start location on the screen:

```
import UIKit

class ViewController: UIViewController {

    @IBOutlet weak var xCoord: UILabel!
    @IBOutlet weak var yCoord: UILabel!

    var startPoint: CGPoint?
    .
    .
    .
}
```

50.4 Implementing the touchesBegan Method

When the user first touches the screen the location coordinates need to be saved in the *startPoint* instance variable and those coordinates reported to the user. This can be achieved by implementing the *touchesBegan* method in the *ViewController.swift* file as follows:

```
override func touchesBegan(touches: NSSet, withEvent event: UIEvent) {
    let theTouch = touches.anyObject() as UITouch
    startPoint = theTouch.locationInView(self.view)

    let x = startPoint!.x
    let y = startPoint!.y

    xCoord.text = ("x = \(x)")
    yCoord.text = ("y = \(y)")
}
```

50.5 Implementing the touchesMoved Method

When the user's finger moves across the screen the *touchesMoved* event will be called repeatedly until the motion stops. By implementing the *touchesMoved* method in our view controller, therefore, we can detect the motion and display the revised coordinates to the user:

```
override func touchesMoved(touches: NSSet, withEvent event: UIEvent) {
    let theTouch = touches.anyObject() as UITouch

    var touchLocation = theTouch.locationInView(self.view)
    let x = touchLocation.x
    let y = touchLocation.y

    xCoord.text = ("x = \(x)")
    yCoord.text = ("y = \(y)")
}
```

50.6 Implementing the touchesEnded Method

When the user's finger lifts from the screen the *touchesEnded* method of the first responder is called. The final task, therefore, is to implement this method in our view controller such that it displays the start and end points of the gesture:

```
override func touchesEnded(touches: NSSet, withEvent event: UIEvent) {
    let theTouch = touches.anyObject() as UITouch

    var endPoint = theTouch.locationInView(self.view)
    let x = endPoint.x
    let y = endPoint.y

    xCoord.text = ("x = \(x)")
    yCoord.text = ("y = \(y)")
}
```

50.7 **Building and Running the Gesture Example**

Build and run the application using the run button located in the toolbar of the main Xcode project window. When the application starts (either in the iOS Simulator or on a physical device) touch the screen and drag to a new location before lifting your finger from the screen (or mouse button in the case of the iOS Simulator). During the motion the current coordinates will update in real time. Once the gesture is complete the start and end locations of the movement will be displayed.

50.8 **Summary**

Simply by implementing the standard touch event methods the motion of a gesture can easily be tracked by an iOS application. Much of a user's interaction with applications, however, involves some very specific gesture types such as swipes and pinches. To write code to correlate finger movement on the screen with a specific gesture type would be extremely complex. Fortunately, iOS 8 makes this task easy through the use of *gesture recognizers*. In the next chapter, entitled *Identifying Gestures using iOS 8 Gesture Recognizers*, we will look at this concept in more detail.

51. Identifying Gestures using iOS 8 Gesture Recognizers

In the chapter entitled *Detecting iOS 8 Touch Screen Gesture Motions* we looked at how to track the motion of contact with the touch screen of an iOS device. In practice, an application will need to respond to specific motions that take place during the course of a gesture. The swiping of a finger across the screen might, for example, be required to slide a new view onto the display. Similarly, a pinching motion is typically used in iOS applications to enlarge or reduce an image or view.

Prior to iOS 4, the identification of a gesture was the responsibility of the application developer and typically involved the creation of complex mathematical algorithms. In recognition of this complexity, and given the importance of gestures to user interaction with the iOS device, Apple introduced the UIGestureRecognizer class in iOS 4 thereby making the task of identifying the types of gestures a much easier task for the application developer.

The goal of this chapter, therefore, is to provide an overview of gesture recognition within the context of iOS 8. The next chapter will work through *An iOS 8 Gesture Recognition Tutorial*.

51.1 The UIGestureRecognizer Class

The UIGestureRecognizer class is used as the basis for a collection of subclasses, each designed to detect a specific type of gesture. These subclasses are as follows:

- **UITapGestureRecognizer** – This class is designed to detect when a user taps on the screen of the device. Both single and multiple taps may be detected based on the configuration of the class instance.
- **UIPinchGestureRecognizer** – Detects when a pinching motion is made by the user on the screen. This motion is typically used to zoom in or out of a view or to change the size of a visual component.
- **UIPanGestureRecognizer** – Detects when a dragging or panning gesture is made by the user.
- **UIScreenEdgePanGestureRecognizer** – Detects when a dragging or panning gesture is performed starting near the edge of the display screen.
- **UISwipeGestureRecognizer** – Used to detect when the user makes a swiping gesture across the screen. Instances of this class may be configured to detect motion only in specific directions (left, right, up or down).
- **UIRotationGestureRecognizer** – Identifies when the user makes a rotation gesture (essentially two fingers in contact with the screen located opposite each other and moving in a circular motion).

- **UILongPressGestureRecognizer** – Used to identify when the user touches the screen with one or more fingers for a specified period of time (also referred to as "touch and hold").

These gesture recognizers must be attached to the view on which the gesture will be performed via a call to the view object's *addGestureRecognizer* method. Recognizers must also be assigned an action method that is to be called when the specified gesture is detected. Gesture recognizers may subsequently be removed from a view via a call to the view's *removeGestureRecognizer* method, passing through as an argument the recognizer to be removed.

51.2 **Recognizer Action Messages**

The iOS gesture recognizers use the target-action model to notify the application of the detection of a specific gesture. When an instance of a gesture recognizer is created it is provided with the reference to the method to be called in the event that the corresponding gesture is detected.

51.3 **Discrete and Continuous Gestures**

Gestures fall into two distinct categories – *discrete* and *continuous*. A discrete gesture results in only a single call being made to the corresponding action method. Tap gestures (including multiple taps) are considered to be discrete because they only trigger the action method once. Gestures such as swipes, pans, rotations and pinches are deemed to be continuous in that they trigger a constant stream of calls to the corresponding action methods until the gesture ends.

51.4 **Obtaining Data from a Gesture**

Each gesture action method is passed as an argument a UIGestureRecognizer sender object which may be used to extract information about the gesture. For example, information about the scale factor and speed of a pinch gesture may be obtained by the action method. Similarly, the action method assigned to a rotation gesture recognizer may ascertain the amount of rotation performed by the user and the corresponding velocity.

51.5 **Recognizing Tap Gestures**

Tap gestures are detected using the UITapGestureRecognizer class. This must be allocated and initialized with an action selector referencing the method to be called when the gesture is detected. The number of taps that must be performed to constitute the full gesture may be defined by setting the *numberOfTapsRequired* property of the recognizer instance. The following code, for example, will result in a call to the *tapsDetected* method when two consecutive taps are detected on the corresponding view:

```
let doubleTap = UITapGestureRecognizer(target: self,
                        action: "tapDetected")
doubleTap.numberOfTapsRequired = 2

self.view.addGestureRecognizer(doubleTap)
```

A template method for the action method for this and other gesture recognizers is as follows:

```
func tapDetected() {
        // Code to respond to gesture here
}
```

51.6 Recognizing Pinch Gestures

Pinch gestures are detected using the UIPinchGestureRecognizer class. For example:

```
let pinchRecognizer = UIPinchGestureRecognizer(target: self,
                                    action: "pinchDetected")

self.view.addGestureRecognizer(pinchRecognizer)
```

51.7 Detecting Rotation Gestures

Rotation gestures are recognized by the UIRotationGestureRecognizer, the sample code for which is as follows:

```
let rotationRecognizer = UIRotationGestureRecognizer(target: self,
                                       action: "rotationDetected")

self.view.addGestureRecognizer(rotationRecognizer)
```

51.8 Recognizing Pan and Dragging Gestures

Pan and dragging gestures are detected using the UIPanGestureRecognizer class. Pan gestures are essentially any *continuous* gesture. For example, the random meandering of a finger across the screen will generally be considered by the recognizer as a pan or drag operation:

```
let panRecognizer = UIPanGestureRecognizer(target: self,
                                  action: "panDetected")

self.view.addGestureRecognizer(panRecognizer)
```

If both swipe and pan recognizers are attached to the same view it is likely that most swipes will be recognized as pans. Caution should be taken, therefore, when mixing these two gesture recognizers on the same view.

51.9 Recognizing Swipe Gestures

Swipe gestures are detected using the UISwipeGestureRecognizer class. All swipes, or just those in a specific direction, may be detected by assigning one of the following constants to the *direction* property of the class:

- UISwipeGestureRecognizerDirection.Right
- UISwipeGestureRecognizerDirection.Left
- UISwipeGestureRecognizerDirection.Up

- UISwipeGestureRecognizerDirection.Down

Note that when programming in swift, the above constants may be abbreviated to *.Right*, *.Left*, *.Up*, and *.Down*.

If no direction is specified the default is to detect rightward swipes. The following code configures a UISwipeGestureRecognizer instance to detect upward swipes:

```
let swipeRecognizer = UISwipeGestureRecognizer(target: self,
                              action: "swipeDetected")
swipeRecognizer.direction = .Up

self.view.addGestureRecognizer(swipeRecognizer)
```

51.10 **Recognizing Long Touch (Touch and Hold) Gestures**

Long touches are detected using the UILongPressGestureRecognizer class. The requirements for the gesture may be specified in terms of touch duration, number of touches, number of taps and allowable movement during the touch. These requirements are specified by the *minimumPressDuration*, *numberOfTouchesRequired*, *numberOfTapsRequired* and *allowableMovement* properties of the class respectively. The following code fragment configures the recognizer to detect long presses of 3 seconds or more involving one finger. The default allowable movement is not set and therefore defaults to 10 pixels:

```
let longPressRecognizer = UILongPressGestureRecognizer(target: self,
                              action: "longPressDetected")
longPressRecognizer.minimumPressDuration = 3
longPressRecognizer.numberOfTouchesRequired = 1

self.view.addGestureRecognizer(longPressRecognizer)
```

51.11 **Summary**

In this chapter we have provided an overview of gesture recognizers and outlined some examples of how to detect the various types of gesture typically used by iOS device users. In the next chapter we will work step-by-step through a tutorial designed to show these theories in practice.

52. An iOS 8 Gesture Recognition Tutorial

Having covered the theory of gesture recognition on iOS in the chapter entitled *Identifying Gestures using iOS 8 Gesture Recognizers*, the purpose of this chapter is to work through an example application intended to demonstrate the use of the various UIGestureRecognizer subclasses.

The application created in this chapter will configure recognizers to detect a number of different gestures on the iPhone or iPad display and update a status label with information about each recognized gesture.

52.1 Creating the Gesture Recognition Project

Begin by invoking Xcode and creating a new iOS *Single View Application* project named *Recognizer* using Swift as the programming language and with the devices menu set to *Universal*.

52.2 Designing the User Interface

The only visual component that will be present on our UIView object will be the label used to notify the user of the type of gesture detected. Since the text displayed on this label will need to be updated from within the application code it will need to be connected to an outlet. In addition, the view controller will also contain five gesture recognizer objects to detect pinches, taps, rotations, swipes and long presses. When triggered, these objects will need to call action methods in order to update the label with a notification to the user that the corresponding gesture has been detected.

Select the *Main.storyboard* file and drag a Label object from the Object Library panel to the center of the view. Once positioned, use the Auto Layout *Align* menu to enable horizontal and vertical "Center in Container" constraints as illustrated in Figure 52-1:

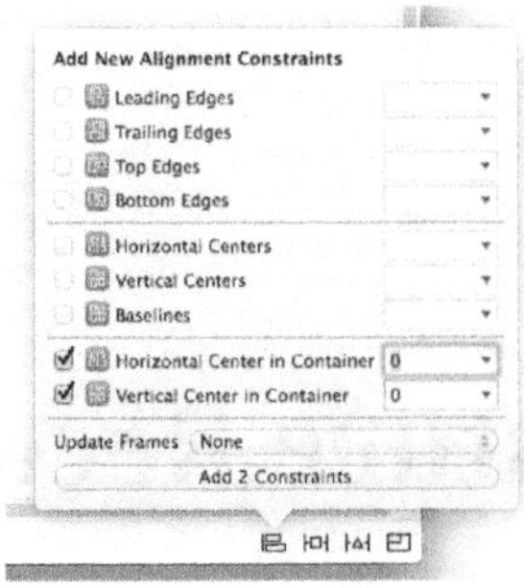

Figure 52-1

Select the label object in the view canvas, display the Assistant Editor panel and verify that the editor is displaying the contents of the *ViewController.swift* file. Ctrl-click on the same label object and drag to a position just below the class declaration line in the Assistant Editor. Release the line and, in the resulting connection dialog, establish an outlet connection named *statusLabel*.

Next, the non-visual gesture recognizer objects need to be added to the design. Scroll down the list of objects in the Object Library panel until the *Tap Gesture Recognizer* object comes into view. Drag and drop the object onto the View in the design area (if the object is dropped outside the view, the connection between the recognizer and the view on which the gestures are going to be performed will not be established). Repeat these steps to add Pinch, Rotation, Swipe and Long Press Gesture Recognizer objects to the design. Note that the document outline panel (which can be displayed by clicking on the panel button in the lower left hand corner of the storyboard panel) has updated to reflect the presence of the gesture recognizer objects as illustrated in Figure 52-2. An icon for each recognizer added to the view also appears within the toolbar across the top of the storyboard scene.

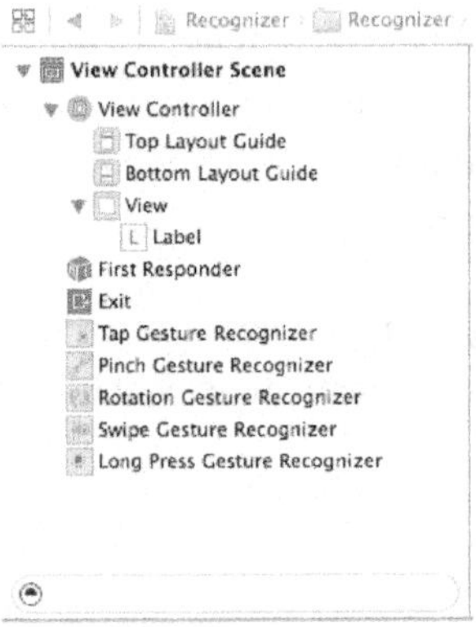

Figure 52-2

Within the document outline panel, select the Tap Gesture Recognizer instance and display the Attributes Inspector (*View -> Utilities -> Show Attributes Inspector*). Within the attributes panel, change the *Taps* value to 2 so that only double taps are detected.

Similarly, select the Long Press Recognizer object and change the *Min Duration* attribute to 3 seconds.

Having added and configured the gesture recognizers, the next step is to connect each recognizer to its corresponding action method.

Display the Assistant Editor and verify that it is displaying the content of *ViewController.swift*. Ctrl-click on the *Tap Gesture Recognizer* object either in the document outline panel or in the scene toolbar and drag the line to the area immediately beneath the *viewDidLoad* method in the Assistant Editor panel. Release the line and, within the resulting connection dialog, establish an Action method configured to call a method named *tapDetected* with the *Type* value set to *UITapGestureRecognizer* as illustrated in Figure 52-3:

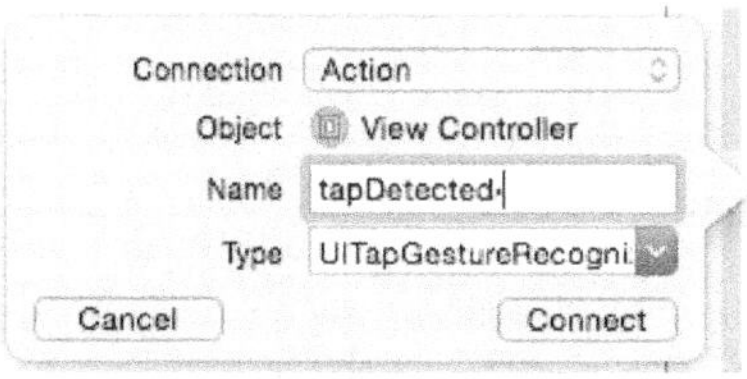

Figure 52-3

Repeat these steps to establish action connections for the pinch, rotation, swipe and long press gesture recognizers to methods named *pinchDetected*, *rotationDetected*, *swipeDetected* and *longPressDetected* respectively, taking care to select the corresponding type value for each action.

52.3 Implementing the Action Methods

Having configured the gesture recognizers, the next step is to add code to the action methods that will be called by each recognizer when the corresponding gesture is detected. The methods stubs created by Xcode reside in the *ViewController.swift* file and will update the status label with information about the detected gesture:

```
@IBAction func tapDetected(sender: UITapGestureRecognizer) {
    statusLabel.text = "Double Tap"
}


@IBAction func pinchDetected(sender: UIPinchGestureRecognizer) {
    let scale = sender.scale
    let velocity = sender.velocity
    let resultString =
        "Pinch - scale = \(scale), velocity = \(velocity)"

    statusLabel.text = resultString
}


@IBAction func rotationDetected(sender: UIRotationGestureRecognizer) {
```

```
    let radians = sender.rotation
    let velocity = sender.velocity
    let resultString =
        "Rotation - Radians = \(radians), velocity = \(velocity)"

    statusLabel.text = resultString
}

@IBAction func swipeDetected(sender: UISwipeGestureRecognizer) {
    statusLabel.text = "Right swipe"
}

@IBAction func longPressDetected(sender: UILongPressGestureRecognizer) {
    statusLabel.text = "Long Press"
}
```

52.4 Testing the Gesture Recognition Application

The final step is to build and run the application. In order to fully test the pinching and rotation recognition it will be necessary to run the application on a physical device (since it is not possible to emulate two simultaneous touches within the iOS Simulator environment). Assuming a provisioned device is attached (see *Testing Apps on iOS 8 Devices with Xcode 6* for more details) simply click on the Xcode run button. Once the application loads on the device, perform the appropriate gestures on the display and watch the status label update accordingly. Note that when testing on an iPhone it will be necessary to rotate the device into landscape orientation in order to be able to see the full text displayed on the label.

52.5 Summary

The iOS SDK includes a set of gesture recognizer classes designed to detect swipe, tap, long press, pan, pinch and rotation gestures. This chapter has worked through the creation of an example application that demonstrates how to implement gesture detection using these classes within the Interface Builder environment.

53. Implementing TouchID Authentication in iOS 8 Apps

In the world of computer security, user authentication falls into the three categories of something you know, something you have and something you are. The "something you know" category typically involves a memorized password or PIN number and is considered the least secure option. A more secure option is the "something you have" approach which usually takes the form of a small authentication token or device which generates one-time access codes on request.

The final category, "something you are", refers to a physical attribute that is unique to the user. This, of course, involves biometrics in the form of a retina scan, voice recognition or fingerprint.

With the iPhone 5s, Apple introduced a built-in fingerprint scanner which enabled users to access the device and make purchases in the iTunes, App and iBooks stores using fingerprint authentication. With the introduction of iOS 8, this biometric authentication capability can now be built into your own applications.

53.1 The Local Authentication Framework

TouchID based authentication for iOS applications is implemented using the Local Authentication Framework. The key class within this framework is the LAContext class which, among other tasks, is used to evaluate the authentication abilities of the device on which the application is running and perform the authentication.

53.2 Checking for TouchID Availability

Not all iOS devices have the fingerprint scanner and, even on devices with a scanner, not all users will have activated the TouchID authentication features. The first step in using TouchID authentication, therefore, is to check that TouchID authentication is a viable option on the device:

```
let context = LAContext()

var error: NSError?

if context.canEvaluatePolicy(
        LAPolicy.DeviceOwnerAuthenticationWithBiometrics,
            error: &error) {
        // TouchID is available on the device
```

```
} else {
        // TouchID is not available on the device
        // No scanner or user has not set up TouchID
}
```

If TouchID authentication is not available, the reason can be identified by accessing the errorCode property of the error parameter and will fall into one of the following categories:

- **LAError.TouchIDNotEnrolled** – The user has not enrolled any fingerprints into TouchID on the device.
- **LAError.PasscodeNotSet** – The user has not yet configured a passcode on the device.
- **LAError.TouchIDNotAvailable** – The device does not have a TouchID fingerprint scanner.

53.3 Evaluating TouchID Policy

In the event that TouchID is available, the next step is to evaluate the policy (which in terms of TouchID involves prompting the user to provide authentication). This task is performed by calling the *evaluatePolicy* method of the LAContext instance, passing through the authentication policy type and a message to be displayed to the user. The task is performed asynchronously and a *reply* closure expression called once the user has provided input:

```
context.evaluatePolicy(
        LAPolicy.DeviceOwnerAuthenticationWithBiometrics,
        localizedReason: "Authentication is required for access",
        reply: {(success, error) in
                // Code to handle reply here
  })
```

The reply closure expression is passed a Boolean value indicating the success or otherwise of the authentication and an NSError object from which the nature of any failure can be identified via the corresponding error code. Failure to authenticate will fall into one of the following three categories:

- **LAError.SystemCancel** – The authentication process was cancelled by the operating system. This error typically occurs when the application is placed in the background.
- **LAError.UserCancel** - The authentication process was cancelled by the user.
- **LAError.UserFallback** – The user opted to authenticate using a password instead of using TouchID.

In the event of the user fallback, it is the responsibility of the application to prompt for and verify a password before providing access.

If the authentication process is successful, however, the application should provide the user with access to whatever screens, data or functionality were being protected.

53.4 **A TouchID Example Project**

Launch Xcode and create a new iOS Universal Single View Application project named *TouchID* using Swift as the programming language.

Select the *Main.storyboard* file and drag and drop a Button view so that it is positioned in the center of the storyboard scene. Double-click on the button and change the text so that it reads "Test TouchID".

With the button still selected, display the Auto Layout Align menu and configure both horizontal and vertical *Center in Container* constraints.

Finally, display the Assistant Editor and Ctrl-click and drag from the button view to a position just beneath the *viewDidLoad* method in the *ViewController.swift* file. Release the line and, in the connection dialog, establish an Action connection to a method named *testTouchID*.

On completion of the user interface design the layout should resemble Figure 53-1:

Figure 53-1

53.5 **Checking for TouchID Availability**

With the user interface designed, the next step is to add some code to the *testTouchID* function to verify that the device can handle TouchID authentication. Select the *ViewController.swift* file, import the LocalAuthentication Framework and add code to the *testTouchID* method as follows:

```
import UIKit
import LocalAuthentication

class ViewController: UIViewController {

    override func viewDidLoad() {
        super.viewDidLoad()
        // Do any additional setup after loading the view, typically from
a nib.
```

```
    }

    @IBAction func testTouchID(sender: AnyObject) {

        let context = LAContext()

        var error: NSError?

        if context.canEvaluatePolicy(
                LAPolicy.DeviceOwnerAuthenticationWithBiometrics,
                    error: &error) {

            // Device can use TouchID

        } else {
            // Device cannot use TouchID
            switch error!.code{

            case LAError.TouchIDNotEnrolled.rawValue:
                notifyUser("TouchID is not enrolled",
                        err: error?.localizedDescription)

            case LAError.PasscodeNotSet.rawValue:
                notifyUser("A passcode has not been set",
                        err: error?.localizedDescription)

            default:
                notifyUser("TouchID not available",
                        err: error?.localizedDescription)

            }
        }
    }
.
.
}
```

Before proceeding, implement the *notifyUser* method as follows:

```
func notifyUser(msg: String, err: String?) {
    let alert = UIAlertController(title: msg,
            message: err,
            preferredStyle: UIAlertControllerStyle.Alert)
```

```
let cancelAction = UIAlertAction(title: "OK",
          style: .Cancel, handler: nil)

alert.addAction(cancelAction)

self.presentViewController(alert, animated: true,
              completion: nil)
}
```

53.6 Seeking TouchID Authentication

The next task is to attempt to obtain authentication from the user. This involves a call to the *evaluatePolicy* method of the local authentication context:

```
@IBAction func testTouchID(sender: AnyObject) {

    let context = LAContext()

    var error: NSError?

    if context.canEvaluatePolicy(
        LAPolicy.DeviceOwnerAuthenticationWithBiometrics,
            error: &error) {

        // Device can use TouchID

            context.evaluatePolicy(
                LAPolicy.DeviceOwnerAuthenticationWithBiometrics,
                localizedReason: "Access requires authentication",
                    reply: {(success, error) in

            if error != nil {

                switch error!.code {

                    case LAError.SystemCancel.rawValue:
                        self.notifyUser("Session cancelled",
                            err: error?.localizedDescription)

                    case LAError.UserCancel.rawValue:
                    self.notifyUser("Please try again",
                            err: error?.localizedDescription)

                    case LAError.UserFallback.rawValue:
```

```
                    self.notifyUser("Authentication",
                        err: "Password option selected")
                    // Custom code to obtain password here

              default:
                    self.notifyUser("Authentication failed",
                        err: error?.localizedDescription)
              }

          } else {
              self.notifyUser("Authentication Successful",
                  err: "You now have full access")
          }

      })

  } else {
      // Device cannot use TouchID

  .
  .
  .


  }
}
```

The code added to the method initiates the authentication process and displays a message confirming a successful authentication. In the event of an authentication failure, a message is displayed to the user indicating the reason for the failure. Selection of the password option simply confirms that the option was selected. The actual action taken in this situation will be application specific but will likely involve prompting for a password and verifying it against a database of valid passwords.

53.7 Testing the Application

Compile and run the application on a physical iOS device (TouchID is not available on the simulator environment) and tap on the *Test TouchID* button. If the device supports TouchID and has been enabled and configured by the user, the touch request panel will appear as demonstrated in Figure 53-2:

Figure 53-2

Authenticate with a registered fingerprint and wait for the confirmation of successful authentication to appear. Experiment with a variety of failure scenarios to verify that the error handling code covers all events (such as tapping the Cancel button or attempting to authenticate with a non-registered fingerprint).

53.8 **Summary**

Introduced with iOS 7 and the iPhone 5s device, TouchID has been provided to iOS users as a way to gain access to devices and to make Apple related purchases. With the introduction of iOS 8, fingerprint authentication using the TouchID system is now available to application developers. This chapter has outlined the steps involved in using the Local Authentication Framework to implement biometric authentication using the TouchID system.

54. An Overview of iOS 8 Collection View and Flow Layout

The Collection View and Flow Layout combine to provide a flexible way to present content to the user. This is essentially achieved by providing a mechanism by which data driven content can be displayed in cells and the arrangement, appearance and behavior of those cells configured to meet a variety of different layout and organizational needs.

Before the introduction of Collection Views and Flow Layout, the closest iOS came to providing organized data presentation involved the use of the Table View. Whilst still a powerful user interface design option, the Table View was intended to fill a very specific need and, as such, has some limitations in terms of flexibility. Table View, for example, displays data in cells arranged in a single column layout. Collection views, on the other hand, provide a high degree of flexibility, allowing cells to be organized in just about any configuration imaginable, including grids, stacks, tiles and circular arrangements.

The goal of this chapter is to present an overview of the key elements that make up collection views prior to working through a step by step tutorial in the next chapter, entitled *An iOS 8 Storyboard-based Collection View Tutorial*.

54.1 An Overview of Collection Views

In the chapter entitled *Using Xcode 6 Storyboards to Build Dynamic TableViews with Prototype Table View Cells* a Table View layout was used to display a list of tourist destinations and corresponding images. The fact is that whilst this presented the necessary information, the Table View provided very little in the way of customization options. Had the user interface been designed using a collection view, a much more visually appealing user interface could have been implemented. Figure 54-1, for example, illustrates how some images of cars could be organized using a collection view configuration.

Figure 54-1

Whilst not entirely obvious from the previous screenshot, the collection view is actually scrollable, allowing the user to swipe left or right to view other car images. It is also important to note that this example is just the default behavior of a collection view with a flow layout. Customization options far beyond this are possible using collection views.

At an abstract level, a collection view consists of four key elements consisting of *cells*, *supplementary views*, *decoration views* and a *layout object*. A cell is a representation of an item of data to be displayed (for example an image or a set of text based data).

As with the Table View, a collection view may be divided into multiple sections. Supplementary views are objects that provide additional information about a section in a collection view. These are somewhat similar to section headers and footers in table views but are more general purpose and provide a greater level of flexibility in terms of positioning and content.

Decoration views can be used to provide a decorative background for the collection view which scrolls along with the content. The classic example of a decoration view in Apple's own demonstrations involves constructing the image of a bookshelf behind a collection view containing photo images. It is important to note that the standard Flow Layout class does not support decoration views.

In practical terms, a collection view consists of multiple class instances, each of which will be described in more detail in the remainder of this chapter.

54.2 The UICollectionView Class

The UICollectionView class is responsible for managing the data items that are to be displayed to the user. The collection view instance needs a data source object from which to obtain the data items to be displayed, together with a delegate object to handle user interaction with the collection. These objects must implement the UICollectionViewDataSource and UICollectionViewDelegate protocols respectively.

Perhaps the most important requirement for the UICollectionView class is a layout object to control the layout and organization of the cells. By default, the UICollectionViewFlowLayout class is used by instances of the UICollectionView class. In the event that the flow layout does not provide the necessary behavior, this class may also be subclassed and extended to provide additional functionality. Perhaps the most impressive fact, however, is that an entirely new layout class may be created by subclassing UICollectionViewLayout and implementing application specific layout capabilities within that class. The custom layout is then essentially "plugged in" to the UICollectionView instance where it will dictate the layout of the data cells as it has been designed to do.

The UICollectionView class also includes a wide range of methods that can be used to perform such tasks as to add, remove, move, modify and select items.

54.3 **The UICollectionViewCell Class**

As the name suggests, the UICollectionViewCell class is responsible for displaying whatever data is provided to the UICollectionView instance by the data source with one cell corresponding to one data item. In terms of architecture, this class consists of two background views and one content view. The two background views may be used to provide a visual cue to the user when the corresponding cell is selected or highlighted. The content view contains the objects necessary to display the data to the user and can consist of any combination of valid UIKit classes. When adding subviews to a cell it is imperative that those objects be added to the contentView and not the background views, otherwise the objects will not be visible to the user.

There is a clear separation between layout and the contents of a cell. The cell only knows what to display, the sizing and positioning of the cell within the wider context of the collection view is controlled by the layout object assigned to the collection view.

Instances of UICollectionViewCell class are not typically instantiated directly in code. Instead, the class is registered as the cell class for a collection view and is then created internally as needed. Collection views are scrollable and, consequently, at any one time only a subset of the cells in a collection are visible. This enables the system to reuse cell objects that are currently scrolled outside of the viewable area of the screen and only create new ones when necessary. This is achieved using a queuing mechanism and results in improved performance, particularly when dealing with larger data sets.

54.4 **The UICollectionReusableView Class**

The base class from which the UICellCollectionView class is derived, this class is most typically subclassed in application code to create supplementary views.

54.5 **The UICollectionViewFlowLayout Class**

The UICollectionViewFlowLayout class is the default layout class for collection views and is designed to layout cells in a grid-like manner.

This class requires a delegate object that conforms to the UICollectionViewDelegateFlowLayout protocol which is typically the collection view's UICollectionViewDelegate object.

By default, flow is implemented in a manner similar to that of "line wrapping" in a text editor. When one row of cells is full, the cells flow onto the next row and so on until all cells capable of fitting into the currently visible display region are visible. The flow layout class supports both horizontal and vertical scrolling configurable via the *scrollDirection* property. In addition, properties such as the spacing between lines of cells in the grid and cells in a row may be configured, together with default sizes for cells and supplementary views (unless overridden via methods implemented in the delegate object).

54.6 **The UICollectionViewLayoutAttributes Class**

Each item in a collection view, be it a cell or a supplementary view, has associated with it a set of attributes. The UICollectionViewLayoutAttributes class serves as an object into which these attributes can be stored and transferred between objects. A Flow Layout object will, for example, be asked by the collection view object to return the attributes for a cell at a given index in a collection view via a call to the *layoutAttributesForItemAtIndexPath* method. This method, in turn, returns those attributes encapsulated in a UICollectionViewLayoutAttributes object. Similarly, such object instances can be used to apply new attributes to a collection view element. The attributes stored by the UICollectionViewLayoutAttributes class are as follows (keeping in mind that this class may be subclassed and extended to allow the storage of other values):

- **alpha** – the transparency of the item.
- **center** – the location of the center of the item.
- **frame** – the CGRect frame in which the item is displayed.
- **hidden** – whether or not the item is currently visible.
- **indexPath** – the index path location of the item in the collection view.
- **representedElementCategory** – The type of item for which the attributes apply (i.e. for a cell, supplementary or decoration view).
- **size** – the size of the item.
- **transform3D** – the current transform of the item. This attribute can be used to perform tasks such as rotating or scaling the item.
- **zIndex** – controls the position of the item in the z axis (in other words whether or not it is on top of or below other overlapping items).

54.7 **The UICollectionViewDataSource Protocol**

The UICollectionViewDataSource protocol needs to be implemented by the class responsible for supplying the collection view with the pre-configured cells and supplementary views to be displayed to the user. This basically consists of a number of methods that define information such as how many items of data are to be displayed, how the data is divided into different sections and, most importantly, supplies the collection view with the cell objects to be displayed.

Mandatory methods in the protocol are as follows:

- **collectionView(_:numberOfItemsInSection:)** - Returns the number of items to be displayed in the specified section of the collection view.
- **collectionView(_:cellForItemAtIndexPath:)** - This method is called by the collection view when it is ready to display a cell at the specified index path location in the collection view. It is required to return a cell object configured appropriately for the referenced index.

Optional methods in the protocol are as follows:

- **numberOfSectionsInCollectionView(_:)** - Indicates to the collection view the number of sections into which the collection view is to be divided.
- **collectionView(_:viewForSupplementaryElementOfKind:atIndexPath:)** - Called by the collection view to request a supplementary view of the specified kind. Returns an appropriately configured object to be displayed. In terms of the UICollectionViewFlowLayout class, the layout will request a supplementary view for either a header (UICollectionElementKindSectionHeader) or footer (UICollectionElementKindSectionFooter).

54.8 **The UICollectionViewDelegate Protocol**

The UICollectionViewDelegate protocol defines a set of optional methods which, if implemented, will be called when certain events take place within the corresponding collection. These methods relate primarily to handling user interaction with the collection view elements (such as selecting a specific cell). Some of the key methods in this protocol include:

- **collectionView(_:shouldSelectItemAtIndexPath:)** - Returns a boolean value indicating whether the specified item is selectable by the user.
- **collectionView(_:didSelectItemAtIndexPath:)** - Called by the collection view when the specified item has been selected by the user.
- **collectionView(_:shouldDeselectItemAtIndexPath:)** - Returns a boolean value to indicate whether the specified item may be deselected by the user.
- **collectionView(_:didDeselectItemAtIndexPath:)** - Called by the collection view when the specified item has been selected by the user.
- **collectionView(_:shouldHighlightItemAtIndexPath:)** - Returns a boolean value indicating whether the specified item should be highlighted as a pre-cursor to possible selection by the user.

- **collectionView(_:didHighlightItemAtIndexPath:)** - Called by the collection view when the specified item has been highlighted.
- **collectionView(_:didUnhighlightItemAtIndexPath:)** - Called by the collection view when the specified item has been un-highlighted.
- **collectionView(_:didEndDisplayingCell:forItemAtIndexPath:)** - Called by the collection view when the specified cell has been removed from the collection view.
- **collectionView(_:didEndDisplayingSupplementaryView:forElementOfKind:atIndexPath:)** - Called by the collection view when the specified supplementary view has been removed from the collection view.

54.9 **The UICollectionViewDelegateFlowLayout Protocol**

The UICollectionViewFlowLayout class has a number of properties that can be set to globally set default characteristics for items within a collection view (for example section inset, item spacing, line spacing, inter-cell spacing, supplementary view header and footer sizing etc). Alternatively, these values may be overridden on a per-cell and per-section basis by implementing the following delegate methods in a class which conforms to the UICollectionViewDelegateFlowLayout protocol. In most cases, this will be the same class as that implementing the UICollectionViewDelegate protocol. Note that in each case, the method is passed a reference either to the cell or section for which information is required:

- **collectionView(_:layout:sizeForItemAtIndexPath:)** - Required to return to the flow layout object the size attributes for the item at the specified index path.
- **collectionView(_:layout:insetForSectionAtIndex:)** - Required to return the inset value for the specified collection view section.
- **collectionView(_:layout:minimumLineSpacingForSectionAtIndex:)** - Required to return the inset value for the specified collection view section.
- **collectionView(_:layout:minimumInteritemSpacingForSectionAtIndex:)** - Required to return the interim spacing between cells in a row for the specified collection view section.
- **collectionView(_:layout:referenceSizeForHeaderInSection:)** - Required to return the size for the header supplementary view for specified collection view section. Note that if a size is not specified, the view will not appear.
- **collectionView(_:layout:referenceSizeForFooterInSection:)** - Required to return the size for the footer supplementary view for specified collection view section. Note that if a size is not specified, the view will not appear.

54.10 **Cell and View Reuse**

As previously discussed, the code for a typical application using a collection view will not directly create instances of either the cell or supplementary view classes. The reasoning behind this becomes evident when performance and memory requirements are taken into consideration. Consider, for example, a collection view that is required to display 1000 photo images. It can be assumed with a reasonable degree of certainty that only a small percentage of cells will be visible to the user at any one time. If the application were permitted to create each of the 1000 cells in advance the device would very quickly run into memory limitations.

Instead, the application begins by registering with the collection view the class to be used for cell objects, along with a *reuse identifier*. If the cell class was written in code, the registration is performed using the *registerClass* method of UICollectionView. For example:

```
self.collectionView?.registerClass(UICollectionViewCell.self,
            forCellWithReuseIdentifier: "MyCell")
```

In the event that the cell is contained within an Interface Builder NIB file, the *registerNib* method is used instead.

The same concept applies to supplementary views which must also be registered with the collection view using either the *registerClass:forSupplementaryViewOfKind:* and *registerNib:forSupplementaryViewOfKind* methods.

Perhaps the most important point to remember from this chapter is that if the cell or supplementary views are created using prototypes within a storyboard it is not necessary to register the class in code and, in fact, doing so will prevent the cell or view from appearing when the application runs and may cause the application to crash.

As the collection view initializes, it calls the *cellForItemAtIndexPath* method of the datasource class passing through the index path for which a cell object is required. This method will then call the *dequeueReusableCellWithReuseIdentifier* method of the collection view, passing through both the index path and the reuse ID assigned to the cell class when it was registered, to find out if there is a reusable cell object in the queue that can be used for this new cell. Since this is the initialization phase and no cells have been deemed eligible for reuse, the method will create a new cell and return it. Once all the visible cells have been created the collection view will stop asking for more cells. The code for *cellForItemAtIndexPath* will typically read as follows (though the code to customize the cell before returning it will be implementation specific):

```
override func collectionView(collectionView: UICollectionView!,
        cellForItemAtIndexPath indexPath: NSIndexPath!) ->
            UICollectionViewCell! {

    let cell =
collectionView.dequeueReusableCellWithReuseIdentifier(reuseIdentifier,
        forIndexPath: indexPath)

    // Configure the cell
    let image = UIImage(named: myImages[indexPath.row])
    cell.cellImage.image = image

    return cell
}
```

As the user scrolls through the collection view, some cells will move out of the visible frame. When this happens, the collection view places them on the reuse queue. As cells are moving out of view, new ones are likely to be coming into view. For each cell moving into the view area, the collection view will call *cellForItemAtIndexPath*. This time, however, when a call to *dequeueReusableCellWithReuseIdentifier* is made, it is most likely that an existing cell object will be returned from the reuse queue, thereby avoiding the necessity to create a new object.

These same reuse concepts apply equally to supplementary views, with the exception that the collection view will call the *viewForSupplementaryElementOfKind* method of the data source when seeking a view object which must, in turn, call *dequeueReusableSupplementaryViewOfKind*.

54.11 **Summary**

Collection view and the flow layout were introduced into iOS 6 to provide a flexible approach to displaying data items to the user. The key objectives of collection views are flexibility and performance.

This chapter has outlined the overall concepts behind collection views and flow layout before looking in some detail at the different classes that can be brought together to implement collection views in iOS 8 applications. Finally, the chapter provided an explanation of cell and supplementary view object reuse.

The next chapter will work through the creation of an example application that utilizes collection views to present a gallery of images to the user.

55. An iOS 8 Storyboard-based Collection View Tutorial

The primary goal of this chapter is to demonstrate, in a tutorial format, the steps involved in implementing a collection view based application user interface and, in doing so, serve to re-enforce the collection view concepts outlined in the previous chapter. By far the most productive way to implement collection views (and the approach used in this tutorial) is to take advantage of the Storyboard feature of Xcode and, in particular, the collection view cell and supplementary view prototyping options of Interface Builder.

55.1 Creating the Collection View Example Project

Launch Xcode and create a new project by selecting the options to create a new iOS application based on the *Single View Application* template. Enter *CollectionDemo* as the product name, choose Swift as the programming language and set the device menu to *Universal*.

55.2 Removing the Template View Controller

Based on the template selection made when the project was set up, Xcode has created a generic UIViewController based subclass for the application. For the purposes of this tutorial, however, this needs to be replaced with a UICollectionViewController subclass. Begin, therefore, by selecting the *ViewController.swift* file in the project navigator and pressing the keyboard delete key. When prompted, click the button to move the file to trash.

Next, select the *Main.storyboard* file and, in the storyboard canvas, select the view controller so that it is outlined in blue (the view controller is selected by clicking on the toolbar area at the top of the layout view) and tap the keyboard delete key to remove the controller and leave a blank storyboard.

55.3 Adding a Collection View Controller to the Storyboard

The first element that needs to be added to the project is a UICollectionViewController subclass. To add this, select the Xcode *File -> New -> File...* menu option. In the resulting panel, select *Source* listed under *iOS* in the left hand panel, followed by *Cocoa Touch Class* in the main panel before clicking *Next*.

On the subsequent screen, name the new class *MyCollectionViewController* and, from the *Subclass of* drop down menu, choose *UICollectionViewController*. Verify that the option to create an XIB file is switched off before clicking *Next*. Choose a location for the files and then click *Create*.

The project now has a new file named *MyCollectionViewController.swift* which represents a new class named *MyCollectionViewController* which is itself a subclass of *UICollectionViewController*.

The next step is to add a UICollectionViewController instance to the storyboard and then associate it with the newly created class. Select the *Main.storyboard* file and drag and drop a Collection View Controller object from the Object Library panel onto the storyboard canvas as illustrated in Figure 55-1.

Note that the UICollectionViewController added to the storyboard has also brought with it a UICollectionView instance (indicated by the black background) and a prototype cell (represented by the white square outline located in the top left hand corner of the collection view).

Figure 55-1

With the new view controller selected in the storyboard, display the Identity Inspector either by selecting the toolbar item in the Utilities panel or via the View -> Utilities -> Show Identity Inspector menu option and change the Class setting (Figure 55-2) from the generic UICollectionViewController class to the newly added *MyCollectionViewController* class.

Figure 55-2

With the view controller scene still selected, display the Attributes Inspector and enable the *Is Initial View Controller* option so that the view controller is loaded when the app starts.

55.4 **Adding the Collection View Cell Class to the Project**

With a subclass of UICollectionViewController added to the project, a new class must now be added which subclasses UICollectionViewCell.

Once again, select the Xcode *File -> New -> File...* menu option. In the resulting panel, select the iOS *Source* option from the left hand panel, followed by *Cocoa Touch Class* in the main panel before clicking *Next.*

On the subsequent screen, name the new class *MyCollectionViewCell* and from the *Subclass of* drop down menu choose *UICollectionViewCell*. Click *Next*, choose a location for the files and then click *Create*.

Return to the *Main.storyboard* file and select the white square in the collection view. This is the prototype cell for the collection view and needs to be assigned a reuse identifier and associated with the new class. With the cell selected, open the Identity Inspector panel and change the Class to *MyCollectionViewCell*. Remaining in the Utilities panel, display the Attributes Inspector (Figure 55-3) and enter *MyCell* as the reuse identifier.

Figure 55-3

55.5 **Designing the Cell Prototype**

With the basic collection view classes implemented and associated with the storyboard objects, it is now time to design the cell. This is, quite simply, a matter of dragging and dropping items from the Object Library onto the prototype cell in the storyboard view. Additionally the size of the cell may be modified by selecting it and using the resulting resize handles. The exact design of the cell is entirely dependent on what is to be displayed. For the purposes of this example, however, each cell is simply going to display an image.

Begin by resizing the cell to a slightly larger size, locating the Image View object in the Object Library panel and dragging and dropping it into the prototype cell as shown in Figure 55-4.

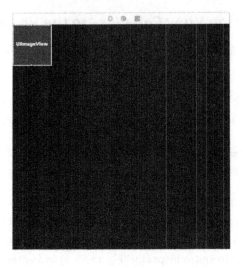

Figure 55-4

With the Image View object selected in the storyboard scene, select the *Pin* menu from the toolbar located in the lower right hand corner of the storyboard panel and set up *Spacing to nearest neighbor* constraints on all four sides of the view with the *Constrain to margins* option turned off as illustrated in Figure 55-5:

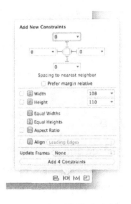

Figure 55-5

Once configured, click on the *Add 4 Constraints* button to establish the constraints.

Since it will be necessary to assign an image when a cell is configured, an outlet to the Image View will be needed. Display the Assistant Editor, make sure it is listing the code for the *MyCollectionViewCell.swift* file then Ctrl-click and drag from the Image View object to a position immediately beneath the class declaration line. Release the line and, in the resulting connection panel, establish an outlet connection named *imageView*. On completion of the connection, select *MyCollectionViewCell.swift* in the project navigator and verify that it reads as follows:

```
import UIKit
```

```
class MyCollectionViewCell: UICollectionViewCell {

    @IBOutlet weak var imageView: UIImageView!
}
```

With the connection established, the prototype cell implementation is complete.

55.6 Implementing the Data Model

The data model for this example application is going to consist of a set of images, each of which will be displayed in a cell within the collection view. The first step in creating this model is to load the images into the project. These images can be found in the *carImagesSmall* folder of the sample code archive which is downloadable from the following URL:

http://www.ebookfrenzy.com/print/ios8

Once downloaded, unzip the archive and drag and drop the 12 image files onto the *Supporting Files* section of the Xcode project navigator panel.

Next, select the *MyCollectionViewController.swift* file and declare an array into which will be stored the image file names. Also change the *reuseIdentifier* constant to match the identifier assigned to the cell in Interface Builder:

```
import UIKit

let reuseIdentifier = "MyCell"

class MyCollectionViewController: UICollectionViewController {

    var carImages = [String]()
    .
    .
    .
}
```

Finally, edit the *MyCollectionViewController.swift* file and modify the *viewDidLoad* method to initialize the array with the names of the car image files. Also comment out or delete the following line so that it is no longer executed when the application runs. As outlined in the previous chapter, it is not necessary to register cell classes when using Storyboard prototypes:

```
self.collectionView?.registerClass(UICollectionViewCell.self,
            forCellWithReuseIdentifier: reuseIdentifier)
```

The completed *viewDidLoad* method should read as follows:

```
override func viewDidLoad() {
```

```
    super.viewDidLoad()

    // Uncomment the following line to preserve selection between
presentations
    // self.clearsSelectionOnViewWillAppear = false

    // Register cell classes
    self.collectionView?.registerClass(UICollectionViewCell.self,
            forCellWithReuseIdentifier: reuseIdentifier)

    // Do any additional setup after loading the view.
    carImages = ["chevy_small.jpg",
                "mini_small.jpg",
                "rover_small.jpg",
                "smart_small.jpg",
                "highlander_small.jpg",
                "venza_small.jpg",
                "volvo_small.jpg",
                "vw_small.jpg",
                "ford_small.jpg",
                "nissan_small.jpg",
                "honda_small.jpg",
                "jeep_small.jpg"]
}
```

55.7 Implementing the Data Source

As outlined in the chapter entitled *An Overview of iOS 8 Collection View and Flow Layout*, a collection view needs a data source and a delegate in order to provide all the functionality it is capable of providing. By default, Xcode has designated the *MyCollectionViewController* class as both the delegate and data source for the UICollectionView in the user interface. To verify this, select the black background of the collection view controller in the storyboard to select the UICollectionView subclass instance and display the Connections Inspector (select the far right item at the top of the Utilities panel or use the *View -> Utilities -> Show Connection Inspector* menu option). Assuming that the connections have been made, the *Outlets* section of the panel will be configured as shown in Figure 55-6.

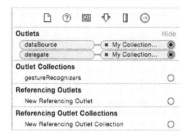

Figure 55-6

The next step is to declare which protocols the MyCollectionViewController class is going to implement. Select the *MyCollectionViewController.swift* file and modify it so that it reads as outlined in the following listing:

```
import UIKit

let reuseIdentifier = "MyCell"

class MyCollectionViewController: UICollectionViewController,
    UICollectionViewDataSource, UICollectionViewDelegate {

    var carImages = [String]()
```

A number of data source methods will now need to be modified to conform with the UICollectionViewDataSource protocol. The first lets the collection view know how many sections are to be displayed. For the purposes of this example there is only going to be one section, so locate the *numberOfSectionsInCollectionView* method generated by Xcode and modify it to return a value of 1.

```
override func numberOfSectionsInCollectionView(collectionView:
            UICollectionView!) -> Int {
    return 1
}
```

The next method is called by the collection view to identify the number of items that are to be displayed in each section. In this case, the sole collection view section will be required to display a cell for each element in the *carImages* array. Locate the template method and modify it as follows:

```
override func collectionView(collectionView: UICollectionView!,
            numberOfItemsInSection section: Int) -> Int {
    return carImages.count
}
```

The *cellForItemAtIndexPath* method will be called by the collection view in order to obtain cells configured based on the indexPath value passed to the method. This method will request a cell object from the reuse queue and then set the image on the Image View object which was configured in the cell prototype earlier in this chapter, using the index path row as the index into the *carImages* array:

```
override func collectionView(collectionView: UICollectionView!,
        cellForItemAtIndexPath indexPath: NSIndexPath!) ->
            UICollectionViewCell! {

    let cell =
collectionView.dequeueReusableCellWithReuseIdentifier(reuseIdentifier,
        forIndexPath: indexPath) as MyCollectionViewCell

    // Configure the cell
    let image = UIImage(named: carImages[indexPath.row])
    cell.imageView.image = image

    return cell
}
```

55.8 Testing the Application

Compile and run the application, either on a physical iPhone device or using the iOS Simulator. Once loaded, the collection view will appear as illustrated in Figure 55-7. Clearly, each cell has been displayed at a fixed size causing the images to be compressed to fit into the containing cell. In order to improve the visual experience, some work is clearly still needed.

Figure 55-7

55.9 **Setting Sizes for Cell Items**

When the prototype cell was designed, it was set to a specific size. Unless additional steps are taken, each cell within the collection view will appear at that size. This means that images are not displayed at their original size. In actual fact, all of the car images differ in size from each other. What is needed is a way to set the size of each cell based on the size of the content it is required to display (in this instance the dimensions of the corresponding image). As outlined in the previous chapter, if a method named *sizeForItemAtIndexPath* is implemented in the UICollectionViewFlowLayoutDelegate protocol class (which by default is the same class as the UICollectionViewDelegate delegate), it will be called for each cell to request size information. Clearly, by implementing this method it will be possible to have each image displayed at its own size. Remaining in *MyCollectionViewController.swift*, implement this method to identify the size of the current image and return the result to the collection view:

```
// MARK: UICollectionViewFlowLayoutDelegate

func collectionView(collectionView: UICollectionView,
    layout collectionViewLayout: UICollectionViewLayout,
    sizeForItemAtIndexPath indexPath: NSIndexPath) -> CGSize {

    let image = UIImage(named: carImages[indexPath.row])
    return image!.size
}
```

Run the application once again and note that, as shown in Figure 55-8, the images are now displayed at their original sizes.

Figure 55-8

55.10 **Changing Scroll Direction**

As currently configured, the flow layout object assigned to the collection view is in vertical scrolling mode. As a demonstration of both one of the delegate methods for handling user interaction and the effects of horizontal scrolling, the example will now be extended to switch to horizontal scrolling when any cell in the view is selected.

When making changes to the flow layout assigned to a collection view, it is not possible to directly change properties on the layout object. Instead, and as illustrated in the following code, a new layout object must be created, configured and then set as the current layout object for the collection view. Within the *MyCollectionViewController.swift* file, implement the *didSelectItemAtIndexPath* delegate method as follows:

```
// MARK: UICollectionViewDelegate

override func collectionView(collectionView: UICollectionView,
didSelectItemAtIndexPath indexPath: NSIndexPath) {

    let myLayout = UICollectionViewFlowLayout()

    myLayout.scrollDirection =
            UICollectionViewScrollDirection.Horizontal

    self.collectionView?.setCollectionViewLayout(myLayout,
                        animated: true)
}
```

Compile and run the application and select an image once the collection view appears. Notice how the layout smoothly animates the transition from vertical to horizontal scrolling.

Note also that the layout adjusts automatically when the orientation of the device is rotated. Figure 55-9, for example shows the collection view in landscape orientation with horizontal scrolling enabled.

Figure 55-9

55.11 Implementing a Supplementary View

The next task in this tutorial is to demonstrate the implementation of supplementary views in the form of a header for the car image gallery. The first step is to ask Interface Builder to add a prototype header supplementary view to the UICollectionView. To do this, select the *Main.storyboard* file and click on the black background of the collection view controller canvas representing the UICollectionView object. Display the Attributes Inspector in the Utilities panel, locate the *Accessories* section listed under *Collection View* and set the *Section Header* check box as illustrated in Figure 55-10.

Figure 55-10

Once the header section has been enabled, a header prototype object will have been added to the storyboard view canvas. As with the prototype cell, this header can be configured using any combination of view objects from the Object Library panel. For this example, drag a Label object onto the prototype header and position it so the horizontal and vertical center guidelines appear. Using the Auto Layout Align menu, set constraints on the label so that it is positioned in the horizontal and vertical center of the containing view as shown in Figure 55-11:

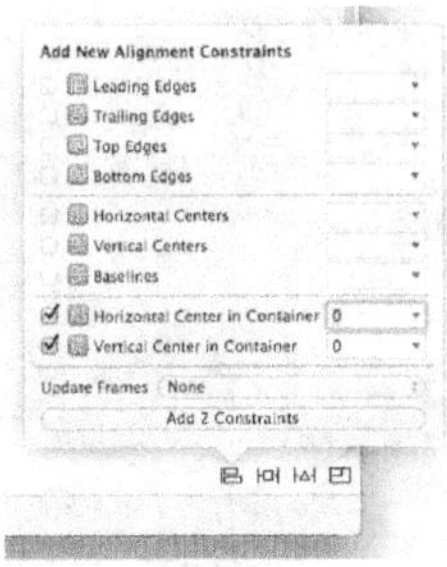

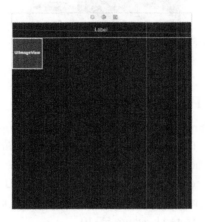

Figure 55-11

By default, labels have a black foreground so the text in the label will not be visible until a different color is selected. With the label still selected, move to the Attributes Inspector and change the Color property to white. Once completed, the layout should now resemble that of Figure 55-12.

Figure 55-12

With a header prototype added to the storyboard, a new class needs to be added to the project to serve as the class for the header. Select *File -> New -> File...* and add a new iOS Cocoa Touch class named MySupplementaryView subclassed from UICollectionReusableView. Select the header in the storyboard and, using the Identity Inspector, change the class from UICollectionReusableView to MySupplementaryView.

As with cells, supplementary views are reused, so select the Attributes Inspector in the Utilities panel and enter *MyHeader* as the reuse identifier.

The text displayed on the header will be set within a data source method of the view controller. As such, an outlet to the label will be needed. Display the Assistant Editor and make sure that it is displaying the code for *MySupplementaryView.swift*. With the *MySupplementaryView.swift* file displayed in the Assistant Editor, establish an outlet connection from the label in the header and name it *headerLabel*. On completion of the connection, the content of the file should read as follows:

```
import UIKit
```

```
class MySupplementaryView: UICollectionReusableView {

    @IBOutlet weak var headerLabel: UILabel!
}
```

55.12 Implementing the Supplementary View Protocol Methods

In order for the supplementary header view to work, a data source method needs to be implemented. When the collection view is ready to display a supplementary view it will call the *viewForSupplementaryElementOfKind* method of the data source and expect, in return, a configured object ready to be displayed. Passed through as an argument to this method is a value indicating whether this is a header or footer which can be checked by the code to return the appropriate object. Note also that supplementary views use a dequeuing mechanism similar to cells. For this example, implement the *viewForSupplementaryElementOfKind* method as follows in the *MyCollectionViewController.swift* file:

```
override func collectionView(collectionView: UICollectionView,
    viewForSupplementaryElementOfKind kind: String,
    atIndexPath indexPath: NSIndexPath)
            -> UICollectionReusableView {

    var header: MySupplementaryView?

    if kind == UICollectionElementKindSectionHeader {
        header =
          collectionView.dequeueReusableSupplementaryViewOfKind(kind,
          withReuseIdentifier: "MyHeader", forIndexPath: indexPath)
            as? MySupplementaryView

        header?.headerLabel.text = "Car Image Gallery"
    }
        return header!
}
```

Compile and run the application once again and note that the header supplementary view is now visible in the collection view.

55.13 Summary

The previous chapter covered a considerable amount of ground in terms of the theory behind collection views in iOS 8. This chapter has put much of this theory into practice through the implementation of an example application that uses a collection view to display a gallery of images.

56. Subclassing and Extending the iOS 8 Collection View Flow Layout

In this, the final chapter on the subject of collection views in iOS 8, the UICollectionViewFlowLayout class will be extended to provide custom layout behavior for the *CollectionDemo* application created in the previous chapter.

As previously described, whilst the collection view is responsible for displaying data elements in the form of cells, it is the layout object that controls how those cells are to be arranged and positioned on the screen. One of the most powerful features of collection views is the ability to switch out one layout object for another in order to change both the way in which cells are presented to the user, and the way in which that layout responds to user interaction.

In the event that the UICollectionViewFlowLayout class does not provide the necessary behavior for an application, therefore, it can be replaced with a custom layout object that does. By far the easiest way to achieve this is to subclass the UICollectionViewFlowLayout class and extend it to provide the desired layout behavior.

56.1 About the Example Layout Class

This chapter will work step-by-step through the process of creating a new collection view layout class by subclassing and extending UICollectionViewFlowLayout. The purpose of the new layout class will be to allow the user to move and stretch cells in the collection view by pinching and dragging cells. As such, the example will also demonstrate the use of gesture recognizers with collection views.

Begin by launching Xcode and loading the *CollectionDemo* project created in the previous chapter.

56.2 Subclassing the UICollectionViewFlowLayout Class

The first step is to create a new class that is itself a subclass of UICollectionViewFlowLayout. Begin, therefore, by selecting the *File -> New -> File...* menu option in Xcode and in the resulting panel, create a new iOS Cocoa Touch class file named *MyFlowLayout* that subclasses from UICollectionViewFlowLayout.

56.3 **Extending the New Layout Class**

The new layout class is now created and ready to be extended to add the new functionality. Since the new layout class is going to allow cells to be dragged around and resized by the user, it will need some properties to store a reference to the cell being manipulated, the scale value by which the cell is being resized and, finally, the current location of the cell on the screen. With these requirements in mind, select the *MyFlowLayout.swift* file and modify it as follows:

```
import UIKit

class MyFlowLayout: UICollectionViewFlowLayout {

    var currentCellPath: NSIndexPath?
    var currentCellCenter: CGPoint?
    var currentCellScale: CGFloat?
}
```

When the scale and center properties are changed, it will be necessary to invalidate the layout so that the collection view is updated and the cell redrawn at the new size and location on the screen. To ensure that this happens, two methods need to be implemented in the *MyFlowLayout.swift* file for the center and scale properties that invalidate the layout in addition to storing the new property values:

```
func setCurrentCellScale(scale: CGFloat)
{
    currentCellScale = scale
    self.invalidateLayout()
}

func setCurrentCellCenter(origin: CGPoint)
{
    currentCellCenter = origin
    self.invalidateLayout()
}
```

56.4 **Implementing the layoutAttributesForItemAtIndexPath Method**

The collection view object makes calls to a datasource delegate object to obtain cells to be displayed within the collection, passing through an index path object to identify the cell that is required. When a cell is returned by the datasource, the collection view object then calls the layout object and expects in return a set of layout attributes in the form of a UICollectionViewLayoutAttributes object for that cell indicating how and where it is to be displayed on the screen.

The method of the layout object called by the collection view will be one of either *layoutAttributesForItemAtIndexPath* or *layoutAttributesForElementsInRect*. The former method is passed the index path to the specific cell for which layout attributes are required. It is the job of this method to calculate these attributes based on internal logic and return the attributes object to the collection view.

The *layoutAttributesForElementsInRect* method, on the other hand, is passed a CGRect object representing a rectangular region of the device display and expects, in return, an array of attribute objects for all cells that fall within the designated region.

In order to modify the behavior of the flow layout subclass, these methods need to be overridden to apply the necessary layout attribute changes to the cell items.

The first method to be implemented in this example is the *layoutAttributesForItemAtIndexPath* method which should be implemented in the *MyFlowLayout.swift* file as follows:

```
override func layoutAttributesForItemAtIndexPath(indexPath:
        NSIndexPath) -> UICollectionViewLayoutAttributes {

    let attributes =
                super.layoutAttributesForItemAtIndexPath(indexPath)

    self.modifyLayoutAttributes(attributes)
    return attributes
}
```

Before the attributes for the requested cell can be modified, the method needs to know what those attributes would be for an unmodified UICollectionViewFlowLayout instance. Since this class is a subclass of UICollectionViewFlowLayout, we can obtain this information, as performed in the above method, via a call to the *layoutAttributesForItemAtIndexPath* method of the superclass:

```
let attributes = super.layoutAttributesForItemAtIndexPath(indexPath)
```

Having ascertained what the attributes would normally be, the method then calls a custom method named *modifyLayoutAttributes* and then returns the modified attributes to the collection view. It will be the task of the *modifyLayoutAttributes* method (which will be implemented later) to apply the resize and movement effects to the attributes of the cell over which the pinch gesture is taking place.

56.5 Implementing the layoutAttributesForElementsInRect Method

The *layoutAttributesForElementsInRect* method will need to perform a similar task to the previous method in terms of getting the attributes values for cells in the designated display region from the superclass, calling the *modifyLayoutAttributes* method and returning the results to the collection view object:

```
override func layoutAttributesForElementsInRect(rect: CGRect) ->
    [AnyObject] {

    let allAttributesInRect =
```

```
                    super.layoutAttributesForElementsInRect(rect)

    for cellAttributes in allAttributesInRect! {
        self.modifyLayoutAttributes(cellAttributes as
                            UICollectionViewLayoutAttributes)
    }

    return allAttributesInRect!
}
```

56.6 Implementing the modifyLayoutAttributes Method

By far the most interesting method to be implemented is the *modifyLayoutAttributes* method. This is where the layout attributes for the cell the user is currently manipulating on the screen are modified. This method should now be implemented as outlined in the following listing:

```
func modifyLayoutAttributes(layoutattributes:
                    UICollectionViewLayoutAttributes) {

    if layoutattributes.indexPath == currentCellPath? {
        layoutattributes.transform3D =
            CATransform3DMakeScale(currentCellScale!,
                                    currentCellScale!, 1.0)
        layoutattributes.center = currentCellCenter!
        layoutattributes.zIndex = 1
    }
}
```

In completing the example application, a pinch gesture recognizer will be attached to the collection view object and configured to set the *currentCellPath*, *currentCellScale* and *currentCellCenter* values of the layout object in real-time as the user pinches and moves a cell. As is evident from the above code, use is made of these settings during the attribute modification process.

Since this method will be called for each cell in the collection, it is important that the attribute modifications only be applied to the cell the user is currently moving and pinching. This cell is stored in the currentCellPath property as updated by the gesture recognizer:

```
if layoutattributes.indexPath == currentCellPath?
```

If the cell matches that referenced by the currentCellPath property, the attributes are transformed via a call to the *CATransform3DMakeScale* function of the QuartzCore Framework, using the currentCellScale property value which is updated by the gesture recognizer during a pinching motion:

```
layoutattributes.transform3D =
    CATransform3DMakeScale(currentCellScale!, currentCellScale!, 1.0)
```

Finally, the center location of the cell is set to the currentCellCenter property value and the zIndex property set to 1 so that the cell appears on top of overlapping collection view contents.

The implementation of a custom collection layout is now complete. All that remains is to implement the gesture recognizer in the application code so that the flow layout knows which cell is being pinched and moved, and by how much.

56.7 Adding the New Layout and Pinch Gesture Recognizer

In order to detect pinch gestures, a pinch gesture recognizer needs to be added to the collection view object. Code also needs to be added to replace the default layout object with our new custom flow layout object.

Select the *MyCollectionViewController.swift* file and modify the *viewDidLoad* method to change the layout to our new layout class and to add a pinch gesture recognizer configured to call a method named *handlePinch*:

```
override func viewDidLoad() {
    super.viewDidLoad()

    let myLayout = MyFlowLayout()

    self.collectionView?.setCollectionViewLayout(myLayout,
                        animated: true)

    let pinchRecognizer = UIPinchGestureRecognizer(target: self,
                        action: "handlePinch:")

    self.collectionView?.addGestureRecognizer(pinchRecognizer)

    // Uncomment the following line to preserve selection between
presentations
    // self.clearsSelectionOnViewWillAppear = false

    // Register cell classes
    // self.collectionView?.registerClass(UICollectionViewCell.self,
forCellWithReuseIdentifier: reuseIdentifier)

    // Do any additional setup after loading the view.
    carImages = ["chevy_small.jpg",
                "mini_small.jpg",
                "rover_small.jpg",
                "smart_small.jpg",
                "highlander_small.jpg",
                "venza_small.jpg",
                "volvo_small.jpg",
```

```
                "vw_small.jpg",
                "ford_small.jpg",
                "nissan_small.jpg",
                "honda_small.jpg",
                "jeep_small.jpg"]
    }
```

56.8 Implementing the Pinch Recognizer

Remaining within the *MyCollectionViewController.swift* file, the last coding related task before testing the application is to write the pinch handler method, the code for which reads as follows:

```
func handlePinch(gesture: UIPinchGestureRecognizer) {

    let layout = self.collectionView?.collectionViewLayout
                    as MyFlowLayout

    if gesture.state == UIGestureRecognizerState.Began
    {
        // Get the initial location of the pinch?
        let initialPinchPoint =
                    gesture.locationInView(self.collectionView)

        // Convert pinch location into a specific cell
        let pinchedCellPath =
         self.collectionView?.indexPathForItemAtPoint(initialPinchPoint)

        // Store the indexPath to cell
        layout.currentCellPath = pinchedCellPath
    }
    else if gesture.state == UIGestureRecognizerState.Changed
    {
        // Store the new center location of the selected cell
        layout.currentCellCenter =
                    gesture.locationInView(self.collectionView)
        // Store the scale value
        layout.setCurrentCellScale(gesture.scale)
    }
    else
    {
        self.collectionView?.performBatchUpdates({
            layout.currentCellPath = nil
            layout.currentCellScale = 1.0}, completion:nil)
    }
}
```

```
}
```

The method begins by getting a reference to the layout object associated with the collection view:

```
let layout = self.collectionView?.collectionViewLayout as MyFlowLayout
```

Next, it checks to find out if the gesture has just started. If so, the method will need to identify the cell over which the gesture is taking place. This is achieved by identifying the initial location of the gesture and then passing that location through to the *indexPathForItemAtPoint* method of the collection view object. The resulting indexPath is then stored in the currentCellPath property of the layout object where it can be accessed by the *modifyLayoutAttributes* method previously implemented in the MyFlowLayout class:

```
if gesture.state == UIGestureRecognizerState.Began
{
    // Get the initial location of the pinch?
    let initialPinchPoint = gesture.locationInView(self.collectionView)

    // Convert pinch location into a specific cell
    let pinchedCellPath =
        self.collectionView?.indexPathForItemAtPoint(initialPinchPoint)

    // Store the indexPath to cell
    layout.currentCellPath = pinchedCellPath
}
```

In the event that the gesture is in progress, the current scale and location of the gesture need to be stored in the layout object:

```
else if gesture.state == UIGestureRecognizerState.Changed
{
    // Store the new center location of the selected cell
    layout.currentCellCenter =
                    gesture.locationInView(self.collectionView)
    // Store the scale value
    layout.setCurrentCellScale(gesture.scale)
}
```

Finally, if the gesture has just ended, the scale needs to be returned to 1 and the currentCellPath property reset to *nil*:

```
else
{
    self.collectionView?.performBatchUpdates({
        layout.currentCellPath = nil
        layout.currentCellScale = 1.0}, completion:nil)
```

}

This task is performed as a batch update so that the changes take place in a single animated update.

56.9 Avoiding Image Clipping

When the user pinches on a cell in the collection view and stretches the cell, the image contained therein will stretch with it. In order to avoid the enlarged image from being clipped by the containing cell when the gesture ends, a property on the MyCollectionViewCell class needs to be modified.

Within Xcode, select the *Main.storyboard* file followed by the *MyCell* entry in the Document Outline panel to the left of the storyboard canvas. Display the Attributes Inspector and, in the *Drawing* section of the panel, unset the checkbox next to *Clip Subviews*.

56.10 Testing the Application

With a suitably provisioned iOS device attached to the development system, run the application. Once running, use pinching motions on the display to resize an image in a cell, noting that the cell can also be moved during the gesture. On ending the gesture, the cell will spring back to the original location and size. Figure 56-1 shows the collection view during the resizing of a cell.

Figure 56-1

56.11 Summary

Whilst the UICollectionViewFlowLayout class provides considerable flexibility in terms of controlling the way in which data is presented to the user, additional functionality can be added by subclassing and extending this class. In most cases the changes simply involve overriding two methods and modifying the layout attributes within those methods to implement the required layout behavior.

This chapter has worked through the implementation of a custom layout class that extends UICollectionViewFlowLayout to allow the user to move and resize the images contained in collection view cells. The chapter also looked at the use of gesture recognizers within the context of collection views.

57. Drawing iOS 8 2D Graphics with Core Graphics

The ability to draw two dimensional graphics on the iPhone and iPad is provided as part of the Core Graphics Framework in the form of the Quartz 2D API. The iOS implementation of Quartz on iOS is the same implementation as that provided with Mac OS X and provides a set of C functions designed to enable the drawing of 2D graphics in the form of images, lines and shapes together with a range of fill patterns and gradients.

In this chapter we will provide an overview of Quartz 2D. A later chapter, entitled, *An iOS 8 Graphics Tutorial using Core Graphics and Core Image* provides a step-by-step tutorial designed to teach the basics of two dimensional drawing on iOS.

57.1 Introducing Core Graphics and Quartz 2D

Quartz 2D is a two dimensional graphics drawing engine that makes up the bulk of the UIKit Core Graphics Framework. It is a C based application programming interface (API) and as such is utilized primarily through calls to a range of C functions. Quartz 2D drawing typically takes place on a UIView object (or, more precisely a subclass thereof). Drawings are defined in terms of the paths that a line must follow and rectangular areas into which shapes (rectangles, ellipses etc) must fit.

57.2 The drawRect Method

The first time a view is displayed, and each time part of that view needs to be redrawn as a result of another event, the *drawRect* method of the view is called. Drawing is achieved, therefore, by subclassing the UIView class, implementing the *drawRect* method and placing within that method the Quartz 2D API calls to draw the graphics.

In instances where the *drawRect* method is not automatically called, a redraw may be forced via a call to the *setNeedsDisplay* or *setNeedsDisplayInRect* methods.

57.3 Points, Coordinates and Pixels

The Quartz 2D API functions work on the basis of *points*. These are essentially the x and y coordinates of a two dimensional coordinate system on the device screen with 0, 0 representing the top left hand corner of the display. These coordinates are stored in the form of CGFloat variables.

An additional C structure named CGPoint is used to contain both the x and y coordinates to specify a point on the display. Similarly, the CGSize structure stores two CGFloat values designating the width and height of an element on the screen.

Further, the position and dimension of a rectangle can be defined using the CGRect structure which contains a CGPoint (the location) and CGSize (the dimension) of a rectangular area.

Of key importance when working with points and dimensions is that these values do not correspond directly to screen pixels. In other words there is not a one to one correlation between pixels and points. Instead the underlying framework decides, based on a *scale factor*, where a point should appear and at what size, relative to the resolution of the display on which the drawing is taking place. This enables the same code to work on both higher and lower resolution screens (for example an iPhone 3GS screen and an iPhone 6 retina display) without the programmer having to worry about it.

For more precise drawing requirements, iOS version 4 and later allows the *scale factor* for the current screen to be obtained from UIScreen, UIView, UIImage, and CALayer classes allowing the correlation between pixels and points to be calculated for greater drawing precision. For iOS 3 or older the scale factor is always returned as 1.0.

57.4 **The Graphics Context**

Almost without exception, all Quartz API function calls require that the *graphics context* be passed as an argument. Each view has its own context which is responsible for performing the requested drawing tasks and subsequently rendering those drawings onto the corresponding view. The graphics context can be obtained with a call to the *UIGraphicsGetCurrentContext()* function which returns a result of type *CGContextRef*:

```
let context = UIGraphicsGetCurrentContext()
```

57.5 **Working with Colors in Quartz 2D**

The Core Graphics CGColorRef data type is used to store colors when drawing with Quartz. This data type holds information about the *colorspace* of the color (RGBA, CMYK or gray scale) together with a set of component values that specify both the color and the transparency of that color. For example, the color red with no transparency would be defined with the RGBA components 1.0, 0.0, 0.0, 1.0.

A *colorspace* can be created via a Quartz API function call. For example, to create an RGB colorspace:

```
let colorSpace = CGColorSpaceCreateDeviceRGB()
```

If the function fails to create a colorspace, it will return a nil value.

Gray scale and CMYK color spaces may similarly be created using the *CGColorSpaceCreateDeviceGray()* and *CGColorSpaceCreateDeviceCMYK()* functions respectively.

Once the colorspace has been created, the next task is to define the components. The following declaration defines a set of RGBA components for a semi-transparent blue color:

```
let components: [CGFloat] = [0.0, 0.0, 1.0, 0.5]
```

With both the colorspace and the components defined, the CGColorRef structure can be created:

```
let color = CGColorCreate(colorSpace, components)
```

The color may then be used to draw using the Quartz 2D drawing API functions.

Another useful method for creating colors involves the UIKit UIColor class. Whilst this class cannot be used directly with the Quartz function since it is a Swift class, it is possible to extract a color in CGColorRef format from the UIColor class by referencing the CGColor property.

The advantage offered by UIColor, in addition to being object oriented, is that it includes a range of convenience methods that can be used to create colors. For example, the following code uses the UIColor class to create the color red, and then accesses the CGColor property for use as an argument to the *CGCreateSetStrokeColorWithColor()* C function:

```
CGContextSetStrokeColorWithColor(context, UIColor.redColor().CGColor)
```

The color selection and transparency can be further refined using this technique simply by specifying additional components. For example:

```
let color = UIColor(red:1.0 green:0.3 blue:0.8 alpha:0.5)
```

As we can see, the use of UIColor avoids the necessity to create colorspaces and components when working with colors. Refer to the Apple documentation for more details of the range of methods provided by the UIColor class.

57.6 **Summary**

This chapter has covered some of the basic principles behind the drawing of two dimensional graphics on iOS 8 using the Quartz 2D API. Topics covered included obtaining the graphics context, implementing the *drawRect* method and the handling of colors and transparency. In *An iOS 8 Graphics Tutorial using Core Graphics and Core Image* this theory will be put into practice with examples of how to draw a variety of shapes and images on an iOS device screen. Before moving on to the drawing tutorial, however, the next chapter will begin by exploring the Live Views feature of Interface Builder. Introduced in Xcode 6, Live Views are particularly useful when writing dynamic user interface code such as drawing graphics.

58. Interface Builder Live Views and iOS 8 Embedded Frameworks

Two related areas of iOS development will be covered in this chapter in the form of Live Views in Interface Builder and Embedded Frameworks, both of which have been introduced with Xcode 6 and iOS 8 to make the tasks of sharing common code between projects and designing dynamic user interfaces easier.

58.1 Embedded Frameworks

A framework is defined by Apple as "a collection of code and resources to encapsulate functionality that is valuable across multiple projects". A typical iOS application project will use a multitude of Frameworks from the iOS SDK. All applications, for example, make use of the Foundation Framework while a game might also make use of the SpriteKit Framework.

Embedded Frameworks is a new feature introduced with iOS 8 and Xcode 6 that allows developers to create their own frameworks. Embedded frameworks are easy to create and provide a number of advantages, the most obvious of which is the ability to share common code between multiple application projects.

Embedded Frameworks are particularly useful when working with extensions. By nature, an extension will inevitably need to share code that already exists within the containing app. Rather than duplicate code between the app and the extension, a better solution is to place common code into an embedded framework.

Another benefit of embedded frameworks is the ability to publish code in the form of 3rd party frameworks that can be downloaded for use by other developers in their own projects.

One of the more intriguing features of embedded frameworks, however, is that they facilitate a powerful new feature of Interface Builder known as Live Views.

58.2 Interface Builder Live Views

Traditionally, designing a user interface layout using Interface Builder has involved placing static representations of view components onto a canvas. The application logic behind these views to implement dynamic behavior is then implemented within the view controller and the application compiled and run on a device or simulator in order to see the live user interface is action.

Live views allow the dynamic code behind the views to be executed from within the Interface Builder storyboard file as the user interface is being designed without the necessity to compile and run the application.

Live views also allow variables within the code behind a view to be exposed in such a way that they can be accessed and modified in the Interface Builder Attributes Inspector panel, with the changes reflected in real-time within the live view.

The reason that embedded frameworks and live views are both covered in this chapter is that a prerequisite for live views is for the underlying code for a live view to be contained within an embedded framework.

The best way to gain a better understanding of both embedded frameworks and live views is to see them in action in an example project.

58.3 Creating the Example Project

Launch Xcode and create a new Single View Application project named LiveViewDemo using Swift as the programming language and with the device family menu set to *Universal*.

When the project has been created, select the *Main.storyboard* file and drag and drop a View object from the Object Library panel onto the view controller canvas. Resize the view, stretching it in each dimension until the blue dotted line appears indicating the recommended margin. Display the Auto Layout *Pin* menu and enable "spacing to nearest neighbor" constraints on all four sides of the view with the *Constrain to margins* option enabled as shown in Figure 58-1 before clicking on the *Add 4 Constraints* button:

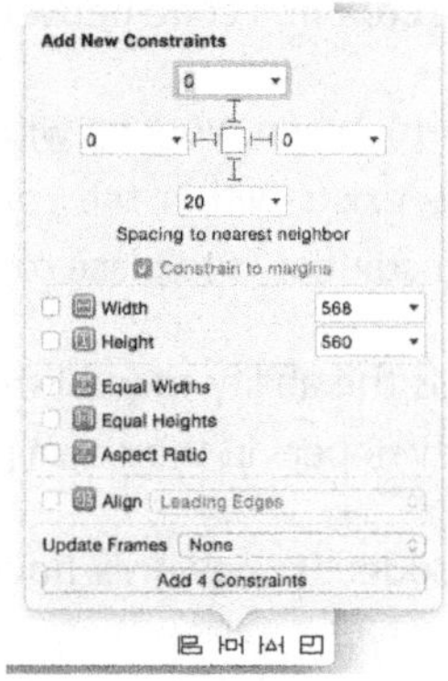

Figure 58-1

Once the above steps are complete, the layout should resemble that illustrated in Figure 58-2 below:

Figure 58-2

With the user interface designed, the next step is to add a framework to the project.

58.4 Adding an Embedded Framework

The framework to be added to the project will contain a UIView subclass containing some graphics drawing code.

Within Xcode, select the *File -> New -> Target...* menu option and, in the template selection panel, choose the *Framework & Library* option listed under *iOS* in the left hand panel and *Cocoa Touch Framework* from the main panel (Figure 58-3):

Figure 58-3

Click on the *Next* button and, on the subsequent screen, enter *MyDrawKit* into the product name field before clicking on the *Finish* button.

Within the project navigator panel, a new folder will have been added named *MyDrawKit* into which will be stored the files that make up the new framework. Ctrl-click on this entry and select the *New File...* menu option. In the template chooser panel, select the *Source* entry listed under *iOS* in the left hand panel and *Cocoa Touch Class* from the main panel before clicking on *Next*.

On the next screen, name the class *MyDrawView* and configure it as a subclass of UIView. Click the *Next* button and save the new class file into the *MyDrawKit* subfolder of the project directory.

Select the *Main.storyboard* file in the project navigator panel and click on the View object that was added in the previous section. Display the Identity Inspector in the utilities panel and change the Class setting from *UIView* to *MyDrawView*:

Figure 58-4

58.5 Implementing the Drawing Code in the Framework

The code to perform the graphics drawing on the View will reside in the *MyDrawView.swift* file which is located in the *Supporting Files* subfolder of the *MyDrawKit* folder. Locate this file in the project navigator panel and double click on it to load it into a separate editing window (thereby allowing the *Main.storyboard* file to remain visible in Interface Builder).

Remove the comment markers (/* and */) from around the template *drawRect* method and implement the code for this method so that it reads as follows:

```
import UIKit
import QuartzCore

class MyDrawView: UIView {

    var startColor: UIColor = UIColor.whiteColor()
    var endColor: UIColor = UIColor.blueColor()
    var endRadius: CGFloat = 200

    override func drawRect(rect: CGRect)
    {
        let context = UIGraphicsGetCurrentContext()

        var colorspace = CGColorSpaceCreateDeviceRGB()
        var locations: [CGFloat] = [ 0.0, 1.0]

        var gradient = CGGradientCreateWithColors(colorspace,
                    [startColor.CGColor, endColor.CGColor],
                        locations)

        var startPoint = CGPoint()
```

```
        var endPoint = CGPoint()

        var startRadius: CGFloat = 0

        startPoint.x = 210
        startPoint.y = 180
        endPoint.x = 210
        endPoint.y = 200

        CGContextDrawRadialGradient (context, gradient,
                        startPoint, startRadius,
                        endPoint, endRadius, 0)
    }
}
```

58.6 Making the View Designable

At this point the code has been added and running the application on a device or simulator will show the view with the graphics drawn on it. The object of this chapter, however, is to avoid the need to compile and run the application to see the results of the code. In order to make the view "live" within Interface Builder, the class needs to be declared as being "Interface Builder designable". This is achieved by adding an *@IBDesignable* directive immediately before the class declaration in the *MyDrawView.swift* file:

```
import UIKit
import QuartzCore

@IBDesignable
class MyDrawView: UIView {

    var startColor: UIColor = UIColor.whiteColor()
    var endColor: UIColor = UIColor.blueColor()
    var endRadius: CGFloat = 200

.
.
.
}
```

As soon as the directive is added to the file, Xcode will compile the class and render it within the Interface Builder storyboard canvas (Figure 58-5):

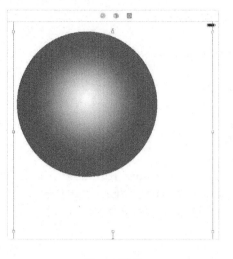

Figure 58-5

From now on, any changes made to the MyDrawView code will be reflected in the Interface Builder live view. To see this in action, change the endColor variable declaration so that it is assigned a different color and observe the color change take effect in the Interface Builder live view:

```
var endColor: UIColor = UIColor.redColor()
```

58.7 Making Variables Inspectable

Although it is possible to modify variables by editing the code in the framework class, it would be easier if they could be changed just like any other property using the Attributes Inspector panel. In fact, this can be achieved simply by prefixing the variable declarations with the *@IBInspectable* directive as follows:

```
@IBDesignable
class MyDrawView: UIView {

    @IBInspectable var startColor: UIColor = UIColor.whiteColor()
    @IBInspectable var endColor: UIColor = UIColor.redColor()
    @IBInspectable var endRadius: CGFloat = 200
    .
    .
    .
}
```

With the changes made to the code, select the View in the storyboard file and display the Attributes Inspector panel. The properties should now be listed for the view (Figure 58-6) and can be modified. Any changes to these variables made through the Attributes Inspector will take effect in real-time without the need for Xcode to recompile the framework code. These settings will also be generated into the application when it is compiled and run on a device or simulator.

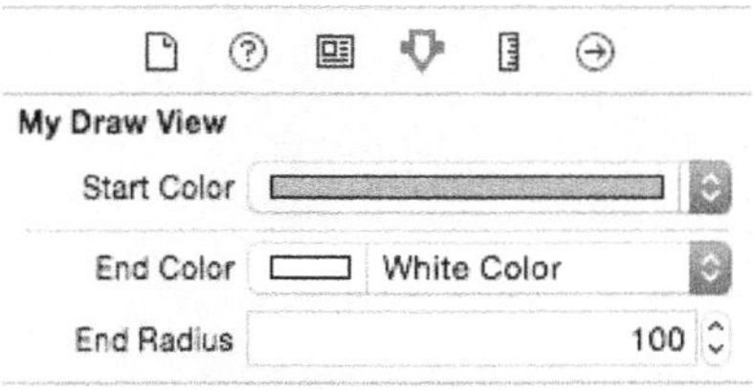

My Draw View

Start Color

End Color　☐　White Color

End Radius　　　　　　　　　　100

Figure 58-6

58.8 **Summary**

Xcode 6 and iOS 8 introduced two new concepts in the form of embedded frameworks and Interface Builder live views. Embedded frameworks allow developers to place source code into frameworks which can then be shared between multiple application projects. Embedded frameworks also provide the basis for the live views feature of Interface Builder. Prior to the introduction of live views, it was necessary to compile and run an application in order to be able to see dynamic user interface behavior in action. With live views, the dynamic behavior of a view can now be seen within Interface Builder, with code changes reflected in real-time.

59. An iOS 8 Graphics Tutorial using Core Graphics and Core Image

As previously discussed in *Drawing iOS 8 2D Graphics with Core Graphics* the Quartz 2D API is the primary mechanism by which 2D drawing operations are performed within iOS applications. Having provided an overview of Quartz 2D as it pertains to iOS development in that chapter, the focus of this chapter is to provide a tutorial that provides examples of how 2D drawing is performed. If you are new to Quartz 2D and have not yet read *Drawing iOS 8 2D Graphics with Core Graphics* it is recommended that you do so now before embarking on this tutorial.

59.1 The iOS Drawing Example Application

If you are reading this book sequentially and have created the *LiveViewDemo* project as outlined in the chapter entitled *Interface Builder Live Views and iOS 8 Embedded Frameworks*, then the code in this chapter may simply be placed in the *drawRect* method contained within the *MyDrawView.swift* file and the results viewed dynamically within the live view in the *Main.storyboard* file. If you have not yet completed the tutorial in *Interface Builder Live Views and iOS 8 Embedded Frameworks*, follow the steps in the next three sections to create a new project, add a UIView subclass and locate the *drawRect* method.

59.2 Creating the New Project

The application created in this tutorial will contain a subclassed UIView component within which the *drawRect* method will be overridden and used to perform a variety of 2D drawing operations. Create the new project by launching the Xcode development environment and selecting the option to create a new project. When prompted to select a template for the application, choose the *Single View Application* option and name the project *Draw2D* with the Devices menu set to *Universal* and Swift selected as the programming language.

59.3 Creating the UIView Subclass

In order to draw graphics on the view it is necessary to create a subclass of the UIView object and override the *drawRect* method. In the project navigator panel located on the left hand side of the main Xcode window Ctrl-click on the *Draw2D* folder entry and select *New File...* from the resulting menu. In the *New File* window, select the iOS source *Cocoa Touch Class* icon and click *Next*. On the subsequent options screen, change the *Subclass of* menu to *UIView* and the class name to *Draw2D*. Click *Next* and on the final screen click on the *Create* button.

Select the *Main.storyboard* file and select the UIView component in either the view controller canvas or the document outline panel. Display the Identity Inspector (*View -> Utilities -> Show Identity Inspector*) and change the *Class* setting from *UIView* to our new class named *Draw2D:*

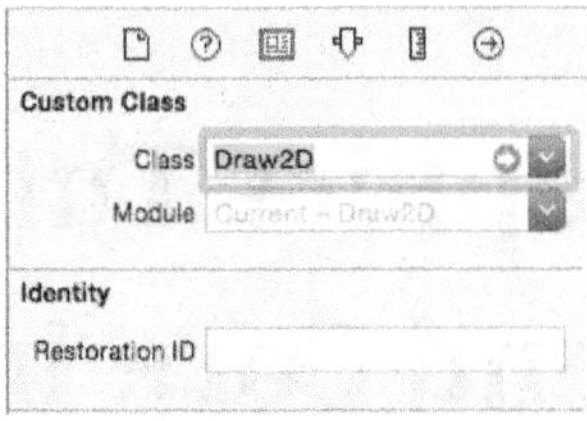

Figure 59-1

59.4 Locating the drawRect Method in the UIView Subclass

Now that we have subclassed our application's UIView the next step is to implement the *drawRect* method in this subclass. Fortunately Xcode has already created a template of this method for us. To locate this method, select the *Draw2D.swift* file in the project navigator panel. Having located the method in the file, remove the comment markers (/* and */) within which it is currently encapsulated:

```
import UIKit

class Draw2D: UIView {

    // Only override drawRect: if you perform custom drawing.
    // An empty implementation adversely affects performance during
animation.
    override func drawRect(rect: CGRect) {
        // Drawing code
    }
}
```

In the remainder of this tutorial we will modify the code in the *drawRect* method to perform a variety of different drawing operations.

59.5 Drawing a Line

In order to draw a line on a device screen using Quartz 2D we first need to obtain the graphics context for the view:

```
let context = UIGraphicsGetCurrentContext()
```

Once the context has been obtained, the width of the line we plan to draw needs to be specified:

```
CGContextSetLineWidth(context, 2.0)
```

Next, we need to create a color reference. We can do this by specifying the RGBA components of the required color (in this case opaque blue):

```
let colorSpace = CGColorSpaceCreateDeviceRGB()
let components: [CGFloat] = [0.0, 0.0, 1.0, 1.0]
let color = CGColorCreate(colorSpace, components)
```

Using the color reference and the context we can now specify that the color is to be used when drawing the line:

```
CGContextSetStrokeColorWithColor(context, color)
```

The next step is to move to the start point of the line that is going to be drawn:

```
CGContextMoveToPoint(context, 30, 30)
```

The above line of code indicates that the start point for the line is the top left hand corner of the device display. We now need to specify the end point of the line, in this case 300, 400:

```
CGContextAddLineToPoint(context, 300, 400)
```

Having defined the line width, color and path, we are ready to draw the line:

```
CGContextStrokePath(context)
```

Bringing this all together gives us a *drawRect* method that reads as follows:

```
override func drawRect(rect: CGRect)
{
    let context = UIGraphicsGetCurrentContext()
    CGContextSetLineWidth(context, 2.0)
    let colorSpace = CGColorSpaceCreateDeviceRGB()
    let components: [CGFloat] = [0.0, 0.0, 1.0, 1.0]
    let color = CGColorCreate(colorSpace, components)
    CGContextSetStrokeColorWithColor(context, color)
    CGContextMoveToPoint(context, 30, 30)
    CGContextAddLineToPoint(context, 300, 400)
    CGContextStrokePath(context)
}
```

When compiled and run, the application should display as illustrated in Figure 59-2:

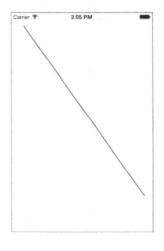

Figure 59-2

Note that in the above example we manually created the colorspace and color reference. As described in *Drawing iOS 8 2D Graphics with Core Graphics* colors can also be created using the UIColor class. For example, the same result as outlined above can be achieved with fewer lines of code as follows:

```
override func drawRect(rect: CGRect)
{
    let context = UIGraphicsGetCurrentContext()
    CGContextSetLineWidth(context, 2.0)
    CGContextSetStrokeColorWithColor(context,
                            UIColor.blueColor().CGColor)
    CGContextMoveToPoint(context, 30, 30)
    CGContextAddLineToPoint(context, 300, 400)
    CGContextStrokePath(context)
}
```

59.6 Drawing Paths

As you may have noticed, in the above example we draw a single line by essentially defining the path between two points. Defining a path that comprises multiple points allows us to draw using a sequence of straight lines all connected to each other using repeated calls to the *CGContextAddLineToPoint()* function. Non-straight lines may also be added to a shape using calls to, for example, the *CGContextAddArc()* function.

The following code, for example, draws a diamond shape:

```
override func drawRect(rect: CGRect)
{
    let context = UIGraphicsGetCurrentContext()
    CGContextSetLineWidth(context, 2.0)
    CGContextSetStrokeColorWithColor(context,
```

```
        UIColor.blueColor().CGColor)
        CGContextMoveToPoint(context, 100, 100)
        CGContextAddLineToPoint(context, 150, 150)
        CGContextAddLineToPoint(context, 100, 200)
        CGContextAddLineToPoint(context, 50, 150)
        CGContextAddLineToPoint(context, 100, 100)
        CGContextStrokePath(context)
}
```

When executed, the above code should produce output that appears as shown in Figure 59-3:

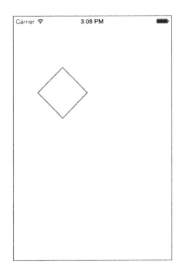

Figure 59-3

59.7 Drawing a Rectangle

Rectangles are drawn in much the same way as any other path is drawn, with the exception that the path is defined by specifying the x and y co-ordinates of the top left hand corner of the rectangle together with the rectangle's height and width. These dimensions are stored in a CGRect structure and passed through as an argument to the *CGContextAddRect* function:

```
override func drawRect(rect: CGRect)
{
    let context = UIGraphicsGetCurrentContext()
    CGContextSetLineWidth(context, 4.0)
    CGContextSetStrokeColorWithColor(context,
            UIColor.blueColor().CGColor)
    let rectangle = CGRectMake(60,170,200,80)
    CGContextAddRect(context, rectangle)
    CGContextStrokePath(context)
}
```

The above code will result in the following display when compiled and executed:

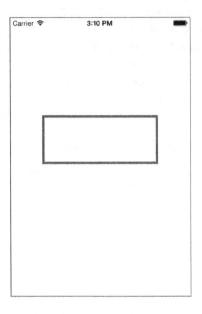

Figure 59-4

59.8 Drawing an Ellipse or Circle

Circles and ellipses are drawn by defining the rectangular area into which the shape must fit and then calling the *CGContextAddEllipseInRect()* function:

```
override func drawRect(rect: CGRect)
{
    let context = UIGraphicsGetCurrentContext()
    CGContextSetLineWidth(context, 4.0)
    CGContextSetStrokeColorWithColor(context,
            UIColor.blueColor().CGColor)
    let rectangle = CGRectMake(60,170,200,80)
    CGContextAddEllipseInRect(context, rectangle)
    CGContextStrokePath(context)
}
```

When compiled, the above code will produce the following graphics:

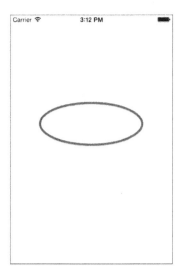

Figure 59-5

In order to draw a circle simply define a rectangle with equal length sides (a square in other words).

59.9 Filling a Path with a Color

A path may be filled with a color using a variety of Quartz 2D API functions. Rectangular and elliptical paths may be filled using the *CGContextFillRect()* and *CGContextFillEllipse()* functions respectively. Similarly, a path may be filled using the *CGContextFillPath()* function. Prior to executing a fill operation, the fill color must be specified using the *CGContextSetFillColorWithColor()* function.

The following example defines a path and then fills it with the color red:

```
override func drawRect(rect: CGRect)
{
    let context = UIGraphicsGetCurrentContext()
    CGContextMoveToPoint(context, 100, 100)
    CGContextAddLineToPoint(context, 150, 150)
    CGContextAddLineToPoint(context, 100, 200)
    CGContextAddLineToPoint(context, 50, 150)
    CGContextAddLineToPoint(context, 100, 100)
    CGContextSetFillColorWithColor(context,
        UIColor.redColor().CGColor)
    CGContextFillPath(context)
}
```

The above code produces the following graphics on the device or simulator display when executed:

Figure 59-6

The following code draws a rectangle with a blue border and then once again fills the rectangular space with red:

```
override func drawRect(rect: CGRect)
{
    let context = UIGraphicsGetCurrentContext()
    CGContextSetLineWidth(context, 4.0)
    CGContextSetStrokeColorWithColor(context,
        UIColor.blueColor().CGColor)
    let rectangle = CGRectMake(60,170,200,80)
    CGContextAddRect(context, rectangle)
    CGContextStrokePath(context)
    CGContextSetFillColorWithColor(context,
        UIColor.redColor().CGColor)
    CGContextFillRect(context, rectangle)
}
```

When added to the example application, the resulting display should appear as follows:

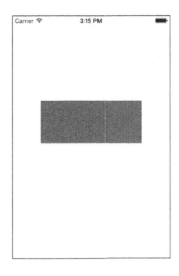

Figure 59-7

59.10 **Drawing an Arc**

An arc may be drawn by specifying two tangent points and a radius using the *CGContextAddArcToPoint()* function, for example:

```
override func drawRect(rect: CGRect)
{
    let context = UIGraphicsGetCurrentContext()
    CGContextSetLineWidth(context, 4.0)
    CGContextSetStrokeColorWithColor(context,
        UIColor.blueColor().CGColor)
    CGContextMoveToPoint(context, 100, 100)
    CGContextAddArcToPoint(context, 100,200, 300,200, 100)
    CGContextStrokePath(context)
}
```

The above code will result in the following graphics output:

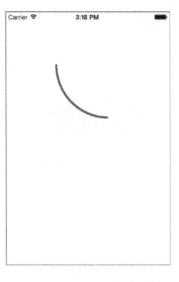

Figure 59-8

59.11 Drawing a Cubic Bézier Curve

A cubic Bézier curve may be drawn by moving to a start point and then passing two control points and an end point through to the *CGContextAddCurveToPoint()* function:

```
override func drawRect(rect: CGRect)
{
    let context = UIGraphicsGetCurrentContext()
    CGContextSetLineWidth(context, 4.0)
    CGContextSetStrokeColorWithColor(context,
            UIColor.blueColor().CGColor)
    CGContextMoveToPoint(context, 10, 10)
    CGContextAddCurveToPoint(context, 0, 50, 300, 250, 300, 400)
    CGContextStrokePath(context)
}
```

The above code will cause the curve illustrated in Figure 59-9 to be drawn when compiled and executed in our example application:

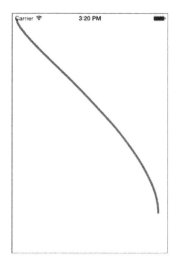

Figure 59-9

59.12 Drawing a Quadratic Bézier Curve

A quadratic Bézier curve is drawn using the *CGContextAddQuadCurveToPoint()* function, providing a control and end point as arguments having first moved to the start point:

```
override func drawRect(rect: CGRect)
{
    let context = UIGraphicsGetCurrentContext()
    CGContextSetLineWidth(context, 4.0)
    CGContextSetStrokeColorWithColor(context,
        UIColor.blueColor().CGColor)
    CGContextMoveToPoint(context, 10, 200)
    CGContextAddQuadCurveToPoint(context, 150, 10, 300, 200)
    CGContextStrokePath(context)
}
```

The above code, when executed, will display a curve that appears as illustrated in the following figure:

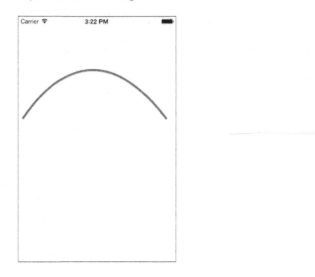

Figure 59-10

59.13 Dashed Line Drawing

So far in this chapter we have performed all our drawing with a solid line. Quartz also provides support for drawing dashed lines. This is achieved via the Quartz *CGContextSetLineDash()* function which takes as its arguments the following:

- **context** – The graphics context of the view on which the drawing is to take place
- **phase** - A floating point value that specifies how far into the dash pattern the line starts
- **lengths** – An array containing values for the lengths of the painted and unpainted sections of the line. For example an array containing 5 and 6 would cycle through 5 painted unit spaces followed by 6 unpainted unit spaces.
- **count** – A count of the number of items in the lengths array

For example, a [2,6,4,2] lengths array applied to a curve drawing of line thickness 5.0 will appear as follows:

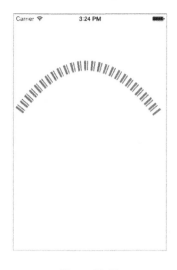

Figure 59-11

The corresponding drawRect code that drew the above line reads as follows:

```
override func drawRect(rect: CGRect)
{
    let context = UIGraphicsGetCurrentContext()
    CGContextSetLineWidth(context, 20.0)
    CGContextSetStrokeColorWithColor(context,
            UIColor.blueColor().CGColor)
    let dashArray:[CGFloat] = [2,6,4,2]
    CGContextSetLineDash(context, 3, dashArray, 4)
    CGContextMoveToPoint(context, 10, 200)
    CGContextAddQuadCurveToPoint(context, 150, 10, 300, 200)
    CGContextStrokePath(context)
}
```

59.14 Drawing Shadows

In addition to drawing shapes, Core Graphics can also be used to create shadow effects. This is achieved using the *CGContextSetShadow* function, passing through a graphics context, offset values for the position of the shadow relative to the shape for which the shadow is being drawn and a value specifying the degree of blurring required for the shadow effect. Colored shadows may similarly be created using the *CGContextSetShadowWithColor* function which takes an additional argument in the form of a CGColor object.

The following code, for example, draws an ellipse with a shadow:

```
override func drawRect(rect: CGRect)
{
    let context = UIGraphicsGetCurrentContext()
```

```
    let myShadowOffset = CGSizeMake (-10,  15)

    CGContextSaveGState (context)

    CGContextSetShadow (context, myShadowOffset, 5)

    CGContextSetLineWidth (context, 4.0)
    CGContextSetStrokeColorWithColor (context,
        UIColor.blueColor() .CGColor)
    let rectangle = CGRectMake (60,170,200,80)
    CGContextAddEllipseInRect (context, rectangle)
    CGContextStrokePath (context)
    CGContextRestoreGState (context)
}
```

When executed, the above code will produce the effect illustrated in Figure 59-12:

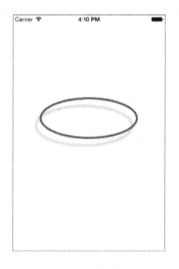

Figure 59-12

The color of the shadow could be changed, for the sake of an example, to red by calling *CGContextSetShadowWithColor* instead of *CGContextSetShadow* as follows:

```
CGContextSetShadowWithColor (context, myShadowOffset, 5,
UIColor.redColor() .CGColor)
```

59.15 Drawing Gradients

Gradients are implemented using the Core Graphics CGGradient class which provides support for linear, radial and axial gradients. Use of the CGGradient class essentially involves the specification of two or more colors together with a set of location values. The location values are used to indicate the points at which the gradient should switch from one color to another as the gradient is drawn along an axis line where 0.0 represents the start of the axis and 1.0 the end point. Assume, for the purposes of an example, that you wish to create a gradient that transitions through three different colors along the gradient axis with each color being given an equal amount of space within the gradient. In this situation, three locations would be specified. The first would be 0.0 to represent the start of the gradient. Two more locations would then need to be specified for the transition points to the remaining colors. In order to equally divide the axis amongst the colors these would need to be set to 0.3333 and 0.6666 respectively.

Having configured a CGGradient instance, a linear gradient is then drawn via a call to the *CGContentDrawLinearGradient* function, passing through the colors, locations and start and end points as arguments.

The following code, for example, draws a linear gradient using four colors with four equally spaced locations:

```
override func drawRect(rect: CGRect)
{
    let context = UIGraphicsGetCurrentContext()

    let locations: [CGFloat] = [ 0.0, 0.25, 0.5, 0.75 ]

    let colors = [UIColor.redColor().CGColor,
                  UIColor.greenColor().CGColor,
                  UIColor.blueColor().CGColor,
                  UIColor.yellowColor().CGColor]

    let colorspace = CGColorSpaceCreateDeviceRGB()

    let gradient = CGGradientCreateWithColors(colorspace,
                  colors, locations)

    var startPoint = CGPoint()
    var endPoint =  CGPoint()

    startPoint.x = 0.0
    startPoint.y = 0.0
    endPoint.x = 600
    endPoint.y = 600

    CGContextDrawLinearGradient(context, gradient,
            startPoint, endPoint, 0)
}
```

When executed, the above code will generate the gradient shown in Figure 59-13:

Figure 59-13

Radial gradients involve drawing a gradient between two circles. When the circles are positioned apart from each other and given different sizes a conical effect is achieved as shown in Figure 59-14:

Figure 59-14

The code to draw the above radial gradient sets up the colors and locations for the gradient before declaring the center points and radius values for two circles. The gradient is then drawn via a call to the *CGContextDrawRadialGradient* function:

```
override func drawRect(rect: CGRect)
{
    let context = UIGraphicsGetCurrentContext()

    let locations: [CGFloat] = [0.0, 0.5, 1.0]

    let colors = [UIColor.redColor().CGColor,
                  UIColor.greenColor().CGColor,
                  UIColor.cyanColor().CGColor]
```

```
    let colorspace = CGColorSpaceCreateDeviceRGB()

    let gradient = CGGradientCreateWithColors(colorspace,
                    colors, locations)

    var startPoint =  CGPoint()
    var endPoint  = CGPoint()

    startPoint.x = 100
    startPoint.y = 100
    endPoint.x = 200
    endPoint.y = 200
    var startRadius: CGFloat = 10
    var endRadius: CGFloat = 75

    CGContextDrawRadialGradient(context, gradient, startPoint,
                    startRadius, endPoint, endRadius, 0)
}
```

Interesting effects may also be created by assigning a radius of 0 to the starting point circle and positioning it within the circumference of the end point circle:

```
override func drawRect(rect: CGRect)
{
    let context = UIGraphicsGetCurrentContext()
    let locations: [CGFloat] = [0.0, 1.0]

    let colors = [UIColor.whiteColor().CGColor,
                    UIColor.blueColor().CGColor]

    let colorspace = CGColorSpaceCreateDeviceRGB()

    let gradient = CGGradientCreateWithColors(colorspace,
                    colors, locations)

    var startPoint = CGPoint()
    var endPoint = CGPoint()
    startPoint.x = 180
    startPoint.y = 180
    endPoint.x = 200
    endPoint.y = 200
    let startRadius: CGFloat = 0
    let endRadius: CGFloat = 75
```

```
CGContextDrawRadialGradient (context, gradient, startPoint,
                      startRadius, endPoint, endRadius,
                      0)
}
```

When executed, the above code creates the appearance of light reflecting on the surface of a shiny blue sphere:

Figure 59-15

59.16 Drawing an Image into a Graphics Context

An image may be drawn into a graphics context either by specifying the coordinates of the top left hand corner of the image (in which case the image will appear full size) or resized so that it fits into a specified rectangular area. Before we can display an image in our example application, however, that image must first be added to the project resources.

Begin by locating the desired image using the Finder and then drag and drop that image onto the *Supporting Files* category of the project navigator panel of the Xcode main project window.

The following example drawRect method code displays the image in a file named *tree.jpg* full size located at 0, 0:

```
override func drawRect(rect: CGRect)
{
    let myImage = UIImage(named: "tree.jpg")
    let imagePoint = CGPointMake(0, 0)
    myImage?.drawAtPoint(imagePoint)
}
```

As is evident when the application is run, the size of the image far exceeds the available screen size:

Figure 59-16

Using the *drawInRect* method of the UIImage object, however, we can scale the image to fit better on the screen. In this instance it is useful to identify the screen size since this changes depending on the device on which the application is running. This can be achieved using the *mainScreen* and *bounds* methods of the UIScreen class. The *mainScreen* method returns another UIScreen object representing the device display. Calling the *bounds* method of that object returns the dimensions of the display in the form of a CGRect object:

```
override func drawRect(rect: CGRect)
{
    let myImage = UIImage(named: "tree.jpg")
    let imageRect = UIScreen.mainScreen().bounds
    myImage?.drawInRect(imageRect)
}
```

This time, the entire image fits comfortably on the screen:

Figure 59-17

59.17 **Image Filtering with the Core Image Framework**

Having covered the concept of displaying images within an iOS application, now is a good time to provide a basic overview of the Core Image Framework.

Core Image was introduced with iOS 5 and provides a mechanism for filtering and manipulating still images and videos. Included with Core Image is a wide range of different filters together with the ability to build custom filters to meet specific requirements. Examples of filters that may be applied include cropping, color effects, blurring, warping, transformations and gradients. A full listing of filters is available in Apple's *Core Image Filter Reference* document which is located in the iOS Developer portal.

A CIImage object is typically initialized with a reference to the image to be manipulated. A CIFilter object is then created and configured with the type of filtering to be performed, together with any input parameters required by that filter. The CIFilter object is then instructed to perform the operation and the modified image is subsequently returned in the form of a CIImage object. The application's CIContext reference may then be used to render the image for display to the user.

By way of an example of Core Image in action we will modify the *drawRect* method of our Draw2D example application to render the previously displayed image in a sepia tone using the CISepiaTone filter. The first step, however, is to add the CoreImage Framework to the project. This is achieved by selecting the *Draw2D* target at the top of the project navigator and then selecting the *Build Phases* tab in the main panel. Unfold the *Link Binary with Libraries* section of the panel, click on the + button and locate and add the *CoreImage.framework* library from the resulting list.

Having added the framework, select the *Draw2D.swift* file and modify *drawRect* as follows:

```
override func drawRect(rect: CGRect)
{
    let myimage = UIImage(named: "tree.jpg")
    let cimage = CIImage(image: myimage)

    let sepiaFilter = CIFilter(name: "CISepiaTone")
    sepiaFilter.setDefaults()
    sepiaFilter.setValue(cimage, forKey: "inputImage")
    sepiaFilter.setValue(NSNumber(float: 0.8),
                forKey: "inputIntensity")

    let image = sepiaFilter.outputImage

    let context = CIContext(options: nil)

    let cgImage = context.createCGImage(image,
                fromRect: image.extent())

    let resultImage = UIImage(CGImage: cgImage)
    let imageRect = UIScreen.mainScreen().bounds
    resultImage?.drawInRect(imageRect)
}
```

The method begins by loading the image .jpg file used in the previous section of this chapter. Since Core Image works on CIImage objects it is then necessary to convert the UIImage to a CIImage. Next a new CIFilter object is created and initialized with the CISepiaTone filter. The filter is then set to the default settings before being configured with the input image (in this case our *cimage* object) and the value of intensity of the filter (0.8).

With the filter object configured, its *outputFile* method is called to perform the manipulation and the resulting modified image assigned to a new CImage object. The CIContext reference for the application is then obtained and used to convert the CImage object to a CGImageRef object. This, in turn, is converted to a UIImage object which is then displayed to the user using the object's *drawInRect* method. When compiled and run the image will appear in a sepia tone.

59.18 Summary

By subclassing the UIView class and overriding the *drawRect* method a variety of 2D graphics drawing functions may be performed on the view canvas. In this chapter we have explored some of the graphics drawing capabilities of Quartz 2D to draw a variety of line types and paths and to present images on the iOS device screen.

Introduced in iOS 5, the Core Image Framework is designed specifically for the filtering and manipulation of images and video. In this chapter we have provided a brief overview of Core Image and worked through a simple example that applied a sepia tone filter to an image.

60. Basic iOS 8 Animation using Core Animation

The majority of the visual effects used throughout the iOS 8 user interface are performed using *Core Animation*. Core Animation provides a simple mechanism for implementing basic animation within an iOS application. If you need a user interface element to gently fade in or out of view, slide smoothly across the screen or gracefully resize or rotate before the user's eyes, these effects can be achieved using Core Animation in just a few lines of code.

In this chapter we will provide an overview of the basics of Core Animation and work through a simple example. While much can be achieved with Core Animation, however, it should be noted that if you plan to develop a graphics intensive 3D style application then it is more likely that OpenGL ES or SceneKit will need to be used, a subject area to which numerous books are dedicated.

60.1 UIView Core Animation Blocks

The concept of Core Animation involves the use of so-called *animation block* methods. Animation block methods are used to mark the beginning and end of a sequence of changes to the appearance of a UIView and its corresponding subviews. Once the end of the block is reached, the animation is performed over a specified duration. For the sake of example, consider a UIView object that contains a UIButton connected to an outlet named *theButton.* The application requires that the button gradually fade from view over a period of 3 seconds. This can be achieved by making the button transparent through the use of the *alpha* property:

```
theButton.alpha = 0
```

Simply setting the alpha property to 0, however, causes the button to immediately become transparent. In order to make it fade out of sight gradually we need to place this line of code in a call to the *animateWithDuration:* animation block method as follows:

```
UIView.animateWithDuration(3.0, animations: {
        self.theButton.alpha = 0
})
```

A variety of properties may also be defined within the animation block. For example, the start of the animation can   be   delayed   using   the   delay   argument   of   the *animateWithDuration(_:delay:options:animations:completion:)* method call. The following example delays the start of the 3 second fade out animation sequence by 5 seconds:

```
UIView.animateWithDuration(3.0, delay: 5.0,
        options: UIViewAnimationOptions.CurveLinear,
        animations: {
                self.theButton.alpha = 0
        },
        completion: nil)
}
```

60.2 Understanding Animation Curves

In addition to specifying the duration of an animation sequence, the linearity of the animation timeline may also be defined by specifying an *animation curve* setting for the *options* argument of the *animateWithDuration* class method. This setting controls whether the animation is performed at a constant speed, whether it starts out slow and speeds up and so on. There are currently four possible animation curve settings:

- **UIViewAnimationOptions.CurveLinear** – The animation is performed at constant speed for the specified duration and is the option declared in the above code example.
- **UIViewAnimationOptions.CurveEaseOut** – The animation starts out fast and slows as the end of the sequence approaches
- **UIViewAnimationOptions.CurveEaseIn** – The animation sequence starts out slow and speeds up as the end approaches.
- **UIViewAnimationOptions.CurveEaseInOut** – The animation starts slow, speeds up and then slows down again.

60.3 Receiving Notification of Animation Completion

Once an animation sequence has been committed and is underway it may be necessary to receive notification when the animation is completed so that the application code can, for example, trigger another animation sequence. This can be achieved by adding a code block to the *completion:* argument of the *animateWithDuration* class method call. The following code, for example, implements a completion handler to fade the button back into view after the fade out animation finishes:

```
UIView.animateWithDuration(3.0, delay: 5.0,
        options: UIViewAnimationOptions.CurveLinear,
        animations: {
                self.theButton.alpha = 0
        },
        completion: ({finished in
                if (finished) {
                        UIView.animateWithDuration(3.0, animations: {
```

```
                     self.theButton.alpha = 1.0
              })
          }
      }))
```

60.4 Performing Affine Transformations

Transformations allow changes to be made to the coordinate system of a screen area. This essentially allows the programmer to rotate, resize and translate a UIView object. A call is made to one of a number of transformation functions and the result assigned to the *transform* property of the UIView object.

For example, to change the scale of a UIView object named *myView* by a factor of 2 in both height and width:

```
myView.transform = CGAffineTransformMakeScale(2, 2)
```

Similarly, the UIView object may be rotated using the *CGAffineTransformMakeRotation()* function which takes as an argument the angle (in radians) by which the view is to be rotated. The following code, for example, rotates a view by 90 degrees:

```
let angle = CGFloat(90 * M_PI / 180)
myView.transform = CGAffineTransformMakeRotation(angle)
```

The key point to keep in mind with transformations is that they become animated effects when performed within an animation block. The transformations evolve over the duration of the animation and follow the specified animation curve in terms of timing.

60.5 Combining Transformations

Two transformations may be combined to create a single transformation effect via a call to the *CGAffineTransformConcat()* function. This function takes as arguments the two transformation objects that are to be combined. The result may then be assigned to the transform property of the UIView object to be transformed. The following code fragment, for example, both scales and rotates a UIView object named *myView*:

```
let scaleTrans = CGAffineTransformMakeScale(2, 2)
let angle = CGFloat(90 * M_PI / 180)
let rotateTrans = CGAffineTransformMakeRotation(angle)

myView.transform = CGAffineTransformConcat(scaleTrans, rotateTrans)
```

Affine transformations offer an extremely powerful and flexible mechanism for creating animations and it is just not possible to do justice to these capabilities in a single chapter. In order to learn more about affine transformations, a good starting place is the *Transforms* chapter of Apple's *Quartz 2D Programming Guide*.

60.6 **Creating the Animation Example Application**

The remainder of this chapter is dedicated to the creation of an iOS application intended to demonstrate the use of Core Animation. The end result is a simple application on which a blue square appears. When the user touches a location on the screen the box moves to that location. Through the use of affine transformations, the box will rotate 180 degrees as it moves to the new location whilst also changing in size.

Begin by launching Xcode and creating a new Single View Application project named *Animate* using Swift as the programming language and with the *Universal* device option selected.

60.7 **Implementing the Variables**

For the purposes of this application we will need a UIView to represent the blue square and variables to contain the rotation angle and scale factor by which the square will be transformed. These need to be declared in the *ViewController.swift* file as follows:

```
import UIKit

class ViewController: UIViewController {

    var scaleFactor: CGFloat = 2
    var angle: Double = 180
    var boxView: UIView?
    .
    .
    .
```

60.8 **Drawing in the UIView**

Having declared the UIView reference, we now need to initialize an instance object and draw a blue square located at a specific location on the screen. We also need to add *boxView* as a subview of the application's main view object. These tasks only need to be performed once when the application first starts up so a good option is to use the *viewDidLoad* method in the *ViewController.swift* file:

```
override func viewDidLoad() {
    super.viewDidLoad()

    let frameRect = CGRectMake(20, 20, 45, 45)

    boxView = UIView(frame: frameRect)
    boxView?.backgroundColor = UIColor.blueColor()
    self.view.addSubview(boxView!)
}
```

60.9 Detecting Screen Touches and Performing the Animation

When the user touches the screen the blue box needs to move from its current location to the location of the touch. During this motion, the box will rotate 180 degrees and change in size. The detection of screen touches was covered in detail in *An Overview of iOS 8 Multitouch, Taps and Gestures*. For the purposes of this example we want to initiate the animation at the point that the user's finger is lifted from the screen so we need to implement the *touchesEnded* method in the *ViewController.swift* file:

```swift
override func touchesEnded(touches: NSSet, withEvent event: UIEvent) {
    let touch = touches.anyObject() as UITouch
    let location = touch.locationInView(self.view)

    UIView.animateWithDuration(2.0, delay: 0.0,
        options: UIViewAnimationOptions.CurveEaseInOut, animations: {
            let scaleTrans =
                CGAffineTransformMakeScale(self.scaleFactor,
                                                self.scaleFactor)
            let rotateTrans = CGAffineTransformMakeRotation(
                                    CGFloat(self.angle * M_PI / 180))

            self.boxView!.transform =
                CGAffineTransformConcat(scaleTrans, rotateTrans)

            self.angle = (self.angle == 180 ? 360 : 180)
            self.scaleFactor = (self.scaleFactor == 2 ? 1 : 2)
            self.boxView?.center = location
        }, completion: nil)
}
```

Before compiling and running the application we need to take some time to describe the actions performed in the above method. First, the method gets the UITouch object from the *touches* argument and the *locationInView* method of this object is called to identify the location on the screen where the touch took place:

```swift
let touch = touches.anyObject() as UITouch
let location = touch.locationInView(self.view)
```

The animation block class method is then called with an animation duration of 2 seconds and the curve set to ease in/ease out:

```swift
UIView.animateWithDuration(2.0, delay: 0.0,
    options: UIViewAnimationOptions.CurveEaseInOut, animations: {
.
.
.
```

Two transformations are then generated for the view, one to scale the size of the view and one to rotate it 180 degrees. These transformations are then combined into a single transformation and applied to the UIView object:

```
let scaleTrans = CGAffineTransformMakeScale(self.scaleFactor,
                                             self.scaleFactor)
let rotateTrans = CGAffineTransformMakeRotation(
                              CGFloat(self.angle * M_PI / 180))

self.boxView!.transform = CGAffineTransformConcat(scaleTrans,
                                                  rotateTrans)
```

Ternary operators are then used to switch the scale and rotation angle variables ready for the next touch. In other words, after rotating 180 degrees on the first touch the view will need to be rotated to 360 degrees on the next animation. Similarly, once the box has been scaled by a factor of 2 it needs to scale back to its original size on the next animation:

```
self.angle = (self.angle == 180 ? 360 : 180)
self.scaleFactor = (self.scaleFactor == 2 ? 1 : 2)
```

Finally, the location of the view is moved to the point on the screen where the touch occurred:

```
self.boxView?.center = location
```

Once the *touchesEnded* method has been implemented it is time to try out the application.

60.10 Building and Running the Animation Application

Once all the code changes have been made and saved, click on the run button in the Xcode toolbar. Once the application has compiled it will load into the iOS Simulator (refer to *Testing Apps on iOS 8 Devices with Xcode 6* for steps on how to run the application on a physical iOS device).

When the application loads the blue square should appear near the top left hand corner of the screen. Click (or touch if running on a device) the screen and watch the box glide and rotate to the new location, the size of the box changing as it moves:

iOS Simulator – iPhone 5s – iPhone 5s / iOS 8...

Carrier 🔋   5:26 PM

Figure 60-1

60.11 **Summary**

Core Animation provides an easy to implement interface to animation within iOS 8 applications. From the simplest of tasks such as gracefully fading out a user interface element to basic animation and transformations, Core Animation provides a variety of techniques for enhancing user interfaces. This chapter covered the basics of Core Animation before working step-by-step through an example to demonstrate the implementation of motion, rotation and scaling animation.

61. iOS 8 UIKit Dynamics – An Overview

U IKit Dynamics provides a powerful and flexible mechanism for combining user interaction and animation into iOS user interfaces. What distinguishes UIKit Dynamics from other approaches to animation is the ability to declare animation behavior in terms of real-world physics.

Before moving on to a detailed tutorial in the next chapter, this chapter will provide an overview of the concepts and methodology behind UIKit Dynamics in iOS 8.

61.1 Understanding UIKit Dynamics

UIKit Dynamics allows for the animation of user interface elements (typically view items) to be implemented within a user interface, often in response to user interaction. In order to fully understand the concepts behind UIKit Dynamics, it helps to visualize how real world objects behave.

Holding an object in the air and then releasing it, for example, will cause it to fall to the ground. This behavior is, of course, the result of gravity. Whether or not, and by how much, an object bounces upon impact with a solid surface is dependent upon that object's elasticity and its velocity at the point of impact.

Similarly, pushing an object positioned on a flat surface will cause that object to travel a certain distance depending on the magnitude and angle of the pushing force combined with the level of friction at the point of contact between the two surfaces.

An object tethered to a moving point will react in a variety of ways such as following the anchor point, swinging in a pendulum motion or even bouncing and spinning on the tether in response to more aggressive motions. An object similarly attached using a spring, however, will behave entirely differently in response to the movement of the point of attachment.

Having considered how objects behave in the real world, imagine the ability to selectively apply these same physics related behaviors to view objects in a user interface and you will begin to understand the basic concepts behind UIKit Dynamics. Not only does UIKit Dynamics allow user interface interaction and animation to be declared using concepts with which we are all already familiar, but in most cases it allows this to be achieved with just a few simple lines of code.

61.2 **The UIKit Dynamics Architecture**

Before looking at the details of how UIKit Dynamics are implemented in application code, it helps to first gain an understanding of the different elements that comprise the dynamics architecture.

The UIKit Dynamics implementation comprises four key elements consisting of a *dynamic animator*, a set of one or more *dynamic behaviors*, one or more *dynamic items* and a *reference view*.

61.2.1 Dynamic Items

The dynamic items are the view elements within the user interface that are to be animated in response to specified dynamic behaviors. A dynamic item is any view object that implements the *UIDynamicItem* protocol which includes the UIView and UICollectionView classes and any subclasses thereof (such as UIButton and UILabel). Any custom view item can be made to work with UIKit Dynamics by making it conform to the UIDynamicItem protocol.

61.2.2 Dynamic Behaviors

Dynamic behaviors are used to configure the behavior which is to be applied to one or more dynamic items. A range of predefined dynamic behavior classes is available, including *UIAttachmentBehavior*, *UICollisionBehavior*, *UIGravityBehavior*, *UIDynamicItemBehavior*, *UIPushBehavior* and *UISnapBehavior*. Each of which is a subclass of the *UIDynamicBehavior* class which will be covered in detail later in this chapter.

In general, an instance of the class corresponding to the desired behavior (UIGravityBehavior for gravity, for example) will be created and the dynamic items for which the behavior is to be applied added to that instance. Dynamic items can be assigned to multiple dynamic behavior instances at the same time and may be added to, or removed from a dynamic behavior instance during runtime.

Once created and configured, behavior objects are then added to the *dynamic animator* instance. Once added to a dynamic animator, the behavior may be removed at any time.

61.2.3 The Reference View

The reference view dictates the area of the screen within which the UIKit Dynamics animation and interaction are to take place. This is typically the parent superclass view or collection view of which the dynamic item views are children.

61.2.4 The Dynamic Animator

The dynamic animator is responsible for coordinating the dynamic behaviors and items, and working with the underlying physics engine to perform the animation. The dynamic animator is represented by an instance of the *UIDynamicAnimator* class, and is initialized with the corresponding reference view at creation time. Once created, suitably configured dynamic behavior instances can be added and removed as required to implement the desired user interface behavior.

The overall architecture for an example UIKit Dynamics implementation can be represented visually using the diagram outlined in Figure 61-1:

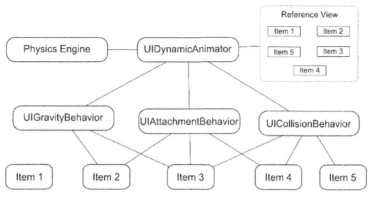

Figure 61-1

In the above example three dynamic behaviors have been added to the dynamic animator instance. The reference view contains 5 dynamic items, all but one of which have been added to at least one dynamic behavior instance.

61.3 Implementing UIKit Dynamics in an iOS 8 Application

The implementation of UIKit Dynamics in an application requires three very simple steps:

1. Create an instance of the *UIDynamicAnimator* class to act as the dynamic animator and initialize it with a reference to the reference view.

2. Create and configure a dynamic behavior instance and assign to it the dynamic items on which the specified behavior is to be imposed.

3. Add the dynamic behavior instance to the dynamic animator.

4. Repeat from step 2 to create and add additional behaviors.

61.4 Dynamic Animator Initialization

The first step in implementing UIKit Dynamics is to create and initialize an instance of the UIDynamicAnimator class. The first step is to declare an instance variable for the reference:

```
var animator: UIDynamicAnimator?
```

Next, the dynamic animator instance can be created. The following code, for example, creates and initializes the animator instance within the *viewDidLoad* method of a view controller, using the view controller's parent view as the reference view:

```
override func viewDidLoad() {
```

```
    super.viewDidLoad()
    animator = UIDynamicAnimator(referenceView: self.view)
}
```

With the dynamic animator created and initialized, the next step is to begin to configure behaviors, the details for which differ slightly depending on the nature of the behavior.

61.5 Configuring Gravity Behavior

Gravity behavior is implemented using the UIGravityBehavior class, the purpose of which is to cause view items to want to "fall" within the reference view as though influenced by gravity. UIKit Dynamics gravity is slightly different from real world gravity in that it is possible to define a vector for the direction of the gravitational force using x and y components (x, y) contained within a CGVector instance. The default vector for this class is (0.0, 1.0) which corresponds to downwards motion at a speed of 1000 points per second[2]. A negative x or y value will reverse the direction of gravity.

A UIGravityBehavior instance can be initialized as follows, passing through an array of dynamic items on which the behavior is to be imposed (in this case two views named view1 and view2):

```
let gravity = UIGravityBehavior(items: [view1, view2])
```

Once created, the default vector can be changed if required at any time:

```
let vector = CGVectorMake(0.0, 0.5)
gravity.gravityDirection = vector
```

Finally, the behavior needs to be added to the dynamic animator instance:

```
animator?.addBehavior(gravity)
```

At any point during the application lifecycle, dynamic items may be added to, or removed from, the behavior:

```
gravity.addItem(view3)
gravity.removeItem(view)
```

Similarly, the entire behavior may be removed from the dynamic animator:

```
animator?.removeBehavior(gravity)
```

When gravity behavior is applied to a view, and in the absence of opposing behaviors, the view will immediately move in the direction of the specified gravity vector. In fact, as currently defined, the view will fall out of the bounds of the reference view and disappear. This can be prevented by setting up a collision behavior.

61.6 **Configuring Collision Behavior**

UIKit Dynamics is all about making items move on the device display. When an item moves there is a high chance it will collide either with another item or with the boundaries of the encapsulating reference view. As previously discussed, in the absence of any form of collision behavior, a moving item can move out of the visible area of the reference view. Such a configuration will also cause a moving item to simply pass over the top of any other items that happen to be in its path. Collision behavior (defined using the UICollisionBehavior class) allows for such collisions to behave in ways more representative of the real world.

Collision behavior can be implemented between dynamic items (such that certain items can collide with others) or within boundaries (allowing collisions to occur when a designated boundary is reached by an item). Boundaries can be defined such that they correspond to the boundaries of the reference view, or entirely new boundaries can be defined using lines and Bezier paths.

As with gravity behavior, a collision is generally created and initialized with an array object containing the items to which the behavior is to be applied. For example:

```
let collision = UICollisionBehavior(items: [view1, view2])
animator?.addBehavior(collision)
```

As configured, view1 and view2 will now collide when coming into contact with each other. What then happens will be decided by the physics engine depending on the elasticity of the items, and the angle and speed of the collision. In other words, the engine will animate the items so that they behave as if they were physical objects subject to the laws of physics.

By default, an item under the influence of a collision behavior will collide both with other items in the same collision behavior set, and also with any boundaries set up. To declare the reference view as a boundary, simply set the *translatesReferenceBoundsIntoBoundary* property of the behavior instance to *true*:

```
collision.translatesReferenceBoundsIntoBoundary = true
```

A boundary inset from the edges of the reference view may be defined using the *setsTranslateReferenceBoundsIntoBoundaryWithInsets* method, passing through the required insets as an argument in the form of a *UIEdgeInsets* object.

The *collisionMode* property may be used to change default collision behavior by assigning one of the following constants:

- **UICollisionBehaviorMode.Items** – Specifies that collisions only occur between items added to the collision behavior instance. Boundary collisions are ignored.
- **UICollisionBehaviorMode.Boundaries** – Configures the behavior to ignore item collisions, recognizing only collisions with boundaries.
- **UICollisionBehaviorMode.Everything** – Specifies that collisions occur between items added to the behavior and all boundaries. This is the default behavior.

The following code, for example, enables collisions only for items:

```
collision.collisionMode = UICollisionBehaviorMode.Items
```

In the event that an application needs to react to a collision, simply declare a class instance that conforms to the UICollisionBehaviorDelegate class by implementing the following methods and assign it as the delegate for the UICollisionBehavior object instance.

- collisionBehavior(_:beganContactForItem:withBoundaryIdentifier:atPoint:)
- collisionBehavior(_:beganContactForItem:withItem:atPoint:)
- collisionBehavior(_:endedContactForItem:withBoundaryIdentifier:)
- collisionBehavior(_:endedContactForItem:withItem:)

When implemented, the application will be notified when collisions begin and end. Note that in most cases the delegate methods will be passed information about the collision such as the location and the items or boundaries involved.

In addition, aspects of the collision behavior such as friction and the elasticity of the colliding items (such that they bounce on contact) may be configured using the UIDynamicBehavior class. This class will be covered in detail later in this chapter.

61.7 Configuring Attachment Behavior

As the name suggests, the UIAttachmentBehavior class allows dynamic items to be configured such that they behave as if attached. These attachments can take the form of two items attached to each other or an item attached to an anchor point at specific coordinates within the reference view. The attachment can take the form of an imaginary piece of cord that does not stretch, or a spring attachment with configurable damping and frequency properties that control how "bouncy" the attached item is in response to motion.

By default, the attachment point within the item itself is positioned at the center of the view. This can, however, be changed to a different position causing the real world behavior outlined in Figure 61-2 to occur:

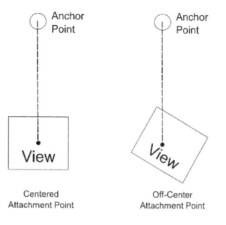

Figure 61-2

In general, the physics engine will simulate animation to match what would typically happen in the real world. As illustrated above, the item will tilt when not attached in the center. In the event that the anchor point moves, the attached view will also move. Depending on the motion, the item will swing in a pendulum motion and, assuming appropriate collision behavior configuration, bounce off any boundaries it collides with as it swings.

As with all UIKit Dynamics behavior, all the work to achieve this is performed for us by the physics engine. The only effort required by the developer is to write a few lines of code to set up the behavior before adding it to the dynamic animator instance. The following code, for example, sets up an attachment between two dynamic items:

```
let attachment = UIAttachmentBehavior(item: view1,
                                      attachedToItem: view2)
animator?.addBehavior(attachment)
```

The following code, on the other hand, specifies an attachment between view1 and an anchor point with the frequency and damping values set to configure a spring effect:

```
let anchorpoint = CGPointMake(100, 100)
let attachment = UIAttachmentBehavior(item: view1,
                    attachedToAnchor: anchorPoint)
attachment.frequency = 4.0
attachment.damping = 0.0
```

The above examples attach to the center point of the view. The following code fragment sets the same attachment as above, but with an attachment point offset 20, 20 points relative to the center of the view:

```
let anchorpoint = CGPointMake(100, 100)
let offset = UIOffsetMake(20, 20)

let attachment = UIAttachmentBehavior(item: view1,
```

```
                    offsetFromCenter: offset,
                attachedToAnchor: anchorPoint)
```

61.8 Configuring Snap Behavior

The UISnapBehavior class allows a dynamic item to be "snapped" to a specific location within the reference view. When implemented, the item will move toward the snap location as though pulled by a spring and, depending on the damping property specified, will oscillate a number of times before finally snapping into place. Until the behavior is removed from the dynamic animator, the item will continue to snap to the location when subsequently moved to another position.

The damping property can be set to any value between 0.0 and 1.0 with 1.0 specifying maximum oscillation. The default value for damping is 0.5.

The following code configures snap behavior for dynamic item view1 with damping set to 1.0:

```
let point = CGPointMake(100, 100)
let snap = UISnapBehavior(item: view1, snapToPoint: point)

animator?.addBehavior(snap)
```

61.9 Configuring Push Behavior

Push behavior, defined using the UIPushBehavior class, simulates the effect of pushing one or more dynamic items in a specific direction with a specified force. The force can be specified as continuous or instantaneous. In the case of a continuous push, the force is continually applied causing the item to accelerate over time. The instantaneous push is more like a "shove" than a push in that the force is applied for a short pulse causing the item to quickly gain velocity, but gradually lose momentum and eventually stop. Once an instantaneous push event has completed, the behavior is disabled (though it can subsequently be re-enabled).

The direction of the push can be defined in radians or using x and y components. By default, the pushing force is applied to the center of the dynamic item, though as with attachments, this can be changed to an offset relative to the center of the view.

A force of magnitude 1.0 is defined as being a force of one UIKit Newton which equates to a view sized at 100 x 100 points with a density of value 1.0 accelerating at a rate of 100 points per second[2]. The density of a view can, as will be explained in the next section, be configured using the UIDynamicItemBehavior class.

The following code pushes an item with instantaneous force at a magnitude of 0.2 applied on both the x and y axes, causing the view to move diagonally down and to the right.

```
let push = UIPushBehavior(items: [view1],
                        mode: UIPushBehaviorMode.Instantaneous)
let vector = CGVectorMake(0.2, 0.2)
push.pushDirection = vector
```

Continuous push behavior can be achieved by changing the *mode* in the above code property to *UIPushBehaviorMode.Continuous*.

To change the point where force is applied, configure the behavior using the *setTargetOffsetFromCenter(_:forItem:)* method of the behavior object, specifying an offset relative to the center of the view. For example:

```
let offset = UIOffsetMake(20, 20)
push.setTargetOffsetFromCenter(offset, forItem:view1)
```

In most cases, an off-center target for the pushing force will cause the item to rotate as it moves as indicated in Figure 61-3:

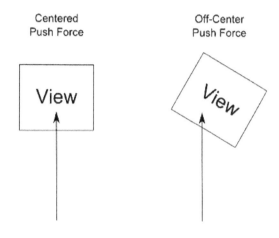

Figure 61-3

61.10 **The UIDynamicItemBehavior Class**

The UIDynamicItemBehavior class allows additional behavior characteristics to be defined that complement a number of the above primitive behaviors. This class can, for example, be used to define the density, resistance and elasticity of dynamic items so that they do not move as far when subjected to an instantaneous push, or bounce to a greater extent when involved in a collision. Dynamic items also have the ability to rotate by default. In the event that rotation is not required for an item, this behavior can be turned off using a UIDynamicItemBehavior instance.

Behavioral properties of dynamic items that can be governed by the UIDynamicItemBehavior class are as follows:

- **allowsRotation** – Controls whether or not the item is permitted to rotate during animation.
- **angularResistence** – The amount by which the item resists rotation. The higher the value, the faster the item will stop rotating.
- **density** – The mass of the item.

- **elasticity** – The amount of elasticity an item will exhibit when involved in a collision. The greater the elasticity the more the item will bounce.
- **friction** – The resistance exhibited by an item when it slides against another item.
- **resistence** – The overall resistance that the item exhibits in response to behavioral influences. The greater the value the sooner the item will come to a complete stop during animation.

In addition, the class includes the following methods that may be used to increase or decrease the angular or linear velocity of a specified dynamic item:

- **angularVelocityForItem()** – Increases or decreases the angular velocity of the specified item. Velocity is specified in radians per second where a negative value reduces the angular velocity.
- **linearVelocityForItem()** – Increases or decreases the linear velocity of the specified item. Velocity is specified in points per second where a negative value reduces the velocity.

The following code example creates a new UIDynamicItemBehavior instance and uses it to set resistance and elasticity for two views before adding the behavior to the dynamic animator instance:

```
let behavior = UIDynamicItemBehavior(items: [view1, view2])
behavior.elasticity = 0.2
behavior.resistance = 0.5
animator?.addBehavior(behavior)
```

61.11 Combining Behaviors to Create a Custom Behavior

Multiple behaviors may be combined to create a single custom behavior using an instance of the UIDynamicBehavior class. The first step is to create and initialize each of the behavior objects. An instance of the UIDynamicBehavior class is then created and each behavior added to it via calls to the *addChildBehavior* method. Once created, only the UIDynamicBehavior instance needs to be added to the dynamic animator. For example:

```
// Create multiple behavior objects here

let customBehavior = UIDynamicBehavior()

customBehavior.addChildBehavior(behavior)
customBehavior.addChildBehavior(attachment)
customBehavior.addChildBehavior(gravity)
customBehavior.addChildBehavior(push)

animator?.addBehavior(customBehavior)
```

61.12 Summary

UIKit Dynamics, introduced as part of iOS 7, provides a new way to bridge the gap between user interaction with an iOS device and corresponding animation within an application user interface. UIKit Dynamics takes a novel approach to animation by allowing view items to be configured such that they behave in much the same way as physical objects in the real world. This chapter has covered an overview of the basic concepts behind UIKit Dynamics and provided some details on how such behavior is implemented in terms of coding. The next chapter will work through a tutorial that demonstrates many of these concepts in action.

Chapter 62

62. An iOS 8 UIKit Dynamics Tutorial

With the basics of UIKit Dynamics covered in the previous chapter, this chapter will take this knowledge and apply it to the creation of an example application designed to show UIKit Dynamics in action. The example application created in this chapter will make use of the gravity, collision, elasticity and attachment features in conjunction with touch handling to demonstrate how these key features are implemented.

62.1 Creating the UIKit Dynamics Example Project

Begin by launching Xcode and selecting the option to create a new project from the welcome screen (or select the *File -> New -> Project...* menu option if the welcome screen is not visible). From the resulting template selection screen, choose the *Single View Application* option before clicking *Next* to proceed. Enter *UIKitDynamics* into the Product Name field and select *Swift* and *Universal* from the Language and Devices fields respectively. Click on *Next* once again and, in the file selection screen, navigate to a suitable location for the project files before clicking on *Create*.

62.2 Adding the Dynamic Items

The user interface for the application is going to consist of two view objects which will be drawn in the form of squares colored blue and red respectively. The first step in the tutorial, therefore, is to implement the code to create and draw these views. Within the project navigator panel, locate and select the *ViewController.swift* file and add variables for these two views so that the file reads as follows:

```
import UIKit

class ViewController: UIViewController {

    var blueBoxView: UIView?
    var redBoxView: UIView?
```

With the references declared, select the *ViewController.swift* file and add code to the *viewDidLoad* method to draw the views, color them appropriately and then add them to the parent view so that they appear within the user interface:

```
override func viewDidLoad() {
    super.viewDidLoad()
```

```
    var frameRect = CGRectMake(10, 20, 80, 80)
    blueBoxView = UIView(frame: frameRect)
    blueBoxView?.backgroundColor = UIColor.blueColor()

    frameRect = CGRectMake(150, 20, 60, 60)
    redBoxView = UIView(frame: frameRect)
    redBoxView?.backgroundColor = UIColor.redColor()

    self.view.addSubview(blueBoxView!)
    self.view.addSubview(redBoxView!)
}
```

Perform a test run of the application on either a simulator or physical iOS device and verify that the new views appear as expected within the user interface (Figure 62-1):

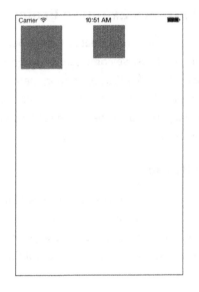

Figure 62-1

62.3 Creating the Dynamic Animator Instance

As outlined in the previous chapter, a key element in implementing UIKit Dynamics is an instance of the UIDynamicAnimator class. Select the *ViewController.swift* file and add an instance variable for a UIDynamicAnimator object within the application code:

```
import UIKit

class ViewController: UIViewController {

    var blueBoxView: UIView?
    var redBoxView: UIView?
```

```
var animator: UIDynamicAnimator?
```

Next, modify the *viewDidLoad* method within the *ViewController.swift* file once again to add code to create and initialize the instance, noting that the top level view of the view controller is passed through as the reference view:

```
override func viewDidLoad() {
    super.viewDidLoad()

    var frameRect = CGRectMake(10, 20, 80, 80)
    blueBoxView = UIView(frame: frameRect)
    blueBoxView?.backgroundColor = UIColor.blueColor()

    frameRect = CGRectMake(150, 20, 60, 60)
    redBoxView = UIView(frame: frameRect)
    redBoxView?.backgroundColor = UIColor.redColor()

    self.view.addSubview(blueBoxView!)
    self.view.addSubview(redBoxView!)

    animator = UIDynamicAnimator(referenceView: self.view)
}
```

With the dynamic items added to the user interface and an instance of the dynamic animator created and initialized, it is now time to begin creating dynamic behavior instances.

62.4 Adding Gravity to the Views

The first behavior to be added to the example application is going to be gravity. For the purposes of this tutorial, gravity will be added to both views such that a force of gravity of 1.0 UIKit Newton is applied directly downwards along the y axis of the parent view. To achieve this, the *viewDidLoad* method needs to be further modified to create a suitably configured instance of the UIGravityBehavior class and to add that instance to the dynamic animator:

```
override func viewDidLoad() {
    super.viewDidLoad()

    var frameRect = CGRectMake(10, 20, 80, 80)
    blueBoxView = UIView(frame: frameRect)
    blueBoxView?.backgroundColor = UIColor.blueColor()

    frameRect = CGRectMake(150, 20, 60, 60)
    redBoxView = UIView(frame: frameRect)
    redBoxView?.backgroundColor = UIColor.redColor()
```

```
self.view.addSubview(blueBoxView!)
self.view.addSubview(redBoxView!)

animator = UIDynamicAnimator(referenceView: self.view)

let gravity = UIGravityBehavior(items: [blueBoxView!,
                                                   redBoxView!])

let vector = CGVectorMake(0.0, 1.0)
gravity.gravityDirection = vector

animator?.addBehavior(gravity)
}
```

Compile and run the application once again. Note that after launching, the gravity behavior causes the views to fall from the top of the reference view and out of view at the bottom of the device display. In order to keep the views within the bounds of the reference view, it is necessary to set up a collision behavior.

62.5 Implementing Collision Behavior

In terms of collision behavior, the example requires that collisions occur both when the views impact each other and when making contact with the boundaries of the reference view. With these requirements in mind, the collision behavior needs to be implemented as follows:

```
override func viewDidLoad() {
    super.viewDidLoad()

    var frameRect = CGRectMake(10, 20, 80, 80)
    blueBoxView = UIView(frame: frameRect)
    blueBoxView?.backgroundColor = UIColor.blueColor()

    frameRect = CGRectMake(150, 20, 60, 60)
    redBoxView = UIView(frame: frameRect)
    redBoxView?.backgroundColor = UIColor.redColor()

    self.view.addSubview(blueBoxView!)
    self.view.addSubview(redBoxView!)

    animator = UIDynamicAnimator(referenceView: self.view)

    let gravity = UIGravityBehavior(items: [blueBoxView!,
                                                   redBoxView!])

    let vector = CGVectorMake(0.0, 1.0)
    gravity.gravityDirection = vector
```

```
    let collision = UICollisionBehavior(items: [blueBoxView!,
                                                  redBoxView!])
    collision.translatesReferenceBoundsIntoBoundary = true

    animator?.addBehavior(collision)
    animator?.addBehavior(gravity)
}
```

Running the application should now cause the views to stop at the bottom edge of the reference view and bounce slightly after impact. The amount by which the views bounce in the event of a collision can be changed by creating a UIDynamicBehavior class instance and changing the elasticity property. The following code, for example, changes the elasticity of the blue box view so that it bounces to a higher degree than the red box:

```
override func viewDidLoad() {
    super.viewDidLoad()
    .
    .
    .
    let collision = UICollisionBehavior(items: [blueBoxView!,
                                                  redBoxView!])
    collision.translatesReferenceBoundsIntoBoundary = true

    let behavior = UIDynamicItemBehavior(items: [blueBoxView!,
                                                   redBoxView!])

    behavior.elasticity = 0.5

    animator?.addBehavior(behavior)
    animator?.addBehavior(collision)
    animator?.addBehavior(gravity)
}
```

62.6 Attaching a View to an Anchor Point

So far in this tutorial we have added some behavior to the application but have not yet implemented any functionality that connects UIKit Dynamics to user interaction. In this section, however, the example will be modified such that an attachment is created between the blue box view and the point of contact of a touch on the screen. This anchor point will be continually updated as the user's touch moves across the screen, thereby causing the blue box to follow the anchor point. The first step in this process is to declare within the *ViewController.swift* file some instance variables within which to store both the current location of the anchor point and a reference to a UIAttachmentBehavior instance:

```
import UIKit

class ViewController: UIViewController {
```

```
var blueBoxView: UIView?
var redBoxView: UIView?
var animator: UIDynamicAnimator?
var currentLocation: CGPoint?
var attachment: UIAttachmentBehavior?
```

As outlined in the chapter entitled *An Overview of iOS 8 Multitouch, Taps and Gestures*, touches can be detected by overriding the *touchesBegan*, *touchesMoved* and *touchesEnded* methods. The *touchesBegan* method in the *ViewController.swift* file now needs to be implemented to obtain the coordinates of the touch and to add an attachment behavior between that location and the blue box view to the animator instance:

```
override func touchesBegan(touches: NSSet, withEvent event: UIEvent) {

    let theTouch = touches.anyObject() as UITouch
    currentLocation = theTouch.locationInView(self.view)

    attachment = UIAttachmentBehavior(item: blueBoxView!,
                         attachedToAnchor: currentLocation!)

    animator?.addBehavior(attachment)
}
```

As the touch moves around within the reference view, the anchorPoint property of the attachment behavior needs to be modified to track the motion. This involves overriding the *touchesMoved* method as follows:

```
override func touchesMoved(touches: NSSet, withEvent event: UIEvent) {
    let theTouch = touches.anyObject() as UITouch

    currentLocation = theTouch.locationInView(self.view)
    attachment?.anchorPoint = currentLocation!
}
```

Finally, when the touch ends, the attachment needs to be removed so that the view will be pulled down to the bottom of the reference view by the previously defined gravity behavior. Remaining within the *ViewController.swift* file, implement the *touchesEnded* method as follows:

```
override func touchesEnded(touches: NSSet, withEvent event: UIEvent) {
    animator?.removeBehavior(attachment)
}
```

Compile and run the application and touch the display. As the touch is moved, note that the blue box view moves as though tethered to the touch point. Move the touch such that the blue and red boxes collide and observe that the red box will move in response to the collision whilst the blue box will rotate on the attachment point as illustrated in Figure 62-2:

Figure 62-2

Release the touch and note that gravity causes the blue box to fall once again and settle at the bottom edge of the reference view.

The code that creates the attachment currently attaches to the center point of the blue box view. Modify the *touchesBegan* method to adjust the attachment point so that it is off center:

```
override func touchesBegan(touches: NSSet, withEvent event: UIEvent) {
    let theTouch = touches.anyObject() as UITouch

    currentLocation = theTouch.locationInView(self.view)
    let offset = UIOffsetMake(20, 20)
    attachment = UIAttachmentBehavior(item: blueBoxView!,
                    offsetFromCenter: offset,
                    attachedToAnchor: currentLocation!)

    animator?.addBehavior(attachment)
}
```

When the blue box view is now suspended by the anchor point attachment, it will tilt in accordance with the offset attachment point.

62.7 Implementing a Spring Attachment Between two Views

The final step in this tutorial is to attach the two views together using a spring-style attachment. All that this involves is a few lines of code within the *viewDidLoad* method to create the attachment behavior, set the frequency and damping values to create the springing effect and then add the behavior to the animator instance:

```
override func viewDidLoad() {
    super.viewDidLoad()

    .

    .

    .

    let behavior = UIDynamicItemBehavior(items: [blueBoxView!,
                                                 redBoxView!])

    behavior.elasticity = 0.5

    let boxAttachment = UIAttachmentBehavior(item: blueBoxView!,
                                 attachedToItem: redBoxView!)

    boxAttachment.frequency = 4.0
    boxAttachment.damping = 0.0

    animator?.addBehavior(boxAttachment)
    animator?.addBehavior(behavior)
    animator?.addBehavior(collision)
    animator?.addBehavior(gravity)
}
```

When the application is now run, the red box will move in relation to the blue box as though connected by a spring (Figure 62-3). The views will even spring apart when pushed together before the touch is released.

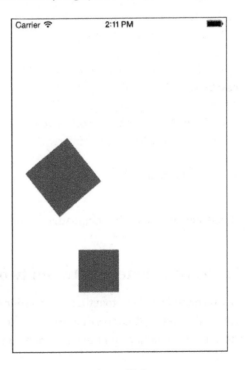

Figure 62-3

62.8 **Summary**

The example created in this chapter has demonstrated the steps involved in implementing UIKit Dynamics within an iOS 8 application in the form of gravity, collision and attachment behaviors. Perhaps the most remarkable fact about the animation functionality implemented in this tutorial is that it was achieved in approximately 40 lines of UIKit Dynamics code, a fraction of the amount of code that would have been required to implement such behavior in the absence of UIKit Dynamics.

63. An Introduction to iOS 8 Sprite Kit Programming

If you have ever had an idea for a game, but didn't create it because you lacked the skills or time to write complex game code and logic, then look no further than Sprite Kit. Introduced as part of the iOS 8 SDK, Sprite Kit provides a way for 2D games to be developed with relative ease.

Sprite Kit provides just about everything needed to create 2D games for iOS and Mac OS X with a minimum amount of coding. Some of the features provided by Sprite Kit include animation, physics, collision detection and special effects. Most of these features can be harnessed within a game with just a few method calls.

In this, and the next three chapters, the topic of games development with Sprite Kit will be covered with the objective of bringing the reader up to a level of competence to begin creating games whilst also providing a knowledge base on which to develop further Sprite Kit development skills.

63.1 What is Sprite Kit?

Sprite Kit is a programming framework that makes it easy for the developer to implement 2D based games that run on iOS and OS X. It provides a range of classes that support the rendering and animation of graphical objects (otherwise known as *sprites*) that can be configured to behave in specific programmer defined ways within a game. Through use of *actions,* a wide variety of activities can be run on sprites such as animating a character so that it appears to be walking, making a sprite follow a specific path within a game scene or changing the color and texture of a sprite in real-time.

Sprite Kit also includes a physics engine allowing physics related behavior to be imposed on sprites. A sprite can, amongst other things, be made to move by subjecting it to a pushing force, configured to behave as though affected by gravity, or to bounce back from another sprite as the result of a collision.

In addition, the Sprite Kit particle emitter class provides a useful mechanism for creating special effects within a game such as smoke, rain, fire and explosions. A range of templates for existing special effects is provided with Sprite Kit along with an editor built into Xcode for creating custom particle emitter based special effects.

63.2 The Key Components of a Sprite Kit Game

A Sprite Kit game will typically consist of a number of different elements.

63.2.1 Sprite Kit View

Every Sprite Kit game will have at least one SKView class. An SKView instance sits at the top of the component hierarchy of a game and is responsible for displaying the game content to the user. It is a subclass of the UIView class and, as such, has many of the traits of that class including an associated view controller.

63.2.2 Scenes

A game will also contain one or more scenes. One scene might, for example, display a menu when the game first starts while additional scenes may represent multiple levels within the game. Scenes are represented in a game by the SKScene class which is a subclass of the SKNode class.

63.2.3 Nodes

Each scene within a Sprite Kit game will have a number of Sprite Kit node children. These nodes fall into a number of different categories, each of which has associated with it a dedicated Sprite Kit node class. These node classes are all subclasses of the SKNode class and can be summarized as follows:

- **SKSpriteNode** – Draws a sprite with a texture. This will typically be used for creating image based characters or objects in a game, such as a spaceship, animal or monster.
- **SKLabelNode** – Used to display text within a game such as menu options, the prevailing score or a "game over" message.
- **SKShapeNode** – Allows nodes to be created containing shapes defined using Core Graphics paths. If a sprite is required to display a circle, for example, the SKShapeNode class could be used to draw the circle as an alternative to texturing an SKSpriteNode with an image of a circle.
- **SKEmitterNode** – The node responsible for managing and displaying particle emitter based special effects.
- **SKVideoNode** – Allows video playback to be performed within a game node.
- **SKEffectNode** – Allows Core Image filter effects to be applied to child nodes. A sepia filter effect, for example, could be applied to all child nodes of an SKEffectNode.
- **SKCropNode** – Allows the pixels in a node to be cropped subject to a specified mask.
- **SKLightNode** – The lighting node is provided as a way to add light sources to a SpriteKit scene, including the casting of shadows when the light falls on other nodes in the same scene.
- **SK3DNode** – The SK3DNode allows 3D assets created using the Scene Kit Framework to be embedded into 2D Sprite Kit games.

63.2.4 Physics Bodies

Each node within a scene has the option to have associated with it a physics body. Physics bodies are represented by the SKPhysicsBody class. Assignment of a physics body to a node brings a wide range of additional possibilities in terms of the behavior that can be associated with a node. When a node is assigned a physics body it will, by default, behave as though subject to the prevailing forces of gravity within the scene. In addition, the node can be configured to behave as though having a physical boundary. This boundary can be defined as a circle, a rectangle or a polygon of any shape.

Once a node has a boundary, collisions between other nodes can be detected and the physics engine used to apply real-world physics to the node such as causing it to bounce when hitting other nodes. The use of contact bit masks can be employed to specify the types of nodes for which contact notification is required.

The physics body also allows forces to be applied to nodes, such as propelling a node in a particular direction across a scene using either a constant or one time impulse force. Physical bodies can also be joined together using a variety of different join types (such as sliding, fixed, hinged and spring based attachments).

The properties of a physics body (and therefore the associated node) may also be changed. Mass, density, velocity and friction are just a few of the properties of a physics body available for modification by the game developer.

63.2.5 Physics World

Each scene in a game has its own *physics world* object in the form of an instance of the SKPhysicsWorld class. A reference to this object, which is created automatically when the scene is initialized, may be obtained by accessing the *physicsWorld* property of the scene. The physics world object is responsible for managing and imposing the rules of physics on any nodes in the scene with which a physics body has been associated. Properties are available on the physics world instance to change the default gravity settings for the scene and also to change the speed at which the physics simulation runs.

63.2.6 Actions

An action is an activity that is performed by a node in a scene. Actions are the responsibility of SKAction class instances which are created and configured with the action to be performed. That action is then run on one or more nodes. An action might, for example, be configured to perform a rotation of 90 degrees. That action would then be run on a node to make it rotate within the scene. The SKAction class includes a wide range of action types including fade in, fade out, rotation, movement and scaling. Perhaps the most interesting action involves animating a sprite node through a series of texture frames.

Actions can be categorized as *sequence*, *group* or *repeating* actions. An action sequence specifies a series of actions that are to be performed consecutively whilst group actions specify a set of actions to be performed in parallel. Repeating actions are configured to restart after completion. An action may be configured either to repeat a set number of times or to repeat indefinitely.

63.2.7 Transitions

Transitions occur when a game changes from one scene to another. Whilst it is possible to immediately switch from one scene to another, a more visually pleasing result might be achieved by animating the transition in some way. This can be implemented using the SKTransition class which provides a number of different pre-defined transition animations such as sliding the new scene down over the top of the old scene, or presenting the effect of doors opening to reveal the new scene.

63.2.8 Texture Atlas

A large part of developing games involves handling images. Many of these images serve as textures for sprites. Whilst it is possible to add images to a project individually, Sprite Kit also allows images to be grouped together into a texture atlas. Not only does this make it easier to manage the images, but it also brings efficiencies in terms of image storage and handling. Typically the texture images for a particular sprite animation sequence would be stored in a single texture atlas whilst another atlas might store the images for the background of a particular scene.

63.2.9 Constraints

Constraints allow restrictions to be imposed on nodes within a scene in terms of distance and orientation in relation to a point or another node. A constraint can, for example, be applied to a node such that its movement is restricted to within a certain distance of another node. Similarly, a node can be configured so that it is oriented to point towards either another node or a specified point within the scene. A constraint is represented by an instance of the SKConstraint class and are group together into an array and assigned to the *constraints* property of the node to which they are to be applied.

63.3 **An Example Sprite Kit Game Hierarchy**

To aid in visualizing how the various Sprite Kit components fit together, Figure 63-1 outlines the hierarchy for a simple game:

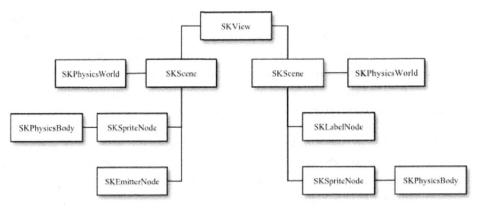

Figure 63-1

In this hypothetical game, a single SKView instance has two SKScene children, each of which has its own SKPhysicsWorld object. Each scene, in turn, has two node children. In the case of both scenes, the SKSpriteNode instances have been assigned SKPhysicsBody instances.

63.4 **The Sprite Kit Game Rendering Loop**

When working with Sprite Kit, it helps to have a basic understanding of the way in which the animation and physics simulation process works. This can best be described by looking at the Sprite Kit frame rendering loop.

Sprite Kit performs the work of rendering a game using a *game rendering loop*. Within this loop, Sprite Kit performs a variety of tasks to render the visual and behavioral elements of the currently active scene, with an iteration of the loop being performed for each successive frame displayed to the user.

Figure 63-2 provides a visual representation of the frame rendering sequence performed in the loop:

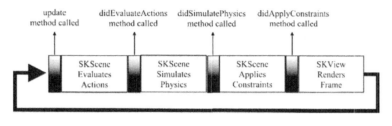

Figure 63-2

When a scene is displayed within a game, Sprite Kit enters the rendering loop and repeatedly performs the same sequence of steps as shown above. At a number of points in this sequence, the loop will make calls to your game providing the opportunity for the game logic to respond when necessary.

Before performing any other tasks, the loop begins by calling the *update* method of the corresponding SKScene instance. It is within this method that the game should perform any tasks prior to the frame being updated, such as adding additional sprites or updating the current score.

The loop then evaluates and implements any actions that are pending on the scene, after which the game is given the opportunity to perform more tasks via a call to the *didEvaluateActions* method.

Next, physics simulations are performed on the scene followed by a call to the scene's *didSimulatePhysics* method where the game logic may react where necessary to any changes as a result of the physics simulation.

The scene then applies any constraints that have been configured on the nodes in the scene. Once this task has been completed a call is made to the scene's *didApplyConstraints* method if it has been implemented.

Finally, the SKView instance renders the new scene frame before the loop sequence repeats once again.

63.5 The Sprite Kit Level Editor

Prior to the introduction of Xcode 6, the development of Sprite Kit game scenes was almost entirely a matter of writing code to use the SpriteKit framework. Xcode 6, however, has introduced the Sprite Kit Level Editor tool. This editor allows scenes to be designed by dragging and dropping nodes onto a scene canvas and setting properties on those nodes using the SKNode Inspector. Whilst code writing is still required for anything but the most basic of scene requirements, the Level Editor provides a useful alternative to writing code for some of the less complex aspects of SpriteKit game development.

63.6 **Summary**

Sprite Kit provides a platform for the creation of 2D games on iOS and Mac OS X. Games are comprised of an SKView instance with an SKScene object for each scene of the game. Scenes contain nodes that represent the characters, objects and items in the game. A variety of node types are available, all of which are subclassed from the SKNode class. Each node can have associated with it a physics body in the form of an SKPhysicsBody instance. A node with a physics body will be subject to physical forces such as gravity and, when given a physical boundary, collisions with other nodes may also be detected. Actions are configured using the SKAction class, instances of which are then run by the nodes on which the action is to be performed.

The orientation and movement of a node can be restricted through the implementation of constraints using the SKConstraint class.

The rendering of a Sprite Kit game takes place within the *game loop* with one loop being performed for each frame of the game. At a variety of points in this loop, the application will be given the opportunity to perform tasks as needed to implement and manage the underlying game logic.

Having provided a high level overview in this chapter, the next three chapters will take a more practical approach to exploring the capabilities of Sprite Kit through the creation of a simple game.

64. An iOS 8 Sprite Kit Level Editor Game Tutorial

In this chapter of iOS 8 App Development Essentials, many of the Sprite Kit Framework features outlined in the previous chapter will be used to create a game based application. In particular, this tutorial will demonstrate practical use of scenes, textures, sprites, labels and actions. In addition, the application created in this chapter will also make use of physics bodies to demonstrate the use of collisions and simulated gravity.

This tutorial will also demonstrate the use of the Sprite Kit Level Editor combined with Swift code to create a Sprite Kit based game.

64.1 About the Sprite Kit Demo Game

The game created in this chapter consists of a single animated character that shoots arrows across the scene when the screen is tapped. For the duration of the game, balls fall from the top of the screen with the objective being to hit as many balls as possible with the arrows. When an arrow hits a ball, the texture of the arrow is changed to make it appear as though the tip of the arrow is embedded in the ball. A physical join is also established at the point of collision so that the arrow sprite remains stuck into the side of the ball as it continues to fall off the bottom of the screen.

The completed game will comprise the following two scenes:

- **GameScene** – The scene which appears when the game is first launched. The scene will announce the name of the game and invite the user to touch the screen to begin the game. The game will then transition to the second scene.
- **ArcheryScene** – The scene where the game play takes place. Within this scene the archer and ball sprites are animated and the physics behavior and collision detection implemented to make the game work.

In terms of sprite nodes, the game will include the following:

- **Welcome Node** – An SKLabelNode instance that displays a message to the user on the Welcome Scene.
- **Archer Node** – An SKSpriteNode instance to represent the archer game character. The animation frames that cause the archer to load and launch an arrow are provided via a sequence of image files contained within a texture atlas.

- **Arrow Node** – An SKSpriteNode instance used to represent the arrows as they are shot by the archer character. This node is initially assigned a texture showing the entire arrow. This texture is then changed on collision with a ball to show the arrow embedded into the target. This node has associated with it a physics body so that collisions can be detected and to make sure it responds to gravity.
- **Ball Node** – An SKSpriteNode used to represent the balls that fall from the sky. The ball has associated with it a physics body for gravity and collision detection purposes.
- **Game Over Node** – An SKLabelNode instance that displays the score to the user at the end of the game.

The overall architecture of the game can be represented hierarchically as outlined in Figure 64-1:

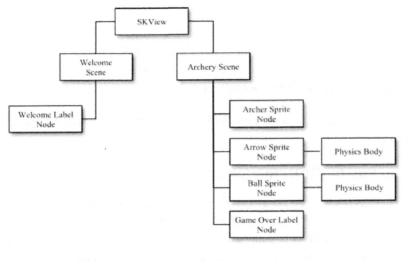

Figure 64-1

64.2 **Creating the SpriteKitDemo Project**

To create the project, launch Xcode and select the *Create a new Xcode project* option from the welcome screen (or use the *File -> New -> Project...*) menu option. On the template selection panel make sure that the *Application* category is selected under *iOS* in the left hand pane before choosing the *Game* template option.

Click on the *Next* button to proceed and on the resulting options screen, name the product *SpriteKitDemo* and choose *Swift* as the language in which the application will be developed. Finally, set the Game Technology and Devices menus to *SpriteKit* and *Universal* respectively. Click *Next* and choose a suitable location for the project files. Once selected, click *Create* to create the project.

64.3 **Reviewing the SpriteKit Game Template Project**

Selection of the SpriteKit Game template has caused Xcode to create a template project with a demonstration incorporating some pre-built Sprite Kit behavior. This consists of a View Controller class (*GameViewController.swift*), an Xcode Sprite Kit scene file (*GameScene.sks*) and corresponding GameScene class file (*GameScene.swift*). The code within the *GameViewController.swift* file loads the scene design contained within the *GameScene.sks* file and presents it on the view so that it is visible to the user. This, in turn, triggers a call to the *didMoveToView* method of the GameScene class as implemented in the *GameScene.swift* file. This method creates an SKLabelNode displaying text that reads "Hello, World!".

The GameScene class also includes a *touchesBegan* method implementation which, when triggered, creates an SKSpriteNode instance textured with the *Spaceship.png* image file and displays it at the location at which the screen was touched. A rotation SKAction is then created and run on the space ship sprite node so that the sprite spins in place. To see the template project in action (Figure 64-2), run it on a physical device or the iOS simulator.

Figure 64-2

As impressive as this may be given how little code is involved, this bears no resemblance to the game that will be created in this chapter, so some of this functionality needs to be removed to provide a clean foundation on which to build. Begin the tidying process by selecting and editing the *GameScene.swift* file to remove the code to create and present nodes in the scene:

```
import SpriteKit

class GameScene: SKScene {
    override func didMoveToView(view: SKView) {
        /* Setup your scene here */
        let myLabel = SKLabelNode(fontNamed:"Chalkduster")
        myLabel.text = "Hello, World!"
        myLabel.fontSize = 65
        myLabel.position = CGPoint(x:CGRectGetMidX(self.frame),
y:CGRectGetMidY(self.frame))

        self.addChild(myLabel)
    }
```

```
    override func touchesBegan(touches: NSSet, withEvent event: UIEvent)
{
        /* Called when a touch begins */

        for touch: AnyObject in touches {
            let location = touch.locationInNode(self)

            let sprite = SKSpriteNode(imageNamed:"Spaceship")

            sprite.xScale = 0.5
            sprite.yScale = 0.5
            sprite.position = location

            let action = SKAction.rotateByAngle(CGFloat(M_PI),
duration:1)

            sprite.runAction(SKAction.repeatActionForever(action))

            self.addChild(sprite)
        }
    }
    .
    .
    .
}
```

With these changes made, it is time to start creating the SpriteKitDemo game.

64.4 Restricting Interface Orientation

The game created in this tutorial assumes that the device on which it is running will be in landscape orientation. To prevent the user from attempting to play the game with a device in portrait orientation, the *supportedInterfaceOrientations* method located in the *GameViewController.swift* file needs to be modified to only allow Landscape Left orientation as follows:

```
override func supportedInterfaceOrientations() -> Int {
        return Int(UIInterfaceOrientationMask.LandscapeLeft.rawValue)
}
```

64.5 Modifying the GameScene SpriteKit Scene File

As previously outlined, Xcode has provided a SpriteKit scene file (*GameScene.sks*) for a scene named GameScene together with a corresponding class declaration contained within the *GameScene.swift* file. The next task is to repurpose this scene to act as the welcome screen for the game. Begin by selecting the *GameScene.sks* file so that it loads into the SpriteKit Level Editor as shown in Figure 64-3:

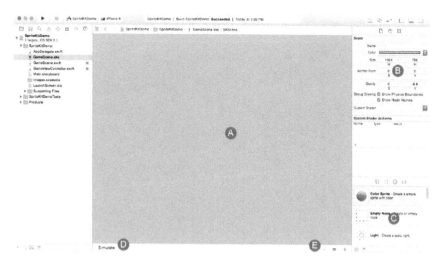

Figure 64-3

When working with the Level Editor to design SpriteKit scenes there are a number of key areas of importance, each of which has been labelled in the above figure:

- **A – Scene Canvas** - This is the canvas onto which nodes may be placed, positioned and configured.
- **B – SKNode Inspector Panel** - This panel provides a range of configuration options for the currently selected node in the scene canvas.
- **C – Object Library** - The Object Library panel contains a range of node and effect types that can be dragged and dropped onto the scene. Clicking on the far right button in the Object Library toolbar displays the Media Library containing items such as textures for sprites. At this stage in the tutorial, the only item in the Media Library is the Spaceship texture.
- **D – Simulate/Edit Button** - Toggles between the editor's simulate and edit modes. Simulate mode provides a useful mechanism for previewing the scene behavior without the need to compile and run the application.
- **E – Zoom Buttons** – Buttons to zoom in and out of the scene canvas.

With the scene selected in the scene canvas, click on the *Color* swatch in the SKNode Inspector panel and use the color selection dialog to change the scene color to a shade of green.

From within the Object Library panel, locate the Label node object and drag and drop an instance onto the center of the scene canvas. With the label still selected, change the *Text* property in the inspector panel to read "SpriteKitDemo – Tap Screen to Play". Remaining within the inspector panel, click on the T next to the font name and use the font selector to assign a 24-point *Marker Felt Wide* font to the label from the *Fun* font category. Finally, set the *Name* property for the label node to "welcomeNode". Save the scene file before proceeding.

With these changes complete, the scene should resemble that of Figure 64-4:

Figure 64-4

64.6 Creating the Archery Scene

As previously outlined, the first scene of the game is a welcome screen on which the user will tap to begin playing. Add a new class to the project to represent this second scene by selecting the *File -> New -> File...* menu option. In the file template panel, make sure that the *iOS Source* option is selected in the left hand panel and that the *Cocoa Touch Class* template is selected in the main panel. Click on the *Next* button and configure the new class to be a subclass of *SKScene* named *ArcheryScene*. Click on the *Next* button and create the new class file within the project folder.

The new scene class will also require a corresponding SpriteKit scene file. Select *File -> New -> File...* once again, this time selecting the *iOS Resource* option from the left hand panel and *SpriteKit Scene* from the main panel (Figure 64-5). Click *Next*, name the scene *ArcheryScene* and click on the *Create* button to add the scene file to the project.

Figure 64-5

Edit the newly added *ArcheryScene.swift* file and modify it to import the SpriteKit Framework as follows:

```
import UIKit
import SpriteKit

class ArcheryScene: SKScene {

}
```

64.7 Transitioning to the Archery Scene

Clearly having instructed the user to tap the screen in order to play the game, some code now needs to be written to make this happen. This behavior will be added by implementing the *touchesBegan* method in the GameScene class. Rather than move directly to ArcheryScene, however, some effects will be added in the form of an action and a transition.

When implemented, the SKAction will cause the node to fade away from view whilst an SKTransition instance will be used to animate the transition from the current scene to the archery scene using a "doorway" style of animation. Implement these requirements by adding the following code to the *touchesBegan* method in the *GameScene.swift* file:

```
override func touchesBegan(touches: NSSet, withEvent event: UIEvent) {
    /* Called when a touch begins */
    let welcomeNode = childNodeWithName("welcomeNode")

    if (welcomeNode != nil) {
        let fadeAway = SKAction.fadeOutWithDuration(1.0)

        welcomeNode?.runAction(fadeAway, completion: {
            let doors = SKTransition.doorwayWithDuration(1.0)
            let archeryScene = ArcheryScene(fileNamed: "ArcheryScene")
            self.view?.presentScene(archeryScene, transition: doors)
        })
    }
}
```

Before moving on to the next steps, we will take some time to provide more detail on the above code.

From within the context of the *touchesBegan* method we have no direct reference to the *welcomeNode* instance. We do know, however, that when it was added to the scene in the SpriteKit Level Editor that it was assigned the name "welcomeNode". Using the *childNodeWithName* method of the scene instance, therefore, a reference to the node is being obtained within the *touchesBegan* method as follows:

```
let welcomeNode = childNodeWithName("welcomeNode")
```

The code then checks that the node was found before creating a new SKAction instance configured to cause the node to fade from view over a one second duration:

```
let fadeAway = SKAction.fadeOutWithDuration(1.0)
```

The action is then executed on the welcomeNode. A completion block is also specified to be executed when the action completes. This block creates an instance of the ArcheryScene class preloaded with the scene contained within the *ArcheryScene.sks* file and an appropriately configured SKTransition object. The transition to the new scene is then initiated:

```
let fadeAway = SKAction.fadeOutWithDuration(1.0)

welcomeNode?.runAction(fadeAway, completion: {
    let doors = SKTransition.doorwayWithDuration(1.0)
    let archeryScene = ArcheryScene(fileNamed: "ArcheryScene")
    self.view?.presentScene(archeryScene, transition: doors)
})
```

Compile and run the application. Once running, touch the screen and note that the label node fades away and that after the transition to the ArcheryScene takes effect we are presented with a grey scene that now needs to be implemented.

64.8 Adding the Texture Atlas

Before textures can be used on a sprite node, the texture images first need to be added to the project. Textures take the form of image files and may be added individually to the *Supporting Files* folder of the project. For larger numbers of texture files, it is more efficient (both for the developer and the application) to create a texture atlas. In the case of the archer sprite, this will require twelve image files to animate the loading and subsequent shooting of an arrow. As such, a texture atlas will be used to store these animation frame images. The images for this project can be found in the sample code download which can be obtained from the following web page:

http://www.ebookfrenzy.com/print/ios8

Within the code sample archive, locate the folder named *SpriteImages*. Located within this folder is the *archer.atlas* sub-folder which contains the animation images for the archer sprite node.

To add the atlas to the project, drag and drop the *archer.atlas* folder into the *Supporting Files* folder in the Xcode project navigator panel so that it appears as shown in the following figure:

archer.atlas
> Supporting Files
> archer.atlas
  archer001.png   A
  archer002.png   A
  archer003.png   A
  archer004.png   A
  archer005.png   A
  archer006.png   A
  archer007.png   A
  archer008.png   A
  archer009.png   A
  archer010.png   A
  archer011.png   A
  archer012.png   A

Figure 64-6

64.9 Designing the Archery Scene

The layout for the archery scene is contained within the *ArcheryScene.sks* file. Select this file so that it loads into the Level Editor environment. With the scene selected in the canvas, use the SKNode Inspector panel to change the color property to white.

From within the SpriteKit Level Editor the next task is to add to the scene the sprite node representing the archer. Referring to the Object Library panel, click on the Media Library toolbar option and locate the *archer001.png* texture image file as outlined in Figure 64-7:

Figure 64-7

Once located, drag and drop the texture onto the canvas and position it so that it is located in the vertical center of the scene at the left hand edge as shown in the following figure:

Figure 64-8

With the archer node selected, use the SKNode Inspector panel to assign the name "archerNode" to the sprite. The next task is to define the outline of the physical outline of the archer sprite. This will be used by the SpriteKit system when deciding whether the sprite has been involved in a collision with another node within the scene. By default, the physical shape is assumed to be a rectangle surrounding the sprite texture (represented by the blue boundary around the node in the scene editor). Another option is to define a circle around the sprite to represent the physical shape. A much more accurate approach, and one that has been introduced in iOS 8, is to have SpriteKit base the physical shape of the node based on the outline of the sprite texture image. With the archer node selected in the scene, scroll down within the SKNode inspector panel until the *Physics Definition* section comes into view. Using the *Body Type* menu, change the setting from *Bounding rectangle* to *Alpha mask*:

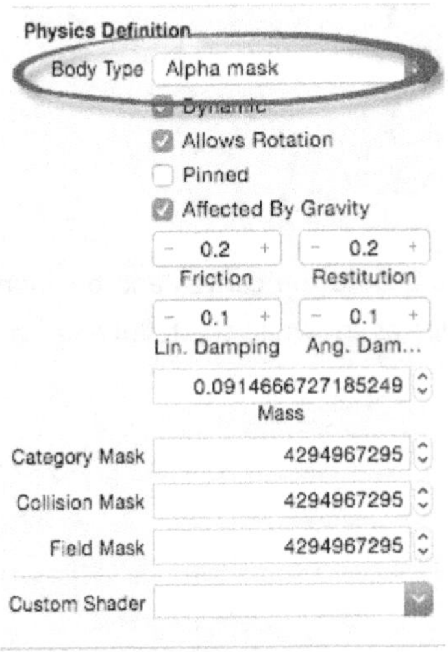

Figure 64-9

Once the change has been made, note that the sprite node is now outlined by a physical body shape matching the texture image:

Figure 64-10

Before proceeding with the next phase of the development process, test that the scene behaves as required by clicking on the *Simulate* button located along the bottom edge of the editor panel. Note that the archer slides down and disappears off the bottom edge of the scene. This is because the sprite is configured to be affected by gravity. For the purposes of the game, the archer is required to be pinned to the same location and not subject to the laws of gravity. Click on the *Edit* button to leave simulation mode, select the archer sprite and within the *Physical Definition* section turn the *Pinned* option on and the *Dynamic*, *Allows Rotation* and *Affected by Gravity* options off. Re-run the simulation to verify that the archer sprite now remains in place.

Save the scene file before proceeding.

64.10 Preparing the Archery Scene

Select the *ArcheryScene.swift* file and modify it as follows to add some private variables and implement the *didMoveToView* method:

```
import UIKit
import SpriteKit

class ArcheryScene: SKScene {

    var score = 0
    var ballCount = 20

    override func didMoveToView(view: SKView) {
            self.initArcheryScene()
    }
.
.
}
```

The above code calls another method named *initArcheryScene* which now needs to be implemented as follows within the *ArcheryScene.swift* file ready for code which will be added later in the chapter:

```
func initArcheryScene() {
```

}

64.11 Preparing the Animation Texture Atlas

When the user touches the screen, the archer sprite node will launch an arrow across the scene. For the purposes of this example we want the loading and shooting of the arrow by the sprite character to be animated. The texture atlas already contains the animation frames needed to implement this (named sequentially from *archer001.png* through to *archer012.png*), so the next step is to write some code to implement the animation.

In the first instance, an array of the textures in the animation atlas needs to be created. Whilst it is possible to write code to manually reference each texture file, this would quickly become a cumbersome task for animations involving large numbers of textures. A more efficient approach is to write a *for* loop to iterate through the files in the atlas, assigning each file name to the texture array. Since this only needs to be performed once each time the scene is presented, this is best achieved within the *initArcheryScene* method.

Edit the *ArcheryScene.swift* file and modify it as follows to declare and initialize the array:

```
import UIKit
import SpriteKit


class ArcheryScene: SKScene {

    var score = 0
    var ballCount = 20
    var archerAnimation = [SKTexture]()
    .

    .

    .

    func initArcheryScene() {
        let archerAtlas = SKTextureAtlas(named: "archer")

        for index in 1...archerAtlas.textureNames.count {
            let texture = String(format: "archer%03d", index)
            archerAnimation += [archerAtlas.textureNamed(texture)]
        }
    }
}
    .

    .

}
```

The above code begins by obtaining a reference to the archer texture atlas. A loop is then initialized based on the number of textures in the atlas. With knowledge of the naming convention of the image files, a texture file name is created and the *textureNamed* method of the SKTextureAtlas instance used to extract the texture with the corresponding name. The texture is then added to the *archerAnimation* array where it will be referenced later to animate the sprite node.

64.12 Animating the Archer Sprite Node

Now that an array of textures for the animation action has been created and initialized, code now needs to be written to perform the animation. Since this animation is triggered by a touch on the screen, this code needs to go in the *touchesBegan* method of the *ArcheryScene* class. Edit the *ArcheryScene.swift* file and implement this method as follows:

```
override func touchesBegan(touches: NSSet, withEvent event: UIEvent) {

    let archerNode = self.childNodeWithName("archerNode")

    if archerNode != nil {
        let animate = SKAction.animateWithTextures(archerAnimation,
                                    timePerFrame: 0.05)
        archerNode?.runAction(animate)
    }
}
```

The method obtains a reference to the sprite node representing the archer character in the game, creates an SKAction object configured to animate the texture frames in the archerAnimation array and then runs the action on the archer node.

Run the application and touch the screen within the Archery Scene. Each time a touch is detected, the archer sprite will run through the animation sequence of shooting an arrow.

64.13 Creating the Arrow Sprite Node

At this point in the tutorial, the archer sprite node goes through an animation sequence of loading and shooting an arrow but no actual arrow is being launched across the scene. In order to implement this, a new sprite node needs to be added to the ArcheryScene. This node will be textured with an image of an arrow and will be placed to the right of the archer sprite at the end of the animation sequence. A physics body will be associated with the arrow and an impulse force applied to it to propel it across the scene as though shot by the archer's bow.

Begin by locating the *ArrowTexture.png* file in the SpriteImages folder of the sample code archive and drag and drop it onto the *Supporting Files* folder in the Xcode project navigator panel. Next, add a new method named *createArrowNode* within the *ArcheryScene.swift* file so that it reads as follows:

```
func createArrowNode() -> SKSpriteNode {
    let archerNode = self.childNodeWithName("archerNode")
    let archerPosition = archerNode?.position
    let archerWidth = archerNode?.frame.size.width
```

```
let arrow = SKSpriteNode(imageNamed: "ArrowTexture.png")
arrow.position = CGPointMake(archerPosition!.x + archerWidth!,
                            archerPosition!.y)

arrow.name = "arrowNode"

arrow.physicsBody = SKPhysicsBody(rectangleOfSize:
            arrow.frame.size)

arrow.physicsBody?.usesPreciseCollisionDetection = true

return arrow
}
```

The code creates a new SKSpriteNode object, positions it to the right of the archer sprite node and assigns it the name *arrowNode*. A physics body is then assigned to the node, using the size of the node itself as the boundary of the body and enabling precision collision detection. Finally the node is returned.

64.14 Shooting the Arrow

In order to propel the arrow across the scene, a physical force needs to be applied to it. The creation and propulsion of the arrow sprite needs to be timed to occur at the end of the archer animation sequence. This can be achieved via some minor modifications to the *touchesBegan* method:

```
override func touchesBegan(touches: NSSet, withEvent event: UIEvent) {
    let archerNode = self.childNodeWithName("archerNode")

    if archerNode != nil {
        let animate = SKAction.animateWithTextures(archerAnimation,
timePerFrame: 0.05)

        let shootArrow = SKAction.runBlock({
            let arrowNode = self.createArrowNode()
            self.addChild(arrowNode)
            arrowNode.physicsBody?.applyImpulse(CGVectorMake(60.0, 0))
        })

        let sequence = SKAction.sequence([animate, shootArrow])
        archerNode?.runAction(sequence)
    }
}
```

A new SKAction object is created, this time specifying a block of code to be executed. This run block calls the *createArrowNode* method, adds the new node to the scene and then applies an impulse force of 60.0 on the

X axis of the scene. An SKAction sequence is then created comprising the previously created animation action and the new run block action. This sequence is then run on the archer node.

When executed with these changes, touching the screen should now cause an arrow to be launched after the archer animation completes. Note that as the arrow flies across the scene it gradually falls towards the bottom of the display. This is, of course, due to the effect of gravity imposed upon the physics body assigned to the node.

64.15 Adding the Ball Sprite Node

The objective of the game is to score points by hitting balls with arrows. Clearly, the next logical step is to add the ball sprite node to the scene. Begin by locating the *BallTexture.png* file in the *SpriteImages* folder of the sample code package and drag and drop it onto the *Supporting Files* section of the project navigator panel.

Next add the corresponding *createBallNode* method to the *ArcheryScene.swift* file as outlined in the following code fragment:

```
func createBallNode() {
    let ball = SKSpriteNode(imageNamed: "BallTexture.png")
    ball.position = CGPointMake(randomBetween(0, high:
                        self.size.width-200), self.size.height-50)

    ball.name = "ballNode"
    ball.physicsBody = SKPhysicsBody(circleOfRadius:
                        (ball.size.width/2))

    ball.physicsBody?.usesPreciseCollisionDetection = true
    self.addChild(ball)
}
```

This code creates a sprite node using the ball texture and then sets the initial position at the top of the scene but a random position on the X axis. The node is assigned a name and a circular physics body that is slightly less than the radius of the ball texture image (this will ensure that there is no gap when the arrow is made to stick into the ball in the next chapter). Precision collision detection is enabled and the ball node is added to the scene.

Before proceeding, add the following method to facilitate the random number generation used in calculating the X coordinate of the ball sprite node:

```
func randomBetween(low: CGFloat, high: CGFloat) -> CGFloat
{
    let lowInt = UInt32(low)
    let highInt = UInt32(high) - UInt32(low)
    let result = arc4random_uniform(highInt) + UInt32(low)
```

```
    return CGFloat(result)
}
```

Next, modify the *initArcheryScene* method to create an action to release a total of 20 balls at one second intervals:

```
func initArcheryScene() {
    let archerAtlas = SKTextureAtlas(named: "archer")

    for index in 1...archerAtlas.textureNames.count {
        let texture = String(format: "archer%03d", index)
        archerAnimation += [archerAtlas.textureNamed(texture)]
    }

    let releaseBalls = SKAction.sequence([SKAction.runBlock({
            self.createBallNode() }),
        SKAction.waitForDuration(1)])

    self.runAction(SKAction.repeatAction(releaseBalls,
            count: ballCount), completion: nil)
}
```

Run the application and verify that the balls now fall from the top of the scene. Attempt to hit the balls as they fall by tapping the background to launch arrows. Note, however, that when an arrow hits a ball it simply bounces off:

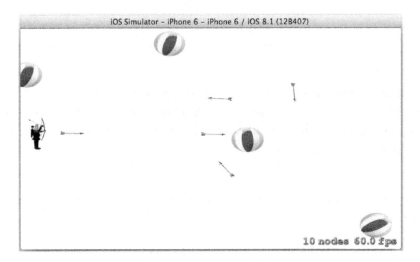

Figure 64-11

The goal for the completed game is to have the arrows stick into the balls on collision and for a score to be updated for each hit. The steps to implement this behavior will be covered in the next chapter entitled *An iOS 8 Sprite Kit Collision Handling Tutorial*.

The balls fall from the top of the screen because they have been assigned a physics body and are subject to the simulated forces of gravity within the Sprite Kit physical world. To reduce the effects of gravity on both the arrows and balls, modify the *didMoveToView* method to change the current gravity setting on the scene's *physicsWorld* object:

```
override func didMoveToView(view: SKView) {
    self.physicsWorld.gravity = CGVectorMake(0, -1.0)
    self.initArcheryScene()
}
```

64.16 Summary

The goal of this chapter has been to create a simple game for iOS 8 using the Sprite Kit framework. In the course of creating this game topics such as using sprite nodes, actions, textures, sprite animations and physical forces have been put to practical use.

In the next chapter, this game example will be further extended to demonstrate the detection of collisions and the use of physical joins.

65. An iOS 8 Sprite Kit Collision Handling Tutorial

In this chapter, the game created in the previous chapter entitled *An iOS 8 Sprite Kit Level Editor Game Tutorial* will be extended to implement collision detection. The objective is to detect when an arrow node collides with a ball node and, in the event of such a collision, implement a join between those two nodes so that the arrow appears to embed into the ball.

65.1 Defining the Category Bit Masks

If not already loaded, start Xcode and open the SpriteKitDemo project created in the previous chapter.

When detecting collisions within a Sprite Kit scene, a delegate method is called each time a collision is detected. This method will only be called, however, if the colliding nodes are configured appropriately using *category bit masks*.

For the purposes of this demonstration game, only collisions between arrow and ball sprite nodes are of interest. The first step, therefore, is to declare collision masks for these two node categories. Begin by editing the *ArcheryScene.swift* file and adding these declarations at the top of the class implementation:

```
import UIKit
import SpriteKit

class ArcheryScene: SKScene {

    let arrowCategory: UInt32 = 0x1 << 0
    let ballCategory: UInt32 = 0x1 << 1
.
.
```

65.2 Assigning the Category Masks to the Sprite Nodes

Having declared the masks, these need to be assigned to the respective node objects when they are created within the game. This is achieved by assigning the mask to the *categoryBitMask* property of the physics body assigned to the node. In the case of the ball node, this code can be added in the *createBallNode* method as follows:

```
func createBallNode() {
    let ball = SKSpriteNode(imageNamed: "BallTexture.png")
    ball.position = CGPointMake(self.randomBetween(0, high:
self.size.width-200), self.size.height-50)
    ball.name = "ballNode"
    ball.physicsBody = SKPhysicsBody(circleOfRadius:
                             (ball.size.width/2))
    ball.physicsBody?.usesPreciseCollisionDetection = true
    ball.physicsBody?.categoryBitMask = ballCategory
    self.addChild(ball)
}
```

Repeat this step to assign the appropriate category mask to the arrow node in the *createArrowNode* method:

```
func createArrowNode() -> SKSpriteNode {

    let archerNode = self.childNodeWithName("archerNode")
    let archerPosition = archerNode?.position
    let archerWidth = archerNode?.frame.size.width

    let arrow = SKSpriteNode(imageNamed: "ArrowTexture.png")
    arrow.position = CGPointMake(archerPosition!.x + archerWidth!,
                             archerPosition!.y)
    arrow.name = "arrowNode"
    arrow.physicsBody = SKPhysicsBody(rectangleOfSize:
                             arrow.frame.size)
    arrow.physicsBody?.usesPreciseCollisionDetection = true
    arrow.physicsBody?.categoryBitMask = arrowCategory
    return arrow
}
```

65.3 Configuring the Collision and Contact Masks

Having assigned category masks to the arrow and ball nodes, these nodes are ready to be included in collision detection handling. Before this can be implemented however, code needs to be added to indicate whether the application needs to know about *collisions*, *contacts* or both. When a contact occurs, two nodes are able to touch or even occupy the same space in a scene. It might be valid, for example, for one sprite node to pass over another node and the game logic needs to be notified when this happens. A collision involves contact between two nodes that cannot occupy the same space in the scene. In such a situation (and subject to prevailing physics body properties) the two nodes will typically bounce away from each other.

The type of contact for which notification is required is specified by assigning contact and collision bit masks to the physics body of one of the node categories involved in the contact. For the purposes of this example, we will specify that notification is required for both contact and collision between the arrow and ball categories:

```
func createArrowNode() -> SKSpriteNode {

    let archerNode = self.childNodeWithName("archerNode")
    let archerPosition = archerNode?.position
    let archerWidth = archerNode?.frame.size.width

    let arrow = SKSpriteNode(imageNamed: "ArrowTexture.png")
    arrow.position = CGPointMake(archerPosition!.x + archerWidth!,
                                 archerPosition!.y)
    arrow.name = "arrowNode"
    arrow.physicsBody = SKPhysicsBody(rectangleOfSize:
                                 arrow.frame.size)
    arrow.physicsBody?.usesPreciseCollisionDetection = true
    arrow.physicsBody?.categoryBitMask = arrowCategory
    arrow.physicsBody?.collisionBitMask = arrowCategory | ballCategory
    arrow.physicsBody?.contactTestBitMask =
                                 arrowCategory | ballCategory
    return arrow
}
```

65.4 Implementing the Contact Delegate

When the Sprite Kit physics system detects a collision or contact for which appropriate masks have been configured it needs a way to notify the application code that such an event has occurred.

It does this by calling methods on the class instance that has been registered as the *contact delegate* for the physics world object associated with the scene in which the contact took place. In actual fact, the system is able to notify the delegate at both the beginning and end of the contact if both the *didBeginContact* and *didEndContact* methods are implemented. Passed as an argument to these methods is an SKPhysicsContact object containing information about the location of the contact and references to the physical bodies of the two nodes involved in the contact.

For the purposes of this tutorial we will use the ArcheryScene instance as the contact delegate and implement only the *didBeginContact* method. Begin, therefore, by modifying the *didMoveToView* method in the *ArcheryScene.swift* file to declare the class as the contact delegate:

```
override func didMoveToView(view: SKView) {
    self.physicsWorld.gravity = CGVectorMake(0, -1.0)
    self.physicsWorld.contactDelegate = self
    self.initArcheryScene()
}
```

Having made the ArcheryScene class the contact delegate the *ArcheryScene.swift* file needs to be modified to indicate that the class now implements the SKPhysicsContactDelegate protocol:

```
import UIKit
import SpriteKit

class ArcheryScene: SKScene, SKPhysicsContactDelegate {
.

.

.
```

Remaining within the *ArcheryScene.swift* file, implement the *didBeginContact* method as follows:

```
func didBeginContact(contact: SKPhysicsContact) {
    let firstNode = contact.bodyA.node as SKSpriteNode
    let secondNode = contact.bodyB.node as SKSpriteNode

    if (contact.bodyA.categoryBitMask == arrowCategory) &&
            (contact.bodyB.categoryBitMask == ballCategory) {

        let contactPoint = contact.contactPoint
        let contact_y = contactPoint.y
        let target_y = secondNode.position.y
        let margin = secondNode.frame.size.height/2 - 25

        if (contact_y > (target_y - margin)) &&
            (contact_y < (target_y + margin)) {
            println("Hit")
            score++
        }
    }
}
```

The code starts by extracting references to the two nodes that have collided. It then checks that the first node was an arrow and the second a ball (no points are scored if a ball falls onto an arrow). Next, the point of contact is identified and some rudimentary mathematics used to check that the arrow struck the side of the ball (for a game of app store quality more rigorous checking might be required to catch all cases). Assuming that the hit was within the defined parameters, a message is output to the console and the game score variable is incremented.

Run the game and test the collision handling by making sure that the "Hit" message appears in the Xcode console when an arrow hits the side of a ball.

65.5 **Implementing a Physics Joint Between Nodes**

When a valid hit is detected, the arrow needs to appear to embed partway into the ball and stick there as the ball continues its descent. In order to achieve this, a new texture will be applied to the arrow sprite node that makes the arrow appear without a tip and slightly shorter.

The joining of the arrow node and ball will be achieved by implementing a *physics joint* at the point of contact between the two nodes. A number of different joint types are available, but for the purposes of this game, a fixed joint provides the exact behavior required.

The embedded arrow texture is contained in the *ArrowHitTexture.png* file. Locate this file in the *SpriteImages* folder of the sample code download and drag and drop it onto the *Supporting Files* folder in the project navigator.

Within the *ArcheryScene.swift* file, modify the *didBeginContact* method to establish a fixed joint between the two nodes and to change the texture of the arrow:

```
func didBeginContact(contact: SKPhysicsContact) {
    let firstNode = contact.bodyA.node as SKSpriteNode
    let secondNode = contact.bodyB.node as SKSpriteNode

    if (contact.bodyA.categoryBitMask == arrowCategory) &&
            (contact.bodyB.categoryBitMask == ballCategory) {

        let contactPoint = contact.contactPoint
        let contact_x = contactPoint.x
        let contact_y = contactPoint.y
        let target_y = secondNode.position.y
        let margin = secondNode.frame.size.height/2 - 25

        if (contact_y > (target_y - margin))
                && (contact_y < (target_y + margin)) {
            let texture = SKTexture(imageNamed: "ArrowHitTexture")
            firstNode.texture = texture
            let joint =
                SKPhysicsJointFixed.jointWithBodyA(contact.bodyA,
                        bodyB: contact.bodyB,
                        anchor: CGPointMake(contact_x, contact_y))
            self.physicsWorld.addJoint(joint)
            score++
        }
    }
}
```

Compile and run the application. When an arrow scores a hit on a ball the arrow will now appear to stick into the ball. Note that the attachment of the arrow to the ball causes the ball to rotate and change course as a result of the impact and shift in center of gravity (Figure 65-1). All of this is provided automatically by the Sprite Kit physics world.

Figure 65-1

65.6 Game Over

All that now remains is to display the score to the user when all of the balls have been released. This will require a new label node and a small change to an action sequence followed by a transition to the welcome scene so the user can start a new game. Begin by adding the method to create the label node in the *ArcheryScene.swift* file:

```
func createScoreNode() -> SKLabelNode {
    let scoreNode = SKLabelNode(fontNamed: "Bradley Hand")
    scoreNode.name = "scoreNode"

    let newScore = "Score \(score)"

    scoreNode.text = newScore
    scoreNode.fontSize = 60
    scoreNode.fontColor = SKColor.redColor()
    scoreNode.position = CGPointMake(CGRectGetMidX(self.frame),
            CGRectGetMidY(self.frame))
    return scoreNode
}
```

Next, implement the *gameOver* method which will display the score label node and then transition back to the welcome scene:

```
func gameOver() {
    let scoreNode = self.createScoreNode()
    self.addChild(scoreNode)
    let fadeOut = SKAction.sequence([SKAction.waitForDuration(3.0),
            SKAction.fadeOutWithDuration(3.0)])

    let welcomeReturn =  SKAction.runBlock({
        let transition = SKTransition.revealWithDirection(
            SKTransitionDirection.Down, duration: 1.0)
```

```
        let welcomeScene = GameScene(fileNamed: "GameScene")
        self.scene!.view?.presentScene(welcomeScene,
                               transition: transition)
    })

    let sequence = SKAction.sequence([fadeOut, welcomeReturn])

    self.runAction(sequence)
}
```

Finally, add a completion handler that calls the *gameOver* method to the ball release action in the *initArcheryScene* method:

```
func initArcheryScene() {

.

.

.

    let releaseBalls = SKAction.sequence([SKAction.runBlock({
            self.createBallNode() }),
                    SKAction.waitForDuration(1)])

    self.runAction(SKAction.repeatAction(releaseBalls,
                    count: ballCount), completion: {
        let sequence =
                SKAction.sequence([SKAction.waitForDuration(5.0),
                    SKAction.runBlock({ self.gameOver() })])
        self.runAction(sequence)
    })
}
```

Compile, run and test. Also feel free to experiment by adding other features to the game to gain familiarity with the capabilities of Sprite Kit. The next chapter, entitled *An iOS 8 Sprite Kit Particle Emitter Tutorial* will cover the use of the Particle Emitter to add special effects to Sprite Kit games.

65.7 Summary

The Sprite Kit physics engine provides a mechanism for detecting when two nodes within a scene come into contact with each other. Collision and contact detection is configured through the use of category masks together with contact and collision masks. When appropriately configured, the *didBeginContact* and *didEndContact* methods of a designated delegate class are called at the start and end of a contact between two nodes for which detection is configured. These methods are passed references to the nodes involved in the contact so that appropriate action can be taken within the game.

Sprite Kit also allows joints to be formed between nodes. In this chapter a fixed joint was implemented to attach arrow nodes to the ball nodes in the event of contacts being detected.

66. An iOS 8 Sprite Kit Particle Emitter Tutorial

In this, the last chapter dedicated to the Sprite Kit framework, the use of the Particle Emitter class and editor to add special effects to Sprite Kit based games will be covered. Having provided an overview of the various elements that make up particle emitter special effects, the SpriteKitDemo application will be extended using particle emitter features to make the balls burst when hit by an arrow.

66.1 What is the Particle Emitter?

The Sprite Kit particle emitter is essentially a mechanism designed to add special effects to games. It comprises the SKEmitterNode class and the Particle Emitter Editor bundled with Xcode. A particle emitter special effect begins with an image file that is to represent the particle. The emitter is then responsible for generating multiple instances of the particle on the scene and animating each particle subject to a set of properties. These properties control aspects of the special effect such as the rate of particle generation, the angle and speed of motion of particles, whether or not particles rotate and the way in which the particles blend in with the background.

With some time and experimentation, a wide range of special effects ranging from smoke to explosions can be created using particle emitters.

66.2 The Particle Emitter Editor

The Particle Emitter Editor is built into Xcode and provides a visual environment in which to design particle emitter effects. In addition to providing a platform for developing custom effects, the editor also offers a collection of pre-built particle based effects including rain, fire, magic, snow and sparks. These template effects also provide an excellent starting point on which to base other special effects.

Within the editor environment, a canvas displays the current particle emitter configuration. A settings panel allows the various properties of the emitter node to be changed, with each modification reflected in the canvas in real-time, thereby making the task of creating and refining special effects much easier. Once the design of the special effect is complete, the effect is saved in a Sprite Kit particle file. This file actually contains an archived SKEmitterNode object configured to run the particle effects designed in the editor.

66.3 **The SKEmitterNode Class**

The SKEmitterNode is responsible for displaying and running the particle emitter effect within a Sprite Kit game. As with other Sprite Node classes, the SKEmitterNode class has many of the properties and behaviors of other classes in the Sprite Kit family. Generally an SKEmitterNode class is created and initialized with a Sprite Kit particle file created using the Particle Emitter editor. The following code fragment, for example, obtains the path to a specific particle file from the application main bundle and then unarchives the SKEmitterNode instance saved in that particle file. The unarchived node is then configured to appear at a specific position within the current scene before being added to the scene so that it appears within the game:

```
let burstPath = NSBundle.mainBundle().pathForResource("Burst",
                                ofType: "sks")

let burstNode = NSKeyedUnarchiver.unarchiveObjectWithFile(burstPath!)
                        as SKEmitterNode

burstNode.position = CGPointMake(100, 400)

self.addChild(burstNode)
```

Once created, all of the emitter properties that are available within the Particle Emitter Editor are also controllable from within the code allowing the behavior of the effect to be changed in real-time. The following code, for example, adjusts the number of particles the emitter is to emit before ending:

```
burstEmitter.numParticlesToEmit = 400
```

In addition, actions may be assigned to particles from within the application code to add additional behavior to a special effect. The particles can, for example, be made to display an animation sequence.

66.4 **Using the Particle Emitter Editor**

By far the easiest and most productive approach to designing particle emitter based special effects is to use the Particle Emitter Editor tool bundled with Xcode. To experience the editor in action, launch Xcode and create a new SpriteKit Game-based application project named *ParticleDemo* with the Devices and Language menus set to *Universal* and *Swift* respectively.

Once the new project has been created, select the *File -> New -> File...* menu option. In the resulting panel, select the *Resource* option located beneath the *iOS* heading in the left hand panel before choosing the *SpriteKit Particle File* template option as outlined in Figure 66-1:

Choose a template for your new file:

iOS				
Source	GeoJSON File	GPX File	Asset Catalog	Settings Bundle
User Interface				
Core Data				
Resource				
Other				
OS X	Property List	Rich Text File	SceneKit Particle System	SpriteKit Particle File
Source				
User Interface				
Core Data				
Resource				
Other				

SpriteKit Particle File

A particle effect template for SpriteKit particle emitter.

Cancel   Previous   Next

Figure 66-1

Click *Next* and choose a Particle template on which to base the special effect. For the purposes of this example we will use the *Fire* template. Click *Next* and name the file *RocketFlame* before clicking on *Create*.

At this point, Xcode will have added two files to the project. One is an image file named *spark.png* representing the particle and the other is the *RocketFlame.sks* file containing the particle emitter configuration. Xcode should also have pre-loaded the Particle Emitter Editor panel with the fire effect playing in the canvas as shown in Figure 66-2 (the editor can be accessed at any time by selecting the corresponding sks file in the project navigator panel).

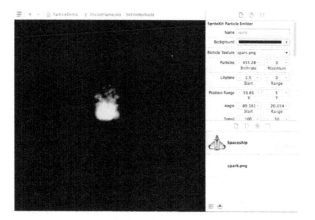

Figure 66-2

The right hand panel of the editor provides access to, and control of, all of the properties associated with the emitter node. To access these property settings, click on the right hand toolbar button in the right hand panel.

Much about particle emitter special effects can be learned through experimentation with the particle editor. Before modifying the fire effects in this example, however, it will be helpful to provide an overview of what these properties do.

66.5 **Particle Emitter Node Properties**

The behavior of a particle emitter and associated particles is controlled by a range of property settings. These properties can be summarized as follows:

66.5.1 Background

Though presented as an option within the editor, this is not actually a property of the emitter node. This option is provided so that the appearance of the effect can be tested against different backgrounds. This is of particular importance when the particles are configured to blend with the background. Use this setting to test the particle effects against any background colors the effect is likely to appear with within the game.

66.5.2 Particle Texture

The image file containing the texture that will be used to represent the particles within the emitter.

66.5.3 Particle Birthrate

The birthrate defines the rate at which new particles are emitted by the node. The greater the value the faster new particles are generated, though it is recommended that the minimum number of particles needed to achieve the desired effect be used to avoid performance degradation. The total number of particles to be emitted may also be specified. A value of zero causes particles to be emitted indefinitely. If a limit is specified the node will stop emitting particles when that value is reached.

66.5.4 Particle Life Cycle

The lifetime property controls the length of time in seconds that a particle lives (and is therefore visible) before disappearing from view. The range property may be used to introduce variance in the lifetime from one particle to the next based on a random time value between 0 and the specified range value.

66.5.5 Particle Position Range

The position properties define the location from which particles are created. The X and Y values can be used to declare an area around the center of the node location from which particles will be created randomly.

66.5.6 Angle

The angle at which a newly emitted particle will travel away from the creation point in counterclockwise degrees, where a value of 0 degrees equates to rightward movement. Random variance in direction can be introduced via the range property.

66.5.7 Particle Speed

The speed property specifies the initial speed of the particles at time of creation. The speed can be randomized by specifying a range value.

66.5.8 Particle Acceleration

The acceleration properties control the degree to which a particle accelerates or decelerates after emission in terms of both X and Y directions.

66.5.9 Particle Scale

The size of the particles can be configured to change using the scale properties. These settings cause the particles to grow or shrink over the course of their lifetimes. Random resizing behavior can be implemented by specifying a range value. The speed setting controls the speed with which the size changes take place.

66.5.10 Particle Rotation

The rotation properties control the speed and amount of rotation applied to the particles after creation. Values are specified in degrees with positive and negative values correlating to clockwise and counter-clockwise rotation respectively. The speed of rotation may be specified in degrees per second.

66.5.11 Particle Color

The particles created by an emitter can be configured to transition through a range of colors during a lifetime. To add a new color in the lifecycle timeline, click on the color ramp at the location where the color is to change and select a new color. Change an existing color by double clicking on the marker to display the color selection dialog. Figure 66-3, for example, shows a color ramp with three color transitions specified:

Figure 66-3

To remove a color from the color ramp, click and drag it downward out of the editor panel.

The color blend settings control the amount by which the colors in the particle's texture blend with the prevailing color in the color ramp at any given time during the life of the particle. The greater the Factor property, the greater the colors blend, with 0 indicating no blending. The blending factor can be randomized by specifying a range, and the speed at which the blend is performed by adjusting the speed property.

66.5.12 Particle Blend Mode

The Blend Mode property governs the way in which particles blend with other images, colors and graphics in Sprite Kit game scenes. Options available are as follows:

- **Alpha** – Blends transparent pixels in the particle with the background.
- **Add** – Adds the particle pixels to the corresponding background image pixels.
- **Subtract** – Subtracts the particle pixels from the corresponding background image pixels.
- **Multiply** - Multiplies the particle pixels by the corresponding background image pixels. Results in a darker particle effect.

- **MultiplyX2** – Creates a darker particle effect than the standard Multiply mode.
- **Screen** – Inverts pixels, multiplies and inverts a second time. Results in lighter particle effects.
- **Replace** – No blending with the background. Only the particle's colors are used.

66.6 Experimenting with the Particle Emitter Editor

Creating compelling special effects with the particle emitter is largely a case of experimentation. As an example of adapting a template effect for another purpose we will now modify the fire effect in the *RocketFlame.sks* file so that instead of resembling a camp fire it could instead be attached to the back of a sprite to represent the flame of a rocket launching into space.

Within Xcode, select the previously created *RocketFlame.sks* file so that it loads into the Particle Emitter Editor. The animation should appear and resemble a camp fire as illustrated in Figure 66-2.

1. The first step in modifying the effect is to change the angle of the flames so that they burn downwards. To achieve this, change the *Start* property of the *Angle* setting to 270 degrees. The fire should now be inverted.

2. Change the X value of the *Position Range* property to 5 so that the flames become narrower and more intense.

3. Increase the *Start* value of the *Speed* property to 450.

4. Change the *Lifetime* start property to 7.

The effect now resembles the flames a user might expect to see shooting out of the back of a rocket against a nighttime sky (Figure 66-4).

Figure 66-4

Note also that the effects of motion of the emitter node may be simulated by clicking and dragging the node around the canvas.

66.7 Bursting a Ball using Particle Emitter Effects

The final task is to update the SpriteKitDemo game so that the balls burst when they are hit by an arrow shot by the archer sprite.

The particles for the bursting ball will be represented by the *BallFragment.png* file located in the sample code download archive in the *SpriteImages* folder. Open the SpriteKitDemo project within Xcode, locate the *BallFragment.png* file in a Finder window and drag and drop it onto the Supporting Files folder of the Xcode project navigator panel.

Select the *File -> New -> File…* menu option and, in the resulting panel, select the *Resource* option located beneath the *iOS* heading in the left hand panel before choosing the *SpriteKit Particle File* template option. Click *Next* and on the template screen select the *Spark* template. Click *Next*, name the file *BurstParticle* and click *Create*.

The Particle Emitter Editor will appear with the spark effect running. Since the scene on which the effect is going to run has a white background, click on the black swatch next to *Background* in the SKNode Inspector panel and change the Palette to *Apple* and the color to *White* as shown in Figure 66-5:

Figure 66-5

Click on the Particle Texture drop down menu and select the *BallFragment.png* file and change the *Blend Mode* menu to *Alpha*.

A large number of ball fragments should now be visible all blended with the yellow color specified in the color ramp. Set the *Birthrate* property to 15 to reduce the number of particles emitted. Click on the yellow marker at the start of the color ramp and change the color to *White* in the resulting color dialog. The particles should now begin to look like fragments of the ball used in the game.

The fragments of a bursting ball would be expected to originate from any part of the ball. As such the Position Range X and Y values need to match the dimensions of the ball. Set both of these values to 86 accordingly.

Finally, limit the total number of particles by changing the *Maximum* property in the Particles section to 8.

The burst particle effect is now ready to be incorporated into the game logic.

66.8 Adding the Burst Particle Emitter Effect

When an arrow now scores a hit on a ball node, the ball node will be removed from the scene and replaced with a *BurstParticle* SKEmitterNode instance. To implement this behavior, edit the *ArcherScene.swift* file and modify the *didBeginContact* method to remove the code that embeds the arrow into the ball:

```
func didBeginContact(contact: SKPhysicsContact) {
    let firstNode = contact.bodyA.node as SKSpriteNode
    let secondNode = contact.bodyB.node as SKSpriteNode

    if (contact.bodyA.categoryBitMask == arrowCategory) &&
            (contact.bodyB.categoryBitMask == ballCategory) {

        let contactPoint = contact.contactPoint
        let contact_x = contactPoint.x
        let contact_y = contactPoint.y
        let target_y = secondNode.position.y
        let margin = secondNode.frame.size.height/2 - 25

        if (contact_y > (target_y - margin))
                && (contact_y < (target_y + margin)) {
            let texture = SKTexture(imageNamed: "ArrowHitTexture")
            firstNode.texture = texture
            let joint =
                    SKPhysicsJointFixed.jointWithBodyA(contact.bodyA,
                            bodyB: contact.bodyB,
                            anchor: CGPointMake(contact_x, contact_y))
            self.physicsWorld.addJoint(joint)
            score++
        }
    }
}
```

Having removed the code, add a new method call to extract the SKEmitterNode from the archive in the *BurstParticle* file, remove the ball node from the scene and replace it at the same position with the emitter:

```
func didBeginContact(contact: SKPhysicsContact) {
    let firstNode = contact.bodyA.node as SKSpriteNode
    let secondNode = contact.bodyB.node as SKSpriteNode

    if (contact.bodyA.categoryBitMask == arrowCategory) &&
```

```
                 (contact.bodyB.categoryBitMask == ballCategory) {

        let contactPoint = contact.contactPoint
        let contact_y = contactPoint.y
        let target_x = secondNode.position.x
        let target_y = secondNode.position.y
        let margin = secondNode.frame.size.height/2 - 25

        if (contact_y > (target_y - margin))
              && (contact_y < (target_y + margin)) {

            let burstPath = NSBundle.mainBundle().pathForResource(
                    "BurstParticle", ofType: "sks")

            if burstPath != nil {
                let burstNode =
                  NSKeyedUnarchiver.unarchiveObjectWithFile(burstPath!)
                        as SKEmitterNode
                burstNode.position = CGPointMake(target_x, target_y)
                secondNode.removeFromParent()
                self.addChild(burstNode)
            }
             score++
        }
    }
}
```

Compile and run the application. When a ball is hit by an arrow it should now be replaced by the particle emitter effect:

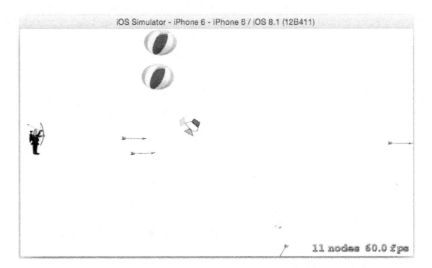

Figure 66-6

66.9 Summary

The particle emitter allows special effects to be added to Sprite Kit games. All that is required is an image file to represent the particles and some configuration of the particle emitter properties. Much of this work can be simplified through the use of the Particle Emitter Editor included with Xcode. The editor is supplied with a set of pre-configured special effects such as smoke, fire and rain which can be used as supplied, or modified to meet many special effects needs.

67. Integrating iAds into an iOS 8 App

In terms of revenue generation options, the iTunes App Store eco-system provides a number of options. Perhaps the most obvious source of revenue for app developers involves charging the user an upfront fee for the application. Another option involves a concept referred to as "in-app purchase" whereby a user buys something from within the installed and running application. This typically takes the form of virtual goods (a packet of seeds in a farming simulation or a faster car in a racing game) or premium content such as access to specific articles in a news application. Yet another option involves the inclusion of advertisements in the application. It is, of course, also common to generate revenue from a mixture of these three options.

The subject of this chapter involves the use of advertising, specifically using Apple's iAds system to incorporate adverts into iOS 8 based applications.

67.1 Preparing to Run iAds within an Application

In order to receive revenue from iAds advertising that you place in your applications it is important to accept the iAd Network terms and conditions. This is achieved by logging into the iTunes Connect portal at itunesconnect.apple.com using your Apple ID, clicking on the *Contracts, Tax and Banking* link and following the instructions to set up the agreements and to enter the necessary tax and banking information.

67.2 iAd Advertisement Formats

The iAds platform supports four different advertising formats consisting of *banner*, *interstitial*, *medium rectangle* and *pre-roll video*, each of which can be implemented within an iOS application using just a few lines of code.

67.2.1 Banner Ads

Banner ads are supported on both iPhone and iPad based applications and are intended to appear at the bottom of the device display while an application view is visible to the user. When a banner ad is tapped, a full screen advert appears until dismissed by the user. For as long as the banner is visible and the device has internet connectivity, the banner will cycle through different ads.

All that is required to make a banner ad appear on a view is to set the *canDisplayBannerAds* property of the corresponding view controller to *true*. For example:

```
override func viewDidLoad() {
    super.viewDidLoad()
```

```
    self.canDisplayBannerAds = true
}
```

When this property is enabled, iAds will rename the *view* property of the view controller to *originalContentView* and request a banner ad from the iAds ad server. In the event that an ad is available from the iAds inventory, the *originalContentView* will be resized to make space for the banner and the banner will be displayed.

Banner ads may be disabled at any time by turning off the *canDisplayBannerAds* property:

```
self.canDisplayBannerAds = false
```

As previously described, when the user taps on a banner a full screen advert will appear obscuring the current view. This advert will remain on the screen until dismissed by the user. Depending on the type of application, it may be necessary to take action when the banner is tapped. If the app is playing a video, for example, it would be prudent to pause playback while the view is obscured by the ad and subsequently resume once the user dismisses the ad. Such functionality can be achieved by overriding the *viewWillDisappear* and *viewWillAppear* delegate methods within the view controller code. These methods will then be called when the ad appears and disappears respectively:

```
override func viewWillAppear(animated: Bool) {
    // View is about to be obscured by an advert.
    // Pause activities if necessary
}

override func viewWillDisappear(animated: Bool) {
    // Advert has been dismissed. Resume paused activities
}
```

67.2.2 Interstitial Ads

Interstitial adverts occupy the full device display and are primarily intended to be displayed when a user transitions from one screen to another within an application. When a transition is taking place from one view controller to another, interstitial ad display can be enabled by setting the *interstitialPresentationPolicy* property of the destination view controller. When using storyboards this is best performed within the *prepareForSegue* method which is called immediately before the transition takes place. Interstitial display can be configured to be automatic or manual. The following code, for example, implements automatic interstitial advertising for a transition using the *prepareForSegue* method:

```
override func prepareForSegue(segue: UIStoryboardSegue,
                       sender: AnyObject?) {

    let destination = segue.destinationViewController
                            as UIViewController
    destination.interstitialPresentationPolicy =
```

```
                ADInterstitialPresentationPolicy.Automatic
}
```

The following code, on the other hand, demonstrates how to manually display an interstitial ad:

```
destination.interstitialPresentationPolicy =
            ADInterstitialPresentationPolicy.Manual

destination.requestInterstitialAdPresentation()
```

When using interstitial ads, it is recommended that the application be given an opportunity in advance of the transition to make ad requests to the iAds system. This prevents any delays when the time comes to display the ad during the transition. This can be achieved by making a call to the *prepareInterstitialAds* method of the UIViewController class. An ideal place to perform this task is within the *didFinishLaunchingWithOptions* method of the application delegate class, for example:

```
import UIKit
import iAd

@UIApplicationMain
class AppDelegate: UIResponder, UIApplicationDelegate {

    var window: UIWindow?

    func application(application: UIApplication,
didFinishLaunchingWithOptions launchOptions: [NSObject: AnyObject]?) ->
Bool {
        UIViewController.prepareInterstitialAds()
        return true
    }
    .
    .
}
```

67.2.3 Medium Rectangle Ads

The medium rectangle ad is presented to the user in the form of a 300x250 pixel rectangle and is designed to be used within the content of a view. Medium rectangle ads are represented by instances of the *AdBannerView* class which must be assigned a delegate that conforms to the ADBannerViewDelegate protocol. These delegate methods are called to notify the application of whether or not an ad is ready to be displayed. It is the responsibility of these methods to position, display and hide the ad within the view as needed. For as long as the banner is visible and the device has internet connectivity, the banner will cycle through different ads.

The following code, for example, creates a medium rectangle ad instance and assigns the current class as the delegate:

```
let rectangleAdView = ADBannerView(adType: ADAdType.MediumRectangle)
rectangleAdView?.delegate = self
```

When an ad is ready to be displayed, the *bannerViewDidLoadAd* method of the delegate will be called, the responsibility of which is to display the ad within the current view. For example:

```
func bannerViewDidLoadAd(banner: ADBannerView!) {
    self.view.addSubview(banner)
    self.view.layoutIfNeeded()
}
```

Note that the above code does not attempt to position the ad rectangle. In a real world application code will need to be added so that the ad appears in the appropriate location on the view.

The rectangle ad will rotate through different ads as long as inventory is available. In the event that an ad is not available, or the device loses connectivity, the *didFailToReceiveAdWithError:* delegate method will be called so that the advert can be removed from the view until another ad is available to be displayed:

```
func bannerView(banner: ADBannerView!, didFailToReceiveAdWithError
                                        error: NSError!) {

    banner.removeFromSuperview()
    self.view.layoutIfNeeded()
}
```

As with the banner ad format, a full screen advertisement will be displayed in the event that the user taps on the rectangle ad. Once again, the *viewWillDisappear* and *viewWillAppear* delegate methods may be used to pause and resume the application if appropriate.

67.2.4 Pre-Roll Video Ads

For applications that make use of the iOS MediaPlayer Framework to play videos, this feature allows advertisement videos to be played before the actual video is played to the user. This simply involves calling the *playPrerollAdWithCompletionHandler* method of the media player instance. A completion handler is then called so that the playback of the actual video can be initiated when the ad has finished running. For example:

```
let url = NSURL(string:
                "http://www.ebookfrenzy.com/ios_book/movie/movie.mov")

let player = AVPlayer(URL: url)
let playerController = AVPlayerViewController()
playerController.player = player

self.presentViewController(playerController, animated: true,
```

```
                                              completion: nil)

playerController.playPrerollAdWithCompletionHandler({error in
    player.play()
})
```

As with the interstitial ad format, Apple recommends preparing the application for pre-roll video ads at application launch time:

```
    .
    .
import AVKit
    .
    .
func application(application: UIApplication,
didFinishLaunchingWithOptions launchOptions: [NSObject: AnyObject]?) ->
Bool {

    AVPlayerViewController.preparePrerollAds()
    return true
}
```

67.3 Creating an Example iAds Application

In the remainder of this chapter we will work step by step through the creation of a simple iOS 8 application that includes banner, interstitial and rectangle based iAd advertisements. Begin this tutorial by launching Xcode and creating a new iOS application project named *iAdDemo* using the *Single View Application* template using the Swift language and with the Devices menu set to *Universal*.

67.4 Adding the iAds Framework to the Xcode Project

Once the new project has been created, the first step is to make sure the iAds Framework is included in the project. Failure to add this framework will result in the application crashing at runtime.

To add the iAds framework, select the *iAdDemo* target located at the top of the project navigator panel. In the center pane, select the *Build Phases* tab and unfold the *Link Binary With Libraries* panel. Click on the '+' button to display a list of existing frameworks, locate and select *iAd.framework* and click the *Add* button. The iAd.framework will now appear in the frameworks list along with the other frameworks already included in the project.

67.5 Enabling Banner Ads

To enable banner ads, begin by selecting the *ViewController.swift* file, importing the iAd Framework and modifying the *viewDidLoad* method to enable banner ads on the view controller class:

```
import UIKit
import iAd

class ViewController: UIViewController {


    override func viewDidLoad() {
        super.viewDidLoad()
        self.canDisplayBannerAds = true
    }
    .
    .
    .
}
```

Run the application to verify that a banner ad appears along the bottom edge of the view as illustrated in Figure 67-1:

Figure 67-1

When the banner appears, tap on it to see the full screen advertisement, then close the advert to revert to the application.

67.6 Adding a Medium Rectangle Ad

To add the medium rectangle, begin by selecting the *ViewController.swift* file and modifying it to reflect the fact that this class will now be implementing the ADBannerViewDelegate protocol and to declare a reference to an ADBannerView instance:

```
import UIKit
import iAd
```

```
class ViewController: UIViewController, ADBannerViewDelegate {

    var rectangleAdView: ADBannerView?
    .
    .
    .
}
```

Return to the *viewDidLoad* method and add code to create the ad instance and to designate the view controller as the delegate:

```
override func viewDidLoad() {
    super.viewDidLoad()
    self.canDisplayBannerAds = true

    rectangleAdView = ADBannerView(adType: ADAdType.MediumRectangle)
    rectangleAdView?.delegate = self
}
```

Next, implement the delegate methods to add and remove the ad rectangle from the view:

```
func bannerViewDidLoadAd(banner: ADBannerView!) {
    self.view.addSubview(banner)
    self.view.layoutIfNeeded()
}

func bannerView(banner: ADBannerView!, didFailToReceiveAdWithError error:
NSError!) {
    banner.removeFromSuperview()
    self.view.layoutIfNeeded()
}
```

Compile and run the application, at which point the medium rectangle ad should appear in the top left hand corner of the display as shown in Figure 67-2:

Figure 67-2

67.7 Implementing an Interstitial Ad

The first step in demonstrating interstitial ads in action is to add a second scene to the storyboard and implement a segue to that scene from the first scene. Begin by selecting the *Main.storyboard* file and dragging and dropping a new View Controller instance from the Object Library so that it is positioned to the right of the existing view controller scene.

Next, drag and drop a Button view onto the center of the first view controller scene. With the button selected, use the Auto Layout Align menu to add horizontal and vertical *Center in Container* constraints.

Ctrl-click on the button and drag the resulting line to the second view controller scene. Release the line and select the *show* option from the resulting menu.

On completion of these settings, the storyboard should resemble that of Figure 67-3:

Figure 67-3

In order to avoid any delay in loading the ad artwork, prepare the application for interstitial ads by modifying the *AppDelegate.swift* file to import the iAd file framework and to perform the preparation method call:

```
import UIKit
import iAd

@UIApplicationMain
class AppDelegate: UIResponder, UIApplicationDelegate {

    var window: UIWindow?

    func application(application: UIApplication,
didFinishLaunchingWithOptions launchOptions: [NSObject: AnyObject]?) ->
Bool {
        UIViewController.prepareInterstitialAds()
        return true
    }
    .
    .
    .
}
```

The last task is to add the *prepareForSegue* method to the *ViewController.swift* file to enable automatic interstitial ads for the transition to the destination view controller:

```
override func prepareForSegue(segue: UIStoryboardSegue, sender:
AnyObject?) {
    let destination = segue.destinationViewController
                    as UIViewController
    destination.interstitialPresentationPolicy =
                    ADInterstitialPresentationPolicy.Automatic
}
```

Compile and run the application and, once loaded, tap on the button to transition to the second scene at which point the interstitial ad should appear (Figure 67-4):

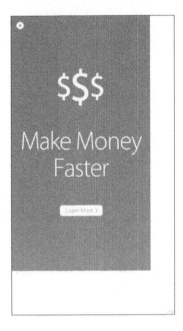

Figure 67-4

67.8 Configuring iAds Test Settings

In the real world, there will be situations where an ad is not available to be displayed to the user. This might be because Apple does not have a suitable ad available in its inventory, or simply because the device does not have an internet connection and cannot connect to the Apple ad server. It is important, therefore, to test that the application gracefully handles such situations. In recognition of this fact, iOS provides a mechanism for simulating the absence of ad inventory (otherwise known as the ad fill rate) while testing an application. These settings are accessible via the *Developer* section of the Settings app on the device. Settings are available to adjust the ad refresh rate and also, as illustrated in Figure 67-5, the fill rate.

In the event that the ad does not appear, keep in mind that it can take a while for the Ad to arrive from the server. If no ad appears after about a minute, it may be worth accessing the Developer settings on the device and changing the fill rate to 100%.

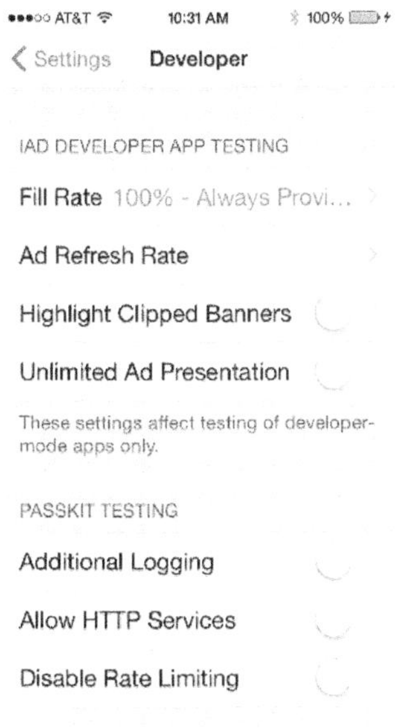

❮ Settings   **Developer**

IAD DEVELOPER APP TESTING

Fill Rate 100% - Always Provi... ❯

Ad Refresh Rate   ❯

Highlight Clipped Banners

Unlimited Ad Presentation

These settings affect testing of developer-
mode apps only.

PASSKIT TESTING

Additional Logging

Allow HTTP Services

Disable Rate Limiting

Figure 67-5

Other options provided on this settings screen include the ability to adjust the frequency with which the ads refresh during testing and a mode to highlight ads that are clipped by other views within the user interface.

67.9 Summary

There are a variety of methods for generating revenue from an iOS application. Perhaps one of the more obvious solutions, aside from charging an upfront fee for the application, is to integrate advertising into the user interface. The iAds Framework provides an easy to use mechanism for the integration of advertisements sourced from Apple's iAds inventory. This chapter has covered the basics of the iAds Framework and worked through the creation of an example application.

68. iOS 8 Multitasking, Background Transfer Service and Fetching

Multitasking refers to the ability of an operating system to run more than one application concurrently. The introduction of iOS version 4.0 was met with much fanfare relating to the fact that the operating system now supported multitasking. In actual fact, iOS has always been able to support multitasking and many of the applications bundled with the device (such as the Mail, Phone and Music apps) have been leveraging the multitasking abilities of iOS since the very first iPhone shipped. What was, in fact, significant about iOS 4 was that many of the multitasking capabilities of the operating system were now being made available to us as third party application developers. These capabilities are, unsurprisingly, still available in iOS 8.

Multitasking in iOS, within the context of third party application development at least, is not without some restrictions however. The goal of this chapter, therefore, is to provide an overview of the capabilities, limitations and implementation of multitasking in iOS 8, including an overview of features such as the background transfer service and background fetch.

68.1 Understanding iOS Application States

At any given time an iOS application can be in one of a number of different states. Applications in the *not running* state have either yet to be launched by the user or were previously launched but have been terminated either by the user or the operating system.

An application is in the *foreground* state when it is the current application displayed to the user. At any one time only one application can be in the foreground state. Applications in the foreground can be in one of two sub-states, namely *active* or *not active*.

When in the *not active* state, the application is running in the foreground but is not actively receiving or handling any events (for example because the system is awaiting a user response to an event such as an incoming phone call or because the screen lock has been activated).

An *active* application, on the other hand, is running in the *foreground* and currently receiving events (perhaps due to interaction with the user or via the network).

An application is considered to be in the *background* state when it is no longer the *foreground* application. Applications in this state are still executing code either because they have requested additional background execution time to complete a task or because they have requested permission to remain running in the background and, in so doing, have met the criteria (discussed later in the chapter) to do so. An application typically enters the background when the user launches another application, or brings another background application into the foreground. With iOS 4.0 or later it is also possible to launch an application directly into the background.

Applications enter the *suspended* state when they have been moved to the background and are no longer executing code. The application is still stored in memory preserving its state at the point of suspension but is neither using any CPU cycles nor is it placing additional load on the battery. This state of suspended animation allows the application to be quickly moved into the foreground and execution resumed at the request of the user thereby providing near instantaneous application switching. Suspended applications may be terminated at any time at the discretion of the operating system (typically in order to free up memory resources) so it is essential that applications save any status information to non-volatile storage prior to entering the suspended state.

68.2 A Brief Overview of the Multitasking Application Lifecycle

The lifecycle of an iOS 8 application primarily involves a series of transitions between the various states outlined in the preceding section. At each stage of the lifecycle, calls are made to specific methods in the application's delegate so that the application can take appropriate action where necessary.

When an application is launched it transitions from *not running* to either the *active* or *background* state. Once the application has loaded the *didFinishLaunchingWithOptions* delegate method is called. If the newly launched application is entering *foreground* mode the *applicationDidBecomeActive* method is then called. If, on the other hand the application is moving directly to the background state (either by design or by necessity), then the *applicationDidEnterBackground* delegate method is triggered.

When a foreground application enters the background the application transitions to the *inactive* state, triggering a call to the application delegate's *applicationWillResignActive* method. This in turn is followed by a transition to *background* status which is accompanied by a call to the *applicationDidEnterBackground* method.

If the application has not indicated that it is eligible to continue running in the background the application is given 5 seconds to complete any tasks before returning from the *applicationDidEnterBackground* method. If these tasks cannot be performed in the time given they may be performed by making a call to the *beginBackgroundTaskWithExpirationHandler* method followed by a call to the *endBackgroundTask* method when the task is complete. Failure to return from the *applicationDidEnterBackground* method within the allocated time will result in the application being terminated. Apple has also introduced a slight change in the way in which extra time is provided to complete a task in iOS 7 which has carried over to iOS 8. In iOS 6, for example, if the user put the device into sleep mode by locking the screen whilst an application was completing tasks, the device would be kept awake until the tasks were complete. With iOS 7 and later releases, however, the tasks are suspended when the device goes to sleep and then given small bursts of time to progress the tasks when the device wakes up to perform other tasks such as checking email. Network based tasks should, therefore, be wrapped in NSURLSession instances in order to handle the intermittent nature of this background execution environment.

When an application is moved from the background to the foreground, the *applicationWillEnterForeground* method is triggered, followed by a call to *applicationDidBecomeActive*.

Finally, when an application is about to be terminated (either by the user or the system) the application delegate's *applicationWillTerminate* method is called.

68.3 Checking for Multitasking Support

Multitasking is only supported on the iPhone 3GS and later devices running iOS 4.0 or newer. In the case of devices where multitasking is not supported, applications are simply terminated rather than being placed in the background.

If you are developing an application that relies on multitasking it is recommended that defensive code be implemented to check for multitasking support so that application behavior can be modified to compensate for the missing functionality. This can be achieved using the following code fragment:

```
func multitaskingSupported() -> Bool {
    let device = UIDevice.currentDevice()
    var backgroundIsSupported = false

    if device.respondsToSelector("isMultitaskingSupported") {
        backgroundIsSupported = device.multitaskingSupported
    }
    return backgroundIsSupported
}
```

When the above method is called it returns either true or false depending on whether or not multitasking is supported on the device.

68.4 Enabling Multitasking for an iOS Application

Multitasking support is disabled by default for all applications developed in Xcode. In situations where an application is required to enter background mode a configuration setting is required in the application's *Info.plist* file. The simplest way to make this configuration change is to select the application target at the top of the project navigator panel, select the *Capabilities* tab and switch the *Background Modes* option from *Off* to *On* as illustrated in Figure 68-1:

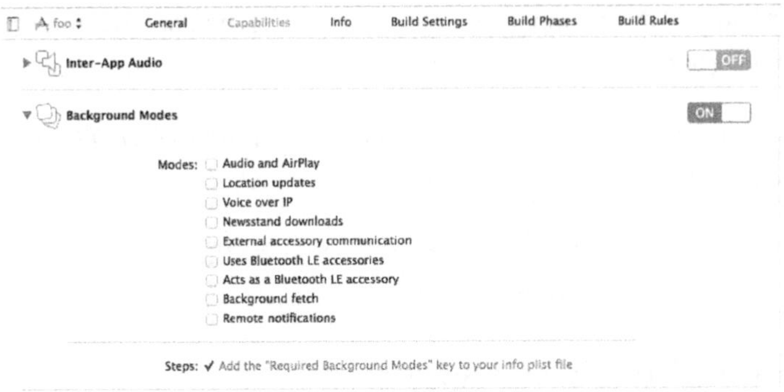

Figure 68-1

Once selected, the appropriate setting will be added to the application's *Info.plist* file to enable multitasking support.

68.5 Supported Forms of Background Execution

So far we have looked primarily at the types of applications for which a suspended background state is acceptable to the user. Apple, however, recognizes nine categories in which application suspension would be detrimental to the user experience, these being audio, location updates, voice over IP (VOIP), Newsstand updates, external and Bluetooth accessory communication, background fetch and remote notifications.

The background execution modes supported by an application are configured in the application's *Info.plist* file using the *UIBackgroundModes* key. The value for the key is actually an array allowing an application to register for more than one background execution mode. To select the background modes, simply enable the checkbox next to the required modes within the *Background Modes* section of the project *Capabilities* panel as outlined in Figure 68-1 above.

68.6 An Overview of Background Fetch

Background fetch provides a way for an application to be woken up in the background to perform content updates. A news application, for example, might benefit from being given opportunities to download new articles in the background so that the next time the user launches the application it is already populated with the latest news headlines and articles. The frequency of background fetch operations can be configured by the application by specifying a time interval, or left at the discretion of the operating system. When the background fetch schedule is left at the discretion of iOS, the operating system will learn the user's pattern of application use and schedule fetch operations so that they occur before those times. If iOS notices, for example, that the application is launched at lunch time each weekday, fetch opportunities will be provided for the application prior to that time.

Background fetch must first be enabled in the background modes settings for the application via the Capabilities panel previously discussed. Once enabled, the background fetch interval must be set. By default this is set to *UIApplicationBackgroundFetchIntervalNever* which will result in no fetch operations being scheduled. To let iOS calculate optimal fetch operations, the application's *setMinimumBackgroundFetchInterval* method may be called within the application delegate as follows:

```
func application(application: UIApplication,
        didFinishLaunchingWithOptions
        launchOptions: [NSObject: AnyObject]?) -> Bool {

    application.setMinimumBackgroundFetchInterval(
            UIApplicationBackgroundFetchIntervalMinimum)
    return true
}
```

Once background fetches have been suitably enabled and configured, the application's *performFetchWithCompletionHandler:* delegate method will be called for each fetch. This method should also be implemented within the application delegate file for example,

```
func application(application: UIApplication,
        performFetchWithCompletionHandler completionHandler:
                (UIBackgroundFetchResult) -> Void) {

    completionHandler(UIBackgroundFetchResult.NewData)
}
```

When called, it is the responsibility of the method to obtain the latest content for the application (such as news articles in the case of a news app). Passed as an argument to the delegate method is the reference to a completion handler which must be called once the fetch is complete. When the handler is called, it must be passed as an argument a value indicating the success or otherwise of the fetch operation. In the example above, the completion handler is notified that new data was received. The method should also be implemented to handle situations where the fetch fails, or no new data was available. This can be achieved by using the *UIBackgroundFetchResult.NoData* and *UIBackgroundFetchResult.Failed* values.

If the application is not already running in the background when a fetch is scheduled to occur, it will be launched in the background by the operating system and the fetch delegate method called. To test this behavior, edit the scheme for the application by clicking on the current scheme in the Xcode toolbar and selecting the *Edit Scheme...* menu option as outlined in Figure 68-2:

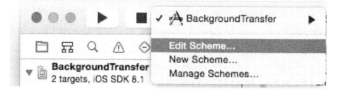

Figure 68-2

Within the Edit Scene panel, select the Run/Debug option in the left hand panel followed by Options in the main panel, enable the check box next to *Launch due to a background fetch* and click on *OK*:

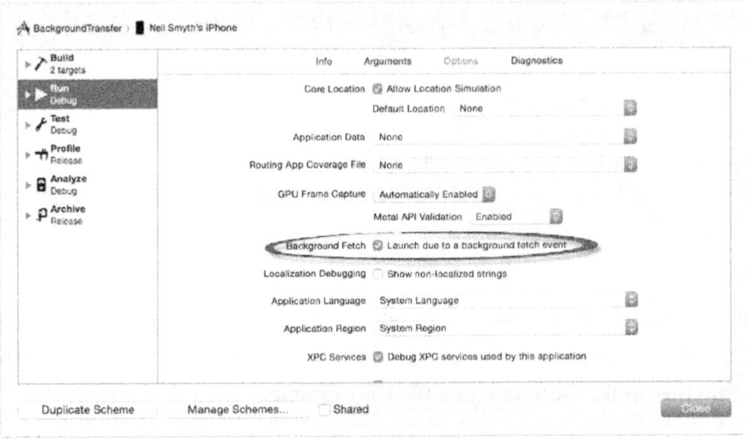

Figure 68-3

When the application is next run, it will launch in the background and the fetch delegate method will be called. Once the testing is complete, re-edit the scheme and turn off the background fetch toggle.

The second scenario to test involves situations where the application is already in the background when the fetch is triggered. To test this, run the application and place it into the background using the home button. Once in the background, select the Xcode *Debug -> Simulate Background Fetch* menu option.

68.7 An Overview of Remote Notifications

Remote Notifications allow applications to receive notifications from a remote server and process that notification in the background. When a notification for the application arrives, the application is woken up and passed the message so that it can act on it. Notifications are typically displayed to the user once they have been handled by the application, though the option is also provided to allow a notification to be silent so that only the application knows it has been received. This allows you, for example, to notify your application via a remote server that some form of new content or data is available for download. The application can then download that data and have it ready for the user next time they access the application.

With *Remote notifications* background mode enabled in the project capabilities panel, and the appropriate notification server set up and configured, the application's *didReceiveRemoteNotification* delegate method will be called when a notification arrives on the device for it. Once the notification has been handled, the completion handler passed to the delegate method then needs to be called.

68.8 An Overview of Local Notifications

Suspended applications and those running in one of the background execution modes do not, by definition, have access to the display of the iOS device. In recognition of the fact that background applications may still need to display alert messages to users, Apple introduced the *Local Notifications* feature in iOS 4. Unlike the *Remote Notifications* functionality, local notifications allow alerts to be triggered from within the local application without the need to rely on a remote server.

A local notification may be triggered at any time by an executing background application. Suspended applications must, however, schedule the notification to be delivered at a future time as part of the clean-up process contained within the *applicationDidEnterBackground* method. A step-by-step example of how to schedule a local notification within an application entering suspended mode is covered in the chapter entitled *Scheduling iOS 8 Local Notifications*.

68.9 **An Overview of Background Transfer Service**

The background transfer service allows applications to perform large file upload and download operations in the background in a way that optimizes battery efficiency. Background transfer services are continued regardless of whether or not the application exits and will automatically resume in the event that the device is rebooted. The application will receive notifications via delegate methods when the download completes, or in the event that an error occurs. If the application exited before the transfer completes, it will be automatically restarted on completion. Download sessions are implemented using the NSURLSession API.

68.10 **The Rules of Background Execution**

Apple recommends that a number of rules be observed when running an application in background execution mode:

*   Only perform the minimum tasks when the application is in background mode. For example, if the application is playing audio content, the application should only perform the tasks necessary to maintaining the audio stream. All other tasks should be placed on hold until the application is returned to the foreground.
*   Do not perform updates to the user interface of the application. Since the application is in the background the user cannot see the user interface. There is nothing, therefore, to be gained (except for unnecessarily using CPU cycles and draining the battery) by continuing to update the UI.
*   Do not perform OpenGL ES calls. Doing so will cause your application to be terminated.
*   Always save the state and data information for the application when notification is received that it is entering the background. Even when suspended, an application may be terminated by the system in order to free up resources.
*   Stop using shared resources such as the address book or calendar when the background notification is received to avoid termination.
*   Attempt to release any memory used by the application that can safely be released without impacting the application's subsequent return to the foreground. The more memory a suspended application is holding on to the more likely it is to be terminated should the system need to free up resources.
*   Cancel Bonjour related services.

68.11 **Summary**

This chapter has provided a summary of the way in which multitasking functions on iOS 8 within the context of an application. The chapter has also looked at some of the tasks that can be performed when an application is in the background, such as receiving notifications, performing transfers of large files and fetching new content.

69. Scheduling iOS 8 Local Notifications

Local Notifications provide a mechanism for an application to schedule an alert to notify the user about an event. These notifications take the form of an alert box or notification panel containing a message accompanied by a sound and the vibration of the device (on devices supporting vibration).

The primary purpose of local notifications is to provide a mechanism for a suspended or background application to gain the attention of the user. For example, an audio streaming app might need to notify the user of the loss of network connection or a calendar based application an approaching appointment. Local notifications are similar to the *push notification* system with the primary difference that notifications are scheduled locally by the application and so do not require the involvement of a remote server.

The goal of this chapter is to build upon the groundwork established in *iOS 8 Multitasking, Background Transfer Service and Fetching* by developing a simple iOS application that, when placed into the background by the user, schedules a local notification event for a future time.

69.1 Creating the Local Notification App Project

The first step in demonstrating the use of local notifications is to create a new Xcode project. Begin by launching Xcode and selecting the options to create a new Swift based Universal project using the *Single View Application* template. When prompted to do so, name the product *LocalNotify*.

69.2 Adding a Sound File to the Project

When a local notification is triggered, the option is available to play a sound to gain the user's attention. If such an audio alert is required the corresponding sound file must be added to the application project resources. If no sound file is specified, the default is for the notification to be silent (though the iPhone device will still vibrate).

For the purposes of this exercise, we will use a public domain sound clip file named *bell_tree.mp3* which can be found in the *audiofiles* folder of the sample code archive which may be downloaded using the following URL:

http://www.ebookfrenzy.com/print/ios8

Once downloaded, drag this file and drop it onto the *Supporting Files* category located in the Xcode project navigator panel and click the *Finish* button in the resulting panel. The audio file should now be included in the list of resources for the project ready to be accessed by the application code.

69.3 Requesting Permission to Trigger Alerts

With the introduction of iOS 8, it is now the responsibility of the application to request permission from the user to display alerts and play sounds when using local notifications. For the purposes of this example, the code to make this request will be placed in the *viewDidLoad* method located in the *ViewController.swift* file as follows:

```
override func viewDidLoad() {
    super.viewDidLoad()
    let app = UIApplication.sharedApplication()

    let notificationSettings = UIUserNotificationSettings(forTypes:
            UIUserNotificationType.Alert |
            UIUserNotificationType.Sound,
            categories: nil)

    app.registerUserNotificationSettings(notificationSettings)
}
```

The first time that the application loads, the user will be prompted to provide the application with permission to deliver notifications as shown in Figure 69-1:

Figure 69-1

69.4 **Locating the Application Delegate Method**

The goal of this exercise is to configure a local notification to be triggered 10 seconds after our application enters the background (for additional information on background and suspended applications refer to *iOS 8 Multitasking, Background Transfer Service and Fetching*). When an application is placed in the background, the application delegate's *applicationDidEnterBackground* method is triggered. It is within this method, therefore, that the code to schedule the local notification must be placed. In the case of this example, a template method can be found in the *AppDelegate.swift* file. Within the main Xcode project navigator panel, select this file and scroll down until the method comes into view.

69.5 **Scheduling the Local Notification**

Local notifications require the use of the UILocalNotification class combined with an NSDate object configured with the date and time that the notification is to be triggered. Properties may also be set to specify the text to be displayed to the user, an optional repeat interval and a message to be displayed to the user in the alert box. With these requirements in mind, the following code creates an NSDate object based on the current date and time plus 10 seconds. This date object is then used to schedule a notification with no repeats, a text message and the sound from the audio file:

```swift
func applicationDidEnterBackground(application: UIApplication) {

    let app = UIApplication.sharedApplication()

    let notificationSettings = UIUserNotificationSettings(forTypes:
            UIUserNotificationType.Alert |
            UIUserNotificationType.Sound,
            categories: nil)

    app.registerUserNotificationSettings(notificationSettings)

    let alertTime = NSDate().dateByAddingTimeInterval(10)

    let notifyAlarm = UILocalNotification()

    notifyAlarm.fireDate = alertTime
    notifyAlarm.timeZone = NSTimeZone.defaultTimeZone()
    notifyAlarm.soundName = "bell_tree.mp3"
    notifyAlarm.alertBody = "Staff Meeting in 30 minutes"
    app.scheduleLocalNotification(notifyAlarm)
}
```

69.6 **Testing the Application**

To test the application, click on the run tool bar button located in the Xcode project window. After compiling and linking the application, it will load and run. Once the application has loaded, press the device home button to place the app into background mode (if using the iOS Simulator, select the *Hardware -> Home* menu option). After 10 seconds have elapsed the notification should appear accompanied by the sound from the audio file as illustrated in Figure 69-2.

Figure 69-2

69.7 **Cancelling Scheduled Notifications**

Previously scheduled notifications may be cancelled by obtaining a list of outstanding notifications. These notifications are provided in the form of an NSArray object, the contents of which may be used to cancel individual notifications using the *cancelLocalNotification* method. All currently scheduled notifications may also be cancelled using the *cancelAllLocalNotifications* method as outlined in the following code fragment:

```
let app = UIApplication.sharedApplication()

let oldNotifications = app.scheduledLocalNotifications

if oldNotifications.count > 0 {
    app.cancelAllLocalNotifications()
}
```

69.8 Immediate Triggering of a Local Notification

In addition to the cancellation of a local notification, previously scheduled notifications may be triggered to present immediately to the user irrespective of the *fireDate* property setting. For example, the following code identifies the list of currently scheduled notifications and then triggers the first notification in the array for immediate presentation:

```
let notifications = app.scheduledLocalNotifications

if notifications.count > 0 {
      app.presentLocalNotificationNow(notifications[0]
                    as UILocalNotification)
}
```

Note that notifications presented using the *presentLocalNotificationNow* method will still trigger again when the specified fireDate is reached unless they are specifically cancelled.

69.9 Summary

Local notifications were introduced in iOS 4.0 alongside multitasking support as a way for iOS applications placed in the background or in a suspended state to notify the user of an event. In this chapter we have worked through an example of scheduling a local notification for a future time when an application receives notification that it is transitioning to the background state. Also covered were the steps necessary to cancel pending notifications and to trigger the immediate presentation of a notification regardless of the scheduled delivery time.

70. An Overview of iOS 8 Application State Preservation and Restoration

Application state preservation and restoration is all about presenting the user with application continuity in terms of appearance and behavior. This is, in part, already provided through support for applications to run in the background. Users have come to expect to be able to switch from one app to another and, on returning to the original app, to find it in the exact state it was in before the switch took place. Unless the application developer took specific steps to save and restore state, however, this continuity did not extend between sessions that involve the application stopping and restarting (usually as a result of the operating system killing a background application to free resources). For most applications available today, such a scenario results in the application starting at the home screen with no consideration being given to the previous state of the application.

Apple feels strongly that the continuity of a user's interaction with an application should extend between the application stopping and restarting. In recognition of this fact, Apple provides a set of features in the UIKit Framework intended to make it easier for developers to save and restore application state.

The topic of this chapter is to introduce the concepts of application state preservation and restoration in iOS 8 and outline the steps that are involved in implementing this behavior.

70.1 The Preservation and Restoration Process

The UIKit preservation and restoration system provides a mechanism by which an application is able to save and restore the state of specific view controllers and views between different application invocations. UIKit achieves this by defining a flexible structure to which the application must conform in terms of providing information on what is to be saved, and implementing methods that are called by UIKit at certain points during the preservation and restoration process.

During the application design process, the developer must decide which view controllers and views that comprise the application need to have state preserved to ensure continuity for the user. Each item for which state is to be saved must then be assigned a *restoration identifier*. Those views and view controllers without a restoration ID will not, by default, be included in the saved state. It should also be noted that if a view controller does not have a restoration ID, none of the controller's child views or view controllers will be saved, irrespective of whether or not those sub-views have a restoration ID.

Each time a running application is placed into the background, UIKit will ask the application whether or not it requires state preservation. In the event that the application requires the state to be saved, UIKit will traverse the view controller hierarchy of the application and save the state of each object that has a restoration ID. As it does this, it will call a method on each eligible object in order to provide that object with an opportunity to encode and return additional data to be included in the saved state. Once the state information has been gathered, it is saved to a file on the local file system of the device.

When the application is next launched (as opposed to being brought out of the background and into the foreground) UIKit will look for a saved state file for the application. In the event that it finds one, it will ask the application if state restoration is required. If the application responds affirmatively, UIKit will use the saved state to guide the application through the process of re-creating the views and view controllers to the previous state. As will be seen later in this chapter, the exact sequence of events for this restoration will depend on the nature of the application, but essentially involves UIKit making calls to specific methods (primarily on the application delegate) asking for the objects to be recreated. Once the view controller and view objects have been recreated, UIKit calls methods on those objects passing through any additional data that was saved during the preservation process.

70.2 Opting In to Preservation and Restoration

By default, UIKit does not attempt to save and restore the state of an application. An application must, instead, "opt-in". This is achieved by implementing methods in the application delegate which return a boolean value to indicate whether or not preservation and restoration are required. The following methods, for example, indicate to UIKit that both state restoration and preservation are required:

```
func application(application: UIApplication,
shouldRestoreApplicationState coder: NSCoder) -> Bool {
    return true
}

func application(application: UIApplication, shouldSaveApplicationState
coder: NSCoder) -> Bool {
    return true
}
```

70.3 Assigning Restoration Identifiers

When UIKit walks the view controller hierarchy of an application to preserve state, only those objects with a restoration ID will be saved.

Restoration IDs can be assigned to objects either in code or from within Interface Builder. The restoration ID can be any valid string and may be assigned in code via the *restorationID* property of the UIView and UIViewController classes. For example:

```
myViewController.restorationIdentifier = "thirdViewController"
```

When using Interface Builder, the restoration ID may be assigned by selecting the object and entering the ID into the *Restoration ID* field located in the *Identity* section of the Identity Inspector as illustrated in Figure 70-1.

In the case of storyboards, the restoration ID can be set to use the storyboard ID if one has already been assigned.

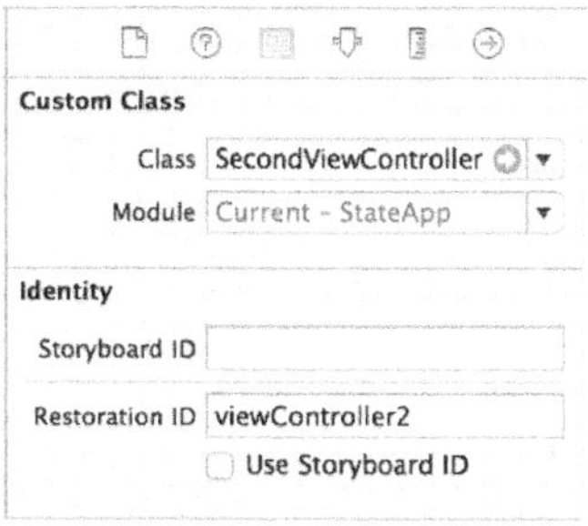

Figure 70-1

When assigning restoration IDs in Interface Builder, it is important to distinguish between views and view controllers. Clicking on the white background of a view in a storyboard, for example, will select the UIView object, not the view controller. Clicking on the status bar containing the battery life indicator will, on the other hand, select the view controller. As a general rule, wherever possible, state preservation should be implemented by saving and restoring the state of the view controller which, in turn, will be responsible for restoring the state of any child view objects. Directly saving and restoring the state of individual view objects in a user interface layout should only be performed when preservation requirements cannot be met using the view controller state.

70.4 Default Preservation Features of UIKit

Once state preservation has been enabled and restoration identifiers assigned appropriately, it is worth being aware that UIKit will preserve certain state information by default and without the need to write any additional code. By default, the following state information is saved and restored automatically for view controllers:

- Currently presented view controller
- Currently selected tab
- State of navigation stacks

In the case of views, the following is preserved by default:

- Current scroll position
- Currently selected cell in a table view
- Current state of an image view (zoom, pan, etc)
- Web history (including scroll position and zoom level)

Additional state preservation will, as will be outlined in the remainder of this chapter, require some coding.

70.5 **Saving and Restoring Additional State Information**

So far we have ascertained that UIKit will store information about which view controllers and views are to be saved based on whether or not those objects have a restoration ID. In many cases, each object will have additional information that it needs to save in order to restore the application exactly as the user left it. This might, for example, relate to a specific item the user has selected, or some text that has been entered into a Text View but not yet been committed to the application's data model. Fortunately, UIKit has a way to handle this.

Once UIKit discovers, for example, that the state of a specific view controller is to be saved, it will check to see if a method named *encodeRestorableStateWithCoder* has been implemented in that object's class. If the method has been implemented, UIKit will call that method, passing through a reference to an NSCoder object. It is then the responsibility of that method to store any additional state data that needs to be preserved into that NSCoder object before returning. UIKit will then save that NSCoder object along with the rest of the application's state.

When UIKit restores the view controller object on a subsequent launch of the application, it will call the *decodeRestorableStateWithCoder* method of that object, passing through the NSCoder object containing the previously stored state data. The method is then responsible for decoding the object and using the data contained therein to restore the view to the previous state. The following code listing shows an example implementation of these two methods for a view controller class intended to save any text that has been entered by the user but not yet saved to the application's data model:

```
override func encodeRestorableStateWithCoder(coder: NSCoder) {
    coder.encodeObject(myTextView.text, forKey:"UnsavedText")
    super.encodeRestorableStateWithCoder(coder)
}

override func decodeRestorableStateWithCoder(coder: NSCoder) {
    myTextView.text = coder.decodeObjectForKey("UnsavedText") as String
    super.decodeRestorableStateWithCoder(coder)
}
```

Note that it is important to call the corresponding method in the superclass before returning from the above methods.

70.6 **Understanding the Restoration Process**

Although UIKit handles the task of remembering which view controllers are to be restored, the actual recreation of those objects is the responsibility of the application code. Restoration can either be performed within the application delegate class, or by implementing a *restoration class* for the view controller.

Restoration classes are useful for restoring view controllers that are not stored in a storyboard file. When attempting to restore a specific view controller, UIKit will first check whether or not a restoration class exists for that controller. If one exists, UIKit instantiates it and calls its *viewControllerWithRestorationIdentifierPath* method and expects the method to create the corresponding view controller object and return it. If the method returns a nil value, however, UIKit assumes the view controller is not to be restored.

In order for a class to qualify as a restoration class it must implement the *UIViewControllerRestoration* protocol. Typically, a view controller not stored in a storyboard file will implement this protocol and act as its own restoration class.

When an application is started and UIKit finds a file containing a preserved state, UIKit makes a call to the *application:willFinishLaunchingWithOptions* method of the application delegate class. This will be followed by repeated calls to an application delegate method named *viewControllerWithRestorationIdentifierPath*. This method will be called once for each saved view controller for which a restoration class cannot be found. Passed through as an argument to this method is an array identifying the *restoration path* explicitly referencing the view controller which is to be recreated.

This restoration path is essentially made up from the restoration IDs of the elements in the view controller hierarchy, starting with the root controller and walking down the tree to the view controller UIKit is looking for. Consider, for example, the view hierarchy illustrated in Figure 70-2 where each tree node is labeled using the restoration ID of the corresponding view or view controller object.

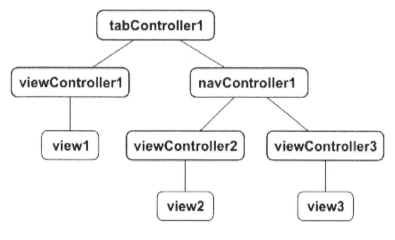

Figure 70-2

In the event that UIKit needs viewController2 to be recreated, the restoration path passed to the application delegate would be:

```
tabController1 / navController1 / viewController2
```

The application delegate method now has two choices. Either it can recreate the view controller object and return it to UIKit or it can return a *nil* value. To recreate a view controller, the application delegate can either instantiate the appropriate view controller class and return it or, if the view controller is stored in a storyboard file, load it and create it from there.

If the *viewControllerWithRestorationIdentifierPath* method returns a nil value, UIKit will continue looking for the view controller object. UIKit will first check to make sure the view controller object has not already been created as part of the application's initialization process. Failing that, if the view controller resides in a storyboard file, UIKit will find it *implicitly* and load and recreate it automatically.

70.7 **Saving General Application State**

So far in this chapter we have focused exclusively on saving the state of the user interface in terms of views and view controllers. There will also be situations where other data may be relevant to the state of the application but not directly associated with the user interface elements. In order to address this need, the following two methods may be implemented within the application delegate class:

*   application:willEncodeRestorableStateWithCoder
*   application:didEncodeRestorableStateWithCoder

The former method is called by UIKit at the start of the preservation process and is passed a reference to an NSCoder object into which state data may be stored. The *application:didEncodeRestorableStateWithCoder* method, on the other hand, is called when UIKit has completed the restoration process and is passed the NSCoder object into which general state data was previously stored.

70.8 **Summary**

A key part of providing an optimal user experience is to ensure that continuity of application appearance and behavior is maintained between one application launch instance and the next. Prior to iOS 6, this involved writing custom code to save and restore state. iOS 6, however, introduced features in the UIKit Framework designed specifically to ease the implementation of state preservation and restoration in iOS applications. In this chapter, the basic concepts of state preservation have been covered. The next chapter, entitled *An iOS 8 State Preservation and Restoration Tutorial*, will work through a practical demonstration of how these concepts are implemented in an application.

71. An iOS 8 State Preservation and Restoration Tutorial

In the previous chapter, a significant amount of information was conveyed relating to preserving and restoring application state when an application currently placed into the background is terminated by the operating system and needs to be restarted.

The knowledge covered in the previous chapter will now be re-enforced through the creation of an example application that demonstrates exactly how to implement state preservation and restoration in iOS 8.

71.1 Creating the Example Application

Begin by launching Xcode and selecting the options to create a new Swift-based Universal application using the *Tabbed Application* template and enter *StateApp* as the product name.

71.2 Trying the Application without State Preservation

The Tabbed Application template has provided enough functionality to experience some of the default effects of state preservation and restoration. First, run the application without opting in to state preservation. To do so, simply select a target of either the iOS Simulator or a physical device in the Xcode toolbar and click on the run button. When the application has loaded, select the *Second* tab so that the *Second View* is visible before pressing the round home button at the bottom of the device to place the application into the background (if using the simulator, select the *Hardware -> Home* menu option).

The easiest way to test state preservation is to simulate the application being terminated by the operating system whilst in the background. To achieve this, simply click on the stop button in the Xcode toolbar. Once the application has stopped running, launch it a second time by clicking on the run button. When the application launches, the *First* tab will be selected instead of the *Second* tab. Clearly no application state has been preserved between application launches. This is because the application has not "opted-in" to state preservation and restoration.

71.3 Opting-in to State Preservation

Before any kind of state preservation and restoration will become effective, the application must first opt in to the system. Within the project navigator panel, select the application delegate implementation source file

(*AppDelegate.swift*) and modify it to add the two methods required to opt in to both the saving and restoration of application state:

```
func application(application: UIApplication,
        shouldRestoreApplicationState coder: NSCoder) -> Bool {
    return true
}

func application(application: UIApplication,
        shouldSaveApplicationState coder: NSCoder) -> Bool {
    return true
}
```

With the above code changes implemented, once again run the application and perform the previous test to verify that the application is restored to the *Second* tab. Yet again, the application will re-launch with the *First* tab selected. This is because, although the application opted in to state preservation, restoration IDs have not been assigned. As far as UIKit is concerned, therefore, no state needed to be preserved.

71.4 Setting Restoration Identifiers

So far the application storyboard consists of a Tab Bar Controller, two view controllers and a view for each controller (each of which in turn currently contains labels added by Xcode when the Tabbed Application template was selected). In order for any kind of application state to be saved, restoration IDs must be assigned to appropriate objects. The rules of state preservation dictate that any view or view controller object, and its direct ancestors up to and including the root view controller must have a restoration ID in order to be included in the state save file. In the case of this application, restoration IDs need to be added to the Tab Controller and the two view controllers. Since the view controllers will be responsible for the state of the views, these views do not need restoration IDs.

Select the *Main.storyboard* file in the project navigator panel and locate the Tab Bar Controller in the storyboard canvas. Display the Identity Inspector and enter *tabController1* into the *Restoration ID* field as illustrated in Figure 71-1:

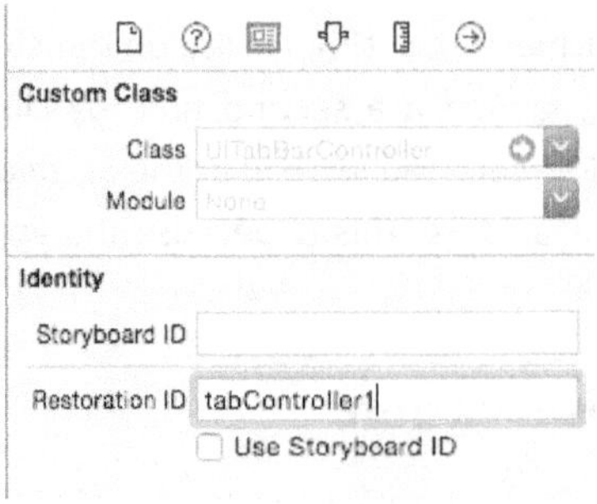

Figure 71-1

Repeat these steps to assign restoration IDs of *viewController1* and *viewController2* to the first and second view controllers respectively. When doing so, make sure that it is the view controllers, and not the view objects, that are being selected by clicking on the status bar at the top of the view above the battery status indicator and not the white background of the view.

With the restoration IDs assigned, run the application and select the *Second* tab. Put the application into the background and then stop and restart the application. This time the application will re-launch and restore the second view as the current view. The default state saving features of UIKit in iOS 8 are now working and more advanced examples of state preservation can be explored.

71.5 Encoding and Decoding View Controller State

The next phase of this tutorial will extend the example application to demonstrate encoding and decoding the state of a view controller. In order to do so, however, some design changes will need to be made to the second view controller.

With the *Main.storyboard* file still selected, locate the second view controller and select and delete the two Label views currently present in the layout. With a blank view object to work with, drag and drop a new TextView object onto the layout. Using the resize handles, reduce the height of the Text View so that it is approximately a quarter of the height of the containing view. Next, add a button, change the label to "Press Me" and position it beneath the Text View as illustrated in Figure 71-2. With the Button view selected, use the Auto Layout Align menu in the lower right hand corner of the storyboard canvas to enable both the Horizontal and Vertical *Center in Container* constraints. Next, select the Text View object and use the Pin menu to establish *Spacing to nearest neighbor* constraints on all four sides of the view using the currently displayed values and with the *Constrain to margins* option enabled.

Select the Text View object, display the Assistant Editor, select the *SecondViewController.swift* file from the toolbar panel if necessary and click and drag from the Text View object to the space beneath the class declaration line. Release the line and, in the resulting panel, establish a new outlet connection named *myTextView*. Close the Assistant Editor.

With the Text View object selected in the Storyboard, display the Attributes Inspector and delete the sample Latin text from the *Text* property.

Build and run the application and, once running, select the second tab and then select and enter some text into the Text View object. Place the application into the background and stop the application using the Xcode stop button. Click on run to launch the application again. Whilst the selection of the second tab has been preserved, the text entered into the Text View has been lost.

In order to preserve the text entered by the user, it will be necessary to implement the *encodeRestorableStateWithCoder* and *decodeRestorableStateWithCoder* methods in the parent view controller of the Text View (in this case *SecondViewController*).

Figure 71-2

Select the *SecondViewController.swift* file and add the encoding methods as follows:

```
override func encodeRestorableStateWithCoder(coder: NSCoder) {
    coder.encodeObject(myTextView.text, forKey:"UnsavedText")
    super.encodeRestorableStateWithCoder(coder)
}
```

This code is actually very straightforward. The method is called by UIKit while the state of the view controller is being saved and is passed an NSCoder object. The *encodeObject* method of the coder (methods exist for other types of data as documented in Apple documentation for the NSCoder class) is then used to encode the text that is currently held in the myTextView object using a key that will be used to decode the data later. The superclass method is then called and the method returns.

The corresponding decode method also needs to be added:

```
override func decodeRestorableStateWithCoder(coder: NSCoder) {
    myTextView.text = coder.decodeObjectForKey("UnsavedText") as String
    super.decodeRestorableStateWithCoder(coder)
}
```

This method simply does the reverse of the encode method. It is called by UIKit during the view controller restoration process and passed the NSCoder object containing the saved data. The method decodes the text using the previously assigned key and assigns it to the Text View.

Compile and run the application once again, enter some text into the Text View object. Place the application into the background before stopping and restarting the application. The previously entered text should now be restored and any work entered by the user but not saved has not been lost between application invocations, a key objective of iOS state preservation.

71.6 **Adding a Navigation Controller to the Storyboard**

Up until this point in the tutorial all view controllers have resided within a storyboard file. As such, UIKit has been able to implicitly find and load the controllers at run time. The tutorial has so far, therefore, failed to demonstrate the use of a restoration class to restore a view controller that was created in code as opposed to being stored in a storyboard file. The remainder of this chapter will focus on just such a scenario.

Within the storyboard, select the Second view controller and insert a navigation controller using the *Editor -> Embed In -> Navigation Controller* menu option. Once added, the storyboard should match that illustrated in Figure 71-3.

Figure 71-3

Select the new navigation controller in the storyboard canvas, display the Identity Inspector and set the restoration ID to *navController1*. Next, select the Second view controller, display the Assistant Editor and Ctrl-click from the Button object in the second view to a suitable location in the *SecondViewController.swift* file before releasing the line. In the resulting panel, change the Connection type to *Action* and specify *displayVC3* as the method name. It is within this action method that the third view controller will be instantiated and pushed onto the navigation controller stack so that it becomes visible to the user.

71.7 **Adding the Third View Controller**

When the "Press Me" button in the second view is touched by the user, a third view controller needs to be instantiated and presented to the user using the navigation controller. This new view controller class first needs to be created. Since the objective here is to demonstrate the use of a restoration class, the view will be created in code and not in the storyboard file. Begin, therefore, by selecting the *File -> New -> File...* menu option. In the resulting panel, select the options to create an iOS *Cocoa Touch Class* before clicking on the *Next* button.

On the next screen, name the class *ThirdViewController* and configure it to be a subclass of UIViewController. Ensure that the *Also create XIB file* option is selected. Click *Next* before creating the new class.

Select the newly created *ThirdViewController.xib* file to load it into Interface Builder and add a label that indicates this is the view of the third view controller (Figure 71-4):

Figure 71-4

With the label selected, use the Auto Layout Align menu to constrain the label both horizontally and vertically within the container view.

The next step is to write some code in the second view controller to create an instance of the ThirdViewController class and to push it onto the navigation controller stack when the "Press Me" button is touched.

Select the *SecondViewController.swift* file and modify it to declare a property for the corresponding view controller object when it is created:

```
import UIKit

class SecondViewController: UIViewController {

    @IBOutlet weak var myTextView: UITextView!
    var thirdViewController: UIViewController?
```

Remaining in the *SecondViewController.swift* file, modify the *viewDidLoad* method to create a new instance of the third view controller class and the *displayVC3* action method to push the view controller onto the navigation stack so that it appears to the user when the button is touched:

```
@IBAction func displayVC3(sender: AnyObject) {
```

```
self.navigationController?.pushViewController(
                    thirdViewController!, animated: true)
}

override func viewDidLoad() {
    super.viewDidLoad()

    thirdViewController = ThirdViewController(nibName:
                        "ThirdViewController", bundle: nil)

}
```

Finally, the code in the ThirdViewController class needs to be modified so that instances of the class are assigned a restoration ID. Select the *ThirdViewController.swift* file and add a line to the *viewDidLoad* method:

```
override func viewDidLoad() {
    super.viewDidLoad()
    self.restorationIdentifier = "thirdViewController"
}
```

Build and run the application, navigate to the third view controller in the user interface and then perform the usual background/kill/run cycle. Note that the application returned to the second view controller screen and not the third view controller. Because the third view controller was created in code, UIKit is unable to find a way to recreate it when the application state is restored. This is where it becomes necessary to implement and register a restoration class for the ThirdViewController class.

71.8 Creating the Restoration Class

There are three very simple rules for implementing a restoration class. Firstly, the class must implement the *UIViewControllerRestoration* protocol. Secondly, in doing so, it must implement the *viewControllerWithRestorationIdentifierPath* class method which, in turn, must return an instance of the view controller for which it is acting as the restoration class. Lastly, the restoration class must be assigned to the *restorationClass* property of the view controller it is designed to restore.

In this instance, the ThirdViewController class is going to act as its own restoration class. Select the *ThirdViewController.swift* file, therefore, and modify it to declare that the class now implements the view controller restoration protocol:

```
import UIKit

class ThirdViewController: UIViewController, UIViewControllerRestoration
{
.
.
.
```

Next, implement the *viewControllerWithRestorationIdentifierPath* class method in the *ThirdViewController.swift* file:

```
class func viewControllerWithRestorationIdentifierPath(
identifierComponents: [AnyObject], coder: NSCoder) -> UIViewController? {

    let myViewController = ThirdViewController(nibName:
                            "ThirdViewController", bundle: nil)
    return myViewController
}
```

All this class method does is create a new instance of the ThirdViewController class initialized with the user interface XIB file and returns it to UIKit.

The last task is to make sure the restoration class is assigned to the view controller. This is achieved by adding a single line to the *viewDidLoad* method, referencing the ThirdViewController class since the class is acting as its own restoration class and using *self* to indicate that we are referencing the class *type* and not an instance of the class:

```
override func viewDidLoad() {
    super.viewDidLoad()

    self.restorationIdentifier = "thirdViewController"
    self.restorationClass = ThirdViewController.self
}
```

Compile and run the application, navigate to the third view controller and background, stop and rerun the application. On the second run, the application should now be restored to the view of the third view controller, a clear sign that the restoration class worked.

71.9 **Summary**

The objective of this chapter has been to work through the creation of an example application designed to demonstrate the practical implementation of state preservation and restoration using the features of the UIKit Framework in the iOS 8 SDK.

Chapter 72

72. Integrating Maps into iOS 8 Applications using MKMapItem

If there is one single fact about Apple that we can state with any degree of certainty, it is that the company is fanatical about retaining control of its own destiny. One glaring omission in this overriding corporate strategy has been the reliance on a competitor (in the form of Google) for mapping data in iOS. This dependency officially ended with iOS 6 through the introduction of Apple Maps.

Apple Maps officially replaces the Google-based map data of previous iOS releases with data provided primarily by a company named TomTom (but also including technology from other companies, including some acquired by Apple for this purpose). Headquartered in the Netherlands, TomTom specializes in mapping and GPS systems. Of particular significance, however, is that TomTom (unlike Google) does not make smartphones, nor does it develop an operating system that competes with iOS, making it a more acceptable partner for Apple.

Political issues aside, there are also technological advantages to the change. Of particular significance is the fact that Google maps were assembled from collections of static images. This led to fuzzy images when zooming in and out and a lack of precision when declaring map regions. Apple maps are dynamically rendered, vector-based images making them both scalable and more precise.

As part of the iOS 6 revamp of mapping, the SDK also introduced a class in the form of MKMapItem, designed solely for the purpose of easing the integration of maps and turn-by-turn directions into iOS applications.

For more advanced mapping requirements, the iOS SDK also includes the original classes of the MapKit framework, details of which will be covered in later chapters.

72.1 MKMapItem and MKPlacemark Classes

The purpose of the MKMapItem class is to make it easy for applications to launch maps without having to write significant amounts of code. MKMapItem works in conjunction with the MKPlacemark class, instances of which are passed to MKMapItem to define the locations that are to be displayed in the resulting map. A range of options are also provided with MKMapItem to configure both the appearance of maps and the nature of turn-by-turn directions that are to be displayed (i.e. whether directions are to be for driving or walking).

72.2 **An Introduction to Forward and Reverse Geocoding**

It is difficult to talk about mapping, in particular when dealing with the MKPlacemark class, without first venturing into the topic of geocoding. Geocoding can best be described as the process of converting a textual based geographical location (such as a street address) into geographical coordinates expressed in terms of longitude and latitude.

Within the context of iOS development, geocoding may be performed by making use of the CLGeocoder class which is used to convert a text based address string into a CLLocation object containing the coordinates corresponding to the address. The following code, for example, converts the street address of the Empire State Building in New York to longitude and latitude coordinates:

```
let geoCoder = CLGeocoder()

geoCoder.geocodeAddressString("350 5th Avenue New York, NY",
        completionHandler:
            {(placemarks: [AnyObject]!, error: NSError!) in

        if error != nil {
            println("Geocode failed with error:
\(error.localizedDescription)")
        }

        if placemarks.count > 0 {
            let placemark = placemarks[0] as CLPlacemark
            let location = placemark.location
            self.coords = location.coordinate

            println("\(self.coords?.latitude) \(self.coords?.longitude)")
        }

    })
```

The code simply calls the *geocodeAddressString* method of a CLGeocoder instance, passing through a string object containing the street address and a completion handler to be called when the translation is complete. Passed as arguments to the handler are an array of CLPlacemark objects (one for each match for the address) together with an Error object which may be used to identify the reason for any failures.

For the purposes of this example the assumption is made that only one location matched the address string provided. The location information is then extracted from the CLPlacemark object at location 0 in the array and the coordinates displayed on the console.

The above code is an example of *forward-geocoding* in that coordinates are calculated based on a text address description. *Reverse-geocoding*, as the name suggests, involves the translation of geographical coordinates into a human readable address string. Consider, for example, the following code:

```
let geoCoder = CLGeocoder()
let newLocation = CLLocation(latitude: 40.74835, longitude: -73.984911)

geoCoder.reverseGeocodeLocation(newLocation, completionHandler:
        {(placemarks: [AnyObject]!, error: NSError!) in

    if error != nil {
        println("Geocode failed with error:
\(error.localizedDescription)")
    }

    if placemarks.count > 0 {
        let placemark = placemarks[0] as CLPlacemark
        let addressDictionary = placemark.addressDictionary

        let address = addressDictionary[kABPersonAddressStreetKey]
                    as NSString
        let city = addressDictionary[kABPersonAddressCityKey]
                    as NSString
        let state = addressDictionary[kABPersonAddressStateKey]
                    as NSString
        let zip = addressDictionary[kABPersonAddressZIPKey]
                    as NSString

        println("\(address) \(city) \(state) \(zip)")
    }
})
```

In this case, a CLLocation object is initialized with longitude and latitude coordinates and then passed through to the *reverseGeocodeLocation* method of a CLGeocoder object. The method passes through to the completion handler an array of matching addresses in the form of CLPlacemark objects. Each object contains an NSDictionary object which, in turn, contains the address information for the matching location. Once again, the code assumes a single match is contained in the array and uses the dictionary keys to access and display the address, city, state, zip and country values. The address dictionary keys follow the standard defined in the *Address Property* section of the iOS SDK Address Book Person reference.

When executed, the above code results in output which reads:

```
338 5th Ave New York New York 10001, United States
```

It should be noted that the geocoding is not actually performed on the iOS device, but rather on a server to which the device connects when a translation is required and the results subsequently returned when the translation is complete. As such, geocoding can only take place when the device has an active internet connection.

72.3 Creating MKPlacemark Instances

Each location that is to be represented when a map is displayed using the MKMapItem class must be represented by an MKPlacemark object. When MKPlacemark objects are created, they must be initialized with the geographical coordinates of the location together with an NSDictionary object containing the address property information. Continuing the example for the Empire State Building in New York, an MKPlacemark object would be created as follows:

```
let coords = CLLocationCoordinate2DMake(40.7483, -73.984911)

let address = [kABPersonAddressStreetKey: "350 5th Avenue",
               kABPersonAddressCityKey: "New York",
               kABPersonAddressStateKey: "NY",
               kABPersonAddressZIPKey: "10118",
               kABPersonAddressCountryCodeKey: "US"]

let place = MKPlacemark(coordinate: coords, addressDictionary: address)
```

Whilst it is possible to initialize an MKPlacemark object passing through a *nil* value for the address dictionary, this will result in the map appearing, albeit with the correct location marked, but it will be tagged as "Unknown" instead of listing the address. The coordinates are, however, mandatory when creating an MKPlacemark object. In the event that the application knows the text address but not the coordinates of a location, geocoding will need to be used to obtain the coordinates prior to creating the MKPlacemark instance.

72.4 Working with MKMapItem

Given the tasks that it is able to perform, the MKMapItem class is actually extremely simple to use. In its simplest form, it can be initialized by passing through a single MKPlacemark object as an argument, for example:

```
let mapItem = MKMapItem(placemark: place)
```

Once initialized, the *openInMapsWithLaunchOptions* method will open the map positioned at the designated location with an appropriate marker as illustrated in Figure 72-1:

```
mapItem.openInMapsWithLaunchOptions(nil)
```

Figure 72-1

Similarly, the map may be initialized to display the current location of the user's device via a call to the *mapItemForCurrentLocation* method:

```
let mapItem = MKMapItem.mapItemForCurrentLocation()
```

Multiple locations may be tagged on the map by placing two or more MKMapItem objects in an array and then passing that array through to the *openMapsWithItems* class method of the MKMapItem class. For example:

```
let mapItems = [mapItem1, mapItem2, mapItem3]

MKMapItem.openMapsWithItems(mapItems, launchOptions: nil)
```

72.5 MKMapItem Options and Enabling Turn-by-Turn Directions

In the example code fragments presented in the preceding sections, a *nil* value was passed through as the options argument to the MKMapItem methods. In actual fact, there are a number of configuration options that are available for use when opening a map. These values need to be set up within an NSDictionary object using a set of pre-defined keys and values:

- **MKLaunchOptionsDirectionsModeKey** – Controls whether turn-by-turn directions are to be provided with the map. In the event that only one placemarker is present, directions from the current location to the placemarker will be provided. The mode for the directions should be one of either *MKLaunchOptionsDirectionsModeDriving* or *MKLaunchOptionsDirectionsModeWalking*.
- **MKLaunchOptionsMapTypeKey –** Indicates whether the map should display satellite, hybrid or standard map images.

- **MKLaunchOptionsMapCenterKey** – Corresponds to a CLLocationCoordinate2D structure value containing the coordinates of the location on which the map is to be centered.
- **MKLaunchOptionsMapSpanKey** – An MKCoordinateSpan structure value designating the region that the map should display when launched.
- **MKLaunchOptionsShowsTrafficKey** – A Boolean value indicating whether or not traffic information should be superimposed over the map when it is launched.

The following code, for example, opens a map with traffic data displayed and includes turn-by-turn driving directions between two map items:

```
let mapItems = [mapItem, mapItem]

let options = [MKLaunchOptionsDirectionsModeKey:
                    MKLaunchOptionsDirectionsModeDriving,
          MKLaunchOptionsShowsTrafficKey: true]

MKMapItem.openMapsWithItems(mapItems, launchOptions: options)
```

72.6 Adding Item Details to an MKMapItem

When a location is marked on a map, the address is displayed together with a blue arrow which, when selected, displays an information card for that location.

The MKMapItem class allows additional information to be added to a location through the *name*, *phoneNumber* and *url* properties. The following code, for example, adds these properties to the map item for the Empire State Building:

```
mapItem.name = "Empire State Building"
mapItem.phoneNumber = "+12127363100"
mapItem.url = NSURL(string: "http://esbnyc.com")
mapItem.openInMapsWithLaunchOptions(nil)
```

When the code is executed, the map place marker displays the location name instead of the address and the information card includes the phone number and URL:

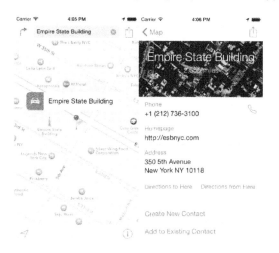

Figure 72-2

72.7 **Summary**

iOS 6 replaced Google Maps with maps provided by TomTom. Unlike Google Maps, which were assembled from static images, the new Apple Maps are dynamically rendered resulting in clear and smooth zooming and more precise region selections. iOS 6 also introduced the MKMapItem class, the purpose of which is to make it easy for iOS application developers to launch maps and provide turn-by-turn directions with the minimum amount of code.

Within this chapter, the basics of geocoding and the MKPlacemark and MKMapItem classes have been covered. The next chapter, entitled *An Example iOS 8 MKMapItem Application*, will work through the creation of an example application that utilizes the knowledge covered in this chapter.

73. An Example iOS 8 MKMapItem Application

The objective of this chapter is to work through the creation of an example iOS 8 application which makes use of reverse geocoding together with the MKPlacemark and MKMapItem classes. The application will consist of a screen into which the user will be required to enter destination address information. When a button is selected by the user, a map will be launched containing turn-by-turn directions from the user's current location to the specified destination.

73.1 Creating the MapItem Project

Launch Xcode and create a new project by selecting the options to create a new iOS application based on the *Single View Application* template. Enter *MapItem* as the product name, set the device menu to *Universal* and choose Swift as the programming language.

73.2 Designing the User Interface

The user interface will consist of four Text Field objects into which the destination address will be entered, together with a Button to launch the map. Select the *Main.storyboard* file in the project navigator panel and, using the Object Library palette, design the user interface layout such that it resembles that of Figure 73-1, taking steps to widen the Text Fields and to configure Placeholder text attributes on each one.

If you reside in a country that is not divided into States and Zip code regions, feel free to adjust the user interface accordingly.

Select all of the view objects within the view canvas, display the Auto Layout Pin menu and configure a Horizontal Center in Container constraint for the views. With the views still selected, display the Auto Resolve Auto Layout issues menu and select the "Add Missing Constraints" option listed under *All Views in View Controller*.

The next step is to connect the outlets for the text views and declare an action for the button. Select the *Street address* Text Field object and display the Assistant Editor and make sure that the editor is displaying the *ViewController.swift* file.

Figure 73-1

Ctrl-click on the *Street address* Text Field object and drag the resulting line to the area immediately beneath the class declaration directive in the Assistant Editor panel. Upon releasing the line, the configuration panel will appear. Configure the connection as an *Outlet* named *address* and click on the *Connect* button. Repeat these steps for the *City*, *State* and *Zip* text fields, connecting them to outlets named *city, state* and *zip* respectively.

Ctrl-click on the *Get Directions* button and drag the resulting line to a position beneath the new outlets declared in the Assistant Editor. In the resulting configuration panel, change the *Connection* type to *Action* and name the method *getDirections*. On completion, the beginning of the *ViewController.swift* file should read as follows:

```
import UIKit

class ViewController: UIViewController {

    @IBOutlet weak var address: UITextField!
    @IBOutlet weak var city: UITextField!
    @IBOutlet weak var state: UITextField!
    @IBOutlet weak var zip: UITextField!

    @IBAction func getDirections(sender: AnyObject) {
    }
```

73.3 Converting the Destination using Forward Geocoding

When the user touches the button in the user interface, the *getDirections* method will be able to extract the address information from the text fields. The objective will be to create an MKPlacemark object to contain this location. As outlined in *Integrating Maps into iOS 8 Applications using MKMapItem*, an MKPlacemark instance requires the longitude and latitude of an address before it can be instantiated. The first step in the *getDirections* method is to perform a forward geocode translation of the address. Before doing so, however, it is necessary to declare a property in the *ViewController.swift* file in which to store these coordinates once they have been calculated. This will, in turn, require that the *CoreLocation* framework be imported. Now is also an opportune time to import the *MapKit* and *AddressBook* frameworks, both of which will be required later in the chapter:

```
import UIKit
import CoreLocation
import AddressBook
import MapKit

class ViewController: UIViewController {

    @IBOutlet weak var address: UITextField!
    @IBOutlet weak var city: UITextField!
    @IBOutlet weak var state: UITextField!
    @IBOutlet weak var zip: UITextField!
    var coords: CLLocationCoordinate2D?
```

Next, select the *ViewController.swift* file, locate the *getDirections* method stub and modify it to convert the address string to geographical coordinates:

```
@IBAction func getDirections(sender: AnyObject) {

    let geoCoder = CLGeocoder()

    let addressString = "\(address.text) \(city.text) \(state.text)
\(zip.text)"

    geoCoder.geocodeAddressString(addressString, completionHandler:
        {(placemarks: [AnyObject]!, error: NSError!) in

        if error != nil {
            println("Geocode failed with error:
\(error.localizedDescription)")
        } else if placemarks.count > 0 {
            let placemark = placemarks[0] as CLPlacemark
            let location = placemark.location
            self.coords = location.coordinate

            self.showMap()

        }
    })
}
```

The steps used to perform the geocoding translation mirror those outlined in *Integrating Maps into iOS 8 Applications using MKMapItem* with one difference in that a method named *showMap* is called in the event that a successful translation took place. All that remains, therefore, is to implement this method.

73.4 Launching the Map

With the address string and coordinates obtained, the final task is to implement the *showMap* method. This method will create a new MKPlacemark instance for the destination address, configure options for the map to request driving directions and then launch the map. Since the map will be launched with a single map item, it will default to providing directions from the current location. With the *ViewController.swift* file still selected, add the code for the *showMap* method so that it reads as follows:

```
func showMap() {
    let addressDict =
            [kABPersonAddressStreetKey as NSString: address.text,
             kABPersonAddressCityKey: city.text,
             kABPersonAddressStateKey: state.text,
             kABPersonAddressZIPKey: zip.text]

    let place = MKPlacemark(coordinate: coords!,
                            addressDictionary: addressDict)

    let mapItem = MKMapItem(placemark: place)

    let options = [MKLaunchOptionsDirectionsModeKey:
                    MKLaunchOptionsDirectionsModeDriving]

    mapItem.openInMapsWithLaunchOptions(options)
}
```

The method simply creates an NSDictionary containing the AddressBook keys and values for the destination address and then creates an MKPlacemark instance using the address dictionary and the coordinates from the forward-geocoding operation. A new MKMapItem object is created using the placemarker object before another dictionary is created and configured to request driving directions. Finally, the map is launched.

73.5 Building and Running the Application

Within the Xcode toolbar, click on the Run button to compile and run the application, either on a physical iOS device or the iOS Simulator. Once loaded, enter an address into the text fields before touching the *Get Directions* button. The map should subsequently appear together with the route between your current location and the destination address. Note that if the app is running in the simulator, the current location will likely default to Apple's headquarters in California.

Figure 73-2

73.6 **Summary**

The goal of this chapter has been to work through the creation of a simple application designed to use a combination of geocoding and the MKPlacemark and MKMapItem classes. The example application created in this chapter has demonstrated the ease with which maps and directions can be integrated into iOS 8 applications.

Chapter 74

74. Getting Location Information using the iOS 8 Core Location Framework

iOS devices are able to employ a number of different techniques for obtaining information about the current geographical location of the device. These mechanisms include GPS, cell tower triangulation and finally (and least accurately), by using the IP address of available Wi-Fi connections. The mechanism that is used by iOS to detect location information is, however, largely transparent to the application developer and the system will automatically use the most accurate solution available at any given time. In fact, all that is needed to integrate location based information into an iOS 8 application is an understanding of how to use the Core Location Framework which, incidentally, is the subject of this chapter.

Once the basics of location tracking with Core Location have been covered in this chapter, the next chapter will provide detailed steps on how to create *An Example iOS 8 Location Application*.

74.1 The Core Location Manager

The key classes contained within the Core Location Framework are CLLocationManager and CLLocation. An instance of the CLLocationManager class can be created using the following Swift code:

```
var locationManager: CLLocationManager = CLLocationManager()
```

Once a location manager instance has been created, it must seek permission from the user to collect location information before it can begin to track data.

74.2 Requesting Location Access Authorization

Before any application can begin to track location data it must first seek permission to do so from the user. This can be achieved by making a call to one of two methods on the CLLocationManager instance depending on the specific requirement. If the application only needs to track location information when the application is in the foreground then a call should be made to the *requestWhenInUseAuthorization* method of the location manager instance. For example:

```
locationManager.requestWhenInUseAuthorization()
```

In the event that tracking is also required when the application is running in the background, the *requestAlwaysAuthorization* method should be used instead:

```
locationManager.requestAlwaysAuthorization()
```

Each method call requires that a specific key-value pair be added to the Information Property List dictionary contained within the application's Info.plist file. The value takes the form of a string and must describe the reason why the application needs access to the user's current location. The keys associated with these values are as follows:

- **NSLocationWhenInUseUsageDescription** – A string value describing to the user why the application needs access to the current location when running in the foreground.
- **NSLocationAlwaysUsageDescription** – A string describing to the user why the application needs access to the current location data all the time that the application is running (including when it is in the background).

74.3 Configuring the Desired Location Accuracy

The level of accuracy to which location information is to be tracked is specified via the *desiredAccuracy* property of the CLLocationManager object. It is important to keep in mind when configuring this property that the greater the level of accuracy selected the greater the drain on the device battery. An application should, therefore, never request a greater level of accuracy than is actually needed.

A number of predefined constant values are available for use when configuring this property:

- **kCLLocationAccuracyBestForNavigation** – Uses the highest possible level of accuracy augmented by additional sensor data. This accuracy level is intended solely for use when the device is connected to an external power supply.
- **kCLLocationAccuracyBest** – The highest recommended level of accuracy for devices running on battery power.
- **kCLLocationAccuracyNearestTenMeters** - Accurate to within 10 meters.
- **kCLLocationAccuracyHundredMeters** – Accurate to within 100 meters.
- **kCLLocationAccuracyKilometer** – Accurate to within one kilometer.
- **kCLLocationAccuracyThreeKilometers** – Accurate to within three kilometers.

The following code, for example, sets the level of accuracy for a location manager instance to "best accuracy":

```
locationManager.desiredAccuracy = kCLLocationAccuracyBest
```

74.4 Configuring the Distance Filter

The default configuration for the location manager is to report updates whenever any changes are detected in the location of the device. The *distanceFilter* property of the location manager allows applications to specify the amount of distance the device location must change before an update is triggered. If, for example, the distance filter is set to 1000 meters the application will only receive a location update when the device travels 1000 meters or more from the location of the last update. For example, to specify a distance filter of 1500 meters:

```
locationManager.distanceFilter = 1500.0
```

The distance filter may be cancelled, thereby returning to the default setting, using the kCLDistanceFilterNone constant:

```
locationManager.distanceFilter = kCLDistanceFilterNone
```

74.5 **The Location Manager Delegate**

Location manager updates and errors result in calls to two delegate methods defined within the CLLocationManagerDelegate protocol. Templates for the two delegate methods that must be implemented to comply with this protocol are as follows:

```
func locationManager(manager: CLLocationManager!,
    didUpdateLocations locations: [AnyObject]!)
{
    // Handle location updates here
}

func locationManager(manager: CLLocationManager!,
    didFailWithError error: NSError!)
{
    // Handle errors here
}
```

Each time the location changes, the *didUpdateLocations* delegate method is called and passed as an argument an array of CLLocation objects with the last object in the array containing the most recent location data.

Changes to the location tracking authorization status of an application are reported via a call to the optional *didChangeAuthorizationStatus* delegate method:

```
func locationManager(manager: CLLocationManager!,
    didChangeAuthorizationStatus status: CLAuthorizationStatus) {

        // App may no longer be authorized to obtain location
        //information. Check status here and respond accordingly.

}
```

Once a class has been configured to act as the delegate for the location manager, that object must be assigned to the location manager instance. In most cases, the delegate will be the same view controller class in which the location manager resides, for example:

```
locationManager.delegate = self
```

74.6 **Starting Location Updates**

Once suitably configured and authorized, the location manager can then be instructed to start tracking location information:

```
locationManager.startUpdatingLocation()
```

With each location update, the *didUpdateToLocation* delegate method is called by the location manager and passed information about the current location.

74.7 **Obtaining Location Information from CLLocation Objects**

Location information is passed through to the *didUpdateLocation* delegate method in the form of CLLocation objects. A CLLocation object encapsulates the following data:

- Latitude
- Longitude
- Horizontal Accuracy
- Altitude
- Altitude Accuracy

74.7.1 Longitude and Latitude

Longitude and latitude values are stored as type CLLocationDegrees and may be obtained from a CLLocation object as follows:

```
let currentLatitude: CLLocationDistance =
                    location.coordinate.latitude

let currentLongitude: CLLocationDistance =
                    location.coordinate.longitude
```

74.7.2 Accuracy

Horizontal and vertical accuracy are stored in meters as CLLocationAccuracy values and may be accessed as follows:

```
let verticalAccuracy: CLLocationAccuracy =
                    location.verticalAccuracy

let horizontalAccuracy: CLLocationAccuracy =
                    location.horizontalAccuracy
```

74.7.3 Altitude

The altitude value is stored in meters as a type CLLocationDistance value and may be accessed from a CLLocation object as follows:

```
let altitude: CLLocationDistance = location.altitude
```

74.8 Calculating Distances

The distance between two CLLocation points may be calculated by calling the *distanceFromLocation* method of the end location and passing through the start location as an argument. For example, the following code calculates the distance between the points specified by *startLocation* and *endLocation*:

```
var distance: CLLocationDistance =
        endLocation.distanceFromLocation(startLocation)
```

74.9 Location Information and Multitasking

Location based iOS applications are one of the three categories of application that are permitted to continue executing when placed into the background (for a detailed description of multitasking refer to *iOS 8 Multitasking, Background Transfer Service and Fetching*). If location updates are required when the application is in the background state it is strongly recommended that the desired accuracy setting be reduced within the *applicationDidEnterBackground* method by making a call to the *startMonitoringSignificantLocationChanges* method of the location manager object. This will ensure that the application is only notified of significant changes to the location of the device thereby reducing the load on the battery.

74.10 Summary

This chapter has provided an overview of the use of the iOS Core Location Framework to obtain location information within an iOS application. This theory will be put into practice in the next chapter entitled *An Example iOS 8 Location Application.*

Chapter 75

75. An Example iOS 8 Location Application

Having covered the basics of location management in iOS 8 applications in the previous chapter it is now time to put theory into practice and work step-by-step through an example application. The objective of this chapter is to create a simple iOS application that tracks the latitude, longitude and altitude of an iOS device. In addition, the level of location accuracy will be reported, together with the distance between a selected location and the current location of the device.

75.1 Creating the Example iOS 8 Location Project

The first step, as always, is to launch the Xcode environment and start a new project to contain the location application. Once Xcode is running, select the *File -> New -> Project...* menu option and configure a new iOS project named *Location* using the *Single View Application* template with the language set to Swift and the Devices menu set to *Universal*.

75.2 Designing the User Interface

The user interface for this example location app is going to consist of a number of labels and a button that will be connected to an action method. Initiate the user interface design process by selecting the *Main.storyboard* file. Once the view has loaded into the Interface Builder editing environment, create a user interface that resembles as closely as possible the view illustrated in Figure 75-1.

In the case of the five labels in the right hand column which will display location and accuracy data, make sure that the labels are stretched to the right until the blue margin guideline appears. The data will be displayed to multiple levels of decimal points requiring space beyond the default size of the label.

Select the label object to the right of the "Current Latitude" label in the view canvas, display the Assistant Editor panel and verify that the editor is displaying the contents of the *ViewController.swift* file. Ctrl-click on the same Label object and drag to a position just below the class declaration line in the Assistant Editor. Release the line and in the resulting connection dialog establish an outlet connection named *latitude*. Repeat these steps for the remaining labels, connecting then to properties named *longitude, horizontalAccuracy, altitude, verticalAccuracy* and *distance* respectively.

Current Latitude   Label
Current Longitude   Label
Horizontal Accuracy (m)   Label
Current Altitude   Label
Vertical Accuracy (m)   Label

Label
Reset Distance

Figure 75-1

The final step of the user interface design process is to connect the button object to an action method. Ctrl-click on the button object and drag the line to the area immediately beneath the *viewDidLoad* method in the Assistant Editor panel. Release the line and, within the resulting connection dialog, establish an Action method on the *Touch Up Inside* event configured to call a method named *resetDistance*.

Close the Assistant Editor and add a variable to the ViewController class in which to store the start location coordinates and the location manager object. Now is also an opportune time to import the CoreLocation framework and to declare the class as implementing the CLLocationManagerDelegate protocol:

```
import UIKit
import CoreLocation

class ViewController: UIViewController, CLLocationManagerDelegate {

    @IBOutlet weak var latitude: UILabel!
    @IBOutlet weak var longitude: UILabel!
    @IBOutlet weak var horizontalAccuracy: UILabel!
    @IBOutlet weak var altitude: UILabel!
    @IBOutlet weak var verticalAccuracy: UILabel!
    @IBOutlet weak var distance: UILabel!

    var locationManager: CLLocationManager = CLLocationManager()
    var startLocation: CLLocation!

    .
    .
    .
}
```

75.3 **Configuring the CLLocationManager Object**

The next task is to configure the instance of the CLLocationManager class and to make sure that the application requests permission from the user to track the current location of the device. Since this needs to occur when the view loads, an ideal location is in the view controller's *viewDidLoad* method in the *ViewController.swift* file:

```
override func viewDidLoad() {
    super.viewDidLoad()

    locationManager.desiredAccuracy = kCLLocationAccuracyBest
    locationManager.delegate = self
    locationManager.requestWhenInUseAuthorization()
    locationManager.startUpdatingLocation()
    startLocation = nil
}
```

The above code changes configure the CLLocationManager object instance to use the "best accuracy" setting. The code then declares the view controller instance as the application delegate for the location manager object. The application then requests permission from the user for the application to track location information while the application is in the foreground prior to starting location updating via a call to the *startUpdatingLocation* method. Since location tracking has just begun at this point, the *startLocation* variable is also set to nil.

75.4 **Setting up the Usage Description Key**

The above code changes included a method call to request permission from the user to track location information when the application is running in the foreground. This method call must be accompanied by a usage description string which needs to be added to the project's *Info.plist* file and assigned to the NSLocationWhenInUseUsageDescription key. Within the project navigator panel, load the *Info.plist* file (located under *Supporting Files*) into the editor. The key-value pair needs to be added to the *Information Property List* dictionary. Select this entry in the list and click on the + button to add a new entry to the dictionary. Within the new entry, enter NSLocationWhenInUseUsageDescription into the key column and, once the key has been added, double-click in the corresponding value column and enter the following text so that the entry matches that of Figure 75-2:

```
The application uses this information to show you your location
```

Key	Type	Value
▼ Information Property List	Dictionary	(16 items)
NSLocationWhenInUseUsageDescription ⇕ ◯ ⊖	String	⇕ The application uses this information to show you your location

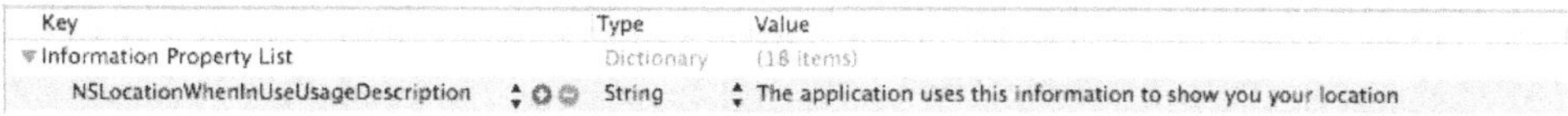

Figure 75-2

75.5 **Implementing the Action Method**

The button object in the user interface is connected to the *resetDistance* action method so the next task is to implement that action. All this method needs to do is set the *startlocation* variable to nil:

```
@IBAction func resetDistance(sender: AnyObject) {
    startLocation = nil
}
```

75.6 **Implementing the Application Delegate Methods**

When the location manager detects a location change, it calls the *didUpdateToLocation* delegate method. Since the view controller was declared as the delegate for the location manager in the *viewDidLoad* method, it is necessary to now implement this method in the *ViewController.swift* file:

```
func locationManager(manager: CLLocationManager!,
            didUpdateLocations locations: [AnyObject]!)
{
    var latestLocation: AnyObject = locations[locations.count - 1]

    latitude.text = String(format: "%.4f",
                        latestLocation.coordinate.latitude)
    longitude.text = String(format: "%.4f",
                        latestLocation.coordinate.longitude)
    horizontalAccuracy.text = String(format: "%.4f",
                        latestLocation.horizontalAccuracy)
    altitude.text = String(format: "%.4f",
                        latestLocation.altitude)
    verticalAccuracy.text = String(format: "%.4f",
                        latestLocation.verticalAccuracy)


    if startLocation == nil {
        startLocation = latestLocation as CLLocation
    }

    var distanceBetween: CLLocationDistance =
            latestLocation.distanceFromLocation(startLocation)

    distance.text = String(format: "%.2f", distanceBetween)
}
```

When the delegate method is called it is passed an array of location objects containing the latest updates, with the last item in the array representing the most recent location information. To begin with, the delegate method extracts the last location object from the array and works through the data contained in the object.

In each case, it creates a string containing the extracted value and displays it on the corresponding user interface label.

If this is the first time that the method has been called either since the application was launched or the user last pressed the *Reset Distance* button, the *startLocation* variable is set to the current location. The *distanceFromLocation* method of the location object is then called, passing through the *startLocation* object as an argument in order to calculate the distance between the two points. The result is then displayed on the distance label in the user interface.

The *didFailWithError* delegate method is called when an error is encountered by the location manager instance. This method should also, therefore, be implemented:

```
func locationManager(manager: CLLocationManager!,
        didFailWithError error: NSError!) {

}
```

The action taken within this method is largely up to the application developer. The method, might, for example, simply display an alert to notify the user of the error.

75.7 Building and Running the Location Application

Click on the run button located in the Xcode project window toolbar. Once the application has compiled and linked it will launch into the iOS Simulator. Before location information can be gathered, the user is prompted to grant permission as outlined in Figure 75-3:

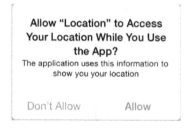

Figure 75-3

Once permission is granted, the application will begin tracking location information. By default, the iOS Simulator will be configured to have no current location causing the labels to remain unchanged. In order to simulate a location, select the iOS Simulator *Debug -> Location* menu option and select either one of the pre-defined locations or journeys (such as City Bicycle Ride), or *Custom Location…* to enter a specific latitude and longitude. The following figure shows the application running in the iOS Simulator after the *Apple* location has been selected from the menu:

Figure 75-4

To experience the full functionality of the application it will be necessary to install it on a physical iOS device, a process that is outlined in the chapter entitled *Testing Apps on iOS 8 Devices with Xcode 6*. Once the application is running on the device, location data will update as you change location.

One final point to note is that the distance data relates to the distance between two points, not the distance travelled. For example, if the device accompanies the user on a 10 mile trip that returns to the start location the distance will be displayed as 0 (since the start and end points are the same).

76. Working with Maps on iOS 8 with MapKit and the MKMapView Class

In the preceding chapters we spent some time looking at handling raw geographical location information in the form of longitude, latitude and altitude data. The next step is to learn about the presentation of location information to the user in the form of maps and satellite images. The goal of this chapter, therefore, is to provide an overview of the steps necessary to present the application user with location, map and satellite imagery using the MapKit Framework and, in particular, the MKMapView class. In the next chapters, this example application will be extended to make use of the Map Kit local search and directions features.

76.1 About the MapKit Framework

The MapKit Framework is based on the Apple Maps data and APIs and provides iOS developers with a simple mechanism for integrating detailed and interactive mapping capabilities into any application.

The core element of the MapKit Framework from the point of view of the app developer is the MKMapView class. This class is a subclass of UIView and provides a canvas onto which map and satellite information may be presented to the user. Information may be presented in map, satellite or hybrid (whereby the map is superimposed onto the satellite image) form. The displayed geographical region may be changed manually by the user via a process of pinching stretching and panning gestures, or programmatically from within the application code via method calls and property manipulation on the MkMapView instance. The current location of the device may also be displayed and tracked on the map view.

The MapKit Framework also includes support for adding annotations to a map. This takes the form of a pin or custom image, title and subview that may be used to mark specific locations on a map.

Implementation of the MKMapViewDelegate protocol allows an application to receive notifications of events relating to the map view such as a change in either the location of the user or region of the map displayed or the failure of the device to identify the user's current location or to download map data.

76.2 Understanding Map Regions

The area of the map that is currently displayed to the user is referred to as the *region*. This is defined in terms of a *center location* (declared by longitude and latitude) and span of the surrounding area to be displayed. Adjusting the span has the effect of zooming in and out of the map relative to the specified center location. The region's span may be specified using either distance (in meters) or coordinate based degrees. When using degrees, one degree of latitude is equivalent to 111 km. Latitude, however, varies depending on the longitudinal distance from the equator. Given this complexity, the map view tutorial in this chapter will declare the span in terms of distance.

76.3 **About the MKMapView Tutorial**

The objective of this tutorial is to develop an iOS application designed to display a map with a marker indicating the user's current location. Buttons located in a navigation bar are provided to allow the user to zoom in on the current location and to toggle between map and satellite views. Through the implementation of the MKMapViewDelegate protocol the map will update as the user's location changes so that the current location marker is always the center point of the displayed map region.

76.4 **Creating the Map Project**

Begin by launching Xcode and creating a new iOS project named *MapSample* using the *Single View Application* template configured with the *Universal* device option and the Swift programming language.

76.5 **Adding the MapKit Framework to the Xcode Project**

Since we will be making use of the MapKit Framework during this tutorial the first step is to add the framework to the project. To achieve this, select the application target at the top of the project navigator panel. In the resulting project settings panel, select the *Build Phases* tab and unfold the *Link Binary with Libraries* section. Click on the '+' button, locate the *MapKit.framework* entry from the resulting list and click *Add*.

76.6 **Adding the Navigation Controller**

Later stages of this tutorial will require the services of a navigation controller. Since the presence of the navigation bar will have implications for the layout of the user interface of the main view, it makes sense to add the controller now. Select the *Main.storyboard* file from the project navigator panel and select the view controller view so that it highlights in blue and use the *Editor -> Embed In -> Navigation Controller* menu option to embed a controller into the storyboard as illustrated in Figure 76-1:

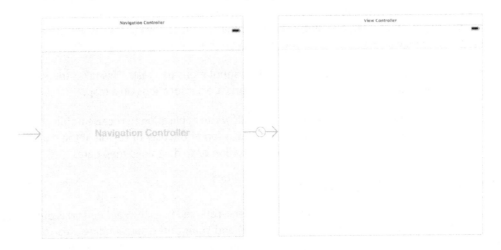

Figure 76-1

76.7 **Creating the MKMapView Instance and Toolbar**

The next step is to create an instance of the MKMapView class we will be using in our application and to add a toolbar instance to the user interface. Remaining in the *Main.storyboard* file, drag a *Toolbar* from the Object Library and place it at the bottom of the view canvas.

Next, drag and drop a Map View object onto the canvas and resize and position it so that it takes up the remaining space in the view above the toolbar and below the navigation bar. By default the Interface Builder tool will have added a single *Bar Button Item* to the new toolbar. For the purposes of this example, however, two buttons will be required so drag and drop a second Bar Button Item from the Object Library panel onto the toolbar. Double click on the toolbar button items and change the text to "Zoom" and "Type" respectively:

Figure 76-2

Select the MKMapView option in the scene and use the Auto Layout Pin menu located in the lower right hand corner of the Interface Builder panel to configure *Spacing to nearest neighbor* constraints of 0 on all four sides of the view with the *Constrain to margins* option switched off. Once the four constraints have been added to the MKMapView object, repeat these steps with the Toolbar view selected.

Select the MKMapView object in the view canvas, display the Assistant Editor panel and verify that the editor is displaying the contents of the *ViewController.swift* file. Ctrl-click on the MKMapView object and drag to a position just below the class declaration line in the Assistant Editor. Release the line and in the resulting connection dialog establish an outlet connection named *mapView*.

Click on the "Zoom" button to select it (note that in order to select a toolbar button item it may be necessary to click on it twice since the first click selects the toolbar parent). With the button item selected, Ctrl-click on the button object and drag the line to the area immediately beneath the *viewDidLoad* method in the Assistant Editor panel. Release the line and, within the resulting connection dialog, establish an Action method on the *Touch Up Inside* event configured to call a method named *zoomIn*. Repeat this step to connect the "Type" button to a method named *changeMapType*.

Working with Maps on iOS 8 with MapKit and the MKMapView Class

Select the *ViewController.swift* file from the project navigator panel and verify that the outlets and actions have been set up correctly. Also take this opportunity to import the MapKit framework and to declare the class as implementing the MKMapViewDelegate protocol:

```
import UIKit
import MapKit

class ViewController: UIViewController, MKMapViewDelegate {

    @IBOutlet weak var mapView: MKMapView!

    override func viewDidLoad() {
        super.viewDidLoad()
    }

    @IBAction func zoomIn(sender: AnyObject) {
    }


    @IBAction func changeMapType(sender: AnyObject) {
    }
.

.

.

}
```

Perform a test run of the application's progress so far by clicking on the run button in the Xcode toolbar. The application should run in the iOS simulator as illustrated in Figure 76-3:

Figure 76-3

76.8 Obtaining Location Information Permission

The next task is to request permission from the user to track the current location of the device. Since this needs to occur when the application loads, an ideal location is in the application delegate *didFinishLaunchingWithOptions* method in the *AppDelegate.swift* file:

```
import UIKit
import CoreLocation

@UIApplicationMain
class AppDelegate: UIResponder, UIApplicationDelegate {

    var window: UIWindow?
    var locationManager: CLLocationManager?

    func application(application: UIApplication,
            didFinishLaunchingWithOptions
            launchOptions: [NSObject: AnyObject]?) -> Bool {

        locationManager = CLLocationManager()
        locationManager?.requestWhenInUseAuthorization()

        return true
    }
```

.
.
}

76.9 Setting up the Usage Description Key

The above code changes included a method call to request permission from the user to track location information when the application is running in the foreground. This method call must be accompanied by a usage description string which needs to be added to the project's *Info.plist* file assigned to the NSLocationWhenInUseUsageDescription key. Within the project navigator panel, load the *Info.plist* file (located under *Supporting Files*) into the editor. The key-value pair needs to be added to the *Information Property List* dictionary. Select this entry in the list and click on the + button to add a new entry to the dictionary. Within the new entry, enter NSLocationWhenInUseUsageDescription into the key column and, once the key has been added, double-click in the corresponding value column and enter the following text so that the entry matches that of Figure 76-4:

```
This information is required to show your current location
```

Key	Type	Value
▼ Information Property List	Dictionary	(16 items)
NSLocationWhenInUseUsage... ⬍◎⊖	String	⬍ This information is required to show your current location
Localization native development r... ⬍	String	en

Figure 76-4

76.10 Configuring the Map View

By default the Map View does not indicate the user's current location. By setting the *showsUserLocation* property of the MKMapView class the map is instructed to display a representation of the current location on the map in the form of a blue translucent ball. Before user location information can be obtained, however, it is first necessary to seek permission from the user. In order to achieve these goals, select the *ViewController.swift* file and locate and modify the *viewDidLoad* method as follows:

```
-  (void) viewDidLoad
{
    [super viewDidLoad]
    mapView.showsUserLocation = true


}
```

76.11 Changing the MapView Region

When the Zoom button is tapped by the user the map view region needs to be changed so that the user's current location is set as the center location and the region span needs to be changed to 2000 meters (analogous to zooming in to the map region). The code to implement this belongs in the *zoomIn* method which now needs to be implemented in the *ViewController.swift* file:

```
@IBAction func zoomIn(sender: AnyObject) {
    let userLocation = mapView.userLocation

    let region = MKCoordinateRegionMakeWithDistance(
            userLocation.location.coordinate, 2000, 2000)

    mapView.setRegion(region, animated: true)
}
```

This method performs some very simple operations in order to achieve the desired effect in the mapView object. Firstly, the user's current location is ascertained by accessing the *userLocation* property of the map view object. This is stored in the form of an MKUserLocation object which, in turn, contains the coordinates of the user. Next, the *MKCoordinateRegionMakeWithDistance* function is called in order to generate an MKCoordinateRegion object consisting of the user's location coordinates and a span that stretches 2000 meters both to the North and South of the current location. Finally, this region object is passed through to the *setRegion* method of the mapView object.

Now that the Zoom functionality has been implemented it is time to configure the map type switching feature of the application.

76.12 Changing the Map Type

The map type of a map view is controlled by the object's *mapType* property. Supported values for this property are MKMapTypeStandard, MKMapTypeSatellite and MKMapTypeHybrid. For the purposes of this example application the map will switch between standard and satellite modes. Within the *ViewController.swift* file modify the *changeMapType* action method connected to the Type button as follows:

```
- (IBAction)changeMapType:(id)sender {
    if mapView.mapType == MKMapType.Standard {
        mapView.mapType = MKMapType.Satellite
    } else {
        mapView.mapType = MKMapType.Standard
    }
}
```

This very simple method simply toggles between the two map types when the button is tapped by the user.

76.13 Testing the MapView Application

Now that more functionality has been implemented, it is a good time to build and run the application again so click on the Xcode *Run* button to load the application into the iOS Simulator. Once the application has loaded, a blue dot should appear over Northern California. Since the application is running in the simulator environment, the location information is simulated to match either the coordinates of Apple's headquarters in Cupertino, CA, or another simulated location depending on the current setting of the *Debug -> Location* menu. Select the Type button to display the satellite view and then zoom in to get a better look at the region:

Carrier 📶   12:18 PM   📶 🔋

Zoom Type

Figure 76-5

To get real location information, load the application onto a physical iOS device (details of which can be found in the *Testing Apps on iOS 8 Devices with Xcode 6* chapter of this book).

76.14 **Updating the Map View based on User Movement**

Assuming that you installed the application on a physical iOS device and went somewhere with the device in your possession (or used one of the debug location settings that simulated movement) you may have noticed that the map did not update as your location changed and that the blue dot marking your current location eventually went off the screen (also assuming, of course, that you had zoomed in to a significant degree).

In order to configure the application so that the map automatically tracks the movements of the user, the first step is to make sure the application is notified when the location changes. At the start of this tutorial the view controller was declared as conforming to the MKMapViewDelegate delegate protocol. One of the methods that comprise this protocol is the *didUpdateUserLocation* method. When implemented, this method is called by the map view object whenever the location of the device changes. We must, therefore, first specify that the MapSampleViewController class is the delegate for the mapView object, which can be performed by adding the following line to the *viewDidLoad* method located in the *ViewController.swift* file:

```
mapView.delegate = self
```

The next task involves the implementation of the *didUpdateUserLocation* method in the *ViewController.swift* file:

```
func mapView(mapView: MKMapView!, didUpdateUserLocation
            userLocation: MKUserLocation!) {
    mapView.centerCoordinate = userLocation.location.coordinate
```

}

The delegate method is passed as an argument an MKUserLocation object containing the current location coordinates of the user. This value is simply assigned to the center coordinate property of the mapView object such that the current location remains at the center of the region. When the application is now installed and run on a device the current location will no longer move outside the displayed region as the device location changes. To experience this effect within the simulator, simply select the *Debug -> Location -> Freeway Drive* menu option and then select the Zoom button in the user interface.

76.15 **Summary**

This chapter has demonstrated the basics of using the MKMapView class to display map based information to the user within an iOS 8 application. The example created in the chapter also highlighted the steps involved in zooming into a region of the map, changing the map display type and configuring a map to track the user's current location.

The next chapter will explore the use of the local search feature of the MapKit Framework before extending the example application to mark all the locations of a specified business type on the map.

77. Working with MapKit Local Search in iOS 8

This chapter will explore the use of the iOS MapKit MKLocalSearchRequest class to search for map locations within an iOS 8 application. The example application created in the chapter entitled *Working with Maps on iOS 8 with MapKit and the MKMapView Class* will then be extended to demonstrate local search in action.

77.1 An Overview of iOS 8 Local Search

Local search is implemented using the MKLocalSearch class. The purpose of this class is to allow users to search for map locations using natural language strings. Once the search has completed, the class returns a list of locations within a specified region that match the search string. A search for "Pizza", for example, will return a list of locations for any pizza restaurants within a specified area. Search requests are encapsulated in instances of the MKLocalSearchRequest class and results are returned within an MKLocalSearchResponse object which, in turn, contains an MKMapItem object for each matching location (up to a total of 10 matches).

Local searches are performed asynchronously and a completion handler called when the search is complete. It is also important to note that the search is performed remotely on Apple's servers as opposed to locally on the device. Local search is, therefore, only available when the device has an active internet connection and is able to communicate with the search server.

The following code fragment, for example, searches for pizza locations within the currently displayed region of an MKMapView instance named *mapView*. Having performed the search, the code iterates through the results and outputs the name and phone number of each matching location to the console:

```
let request = MKLocalSearchRequest()
request.naturalLanguageQuery = "Pizza"
request.region = mapView.region

let search = MKLocalSearch(request: request)

search.startWithCompletionHandler({(response: MKLocalSearchResponse!,
                error: NSError!) in

    if error != nil {
```

```
        println("Error occured in search: \(error.localizedDescription)")
    } else if response.mapItems.count == 0 {
        println("No matches found")
    } else {
        println("Matches found")

        for item in response.mapItems as [MKMapItems] {
            println("Name = \(item.name)")
            println("Phone = \(item.phoneNumber)")
        }

    }
})
```

The above code begins by creating an MKLocalSearchRequest request instance initialized with the search string (in this case "Pizza"). The region of the request is then set to the currently displayed region of the map view instance.

```
let request = MKLocalSearchRequest()
request.naturalLanguageQuery = "Pizza"
request.region = mapView.region
```

An MKLocalSearch instance is then created and initialized with a reference to the search request instance and the search then initiated via a call to the object's *startWithCompletionHandler* method.

```
search.startWithCompletionHandler({(response: MKLocalSearchResponse!,
                error: NSError!) in
```

The code in the completion handler checks the response to make sure that matches were found and then accesses the *mapItems* property of the response which contains an array of mapItem instances for the matching locations. The *name* and *phoneNumber* properties of each mapItem instance are then displayed in the console:

```
if error != nil {
    println("Error occured in search: \(error.localizedDescription)")
} else if response.mapItems.count == 0 {
    println("No matches found")
} else {
    println("Matches found")

    for item in response.mapItems as [MKMapItems] {
        println("Name = \(item.name)")
        println("Phone = \(item.phoneNumber)")
    }

  }
})
```

77.2 **Adding Local Search to the MapSample Application**

In the remainder of this chapter, the MapSample application will be extended so that the user can perform a local search. The first step in this process involves adding a text field to the first storyboard scene. Begin by launching Xcode and opening the MapSample project created in the previous chapter.

77.3 **Adding the Local Search Text Field**

With the project loaded into Xcode, select the *Main.storyboard* file and modify the user interface to add a Text Field object to the user interface layout (reducing the height of the map view object accordingly to make room for the new field). With the new Text Field selected, display the Attributes Inspector and enter *Local Search* into the Placeholder property field. When completed, the layout should resemble that of Figure 77-1:

Figure 77-1

Select the Map Sample view controller by clicking on the toolbar at the top of the scene so that the scene is highlighted in blue. Select the *Resolve Auto Layout Issues* menu from the toolbar in the lower right hand corner of the storyboard canvas and select the *Clear Constraints* menu option.

Select the Text Field object and display the Auto Layout Pin menu. Within the Spacing to Nearest Neighbor section, configure constraints on all four sides of the view with the *Constrain to margins* option disabled and leaving the default settings unchanged as shown in Figure 77-2:

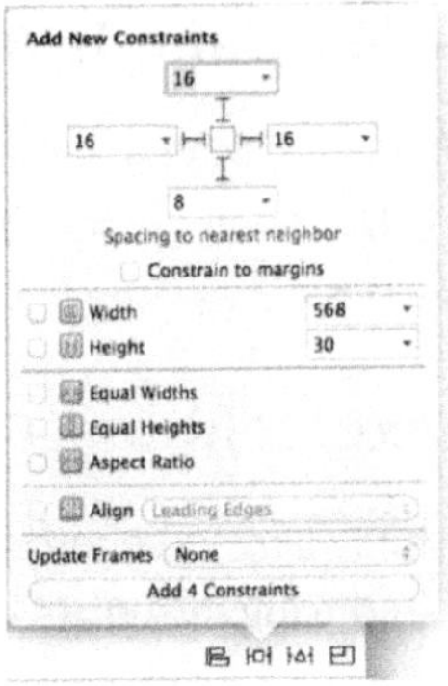

Figure 77-2

Repeat the above steps to apply constraints on the Map View and Toolbar objects.

When the user touches the text field, the keyboard will appear. By default this will display a "Return" key. For the purposes of this application, however, a "Search" key would be more appropriate. To make this modification, select the new Text Field object, display the Attributes Inspector and change the *Return Key* setting from *Default* to *Search*.

Next, display the Assistant Editor panel and make sure that it is displaying the content of the *ViewController.swift* file. Ctrl-click on the Text Field object and drag the resulting line to the Assistant Editor panel and establish an outlet named *searchText*.

Repeat the above step, this time setting up an Action for the Text Field to call a method named *textFieldReturn* for the *Did End on Exit* event.

The *textFieldReturn* method will be required to perform three tasks when triggered. In the first instance it will be required to hide the keyboard from view. When matches are found for the search results, an annotation will be added to the map for each location. The second task to be performed by this method is to remove any annotations created as a result of a previous search.

Finally, the *textFieldReturn* method will initiate the search using the string entered into the text field by the user. Select the *ViewController.swift* file, locate the template *textFieldReturn* method and implement it so that it reads as follows:

```
@IBAction func textFieldReturn(sender: AnyObject) {
    sender.resignFirstResponder()
    mapView.removeAnnotations(mapView.annotations)
    self.performSearch()
}
```

77.4 **Performing the Local Search**

The next task is to write the code to perform the search. When the user touches the keyboard *Search* key, the above *textFieldReturn* method is called which, in turn, has been written such that it makes a call to a method named *performSearch*. Remaining within the *ViewController.swift* file, this method may now be implemented as follows:

```
func performSearch() {

    matchingItems.removeAll()
    let request = MKLocalSearchRequest()
    request.naturalLanguageQuery = searchText.text
    request.region = mapView.region

    let search = MKLocalSearch(request: request)

    search.startWithCompletionHandler({(response:
                        MKLocalSearchResponse!,
                            error: NSError!) in

        if error != nil {
            println("Error occured in search:
\(error.localizedDescription)")
        } else if response.mapItems.count == 0 {
            println("No matches found")
        } else {
            println("Matches found")

            for item in response.mapItems as [MKMapItem] {
                println("Name = \(item.name)")
                println("Phone = \(item.phoneNumber)")

                self.matchingItems.append(item as MKMapItem)
                println("Matching items = \(self.matchingItems.count)")

                var annotation = MKPointAnnotation()
                annotation.coordinate = item.placemark.coordinate
                annotation.title = item.name
                self.mapView.addAnnotation(annotation)
            }
        }
    })
}
```

Next, edit the *ViewController.swift* file to add the declaration for the *matchingItems* array referenced in the above method. This array is used to store the current search matches and will be used later in the tutorial:

```
import UIKit
import MapKit

class ViewController: UIViewController, MKMapViewDelegate {

    @IBOutlet weak var mapView: MKMapView!
    @IBOutlet weak var searchText: UITextField!
    var matchingItems: [MKMapItem] = [MKMapItem]()
.

.
```

The code in the *performSearch* method is largely the same as that outlined earlier in the chapter, the major difference being the addition of code to add an annotation to the map for each matching location:

```
var annotation = MKPointAnnotation()
annotation.coordinate = item.placemark.coordinate
annotation.title = item.name
self.mapView.addAnnotation(annotation)
```

Annotations are represented by instances of the MKPointAnnotation class and are, by default, represented by red pin markers on the map view (though custom icons may be specified). The coordinates of each match are obtained by accessing the placemark instance within each item. The title of the annotation is also set in the above code using the item's *name* property.

77.5 Testing the Application

Compile and run the application on an iOS device and, once running, select the zoom button before entering the name of a type of business into the local search field such as "pizza", "library" or "coffee". Touch the keyboard "Search" button and, assuming such businesses exist within the currently displayed map region, annotation markers will appear for each matching location. Tapping a location marker will display the name of that location (Figure 77-3):

Figure 77-3

Local searches are not limited to business locations. It can also be used, for example, as an alternative to geocoding for finding local addresses.

77.6 **Summary**

The iOS MapKit Local Search feature allows map searches to be performed using free-form natural language strings. Once initiated, a local search will return a response containing map item objects for up to 10 matching locations within a specified map region.

In this chapter the MapSample application was extended to allow the user to perform local searches and to use annotations to mark matching locations on the map view.

In the next chapter, the example will be further extended to cover the use of the Map Kit directions API, both to generate turn-by-turn directions and to draw the corresponding route on a map view.

78. Using MKDirections to get iOS 8 Map Directions and Routes

In this, the final chapter covering the MapKit framework, the use of the MKDirections class to obtain directions and route information from within an iOS 8 application will be explored. Having covered the basics, the MapSample tutorial application will be extended to make use of these features to draw routes on a map view and display turn-by-turn driving directions.

78.1 An Overview of MKDirections

The MKDirections class was introduced into iOS as part of the iOS 7 SDK and is used to generate directions from one geographical location to another. The start and destination points for the journey are passed to an instance of the MKDirections class in the form of MKMapItem objects contained within an MKDirectionsRequest instance. In addition to storing the start and end points, the MKDirectionsRequest class also provides a number of properties that may be used to configure the request, such as indicating whether alternate route suggestions are required and specifying whether the directions should be for driving or walking.

Once directions have been requested, the MKDirections class contacts Apple's servers and awaits a response. Upon receiving a response, a completion handler is called and passed the response in the form of an MKDirectionsResponse object. Depending on whether or not alternate routes were requested (and assuming directions were found for the route), this object will contain one or more MKRoute objects. Each MKRoute object contains the distance, expected travel time, advisory notes and an MKPolyline that can be used to draw the route on a map view. In addition, each MKRoute object contains an array of MKRouteStep objects, each of which contains information such as the text description of a turn-by-turn step in the route and the coordinates at which the step is to be performed. In addition, each MKRouteStep object contains a polyline object for that step and the estimated distance and travel time.

The following code fragment demonstrates an example implementation of a directions request between the user's current location and a destination location represented by an MKMapItem object named *destination*:

```
let request = MKDirectionsRequest()
request.setSource(MKMapItem.mapItemForCurrentLocation())
request.setDestination(destination!)
request.requestsAlternateRoutes = false
```

```
let directions = MKDirections(request: request)

directions.calculateDirectionsWithCompletionHandler({ (response:
            MKDirectionsResponse!, error: NSError!) in

        if error != nil {
            // Handle error
        } else {
            self.showRoute(response)
        }

})
```

The resulting response can subsequently be used to draw the routes on a map view using the following code:

```
func showRoute(response: MKDirectionsResponse) {

    for route in response.routes as [MKRoute] {

        routeMap.addOverlay(route.polyline,
                        level: MKOverlayLevel.AboveRoads)

    }
}
```

The above code simply iterates through the MKRoute objects in the response and adds the polyline for each route alternate as a layer on a map view. In this instance, the overlay is configured to appear above the road names on the map.

Although the layer is added to the map view in the above code, nothing will be drawn until the *rendererForOverlay* delegate method is implemented. This method creates an instance of the MKPolylineRenderer class and then sets properties such as the line color and width:

```
func mapView(mapView: MKMapView!, rendererForOverlay
            overlay: MKOverlay!) -> MKOverlayRenderer! {
    let renderer = MKPolylineRenderer(overlay: overlay)

    renderer.strokeColor = UIColor.blueColor()
    renderer.lineWidth = 5.0
    return renderer
}
```

Note that this method will only be called if the class in which it resides is declared as the delegate for the map view object. For example:

```
routeMap.delegate = self
```

Finally, the turn-by-turn directions for each step in the route can be accessed as follows:

```
for step in route.steps {
    println(step.instructions)
}
```

The above code simply outputs the text instructions for each step of the route. As previously discussed, additional information may also be extracted from the MKRouteStep objects as required by the application.

Having covered the basics of directions and routes in iOS 8, the MapSample application can be extended to put some of this theory into practice.

78.2 Adding Directions and Routes to the MapSample Application

The MapSample application will now be modified to include a *Details* button in the toolbar of the first scene. When selected, this button will display a table view listing the names and phone numbers of all locations matching the most recent local search operation. Selecting a location from the list will display another scene containing a map displaying the route from the user's current location to the selected destination.

78.3 Adding the New Classes to the Project

Load the MapSample application project into Xcode and add a new class to represent the view controller for the table view. To achieve this, select the *File -> New -> File...* menu option and create a new iOS Cocoa Touch Class named *ResultsTableViewController* subclassed from *UITableViewController* with the *Also create XIB file* option disabled.

Since the table view will also need a class to represent the table cells, add another new class to the project named *ResultsTableCell*, this time subclassing from the UITableViewCell class.

Repeat the above steps to add a third class named *RouteViewController* subclassed from UIViewController with the *Also create XIB file* option disabled.

78.4 Configuring the Results Table View

Select the *Main.storyboard* file and drag and drop a Table View Controller object from the Object Library so that it is positioned to the right of the existing *MapSampleViewController* scene in the storyboard canvas (Figure 78-1):

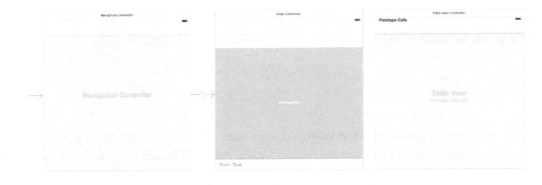

Figure 78-1

With the new controller selected, display the Identity Inspector and change the class from *UITableViewController* to *ResultsTableViewController*.

Select the prototype cell at the top of the table view and change the class setting from *UITableViewCell* to *ResultsTableCell*. With the table cell still selected, switch to the Attributes Inspector and set the *Reuse Identifier* property to *resultCell*.

Drag and drop two Label objects onto the prototype cell and position them as outlined in Figure 78-2, making sure to stretch them so that they extend to the middle of the cell.

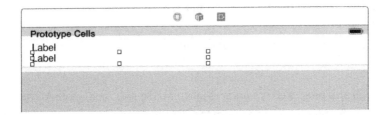

Figure 78-2

Shift-Click on the two Label views so that both are selected, display the Auto Layout *Resolve Auto Layout Issues* menu and select the *Reset to Suggested Constraints* option listed under *Selected Views*.

Display the Assistant Editor, make sure that it is displaying the *ResultsTableCell.swift* file and then establish outlets from the two labels named *nameLabel* and *phoneLabel* respectively.

Next, edit the *ResultsTableViewController.swift* file and modify it to import the MapKit Framework and to declare an array into which will be placed the MKMapItem objects representing the local search results:

```
import UIKit
import MapKit

class ResultsTableViewController: UITableViewController {
```

```
    var mapItems: [MKMapItem]!
    .
    .
    .
}
```

Next, edit the file to modify the data source and delegate methods so that the table is populated with the location information when displayed (removing the #warning lines during the editing process). Note that the comment markers (/* and */) will need to be removed from around the *cellForRowAtIndexPath* method:

```
override func numberOfSectionsInTableView(tableView: UITableView) -> Int
{
    // Return the number of sections.
    return 1
}

override func tableView(tableView: UITableView, numberOfRowsInSection
section: Int) -> Int {
    // Return the number of rows in the section.
    return mapItems.count
}

override func tableView(tableView: UITableView, cellForRowAtIndexPath
indexPath: NSIndexPath) -> UITableViewCell {

    let cell = tableView.dequeueReusableCellWithIdentifier(
        "resultCell", forIndexPath: indexPath) as ResultsTableCell

    // Configure the cell...
    let row = indexPath.row
    let item = mapItems[row]
    cell.nameLabel.text = item.name
    cell.phoneLabel.text = item.phoneNumber
    return cell
}
```

With the results table view configured, the next step is to add a segue from the first scene to this scene.

78.5 Implementing the Result Table View Segue

Select the *Main.storyboard* file and drag and drop an additional Bar Button Item from the Object Library to the toolbar in the Map Sample View Controller scene. Double click on this new button and change the text to *Details*:

Figure 78-3

Click on the Details button to select it (it may be necessary to click twice since the first click will select the Toolbar). Establish a segue by Ctrl-clicking on the Details button and dragging to the Results Table View Controller and select *show* from the *Action Segue* menu.

When the segue is triggered, the *mapItems* property of the ResultsTableViewController instance needs to be updated with the array of locations created by the local search. This can be performed in the *prepareForSegue* method which needs to be implemented in the *ViewController.swift* file as follows:

```
override func prepareForSegue(segue: UIStoryboardSegue,
                            sender: AnyObject?) {

    let destination = segue.destinationViewController as
                                ResultsTableViewController

    destination.mapItems = self.matchingItems
}
```

With the Results scene complete, compile and run the application on an iOS device. Perform a search for a business type that returns valid results before selecting the Details toolbar button. The results table should subsequently appear (Figure 78-4) listing the names and phone numbers for the matching locations:

Figure 78-4

78.6 **Adding the Route Scene**

The last task is to display a second map view and draw on it the route from the user's current location to the location selected from the results table. The class for this scene (RouteViewController) was added earlier in the chapter so the next step is to add a scene to the storyboard and associate it with this class.

Begin by selecting the *Main.storyboard* file and dragging and dropping a View Controller item from the Object Library panel so that it is positioned to the right of the Results Table View Controller scene (Figure 78-5). With the new view controller scene selected (so that it appears with a blue border) display the Identity Inspector and change the class from *UIViewController* to *RouteViewController*.

Figure 78-5

Drag and drop a MapKit View object into the new view controller scene and position it so that it occupies the entire view. Using the Auto Layout Pin menu, set *Spacing to nearest neighbor constraints* of 0 on all four sides of the view with the *Constrain to margins* option switched off.

Display the Assistant Editor, make sure it is displaying the content of the *RouteViewController.swift* file and then establish an outlet from the map view instance named *routeMap*. Remaining in the *RouteViewController.swift* file, add an import directive to the MapKit framework, a property into which will be stored a reference to the destination map item and a declaration that this class implements the MKMapViewDelegate protocol. With these changes implemented, the file should read as follows:

```
import UIKit
import MapKit

class RouteViewController: UIViewController, MKMapViewDelegate {

    var destination: MKMapItem?
    .
    .
}
```

Now that the route scene has been added, it is now time to add some code to it to generate and then draw the route on the map.

78.7 **Getting the Route and Directions**

Remaining within the *RouteViewController.swift* file, modify the *viewDidLoad* method to detect the user's current location and set this class as the delegate for the map view:

```
override func viewDidLoad() {
    super.viewDidLoad()

    routeMap.showsUserLocation = true
    routeMap.delegate = self
    self.getDirections()
}
```

Clearly, the last task performed by the *viewDidLoad* method is to call another method named *getDirections* which now also needs to be implemented:

```
func getDirections() {

    let request = MKDirectionsRequest()
    request.setSource(MKMapItem.mapItemForCurrentLocation())
    request.setDestination(destination!)
    request.requestsAlternateRoutes = false

    let directions = MKDirections(request: request)

    directions.calculateDirectionsWithCompletionHandler({ (response:
            MKDirectionsResponse!, error: NSError!) in

        if error != nil {
            println("Error getting directions")
        } else {
            self.showRoute(response)
        }

    })
}
```

This code largely matches that outlined at the start of the chapter, as is the case with the implementation of the *showRoute* method which also now needs to be implemented in the *RouteViewController.swift* file along with the corresponding *rendererForOverlay* method:

```
func showRoute(response: MKDirectionsResponse) {

    for route in response.routes as [MKRoute] {
```

```
        routeMap.addOverlay(route.polyline,
                level: MKOverlayLevel.AboveRoads)

        for step in route.steps {
            println(step.instructions)
        }
    }
    let userLocation = routeMap.userLocation
    let region = MKCoordinateRegionMakeWithDistance(
            userLocation.location.coordinate, 2000, 2000)

    routeMap.setRegion(region, animated: true)
}

func mapView(mapView: MKMapView!, rendererForOverlay
        overlay: MKOverlay!) -> MKOverlayRenderer! {
    let renderer = MKPolylineRenderer(overlay: overlay)

    renderer.strokeColor = UIColor.blueColor()
    renderer.lineWidth = 5.0
    return renderer
}
```

The *showRoute* method simply adds the polygon for the route as an overlay to the map view, outputs the turn-by-turn steps to the console and zooms in to the user's current location.

78.8 Establishing the Route Segue

All that remains to complete the application is to establish the segue between the results table cell and the route view. This will also require the implementation of the *prepareForSegue* method to pass the map item for the destination to the route scene.

Select the *Main.storyboard* file followed by the table cell in the Result Table View Controller scene (making sure the actual cell and not the view or one of the labels is selected). Ctrl-click on the prototype cell and drag the line to the Route View Controller scene. Release the line and select *show* from the resulting menu.

Finally, edit the *ResultsTableViewController.swift* file and implement the *prepareForSegue* method so that the destination property matches the location associated with the selected table row:

```
override func prepareForSegue(segue: UIStoryboardSegue,
                sender: AnyObject?) {
    let routeViewController = segue.destinationViewController
                                    as RouteViewController
```

```
let indexPath = self.tableView.indexPathForSelectedRow()

let row = indexPath?.row

routeViewController.destination = mapItems![row!]
}
```

78.9 Testing the Application

Build and run the application on a suitable iOS device and perform a local search. Once search results have been returned, select the *Details* button to display the list of locations. Selecting a location from the list should now cause a second map view to appear containing the user's current location and the route from there to the selected location drawn in blue as demonstrated in Figure 78-6:

Figure 78-6

A review of the Xcode console should also reveal that the turn-by-turn directions have also been output, for example:

```
2013-08-07 10:19:27.737 MapSample[184:60b] Proceed to Parkview Dr
2013-08-07 10:19:27.739 MapSample[184:60b] At the end of the road, turn
left onto Parkgreen Ln
2013-08-07 10:19:27.740 MapSample[184:60b] Turn right onto NC Highway 58
2013-08-07 10:19:27.742 MapSample[184:60b] Turn right onto High Meadow Rd
2013-08-07 10:19:27.743 MapSample[184:60b] Turn left onto Wilson Dr
2013-08-07 10:19:27.745 MapSample[184:60b] Turn right onto Morris Pkwy
2013-08-07 10:19:27.789 MapSample[184:60b] Arrive at the destination
```

78.10 Summary

The MKDirections class was added to the MapKit Framework for iOS 7 and allows directions from one location to another to be requested from Apple's mapping servers. Information returned from a request includes the text for turn-by-turn directions, the coordinates at which each step of the journey is to take place and the polygon data needed to draw the route as a map view overlay.

79. An Introduction to Extensions in iOS 8

Extensions are a new feature introduced as part of the iOS 8 release designed to allow certain capabilities of an application to be made available for use within other applications. The developer of a photo editing application might, for example, have devised some unique image filtering capabilities and decide that those features would be particularly useful to users of the iOS Photos app. To achieve this, the developer would implement these features in a Photo Editing extension which would then appear as an option to users when editing an image within the Photos app.

Extensions fall into a variety of different categories and a number of rules and guidelines must be followed in the implementation process. While subsequent chapters will cover in detail the creation of extensions of various types, this chapter is intended to serve as a general overview and introduction to the subject of extensions in iOS.

79.1 iOS Extensions – An Overview

The sole purpose of an extension is to make a specific feature of an existing application available for access within other applications. Extensions are separate executable binaries that run independently of the corresponding application. Although extensions take the form of an individual binary, they must be supplied and installed as part of an application bundle. The application with which an extension is bundled is referred to as the *containing app*. The containing app must provide useful functionality and must not be an empty application provided solely for the purpose of delivering an extension to the user.

Once an extension has been installed, it will be accessible from other applications through a number of different techniques depending on the type of the extension. The application from which an extension is launched and used is referred to as a *host app*.

An application that translates text to a foreign language might, for example, include an extension which can be used to translate the text displayed by a host app. In such a scenario, the user would access the extension via the Share button in the user interface of the host app and the extension would display a view controller displaying the translated text. On dismissing the extension, the user is returned to the host app.

79.2 **Extension Types**

iOS supports a number of different extension types dictated by *extension points*. An extension point is an area of the iOS operating system which has been opened up to allow extensions to be implemented. When developing an extension, it is important to select the extension point that is most appropriate to the features of the extension. The extension types supported by iOS can be summarized as follows:

79.2.1 Today Extension

The Today extension point allows extensions to be made available within the Today view of the iOS Notification Center (the panel that appears when making a swiping motion downward from the top of the device display as shown in Figure 79-1).

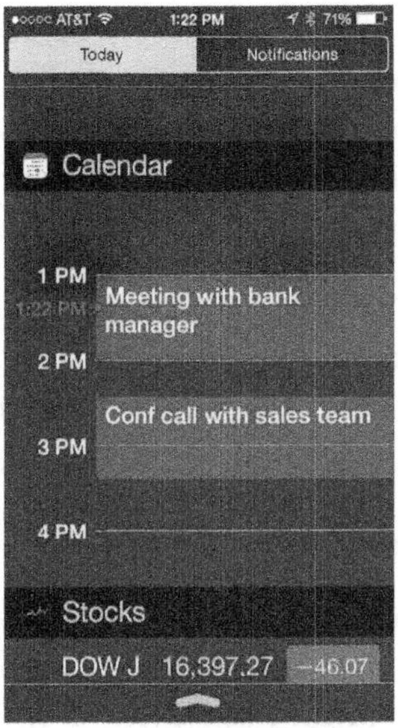

Figure 79-1

By default, the Today view displays information such as calendar appointments for the current day and prevailing stock price information.

Today extensions take the form of *widgets* that display information to the user when the Today view is displayed. Today extensions are covered in detail in the chapter entitled *An iOS 8 Today Extension Widget Tutorial*.

79.2.2 Share Extension

Share extensions provide a quick access mechanism for sharing content such as images, videos, text and web sites within a host app with social network sites or content sharing services. It is important to understand that Apple does not expect developers to write Share extensions designed to post content to destinations such as Facebook or Twitter (such sharing options are already built into iOS) but rather as a mechanism to make sharing easier for developers hosting their own sharing and social sites. Share extensions appear within the activity view controller panel which is displayed when the user taps the Share button from within a host app.

Figure 79-2, for example, shows a Share extension named "Share It" listed alongside the built-in Twitter, Facebook and Flickr share options within the activity view controller.

Figure 79-2

Share extensions can make use of the SLComposeServiceViewController class to implement the interface for posting content. This displays a view (Figure 79-3) containing a preview of the information to be posted and provides the ability to modify the content prior to posting it. For more complex requirements, a custom user interface can be designed using Interface Builder.

Figure 79-3

The actual mechanics of posting the content will be dependent on the way in which the target platform works.

79.2.3 Action Extension

The Action extension point enables extensions to be created that fall into the Action category. Action extensions allow the content within a host app to be transformed or viewed in a different way. As with Share extensions, Action extensions are accessed from the activity view controller via the Share button. Figure 79-4, for example, shows an example Action extension named "Translator" in the activity view controller of the iOS Notes app.

Figure 79-4

Action extensions are context sensitive in that they only appear as an option when the type of content in the host app matches one of the content types for which the extension has declared support. An Action extension that works with images, for example, will not appear in the activity view controller panel for a host app that is displaying text based content.

Action extensions are covered in detail in the chapters entitled *Creating an iOS 8 Action Extension* and *Receiving Data from an iOS 8 Action Extension*.

79.2.4 Photo Editing Extension

The Photo Editing extension point allows the photo editing capabilities of an application to be accessed from within the built-in iOS Photos app. Photo Editing extensions are displayed when the user selects an image in the Photos app, chooses the edit option and taps on the button in the top left hand corner of the Photo editing screen. Figure 79-5 shows the Photos app displaying two Photo Editing extension options:

Figure 79-5

Photo Editing Extensions are covered in detail in the chapter entitled *Creating an iOS 8 Photo Editing Extension*.

79.2.5 Document Provider Extension

The Document Provider extension makes it possible for a containing app to act as a document repository for other applications running on the device. Depending on the level of support implemented in the extension, host apps can import, export, open, and move documents to and from the storage repository provided by the containing app. In most cases the storage repository represented by the containing app will be a third-party cloud storage service providing an alternative to Apple's iCloud service.

A Document Provider extension consists of a Document Picker View Controller extension and an optional File Provider extension. The Document Picker View Controller extension provides a user interface for the extension allowing the user to browse and select the documents available for the Document Provider extension.

The optional File Provider extension provides the host app with access to the documents residing outside of the app's sandbox and is necessary if the extension is to support move and open operations on the documents stored via the containing app.

79.2.6 Custom Keyboard Extension

The Custom Keyboard Extension, as the name suggests, provides the ability to create and install custom keyboards onto iOS devices. Keyboards developed using the Custom Keyboard extension point are available to be used by all applications on the device and, once installed, are selected from within the keyboard settings section of the Settings app on the device.

79.3 Creating Extensions

By far the easiest approach to developing extensions is to use the extension templates provided by Xcode. As previously discussed, extensions must be associated with a containing app. Once the project for a containing app is loaded into Xcode, extensions can be added in the form of new targets by selecting the *File -> New -> Targets...* menu option. This will display the panel shown in Figure 79-6 listing a template for each of the extension types:

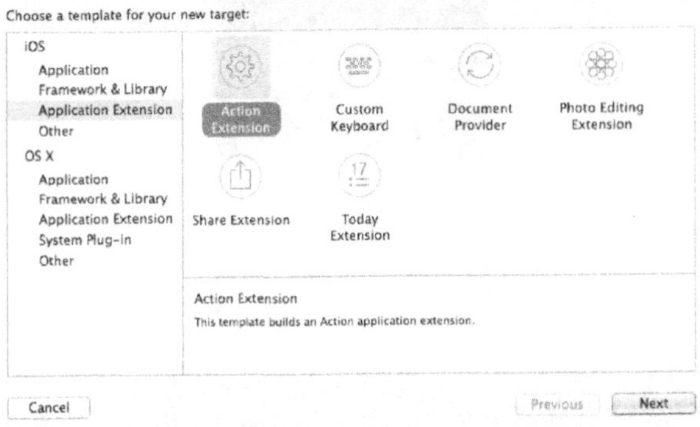

Figure 79-6

Once an extension template has been selected, simply click on *Next* to name and create the template. Once the extension has been created from the template, the steps to implement the extension will differ depending on the type of extension selected. The next few chapters will cover in detail the steps involved in implementing Today, Photo Editing and Action extensions.

79.4 **Summary**

Extensions in iOS provide a way for narrowly defined areas of functionality of one application to be made available from within other applications. iOS 8 currently supports Action, Share, Photo Editing, Document Provider, Today and Custom Keyboard extension types. It is important when developing extensions to select the most appropriate extension point before beginning development work and also to be aware that some application features may not be appropriate candidates to be placed into an extension.

Although extensions run as separate independent binaries, they are only able to be installed as part of an app bundle. The app with which an extension is bundled is called a *containing app*. Apple requires that containing apps provide useful functionality to the user and must not be empty apps intended solely as a delivery platform for an extension. An app from which an extension is launched is referred to as a *host app*.

Having covered the basics of extensions in this chapter, subsequent chapters will focus in detail on the more commonly used extension types.

80. An iOS 8 Today Extension Widget Tutorial

With the basic concepts of extensions covered in the previous chapter, this chapter will work step-by-step through the creation of an example iOS 8 extension widget that will appear within the Today view of the Notifications panel. In the process of creating the example app, key areas of the Today extension implementation process will be covered in detail.

80.1 About the Example Extension Widget

The purpose of the extension created in this tutorial is to display the longitude and latitude of the user's current location within the Today view of the iOS Notification panel. The steps to achieve this will involve the addition of an extension target to an existing container app, the design of the widget user interface and the implementation of the code to obtain, display and update the appropriate location data.

As previously outlined, Apple states that the container app for an extension must itself perform some useful function in addition to serving as the delivery vehicle for an extension. In recognition of this requirement, the tutorial is intended to be implemented as an extension to the Location application created in the chapter of this book entitled *An Example iOS 8 Location Application*. The steps outlined in the chapter may still be followed, however, regardless of whether or not you have completed the location based chapter.

80.2 Creating the Example Project

If you previously completed the Location tutorial as outlined in the *An Example iOS 8 Location Application* chapter of this book, locate the project and load it into Xcode. If, on the other hand, you have yet to complete this tutorial, download the sample code for the examples in this book from the following URL, and locate and load the completed Location example project into Xcode:

http://www.ebookfrenzy.com/print/ios8/

80.3 Adding the Extension to the Project

With the Location project loaded into Xcode, the next step is to add an extension target to the project using one of the extension templates provided by Xcode. From the Xcode menu, select the *File -> New -> Target...* menu option. In the resulting panel, select the *Application Extension* category listed under *iOS* in the left hand panel, and the *Today Extension* template from the main panel as shown in Figure 80-1:

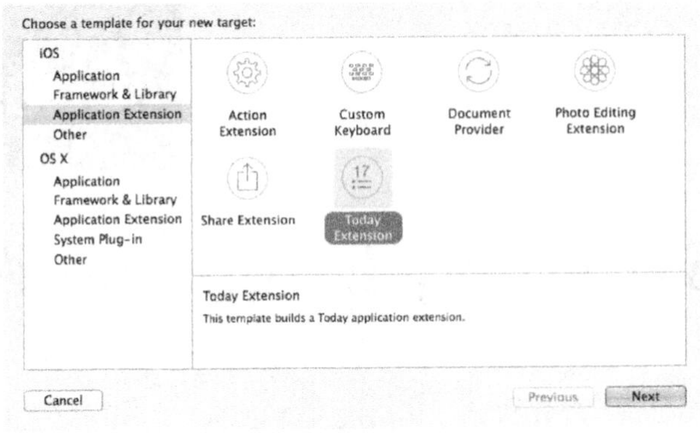

Choose a template for your new target:

iOS				
Application				
Framework & Library	Action	Custom	Document	Photo Editing
Application Extension	Extension	Keyboard	Provider	Extension
Other				
OS X				
Application				
Framework & Library				
Application Extension	Share Extension	Today		
System Plug-in		Extension		
Other				

Today Extension
This template builds a Today application extension.

Cancel   Previous   Next

Figure 80-1

Click on the *Next* button and, on the options panel, enter *MyLocation* into the Product Name field, leaving the remaining settings unchanged from the default values provided by Xcode. Click on *Finish* to create the new extension target.

As soon as the target has been created, a new panel will appear requesting permission to activate the new scheme for the extension target. Every target within an Xcode project has associated with it a scheme which defines how that target is to be built. When an extension target is added to a project, Xcode automatically creates a corresponding scheme so that the extension can be built and run. Activate this scheme now by clicking on the *Activate* button in the request panel.

The Today extension can be tested using the default template settings simply by setting the extension scheme (MyLocation) as the active scheme from the Xcode toolbar as shown in Figure 80-2 , selecting a suitable device or simulator target and clicking on the run button.

Figure 80-2

When an extension is launched it must do so within the context of a *host app*. Xcode will therefore request that a host app be selected for the extension. Since this is a Today extension, select the *Today* application from the list of options (Figure 80-3) prior to clicking on the *Run* button.

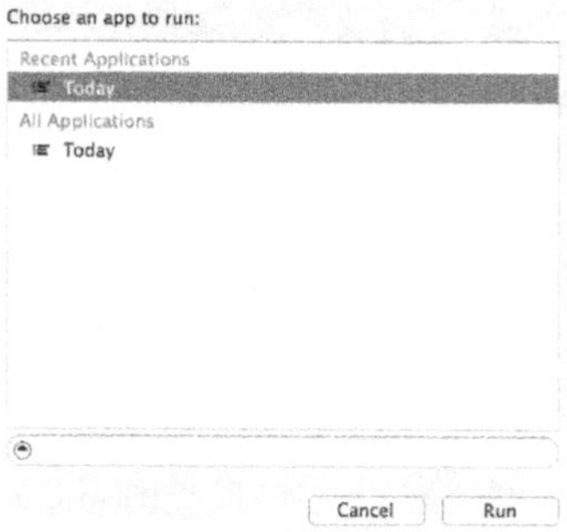

Choose an app to run:

Recent Applications

Today

All Applications

Today

Cancel   Run

Figure 80-3

The default user interface for the Today template consists of a single label displaying text which reads "Hello World". Assuming a successful launch of the extension, the Today view will appear in the Notification panel with the widget displayed as illustrated in Figure 80-4:

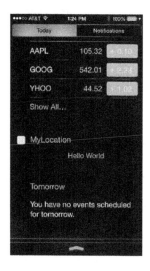

Figure 80-4

If the widget does not appear in the view, it may need to be enabled. Scroll down the Today view and select the *Edit* button when it comes into view. On the edit screen, locate the *MyLocation* widget and tap the green + button located next to it to add it to the view before selecting *Done*:

Figure 80-5

80.4 **Reviewing the Extension Files**

With the extension added to the project it is worth taking time to gain familiarity with the files which have been added to the project. Within the project navigator panel a new folder will have been created entitled *MyLocation*. It is within this folder that all of the files associated with the extension are contained (Figure 80-6):

Figure 80-6

The files that make up a Today extension are as follows:

- **TodayViewController.swift** - Contains the source code for the View Controller representing the widget in the Today view.
- **MainInterface.storyboard** – The storyboard file containing the user interface of the widget as it will appear within the Today view.
- **Info.plist** – The information property list for the extension.

80.5 **Designing the Widget User Interface**

The Today extension template provided the project with a simple storyboard layout containing a single label view. For the purposes of this tutorial, two labels will be required to display both the longitude and latitude of the user's current location. Within the Xcode project navigator panel, locate and select the *MyLocation -> MainInterface.storyboard* file to load it into the Interface Builder environment.

Begin by selecting and deleting the "Hello World" label from the view leaving a clean canvas on which to work. By default, the template has configured the widget view with a height suitable to accommodate a single label. In order to fit two labels onto the widget this height property will need to be increased. Click on the gray background of the widget to select the view and display the Size Inspector. Within the inspector panel, change the *Height* property from 37 to 50 as shown in Figure 80-7:

Figure 80-7

With the height increased, drag and drop two Label views from the object palette onto the view canvas, stretch the labels to fill approximately half of the width of the widget view and use the Attributes Inspector panel to change the foreground colors of the labels to *Light Text Color* so that the layout resembles that of Figure 80-8:

Figure 80-8

If the extension were to be launched on a device or simulator at this point, the labels would not be visible. The reason for this is that the Today view relies on Auto Layout settings within the widget layout, or specific preferred content size settings in the view controller code to decide on the size at which the widget should appear. Since no Auto Layout constraints have been configured, and no code has been added to set the preferred content size, the widget content would appear at zero height.

Select the uppermost Label and display the Auto Layout *Pin* menu (Figure 80-9). Enable the "Spacing to nearest neighbor" constraints on the top and left edges of the label by enabling the red constraint bars and using the current values and with the *Constrain to margins* option disabled.

Figure 80-9

Drop down the menu on the Width constraint setting and select the *Use current canvas value* option. Once the spacing and width constraints have been set, click on the *Add 3 Constraints* button to implement the changes.

Select the bottom Label view and repeat the above steps, this time setting spacing constraints on the left, top and bottom edges of the view, once again using the current spacing values.

Run the extension and verify that the widget layout appears correctly within the Today view, returning to the storyboard file if necessary to make adjustments to the layout.

Once the layout work is complete, display the Assistant Editor panel and make sure that it is showing the source code contained in the *TodayViewController.swift* file. Ctrl-click on the upper Label view and drag the resulting line to a position beneath the class declaration line in the Assistance Editor panel. Release the line and, in the resulting connection dialog, establish an outlet connection named *latitudeLabel*. Repeat this sequence of steps for the bottom label, this time creating an outlet named *longitudeLabel*.

80.6 Setting the Preferred Content Size in Code

Although not necessary in this particular instance (since Auto Layout is being used to influence the height of the widget), it is worth noting that the height of a widget can be set in code using the *setPreferredContentSize* method of the extension view controller instance. For example, the following code changes the height of the widget to 200 before it is displayed to the user:

```
override func viewWillAppear(animated: Bool)
{
    var currentSize: CGSize = self.preferredContentSize
    currentSize.height = 200.0
    self.preferredContentSize = currentSize
}
```

This technique is particularly useful when it is necessary to dynamically change the size of a widget at runtime. A widget might, for example, display some initial information to the user and provide a "More" button to display more detailed information. In this scenario the "More" button would simply change the preferred content size to make additional views visible.

80.7 Modifying the Widget View Controller

The view controller class for the Today extension widget now needs to be implemented such that it obtains the user's current location and updates the labels in the widget accordingly. Select and edit the *TodayViewController.swift* file to import the CoreLocation Framework, declare an optional variable in which to store the current location and to create and initialize a location manager instance. Note also that the TodayViewController class declaration has been modified to indicate that it now implements the CLLocationManagerDelegate protocol:

```
import UIKit
import NotificationCenter
import CoreLocation

class TodayViewController: UIViewController, NCWidgetProviding,
CLLocationManagerDelegate {

    @IBOutlet weak var latitudeLabel: UILabel!
    @IBOutlet weak var longitudeLabel: UILabel!

    var locationManager: CLLocationManager = CLLocationManager()
    var currentLocation: CLLocation?

    override func viewDidLoad() {
        super.viewDidLoad()
        locationManager.desiredAccuracy = kCLLocationAccuracyBest
        locationManager.delegate = self
        locationManager.requestWhenInUseAuthorization()
        locationManager.startUpdatingLocation()
    }
    .
    .
    .
}
```

To meet the conformance requirements of the CLLocationManagerDelegate protocol, and in order to be able to receive location update notifications, the location manager's *didUpdateLocations* delegate method now needs to be implemented. The code within this method will extract the latest location information and assign it to the previously declared *currentLocation* optional variable:

```
func locationManager(manager: CLLocationManager!,
        didUpdateLocations locations: [AnyObject]!)
{
    currentLocation = locations[locations.count - 1]
                                as? CLLocation
}
```

Next, a convenience function needs to be written to update the labels with the latest location data:

```
func performWidgetUpdate()
{
    if currentLocation != nil {
        var latitudeText = String(format: "Lat: %.4f",
                    currentLocation!.coordinate.latitude)
```

```
        var longitudeText = String(format: "Lon: %.4f",
                        currentLocation!.coordinate.longitude)

        latitudeLabel.text = latitudeText
        longitudeLabel.text = longitudeText
    }
}
```

This function verifies that the *currentLocation* optional variable contains a value and, if so, constructs String objects containing the current longitude and latitude values before displaying them on the corresponding widget labels.

The last modification to the widget view controller is to ensure that the *performWidgetUpdate* function is called at the appropriate times so that the user sees the latest location information each time the widget is displayed in the Today view. To make sure the function is called prior to the widget being displayed, the *viewWillAppear* method of the view controller needs to be overridden as follows:

```
override func viewWillAppear(animated: Bool) {
        performWidgetUpdate()
}
```

From time to time, the system will take snapshots of the widget so that information can be presented quickly to the user when the Today view is displayed. To make sure that the latest information is displayed when the system takes snapshots of the widget, it is also necessary to update the widget within the *widgetPerformUpdateWithCompletionHandler* method, a template of which has been provided by Xcode in the *TodayViewController.swift* file. All that needs to be added to this method is a call to our *performWidgetUpdate* method:

```
func widgetPerformUpdateWithCompletionHandler(completionHandler:
        ((NCUpdateResult) -> Void)!) {

        performWidgetUpdate()
        completionHandler(NCUpdateResult.NewData)
}
```

80.8 Testing the Extension

Compile and run the extension using the extension's scheme and select the Today view as the host app when prompted. Once the Today view is visible, use the *Edit* button to enable the widget (if it is not already displayed), at which point it should appear as shown in Figure 80-10:

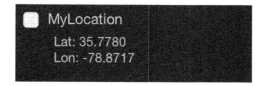

Figure 80-10

80.9 Opening the Containing App from the Extension

When developing extensions it may be useful to provide the user with the ability to open the containing application from within the extension. The MyLocation Today widget, for example, only displays a subset of the data available within the containing Location app.

Every extension has associated with it an *extension context* object, a reference to which can be accessed via the *extensionContext* property of the extension's view controller instance. Among the methods available to be called on the extension context object is the *openURL* method which can be used to launch other, suitably configured applications.

In order for an application to be launchable using the *openURL* method, the *Info.plist* file for that application must define a custom URL scheme. This essentially declares the URL name by which the application is identified (represented by the *CFBundleURLName* key and typically set using a reverse domain name identifier such as com.ebookfrenzy.location) and the schemes it supports (via an array of string values assigned to the *CFBundleURLSchemes* key).

For the purposes of this example, the *Info.plist* file for the Location application will be modified to specify a *CFBundleURLName* value of *com.ebookfrenzy.location* and a URL scheme named *location*. Whilst this can be achieved using the Xcode property list editor, it is actually quicker in this instance to directly edit the XML source of the *Info.plist* file.

Within the project navigator panel Ctrl-click on the *Location -> Supporting Files -> Info.plist* file and select the *Open As -> Source Code* menu option. Once the file has loaded into the editor, modify it to add the URL scheme entries as follows:

```
<?xml version="1.0" encoding="UTF-8"?>
<!DOCTYPE plist PUBLIC "-//Apple//DTD PLIST 1.0//EN"
"http://www.apple.com/DTDs/PropertyList-1.0.dtd">
<plist version="1.0">
<dict>
        <key>CFBundleURLTypes</key>
        <array>
                <dict>
                        <key>CFBundleURLName</key>
                        <string>com.ebookfrenzy.location</string>
                        <key>CFBundleURLSchemes</key>
```

```
                    <array>
                            <string>location</string>
                    </array>
            </dict>
        </array>
        <key>CFBundleDisplayName</key>
        <string></string>
        <key>NSLocationUsageDescription</key>
        <string>The application uses this to display your location in the
Today view</string>
.
.
.
</dict>
</plist>
```

The user interface layout for the MyLocation widget now needs to be modified to include a Button view which, when selected, will open the Location application. Select the *MainInterface.storyboard* file to load it into Interface Builder and add a Button which reads "Open" positioned as shown in Figure 80-11:

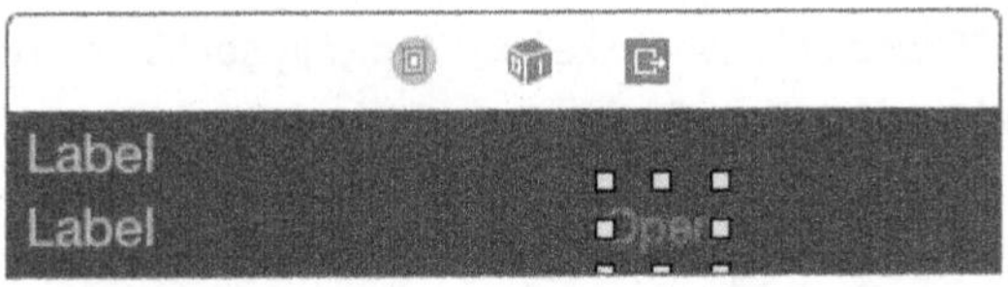

Figure 80-11

Display the Assistant Editor and verify that it is listing the source code for the *TodayViewController.swift* file. Ctrl-click and drag from the newly added Button view to the location within the Swift file where you would like the action method to be placed and release the line. In the resulting panel, change the connection type to *Action* and name the action *openApp* before clicking on the *Connect* button.

Edit the *openApp* method to construct the URL (which is referenced by the CFBundleURLSchemes *location* string) and to call the *openURL* method of the extension context:

```swift
@IBAction func openApp(sender: AnyObject) {

    let url: NSURL? = NSURL(string: "location:")

    if let appurl = url {
        self.extensionContext!.openURL(appurl,
                        completionHandler: nil)
    }
}
```

In order to test this new functionality it will be necessary to build and re-install both the Location containing app and the MyLocation extension. Begin by selecting the Location scheme from the Xcode toolbar and build and run the application on the target device or simulator. Next, change the scheme to MyLocation and build and run the extension using the Today view as the host app.

Once the extension is visible in the Today view, touch the *Open* button to launch the Location container app.

80.10 **Summary**

The Today extension allows widgets to appear within the Today view of the iOS Notification panel. Today widgets are essentially view controllers with the user interface of the widget contained within a storyboard file. It is important when designing a widget to make sure that it is small and lightweight and that either Auto Layout constraints or preferred content size method calls are made to ensure that the widget is sized correctly within the Today view. The system will call the *widgetPerformUpdateWithCompletionHandler* delegate method of the extension view controller at regular intervals in an effort to ensure that recent data is available to be displayed next time the view appears. A widget may provide the option to launch another app from within the Today view using the *openURL* method of the extension context instance.

81. Creating an iOS 8 Photo Editing Extension

The primary purpose of the iOS 8 Photo Editing extension is to allow the photo editing capabilities of an application to be made available from within the standard iOS Photos application. Consider, for example, a scenario where a developer has published an app that allows users to apply custom changes and special effects to videos or photos. Prior to iOS 8, the only way for a user to access these capabilities would have been to launch and work within that application. By placing some of the functionality of the application into a Photo Editing extension, the user is now able to select videos or photos from within the Photos app and choose the extension from a range of editing options available on the device. Once selected, the user interface for the extension is displayed to the user so that changes can be made to the chosen image or video. Once the user has finished making the changes and exits the extension, the modified image or video is returned to the Photos app.

81.1 Creating a Photo Editing Extension

As with all extension types, by far the easiest starting point when creating a Photo Editing extension is to use the template provided by Xcode. For the purposes of this chapter, create a new Xcode project named PhotoDemo using the Single View Application template, the Swift programing language and with the Devices menu set to *Universal*.

Once the application project has been created, a new target will need to be added for the Photo Editing extension. To achieve this, select the *File -> New -> Target...* menu option and, in the resulting panel, select the *Application Extension* option listed under *iOS* in the left hand column and *Photo Editing Extension* from the main panel as shown in Figure 81-1:

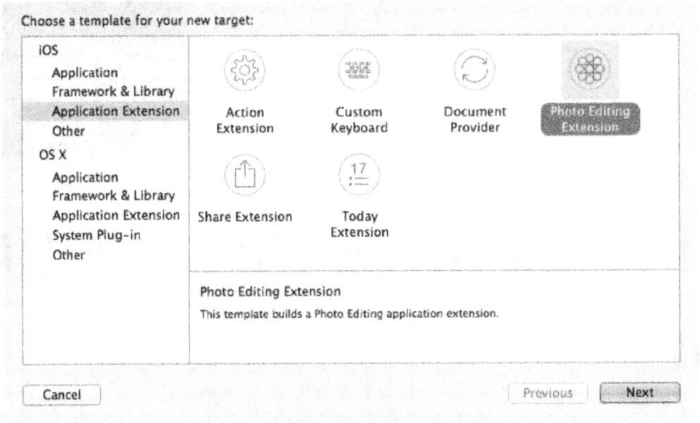

Choose a template for your new target:

iOS				
Application Framework & Library **Application Extension** Other	Action Extension	Custom Keyboard	Document Provider	Photo Editing Extension
OS X				
Application Framework & Library Application Extension System Plug-in Other	Share Extension	Today Extension		

Photo Editing Extension

This template builds a Photo Editing application extension.

Cancel   Previous   Next

Figure 81-1

With the appropriate options selected, click on the Next button and enter *MyPhotoExt* into the Product Name field. Leave the remaining fields set to the default values and click on Finish to complete the extension creation process. When prompted, click on the *Activate* button to activate the scheme created by Xcode to enable the extension to be built and run.

Once the extension has been added, it will appear in the project navigator panel under the *MyPhotoExt* folder. This folder will contain both the Swift source code file for the extension's view controller named *PhotoEditingViewController.swift* and the corresponding user interface storyboard file named *MainInterface.storyboard*. In addition, an *Info.plist* file will be present in the *Supporting Files* sub-folder.

81.2 Accessing the Photo Editing Extension

Before beginning work on implementing the functionality of the extension, it is important to learn how to access such an extension from within the iOS Photos app. Begin by verifying that the *MyPhotoExt* build scheme is selected in the Xcode toolbar as illustrated in Figure 81-2.

Figure 81-2

If the extension is not currently selected, click on the current scheme name and select *MyPhotoExt* from the drop down menu. Also make sure that a physical iOS device is connected to the development system and selected within Xcode as the destination for the running application.

Having verified that the appropriate scheme is selected, click on the toolbar run button. Since this is an extension, it can only be run within the context of a host application. As a result, Xcode will display a panel listing the applications installed on the attached device. From this list of available applications (Figure 81-3), select the *Photos* app and click on the *Run* button.

Figure 81-3

After the extension and containing application have been compiled and installed on the device, the Photos app will automatically launch. Once the Photos app appears, select a photo from those stored on the device and, once selected, tap on the *Edit* button located in the top right hand corner of the screen to enter the standard editing interface of the Photos app. Within the top left hand corner of the Photos editing tool is a small round button containing three dots (referenced as item A in Figure 81-4):

Figure 81-4

Tapping this button will display the action panel (item B in Figure 81-4) where Photo Editing extensions may be chosen and used to edit videos and images. Assuming that the extension for our *PhotoDemo* application is displayed, select it and wait for the extension to launch. Once the extension has loaded it will appear in the form of the user interface as defined in the *MyPhotoExt -> MainInterface.storyboard* file.

81.3 **Configuring the Info.plist File**

A Photo Editing extension must declare the type of media it is able to edit. This is specified via the *PHSupportedMediaTypes* key within the *NSExtension* section of the extension's *Info.plist* file. By default, the Photo Editing template declares that the extension is capable of editing only images as follows:

```
<plist version="1.0">
.
.
.
        <key>NSExtension</key>
         <dict>
                <key>NSExtensionAttributes</key>
                <dict>
                        <key>PHSupportedMediaTypes</key>
                        <array>
                                <string>Image</string>
                        </array>
                </dict>
                <key>NSExtensionMainStoryboard</key>
                <string>MainInterface</string>
                <key>NSExtensionPointIdentifier</key>
                <string>com.apple.photo-editing</string>
        </dict>
</dict>
</plist>
```

If the extension is also able to edit video files, the *PHSupportedMediaTypes* entry within the file would be modified as follows:

```
<key>PHSupportedMediaTypes</key>
      <array>
            <string>Video</string>
            <string>Image</string>
      </array>
```

For the purposes of this example, leave the *Info.plist* file unchanged with support for images only.

81.4 **Designing the User Interface**

The user interface for the extension is going to consist of an Image View and a Toolbar containing three Bar Button Items. Within the Xcode project navigator panel, locate and load the *MyPhotoExt ->*

MainInterface.storyboard file into Interface Builder and select and delete the "Hello World" Label view. With a clean canvas, design and configure the layout so that it matches that of Figure 81-5:

Sepia Mono Invert

Figure 81-5

Select the Image View, display the Attributes Inspector panel and change the Mode setting to *Aspect Fit*.

With the Image View still selected, display the Auto Layout Pin menu and set *Spacing to nearest neighbor* constraints on all four sides of the view with the *Constrain to margins* option switched off.

Click to select the Toolbar view and use the Auto Layout Pin menu once again to apply *Spacing to nearest neighbor* constraints on the left, right and bottom edges of the view with the *Constrain to margins* option still switched off. Before adding the constraints, also enable the *Height* constraint option using the currently displayed value.

Display the Assistant Editor and verify that it is displaying the source code for the *PhotoEditingViewController.swift* file. Select the Bar Button Item displaying the "Sepia" text (note that it may be necessary to click twice since the first click will select the parent Toolbar view). With the item selected, Ctrl-click on the item and drag the resulting line to a position immediately beneath the end of the implementation of the *viewDidLoad* method in the Assistant Editor panel. Release the line and, in the connection dialog, establish an Action named *sepiaSelected*. Repeat these steps for the "Mono" and "Invert" Bar Button Items, naming the Actions *monoSelected* and *invertSelected* respectively.

Finally, Ctrl-click on the Image View and drag the resulting line to a position beneath the "class PhotoEditingViewController" declaration. Release the line and establish an Outlet for the Image View named *imageView*.

81.5 **The PHContentEditingController Protocol**

When Xcode created the template for the Photo Editing extension it created a View Controller class named PhotoEditingViewController and declared it as implementing the PHContentEditingController protocol. It also generated stub methods for each of the methods that must be implemented in order for the class to conform with the protocol. The remainder of implementing a Photo Editing extension primarily consists of writing the code for these methods to implement the required editing behavior. One of the first methods that will need to be implemented relates to the issue of adjustment data.

81.6 **Photo Extensions and Adjustment Data**

When a Photo Extension is selected by the user, a method named *canHandleAdjustmentData* is called on the view controller class of the extension. The method must return a true or false value depending on whether or not the extension supports adjustment data.

If an extension supports adjustment data, it is passed a copy of the original image or video together with a set of data outlining any earlier modifications made to the media during previous editing sessions. The extension then re-applies those changes to the file or video to get it back to the point where it was at the end of the last editing session. The advantage of this approach is that the extension is able to offer the user the ability to undo any previous editing operations performed within previous sessions using the extension. When editing is completed, the extension returns the modified image or video file, together with any new adjustment data reflecting edits that were performed during the current session.

If an image editing extension indicates that it does not support adjustment data, it is passed a copy of the modified image as it appeared at the end of the last editing session. This enables the user to perform additional editing tasks but does not allow previous edits to be undone. In the case of video editing extensions that do not support adjustment data, the extension will be passed the original video and previous edits will be lost. Clearly, therefore, supporting adjustment data is an important requirement for video editing.

Whilst the example contained within this tutorial will store and return adjustment data to the Photos app allowing for future improvements to the extension it will not handle incoming adjustment data. Within the *PhotoEditingViewController.swift* file, therefore, locate and review the *canHandleAdjustmentData* method and verify that it is configured to return a *false* value:

```
func canHandleAdjustmentData(adjustmentData: PHAdjustmentData?) -> Bool {
        return false
}
```

81.7 **Receiving the Content**

The next method that will be called on the extension View Controller class is *startContentEditingWithInput*.

This method is passed as arguments a *PHContentEditingInput* object and a placeholder image. For images, this object contains a compressed version of the image suitable for displaying to the user, a URL referencing the location of the full size image, information about the orientation of the image and, in the case of extensions with adjustment data support, a set of adjustment data from previous edits.

As previously discussed, image extensions with adjustment data support implemented are passed the original image and a set of adjustments to be made to reach parity with the latest state of editing. Since it can take time to render these changes, the placeholder argument contains a snapshot of the image as it currently appears. This can be displayed to the user while the adjustment data is applied and the image rendered in the background.

For this example, the *startContentEditingWithInput* method will be implemented as follows:

```
import UIKit
import Photos
import PhotosUI

class PhotoEditingViewController: UIViewController,
PHContentEditingController {

    @IBOutlet weak var imageView: UIImageView!

    var input: PHContentEditingInput?
    var displayedImage: UIImage?
    var imageOrientation: Int32?

    .

    .

    .

    func startContentEditingWithInput(contentEditingInput:
        PHContentEditingInput?, placeholderImage: UIImage) {

        input = contentEditingInput

        if input != nil {
            displayedImage = input!.displaySizeImage
            imageOrientation = input!.fullSizeImageOrientation
            imageView.image = displayedImage
        }
    }

    .

    .

    .

}
```

The above changes declare two optional variables to contain a reference to the display sized image and the image orientation. The code in the method then assigns the display sized image from the

PHContentEditingInput object passed to the method to the *displayedImage* variable and also stores the orientation setting in the *imageOrientation* variable. Finally, the display sized image is displayed on the Image View in the user interface so that it is visible to the user.

Compile and run the extension, selecting the Photos app as the host application, and verify that the extension displays a copy of the image in the Image View of the extension View Controller.

81.8 Implementing the Filter Actions

The actions connected to the Bar Button Items will change the image by applying Core Image sepia, monochrome and invert filters. Until the user commits the edits made in the extension, any filtering will be performed only on the display sized image to avoid the rendering delays that are likely to be incurred working on the full sized image. Having performed the filter, the modified image will be displayed on the image view instance.

Remaining within the *PhotoEditingViewController.swift* file, implement the three action methods as follows:

```swift
class PhotoEditingViewController: UIViewController,
PHContentEditingController {

    @IBOutlet weak var imageView: UIImageView!

    var input: PHContentEditingInput?
    var displayedImage: UIImage?
    var imageOrientation: Int32?
    var currentFilter = "CIColorInvert"

    override func viewDidLoad() {
        super.viewDidLoad()
        // Do any additional setup after loading the view.
    }

    @IBAction func sepiaSelected(sender: AnyObject) {
        currentFilter = "CISepiaTone"

        if displayedImage != nil {
            imageView.image = performFilter(displayedImage!,
                                    orientation: nil)
        }
    }

    @IBAction func monoSelected(sender: AnyObject) {
        currentFilter = "CIPhotoEffectMono"
```

```
        if displayedImage != nil {
            imageView.image = performFilter(displayedImage!,
                                        orientation: nil)
        }
    }

    @IBAction func invertSelected(sender: AnyObject) {
        currentFilter = "CIColorInvert"

        if displayedImage != nil {
            imageView.image = performFilter(displayedImage!,
                                        orientation: nil)
        }
    }
.
.
.
}
```

In each case, a method named *performFilter* is called to perform the image filtering task. The next step, clearly, is to implement this method using the techniques outline in the chapter entitled *An iOS 8 Graphics Tutorial using Core Graphics and Core Image*:

```
func performFilter(inputImage: UIImage, orientation: Int32?)
                                            -> UIImage?
{
    var cimage: CIImage
    cimage = CIImage(image: inputImage)

    if orientation != nil {
        cimage = cimage.imageByApplyingOrientation(orientation!)
    }

    var filter = CIFilter(name: currentFilter)
    filter.setDefaults()
    filter.setValue(cimage, forKey: "inputImage")

    switch currentFilter {

        case "CISepiaTone", "CIEdges":
            filter.setValue(0.8, forKey: "inputIntensity")

        case "CIMotionBlur":
            filter.setValue(25.00, forKey:"inputRadius")
```

```
            filter.setValue(0.00, forKey:"inputAngle")

    default:
        break
}

var ciFilteredImage = filter.outputImage
var context = CIContext(options: nil)
var cgImage = context.createCGImage(ciFilteredImage,
                        fromRect: ciFilteredImage.extent())
var resultImage = UIImage(CGImage: cgImage)

return resultImage
}
```

The above method takes the image passed through as a parameter, takes steps to maintain the original orientation and performs an appropriately configured filter operation on the image based on the current value assigned to the *currentFilter* variable. The filtered image is then returned to the calling method.

Compile and run the extension once again, this time using the filter buttons to change the appearance of the displayed image.

81.9 Returning the Image to the Photos App

When the user has finished making changes to the image and touches the *Done* button located in the extension toolbar, the *finishContentEditingWithCompletionHandler* method of the View Controller is called. This is passed a reference to a completion handler which must be called once the image has been rendered and is ready to be returned to the Photos app.

Before calling the completion handler, however, this method performs the following tasks:

1. Obtains a copy of the full size version of the image.
2. Ensures that the original orientation of the image is preserved through the rendering process.
3. Applies to the full sized image all of the editing operations previously performed on the display sized image.
4. Renders the new version of the full sized image.
5. Packages up the adjustment data outlining the edits performed during the session.

Since the above tasks (particularly the rendering phase) are likely to take time, these must be performed within a separate asynchronous thread. The code to complete this example extension can now be implemented within the template stub of the method as follows:

```
func finishContentEditingWithCompletionHandler(completionHandler:
            ((PHContentEditingOutput!) -> Void)!) {
```

```
dispatch_async(dispatch_get_global_queue
    (CLong(DISPATCH_QUEUE_PRIORITY_DEFAULT), 0)) {

    let output =
        PHContentEditingOutput(contentEditingInput: self.input)

    let url = self.input?.fullSizeImageURL

    if let imageUrl = url {
        let fullImage = UIImage(contentsOfFile:
                            imageUrl.path!)

        var resultImage = self.performFilter(fullImage!,
            orientation: self.imageOrientation)

        let renderedJPEGData =
            UIImageJPEGRepresentation(resultImage, 0.9)


        renderedJPEGData.writeToURL(
                    output.renderedContentURL,
                atomically: true)

        let archivedData =
                    NSKeyedArchiver.archivedDataWithRootObject(
                        self.currentFilter)

        let adjustmentData =
                    PHAdjustmentData(formatIdentifier:
                        "com.ebookfrenzy.photoext",
                        formatVersion: "1.0",
                    data: archivedData)

        output.adjustmentData = adjustmentData
    }
    completionHandler?(output)
    }
}
```

The code begins by creating a new instance of the *PHContentEditingOutput* class, initialized with the content
of the input object originally passed into the extension:

```
let output =
```

```
PHContentEditingOutput(contentEditingInput: self.input)
```

Next, the URL of the full sized version of the image is extracted from the original input object and the corresponding image loaded into a UIImage instance. The full sized image is then filtered via a call to the *performFilter* method:

```
let url = self.input?.fullSizeImageURL

if let imageUrl = url {
        let fullImage = UIImage(contentsOfFile: imageUrl.path!)

var resultImage = self.performFilter(fullImage!,
                    orientation: self.imageOrientation)
```

With the editing operations now applied to the full sized image, it is rendered into JPEG format and written out to a location specified by the URL assigned to the *renderedContentURL* property of the previously created *PHContentEditingOutput* instance:

```
let renderedJPEGData =
            UIImageJPEGRepresentation(resultImage, 0.9)

            renderedJPEGData.writeToURL(output.renderedContentURL,
                atomically: true)
```

Although the extension had previously indicated that it was not able to accept adjustment data, returning adjustment data reflecting the edits performed on the image to the Photos app is mandatory. For this tutorial, the name of the Core Image filter used to modify the image is archived into an NSData instance together with a revision number and a unique identifier. This object is then packaged into a *PHAdjustmentData* instance and assigned to the *adjustmentData* property of the output object:

```
let archivedData =
        NSKeyedArchiver.archivedDataWithRootObject(
                                        self.currentFilter)

let adjustmentData = PHAdjustmentData(formatIdentifier:
            "com.ebookfrenzy.photoext", formatVersion: "1.0", data:
                archivedData)

output.adjustmentData = adjustmentData
```

If the extension were to be enhanced to handle adjustment data, code would need to be added to the *canHandleAdjustmentData* method to compare the *formatVersion* and *formatIdentifier* values from the incoming adjustment data with those specified in the outgoing data to verify that the data is compatible with the editing capabilities of the extension.

Finally, the completion handler is called and passed the fully configured output object. At this point, control will return to the Photos app and the modified image will appear in the Photos editing screen.

81.10 **Testing the Application**

Build and run the extension using the Photos app as the host and take the, by now familiar, steps to select an image and invoke the newly created Photo Editing extension. Use a toolbar button to change the appearance of the image before tapping the *Done* button. The modified image will subsequently appear within the Photos app editing screen (Figure 81-6 shows the results of the invert filter) where the changes can be committed or discarded:

Figure 81-6

81.11 **Summary**

The Photo Editing extension allows the image editing capabilities of a containing app to be accessed from within the standard iOS Photos app. A Photo Editing extension takes the form of a view controller which implements the PHContentEditingController protocol and the protocol's associated delegate methods.

82. Creating an iOS 8 Action Extension

As with other extension types, the purpose of the Action extension is to extend elements of functionality from one application so that it is available for use within other applications. In the case of Action extensions, this functionality generally must fit the narrow definition of enabling the user to either transform the content within a host application, or view it in a different way. An application designed to translate text into different languages might, for example, provide an extension to allow the content of other applications to be similarly translated.

This chapter will introduce the concept of Action extensions in greater detail and put theory into practice through the creation of an example application and Action extension.

82.1 An Overview of Action Extensions

Action extensions appear within the activity view controller which is the panel that appears when the user taps the Share button within a running application. Figure 82-1, for example, shows the activity view controller panel as it appears from within the Safari web browser running on an iPhone. Action extensions appear within the action area of this panel alongside the built-in actions such as printing and copying of content.

Figure 82-1

When an Action extension is created, it must declare the types of content with which it is able to work. The appearance or otherwise of the Action extension within the activity view controller is entirely context sensitive. In other words, an Action extension that is only able to work with text based content will not appear as an option in the activity view controller when the user is currently working with or viewing image or video content within a host app.

Unlike other extension types, there are two sides to an Action extension. In the first instance, there is the Action extension itself. As with other extension types, this must be bundled with a containing application which must, in turn, provide some useful and meaningful functionality to the user. The other possibility is for host apps to be able to move beyond simply displaying the Action extension as an option within the activity view controller. With the appropriate behavior implemented, a host app can receive modified content from an Action extension and make constructive use of it on the user's behalf. In the remainder of this chapter and the next chapter, both of these concepts will be implemented through the creation of an example Action extension and host app.

82.2 About the Action Extension Example

The tutorial in the remainder of this and the next chapter is divided into two distinct phases. The initial phase involves the creation of an Action extension named "Change it Up" designed to display the text content of host apps in upper case and using a larger font so that it is easier to read. For the sake of brevity, the containing app will not provide any additional functionality beyond containing the extension, though it is important to remember that in the real world it will need to do so.

The second phase of the tutorial involves the creation of a host app that is able to receive modified content back from the Action extension and use it to replace the original content. This will be covered in the next chapter entitled *Receiving Data from an iOS 8 Action Extension*.

82.3 Creating the Action Extension Project

An Action extension is created by adding an extension target to a containing app. Begin by launching Xcode and creating a new Single View Application project named ActionDemo configured for universal device deployment and using Swift as the programming language.

82.4 Adding the Action Extension Target

With the newly created project loaded into Xcode, select the *File -> New -> Target...* menu option and, in the template panel (Figure 82-2), select the options to create an iOS Application Extension using the Action Extension template:

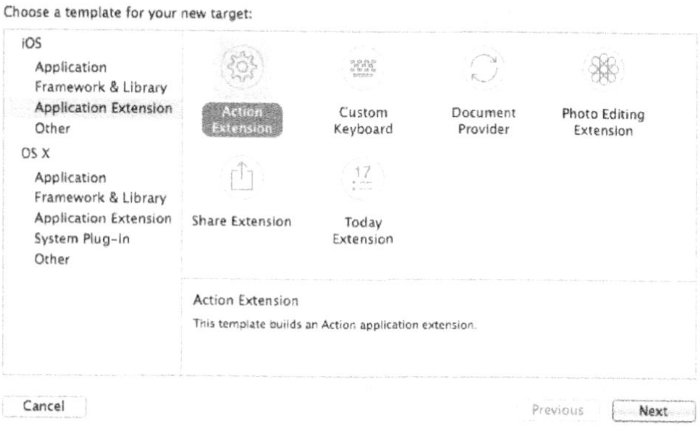

Choose a template for your new target:

iOS
   Application
   Framework & Library
   Application Extension
   Other

           Action Extension   Custom Keyboard   Document Provider   Photo Editing Extension

OS X
   Application
   Framework & Library
   Application Extension   Share Extension   Today Extension
   System Plug-in
   Other

Action Extension
This template builds an Action application extension.

Cancel   Previous   Next

Figure 82-2

With the appropriate options selected, click on the *Next* button and enter *MyActionExt* into the Product Name field. Leave the remaining fields set to the default values and click on *Finish* to complete the extension creation process. When prompted, click on the *Activate* button to activate the scheme created by Xcode to enable the extension to be built and run.

Once the extension has been added, it will appear in the project navigator panel under the *MyActionExt* folder. This folder will contain both the Swift source code file for the extension's view controller named *ActionViewController.swift* and a user interface storyboard file named *MainInterface.storyboard*. In addition, an *Info.plist* file will be present in the *Supporting Files* sub-folder.

82.5 Configuring the Action Extension

It is essential that an Action extension declare the type of content with which it is able to work. This is achieved via key-value settings located in the extension's *Info.plist* file. Select this file within the project navigator panel (*MyActionExt -> Supporting Files -> Info.plist*) and unfold the *NSExtension -> NSExtensionAttributes -> NSExtensionActivationRule* section of the file as shown in Figure 82-3:

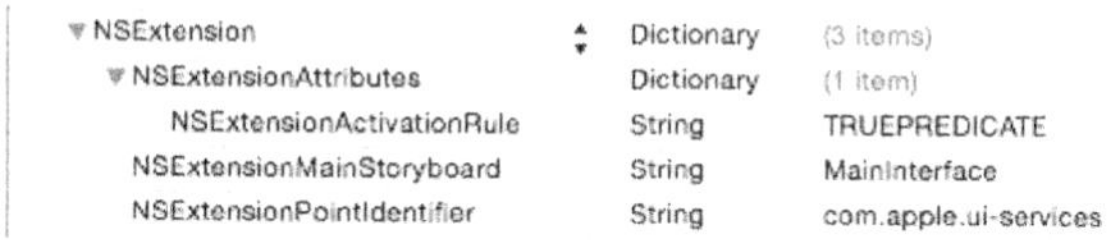

▼ NSExtension	Dictionary	(3 items)
▼ NSExtensionAttributes	Dictionary	(1 item)
NSExtensionActivationRule	String	TRUEPREDICATE
NSExtensionMainStoryboard	String	MainInterface
NSExtensionPointIdentifier	String	com.apple.ui-services

Figure 82-3

The NSExtensionActivationRule defines the conditions under which the Action extension will appear as an option within the activity view controller of a host app. As currently configured, the extension will be activated under any circumstances and, as such, will cause a warning to appear during compilation indicating that the setting will need to be changed before the app will be accepted into the App Store.

Since the extension is intended to be used with text only, the rules need to be changed accordingly to remove the warning. Within the *Info.plist* properties, select the NSExtensionActivationRule line and change the value in the *Type* column from *String* to *Dictionary* as shown in Figure 82-4:

Figure 82-4

With the line still selected, click on the + button to add a new key-value pair to the rule dictionary. In the new item line, enter *NSExtensionActivationSupportsText* into the *Key* column, change the *Type* column to Boolean and select *YES* in the *Value* column. With this modification completed, the NSExtension section of the property list should match that shown in Figure 82-5:

Figure 82-5

One last change that needs to be made concerns the name that will appear beneath the extension icon in the activity view controller. This is dictated by the value assigned to the *Bundle display name* key and currently reads "MyActionExt". Change this value so that it now reads "Change it Up".

82.6 Designing the Action Extension User Interface

The user interface for the Action extension is contained in the *MyActionExt -> MainInterface.storyboard* file. Locate this file in the project navigator panel and load it into Interface Builder.

By default, Xcode has created a template user interface consisting of a toolbar, a "Done" button and an image view. The only change necessary for the purposes of this example is to replace the image view with a text view. Select the image view in the storyboard canvas and remove it using the keyboard delete key. From the Object Library panel drag and drop a Text View object onto the storyboard and position and resize it so that it fills the space previously occupied by the image view.

With the new Text View object still selected, display the *Resolve Auto Layout Issues* menu (indicated in Figure 82-6) and select the *Reset to Suggested Constraints* menu option.

Figure 82-6

Display the Attributes Inspector for the Text View object and delete the default Latin text and, in the *Behavior* section of the panel, turn off the *Editable* option. As previously outlined, one of the features of this extension is that the content is displayed in a larger font so take this opportunity to increase the font setting in the Attribute Inspector from System 14.0 to System 39.0.

Finally, display the Assistant Editor panel and establish an outlet connection for the Text View object named *myTextView*. Remaining within the Assistant Editor, delete the line of code declaring the imageView outlet.

With these changes made, the user interface for the Action extension view controller should resemble that of Figure 82-7:

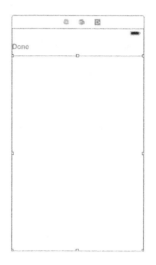

Figure 82-7

82.7 Receiving the Content

The next step in the tutorial is to add some code to receive the content from a host app when the extension is launched. All extension view controllers have an associated *extension context* in the form of an instance of the NSExtensionContext class. A reference to the extension context can be accessed via the *extensionContext* property of the view controller.

Creating an iOS 8 Action Extension

The extension context includes a property named *inputItems* in the form of an array containing objects which provide access to the content from the host app. The input items are, in turn, contained within one or more NSExtensionItem objects.

Within the *ActionViewController.swift* file, locate the *viewDidLoad* method, remove the template code added by Xcode and modify the method to obtain a reference to the first input item object:

```
override func viewDidLoad() {
    super.viewDidLoad()

    let textItem = self.extensionContext!.inputItems[0]
                    as NSExtensionItem
}
```

Each NSExtensionItem object contains an array of *attachment* objects. These attachment objects are of type NSItemProvider and provide access to the data held by the host app. Once a reference to an attachment has been obtained, the *hasItemConformingToTypeIdentifier* method of the object can be called to verify that the host application has data of the type supported by the extension. In the case of this example, the extension supports text based content so the *kUTTypeText* uniform type identifier (UTI) is used to perform this test:

```
override func viewDidLoad() {
    super.viewDidLoad()

    let textItem = self.extensionContext!.inputItems[0]
            as NSExtensionItem

    let textItemProvider = textItem.attachments![0]
            as NSItemProvider

    if textItemProvider.hasItemConformingToTypeIdentifier(
            kUTTypeText as NSString) {

    }
}
```

Assuming that the host app has data of the required type, it can be loaded into the extension via a call to the *loadItemForTypeIdentifier* method of the attachment provider object, once again passing through as an argument the UTI content type supported by the extension. The loading of the data from the host app is performed asynchronously so a completion handler must be specified which will be called when the data loading process is complete:

```
override func viewDidLoad() {
    super.viewDidLoad()
```

```
    let textItem = self.extensionContext!.inputItems[0]
              as NSExtensionItem

    let textItemProvider = textItem.attachments![0]
              as NSItemProvider

    if textItemProvider.hasItemConformingToTypeIdentifier(
                  kUTTypeText as NSString) {
        textItemProvider.loadItemForTypeIdentifier(
            kUTTypeText as NSString,
            options: nil,
            completionHandler: handleCompletion)
    }
}
```

When the above code is executed, the data associated with the attachment will be loaded from the host app and the specified completion handler (in this case a method named *handleCompletion*) will be called. Clearly the next step is to implement this completion handler. Remaining within the *ActionViewController.swift* file, declare an optional variable named *convertString* and implement this handler so that it reads as follows:

```
import UIKit
import MobileCoreServices

class ActionViewController: UIViewController {

    @IBOutlet weak var myTextView: UITextView!
    var convertedString: String?
.
.
.
func handleCompletion(string: NSSecureCoding!, error: NSError!)
{
    convertedString = string as? String

    if convertedString != nil {
        convertedString = convertedString!.uppercaseString

        dispatch_async(dispatch_get_main_queue()) {
            self.myTextView.text = self.convertedString!
        }
    }
}
```

The first parameter to the handler method is an object that conforms to the NSSecureCoding protocol (in this case a string object containing the text loaded from the host app). Within the body of the method, this string is assigned to a new variable before being converted to upper case.

The converted text is then displayed on the Text View object in the user interface. It is important to be aware that because this is a completion handler, the code is being executed in a different thread from the main application thread. As such, any changes made to the user interface must be dispatched to the main thread, hence the *dispatch_async* method wrapper.

82.8 **Returning the Modified Data to the Host App**

The final task in terms of implementing the Action extension is to return the modified content to the host app when the user taps the Done button in the extension user interface. When the Action extension template was created, Xcode connected the Done button to an action method named *done*. Locate this method in the *ActionViewController.swift* file and modify it so that it reads as follows:

```
@IBAction func done() {
    var returnProvider =
            NSItemProvider(item: convertedString,
                    typeIdentifier: kUTTypeText as NSString)

    var returnItem = NSExtensionItem()

    returnItem.attachments = [returnProvider]
    self.extensionContext!.completeRequestReturningItems(
        [returnItem], completionHandler: nil)
}
```

This method essentially reverses the process of unpacking the input items. First a new NSItemProvider instance is created, configured with the modified content (represented by the string value assigned to the *convertedString* variable) and the content type identifier. Next, a new NSExtensionItem instance is created and the NSItemProvider object assigned as an attachment.

Finally, the *completeRequestReturningItems* method of the extension context is called, passing through the NSExtensionItem instance as an argument.

As will be outlined later in this chapter, whether or not the host app does anything with the returned content items is dependent upon whether or not the host app has been implemented to do so.

82.9 **Testing the Extension**

To test the extension, begin by making sure that the *MyExtAction* scheme (and not the *ActionDemo* containing app) is selected in the Xcode toolbar as highlighted in Figure 82-8:

Figure 82-8

With a suitable device connected to the development system, build and run the extension. As with other extension types, Xcode will prompt for a host app to work with the extension. In order for the extension to be activated, an app that works with text content must be selected. Scroll down the list of apps installed on the device to locate and select the standard Notes app (Figure 82-9). Once selected, click on the *Run* button:

Figure 82-9

After the project has compiled and uploaded to the device, the Notes app should automatically load. Select an existing note within the app, or add a new one if none exist then tap the Share button located in the bottom toolbar. If the Action extension does not appear in the activity view controller panel, tap the *More* button and turn on the extension using the switch in the Activities list:

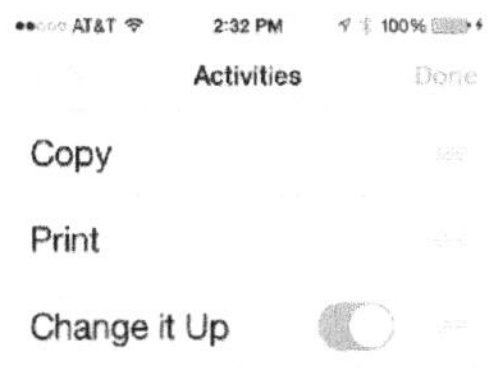

Figure 82-10

Once the extension has been enabled it should appear in the actions section of the activity view controller panel:

Figure 82-11

Once the extension is accessible, select it to launch the action, at which point the extension user interface should appear displaying the text from the note in uppercase using a larger font:

Figure 82-12

Having verified that the Action extension works, tap the Done button to return to the Notes app. Note that the content of the note did not change to reflect the content change to uppercase that was returned from the extension. The reason for this is that the Notes app has not implemented the functionality to accept modified content from an Action extension. As time goes by and Action extensions become more prevalent it will become more common for applications to accept modified content from Action extensions. This, of course, raises the question of how this is implemented, an area that will be covered in the next chapter entitled *Receiving Data from an iOS 8 Action Extension*.

82.10 **Summary**

An Action extension is narrowly defined as a mechanism to transform the content in a host app or display that content to the user in a different way. An Action extension is context sensitive and must declare the type of data with which it is able to work. There are essentially three key elements to an Action extension. First, the extension must load the content data from the host app. Secondly, the extension displays or transforms that content in some, application specific way. Finally, the transformed data is packaged and returned to the host app. Not all host apps are able to handle data returned from an Action extension and in the next chapter we will explore the steps necessary to add such a capability.

83. Receiving Data from an iOS 8 Action Extension

The previous chapter covered the steps involved in creating an Action extension in iOS 8 that was designed to modify and display text content from a host app. In developing the extension, steps were taken to ensure that the modified content was returned to the host app when the user exited the extension. This chapter will work through the creation of an example host application that demonstrates how to receive data from an Action extension.

83.1 Creating the Example Project

Start Xcode and create a new Single View Application project named ActionHostApp with Swift selected as the programming language and the Devices menu set to *Universal*.

The finished application is going to consist of a Text View object and a toolbar containing a Share button that will provide access to the Change it Up Action extension created in the previous chapter. When the Action extension returns, the host app will receive the modified content from the extension and display it to the user.

83.2 Designing the User Interface

Locate and load the *Main.storyboard* file into the Interface Builder tool and drag and drop a Toolbar instance so that it is positioned along the bottom edge of the layout canvas. Next, drag and drop a Text View object onto the canvas and resize and position it so that it occupies the remaining space above the toolbar, stretching the view out horizontally until the blue margin guidelines appear. With the TextView object selected, display the Attributes Inspector and change the displayed text to "This is some sample text".

Finally, hold down the keyboard Shift key and click on both the Text View and Toolbar views in the layout. Once both are selected, display the *Resolve Auto Layout Issues* menu and select the *Reset to Suggested Constraints* option. At this point the layout should resemble Figure 83-1:

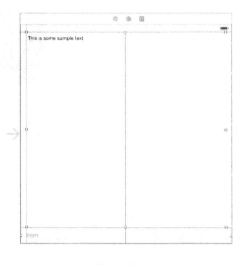

Figure 83-1

Before proceeding, display the Assistant Editor panel and establish an outlet for the Text View object named *myTextView*.

83.3 Importing the Mobile Core Services Framework

The code added to this project will make use of a definition which is declared within the Mobile Core Services framework. To avoid compilation errors, this framework must be imported into the *ViewController.swift* file as follows:

```
import UIKit
import MobileCoreServices

class ViewController: UIViewController {
    .
    .
    .
}
```

83.4 Adding a Share Button to the Application

In order to be able to access the "Change it Up" Action extension from within this host application it will be necessary to implement a Share button. As the user interface currently stands, the toolbar contains a single button item displaying text which reads "Item". To change this to a Share button, select it in the storyboard layout (keeping in mind that it may be necessary to click on it twice since the first click typically selects the parent toolbar rather than the button item).

With the button selected, display the Attributes Inspector and change the *Identifier* menu from *Custom* to *Action*:

Bar Button Item

Style Bordered

Identifier Action

Tint Default

Bar Item

Title

Image

Tag 0

☑ Enabled

Figure 83-2

Once the change has been made, the button item should now have the standard appearance of an iOS Share button as shown in Figure 83-3:

Figure 83-3

Now that the button looks like a Share button, some code now needs to be added to display the activity view controller when it is tapped by the user. With the Assistant Editor displayed, Ctrl-click on the button and drag the resulting line to a suitable location within the *ViewController.swift* file. Release the line and create an Action outlet named *showActionView*. Once created, implement the code in this method so that it reads as follows:

```
@IBAction func showActionView(sender: AnyObject) {

    let activityViewController =
        UIActivityViewController(activityItems:
            [myTextView.text], applicationActivities: nil)

    self.presentViewController(activityViewController,
            animated:true, completion: nil)

    activityViewController.completionWithItemsHandler = myHandler
}
```

The code within the method creates a new UIActivityViewController instance initialized with the content of the Text View in the user interface. The activity view controller is then displayed to the user. Finally, a method is assigned to act as the completion handler to be called when the Action extension returns control to the application. For now this can be implemented as a stub method as follows:

```
func myHandler(activityType:String!, completed: Bool,
```

```
        returnedItems: [AnyObject]!, error: NSError!) {
}
```

Compile and run the application and tap the Share button to test that the activity view controller appears. Select the "Change it Up" extension and verify that it displays the text extracted from the Text View. Finally, tap the Done button to return to the host app, noting that the original text content has not yet been converted to uppercase. This functionality now needs to be implemented within the completion handler method.

83.5 Receiving Data from an Extension

When the user exits from an Action extension, the completion handler assigned to the UIActivityViewController instance will be called and passed a variety of parameters. One of those parameters will be an array of NSExtensionItem objects containing NSItemProvider objects that can be used to load any data that has been returned by the extension.

Using the same techniques described in the previous chapter (*Creating an iOS 8 Action Extension*) this data can be extracted by making the following changes to the *myHandler* method:

```
func myHandler(activityType:String!, completed: Bool,
       returnedItems: [AnyObject]!, error: NSError!) {

    if returnedItems.count > 0 {

        let textItem: NSExtensionItem =
            returnedItems[0] as NSExtensionItem


        let textItemProvider: AnyObject =
            textItem.attachments![0]

        if textItemProvider.hasItemConformingToTypeIdentifier(
            kUTTypeText as NSString) {

            textItemProvider.loadItemForTypeIdentifier(
                kUTTypeText as NSString,
                    options: nil,
                    completionHandler: {(string:
                    NSSecureCoding!, error: NSError!) ->
                     Void in
                        let newtext = string as String
                        self.myTextView.text = newtext
            })
        }
    }
```

```
    }
    .
    .
    .
}
```

The method obtains a reference to the item provider and verifies that at least one item has been returned from the extension. A test is then performed to make sure that it is a text item. If the item is text based, the item is loaded from the extension and a completion handler used to assign the new text to the Text View object.

83.6 Testing the Application

Compile and run the application, select the Share button and launch the "Change it Up" extension. On returning to the host application the original text should now have been updated to be displayed in uppercase as modified within the extension.

83.7 Summary

In addition to providing an alternative view of the content in a host app, Action extensions can also be used to transform that content in some way. Not only can this transformation be performed and viewed within the extension, but a mechanism is also provided to return that modified content to the host app. By default, most host apps will not make use of the returned content. In reality adding this support is a relatively simple task which involves implementing a completion handler method to handle the content returned from the extension into the host app and assigning that handler method to be called when the activity view controller is displayed to the user.

Chapter 84

84. Using iOS 8 Event Kit to Create Date and Location Based Reminders

iOS includes the Reminders application, the purpose of which is to allow users to specify events about which they wished to be reminded. Reminders can be specified for a specific date and time, or even to be triggered when the user either arrives at or leaves a specified location. You might, for example, use the Reminders app to remind you to buy milk on your way home when your iPhone or iPad detects that you are leaving your office. Using the Event Kit Framework, it is possible to create and manage these reminders from within your own applications.

This chapter will cover some of the basics of calendars and reminders before working step-by-step through the creation of an example application that demonstrates the creation of both date and location based reminders.

84.1 An Overview of the Event Kit Framework

The Event Kit Framework consists of a range of classes designed specifically to provide access to the calendar database and to facilitate the management of events, reminders and alarms. In terms of integrating reminders into an iOS application, these classes are EKCalendar, EKEventStore, EKReminder and EKAlarm.

The EKEventStore class provides an interface between applications and the underlying calendar database. The calendar database can, in turn, contain multiple calendars (for example the user may have a work calendar and a personal calendar configured). Each calendar in a database is represented in code in the form of an EKCalendar object.

Within each calendar there are events and reminders, each of which is managed in code using the EKEvent and EKReminder classes respectively.

Finally, the EKAlarm class is used to configure alarms to alert the user at a specified point in the future.

84.2 The EKEventStore Class

In order to work with reminders in an iOS application, an instance of the EKEventStore class must be created. It is important to note that there is system overhead in requesting access to the calendar database so the call to initialize an EKEventStore object should ideally only be performed once within an application. In some situations, the system will prompt the user to allow the application access to the calendar. As such, the

EKEventStore object should only be initialized immediately prior to the point in the code where calendar access is required. A reference to this event store object should then be retained and used for future calendar interaction throughout the lifespan of the application.

An EKEventStore object must request access to the calendar at the point that it is initialized. This request must specify whether access is required for calendar events (EKEntityTypeEvent) or reminders (EKEntityTypeReminder). Whether or not access is granted will depend on the current privacy settings for the application in the Privacy section of the device Settings app. Privacy settings are available for both Calendar and Reminders access. When an application seeks access for the first time, the user will be prompted by the system to allow the application to access either the calendar events or reminders. If the user declines access, the application will need to handle this gracefully. This is achieved via the completion handler of the *requestAccessToEntityType* method of the EKEventStore class. The following code excerpt, for example, seeks access to reminders in the calendar database and reports an error in the console log in the event that access was declined:

```
var eventStore = EKEventStore()

eventStore.requestAccessToEntityType(EKEntityTypeReminder,
    completion: {(granted: Bool, error:NSError!) in
            if !granted {
                println("Access to store not granted")
            }
    })
```

Once access has been accepted or denied by the user, the privacy setting for that application can be viewed and changed by selecting the application in Settings and choosing the Privacy option. Figure 84-1, for example, shows that the access for an application named ReminderApp to Reminders on the system is currently enabled.

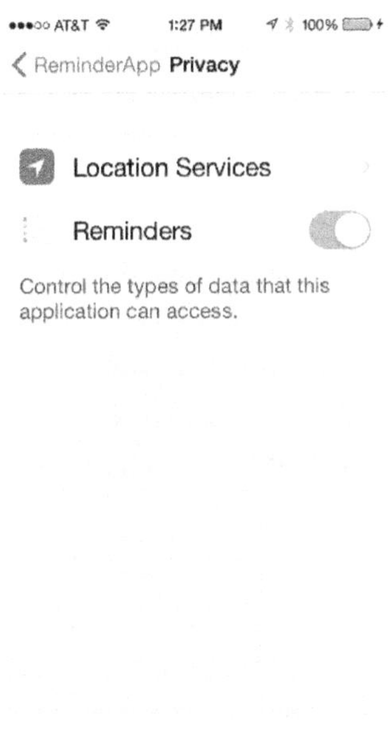

Figure 84-1

In addition, it is worth noting that the message used by the system to request access to the calendar database can be configured by adding an entry to the Info.plist file for the project. By default a message similar to that illustrated in Figure 84-2 will be displayed.

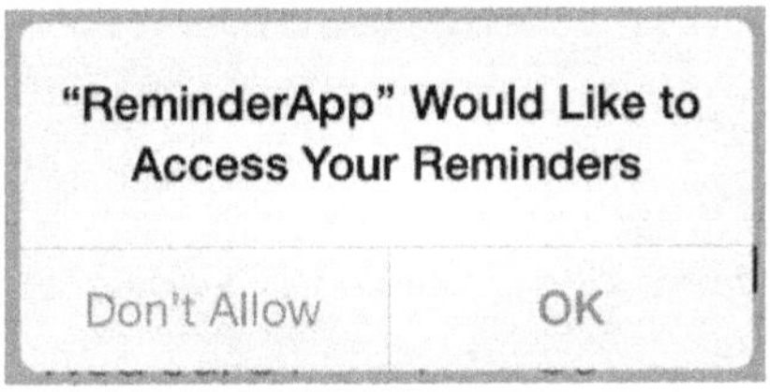

"ReminderApp" Would Like to
Access Your Reminders

Don't Allow   OK

Figure 84-2

By editing the Info.plist file, for example, and adding a "Privacy – Reminders Usage Description" key and value, the message may be augmented to provide the user with additional information as to why access is required. Once defined, the custom message will appear when access is requested from the user.

84.3 Accessing Calendars in the Database

As previously stated, the calendar database on an iOS device can contain multiple calendars, both for the events calendar and for reminders. An array of available calendars can be obtained via a call to the *calendarsForEntityType* method of the event store object, specifying as an argument whether event or reminder calendars are required. The following code outputs a list, by title, of the reminder calendars configured on the device. Note that each calendar entry in the array is represented by an EKCalendar object:

```
let calendars =
```

```
        eventStore.calendarsForEntityType(EKEntityTypeReminder)

for calendar in calendars as [EKCalendar] {
    println("Calendar = \(calendar.title)")
}
```

The Event Kit Framework has the concept of a default calendar for the addition of new reminders and events. This default calendar may be configured by the user within the Settings app on the device *(Settings -> Mail, Contacts, Calendars -> Default Calendar)*. These are represented in code by the *defaultCalendarForNewReminders* and *defaultCalendarForNewEvents* constants. Whilst some applications may need to let the user choose which calendar to use, these defaults can be useful when selection is not necessary.

84.4 Creating Reminders

New reminders are added to the calendar by creating new instances of the EKReminder class, configuring the object according to the requirements of the reminder and then adding it to the event store.

The following example code creates a reminder and adds it to the default calendar for new reminder entries:

```
let reminder = EKReminder(eventStore: self.eventStore)

reminder.title = "Go to the store and buy milk"
reminder.calendar = eventStore.defaultCalendarForNewReminders()

var error: NSError?

eventStore.saveReminder(reminder, commit: true, error: &error)
```

The above code creates a new EKReminder object and, in so doing, associates it with the event store before setting the title of the reminder. Next, the reminder is configured so that it will be added to the user's default reminder calendar before being saved to the event store.

Reminders can be general as in the above example or, as will be demonstrated in the following tutorial, configured to be triggered at a specific date and time, or when the user arrives at or departs from a physical geographical location (a concept known as *geofencing*).

84.5 Creating Alarms

The EKAlarm class can be used to add an alarm to the reminder. Alarms can be specified either using a specific date and time (via a call to *alarmWithAbsoluteDate* and passing through an NSDate object) or using a relative time interval (via a call to *alarmWithRelativeOffset* passing through an NSTimeInterval value).

Once an EKAlarm object has been created and configured it must be added to the EKReminder object with which the alarm is to be associated. When the specified time arrives, the user will be notified of the reminder with sound, vibration and a notification panel.

84.6 Creating the Example Project

Begin by launching Xcode and selecting the options to create a new iOS application based on the *Tabbed Application* template. Enter *ReminderApp* as the product name, set the device menu to *Universal* and choose Swift as the programming language.

In the remainder of this chapter, an application will be constructed to allow the user to add reminders based on either date/time or location factors.

84.7 Designing the User Interface for the Date/Time Based Reminder Screen

Upon reviewing the *Main.storyboard* file, it is clear that Xcode has created a template-based tabbed application consisting of a Tab Bar Controller and two Views, each of which has its own view controller. For the purposes of this example, the first view will be used to implement a screen whereby the user can create a new date and time based reminder. Within the Storyboard canvas, therefore, locate the First View screen and remove the current labels that were added by Xcode. With a clean view, add a Text Field, Date Picker and Button object to the view canvas. Once added, position and configure the user interface layout so that it resembles that of Figure 84-3:

Figure 84-3

Shift-click on all three views so that all of the objects are selected, then use the Auto Layout Align menu to position the views in the horizontal center of the container.

Select the Text Field view and, using the Auto Layout Pin menu, configure a *Spacing to nearest neighbor* constraint on the top edge of the view using the current distance value and with the *Constrain to margins* option switched off. Within the Pin panel, also enable the *Width* constraint using the current value before clicking on the *Add 2 Constraints* button.

Next, select the Button view and add a constraint on the top edge to the nearest neighbor, once again with the *Constrain to margins* option switched off.

Repeat the above step with the Date Picker view selected, this time also enabling the *Height* and *Width* constraints.

Select the Text Field object and display the Assistant Editor using *View -> Assistant Editor -> Show Assistant Editor* menu option, making sure that it is displaying the content of the *FirstViewController.swift* file. If it is not, click on the file name in the bar at the top of the Assistant Editor panel and select the file from the drop down menu.

Ctrl-click on the Text Field object in the view and drag the resulting line to the area immediately beneath the class declaration line in the Assistant Editor panel. Upon releasing the line, the configuration panel will appear. Configure the connection as an *Outlet* named *reminderText* and click on the *Connect* button. Repeat this step to add an outlet connection to the Date Picker object named *myDatePicker*.

Finally, Ctrl-click on the Button object, drag the line to the Assistant Editor and release it beneath the end of the *viewDidLoad* method. In the resulting connection panel, change the connection type to *Action* and name the action *setReminder*.

84.8 Implementing the Reminder Code

With the user interface view designed, the next step is to implement the code in the view controller for the first view to access the event store and set up the reminder. We will need a place to store the event store object once it has been requested and, as previously discussed, it is recommended that access to the event store be requested only once. As such we will need a location to store the reference once it has been obtained, so select the *AppDelegate.swift* file, import the EventKit Framework and declare a variable in which to save the event store reference:

```
import UIKit
import EventKit

@UIApplicationMain
class AppDelegate: UIResponder, UIApplicationDelegate {

    var window: UIWindow?
    var eventStore: EKEventStore?
.

.
```

Next, edit the *FirstViewController.swift* file, import the EventKit Framework and add a variable in which to store a reference to the application delegate:

```
import UIKit
import EventKit

class FirstViewController: UIViewController {

    @IBOutlet weak var reminderText: UITextField!
    @IBOutlet weak var myDatePicker: UIDatePicker!
    var appDelegate: AppDelegate?
.

.
```

Locate the *setReminder* template stub and add the following code:

```
@IBAction func setReminder(sender: AnyObject) {

    appDelegate = UIApplication.sharedApplication().delegate
                        as? AppDelegate

    if appDelegate!.eventStore == nil {
        appDelegate!.eventStore = EKEventStore()
            appDelegate!.eventStore!.requestAccessToEntityType(
                EKEntityTypeReminder, completion: {(granted, error) in
            if !granted {
                println("Access to store not granted")
                println(error.localizedDescription)
            } else {
                    println("Access granted")
            }
        })
    }

    if (appDelegate!.eventStore != nil) {
        self.createReminder()
    }
}
```

The code added to the method verifies that access to the event store has not already been obtained and, in the event that it has not, requests access to the reminder calendars. If access is denied a message is reported to the console. In the event that access is granted, a second method named *createReminder* is called. With *FirstViewController.swift* still in the editing panel, implement this method:

```
func createReminder() {
```

```
    let reminder = EKReminder(eventStore: appDelegate!.eventStore)

    reminder.title = reminderText.text
    reminder.calendar =
        appDelegate!.eventStore!.defaultCalendarForNewReminders()
    let date = myDatePicker.date
    let alarm = EKAlarm(absoluteDate: date)

    reminder.addAlarm(alarm)

    var error: NSError?
    appDelegate!.eventStore!.saveReminder(reminder,
                    commit: true, error: &error)

    if error != nil {
        println("Reminder failed with error
\(error?.localizedDescription)")
    }
}
```

The *createReminder* method creates a new EKReminder object associated with the event store and sets the title property to the content of the Text Field object in the user interface. The code elects the default calendar as the target for the reminder and then creates an EKAlarm object primed with the date value selected by the user in the Date Picker object. The alarm is then added to the reminder which, in turn, is saved in the event store. Errors are output to the console for debugging purposes.

84.9 **Hiding the Keyboard**

Before moving on to the next part of the tutorial, some code will now need to be added to the application so that the keyboard is withdrawn when the user touches the view background.

Within the *FirstViewController.swift* file, override the code in the *touchesBegan* method:

```
override func touchesBegan(touches: NSSet, withEvent event: UIEvent) {
    reminderText.endEditing(true)
}
```

With the time and date based reminder phase of the application completed, the next step is to implement the location based reminder functionality.

84.10 **Designing the Location-based Reminder Screen**

The tab controller created on our behalf by Xcode contains a second view that will be used for the location based reminder creation. The goal of this view will be to allow the user to specify a reminder and alarm that will be triggered when the user moves away from the geographical location at which the reminder was created.

Begin by selecting the *Main.storyboard* file and locating the second view controller scene. Remove the template labels added by Xcode and design a new user interface using a Button and a Text Field as illustrated in Figure 84-4.

Shift-click on both views so that all of the objects are selected, then use the Auto Layout Align menu to position the views in the horizontal center of the container.

Select the Text Field view and, using the Auto Layout Pin menu, configure a *Spacing to nearest neighbor* constraint on the top edge of the view using the current distance value and with the *Constrain to margins* option switched off. Within the Pin panel, also enable the *Width* constraint using the current value before clicking on the *Add 2 Constraints* button.

Next, select the Button view and add a constraint on the top edge to the nearest neighbor, once again with the *Constrain to margins* option switched off.

Using the Assistant Editor (taking care to ensure that the editor displays the code for the *SecondViewController.swift* file and not the file for the first view controller), establish an outlet connection for the Text Field named *locationText*. Next, establish an Action connection from the button to a method named *setLocationReminder*.

Figure 84-4

Finally, add an application delegate property to the *SecondViewController.swift* file and import the Event Kit header:

```
import UIKit
import EventKit

class SecondViewController: UIViewController, CLLocationManagerDelegate {
```

```
@IBOutlet weak var locationText: UITextField!
var appDelegate: AppDelegate?
```

.

.

.

84.11 Creating a Location-based Reminder

The code for accessing the event store is the same as that for the date/time example. Since the application will need to get the user's current location, the CoreLocation framework will need to be imported. The code will require the use of CLLocationManager so a property for the manager instance will also be needed, as will a declaration that the view controller now implements the CLLocationManagerDelegate protocol. The *viewDidLoad* method also needs to be modified to request access to location data on the device and to configure the location manager instance:

```
import UIKit
import EventKit
import CoreLocation

class SecondViewController: UIViewController, CLLocationManagerDelegate {
    @IBOutlet weak var locationText: UITextField!
    var appDelegate: AppDelegate?
    var locationManager: CLLocationManager = CLLocationManager()

    @IBOutlet weak var locationText: UITextField!

    override func viewDidLoad() {
        super.viewDidLoad()

        locationManager.requestWhenInUseAuthorization()
        locationManager.delegate = self
        locationManager.distanceFilter = kCLDistanceFilterNone
        locationManager.desiredAccuracy = kCLLocationAccuracyBest
    }
```

.

.

.

All that remains is to implement the code to access the event store and create the alert and reminder. Still within the *SecondViewController.swift* file, modify the *setLocationReminder* method as follows:

```
@IBAction func setLocationReminder(sender: AnyObject) {

    appDelegate = UIApplication.sharedApplication().delegate as?
AppDelegate
```

```
    if appDelegate!.eventStore == nil {
        appDelegate!.eventStore = EKEventStore()
        appDelegate!.eventStore?.requestAccessToEntityType(
          EKEntityTypeReminder, completion:
                {(granted: Bool, error:NSError!) in
            if !granted {
                println("Access to store not granted")
            } else {
                println("Access granted")
            }
        })
    }

    if (appDelegate!.eventStore != nil) {
        locationManager.startUpdatingLocation()
    }
}
```

As with the previous example, access to the event store is requested. This time, however, a CLLocationManager instance is created and started up. This will result in a call to the *didUpdateLocations* delegate method where the code to obtain the current location and to create the alarm and reminder will need to be implemented:

```
func locationManager(manager: CLLocationManager!, didUpdateLocations
locations: [AnyObject]!) {

    locationManager.stopUpdatingLocation()

    let reminder = EKReminder(eventStore: appDelegate!.eventStore)
    reminder.title = locationText.text
    reminder.calendar =
        appDelegate!.eventStore!.defaultCalendarForNewReminders()

    let location = EKStructuredLocation(title: "Current Location")
    location.geoLocation = locations.last as CLLocation

    let alarm = EKAlarm()

    alarm.structuredLocation = location
    alarm.proximity = EKAlarmProximityLeave

    reminder.addAlarm(alarm)
```

```
    var error: NSError?

    appDelegate!.eventStore?.saveReminder(reminder,
        commit: true, error: &error)

    if error != nil {
        println("Reminder failed with error
\(error?.localizedDescription)")
    }
}
```

Since this code introduces some new concepts a more detailed breakdown is probably warranted. To begin with, the code stops the location manager from sending further updates.

```
locationManager.stopUpdatingLocation()
```

Next, a new EKReminder instance is created and initialized with the text entered by the user into the Text Field.

```
let reminder = EKReminder(eventStore: appDelegate!.eventStore)
reminder.title = locationText.text
```

The default calendar is selected to store the reminder and then an EKStructuredLocation instance created with a location title of "Current Location". This is the title by which the location will be listed in the Reminders app. The most recent location from the location update is extracted from the end of the locations array (see chapter *Getting Location Information using the iOS 8 Core Location Framework* for more details on location awareness) and the coordinates assigned to the EKStructuredLocation object.

```
reminder.calendar =
        appDelegate!.eventStore!.defaultCalendarForNewReminders()

let location = EKStructuredLocation(title: "Current Location")
location.geoLocation = locations.last as CLLocation
```

The location is then added to a newly created alarm instance which is subsequently configured to be triggered when the user moves away from the location proximity:

```
let alarm = EKAlarm()
alarm.structuredLocation = location
alarm.proximity = EKAlarmProximityLeave

reminder.addAlarm(alarm)
```

Finally, the fully configured reminder is saved to the event store.

```
var error: NSError?
```

```
appDelegate!.eventStore?.saveReminder(reminder, commit: true,
            error: &error)

if error != nil {
    println(
        "Reminder failed with error \(error?.localizedDescription)")
}
```

84.12 Setting up the Usage Description Key

The above code changes included a method call to request permission from the user to track location information when the application is running in the foreground. This method call must be accompanied by a usage description string which needs to be added to the project's *Info.plist* file assigned to the NSLocationWhenInUseUsageDescription key. Within the project navigator panel, load the *Info.plist* file (located under *Supporting Files*) into the editor. The key-value pair needs to be added to the *Information Property List* dictionary. Select this entry in the list and click on the + button to add a new entry to the dictionary. Within the new entry, enter NSLocationWhenInUseUsageDescription into the key column and, once the key has been added, double-click in the corresponding value column and enter the following text:

```
This information is required to show your current location
```

84.13 Testing the Application

Since the application will rely on a default calendar having been designated for reminders, the first step is to make sure this has been configured. Launch the Settings application, scroll down to and then select *Reminders*, and make sure that a calendar has been assigned to the *Default List*.

Compile and run the application on a physical device (reminders do not currently work on the iOS Simulator). Select a time a few minutes into the future, and enter some text onto the first screen before touching the Set Reminder button. Put the app into the background and launch the built-in Reminder app where the new reminder should be listed in the default reminder list. When the designated time arrives the alarm should trigger, displaying the text entered by the user.

Using the tab bar, switch to the second screen, enter a message and touch the "When I Leave Here" button. Once again, switch to the built in Reminders app and open the default calendar where the new reminder should now be listed. Select the reminder so that the blue information button appears. Tap on this button to review the reminder details as shown in Figure 84-5:

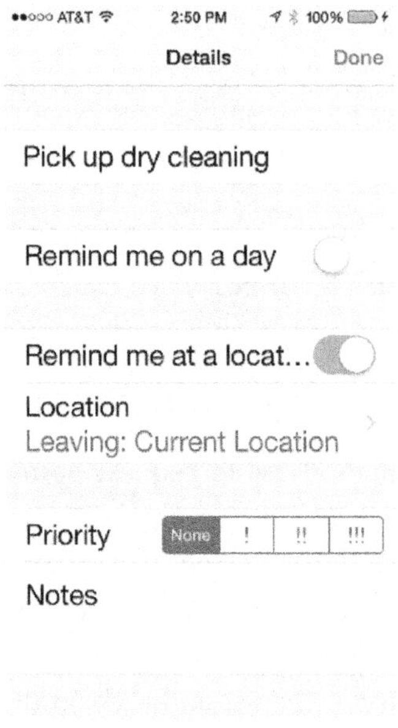

••○○○ AT&T 🔋   2:50 PM   ✈ ✳ 100% ▭ ✦

Details   Done

Pick up dry cleaning

Remind me on a day

Remind me at a locat...

Location
Leaving: Current Location   ›

Priority   None   !   !!   !!!

Notes

Figure 84-5

When you next leave your current location the alarm should trigger.

84.14 Summary

The Event Kit Framework provides a platform for building reminders into iOS applications. Reminders can be triggered based on either a date and time or change of geographical location. This chapter has provided an overview of Event Kit based reminders before working through the creation of an example application.

85. Accessing the iOS 8 Camera and Photo Library

The iOS 8 SDK provides access to both the camera device and photo library through the UIImagePickerController class. This allows videos and photographs to be taken from within an application and for existing photos and videos to be presented to the user for selection.

This chapter will cover the basics and some of the theory behind the use of the UIImagePickerController class before working through the step by step creation of an example application in *An Example iOS 8 iPhone Camera Application*.

85.1 The UIImagePickerController Class

The ultimate purpose of the UIImagePickerController class is to provide applications with either an image or video. It achieves this task by providing the user with access to the camera, camera roll and photo libraries on the device. In the case of the camera, the user is able to either take a photo or record a video depending on the capabilities of the device and the application's configuration of the UIImagePickerController object. In terms of camera roll and library access, the object provides the application with the existing image or video selected by the user. The controller also allows new photos and videos created within the application to be saved to the library.

85.2 Creating and Configuring a UIImagePickerController Instance

In order to use the UIImagePickerController, an instance of the class must first be created. In addition, properties of the instance need to be configured to control the source for the images or videos (camera, camera roll or library). Further, the types of media that are acceptable to the application must also be defined (photos, videos or both). Another configuration option defines whether the user has the option to edit a photo once it has been taken and before it is passed to the application.

The source of the media is defined by setting the *sourceType* property of the UIImagePickerController object to one of the three supported types:

- UIImagePickerControllerSourceType.Camera
- UIImagePickerControllerSourceType.SavedPhotosAlbum
- UIImagePickerControllerSourceType.PhotoLibrary

The types of media acceptable to the application are defined by setting the *mediaTypes* property, an NSArray object that can be configured to support both video and images. The KUTTypeImage and KUTTypeMovie definitions contained in the MobileCoreServices Framework can be used as values when configuring this property.

Whether or not the user is permitted to perform editing before the image is passed on to the application is controlled via the *allowsEditing* Boolean property.

The following code creates a UIImagePickerController instance and configures it for camera use with image support and editing disabled before displaying the controller:

```
let imagePicker = UIImagePickerController()

imagePicker.delegate = self
imagePicker.sourceType = UIImagePickerControllerSourceType.PhotoLibrary
imagePicker.mediaTypes = [kUTTypeImage as NSString]
imagePicker.allowsEditing = false

self.presentViewController(imagePicker, animated: true,
        completion: nil)
```

It should be noted that the above code also configured the current class as the delegate for the UIImagePickerController instance. This is actually a key part of how the class works and is covered in the next section.

85.3 Configuring the UIImagePickerController Delegate

When the user is presented with the UIImagePickerController object user interface the application essentially hands control to that object. That being the case, the controller needs some way to notify the application that the user has taken a photo, recorded a video or made a library selection. It does this by calling delegate methods. The class that instantiates a UIImagePickerController instance should, therefore, declare itself as the object's delegate, conform to the UIImagePickerControllerDelegate and UINavigationControllerDelegate protocols and implement the *didFinishPickingMediaWithInfo* and *imagePickerControllerDidCancel* methods. When the user has selected or created media, the *didFinishPickingMediaWithInfo* method is called and passed an NSDictionary object containing the media and associated data. In the event that the user cancels the operation the *imagePickerControllerDidCancel* method is called. In both cases it is the responsibility of the delegate method to dismiss the view controller:

```
func imagePickerController(picker: UIImagePickerController,
didFinishPickingMediaWithInfo info: [NSObject : AnyObject]) {

    // Code here to work with media

    self.dismissViewControllerAnimated(true, completion: nil)
```

```
}

func imagePickerControllerDidCancel(picker: UIImagePickerController) {
    self.dismissViewControllerAnimated(true, completion: nil)
}
```

The *info* argument passed to the *didFinishPickingMediaWithInfo* method is an NSDictionary object containing the data relating to the image or video created or selected by the user. The first step is typically to identify the type of media:

```
let mediaType = info[UIImagePickerControllerMediaType] as NSString

if mediaType.isEqualToString(kUTTypeImage as NSString) {

        // Media is an image

} else if mediaType.isEqualToString(kUTTypeMovie as NSString) {

        // Media is a video

}
```

The original, unedited image selected or photographed by the user may be obtained from the *info* dictionary as follows:

```
let image = info[UIImagePickerControllerOriginalImage] as UIImage
```

Assuming that editing was enabled on the image picker controller object, the edited version of the image may be accessed via the *UIImagePickerControllerEditedImage* dictionary key:

```
let image = info[UIImagePickerControllerEditedImage] as UIImage
```

If the media is a video, the URL of the recorded media may be accessed as follows:

```
let url = info[UIImagePickerControllerMediaURL]
```

Once the image or video URL has been obtained the application can optionally save the media to the library and either display the image to the user or play the video using the AVPlayer and AVPlayerViewController classes as outlined in the chapter entitled *iOS 8 Video Playback using AVPlayer and AVPlayerViewController*.

85.4 Detecting Device Capabilities

Not all iOS devices provide the same functionality. iPhone models prior to the 3GS model, for example, do not support the recording of video. Some iPod Touch models do not have a camera so neither the camera, nor camera roll are available via the image picker controller. These differences in functionality make it important to detect the capabilities of a device when using the UIImagePickerController class. Fortunately, this may easily be achieved by a call to the *isSourceTypeAvailable* class method of the UIImagePickerController. For example, to detect the presence of a camera:

```
if UIImagePickerController.isSourceTypeAvailable(
            UIImagePickerControllerSourceType.Camera) {
    // Code here
}
```

Similarly, to test for access to the camera roll:

```
if UIImagePickerController.isSourceTypeAvailable(
            UIImagePickerControllerSourceType.SavedPhotosAlbum) {
    // Code here
}
```

Finally, to check for support for photo libraries:

```
if UIImagePickerController.isSourceTypeAvailable(
            UIImagePickerControllerSourceType.PhotoLibrary) {
    // Code here
}
```

85.5 Saving Movies and Images

Once a video or photo created by the user using the camera is handed off to the application it is then the responsibility of the application code to save that media into the library. Photos and videos may be saved via calls to the *UIImageWriteToSavedPhotosAlbum* and *UISaveVideoAtPathToSavedPhotosAlbum* methods respectively. These methods use a *target-action* mechanism whereby the save action is initiated and the application continues to run. When the action is complete a specified method is called to notify the application of the success or otherwise of the operation.

To save an image:

```
UIImageWriteToSavedPhotosAlbum(image, self,
            "image:didFinishSavingWithError:contextInfo:", nil)
```

To save a video:

```
if (UIVideoAtPathIsCompatibleWithSavedPhotosAlbum(videoPath))
{
    UISaveVideoAtPathToSavedPhotosAlbum(videopath, self,
            "image:didFinishSavingWithError:contextInfo:", nil)
}
```

Last, but by no means least, is the *finishedSavingWithError* method which will be called when the action is either complete or failed due to an error:

```
func image(image: UIImage, didFinishSavingWithError
        error: NSErrorPointer, contextInfo:UnsafePointer<Void>) {

    if error != nil {
        // Report error to user
    }
}
```

85.6 Summary

In this chapter we have provided an overview of the UIImagePickerController and looked at how this class can be used either to allow a user to take a picture or record video from within an iOS application or select media from the device photo libraries. Now that the theory has been covered, the next chapter entitled *An Example iOS 8 iPhone Camera Application* will work through the development of an example application designed to implement the theory covered in this chapter.

86. An Example iOS 8 Camera Application

In the chapter entitled *Accessing the iOS 8 Camera and Photo Library* we looked in some detail at the steps necessary to provide access to the iOS camera and photo libraries in an iOS 8 application. The purpose of this chapter is to build on this knowledge by working through an example iOS application designed to access the device's camera and photo libraries.

86.1 An Overview of the Application

The application user interface for this example will consist of an image view and a toolbar containing two buttons. When touched by the user, the first button will display the camera to the user and allow a photograph to be taken which will subsequently be displayed in the image view. The second button will provide access to the camera roll where the user may select an existing photo image. In the case of a new image taken with the camera, this will be saved to the camera roll.

Since we will be covering the playback of video in the next chapter (*iOS 8 Video Playback using AVPlayer and AVPlayerViewController*) the camera roll and camera will be restricted to still images in this example. The addition of video support to this application is left as an exercise for the reader.

86.2 Creating the Camera Project

Begin the project by launching Xcode and creating a new Universal iOS application project named *Camera* using the *Single View Application* template with the Swift language option selected.

86.3 Designing the User Interface

The next step in this tutorial is to design the user interface. This is a very simple user interface consisting of an image view, a toolbar and two bar button items. Select the *Main.storyboard* file and drag and drop components from the Object Library (*View -> Utilities -> Show Object Library*) onto the view. Position and size the components and set the text on the bar button items so that the user interface resembles Figure 86-1.

Figure 86-1

In terms of Auto Layout constraints, begin by selecting the toolbar view and clicking on the *Pin* menu in the toolbar located in the lower right hand corner of the storyboard canvas and establish *Spacing to nearest neighbor* constraints on the bottom and two side edges of the view with the *Constrain to margins* option switched off.

Next, select the Image View object and, once again using the *Pin* menu, establish *Spacing to nearest neighbor* constraints on all four sides of the view, this time with the *Constrain to margins* option enabled.

Finally, with the Image View still selected, display the Attributes Inspector panel and change the *Mode* attribute to *Aspect Fit*.

Select the image view object in the view canvas, display the Assistant Editor panel. Ctrl-click on the image view object and drag to a position just below the class declaration line in the Assistant Editor. Release the line, and, in the resulting connection dialog, establish an outlet connection named *imageView*.

With the Assistant Editor still visible, establish action connections for the two buttons to methods named *useCamera* and *useCameraRoll* respectively (keeping mind that it may be necessary to click twice on each button to select it since the first click will typically select the toolbar parent object).

Close the Assistant Editor, select the *ViewController.swift* file and modify it further to add import and delegate protocol declarations together with a Boolean property declaration that will be required later in the chapter:

```
import UIKit
import MobileCoreServices

class ViewController: UIViewController, UIImagePickerControllerDelegate,
UINavigationControllerDelegate {
```

```
@IBOutlet weak var imageView: UIImageView!
var newMedia: Bool?
```

.

.

86.4 Implementing the Action Methods

The *useCamera* and *useCameraRoll* action methods now need to be implemented. The *useCamera* method first needs to check that the device on which the application is running has a camera. It then needs to create a UIImagePickerController instance, assign the cameraViewController as the delegate for the object and define the media source as the camera. Since we do not plan on handling videos the supported media types property is set to images only. Finally, the camera interface will be displayed. The last task is to set the *newMedia* flag to true to indicate that the image is new and is not an existing image from the camera roll. Bringing all these requirements together gives us the following *useCamera* method:

```
@IBAction func useCamera(sender: AnyObject) {

    if UIImagePickerController.isSourceTypeAvailable(
            UIImagePickerControllerSourceType.Camera) {

        let imagePicker = UIImagePickerController()

        imagePicker.delegate = self
        imagePicker.sourceType =
            UIImagePickerControllerSourceType.Camera
        imagePicker.mediaTypes = [kUTTypeImage as NSString]
        imagePicker.allowsEditing = false

        self.presentViewController(imagePicker, animated: true,
                            completion: nil)
        newMedia = true
    }
}
```

The *useCameraRoll* method is remarkably similar to the previous method with the exception that the source of the image is declared to be UIImagePickerControllerSourceType.PhotoLibrary and the *newMedia* flag is set *to false* (since the photo is already in the library we don't need to save it again):

```
@IBAction func useCameraRoll(sender: AnyObject) {

    if UIImagePickerController.isSourceTypeAvailable(
            UIImagePickerControllerSourceType.SavedPhotosAlbum) {
        let imagePicker = UIImagePickerController()
```

```
        imagePicker.delegate = self
        imagePicker.sourceType =
                UIImagePickerControllerSourceType.PhotoLibrary
        imagePicker.mediaTypes = [kUTTypeImage as NSString]
        imagePicker.allowsEditing = false
        self.presentViewController(imagePicker, animated: true,
                completion: nil)
        newMedia = false
    }
}
```

86.5 Writing the Delegate Methods

As described in *Accessing the iOS 8 Camera and Photo Library*, in order to fully implement an instance of the image picker controller delegate protocol it is necessary to implement some delegate methods. The most important method is *didFinishPickingMediaWithInfo* which is called when the user has finished taking or selecting an image. The code for this method in our example reads as follows:

```
func imagePickerController(picker: UIImagePickerController,
didFinishPickingMediaWithInfo info: [NSObject : AnyObject]) {

    let mediaType = info[UIImagePickerControllerMediaType] as NSString

    self.dismissViewControllerAnimated(true, completion: nil)

    if mediaType.isEqualToString(kUTTypeImage as NSString) {
        let image = info[UIImagePickerControllerOriginalImage]
                            as UIImage

        imageView.image = image

        if (newMedia == true) {
            UIImageWriteToSavedPhotosAlbum(image, self,
                "image:didFinishSavingWithError:contextInfo:", nil)
        } else if mediaType.isEqualToString(kUTTypeMovie as NSString) {
                // Code to support video here
        }

    }
}

func image(image: UIImage, didFinishSavingWithError error:
NSErrorPointer, contextInfo:UnsafePointer<Void>) {
```

```
if error != nil {
    let alert = UIAlertController(title: "Save Failed",
        message: "Failed to save image",
        preferredStyle: UIAlertControllerStyle.Alert)

    let cancelAction = UIAlertAction(title: "OK",
        style: .Cancel, handler: nil)

    alert.addAction(cancelAction)
    self.presentViewController(alert, animated: true,
                    completion: nil)
    }
}
```

The code in this delegate method dismisses the image picker view and identifies the type of media passed from the image picker controller. If it is an image it is displayed on the view image object of the user interface. If this is a new image it is saved to the camera roll. The *finishedSavingWithError* method is configured to be called when the save operation is complete. If an error occurred it is reported to the user via an alert box.

It is also necessary to implement the *imagePickerControllerDidCancel* delegate method which is called if the user cancels the image picker session without taking a picture or making an image selection. In most cases all this method needs to do is dismiss the image picker:

```
func imagePickerControllerDidCancel(picker: UIImagePickerController) {
    self.dismissViewControllerAnimated(true, completion: nil)
}
```

86.6 Building and Running the Application

In order to experience the full functionality of this application it will be necessary to install it on a physical device with a camera. Steps on performing this are covered in *Testing Apps on iOS 8 Devices with Xcode 6*.

Assuming certificates and provisioning are configured, click on the Xcode run button to launch the application. Once the application loads, select the *Camera* button to launch the camera interface.

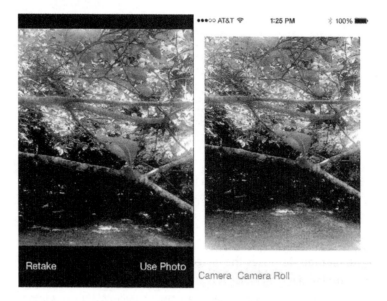

Figure 86-2

Once the picture has been taken and selected for use in the application, it will appear in the image view object of our application user interface.

Selecting the *Camera Roll* button will provide access to the camera roll and photo stream on the device where an image selection can be made:

Figure 86-3

87. iOS 8 Video Playback using AVPlayer and AVPlayerViewController

Whilst the iPhone 3GS model introduced support for recording videos using the built in camera, all iPhone and iPad models and iOS versions have included support for video playback. Video playback support in iOS 8 is provided by combining the AVFoundation AVPlayer and AVKit AVPlayerViewController classes.

This chapter presents an overview of video playback in iOS 8 using these two classes followed by a step by step example.

87.1 The AVPlayer and AVPlayerViewController Classes

The sole purpose of the AVPlayer class is to play media content. An AVPlayer instance is initialized with the URL of the media to be played (either a path to a local file on the device or the URL of network based media). Playback can be directed to a device screen or, in the case of external playback mode, via AirPlay or an HDMI/VGA cable connection to an external screen.

The AVKit Player View Controller (AVPlayerViewController) class provides a view controller environment through which AVPlayer video is displayed to the user together with a number of controls that enable the user to manage the playback experience. Playback may also be controlled from within the application code by calling the *play* and *pause* methods of the AVPlayer instance.

87.2 The iOS Movie Player Example Application

The objective of the remainder of this chapter is to create a simple application that will play back a video when a button is pressed. The video will be streamed over the internet from a movie file located on a web server.

Begin by launching Xcode and creating a new iOS application project based on the *Single View Application* template configured for the Swift language and *Universal* devices, naming the product *AVPlayerDemo*.

87.3 Adding the AVKit Framework to the Xcode Project

Once the new project has been created, the first step is to make sure the AVKit Framework is included in the project. Failure to add this framework will result in the application crashing at runtime.

To add the AVKit framework, select the *AVPlayerDemo* target located at the top of the project navigator panel. In the center pane, select the *Build Phases* tab and unfold the *Link Binary With Libraries* panel. Click on the '+' button to display a list of existing frameworks, locate and select *AVKit.framework* and click the *Add* button. The AVKit.framework will now appear in the frameworks list along with any other frameworks already included in the project.

87.4 **Designing the User Interface**

Select the *Main.storyboard* file and display the Object Library (*View -> Utilities -> Show Object Library*). Drag a single Button instance to the view window and change the text on the button to "Play Movie". With the button selected in the storyboard canvas, display the Auto Layout Align menu and add both horizontal and vertical *Center in Container* constraints to the view.

From the Object Library panel, locate the AVKit Player View Controller object and drag and drop it onto the storyboard to the right of the existing view controller. Ctrl-click on the button in the first view controller and drag the resulting line to the second AVKit Player View Controller. Release the line and select *show* from the segue selection menu. On completion of these tasks, the storyboard should resemble that of Figure 87-1:

Figure 87-1

87.5 **Initializing Video Playback**

When the "Play Movie" button is tapped by the user the application will perform a segue to the AVPlayerViewController scene. Verify that this works by running the application and selecting the button. The AVPlayerViewController will appear and display the video playback controls but as yet no AVPlayer has been configured to play video content. This can be achieved by implementing the *prepareForSegue* method within the *ViewController.swift* file as follows, the code for which relies on the AVKit and AVFoundation frameworks having been imported:

```
import UIKit
```

```
import AVKit
import AVFoundation

class ViewController: UIViewController {
.
.
.

    override func prepareForSegue(segue: UIStoryboardSegue,
                sender: AnyObject?) {
        let destination = segue.destinationViewController as
                            AVPlayerViewController
        let url = NSURL(string:
                "http://www.ebookfrenzy.com/ios_book/movie/movie.mov")
        destination.player = AVPlayer(URL: url)
    }
.
.
.
```

The code in this above method begins by obtaining a reference to the destination view controller, in this case the AVPlayerViewController instance. An NSURL object is then initialized with the URL of a web based video file. Finally a new AVPlayer instance is created, initialized with the video URL and assigned to the *player* property of the AVPlayerViewController object.

Running the application once again should cause the video to be available for playback within the player view controller scene.

87.6 Build and Run the Application

With the design and coding phases complete, all that remains is to build and run the application. Click on the run button located in the toolbar of the main Xcode project window. Assuming that no errors occur, the application should launch within the iOS Simulator or device. Once loaded, touching the *Play Movie* button should launch the movie player in full screen mode and playback should automatically begin:

Figure 87-2

87.7 Creating AVPlayerViewController Instance from Code

The example shown in this chapter used storyboard scenes and a transition to display an AVPlayerViewController instance. Whilst this is a quick approach to working with the AVPlayerViewController and AVPlayer classes, the same result may also be achieved directly by writing code within the application. The following code fragment, for example, initializes and plays video within an application using these two classes without the use of a storyboard scene:

```
let player = AVPlayer(URL: url)
let playerController = AVPlayerViewController()

playerController.player = player
self.addChildViewController(playerController)
self.view.addSubview(playerController.view)
playerController.view.frame = self.view.frame

player.play()
```

87.8 Summary

The basic classes needed to play back video from within an iOS 8 application are provided by the AVFoundation and AVKit frameworks. The purpose of the AVPlayer class is to facilitate the playback of video media files. The AVPlayerViewController class provides a quick and easy way to embed an AVPlayer instance into a view controller environment together with a set of standard on-screen playback controls.

88. Playing Audio on iOS 8 using AVAudioPlayer

The iOS 8 SDK provides a number of mechanisms for implementing audio playback from within an iOS application. The easiest technique from the perspective of the application developer is to use the AVAudioPlayer class which is part of the AV Foundation Framework.

This chapter will provide an overview of audio playback using the AVAudioPlayer class. Once the basics have been covered, a tutorial is worked through step by step. The topic of recording audio from within an iOS application is covered in the next chapter entitled *Recording Audio on iOS 8 with AVAudioRecorder*.

88.1 Supported Audio Formats

The AV Foundation Framework supports the playback of a variety of different audio formats and codecs including both software and hardware based decoding. Codecs and formats currently supported are as follows:

- AAC (MPEG-4 Advanced Audio Coding)
- ALAC (Apple Lossless)
- AMR (Adaptive Multi-rate)
- HE-AAC (MPEG-4 High Efficiency AAC)
- iLBC (internet Low Bit Rate Codec)
- Linear PCM (uncompressed, linear pulse code modulation)
- MP3 (MPEG-1 audio layer 3)
- μ-law and a-law

If an audio file is to be included as part of the resource bundle for an application it may be converted to a supported audio format prior to inclusion in the application project using the Mac OS X *afconvert* command-line tool. For details on how to use this tool, run the following command in a Terminal window:

```
afconvert -h
```

88.2 Receiving Playback Notifications

An application receives notifications from an AVAudioPlayer instance by declaring itself as the object's delegate and implementing some or all of the following AVAudioPlayerDelegate protocol methods:

- **audioPlayerDidFinishPlaying** – Called when the audio playback finishes. An argument passed through to the method indicates whether the playback completed successfully or failed due to an error.

- **audioPlayerDecodeErrorDidOccur** - Called when a decoding error is encountered by the AVAudioPlayer object during audio playback. An error object containing information about the nature of the problem is passed through to this method as an argument.

- **audioPlayerBeginInterruption** – Called when audio playback has been interrupted by a system event such as an incoming phone call. Playback is automatically paused and the current audio session deactivated.

- **audioPlayerEndInterruption** - Called after an interruption ends. The current audio session is automatically activated and playback may be resumed by calling the *play* method of the corresponding AVAudioPlayer instance.

88.3 Controlling and Monitoring Playback

Once an AVAudioPlayer instance has been created the playback of audio may be controlled and monitored programmatically via the methods and properties of that instance. For example, the self-explanatory *play*, *pause* and *stop* methods may be used to control playback. Similarly, the *volume* property may be used to adjust the volume level of the audio playback whilst the *playing* property may be accessed to identify whether or not the AVAudioPlayer object is currently playing audio.

In addition, playback may be delayed to begin at a later time using the *playAtTime* instance method which takes as an argument the number of seconds (as an NSTimeInterval value) to delay before beginning playback.

The length of the current audio playback may be obtained via the *duration* property whilst the current point in the playback is stored in the *currentTime* property.

Playback may also be programmed to loop back and repeatedly play a specified number of times using the *numberOfLoops* property.

88.4 Creating the Audio Example Application

The remainder of this chapter will work through the creation of a simple iOS 8 application which plays an audio file. The user interface of the application will consist of play and stop buttons to control playback and a slider to adjust the playback volume level.

Begin by launching Xcode and creating a new Universal *Single View Application* named *AudioDemo* using the Swift programming language.

88.5 Adding an Audio File to the Project Resources

In order to experience audio playback it will be necessary to add an audio file to the project resources. For this purpose, any supported audio format file will be suitable. Having identified a suitable audio file, drag and drop it into the *Supporting Files* folder of the project navigator panel of the main Xcode window. For the purposes of this tutorial we will be using an MP3 file named *Moderato.mp3* which can be found in the *audiofiles* folder of the sample code archive, downloadable from the following URL:

http://www.ebookfrenzy.com/print/ios8

Having downloaded and unzipped the file, locate it in a Finder window and drag and drop it onto the *Supporting Files* section of the Xcode project navigator panel.

88.6 Designing the User Interface

The application user interface is going to comprise two buttons labeled "Play" and "Stop" and a slider to allow the volume of playback to be adjusted. Select the *Main.storyboard* file, display the Object Library (*View -> Utilities -> Show Object Library*), drag and drop components from the Library onto the View window and modify properties so that the interface appears as illustrated in Figure 88-1:

Figure 88-1

With the scene view selected within the storyboard canvas, display the Auto Layout *Resolve Auto Layout Issues* menu and select the *Reset to Suggested Constraints* menu option listed in the *All Views in View Controller* section of the menu.

Select the slider object in the view canvas, display the Assistant Editor panel and verify that the editor is displaying the contents of the *ViewController.swift* file. Ctrl-click on the slider object and drag to a position just below the class declaration line in the Assistant Editor. Release the line and in the resulting connection dialog establish an outlet connection named *volumeControl*.

Ctrl-click on the "Play" button object and drag the line to the area immediately beneath the *viewDidLoad* method in the Assistant Editor panel. Release the line and, within the resulting connection dialog, establish an Action method on the *Touch Up Inside* event configured to call a method named *playAudio*. Repeat these steps to establish an action on the "Stop" button to a method named *stopAudio*.

Ctrl-click on the slider object and drag the line to the area immediately beneath the newly created actions in the Assistant Editor panel. Release the line and, within the resulting connection dialog, establish an Action method on the *Value Changed* event configured to call a method named *adjustVolume*.

Close the Assistant Editor panel and select the *ViewController.swift* file in the project navigator panel and add an import directive and delegate declaration, together with a property to store a reference to the AVAudioPlayer instance as follows:

```
import UIKit
import AVFoundation

class ViewController: UIViewController, AVAudioPlayerDelegate {

    @IBOutlet weak var volumeControl: UISlider!
    var audioPlayer: AVAudioPlayer?
.

.
```

88.7 Implementing the Action Methods

The next step in our iOS audio player tutorial is to implement the action methods for the two buttons and the slider. Remaining in the *ViewController.swift* file, locate and implement these methods as outlined in the following code fragment:

```
@IBAction func playAudio(sender: AnyObject) {
    if let player = audioPlayer {
        player.play()
    }
}


@IBAction func stopAudio(sender: AnyObject) {
    if let player = audioPlayer {
        player.stop()
    }
}


@IBAction func adjustVolume(sender: AnyObject) {
    if audioPlayer != nil {
        audioPlayer?.volume = volumeControl.value
    }
}
```

88.8 **Creating and Initializing the AVAudioPlayer Object**

Now that we have an audio file to play and appropriate action methods written, the next step is to create an AVAudioPlayer instance and initialize it with a reference to the audio file. Since we only need to initialize the object once when the application launches a good place to write this code is in the *viewDidLoad* method of the *ViewController.swift* file:

```
override func viewDidLoad() {
    super.viewDidLoad()
    let url = NSURL.fileURLWithPath(
               NSBundle.mainBundle().pathForResource("Moderato",
                     ofType: "mp3")!)

    var error: NSError?

    audioPlayer = AVAudioPlayer(contentsOfURL: url, error: &error)

    if let err = error {
        println("audioPlayer error \(err.localizedDescription)")
    } else {
        audioPlayer?.delegate = self
        audioPlayer?.prepareToPlay()
    }
}
```

In the above code we create an NSURL reference using the filename and type of the audio file added to the project resources. Keep in mind that this will need to be modified to reflect the audio file used in your own projects.

Next, an AVAudioPlayer instance is created using the URL of the audio file. Assuming no errors were detected, the current class is designated as the delegate for the audio player object. Finally, a call is made to the audioPlayer object's *prepareToPlay* method. This performs initial buffering tasks so that there is no buffering delay when the play button is subsequently selected by the user.

88.9 **Implementing the AVAudioPlayerDelegate Protocol Methods**

As previously discussed, by declaring our view controller as the delegate for our AVAudioPlayer instance our application will be able to receive notifications relating to the playback. Templates of these methods are as follows and may be placed in the *ViewController.swift* file:

```
func audioPlayerDidFinishPlaying(player: AVAudioPlayer!, successfully
                flag: Bool) {

}
```

```
func audioPlayerDecodeErrorDidOccur(player: AVAudioPlayer!,
                error: NSError!) {
}

func audioPlayerBeginInterruption(player: AVAudioPlayer!) {
}

func audioPlayerEndInterruption(player: AVAudioPlayer!) {
}
```

For the purposes of this tutorial it is not necessary to implement any code for these methods and they are provided solely for completeness.

88.10 Building and Running the Application

Once all the requisite changes have been made and saved, test the application in the iOS simulator or a physical device by clicking on the run button located in the Xcode toolbar. Once the application appears, click on the Play button to begin playback. Adjust the volume using the slider and stop playback using the Stop button. If the playback is not audible on the device, make sure that the switch on the side of the device is not set to silent mode.

88.11 Summary

The AVAudioPlayer class, which is part of the AVFoundation framework, provides a simple way to play audio from within iOS applications. In addition to playing back audio, the class also provides a number of methods that can be used to control the playback in terms of starting, stopping and changing the volume of the playback. Through the implementation of the methods defined by the AVAudioPlayerDelegate protocol, the application may also be configured to receive notifications of events related to the playback such as playback ending or an error occurring during the audio decoding process.

89. Recording Audio on iOS 8 with AVAudioRecorder

In addition to audio playback, the iOS AV Foundation Framework provides the ability to record sound on iOS using the AVAudioRecorder class. This chapter will work step-by-step through a tutorial demonstrating the use of the AVAudioRecorder class to record audio.

89.1 An Overview of the AVAudioRecorder Tutorial

The goal of this chapter is to create an iOS 8 application that will record and playback audio. It will do so by creating an instance of the AVAudioRecorder class and configuring it with a file to contain the audio and a range of settings dictating the quality and format of the audio. Playback of the recorded audio file will be performed using the AVAudioPlayer class which was covered in detail in the chapter entitled *Playing Audio on iOS 8 using AVAudioPlayer*.

Audio recording and playback will be controlled by buttons in the user interface that are connected to action methods which, in turn, will make appropriate calls to the instance methods of the AVAudioRecorder and AVAudioPlayer objects respectively.

The view controller of the example application will also implement the AVAudioRecorderDelegate and AVAudioPlayerDelegate protocols and a number of corresponding delegate methods in order to receive notification of events relating to playback and recording.

89.2 Creating the Recorder Project

Begin by launching Xcode and creating a new *Universal* single view-based application named *Record* using the Swift programming language.

89.3 Designing the User Interface

Select the *Main.storyboard* file and, once loaded, drag Button objects from the Object Library window (*View -> Utilities -> Show Object Library*) and position them on the View window. Once placed in the view, modify the text on each button so that the user interface appears as illustrated in Figure 89-1:

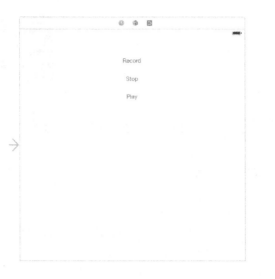

Figure 89-1

With the scene view selected within the storyboard canvas, display the Auto Layout *Resolve Auto Layout Issues* menu and select the *Reset to Suggested Constraints* menu option listed in the *All Views in View Controller* section of the menu.

Select the "Record" button object in the view canvas, display the Assistant Editor panel and verify that the editor is displaying the contents of the *ViewController.swift* file. Ctrl-click on the Record button object and drag to a position just below the class declaration line in the Assistant Editor. Release the line and, in the resulting connection dialog, establish an outlet connection named *recordButton*. Repeat these steps to establish outlet connections for the "Play" and "Stop" buttons named *playButton* and *stopButton* respectively.

Continuing to use the Assistant Editor, establish Action connections from the three buttons to methods named *recordAudio*, *playAudio* and *stopAudio*.

Close the Assistant Editor panel, select the *ViewController.swift* file and modify it to import the AVFoundation framework, declare adherence to some delegate protocols and to add properties to store references to AVAudioRecorder and AVAudioPlayer instances:

```
import UIKit
import AVFoundation

class ViewController: UIViewController, AVAudioPlayerDelegate,
AVAudioRecorderDelegate {

    var audioPlayer: AVAudioPlayer?
    var audioRecorder: AVAudioRecorder?
```

89.4 **Creating the AVAudioRecorder Instance**

When the application is first launched, an instance of the AVAudioRecorder class needs to be created. This will be initialized with the URL of a file into which the recorded audio is to be saved. Also passed as an argument to the initialization method is an NSDictionary object indicating the settings for the recording such as bit rate, sample rate and audio quality. A full description of the settings available may be found in the appropriate *Apple iOS reference materials.*

As is often the case, a good location to initialize the AVAudioRecorder instance is the *viewDidLoad* method of the view controller located in the *ViewController.swift* file. Select the file in the project navigator, locate this method and modify it so that it reads as follows:

```
override func viewDidLoad() {
    super.viewDidLoad()
    playButton.enabled = false
    stopButton.enabled = false

    let dirPaths =
        NSSearchPathForDirectoriesInDomains(.DocumentDirectory,
                                            .UserDomainMask, true)
    let docsDir = dirPaths[0] as String
    let soundFilePath =
                docsDir.stringByAppendingPathComponent("sound.caf")
    let soundFileURL = NSURL(fileURLWithPath: soundFilePath)
    let recordSettings =
                [AVEncoderAudioQualityKey: AVAudioQuality.Min.rawValue,
                 AVEncoderBitRateKey: 16,
                 AVNumberOfChannelsKey: 2,
                 AVSampleRateKey: 44100.0]

    var error: NSError?

    let audioSession = AVAudioSession.sharedInstance()
    audioSession.setCategory(AVAudioSessionCategoryPlayAndRecord,
                                            error: &error)

    if let err = error {
        println("audioSession error: \(err.localizedDescription)")
    }

    audioRecorder = AVAudioRecorder(URL: soundFileURL,
                            settings: recordSettings, error: &error)
```

```
if let err = error {
    println("audioSession error: \(err.localizedDescription)")
} else {
    audioRecorder?.prepareToRecord()
}
}
```

Since no audio has yet been recorded, the above method disables the play and stop buttons. It then identifies the application's documents directory and constructs a URL to a file in that location named *sound.caf*. An NSDictionary object is then created containing the recording quality settings before an audio session and an instance of the AVAudioRecorder class are created. Assuming no errors are encountered, the audioRecorder instance is prepared to begin recording when requested to do so by the user.

89.5 Implementing the Action Methods

The next step is to implement the action methods connected to the three button objects. Select the *ViewController.swift* file and modify it as outlined in the following code excerpt:

```
@IBAction func recordAudio(sender: AnyObject) {
    if audioRecorder?.recording == false {
        playButton.enabled = false
        stopButton.enabled = true
        audioRecorder?.record()
    }
}


@IBAction func stopAudio(sender: AnyObject) {
    stopButton.enabled = false
    playButton.enabled = true
    recordButton.enabled = true

    if audioRecorder?.recording == true {
        audioRecorder?.stop()
    } else {
        audioPlayer?.stop()
    }
}


@IBAction func playAudio(sender: AnyObject) {
    if audioRecorder?.recording == false {
        stopButton.enabled = true
        recordButton.enabled = false
```

```
        var error: NSError?

        audioPlayer = AVAudioPlayer(contentsOfURL: audioRecorder?.url,
                        error: &error)

        audioPlayer?.delegate = self

        if let err = error {
            println("audioPlayer error: \(err.localizedDescription)")
        } else {
            audioPlayer?.play()
        }
    }
}
```

Each of the above methods performs the steps necessary to enable and disable appropriate buttons in the user interface and to interact with the AVAudioRecorder and AVAudioPlayer object instances to record or play back audio.

89.6 Implementing the Delegate Methods

In order to receive notification about the success or otherwise of recording or playback it is necessary to implement some delegate methods. For the purposes of this tutorial we will need to implement the methods to indicate errors have occurred and also when playback finished. Once again, edit the *ViewController.swift* file and add these methods as follows:

```
func audioPlayerDidFinishPlaying(player: AVAudioPlayer!, successfully
flag: Bool) {
    recordButton.enabled = true
    stopButton.enabled = false
}

func audioPlayerDecodeErrorDidOccur(player: AVAudioPlayer!, error:
NSError!) {
    println("Audio Play Decode Error")
}

func audioRecorderDidFinishRecording(recorder: AVAudioRecorder!,
successfully flag: Bool) {
}

func audioRecorderEncodeErrorDidOccur(recorder: AVAudioRecorder!, error:
NSError!) {
    println("Audio Record Encode Error")
```

}

89.7 Testing the Application

Follow the steps outlined in *Testing Apps on iOS 8 Devices with Xcode 6* to configure the application for installation on an iOS device. Configure Xcode to install the application on the connected device and build and run the application by clicking on the run button in the main toolbar. Once loaded onto the device, the operating system will seek permission to allow the app to record audio. Select "OK" and touch the Record button to record some sound. Touch the Stop button when the recording is completed and use the Play button to play back the audio.

90. Integrating Twitter and Facebook into iOS 8 Applications

Social networking services are, for better or for worse, becoming an increasingly prominent aspect of our daily lives. Apple provides support for integrating social elements into iOS apps via the Social Framework with support included for Twitter, Facebook and Sina Weibo.

Within this chapter, the basics of Twitter and Facebook integration will be covered.

90.1 The UIActivityViewController class

Integration of social networks into iOS applications is performed through the use of either the UIActivityViewController class, or the classes of the Social Framework of the iOS SDK. At the time of writing, social networks supported by these classes consist of Facebook, Twitter and Sina Weibo, though it is probable that more will follow in future SDK releases.

For general purpose social network integration, the UIActivityViewController class is the recommended path. When using this class, the user is presented with a screen providing a choice of social network services to which a message may be posted (together with options to print or post via the built-in Mail or Message apps). Once the user of the application has selected a target service, the class then presents the user with a message preview panel where the message may be reviewed and modified prior to being sent. Once the message has been posted, the class handles all aspects of connecting to the user's chosen social network and subsequently posting the update to that service.

90.2 The Social Framework

The Social Framework contains two classes designed to provide more flexible and general purpose mechanisms for social network integration.

The SLComposeViewController class, unlike the UIActivityViewController class, allows a post to be targeted to a specific social network service within the application code, without requiring the user to make a selection from those services available. The target service is simply specified at the point that an instance of the class is created within the application code. The user is then presented with a preview sheet appropriate to the specified service.

The SLRequest class of the Social Framework, on the other hand, is provided for developers with specific needs in terms of social network integration and who are familiar with, or prepared to learn, the corresponding social network APIs. In essence, the SLRequest class allows iOS applications to interact directly with social network APIs through HTTP based requests.

90.3 **Accounts Framework**

The purpose of the Accounts Framework is to provide access to device based system accounts from within iOS applications. Using the Accounts framework, code can be written to access, create and validate social network accounts stored on iOS based devices.

The iOS 8 operating system running on iPhone and iPad devices is able to store multiple Twitter accounts but only one Facebook account at a time. These are accessible both from the device Settings application in addition to using the Accounts Framework within application code.

To manually view and configure Twitter accounts on a device, select the Settings application and choose the *Twitter* option. As illustrated in Figure 90-1, any pre-configured Twitter accounts will be listed together with a button providing the option to add a new Twitter account and switches providing control over which applications may be granted permission to access those Twitter accounts:

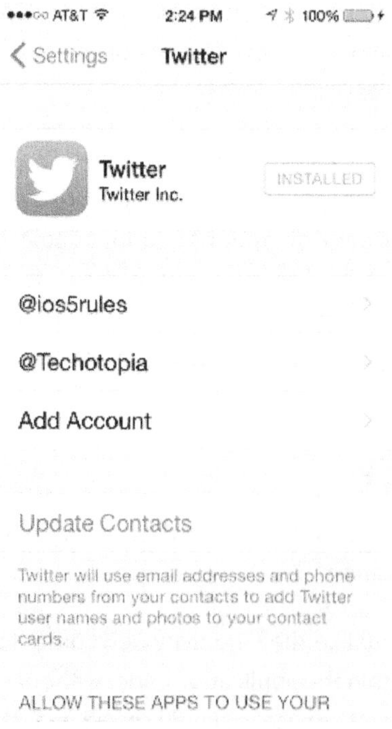

Figure 90-1

The current Facebook account settings on the device may, similarly, be viewed and modified by selecting the Facebook option of the main screen of the Settings application. Options are also provided on the Facebook settings panel to control which applications have access to the Facebook account, and to modify or delete the currently configured Facebook account.

When using the SLRequest class to construct API requests, it will be necessary to use the Accounts Framework to identify and request permission to use the corresponding social network accounts in an application. When using the UIActivityViewController or SLComposeViewController classes, however, the account handling is performed automatically by the class. The remainder of this chapter will focus on the UIActivityViewController and SLComposeViewController classes. The SLRequest class will be covered in detail in the chapter entitled *iOS 8 Facebook and Twitter Integration using SLRequest*.

90.4 **Using the UIActivityViewController Class**

The UIActivityViewController class is instantiated within an application at the point at which a posting is ready to be made to a social network. Once the user takes an action to post an update from within an application, the screen shown in Figure 90-2 will appear listing the options that are available:

Figure 90-2

Once a destination social network has been selected, the preview sheet for the chosen service (Figure 90-3 shows the sheet for a Facebook posting) will appear primed with the content of the update to be sent consisting of text and any optional image attachments. Having reviewed and, optionally, modified the post, the user may then send the message.

Figure 90-3

In the event that the user has not yet configured an account for the selected social network in the Settings application, a dialog will appear providing the option to either set up an account or cancel the post.

The assumption is generally made that at the point an instance of UIActivityViewController is created, the application will already have gathered together the text and images that are to be included in the post. These items need to be placed into an array object and passed to the controller before it is presented to the user. The following code excerpt, for example, instantiates a UIActivityViewController instance primed with text and an image to be included in the post and presents it to the user:

```
let postText = "Great to finally be here on vacation!"
let postImage = UIImage(named: "windsor_castle.jpg")
let activityItems = [postText, postImage]

let activityController = UIActivityViewController(activityItems:
                    activityItems, applicationActivities: nil)

self.presentViewController(activityController,
                    animated: true, completion: nil)
```

90.5 Using the SLComposeViewController Class

In order to use the SLComposeViewController class, a number of steps should be performed in sequence. Firstly, the application may optionally check to verify whether a message can be sent to the specified social network service. This essentially equates to checking if a valid social network account has been configured on the device and is achieved using the *isAvailableForServiceType* class method, passing through as an argument the type of service required from the following options:

- SLServiceTypeFacebook
- SLServiceTypeTwitter
- SLServiceTypeSinaWeibo

The following code, for example, verifies that the Twitter service is available to the application:

```
if SLComposeViewController.isAvailableForServiceType(
                                SLServiceTypeTwitter) {
     // Device is able to send a Twitter message
}
```

This method call is optional and, in the event that an account for the specified social network has yet to be set up, the composer will simply take the user to the device's *Settings* application where a Twitter account may be configured.

The next step is to create an instance of the SLComposeViewController class and supply an optional completion handler to be called when the composer screen is either cancelled by the user or used to send a message. Next, a range of methods may be called on the instance to initialize the object with the content of the message, including the initial text of the message, an image attachment and a URL:

- **setInitialText** - Sets the initial text of the message on the SLComposeViewController instance.
- **addImage** - Adds image files as attachments to the message.
- **addURL** - Adds a URL to the message. The method automatically handles the URL shortening.

Each of the above methods returns a Boolean result indicating whether the addition of content was successful.

Finally, when the message is ready to be presented to the user, the SLComposeViewController object is presented modally by calling the *presentViewController* method of the parent view controller.

The following code excerpt demonstrates the steps to create, configure and present a typical SLComposeViewController instance for posting to Facebook:

```
let composeController = SLComposeViewController(forServiceType:
                                SLServiceTypeFacebook)

composeController.setInitialText("Just found this great web site")
composeController.addImage(UIImage(named: "windsor_castle.jpg"))
composeController.addURL(NSURL(string: "http://www.ebookfrenzy.com"))

self.presentViewController(composeController,
                        animated: true, completion: nil)
```

Once called, this method will present the composer view to the user primed with any text, image and URL contents pre-configured via the method calls. Once displayed, the user has the option to modify the text of the message, cancel the message, add location data or send the message. If a completion handler has been configured it will be called and passed a value indicating the action that was taken by the user within the composer view. Possible values are:

- **SLComposeViewControllerResult.Cancelled** – The user cancelled the composition session by touching the *Cancel* button.
- **SLComposeViewControllerResult.Done** – The user sent the composed message by touching the *Send* button.

90.6 **Summary**

The iOS 8 SDK includes both the UIActivityViewController class and Social Framework, both of which may be used to integrate Twitter, Facebook and Sina Weibo functionality into iOS applications.

For general purpose requirements, both the UIActivityViewController and the SLComposeViewController classes provide an easy to implement path to social network integration. For more complex requirements, however, the SLRequest class may be used in conjunction with the Accounts Framework to access social network accounts and construct and submit HTTP requests to supported social network APIs. This chapter provided an overview of the UIActivityViewController and SLComposeViewController classes and outlined the steps necessary to deploy them in applications. The next chapter, entitled *An iOS 8 Facebook Integration Tutorial using UIActivityViewController* will work through the development of an example application using the UIActivityViewController class to implement Facebook integration into an iOS app. The concepts behind the SLRequest class will be covered in *iOS 8 Facebook and Twitter Integration using SLRequest*.

91. An iOS 8 Facebook Integration Tutorial using UIActivityViewController

With the basics of the Social Framework and UIActivityViewController class covered in the previous chapter, the goal of this chapter will be to create an example application designed to demonstrate the UIActivityViewController class in action. The end result will be an application designed to post status updates to the user's Facebook page, including text and an image.

91.1 Creating the Facebook Social App

Begin by launching Xcode and selecting the options to create a new iOS application based on the *Single View Application* template. Enter *SocialApp* as the product name and set the Device and Language menus to *Universal* and *Swift* respectively.

91.2 Designing the User Interface

Navigate to the *Main.storyboard* file in the project navigator panel and select it to load it into Interface Builder. Click on the background of the view object and change the background color to a light shade of grey using the Attributes Inspector panel.

Drag, position and configure a Text View, Image View and Toolbar onto the view canvas. Drag and drop an additional Bar Button Item onto the Toolbar and set the text on the two items so that the user interface reflects that illustrated in Figure 91-1:

Figure 91-1

Note that the sample Latin text has been removed from the text view object (select the object, display the Attributes Inspector and delete the contents assigned to the *Text* property).

Select the Image View object, display the Attributes Inspector and change the *Mode* setting to *Aspect Fit*. This will ensure that the aspect ratio of the image is preserved when displayed in the image view.

Select the Text View object, display the Auto Layout Pin menu and set *Spacing to nearest neighbor* constraints on all four sides of the view with the *Constrain to margins* option enabled. Select the Image View and repeat this step, this time also enabling the Height constraint on the view.

Finally, select the Toolbar view and set *Spacing to nearest neighbor* constraints of zero on the left, right and bottom edges of the view with the *Constrain to margins* option disabled.

91.3 Creating Outlets and Actions

In order to create the outlets and actions for the application we will, as always, make use of the Assistant Editor. First, select the Text View object and then display the Assistant Editor.

Make sure that the *ViewController.swift* file is displayed in the editor before Ctrl-clicking on the Text View object in the view and dragging the resulting line to the area immediately beneath the class declaration directive in the Assistant Editor panel. Upon releasing the line, the configuration panel will appear. Configure the connection as an *Outlet* named *postText* and click on the *Connect* button. Repeat the above steps to add an outlet for the Image View object named *postImage.*

The application will require three actions. One for each of the button objects and one for the background view that will be used to hide the keyboard when the user has finished entering text. Click on the *Select Image* button (noting that it may be necessary to click on it a second time since the first click will select the parent Toolbar view) and Ctrl-click and drag the resulting line to a position beneath the *viewDidLoad* method in the Assistant Editor. In the resulting configuration panel, change the *Connection* type to *Action* and name the method *selectImage*. Repeat this step to add an action for the *Post Message* button, this time naming the action *sendPost*.

Once the connections have been established, select the *ViewController.swift* file and further modify it to configure the class to act as an image picker delegate and to add some imports that will be required later in the tutorial:

```
import UIKit
import Social
import MobileCoreServices

class ViewController: UIViewController, UIImagePickerControllerDelegate,
UINavigationControllerDelegate {

    @IBOutlet weak var postText: UITextView!
    @IBOutlet weak var postImage: UIImageView!
```

91.4 Implementing the selectImage and Delegate Methods

The purpose of the *selectImage* action method is to provide the user with access to photos on the device and allow one to be selected for inclusion in the Facebook post. With these requirements in mind, select the *ViewController.swift* file, locate the *selectImage* stub added by the Assistant Editor and modify it as follows:

```
@IBAction func selectImage(sender: AnyObject) {
    let imagePicker = UIImagePickerController()
    imagePicker.delegate = self
    imagePicker.sourceType =
            UIImagePickerControllerSourceType.PhotoLibrary
    imagePicker.mediaTypes = [kUTTypeImage as NSString]
    imagePicker.allowsEditing = false
    self.presentViewController(imagePicker, animated: true,
            completion: nil)
}
```

Next, add the other image picker delegate methods so that the picker is dismissed when the user has made a selection:

```
func imagePickerController(picker: UIImagePickerController,
    didFinishPickingMediaWithInfo info: [NSObject : AnyObject]) {
    self.dismissViewControllerAnimated(true, completion: nil)
    let image = info[UIImagePickerControllerOriginalImage] as UIImage
    postImage.image = image
```

```
}

func imagePickerControllerDidCancel(picker:
        UIImagePickerController) {
    self.dismissViewControllerAnimated(true, completion: nil)
}
```

91.5 Hiding the Keyboard

When the user touches the view object in the background of the user interface, we need the keyboard to be removed from view. This will require that code be implemented in the *touchesBegan* method:

```
override func touchesBegan(touches: NSSet, withEvent event: UIEvent) {
    postText.endEditing(true)
}
```

91.6 Posting the Message to Facebook

All that remains is to implement the code to create a UIActivityViewController instance, prime it with the text and image entered by the user and then post the message to the user's Facebook page. These tasks are to be performed within the *sendPost* action method. Within the *ViewController.swift* file, locate the stub for this method and modify it as follows:

```
@IBAction func sendPost(sender: AnyObject) {

    var activityItems: [AnyObject]?
    let image = postImage.image

    if (postImage.image != nil) {
        activityItems = [postText.text, postImage.image!]
    } else {
        activityItems = [postText.text]
    }

    let activityController = UIActivityViewController(activityItems:
                activityItems!, applicationActivities: nil)
    self.presentViewController(activityController, animated: true,
                completion: nil)
}
```

The code simply creates an array of items to be included in the post (in this case the text entered by the user and an image in the event that one was selected), creates a UIActivityViewController instance initialized with that array and presents the controller to the user.

91.7 **Running the Social Application**

With the coding now complete, click on the run button in the Xcode toolbar to launch the application on a device or simulator. When the application appears, enter some text into the text area and select an image from the device. Touch the *Post Message* button to display the target selection screen shown in Figure 91-2:

Figure 91-2

Select the Facebook button to display the preview sheet (Figure 91-3) and then, assuming no changes to the post need to be made, touch the *Post* button to send the message to your Facebook page.

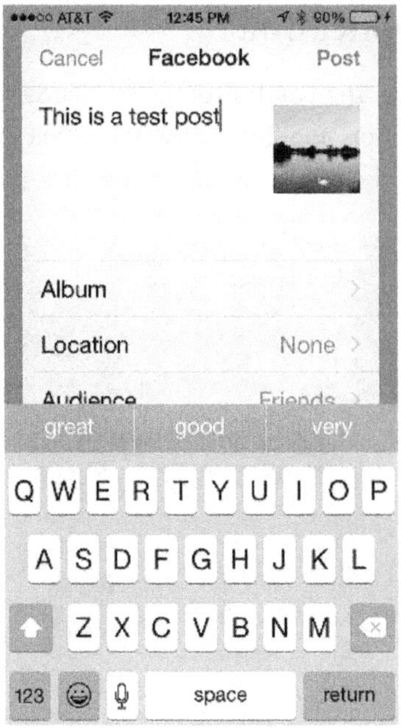

Figure 91-3

91.8 **Summary**

This chapter has worked through the creation of an example application that uses the UIActivityViewController class to post updates to the user's Facebook page. The next chapter will look in more detail at using both the Accounts and Social Frameworks to implement social network integration using the SLRequest class.

92. iOS 8 Facebook and Twitter Integration using SLRequest

Whilst the UIActivityViewController and SLComposeViewController classes provide a quick and easy way to integrate social network interaction into iOS applications, these classes lack the flexibility that might be required to implement more advanced integration. Perhaps the most significant shortcoming of these classes is the fact that they implement one-way communication with social networks. In other words, they can be used to post information to a social network, but do not provide a way to receive information, such as the entries in the timeline of a Twitter or Facebook account.

In recognition of this fact, Apple introduced the SLRequest class as part of the Social Framework included with iOS 7. Using the SLRequest class, in conjunction with the Accounts framework, it is possible to construct HTTP based requests and send them to the application programming interfaces (APIs) of Twitter, Facebook and Sina Weibo and receive data in response. This, in essence, allows an iOS application to perform just about any task allowed by the API of the respective social network service.

This chapter will provide an overview of the way in which the SLRequest class and the Accounts Framework interact to provide social media integration. Once these basics have been covered, the next chapter will work through the implementation of an example application that uses SLRequest to query the entries in a Twitter timeline.

92.1 Using SLRequest and the Account Framework

Both the SLRequest class and the Accounts Framework are required in order to interact with the API of a social network. Implementation follows a standard sequence of events which can be summarized as follows:

1. The application requests access to one of the user's social network accounts as configured in the Settings app. This is achieved via a call to the *requestAccessToAccountsWithType* method of the ACAccountStore class, passing through as an argument the type of social network for which access is being requested together with a range of options depending on the target service.

2. An SLRequest instance is created and initialized with the URL required by the service for interaction, the HTTP request type to be used (GET, POST etc) and any additional parameters required by the API of the service.

3. The *account object* created in step 1 above is assigned to the *account* property of the SLRequest object created in step 2.

4. The request is sent to the target social network service via a call to the *performRequestWithHandler* method of the SLRequest object. The results from the request are passed to the handler code together with an NSError object containing information about the reason for any failure.

92.2 **Twitter Integration using SLRequest**

Integration with the Twitter API begins with gaining access to an account, and is based on the assumption that at least one Twitter account has been configured via the Settings app on the device. Since iOS supports different social networks, the request must also include the type of social network for which access is being requested. This, in turn, is represented by an appropriately configured ACAccountType object.

The following code, for example, seeks access to the Twitter accounts configured on the device:

```
let account = ACAccountStore()
let accountType = account.accountTypeWithAccountTypeIdentifier(
            ACAccountTypeIdentifierTwitter)

account.requestAccessToAccountsWithType(accountType, options: nil,
    completion: {(success: Bool, error: NSError!) -> Void in

        if success {
                // Get account and communicate with Twitter API
        }
    })
```

In the event that access is granted, an array of Twitter accounts on the device can be obtained via a subsequent call to the *accountsWithAccountType* method of the account object used for the request. The required account may then be extracted from the array of accounts for use in constructing an SLRequest object. The following code accesses the array of accounts, selects the last account entry and assigns it to *twitterAccount*:

```
let account = ACAccountStore()
let accountType = account.accountTypeWithAccountTypeIdentifier(
            ACAccountTypeIdentifierTwitter)

account.requestAccessToAccountsWithType(accountType, options: nil,
        completion: {(success: Bool, error: NSError!) -> Void in

    if success {
        let arrayOfAccounts =
                account.accountsWithAccountType(accountType)
```

```
        if arrayOfAccounts.count > 0 {
            let twitterAccount = arrayOfAccounts.last as ACAccount
        }
    }
})
```

The next task is to request an SLRequest object for Twitter access. This is achieved via a call to the *requestForServiceType* class method of the SLRequest class, passing through the following values:

- The type of social network service for which the SLRequest will be used (in this case SLServiceTypeTwitter).
- The HTTP request method type (SLRequestMethodPOST, SLRequestMethodGET or SLRequestMethodDELETE).
- The URL required by the social network API for interaction.
- An NSDictionary object containing any parameters required by the social network API to complete the transaction.

The following code changes request an SLRequest instance configured for sending a Twitter update containing the text "My first post from iOS 8":

```
let account = ACAccountStore()
let accountType = account.accountTypeWithAccountTypeIdentifier(
            ACAccountTypeIdentifierTwitter)

account.requestAccessToAccountsWithType(accountType, options: nil,
        completion: {(success: Bool, error: NSError!) -> Void in

    if success {
        let arrayOfAccounts =
            account.accountsWithAccountType(accountType)

        if arrayOfAccounts.count > 0 {
            let twitterAccount = arrayOfAccounts.last as ACAccount
                let message = ["status" : "My first post from iOS 8"]
                let requestURL = NSURL(string:
                  "https://api.twitter.com/1.1/statuses/update.json")

                let postRequest = SLRequest(forServiceType:
                        SLServiceTypeTwitter,
                        requestMethod: SLRequestMethod.POST,
                        URL: requestURL,
                        parameters: message)
        }
```

```
        }
})
```

Finally, the account object needs to be assigned to the SLRequest object, and the request posted to the Twitter API:

```
let account = ACAccountStore()
let accountType = account.accountTypeWithAccountTypeIdentifier(
                    ACAccountTypeIdentifierTwitter)

account.requestAccessToAccountsWithType(accountType, options: nil,
        completion: {(success: Bool, error: NSError!) -> Void in

    if success {
        let arrayOfAccounts =
                account.accountsWithAccountType(accountType)

        if arrayOfAccounts.count > 0 {
            let twitterAccount = arrayOfAccounts.last as ACAccount
            let message = ["status" : "My first post from iOS 8"]
            let requestURL = NSURL(string:
                "https://api.twitter.com/1.1/statuses/update.json")
            let postRequest = SLRequest(forServiceType:
                    SLServiceTypeTwitter,
                    requestMethod: SLRequestMethod.POST,
                    URL: requestURL,
                    parameters: message)

        postRequest.account = twitterAccount

        postRequest.performRequestWithHandler({
                (responseData: NSData!,
                 urlResponse: NSHTTPURLResponse!,
                 error: NSError!) -> Void in

            if let err = error {
                println("Error : \(err.localizedDescription)")
            }
            println("Twitter HTTP response
\(urlResponse.statusCode)")
        })
        }
    }
})
```

For the purposes of this example, the handler for the *performRequestWithHandler* method simply outputs the HTTP response code for the request to the console.

The above coding example demonstrates the steps involved in posting an update to a Twitter account using SLRequest. In the next chapter, an example application will be created that requests entries from the timeline of a Twitter account and displays those results in the TableView object.

For more information about the Twitter API, refer to the online documentation at:

https://dev.twitter.com/docs

92.3 Facebook Integration using SLRequest

To all intents and purposes, the steps to integrate with Facebook are the same as those for accessing Twitter with one or two significant differences. Firstly, any iOS application requiring access to the Facebook API must first be registered in the Facebook developer portal (*http://developers.facebook.com*). Registration includes providing the iOS bundle ID of the application (as defined when the application was created in Xcode). Once registered, the app will be assigned a Facebook App ID key which must be referenced when seeking account access.

Additionally, the application may also declare the access permissions it requires whilst interacting with the API. A full list of permission options is available in the Facebook developer documentation online at:

https://developers.facebook.com/docs/authentication/permissions/

These permissions are declared using the ACFacebookPermission key. When defining permissions, the ACFacebookAudienceKey value must also be declared and set to one of the following values:

- ACFacebookAudienceEveryone
- ACFacebookAudienceFriends
- ACFacebookAudienceOnlyMe.

The following code demonstrates the steps involved in posting a message to the user's Facebook page:

```
var accountStore = ACAccountStore()
var accountType = accountStore.accountTypeWithAccountTypeIdentifier(
                    ACAccountTypeIdentifierFacebook)

var postingOptions = [ACFacebookAppIdKey:
        "<YOUR FACEBOOK APP ID KEY HERE>",
                ACFacebookPermissionsKey: ["email"],
                ACFacebookAudienceKey: ACFacebookAudienceFriends]

accountStore.requestAccessToAccountsWithType(accountType,
        options: postingOptions) {
```

```
    success, error in
    if success {

        var options = [ACFacebookAppIdKey:
                    "<YOUR FACEBOOK APP ID KEY HERE>",
                    ACFacebookPermissionsKey: ["publish_actions"],
                    ACFacebookAudienceKey: ACFacebookAudienceFriends]

        accountStore.requestAccessToAccountsWithType(accountType,
                    options: options) {
            success, error in
            if success {
                var accountsArray =
                    accountStore.accountsWithAccountType(accountType)

                if accountsArray.count > 0 {
                    var facebookAccount = accountsArray[0] as ACAccount

                    var parameters = Dictionary<String, AnyObject>()
                    parameters["access_token"] =
                        facebookAccount.credential.oauthToken
                    parameters["message"] = "My first Facebook post from
iOS 8"

                    var feedURL = NSURL(string:
                            "https://graph.facebook.com/me/feed")

                    let postRequest = SLRequest(forServiceType:
                        SLServiceTypeFacebook,
                        requestMethod: SLRequestMethod.POST,
                        URL: feedURL,
                        parameters: parameters)
                    postRequest.performRequestWithHandler(
                        {(responseData: NSData!,
                          urlResponse: NSHTTPURLResponse!,
                          error: NSError!) -> Void in
                                println("Twitter HTTP response
\(urlResponse.statusCode)")
                    })
                }
            } else {
                println("Access denied")
                println(error.localizedDescription)
            }
```

```
        }
    } else {
        println("Access denied")
        println(error.localizedDescription)
    }
}
```

When incorporated into an iOS application, the above code will cause a message to be posted to the user's Facebook account which reads "My first Facebook post from iOS 8".

Additional information on the Facebook API can be found online at:

https://developers.facebook.com/docs

92.4 **Summary**

Whilst the SLComposeViewController and UIActivityViewController classes provide an easy path to social network integration, they lack the flexibility and two-way communication needed by many applications. In order to gain greater flexibility in terms of integration, iOS includes the SLRequest class.

The goal of this chapter has been to provide a low level overview of the way in which the Accounts Framework and SLRequest class can be used together to access and interact with Twitter and Facebook accounts using the service APIs of those social networks.

93. An iOS 8 Twitter Integration Tutorial using SLRequest

Having covered much of the theory of using the Accounts Framework and SLRequest class to integrate social networks into iOS applications in the previous chapter, this chapter will put this theory into practice by creating an application to request and display the entries in the timeline of a Twitter account.

93.1 Creating the TwitterApp Project

Begin by launching Xcode and selecting the options to create a new iOS application based on the *Single View Application* template with the product name set to *TwitterApp*. Set the Devices menu to *Universal* and the Language menu to *Swift* before creating the new project.

93.2 Designing the User Interface

Navigate to the *Main.storyboard* file in the project navigator panel and select it to load it into the Interface Builder. From the Object Library panel, drag and drop a Table View component onto the view canvas and position it so that it fills the entire view space as shown in Figure 93-1. With the Table View selected in the storyboard canvas, use the Auto Layout Pin menu to configure *Spacing to nearest neighbor* constraints on all four sides of the view with the *Constrain to margins* option disabled.

Select the Table View object and display the Assistant Editor using *View -> Assistant Editor -> Show Assistant Editor* menu option and make sure that it is displaying the content of the *ViewController.swift* file. Ctrl-click on the Table View object in the view and drag the resulting line to the area immediately beneath the class declaration line in the Assistant Editor panel. Upon releasing the line, the connection panel will appear. Configure the connection as an *Outlet* named *tweetTableView* and click on the *Connect* button.

Figure 93-1

With the Table View still selected, display the Connections Inspector (*View -> Utilities -> Show Connections Inspector*). Click on the circle to the right of the *dataSource* outlet and drag the line to the *Twitter App View Controller* icon in the bar along the top of the view canvas as outlined in Figure 93-2:

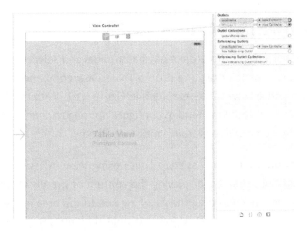

Figure 93-2

Repeat the steps to establish the same connection for the *delegate* outlet.

93.3 Modifying the View Controller Class

Before writing code to talk to the Twitter API, some additional frameworks need to be imported to avoid undefined symbols when we start working with the Accounts and SLRequest classes. In addition, an array is going to be needed to act as the data source for the application which will ultimately contain the tweets that are returned by the Twitter API. The compiler also needs to be notified that this class is acting as both the data source and delegate for the Table View.

Select the *ViewController.swift* file and modify it as follows:

```
import UIKit
import Social
import Accounts

class ViewController: UIViewController, UITableViewDataSource,
UITableViewDelegate {

    @IBOutlet weak var tweetTableView: UITableView!

    var dataSource = [AnyObject]()
.
.
.
```

93.4 Accessing the Twitter API

The code to access the Twitter account and extract the posts from the account timeline will reside in a method named *getTimeLine* located in the *ViewController.swift* file. Select this file and modify it to add the code for this new method:

```
func getTimeLine() {

    let account = ACAccountStore()
    let accountType = account.accountTypeWithAccountTypeIdentifier(
            ACAccountTypeIdentifierTwitter)

    account.requestAccessToAccountsWithType(accountType, options: nil,
            completion: {(success: Bool, error: NSError!) -> Void in

        if success {
            let arrayOfAccounts =
                account.accountsWithAccountType(accountType)

            if arrayOfAccounts.count > 0 {
                let twitterAccount = arrayOfAccounts.last as ACAccount

                let requestURL = NSURL(string:
        "https://api.twitter.com/1.1/statuses/user_timeline.json")

                let parameters = ["screen_name" : "@techotopia",
                    "include_rts" : "0",
                    "trim_user" : "1",
```

```
                        "count" : "20"]

            let postRequest = SLRequest(forServiceType:
                    SLServiceTypeTwitter,
                    requestMethod: SLRequestMethod.GET,
                    URL: requestURL,
                    parameters: parameters)

            postRequest.account = twitterAccount

            postRequest.performRequestWithHandler(
                    {(responseData: NSData!,
                        urlResponse: NSHTTPURLResponse!,
                        error: NSError!) -> Void in
                    var err: NSError?
                    self.dataSource =
NSJSONSerialization.JSONObjectWithData(responseData, options:
NSJSONReadingOptions.MutableLeaves, error: &err) as [AnyObject]

                    if self.dataSource.count != 0 {
                        dispatch_async(dispatch_get_main_queue()) {
                            self.tweetTableView.reloadData()
                        }
                    }
            })
        }
    } else {
        println("Failed to access account")
        }
    })
}
```

Much of the code in this method will be familiar from the previous chapter. There are, however, some notable exceptions. First, the URL used in the request is intended to return the entries in the time line for a specific user's Twitter account:

```
let requestURL = NSURL(string:
        "https://api.twitter.com/1.1/statuses/user_timeline.json")
```

The URL specified requires additional parameters specifying the Twitter user's screen name and how much data is to be returned. In this case the request is limited to the 20 most recent posts and configured to include the tweet entities for a user with the screen name @techotopia:

```
let parameters = ["screen_name" : "@techotopia",
```

```
              "include_rts" : "0",
              "trim_user" : "1",
              "count" : "20"]
```

The SLRequest object is primed to use the *SLRequestMethod.GET* HTTP request method. This is appropriate since this time we are *getting*, as opposed to *posting*, data:

```
let postRequest = SLRequest(forServiceType:
                       SLServiceTypeTwitter,
                       requestMethod: SLRequestMethod.GET,
                       URL: requestURL,
                       parameters: parameters)
```

Finally, the handler code for the *postRequest* method call now accesses the returned NSData object. The NSJSONSerialization class is then used to parse and serialize the data returned and assign it to the dataSource NSArray object. The Table View object is then told to reload the data it is displaying, causing it to re-read the data in the dataSource array and display it to the user. An important point to note here is that iOS performs the Twitter API request in a different thread from the main thread of the application. Threads are the cornerstone of any multitasking operating system and can be thought of as mini-processes running within a main process, the purpose of which is to enable at least the appearance of parallel execution paths within applications.

Since user interface updates take place in the main thread of the application, code has been added to ensure that the Table View reload call is made in the main thread as opposed to the thread used for the post request:

```
postRequest.performRequestWithHandler(
        {(responseData: NSData!,
          urlResponse: NSHTTPURLResponse!,
          error: NSError!) -> Void in

     var err: NSError?
     self.dataSource =
             NSJSONSerialization.JSONObjectWithData(responseData,
                     options: NSJSONReadingOptions.MutableLeaves,
                         error: &err) as [AnyObject]

     if self.dataSource.count != 0 {
         dispatch_async(dispatch_get_main_queue()) {
             self.tweetTableView.reloadData()
         }
     }
  })
```

All that remains is to implement the delegate methods for the Table View so that the tweets are displayed to the user.

93.5 Calling the getTimeLine Method

Having implemented the *getTimeLine* method we need to make sure it gets called when the application is launched. This involves the addition of a method call to the *viewDidLoad* method located in the *ViewController.swift* file. Now is also an opportune time to register the identifier of the table view cell that will be used to display the tweets:

```
override func viewDidLoad() {
    super.viewDidLoad()
    self.tweetTableView.registerClass(UITableViewCell.self,
            forCellReuseIdentifier: "Cell")
    self.getTimeLine()
}
```

93.6 The Table View Delegate Methods

At a minimum, the delegate for a Table View must implement the *numberOfRowsInSection* and *cellForRowAtIndexPath* delegate methods. In terms of this example application, the former simply needs to return the number of items in the dataSource array. Remaining within the *ViewController.swift* file, therefore, implement this method as follows:

```
func tableView(tableView: UITableView, numberOfRowsInSection section:
Int) -> Int {
    return dataSource.count
}
```

The *cellForRowAtIndexPath* method, on the other hand, needs to extract the text of the tweet corresponding to the current table row from the dataSource array and assign it to the table cell. Since each tweet is stored in the array in the form of an NSDictionary object, the tweet object first needs to be extracted and then the entry matching the "text" key in the dictionary used to access the text:

```
func tableView(tableView: UITableView, cellForRowAtIndexPath indexPath:
NSIndexPath) -> UITableViewCell {

    let cell =
        self.tweetTableView.dequeueReusableCellWithIdentifier("Cell")
                as UITableViewCell
    let row = indexPath.row
    let tweet = self.dataSource[row] as NSDictionary
    cell.textLabel.text = tweet.objectForKey("text") as NSString
    cell.textLabel.numberOfLines = 0
    return cell
}
```

An additional point to note in the above method is the line which assigns a zero value to the *numberOfLines* property cell UILabel instance object. This ensures that the tweet text is displayed using line wrapping in the event that the tweet is longer than the width of the cell by informing the label that it can use as many lines as needed to display the text.

93.7 **Building and Running the Application**

Click on the run button located in the Xcode toolbar and wait for the application to launch. The application will then display the 20 most recent tweets posted to the specified account.

Figure 93-3

93.8 **Summary**

In addition to posting entries, the SLRequest class can be used to retrieve information from supported social networks. In this chapter, a list of tweets posted to a Twitter account have been requested using the SLRequest class and displayed to the user within a Table View. The example also introduced the use of the NSJSONSerialization class to serialize the data returned from a Twitter API request.

Chapter 94

94. Making Store Purchases with the SKStoreProductViewController Class

For quite some time, the iOS SDK has included the Store Kit Framework, the purpose of which is to enable applications to implement what are referred to as "in-app purchases". This typically provides a mechanism for application developers to charge users for additional items and services over and above the initial purchase price of the application. Typical examples include purchasing access to higher levels in a game or a monthly subscription to premium content.

The Store Kit Framework has also traditionally provided the ability to enable users to purchase items from Apple's iTunes, App and iBook stores. Prior to the introduction of iOS 6, the Store Kit Framework took the user out of the current application and into the iTunes application to initiate and complete an iTunes Store purchase. iOS 6, however, introduced a view controller class (SKStoreProductViewController) which presents the store product directly within the application using a pre-configured view.

This chapter will provide an overview of the SKStoreProductViewController class before working through an example implementation of this class in an iOS application.

94.1 The SKStoreProductViewController Class

The SKStoreProductViewController class makes it possible to integrate purchasing from Apple's iTunes, App and iBooks stores directly into iOS applications with minimal coding work. The developer of a music review application, might, for example want to provide the user with the option to purchase an album from iTunes after reading a review in the application. The developer of multiple applications may want to encourage users of one of those applications to purchase related applications.

All that is required to implement the SKStoreProductViewController functionality is to initialize an instance of the class with an item ID for the product to be purchased from the store and then to load the product details. Once product details have been loaded, the view controller is presented to the user.

Product item IDs can be obtained a number of ways. For specific items, the ID can be obtained by locating the product in iTunes and Ctrl-clicking (or right-clicking on Windows) on the product image. In the resulting menu, select the option to copy the URL. Paste the URL into a text editor and extract the ID from the end. The ID from the following URL, for example, is 527049179.

http://itunes.apple.com/us/movie/the-pirates!-band-of-misfits/id527049179

Alternatively, searches may be performed on a variety of criteria using the Apple Search API, details of which can be found at the following URL:

http://www.apple.com/itunes/affiliates/resources/documentation/itunes-store-web-service-search-api.html

When the user has finished in the store view, a delegate method is called to notify the application, at which point the store view controller can be dismissed.

The remainder of this chapter will work through the creation of a simple example application to demonstrate the use and implementation of the SKStoreProductViewController class.

94.2 Creating the Example Project

The example application created in this chapter will consist of a single button which, when touched, will display the store kit view controller primed with a specified product.

Launch Xcode and create a new project by selecting the options to create a new iOS application based on the *Single View Application* template. Enter *StoreKitDemo* as the product name, choose Swift as the programming language and set the Devices menu to *Universal*.

94.3 Creating the User Interface

Within the project navigator panel, select the *Main.storyboard* file and drag and drop a Button from the Object Library to the center of the view. Double click on the button text and change it to "Buy Now" so that the layout matches Figure 94-1. With the Button view selected, display the Auto Layout Align menu and enable the horizontal and vertical *Center in Container* constraints.

Display the Assistant Editor and make sure it is showing the code for the *ViewController.swift* file. Select the button in the view and then Ctrl-click on it and drag the resulting line to a location just beneath the *viewDidLoad* method in the Assistant Editor panel. Release the line and in the resulting panel change the connection type to *Action* and name the method *showStoreView*. Click on the *Connect* button and close the Assistant Editor panel.

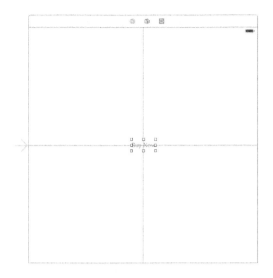

Figure 94-1

94.4 Displaying the Store Kit Product View Controller

When the user touches the *Buy Now* button, the SKStoreProductViewController instance needs to be created, configured and displayed. Before writing this code, however, it will be necessary to declare the StoreKitDemoViewController class as implementing the SKStoreProductViewControllerDelegate protocol. The StoreKit framework also needs to be imported. Both of these tasks need to be performed in the *ViewController.swift* file which should be modified to read as follows:

```
import UIKit
import StoreKit

class ViewController: UIViewController,
        SKStoreProductViewControllerDelegate {
.
.
.
```

Remaining within the *ViewController.swift* file, locate the stub *showStoreView* method and implement the code as outlined in the following listing:

```
@IBAction func showStoreView(sender: AnyObject) {
    let storeViewController = SKStoreProductViewController()
    storeViewController.delegate = self

    let parameters = [SKStoreProductParameterITunesItemIdentifier :
                    NSNumber(integer: 676059878)]
```

```
storeViewController.loadProductWithParameters(parameters,
        completionBlock: {result, error in
    if result {
        self.presentViewController(storeViewController,
                animated: true, completion: nil)
    }

})
}
```

The code begins by creating and initializing a new SKStoreProductViewController instance:

```
let storeViewController = SKStoreProductViewController()
```

Next, the view controller class assigns itself as the delegate for the storeViewController instance:

```
storeViewController.delegate = self
```

A Dictionary is then created and initialized with a key of *SKStoreProductParameterITunesItemIdentifier* associated with an NSNumber value representing a product in a Store (in this case an album in the iTunes store).

```
let parameters = [SKStoreProductParameterITunesItemIdentifier :
                NSNumber(integer: 676059878)]
```

Finally, the product is loaded into the view controller and, in the event that the load was successful, the view controller is presented to the user:

```
storeViewController.loadProductWithParameters(parameters,
        completionBlock: {result, error in
    if result {
        self.presentViewController(storeViewController,
                animated: true, completion: nil)
    }

})
```

94.5 Implementing the Delegate Method

All that remains is to implement the delegate method that will be called when the user has either completed or cancelled the product purchase. Since the StoreKitDemoViewController class was designated as the delegate for the SKStoreProductViewController instance, the method needs to be implemented in the *ViewController.swift* file:

```
func productViewControllerDidFinish(viewController:
        SKStoreProductViewController!) {
```

```
viewController.dismissViewControllerAnimated(true,
                    completion: nil)
}
```

For the purposes of this example, all the method needs to do is to tell the view controller to dismiss itself.

94.6 Testing the Application

Build and run the application on a physical iOS device. Touch the button and wait until the store kit product view controller appears as illustrated in Figure 94-2. Note that there may be a short delay while the store kit contacts the iTunes store to request and download the product information.

Touching the *Cancel* button should trigger the delegate, dismissing the view controller and returning the user to the original view controller screen containing the button.

Figure 94-2

94.7 Summary

The SKStoreProductViewController class provides an easy and visually appealing interface for allowing Apple-based store purchases such as movies, books, music and apps to be made directly from within an iOS application. As demonstrated, this functionality can be added to an application with a minimal amount of code.

95. Building In-App Purchasing into iOS 8 Applications

The previous chapter explored the mechanism for allowing users to purchase items from Apple's iTunes, App and iBooks stores from within an application. A far more common requirement for application developers, however, is the need to generate revenue by charging users to unlock additional functionality or to gain access to some form of premium content. This is a concept referred to as "In-App Purchase" (IAP) and is made possible by a collection of classes within the Store Kit Framework combined with settings configured using the iTunes Connect web portal.

Whilst in-app purchasing has been available for a while, iOS 6 introduced the option to host content associated with purchases on Apple's own servers.

95.1 In-App Purchase Options

In-app purchase allows digital or virtual items to be purchased from within applications. These typically take the form of additional content (such as an eBook or digital magazine edition), access to more advanced levels in a game or the ability to buy virtual goods or property (such as crop seeds in a farming game).

Purchases fall into the categories of *consumable* (the item must be purchased each time it is required by the user such as virtual currency in a game), *non-consumable* (only needs to be purchased once by the user such as content access) and *subscription* based.

In the case of subscription based purchases, these can be *non-renewing* (item remains active for a specified amount of time), *auto-renewing* (the subscription is renewed automatically at specified intervals until cancelled by the user) or *free subscription* based (allowing free access to content for Newsstand based applications).

Non-consumable and auto-renewable purchases should be configured such that they can be restored, at the request of the user, on any of the user's iOS devices.

The item purchased by the user can either be *built-in* or *server* based. The term "built-in" refers to content or functionality that is already present in the application, but currently locked in some way. Once the purchase has been made, the functionality is unlocked. Server based purchases involve downloading of the item from a remote server. This might, for example, be a new background image for a game or a file containing additional content, hosted either on the developer's own server or placed on an Apple hosted server (a concept referred to as *App Store hosted content*).

95.2 Uploading App Store Hosted Content

In the event that a purchase involves the download of additional content hosted on the App Store, this content must first be uploaded. The files containing the content are placed in a structured folder. The root level of the folder must contain a *ContentInfo.plist* XML file that contains two keys:

- **ContentVersion** – The version number of the content.
- **IAPProductIdentifier** – The product identifier of the product with which the content is associated.

The actual content files must be placed in a subfolder named *Contents*.

In practice, much of the work involved in packaging and uploading content can be performed using either Xcode or the Application Loader tool as outlined in the chapter entitled *Configuring and Creating App Store Hosted Content for iOS 8 In-App Purchases*.

95.3 Configuring In-App Purchase Items

The application developer is responsible for defining the products that are available for purchase. This involves assigning product identifiers, descriptions and pricing to each item and is performed using iTunes Connect.

95.4 Sending a Product Request

When the user needs to purchase one or more items, the application uses the Store Kit Framework to send a product request. The request is packaged in the form of an SKProductRequest object configured with product identifiers of one or more items to be purchased. The application should also check whether or not the user has used the Settings app to disable in-app purchases on the device before initiating the purchase:

```
if SKPaymentQueue.canMakePayments() {
    let request = SKProductsRequest(productIdentifiers:
                NSSet(objects: "com.ebookfrenzy.consumable"))
    request.delegate = self
    request.start()
} else {
    // Tell user that In-App Purchase is disabled in Settings
}
```

When the App Store has located and returned the product information, the Store Kit Framework calls the application's *didReceiveResponse* delegate method passing it an object of type SKProductsResponse. This object contains an SKProduct object for each product that matched the request, along with a list of any product items for which a match could not be found in the store. If, on the other hand, the Store Kit was unable to contact the App Store, the *didFailWithError* delegate method will be called to notify the application:

```
func productsRequest(request: SKProductsRequest!, didReceiveResponse
response: SKProductsResponse!) {

    var products = response.products

    if (products.count != 0) {
        // Display the a "buy product" screen containing details
        // from product object
    }

    products = response.invalidProductIdentifiers

    for product in products
    {
        // Handle invalid product IDs if required
    }
}
```

Each SKProduct object will contain product information (name, description and price) and a Boolean property indicating whether the product has associated with it downloadable content hosted on the App Store.

There is no SKStoreProductViewController equivalent for in-app purchasing. It is the responsibility of the application, therefore, to create and display a view where the user can review the product details (which should be extracted from the SKProduct object rather than hard coded into the application code) and initiate or cancel the purchase.

95.5 Accessing the Payment Queue

In order to process the purchase in the event that the user decides to buy the product, it will be necessary for the application to place requests on the application's *payment queue*. The SKPaymentQueue instance is not an object that is created by the application, but rather an existing object on which the application makes method calls. One such method call must be made in order to assign a *transaction observer object* to the queue:

```
SKPaymentQueue.defaultQueue().addTransactionObserver(self)
```

Since the payment queue continues to process requests independently of the application (and even in the event that the application exits) it is recommended that access to the payment queue and transaction observer object assignment takes place when the application is first launched. This will ensure that the application will be notified immediately of any payment transactions that were completed after the application last exited.

95.6 **The Transaction Observer Object**

The transaction observer object assigned to the payment queue can be an instance of any class within the application that implements the SKPaymentTransactionObserver protocol. Compliance with the protocol involves, at a minimum, implementing the *updatedTransactions* method. If the application is required to download App Store hosted content, the *updatedDownloads* method also needs to be implemented.

In the event that downloads are to be performed, the *updatedDownloads* method will be called at regular intervals, providing status updates on the download progress.

95.7 **Initiating the Purchase**

In order to process the purchase, the application creates a payment request in the form of an SKPayment object containing the matching SKProduct object for the item (this is usually just a case of using the object passed through to the *productsRequest* method). The payment request is then placed into the SKPaymentQueue which is then responsible for communicating with the App Store to process the purchase.

```
let payment = SKPayment(product: product)
SKPaymentQueue.defaultQueue().addPayment(payment)
```

95.8 **The Transaction Process**

The payment queue will call the *updatedTransactions* method on the observer object when the purchase is complete, passing through as an argument an array of SKPaymentTransaction objects (one for each item purchased). The method will need to check the *transactionState* property of each transaction object to verify the success or otherwise of the payment and, in the event of a successful transaction, either download or unlock the purchased content or feature.

Each SKPaymentTransaction object contains a *downloads* property. This is an array containing an entry for each content package hosted on the App Store server that needs to be downloaded as part of the purchase. In the event that the purchase requires content downloads, these downloads can be initiated via a call to the *startDownloads* method of the SKPaymentQueue instance.

```
func paymentQueue(queue: SKPaymentQueue!, updatedTransactions
transactions: [AnyObject]!) {

    for transaction in transactions as [SKPaymentTransaction] {

        switch transaction.transactionState {

            case SKPaymentTransactionState.Purchased:
                if (transaction.downloads != nil) {
                    SKPaymentQueue.defaultQueue().startDownloads(
                        transaction.downloads)
                } else {
```

```
                    // Unlock feature or content here before
                    // finishing transaction
                    SKPaymentQueue.defaultQueue().finishTransaction(
                            transaction)
            }

        case SKPaymentTransactionState.Failed:
            SKPaymentQueue.defaultQueue().finishTransaction(
                            transaction)

        default:
            break
        }
    }
}
```

Once started, the system will perform any necessary downloads in the background. As the download progresses, the *updatedDownloads* method of the observer object will be called at regular intervals. Each time the method is called, it will be passed an array of SKDownload objects (one for each download currently in progress) containing information such as download progress, estimated time to completion and state.

Download state can be one of a number of values including active, waiting, finished, failed, paused or cancelled. When the download is completed, the file URL of the downloaded file is accessible via the *contentURL* property of the SKDownload object. At this point, the file is in temporary cache so should be moved to a permanent location (such as the Documents directory).

```
func paymentQueue(queue: SKPaymentQueue!, updatedDownloads downloads:
[AnyObject]!) {

    for download in downloads as [SKDownload]
    {
        switch download.downloadState {
            case SKDownloadState.Active:
                println("Download progress \(download.progress)")
                println("Download time = \(download.timeRemaining)")
                break
            case SKDownloadState.Finished:
                // Download is complete. Content file URL is at
                // path referenced by download.contentURL. Move
                // it somewhere safe, unpack it and give the user
                // access to it
                 break
            default:
                break
```

```
            }
        }

    }
```

Finally, for each transaction returned by the payment queue, and after the purchased feature or content access has been granted to the user, the application must call the queue's *finishTransaction* method in order to complete the transaction. In the case of content downloads, any downloaded files must be moved from temporary cache to a safe location before this method call is made.

The hosted content package is downloaded in the form of a Zip file which may then be unpacked using one of a variety of freely available source code packages for iOS. One such package is SSZipArchive, details of which can be found at:

https://github.com/samsoffes/ssziparchive

95.9 **Transaction Restoration Process**

As previously mentioned, purchases that fall into the categories of non-consumable or auto-renewable subscription should be made available on any other iOS devices on which the user has installed the corresponding application. This can be achieved using the transaction restoration feature of the Store Kit Framework.

In order to restore transactions, the application makes a call to the *restoreCompletedTransactions* method of the payment queue. The queue will then contact the App Store and return to the application (via the observer object) an array of SKPaymentTransaction objects for any previous purchases. Each object will contain a copy of the original transaction object which is accessible via the *originalTransaction* property. This may then be used to reactivate the purchase within the application and, if appropriate, download any associated content files hosted on the App Store.

It is important to be aware that restoration should not be performed automatically at application launch time. This should, instead, be implemented by providing the user with an option within the application to restore previous purchases.

95.10 **Testing In-App Purchases**

Clearly it would be less than ideal if the only way to test in-app purchasing was to spend real money to purchase the items. Fortunately, Apple provides what it calls a "sandbox" environment via which purchasing can be tested without spending any money.

By default, applications signed with a development certificate will automatically connect to the sandbox when purchases are made.

In order for the sandbox to be operable, it is necessary to create a test user using iTunes Connect and set up the products that are to be made available for in-app purchase.

95.11 **Summary**

In-app purchases present the application developer with additional sources of revenue by charging the user for content or to unlock additional features from within an application. In-app purchases can be consumable, non-consumable or subscription-based.

The item purchased by the user can be built-in, in that the functionality is unlocked internally within the application, or server based, whereby content is downloaded from a server. In terms of server based purchases, Apple provides the option to host the content on Apple's own servers.

96. Preparing an iOS 8 Application for In-App Purchases

The previous chapter provided an overview of the mechanism by which in-app purchasing can be implemented within iOS applications. The next few chapters will take this knowledge and put it into practice by working through the creation of an example application containing locked content that can only be accessed by the user after making an in-app purchase.

An important part of supporting in-app purchases occurs before any code is written and is the topic of this chapter. These steps involve the creation of an App ID with in-app purchases enabled, configuration of code signing within Xcode and the use of iTunes Connect to create a test user, application and in-app purchase item. Once these steps have been outlined, the next chapter, entitled *An iOS 8 In-App Purchase Tutorial*, will focus on the application development process.

96.1 About the Example Application

The example application created in this chapter will simulate the requirements of a fictitious, multi-level game whereby the user is provided with access to level 1 when the game is first installed, but must make an in-app purchase to unlock access to a second level.

For ease of testing, the in-app purchase must be performed each time the application runs. In a real world situation, however, a purchase of this type would be considered to be a non-consumable purchase and the application would need to check at startup whether the purchase had been made and unlock the premium level appropriately.

96.2 Creating the Xcode Project

Launch Xcode and create a new project based on the *Single View Application* template. Enter *InAppDemo* as the product name and set the Devices and Language menus to *Universal* and *Swift* respectively.

96.3 Registering and Enabling the App ID for In App Purchasing

In order to use in-app purchases, an application must be associated with an *explicit* App ID rather than a wildcard ID. For example, *com.ebookfrenzy.MyApp* is a valid App ID for in-app purchase, whilst *com.ebookfrenzy.** is not. In addition, the App ID must have In-App Purchase support enabled.

To register the application's explicit App ID with the iOS provisioning portal and enable In-App Purchasing for that ID, load the project into Xcode and select the application name target from the top of the project navigator panel. From the resulting project settings panel, select the *Capabilities* tab and locate and switch on *In-App Purchase* support as outlined in Figure 96-1, selecting a Development Team to use for the provisioning profile if prompted to do so:

Figure 96-1

96.4 **Configuring the Application in iTunes Connect**

Enrollment in the Apple Developer program automatically results in the creation of an iTunes Connect account using the same login credentials. iTunes Connect is a web portal where developers enter tax and payment information, input details about applications and track the status of those applications in terms of sales and revenues.

Access iTunes Connect by navigating to *http://itunesconnect.apple.com* in a web browser and entering your Apple Developer program login and password details.

First time users should click on the *Contracts, Taxes and Banking* link and work through the various tasks to accept Apple's terms and conditions and to input appropriate tax and banking information for the receipt of sales revenue. Failure to complete these steps in advance may prevent in-app purchases from working.

In order to test in-app purchases using the sandbox feature, it is first necessary to create a test user account. These are the account details that will be entered on the device when testing in-app purchases. Within iTunes Connect, click on the *Users and Roles* option. On the Users and Roles screen, select the *Sandbox Testers* category then click on the blue + button to add a new test user. When prompted, enter the credentials for the test user, taking care not to try to use an email address already associated with an active iTunes account.

Once the administrative tasks are complete, select the *My Apps* option followed by the blue + button to add a new iOS app. Provide an App Name (this must be a name that has not been used by another developer so may involve some trial and error) and a SKU Number (which can be any sequence of characters involving letters, numbers, hyphens, underscores and periods). From the Bundle ID menu, select the *InAppDemo* Xcode iOS App ID bundle created previously. Once the information has been entered, click on the *Create* button to add the app to the portal.

96.5 **Creating an In-App Purchase Item**

With the application configured, the next step is to add an in-app purchase item to it. Within iTunes Connect, select the newly created app from the *My Apps* screen and click on the *In-App Purchases* option. In the resulting screen, select the *Create New* button. From the list of in-app purchase types, select the *Non-consumable* option to move to the *In-App Summary* screen where the following information will be required:

- **Reference Name** – The name by which the item will be listed in iTunes Connect and in sales reports.
- **Product ID** – The unique product ID for the item. This is usually constructed using the bundle identifier of the application with which the purchase is associated and must be unique. Make a note of the product ID you enter as it will be needed later in the example.
- **Price and Availability** – The price of the item and whether the item is available for sale. For this tutorial, set the *Price Tier* to 1 and *Cleared for Sale* to *true.*
- **In-App Purchase Details** – For each language the application is required to support, enter a Display Name and a Description for the item. Whatever you enter here will appear in the application later when the user is prompted to make an in-app purchase.
- **Hosting Content with Apple** – Indicates whether or not content will be hosted on Apple's servers for this purchase. For this example no content will be stored.

Once the settings have been configured, click on the *Save* button. Upon returning to the in-app purchases list, the new purchase item should be listed as *Waiting for Screenshot* and we are ready to start developing the application in the next chapter.

96.6 **Summary**

Before any code is written for the application, a number of important steps must first be performed in order to support in-app purchases. This includes creating an appropriately configured App ID for the application. The iTunes Connect portal is then used to create a test account for testing of purchases, an entry in the App Store for the application and to declare and create items for the user to purchase. All of these steps are important and, if not completed accurately, can lead to problems occurring in the purchasing process.

97. An iOS 8 In-App Purchase Tutorial

This chapter assumes that the steps outlined in the previous chapter (*Preparing an iOS 8 Application for In-App Purchases*) have been followed and implemented carefully. This chapter will continue the development of the *InAppDemo* project to demonstrate the application side of in-app purchasing.

97.1 The Application User Interface

When completed, the application will consist of three views (Figure 97-1). The goal is for the Level 2 view to be inaccessible from the Level 1 view until the user has made an in-app purchase using the product purchase view:

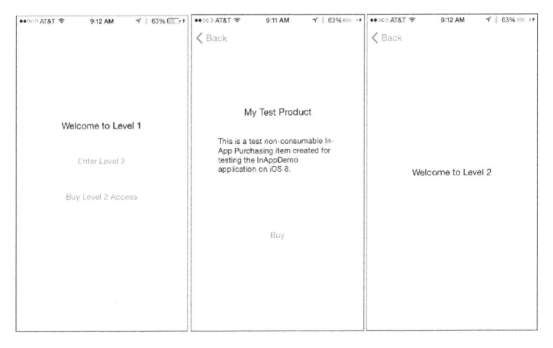

Figure 97-1

97.2 **Designing the Storyboard**

Load the *InAppDemo* project into Xcode, select the *Main.storyboard* file, select the View Controller scene and choose the *Editor -> Embed In -> Navigation Controller* menu option to add a navigation controller to the storyboard.

Next, design the user interface for the Level 1 screen as illustrated in the far left view of Figure 97-1. Using the Assistant Editor with the *ViewController.swift* file selected, establish an *Outlet* connection for the "Enter Level 2" button named *level2Button*.

Select all the views in the storyboard and use the Auto Layout Align menu to configure *Horizontal Center in Container* constraints for the three objects. Select the uppermost label and use the Pin menu to establish a *Spacing to nearest neighbor* constraint in the top edge of the view. Repeat this step for the two buttons.

Add another scene to the storyboard by dragging and dropping a View Controller object from the Object Library onto the canvas. Add a label to the view of the new scene and change the label's text to "Welcome to Level 2". With the label selected, use the Auto Layout Align menu to enable horizontal and vertical *Center in Container* constraints for the view.

Establish a segue from the "Enter Level 2" button to the Level 2 scene by Ctrl-clicking and dragging from the button to the new scene. Release the line and select *show* from the resulting menu.

Select the "Enter Level 2" button, display the Attributes Inspector and turn off the *Enabled* checkbox in the *Control* section. This will ensure that the button is disabled until the user has purchased access to level 2.

Finally, drag and drop a third View Controller onto the storyboard canvas to represent the purchasing screen. Ctrl-click on the *Buy Level 2 Access* button and drag to the newly added view controller. On releasing the line, select *show* from the resulting menu.

The storyboard should appear as shown in Figure 97-2.

Figure 97-2

97.3 **Creating the Purchase View Controller Class**

Select *File -> New -> File...* and create a new iOS *Cocoa Touch Class* named *PurchaseViewController* subclassed from UIViewController with the *Also create XIB file* option deselected.

Within the *Main.storyboard* file, select the blank view controller scene, display the *Identity Inspector* and change the class of the View Controller to the newly created *PurchaseViewController* class.

With the PurchaseViewController scene selected in the storyboard canvas, add a Label, Text View and Button to the layout and configure the user interface design so that it resembles that of Figure 97-3:

Figure 97-3

Ctrl-click on each of the three views so that all are selected and use the Auto Layout Align menu to add *Horizontal Center in Container* constraints to all of the views. Select the Label view and use the Pin menu to add a *Spacing to nearest neighbor* constraint on the top edge using the current value. Repeat this step for the Text View and Button view.

Select the Text View, display the Auto Layout Pin menu and set both Height and Width constraints using the current values.

Finally, remove the sample Latin text from the Text View object using the Attributes Inspector.

Using the Assistant Editor with the *PurchaseViewController.swift* file selected, establish outlets for the Label, Text View and Button named *productTitle, productDescription* and *buyButton* respectively.

Next, establish an Action connection from the Buy button to a method named *buyProduct*.

Remaining within the *PurchaseViewController.swift* file, verify the outlets and action are correctly implemented, then add additional properties and declarations that will be needed later in the chapter (*<YOUR PRODUCT ID GOES HERE>* is replaced by the identifier for the In App Purchase product created using the iTunes Connect portal in the previous chapter):

```
import UIKit
import StoreKit

class PurchaseViewController: UIViewController,
SKPaymentTransactionObserver, SKProductsRequestDelegate {
```

```
@IBOutlet weak var productTitle: UILabel!
@IBOutlet weak var productDescription: UITextView!
@IBOutlet weak var buyButton: UIButton!

var product: SKProduct?
var productID = "<YOUR PRODUCT ID GOES HERE>"
```

.
.
.

Note that purchase attempts will fail if the product ID specified does not match that defined for the in-app purchase item created using iTunes Connect.

The class is also going to act as the transaction observer and products request delegate so this fact is declared. Properties have been added to allow the class to keep track of the product ID and SKProduct object.

97.4 Storing the Home View Controller in the App Delegate Class

The PurchaseViewController class is responsible for handling the purchase of access to the level 2 scene within the application. As such, it will be the responsibility of the PurchaseViewController to enable the *Enter Level 2* button in the first view controller when a purchase has been completed. This will be achieved by making a call to a method in the first view controller. In order to be able to access this method, a reference to the first view controller needs to be accessible to the PurchaseViewController instance. For the purposes of this example, this will be achieved by placing a reference to the first view controller in the application's delegate class where it can be accessed when needed within the PurchaseViewController instance. Select the *AppDelegate.swift* file and edit it to add this variable:

```
import UIKit

@UIApplicationMain
class AppDelegate: UIResponder, UIApplicationDelegate {

    var window: UIWindow?
    var homeViewController: ViewController?
```

.
.

97.5 Completing the ViewController Class

In order to complete the ViewController class implementation, select the *ViewController.swift* file and modify it to import the StoreKit framework. Also, code needs to be added to assign a reference to the view controller instance to the *homeViewController* variable previously added to the app delegate class so that it can be accessed from the PurchaseViewController:

```
import UIKit
import StoreKit

class ViewController: UIViewController {

    @IBOutlet weak var level2Button: UIButton!

    override func viewDidLoad() {
        super.viewDidLoad()
        let appdelegate = UIApplication.sharedApplication().delegate
                                    as AppDelegate

        appdelegate.homeViewController = self
    }
.
.
.
```

Finally, implement the *enableLevel2* method which will be called by the PurchaseViewController instance to enable the Level 2 access button once the purchase is complete:

```
func enableLevel2() {
    level2Button.enabled = true
}
```

The ViewController class is now complete.

97.6 **Completing the PurchaseViewController Class**

The first steps in completing the PurchaseViewController class are to add some code to the *viewDidLoad* method. To begin with, until product information has been obtained and displayed to the user, the buy button should be disabled. The class also needs to be configured as the transaction observer for the purchase operation. Finally, a method needs to be called to obtain the product information for the purchase and display it to the user. To achieve these tasks, edit the *PurchaseViewController.swift* file and modify the *viewDidLoad* method accordingly:

```
override func viewDidLoad() {
    super.viewDidLoad()
    buyButton.enabled = false
    SKPaymentQueue.defaultQueue().addTransactionObserver(self)
    getProductInfo()
}
```

It will be the job of the *getProductInfo* method called from the *viewDidLoad* method above to contact the App Store and get product information for the specified ID and display it. The code for this method belongs in the *PurchaseViewController.swift* file and reads as follows:

```
func getProductInfo()
{
    if SKPaymentQueue.canMakePayments() {
        let request = SKProductsRequest(productIdentifiers:
                                NSSet(objects: self.productID))
        request.delegate = self
        request.start()
    } else {
        productDescription.text =
                        "Please enable In App Purchase in Settings"

    }
}
```

The request for product information will result in a call to the *didReceiveResponse* delegate method which should be implemented as follows:

```
func productsRequest(request: SKProductsRequest!, didReceiveResponse
response: SKProductsResponse!) {

    var products = response.products

    if (products.count != 0) {
        product = products[0] as? SKProduct
        buyButton.enabled = true
        productTitle.text = product!.localizedTitle
        productDescription.text = product!.localizedDescription

    } else {
            productTitle.text = "Product not found"
    }

    products = response.invalidProductIdentifiers

    for product in products
    {
        println("Product not found: \(product)")
    }
}
```

Note that the above code displays the product information to the user and enables the Buy button. This is configured to call the *buyProduct* method, the stub for which now needs to be completed:

```
@IBAction func buyProduct(sender: AnyObject) {
    let payment = SKPayment(product: product)
    SKPaymentQueue.defaultQueue().addPayment(payment)
}
```

This code will initiate the purchasing process and cause calls to be made to the *updatedTransactions* method of the transaction observer object. Since the PurchaseViewController instance was declared as the transaction observer, this method also needs to be implemented in *PurchaseViewController.swift*:

```
func paymentQueue(queue: SKPaymentQueue!, updatedTransactions
transactions: [AnyObject]!) {

    for transaction in transactions as [SKPaymentTransaction] {

        switch transaction.transactionState {

            case SKPaymentTransactionState.Purchased:
                self.unlockFeature()
                SKPaymentQueue.defaultQueue().
                            finishTransaction(transaction)

            case SKPaymentTransactionState.Failed:
                SKPaymentQueue.defaultQueue().
                            finishTransaction(transaction)
            default:
                break
        }
    }
}
```

Regardless of the success or otherwise of the purchase, the code finishes the transaction. In the event of a successful purchase, however, the *unlockFeature* method will be called, and should now be implemented in *PurchaseViewController.swift* as follows:

```
func unlockFeature() {
    let appdelegate = UIApplication.sharedApplication().delegate
                            as AppDelegate

    appdelegate.homeViewController!.enableLevel2()
    buyButton.enabled = false
    productTitle.text = "Item has been purchased"
}
```

This method obtains a reference to the home view controller stored in the application delegate and calls the *enableLevel2* method of that view controller instance. The Buy button is then disabled and the text displayed on the product title label changed to indicate the successful purchase.

97.7 Testing the Application

Connect an iOS device to the development system (in-app purchasing cannot be tested in the iOS Simulator environment). In the Settings application on the device, choose the iTunes & App Store option, select your usual account and choose *Sign Out* from the popup dialog.

Run the application and note that the "Enter Level 2" button is initially disabled. Touch the "Purchase Level 2 Access" button and, after a short delay, note that the product information appears on the purchase screen. Select the Buy button and wait for the purchase confirmation dialog to appear (Figure 97-4). Note that the dialog includes text which reads "[Environment: Sandbox]" to indicate that the sandbox is being used and that this is not a real purchase.

Figure 97-4

Confirm the purchase and, when prompted to do so, enter the test account details configured in the previous chapter. When the purchase is complete Level 2 should now be accessible from the first scene.

97.8 Troubleshooting

By just about any standard, in-app purchasing is a multistep process and, as with any multistep process, implementation of in-app purchases can be susceptible to errors.

In the event that the example application does not work there are few areas that are worthwhile checking:

- Verify that the application bundle ID matches the one used to create the provisioning profile and the app entry in iTunes Connect.
- Make sure that the matching developer profile is being used to sign the application.
- Check that the product ID used in code matches the ID assigned to the in-app purchase item in iTunes Connect.
- Verify that the item was configured as being available for purchase in iTunes Connect.
- Make sure that Tax and Banking details are entered and correct in iTunes Connect.
- Try deleting the application from the device and re-installing it.

97.9 Summary

This chapter has taken the steps to complete a demonstration of in-app purchasing from within an iOS 8 application and provided some guidance in terms of troubleshooting tips in the event that in-app purchasing does not work.

98. Configuring and Creating App Store Hosted Content for iOS 8 In-App Purchases

As discussed in *Building In-App Purchasing into iOS 8 Applications*, iOS provides the option to host the content associated with a server based in-app purchase on Apple's own App Store servers. This service is provided by Apple to application developers at no additional cost. Prior to iOS 6, it was the responsibility of the developer to set up and configure a server system for server based in-app purchases.

The steps involved in implementing hosted content downloads from within application code were covered in the *An iOS 8 In-App Purchase Tutorial* chapter. One area that has yet to be covered in detail, and the main focus of this chapter, involves the mechanism for creating the hosted content package and uploading it to the App Store server.

98.1 Configuring an Application for In-App Purchase Hosted Content

Before a hosted content package is created and uploaded, the corresponding application and in-app purchase product item must be configured in iTunes Connect. Assuming that the application is registered, select the application under the *My Apps* link and, within the App Information screen, click on the *In-App Purchases* tab.

Click on the *Create New* button on the In-App Purchases screen and select the type of purchase to be configured (for hosted content this is most likely to be non-consumable). Enter a reference name for the product (this will be used to list the product in iTunes Connect and within sales reports) and the product ID that will be used when referencing this product in the application code. Mark the product as cleared for sale, set a pricing tier and then specify a product title and description for at least one language.

Finally, set the *Hosting Content with Apple* option to *Yes* before saving the new product to the App Store. Once saved, the purchase will be listed by iTunes Connect as "Waiting for Upload".

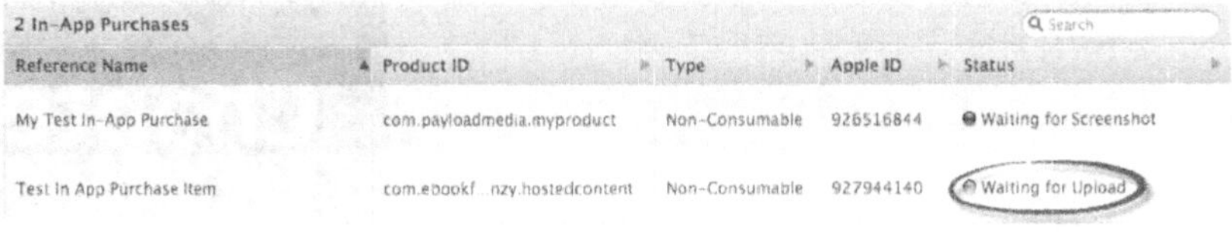

Figure 98-1

98.2 The Anatomy of an In-App Purchase Hosted Content Package

An in-app purchase hosted content package consists of a structured folder, the root level of which must contain a *ContentInfo.plist* file which, in turn, contains two keys:

- **ContentVersion** – The version number of the content.
- **IAPProductIdentifier** – The product identifier of the product with which the content is associated

The folder must also contain a sub-folder named *Contents* in which resides the content files associated with the in-app purchase. App Store hosted content packages are limited to 2GB in size and must not contain executable code or content that violates any of Apple's guidelines.

98.3 Creating an In-App Purchase Hosted Content Package

The easiest way to create a hosted content package is to use Xcode. To do so, launch Xcode and create a new project. When prompted to select a template for the new project, select the *Other* entry listed under *iOS* in the left hand panel of the template screen and, in the main panel, select *In-App Purchase Content* as demonstrated in Figure 98-2:

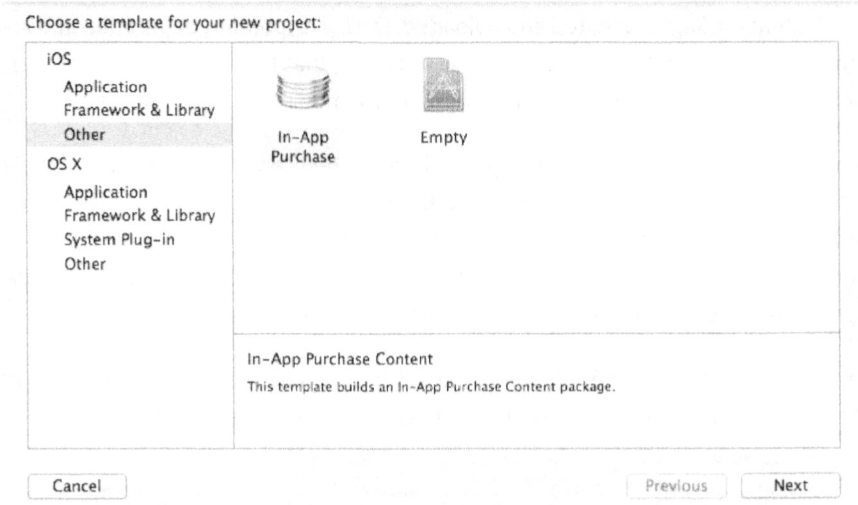

Figure 98-2

Click *Next*, and on the subsequent screen enter a name for the content package which matches the product ID of the purchase item as declared in iTunes Connect. Click *Next* and choose a location for the project before clicking on the *Create* button.

Within the main Xcode screen, unfold the *Supporting Files* section of the project navigator panel and select the *ContentInfo.plist* file. Review the contents of the file and note that the version is set to 1.0 by default. Since this is the first version of the content this can be left unchanged. If the content is modified at any point in the future this version number should be incremented accordingly.

Using a Finder window, locate the content files that are to be hosted on the App Store and drag and drop them onto the *Supporting Files* header in the Xcode project navigator panel and click *Finish* on the resulting panel.

98.4 **Archiving the Hosted Content Package**

With the content configured, the next step is to create the hosted content package file. This is achieved by selecting the Xcode *Product -> Archive* menu option. Once the package has been created, display the Organizer window and select the *Archives* tab as shown in Figure 98-3:

Figure 98-3

98.5 **Validating the Hosted Content Package**

Before the package is uploaded to Apple's servers, it should first be validated to ensure it does not contain ineligible content. To perform the verification, click on the *Validate...* button in the Organizer window and enter your Apple developer program credentials to verify that the content meets Apple's format guidelines. Xcode will then ask that the application for which the content is to be associated be selected from the drop down menu as illustrated in Figure 98-4.

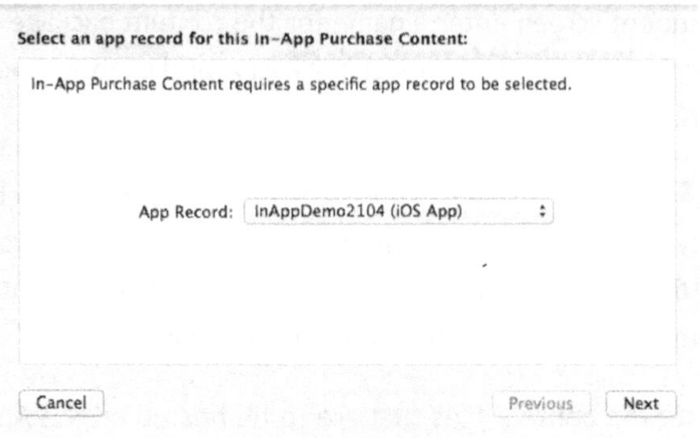

Select an app record for this In–App Purchase Content:

In-App Purchase Content requires a specific app record to be selected.

App Record: InAppDemo2104 (iOS App)   ⇕

Cancel   Previous   Next

Figure 98-4

With the correct Application and In-App Purchase Content items selected, click *Next* to initiate the validation process. If the validation succeeds, the package is ready for upload. In the event that the validation fails, read the error description and make corrections to the content files accordingly.

98.6 **Uploading the Hosted Content Package**

Assuming validation was successful, click on the *Submit* button in the Organizer window and select the option to *Submit in-app purchase content*. Once again, enter your developer program credentials and select both the application and product ID to complete the upload process.

An alternative to submitting the content within Xcode is to export the package from the Organizer window and then use the Application Loader tool to upload it to iTunes Connect. The Application Loader tool can be downloaded from the *Resources and Help* page of the iTunes Connect portal and is known to provide a more flexible and reliable upload process than that offered by Xcode.

Once the upload is complete, the hosted content package will be listed in iTunes Connect.

The content is now available for download as part of an in-app purchase using the steps outlined in *Building In-App Purchasing into iOS 8 Applications*.

98.7 **Summary**

In-app purchases can potentially include additional content that needs to be downloaded to the user's device as part of the purchase process. Prior to the introduction of iOS 6, the hosting of this content on a remote server was the responsibility of the application developer, including the associated security infrastructure to validate purchases prior to download.

iOS 6, however, introduced the ability to upload content packages for hosting on Apple's App Store servers. The steps to initiate in-app purchase downloads from the App Store were covered in the chapter entitled *Building In-App Purchasing into iOS 8 Applications*. This chapter has walked through the steps involved in creating an App Store in-app hosted package and uploading it to the App Store.

99. Preparing and Submitting an iOS 8 Application to the App Store

Having developed an iOS 8 application the final step is to submit it to Apple's App Store. Preparing and submitting an application is a multistep process details of which will be covered in this chapter.

99.1 Verifying the iOS Distribution Certificate

The chapter entitled *Testing Apps on iOS 8 Devices with Xcode 6* covered the steps involved in generating signing certificates. In that chapter, both a development and distribution certificate were generated. Up until this point in the book, applications have been signed using the development certificate so that testing could be performed on physical iOS devices. Before an application can be submitted to the App Store, however, it must be signed using the distribution certificate. The presence of the distribution certificate may be verified from within the Xcode 6 *Preferences* settings.

With Xcode 6 running, select the *Xcode -> Preferences...* menu option and select the *Accounts* category from the toolbar of the resulting window. Assuming that Apple IDs have been configured as outlined in *Testing Apps on iOS 8 Devices with Xcode 6*, a list of one or more Apple IDs will be shown in the accounts panel as illustrated in Figure 99-1:

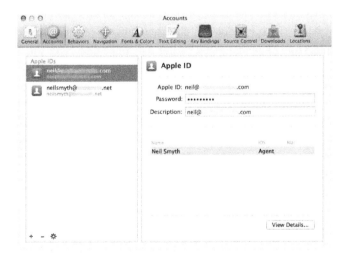

Figure 99-1

Select the Apple ID to be used to sign the application and click on the *View Details* button to display the list of signing identities and provisioning profiles associated with that ID:

Neil Smyth
neil@payloadmedia.com

Signing Identities	Platform	Status
iOS Development	iOS	Valid
iOS Distribution	iOS	Valid

+ ⚙

Provisioning Profiles	Expiration	Entitlements
iOS Team Provisioning Profile: IAPDemo	8/29/15	
iOS Team Provisioning Profile: com.payloadmedia....	8/29/15	
iOSTeam Provisioning Profile: com.ebookfrenzy.Sa...	10/23/15	
iOSTeam Provisioning Profile: com.payloadmedia....	10/23/15	
iOSTeam Provisioning Profile: com.ebookfrenzy.Cl...	10/23/15	
iOS Team Provisioning Profile: com.payloadmedia....	8/29/15	

ⓒ   Done

Figure 99-2

Under the *Signing Identities* heading, check that a valid signing identity is listed for *iOS Distribution.* If a valid distribution certificate is not listed, click on the + button and select *iOS Distribution* from the resulting menu. Xcode will then contact the developer portal and generate and download a new signing certificate suitable for use when signing applications for submission to the App Store.

99.2 Adding App Icons

Before rebuilding the application for distribution it is important to ensure that app icons have been added to the application. The app icons are used to represent your application on the home screen, settings panel and search results on the device. Each of these categories requires a suitable icon in PNG format and formatted for a number of different dimensions. In addition, different variants of the icons will need to be added for retina and non-retina displays and depending on whether the application is for the iPhone or iPad (or both).

App icons are added using the project settings screen of the application project within Xcode. To view these settings, load the project into Xcode and select the application target at the top of the project navigator panel. In the main panel, select the *General* tab and scroll down to the App Icons and Launch Images sections. By default, Xcode will look for the App icon images within an asset catalog named *AppIcon*. Next to the *App Icons Source* menu is a small arrow (as indicated in Figure 99-3) which, when clicked, will provide access to the asset catalog of the App icons.

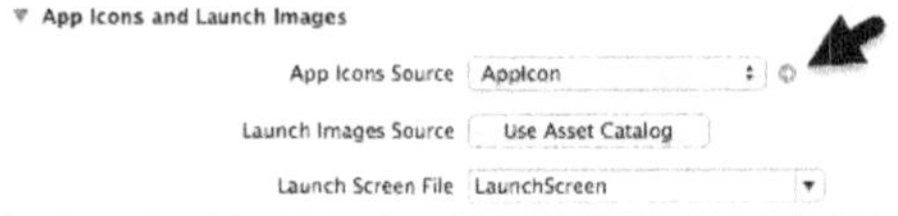

▼ App Icons and Launch Images

App Icons Source   AppIcon   ⫶ ◯

Launch Images Source   Use Asset Catalog

Launch Screen File   LaunchScreen   ▼

Figure 99-3

When selected, the AppIcon asset catalog screen will display showing placeholders for each icon size:

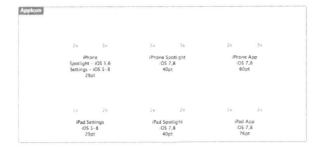

Figure 99-4

To add images, simply drag and drop the missing PNG format image files from a Finder window onto the corresponding placeholders in the asset catalog, or Ctrl-click on the catalog and select *Import* from the menu to import multiple files. At a minimum you will need to add 40 x 40, 76 x 76, 120 x 120 and 152 x 152 PNG icon files in order to pass the archive validate stage.

99.3 Designing the Launch Screen

The launch screen contains the content that appears when the application is starting up. The design for this screen is contained in the *LaunchScreen.xib* Interface Builder file which will have been generated automatically during the project creation process. By default, the screen consists of the application name and some copyright information:

AppStoreDemo

Copyright (c) 2014 Neil Smyth. All rights reserved.

Figure 99-5

Load the file into interface Builder and modify it to meet your requirements, including adding any images that may be required and keeping in mind that the layout must use size classes to ensure that the layout appears correctly on all screen sizes. Note also that the layout is limited to UIKit classes and cannot include a UIWebView object.

99.4 **Assign the Project to a Team**

As part of the submission process, the project must be associated with a development team to ensure that the correct signing credentials are used. In the project navigator panel, select the project name to display the project settings panel. Click the General tab and within the Identity section, select a team from the menu as shown in Figure 99-6:

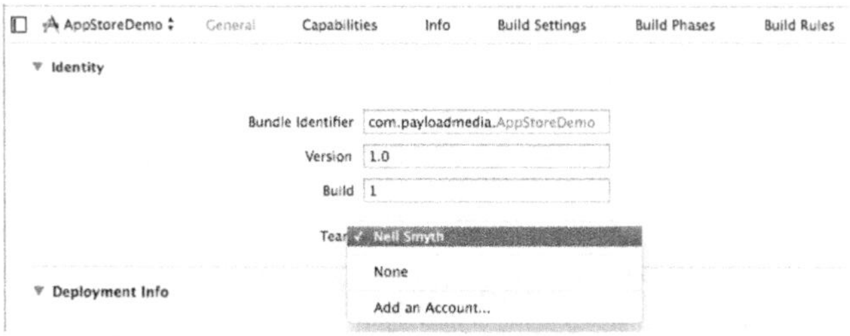

Figure 99-6

99.5 **Archiving the Application for Distribution**

The application must now be rebuilt using the previously installed distribution profile. To generate the archive, select the Xcode *Product -> Archive* menu option. Note that if the Archive menu is disabled this is most likely because a simulator option is currently selected as the run target in the Xcode toolbar. Changing this menu either to a connected device, or the generic *iOS Device* target option should enable the Archive option in the Product menu.

Xcode will proceed to archive the application ready for submission. Once the process is complete the archive will be displayed in the Organizer window ready for upload and distribution:

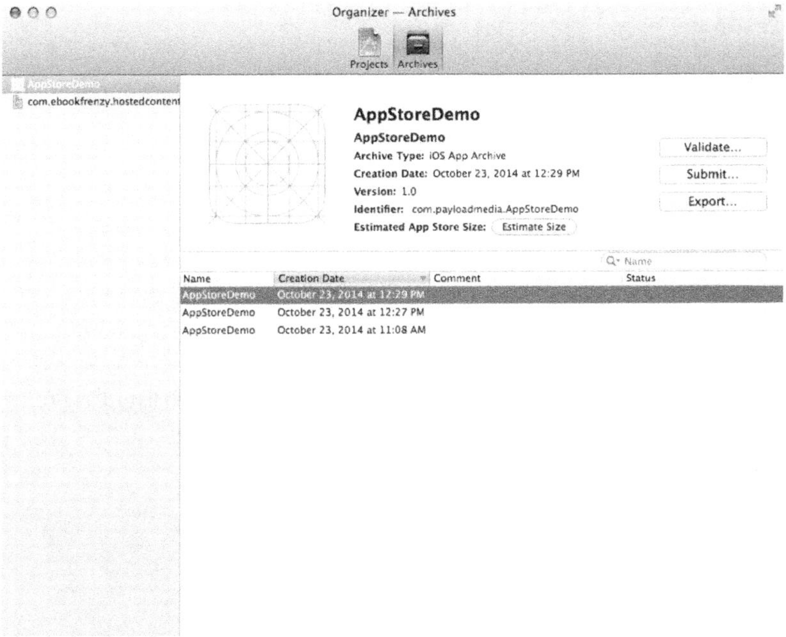

Figure 99-7

99.6 Configuring the Application in iTunes Connect

Before an application can be submitted to the App Store for review it must first be configured in iTunes Connect. Enrollment in the Apple Developer program automatically results in the creation of an iTunes Connect account using the same login credentials. iTunes Connect is a portal where developers enter tax and payment information, input details about applications and track the status of those applications in terms of sales and revenues.

Access iTunes Connect by navigating to *http://itunesconnect.apple.com* in a web browser and entering your Apple Developer program login and password details.

First time users should click on the *Agreements, Tax, and Banking* option and work through the various tasks to accept Apple's terms and conditions and to input appropriate tax and banking information for the receipt of sales revenue.

Once the administrative tasks are complete, select the *My Apps* option and click on the + button followed by *New iOS App* to enter information about the application. Begin by entering a name for the application and an SKU of your own creation. Also select or enter the bundle ID that matches the application that has been prepared for upload in Xcode:

Figure 99-8

Once the application has been added it will appear within the My Apps screen listed as *Prepare for submission*:

Figure 99-9

99.7 **Validating and Submitting the Application**

To validate the application, return to the Archives page of the Xcode Organizer Window, make sure the application archive is selected and click on the *Validate...* button. Enter your iOS Developer program login credentials when prompted to do so. If more than one signing identity is configured within Xcode, select the desired identity from the menu.

Xcode will connect to the iTunes Connect service and perform a validation check on the archived application. Xcode will report any errors identified during the validation process. Correct any reported errors, re-archive the application and validate it again. Repeat these steps until the validation passes:

Figure 99-10

Click on the *Done* button to dismiss the panel. The application is now ready to be uploaded for App Store review.

Make sure the application archive is still selected and click on the *Submit...* button. Enter your developer program login credentials when prompted and wait for the upload process to complete:

Figure 99-11

99.8 Configuring and Submitting the App for Review

On the My Apps screen of the iTunes Connect portal, select the new app entry to display the configuration screen where options are available to set up pre-release test users, designate pricing, enter product descriptions and upload screenshots and preview videos. Once this information has been entered and saved and the app is ready for submission to the App Store, click on the *Submit for Review* button highlighted in Figure 99-12:

Figure 99-12

Once Apple has completed the review process an email will arrive stating whether the application has been accepted or not. In the event that the application has been rejected, reasons for the rejection will be stated and the application may be resubmitted once these issues have been addressed.

Index

C

Index

Index

S

T

U

CPSIA information can be obtained at www.ICGtesting.com
Printed in the USA
LVOW03s1926130215

426960LV00025B/1195/P

9 781505 586411